COLLECTIONS
TOWARDS THE
HISTORY
OF PONTEFRACT.

—II.—
THE SIEGES
OF PONTEFRACT CASTLE.

SITE OF PONTEFRACT CASTLE,

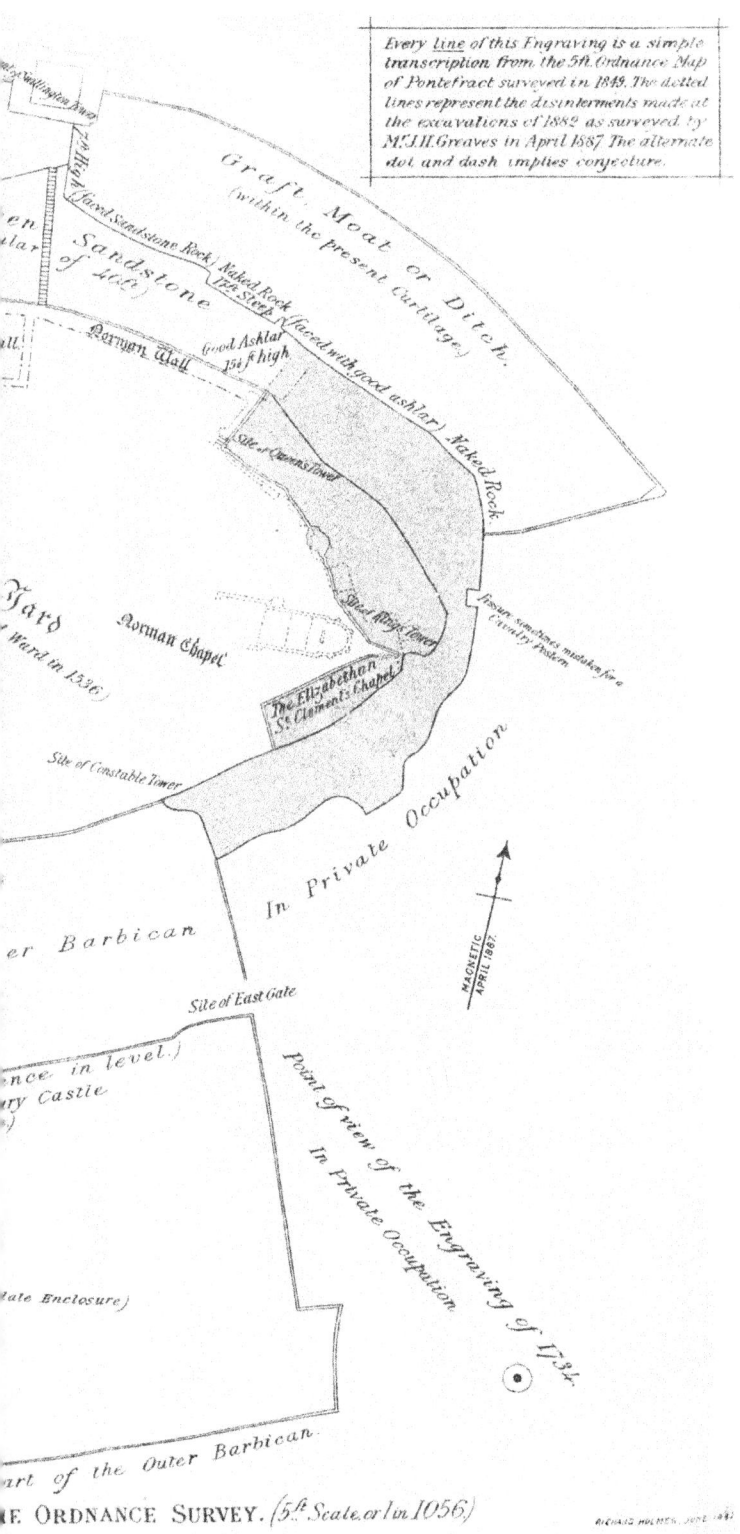

The Sieges
OF
PONTEFRACT CASTLE.

1644-1648.

Edited by
RICHARD HOLMES,

WITH 18 PHOTOGRAPHIC ILLUSTRATIONS.

The Naval & Military Press Ltd

Published by

The Naval & Military Press Ltd
Unit 5 Riverside, Brambleside
Bellbrook Industrial Estate
Uckfield, East Sussex
TN22 1QQ England

Tel: +44 (0)1825 749494

www.naval-military-press.com
www.nmarchive.com

In reprinting in facsimile from the original, any imperfections are inevitably reproduced and the quality may fall short of modern type and cartographic standards.

Living generations thrust aside the mouldering relics of their predecessors for their own convenience, to commemorate their more immediate relatives and friends, or to enhance their own personal importance. But historians do their best to rescue, at least in part, by representation or description, the perishing memorials; and to prove that paper records may be more permanent than those of brass and stone.

My thoughts are with the dead; with them
   I live in long past years;
Their virtues love; their faults condemn;
   Partake their hopes and fears.
      And from their lessons seek and find
      Instruction with a humble mind.

SOUTHEY.

PREFACE.

It is a coincidence entirely unintended that this volume should come at this season before the public as a Jubilee offering, one of the many appropriate commemorations of the happily lengthened reign of Her Most Gracious Majesty.

The volume is the second of a series of Collections towards a History of Pontefract; and although no attempt has been made to weave its contents into a whole, yet as it was hoped that the very comprehensive Index which has been compiled, extending to 41 pages, might to some extent serve the purpose of a record of events, the references under its most important headings have been, where possible, put together in such a way as to form a connected narrative.

But it should go without saying that even such a volume as the present by no means exhausts all the interest of Pontefract Castle. For instance absolutely nothing has been said of one of its most important functions, that of a depository of the official documents of the lords, and of wills and other muniments, which it fulfilled even within a quarter of a century of its demolition, when Thomas Dey, of South Kirkby, ordered his will (proved 1626) to be "deposited among other wills in his Majesty's Castle of Pontefract."

This volume must be considered as treating only of the Civil War sieges and their surroundings. And even so far as these are concerned there is much to be learned. As for instance in respect of the last siege: it is well known that (see pp. 217 and 310) Castilion Morris, the son of the Governor, Colonel John Morris, and who afterwards became Town Clerk of Leeds, wrote its History, of which Thoresby records (Diary I. 462) the perusal during the summer of 1705. A Diary of Castilion Morris, dealing with the events of his own life, and especially during the Revolution of 1688, also passed at the same time, and perhaps as part of the same document, into the hands of that eminent antiquary who copied those parts of it which specially interested him. But whether in one volume or in two, in each case, the MS. itself is lost; let us hope only temporarily, and to be at some time disinterred from the hiding place in which it has been buried nearly two hundred years. A collection of extracts made by Mr Thoresby from the Diary, is, however, still in existence, and was published in the last issued part (January, 1887) of *The Yorkshire Archæological and Topographical Journal*. Unfortunately no corresponding extracts from Morris's History of Pontefract remain, so far as is known with certainty, though there is a probability that some were incorporated into both Boothroyd's and Fox's History of the place; but a Prospectus, probably referring to it, has been discovered by the present compiler, and is

PREFACE.   iii.

printed in Appendix E. And thus this part of the subject rests for the present, serving as an illustration of how much still remains to be discovered and recorded.

In the present volume will also be found a second letter of Capt T. Paulden, narrating the circumstances of the seizure of the Castle in 1648, and the attempt upon Rainsborough. This was apparently complementary to his former letter, and elicited by a remark of Clarendon in praise and commendation of the latter adventure. The original document is among the Clarendon State Papers, and having had it copied with care, we have ourselves collated the copy with the original document, in order to ensure verbal and literal accuracy. (See pp. 291-324).

Indeed, whenever it has been possible, this course has been adopted with regard to all the original documents now printed. Every one that is accessible has been examined and compared; in each case they may therefore be taken to be with few exceptions *literatim et verbatim.*

This work was really ready; what was intended for its last page was printed nearly three years ago; but it was withheld from immediate publication (at the suggestion of one to whose fostering patronage and kindly suggestion it owes almost everything of value it possesses) in order that a Supplement might be prepared embodying the results of a comparison of all the known Engravings of the Castle and Plans of its Sieges. This was, however, not to be done in a few weeks; it has in fact been the occupation of the leisure of nearly three years.

PREFACE.

The compiler ventures upon no further recapitulation. The volume will speak for itself to all who can understand how much patient and laborious investigation has been devoted to the task which is now to a certain stage completed.

But so much as has been said is necessary, if only to show how it has come to pass that this account of the local portion of that struggle in which Pontefract Castle bore so distinguished a part, appears as a Jubilee offering from this nursery of the Lancasterian dynasty, this ancient seat of the Duchy of Lancaster, the last place in which during the Civil War coins were struck with the superscription of the old King, and the scene of the first proclamation of his son and successor, with the proud motto, since adopted by the town, of

POST MORTEM PATRIS, PRO FILIO.

PONTEFRACT, JUNE 20, 1887.

LIST OF ILLUSTRATIONS.

PLAN OF SITE OF CASTLE		*Frontispiece*
		PAGE
VIEW OF ALL SAINTS' CHURCH	to face	9
FAC-SIMILE FROM THE DRAKE MS.	,,	17
VIEW OF NEW HALL	,,	25
PORTRAIT OF MAJOR-GENERAL JOHN LAMBERT	,,	152
PORTRAIT OF MAJOR JOHN MORRIS	,,	177
PORTRAIT OF LIEUT-GENERAL OLIVER CROMWELL	,,	189
THE PONTEFRACT SIEGE COINS	,,	212
VIEW OF THE ROUND TOWER	,,	345
THE SOC. ANT. PRINT OF THE CASTLE (1734-5)	,,	397
JOHN MARSDEN'S DO. DO. (1776)	,,	405
PAUL JOLLAGE'S PLAN OF THE TOWN	,,	409
SIEGE PLAN NO. 1 (BASIRE'S)	,,	412
SIEGE PLAN NO. 3 (SURTEES COPY) DO. (LORD GALWAY'S ORIGINAL)	,,	413
MR. FRANK'S PLAN	,,	416
FAC-SIMILE OF GENT'S ENGRAVINGS	,,	417
SIEGE PLAN NO. 2 WITH CORRECTED PLAN OF WORKS	,,	421

The Sieges of Pontefract Castle.

TILL WELL WITHIN the last five years of its existence the strength of Pontefract Castle was never really tested. Built upon a rock, its walls partly composed of the very rock itself, it was practically impregnable to all the array that could be brought against it: fell famine alone could force a passage. And when the assaults of that dire foe had been provided against, the attacks of a beleaguring enemy could be laughed to scorn,—till the supplies failed. Besiegers could effect little by direct attack; their only resource was an effective blockade.

Constructed in the eleventh century, enlarged in the twelfth and thirteenth, strengthened in the fourteenth, used as a palace and a prison, a fortress and a dungeon, the siege of this formidable garrison, the circumstances of which are so graphically chronicled by Nathan Drake,— and with such simplicity that the man's character can be read in his writings,—was the first real leagure the structure had been called upon to endure. And that the circumstances of the contest, so far as it represented itself to the minds and imagination of the besieged, should have been recorded with so minute a particularity is an accident, for which we who seek in the obscurity of modern times to understand the feelings and sentiments of our predecessors, can hardly be too thankful; throwing, as it does, for our benefit and instruction, such singular light upon an episode which would else be represented by a patch of pitch darkness. We are fortunate in obtaining an account by an eye-witness of the circumstances attending the seizure of the Castle before the third siege; but we are much more fortunate in obtaining, in the diary of Nathan Drake, the minute and circumstantial record (in some respects perhaps unique) which has been handed down among his lineal descendants to the present day; and it seems not at all unsuitable to preface his Diary with an account of his family and descendants.

The chronicler of the two earlier sieges of Pontefract Castle must have been a remarkable man. Of a good yeoman family, long settled in Yorkshire, his pedigree could be traced up to the time of Edward I.; and though the ancestry of Nathan Drake claimed to be quite as good as that of his father's renowned contemporary and namesake, Sir Francis Drake, who belonged to the other end of the kingdom, there is no evidence of a connection between the two families. Moreover, no Drake appears in all Yorkshire at the contemporary Kirkby's Inquest, or in the Rotulus Hundredorum, and although there is a John Drake acting as officer to John of Brittany, earl of Richmond, and presented in the time of Edward I. for having accepted 20s. for conniving at a murder, this occurred in the neighbouring county of Lincoln.

In the Northowram section of the Poll Tax of 1379, there is a John Drac, and in Henry VIII's Subsidy of 1524, there is a John Drayk in the same township, taxed 2s. for goods worth £4, though he seems to have had no lands; but we do not trace the connection between these namesakes, which doubtless existed.

With the great grandson of the latter, Nathan the Diarist, the real Drake pedigree commences, as given at some length in Watson's Halifax. From it we learn that Nathan was settled at Godley, in Halifax, but was deprived of his estate there for his support of the Royalist cause. And as we cannot add much to what we find in the historian of Halifax, we refrain from quoting him here, though we append the following additional particulars of local interest, many collected by ourselves, and, as we believe, published for the first time. (See also Appendix A.)

Born in 1587, and baptised at Halifax on Dec. 17 of that year, Nathan Drake took to wife, in or about 1621, one Elizabeth Higgins, a native of Pontefract, nearly thirteen years younger than himself. How he made her acquaintance, or where they were married, we fail to discover; we can only say negatively that the wedding is not recorded in the Pontefract registers. The baptism is, however, registered there in the earliest volume (**A**), as having take place on 8 June, 1600, of "Elizabeth, ye doughter of Francis Higgins"; special attention being afterwards bespoken to the entry, in what appears to be the handwriting of her grandson—the Vicar Francis, himself, who annotates it, "From whom F. Drake, vic', descended."

The mother of Elizabeth Higgins died while she was but an infant, and from the entry of her burial (20 Dec. 1602, Mary the wiff of Frauncis Higgin was buried in church) we gather that her husband was of some position. The widower must have re-married, and speedily; for on 28 Jan., 1603-4, only thirteen months afterwards, there is an entry, "Johan the daughter of Francis Higgins, was buried, a C.C." (Chrissom child, *i.e.* unbaptised.) This was a time of plague, and the addition to the entry of the word *not* was considered necessary, in order to show that the death was *not* a case of the fearful pestilence, then so virulent, that of 49 burials in that and the preceding month,—the usual number was about 10—only six were distinguished by this negative particle.

We do not trace what became of the father of this maternal ancestor of the Pontefract Drakes, but he was probably still living in the parish when Elizabeth would have been sixteen years old, as we find on 26 Dec., 1616, the entry "John Haggishe, Francis Higgin shepheard, was buried."

It may be supposed that Nathan Drake naturally took an interest in the native place of his wife; and hence about the time that his eldest son (born 1622) was reaching man's estate, we find him with the flower of the gentry of the neighbourhood, among the "volunteers" who were preparing to defend the ancient and hereditary stronghold of the Lancastrian branch of the royal family of England. He is sometimes, indeed, absurdly called Captain, but there is not the shadow of a shade of evidence that he ever raised a troop, or, indeed, had any military rank. Singularly enough, throughout his MSS. he never once mentions his own personal share in the exploits of the garrison. His sentiments, his doings, and his experiences during the first and second seiges, are, with that exception, fully recorded in his Diary; and though his strains are never very eloquent, and his diction is sometimes even rugged, he writes without unnecessary redundancy, and there is hardly a line of his jottings down we should care to lose.

It does not appear that he took part in the third siege, though during at least the latter part of the Commonwealth he lived at Pontefract,—perhaps at Spittle Hardwick, which seems to have been the holding of his father-in-law. But his name does not occur in the Fee Farm Book of 1650, as holding any property here, nor is he entered as a householder and ratepayer in the Assessment Book of 1657, (reprinted in "THE BOOKE OF ENTRIES," pp. 54-56.)

His will was made Dec 2nd, 1658 (proved in London

[P.C.C. Pell 131] on the following Feb. 10th) and his death is thus recorded in the Church Books:—

> Dec. 8th, 1658. Nathan Drake, yeoman, aged above 71, departed this life, and his corps was interred in the parish church of Pontefract, the nineth day of the same moneth.

Thus, though he survived the Protector by three months, and was able to see the Commonwealth system tottering to its downfull, he did not live to enjoy the restoration of the old order of things for which he had striven so strenuously. His widow, Mrs Elizabeth Drake, however, survived him by nearly fourteen years, and was buried beside her husband, within the walls of Pontefract Church, on Nov. 17th, 1672.

Nathan's only son, Samuel, actively served the King, and was engaged in the siege at Newark, as his father had been in that of Pontefract. He was born in 1621, and, as his son's tribute to his memory declares, was a fellow of St. John's, Cambridge, at 16; but during the Rebellion, he was deprived of his fellowship, as his father had been of his estate. Besides this son, Nathan Drake had two daughters.

The elder, Elizabeth, it is to be presumed, married Mr. John Stables, son of Zachary Stables, of Pontefract, (buried "very aged," Feb. 13, 1678-9,) for within six weeks of the death of her father,

> The purpose of marriage between John Stables, of Pontefract, in the county of York, yeoman, son of Zachary Stables, of the same town & county, also yeoman, on the one p't; and Elizabeth Drake, spinster, daughter of Nathan Drake, late of Pontefract, aforesaid, yeoman, deceased, on the other p't, was published in the upper Church of Pontefract aforesaid, three several Lords days at the close of morning exercise, vizt, the 16th, 23th, and 30th day of January, 1658(-9).

A foot note "Certified, 10 Feb, 1658," gives no clue to the parish in which the marriage ceremony was about to be performed, and we have not yet met with the entry in any neighbouring Church. The date of the purpose, so soon after her father's death, rather implies that some obstacle to the alliance had then been removed, but we have no key to the character of the difficulty.

His younger daughter, Mary, eight years all but eight days after the certificate of her elder sister's banns, on Candlemas, 1666-7, married Mr Ald. Knowles, also of Pontefract. She died a widow 19th Feb., 1699-1700.

We do not find where Samuel Drake first exercised his ministry, but he was evidently duly ordained, and when little more than thirty years old, was settled at South Kirkby during the Commonwealth, under melancholy circumstances.

During the third siege of Pontefract Castle, Mr George Beaumont, Vicar of South Kirkby, was hanged on a standing gallows at Baghill, by the Parliamentarians, for carrying on a correspondence with the besieged Royalists; and "1648-9, Feb. 18, Mr Beaumont, Vic' of South Kirkby, buried," is recorded there, without mentioning the cause of death. The entries ceased in the Registers of that parish from the beginning of 1651, to the close of 1653; but among the earliest births on record, after the resumption of the registry, is that of "1654, June 11, Francis son of Samuel Drake, cler', of Sth Kirkby," who thus appears for the first time as a settled minister in the parish. He was then 32 years old, and like his Pontefract contemporary, Joseph Ferrett, could have had no legal institution, as there was at the time no Archbishop. He was recognized, however, by the powers that were, as we find from the following report of him in a list of incumbents throughout England and Wales, and the source from which their income is derived: a document of the Long Parliament preserved in the Lansdowne MSS in the British Museum.

SOUTH KIRKBY. Mr Sam. Drake, a painfull preaching minister, is vic'.

But he never arrogated to himself the title of Vicar of that parish, he always called himself "Clerk," only.

He had married Jane, the daughter of Mr Abbot, who afterwards became Town Clerk of Pontefract, and was himself appointed Vicar there in 1661, fifteen months before St. Bartholomew's day, 1662, when his predecessor is alleged, (by those who prefer fiction to truth) to have been ejected. The fact, however, is, that Mr Joseph Ferrett withdrew, his last entry in the Church books being made on 7 April, that of his successor, Mr. Samuel Drake, commencing on the next Sunday, 14 April, 1661.

In 1662, Samuel Drake received the degree of D.D. from his university, by royal letters patent, on account, as it is said, of his own and his father's loyalty and bravery in the sieges at Newark and Pontefract; i.e., his own at Newark, and his father's at Pontefract. One Ri: Drake had been similarly distinguished in 1661, but we fail to trace the connection, if any, between the two, unless indeed Richard was that second cousin half removed, who became shortly afterwards Precentor of Salisbury; though he must, if so, have been a young man to be made a D.D.

There is indeed a Joseph, eldest brother of Nathan the Diarist, whose descendants, being many of them clergymen and one of them beneficed in the diocese, frequently cross this pedigree, and sometimes are confounded with its members. Richard may be the son or grandson of that Joseph, another of whose sons, also Joseph, had by a second wife, a Nathan, who is very frequently mistaken for Nathan, the son of Samuel. The two Nathans graduated at St. John's, Cambridge; Joseph's son as B.A. in 1680 and M.A. in 1684; Samuel's son as B.A. in 1684, and M.A. not till 1691. Joseph's son was master of the Grammar School at Snaith in 1681, when only twenty-one years of age, and instituted to the Vicarage of Market Weighton in 1689, was Vicar of Sheffield from 1695 to 1713, Prebendary of Bilton from 1703, and Rector of Kirkby Overblow from 9 April,

1713, till his death, sixteen years afterwards, in April, 1729. Perhaps as the eldest inheritor of the name Nathan, he was thus the most prosperous of his family.

He had by his wife, Elizabeth Hill, of Mansfield, who was constituted his executrix by his will, dated 15 Dec., 1727, and proved 11 June, 1730; Robert, baptised at Snaith, 24 Oct, 1689, who died at Sheffield, 17 June, 1723; Mary, baptised at Market Weighton, 27 Jan., 1690-1, where she was living married at her father's death; Elizabeth, Nathan, Sarah, and John, who each died in infancy, a second Elizabeth, or Betty, to whom by his will he left £250, and one son, Joseph, baptised at Sheffield, 12 May, 1697, who became vicar of Burleigh, in Rutland, and died in 1754.

Dr Samuel Drake, besides being Vicar of Pontefract, was made Prebendary of Southwell in 1670, and rector of Hansworth or Handsworth, near Sheffield, in 1671. He died in 1678, and is frequently said to have been Vicar of Hemsworth, a mistake for Hansworth, and to have died in 1679, a mistake for 1678. Even in the recent edition of Hunter's Hallamshire, the unaccountable mistake has been made, of giving the date of his successor's institution, 3 April, 1679, as that of Dr Drake's death, and that the date is thus given on two adjacent pages (pp. 485, 486) does not make the fact less surprising.

The date of his burial is, however, clear, being registered with due formality; and perhaps the mistake may have arisen from some one having added his alleged age (57) to his alleged date of birth (1622) without referring. But it may be remarked that his son, the succeeding Vicar, who made the following entry to his memory in the Pontefract Church Books, says of him that he had reached his 57th year, not that he had completed it:—

ALL SAINTS CHURCH, PONTEFRACT FROM THE S.W.

1678.
Deember 28
Dr Samuell
Drake vic:
de
Pontefract.

(added in another hand)
Degat in Perpetua' Hujusce
Memoria.
N.D. Filioru' natu maximo
Tertius Artiu: B:

Deo Opt: Max:
In Ecclesia Parochiali Omnium Sanctorum de Pontefract Requiescit in Deo Reverendus Dom's Doctor Samuel Drake Sacroboscanus hujus Ecclesiæ Vicarius et Rector Ecclesiæ Parochialis de Hansworth, nec non Ecclesiæ Cathedralis Beati Petri apud Southwell in Agro Notingamiensi Prebendarius Decanus Decant' de Pontefract. In Collegio Divi Johannis Evangst: apud Cantabrig: diligenter Studijs incubuit, et in Decimo Sexto Anno ætatis suæ istius Collegij Socius; sed In valescente Rebellione, neqissimo Scot: Fœdore ejectus. Vir, Religionis cultu, morum Probitate, innocuâ Jucunditate, corporis Elegantiâ, affectu'm temperantiâ, ergà Pauperes Caritate et omnes equitate, se charum præbuit. Qui fidelitatem ac fortitudinem Regiæ Majestati ubertim indicavit, et in Newarkiensi obsidione se firmum strenuumq: militem comprobavit. Qui postquam ad A'num ætatis suæ Quinquagesimum septimum attigisset, non sine nobili et vulgari luctu ab hac vita ad meliorem co'migravit vicesimo octavo mensis Decembris An'oq: Dom' 1678 votumq: suum apud Posteros Sacratum esse voluit Filius suus Devotissimus, F.D. V. de Pont: et Success:

The tribute, thus written by Francis and endorsed by Nathan, the two sons of the departed vicar, may be thus rendered:—

To God, the Best, the Greatest.
In the Parish Church of All Saints of Pontefract Rests in God, the Reverend Sir, Doctor Samuel Drake, Spiritual Pastor, of this Church Vicar, and Rector of the Parish Church of Hansworth, also of the Cathedral Church of the Blessed Peter at Southwell in the County of Nottingham, Prebendary, Dean of the Deanery of Pontefract.
In the College of St. John the Evangelist at Cambridge, he inclined diligently to his studies, and in the sixteenth year of his age, (became) Fellow of that College; but in the growing Rebellion (when the Rebellion was gaining strength) was ejected by the most shameful treaty with the Scots. *As a Man, he made himself*

beloved by reverence for religion, by uprightness of character, by harmless pleasantry, by grace of body, by moderation of passions, by charity towards to the poor, and equity to all. Who fruitfully showed his faithfulness and firmness for the King's Majesty, and in the siege of Newark, proved himself a strong and staunch soldier.

Who after he had attained the fifty-seventh year of his age, departed, not without the grief of high and low, from this life to a better, on the twenty-eighth of the month of December, and in the year of our Lord 1678, and that his tablet be honoured among Posterity, his most devoted son, F.D., vicar of Pontefract, and successor, has willed.

The marginal note is in a rather later hand :—
May his memory live for ever. N.D., his third son, B. of Arts.

The children of Dr. Samuel Drake, and Jane, his wife, were at least

1. Francis, baptised at South Kirkby, June 11, 1654, in the name of his grandmother's father. He succeeded his father in the vicarage of Pontefract; though barely of canonical age, if the baptismal register represents approximately the time of his birth.
2. Samuel, also in orders, who is said to have married a daughter of Mr Benson, St. Peter's, Leeds. He might indeed have been the eldest son, for we have hitherto failed to trace his baptism, and there seems hardly room for him between Francis and Elizabeth. He may be the Mr. Samuel Drake buried at Pontefract on 11 Feb., 1688-9; but if so, his wife was named West, not Benson; for on 24 Sept., 1685, Mr. Samuel Drake and Mrs Elizabeth West were married; whose children were Mary, baptised 8 Sept., 1686, and Nathan (posthumous) baptised 14 June, 1689.
3. Elizabeth, baptised at South Kirkby, July 7, 1656, and married William Stappleton, (or Stapylton) D.D., on 14th Sept., 1686. She died 14 December, 1701, aged 58, according to her memorial still in the porch of Sherburn Church; but there must be a mistake in one of these figures, unless there was a considerable interval between her baptism, and her birth, which is very unlikely, comparing the date of her baptism with that of her brother Francis.
4. Jane, baptised at South Kirkby, July 5, 1659, buried at Pontefract, July 22, 1667, the day her brother William was baptised.
5. Nathan, baptised at Pontefract, June 16, 1663, was perhaps Master of the Grammar School in 1689, afterwards Rector of St. Peter's, Nottingham, and died 24 March, 1705. He is doubtless the Nathan "third son B.A.," referred to in his brother's tribute to the memory of their father. He is said to have been, like his father, a prebendary of Southwell, and to have published in 1675, a translation of the Preces Privatæ of Bp Andrewes; in the latter case, at least, there is a mistake either in the date or the fact, for at the time named he was but twelve years old. Hallamshire (page 271) says perhaps correctly that Dr. Richard Drake, Precentor of Sarum, published the volume referred to of Bishop Andrewes's Greek Devotions. He had a large family, at least four being in orders.
6. John, baptised at Pontefract, April 11, 1665, who was possibly the John Drake, admitted apprentice to Wm. Ramsden, of Hull, on 16 July, 1678. But this is uncertain, especially when it is remembered that there were

Drakes at York, apparently of another family altogether, one of whom, named Joshua, a mercer, deceased in 1691, leaving a widow, Jane.
7. William, baptised at Pontefract, July 22, 1667.
8. Edmund, baptised at Pontefract, August 10, 1668.

Dr. Samuel Drake was in his 57th year at the time of his death, and his widow, Jane, survived him 22 years. She was buried at Pontefract, Jan. 31, 1700-1.

Francis Drake, the second vicar of that surname, besides being Vicar of Pontefract in succession to his father, is sometimes said to have been rector of Hansworth. This is, however, one of the numerous errors that have been floated with regard to members of this family. He was, in 1688, collated to the prebendary of Warthill, in the cathedral of York. He married, 1st, Hannah, daughter of Mr. Palin (not Paylin) of York, where his eldest son was born; 2nd, Elizabeth, daughter of Mr. John Dickson (not Dixon), town clerk of Pontefract. By his first wife, he had

1. John, his eldest son, and successor in the vicarage, bapt. 9 Jan., 1677-8, at the church of St. Mary, Bishophill jun., York, born before his grandfather's death; he was also prebend of Holme archiepiscopi, York, and rector of Kirk Smeaton, which he held together with Pontefract.
2. Frances, baptised at Pontefract, Nov 30, 1680. She was the second wife of Rev. Thos. Barnard, master of the Grammar School, Leeds, whose first wife had been Ann, daughter of the Rev. Mr. Benson, of St. Peter's, Leeds, sister of the wife of Rev. Samuel Drake.
3. Thomas, baptised at Pontefract, Feb. 23, 1681-2, buried April 22, 1685.
4. Hannah, baptised at Pontefract, March 6, 1682-3, where she was married July 3, 1715, to Rev. F. Lascelles. They had issue—Mary, buried 24 March, 1715-6, whose baptism was not recorded; Thomas, baptised March 26, 1717; Francis, baptised Jan. 28, 1718-9, buried the following March 25th; Hannah, baptised May 4, 1720; Dorothy, baptised June 7, 1721, buried May 18, 1723; and Francis, baptised 11 July, 1723.
5. Francis, baptised at Pontefract, May 20, 1684, buried July 2, 1689.
6. Anne, baptised at Pontefract, Jan. 31, 1685-6, buried Feb.13, 1686-7.
7. Nathan, baptised at Pontefract, Jan. 6, 1686-7, buried July 5, 1689.
8. Samuel, privately baptised April 23, 1688, (B.A. 1707, M.A. 1711, B.D. 1718, D.D. 1724,) who became rector of Treeton, a parish adjoining Hansworth, in 1728, and had from 1733, a dispensation to hold with it the vicarage of Holme in Spalding-more. This Dr. Samuel Drake published in 1729, or 1730, an elegant edition of Archbishop Parker's *De Antiquitate Britannicæ Ecclesiæ*, originally printed in 1572. A fine copy of the original in the British Museum, bound in embroidered velvet, appears to have been the Queen Elizabeth's presentation copy. Dr. S. Drake died on March 5, 1753.
9. William, "Captain of a Man of War," baptised at Pontefract, June 20, 1689, who was father of Edward Drake, of York, Surgeon, and may have been father also of "Francis, son of Mr. William Drake," who was buried at Pontefract, 10 July, 1721.

Mr. Francis Drake's first wife died within a fortnight of the birth of her last child, this William, and was buried with her son, Francis, on July 2, 1689.

His second wife, Elizabeth Dickson, had been baptised at Pontefract, Sept. 19, 1671, and was consequently only 23 years old at their marriage in 1694, he being 40. By her he had

(1). Francis (his second of that name, and the author of Eboracum), baptised at Pontefract, January 22, 1695-6, married 19 April, 1720, Mary, third and youngest daughter of George Woodyeare, of Crookhill, Doncaster, She died 18 May, 1728, but he survived till 1771, when he died, leaving two sons,—(1) Dr. Francis Drake (baptised June 5, 1721, at St. Michael's, York,) fellow of Magdalen, vicar of Womersley, and first lecturer of Pontefract, who was afterwards both vicar of St. Mary's, Beverley, and rector of Winestead, in Holderness. (2) William, the younger, who went south. He was in succession third master of Westminster, head master of Felstead, and vicar of Isleworth; and married, his second cousin, Mary, daughter of Nathan Drake, a minor canon of Lincoln, one of the sons of the rector of St. Peter's, Nottingham. This William inherited his father's antiquarian tastes.

(2) Margarita Martina, baptised at Pontefract, Nov. 23, 1698.

We trace no arms for either the Drakes or the Dicksons at the Heraldic Visitations, but when Mrs. Francis Drake (née Woodyeare) died, a monumental tablet was placed in St. Michael's Church, York, to her memory, bearing the following shield :—

1 and 4, ARGENT; a wyvern, GULES—for Drake.

2 and 3 GULES; a cross charged with 5 ogresses between 4 eagles, displayed, OR—for Dickson; Impaling,

SABLE; Semée de lis OR, 3 leopard's faces, two and one, ARGENT,—for Woodyeare.

There is no apparent authority for this use of the red wyvern by any of the Yorkshire Drakes; for exactly that bearing was confirmed in 20 James I. to Francis Drake, of Buckland, in the county of Devon, when he was created baronet; and there could be no pretence of a descent or inheritance, by Francis Drake, of York, from Francis Drake, of Buckland. But the arms have been adopted by many of the branches.

Mr. Francis Drake was buried at Pontefract, July 3,

1713, having died in his sixtieth year. He seems to have been an energetic, active and conscientious vicar, and at his death had held the preferment for above 34 years.

John Drake, who succeeded his father as vicar, the third of the name in lineal descent, was born at York, to which city his mother as we have said belonged. He married Elizabeth Parsons, of Colchester, and had by her

(1). Elizabeth, baptised at Pontefract, April 13, 1715 ; married Christopher Fenton, of Hunslet ; died 14 Jan., 1772.

(2). John, baptised at Pontefract, April 7, 1716, buried June 18, same year ; and

(3). Palin, baptised at Pontefract, Aug. 20, 1718, buried the following 11th Oct.

Elizabeth, his wife, was buried at Pontefract Jan. 5, 1718-9, but he himself survived till November, 1742, having been in 1725 presented to the living of Kirk Smeaton, the chancel of which church he, ten years afterwards, "repaired and beautified," in somewhat of the manner in which such reparations and beautifyings were then usually made.

With him ended the Vicar Drake succession, in the last male of the first marriage of Mr. Francis Drake. But ten years after its termination with his decease in 1742, there commenced a secondary succession of, as they may be styled, Lecturer Drakes, who sprang from the second marriage of the vicar Francis, and filled an office, the origin of which was thus occasioned.

The tithes of the parish would have been, as they were very generally in other places, amply sufficient for the maintenance of the services of the church, the distribution of alms, and the other usual calls upon such property, had they remained attached to the benefice. But very shortly after the Conquest, there crept in the practice of "appropriating" the tithes of a parish to some monastery, the monks of which undertook the responsibility of supplying the spiritual wants of the people. In this district the Priory of St. Oswald, Nostell, was the greatest offender in that respect, absorbing a considerable portion of the revenues of most churches in its neighbourhood. But in Pontefract the Priory of St. John received, among others, the " appropriation" of All Saints' Church, with the obligations attached. It may be easily imagined that this led to great abuses, not the least of which would be the appointment of one of the body of the appropriating monks to a perfunctory and comparatively inexpensive discharge of the duties of the cure. As regards Pontefract, as a matter of fact, it is found that in the middle of the thirteenth century the custom had been established here of appointing *vicars* of All Saints; i.e., permanent priests to perform the divine services, in place of the monks *(vice)*, and probably also at whatever starvation pittance these latter chose to allow. But in 1361, in the reign of Edward III, the Archbishop interposed, insisting that the vicar should be resident, and although appointed by the monks, independent of them. The consequence was that an ordination was made that the vicar should receive for ever 30 marks yearly, out of the profits of the benefice; and in 1452, a further ordination was made, which fixed the vicar's stipend at 20 marks, and a house, called Bailey Place, with the garden adjoining.

Now the great evil of all such fixed stipends is that they remain stationary, while the value of the property out of which they rise, and of everything else, advances. Thirty marks (£20) was a large amount in 1361; twenty marks (£13 6s. 8d.) and a house, was not so valuable in 1452; while in 1539, at the suppression of the monastery of St. John, it was still less valuable in proportion. At that time the property of the rectory (which had been appropriated to the monks) being seized by the King, was leased at once for £32 14s, which instead of being devoted to its original purpose, the support of the Church, went into the King's treasury. The vicarage was still worth only its £13 6s. 8d., at which sum it might have remained to this day, had not the "small" tithes been added, by some means not now to be ascertained. These naturally increased in value, though only with the increased value of property. In 1705, they were worth less than £50, and by 1800 their value had increased to £90, with a steady annual improvement, which being about in proportion to the increase in the value of money, was virtually no increase at all. But they were never more than barely enough to provide for the maintenance of the parish clergyman; and manifestly insufficient to enable him to maintain a curate. Their inadequacy naturally led to the introduction of the wretched system of pluralities, here as in other places. While holding the vicarage of Pontefract, Samuel Drake was rector of Hansworth and John Drake was vicar of Smeaton. In such cases, when the two churches were near each other, "single" services, alternately morning and evening, became a frequent practice; the consequent neglect of the people occasioning the spread of dissent which the eighteenth century was destined to witness.

But in Pontefract another provision was shortly made. It was formerly not considered the duty of parish priests to deliver sermons, and even in our present Prayer Book there is no order for any except for one in the course of the Communion Service; but when from the growth of religious enquiry among the people, sermons began to be sought, voluntary efforts to provide additional clergy to supply the want were occasionally made; among other places at Pontefract, by Dr. Marmaduke Fothergill, the then owner of Friar Wood, a non-juror, who seems to have had religious scruples as to retaining the ownership of that property since it had once been dedicated to religious uses. Accordingly, by deed dated Jan. 3, 1716-7, he conveyed it to the Archbishop of York, in trust to support and maintain a catechist in the chapel of St. Giles, or in the parish church of Pontefract, when rebuilt. This, however, was not to take effect until the death of both the donor and his wife, (Mr. Marmaduke Fothergill married Mrs. Dorothy Dickson, Jan. 13th, 1706-7), the survivor of whom was to appoint the first catechist, whose duties, other than catechising, were to be fixed by the Archbishop. There was a further reservation in the original deed that the vicar should not be catechist, nor should the catechist be vicar.

Dr. Fothergill died in 1731, but his widow survived till 1753, and by her will she nominated as the first catechist, Dr. Francis Drake, son of the Eboracum Francis, whose mother was her own sister; and in accordance with the provisions of the deed, the Archbishop ordained that the duty of the Lecturer should be specially to lecture every alternate Sunday evening at St. Giles's Church, which, by that time had come to be considered as the Parish Church, being legally so constituted shortly afterwards. By the name of Lecturer, accordingly, this additional functionary was known as long as his office lasted. This it did till the foundation of a new incumbency for the lower part of the town, when the office of Lecturer merged in that of Incumbent of All Saints'.

Dr. Francis Drake, the first Lecturer, married a daughter of Joshua Wilson, Recorder of Pontefract, by whom he had a son, the Rev. Francis Drake, who became the second Lecturer, and was similarly succeeded by his son Francis, the third Lecturer, who, in 1821, exchanging his lectureship for the living of Frodingham, terminated the clerical connection of the Drakes with Pontefract, which had lasted for six generations, and rather more than a century and a half.

FACSIMILE OF A PORTION OF THE DRAKE M.S.

BY KIND PERMISSION OF F. H. DRAKE ESQ:
OF HEADINGLEY, NEAR LEEDS, A LINEAL DESCENDANT OF THE DIARIST.
The portion selected is under date May 7th & 8th 1645
with fragments belonging to the entries of May 9th, 10th and 11th see pp. 63-65.

NATHAN DRAKE'S MANUSCRIPT is a foolscap folio of 32 pages, written in double columns, in a remarkably close neat handwriting. It is in many places almost illegible from damp, having evidently had some liquid spilt upon it soon after it had been completed. The paper was in sections of five, and the two sections of which the diary consisted—there being four folios unwritten on, were sewn up roughly in part of a sheet of draft, still containing fragments of some legal pleadings. The way in which this wrappering was folded brought the wide margin, usually then as now left between the writing and the edge of the paper, to the top of the folio of the manuscript, and in the blank space thus offering itself, the "first lecturer" of Pontefract inserted the Title which follows :—

" 1644

" A Journal of the first Siege of Pontefract Castle, kept by Nathan Drake, a Gentleman Volunteer in it. I desire that this MS. in my Great Grand Fathers own Hand-Writing may never go out of the Family.

FRANCIS DRAKE."

Singularly enough the writer was great great Grandson to the diarist, not great Grandson, as he appears to think. And it is more than singular that he did not notice that the diary contained the record of two sieges : unless indeed he considered all the proceedings against Pontefract Castle in 1644 and 1645 to be one siege ; and the final siege in 1648-9 to be not as it is generally called, a third siege, but a second. The Diarist himself is, however, very clear and definite on the point.

Inside the cover, evidenced by the paleness of the ink to have been entered during the days not very long preceding the surrender, appears the following summary of the loss of the Besiegers.

Killd the first seege	Wounded	Second seege.		Killd & wounded	
60	40	3	1	1	252
5		3	2	1	123
3		4	7	1	74
30		2	4	40	—
3		2	4	4	459
3		1	4	6	
5		4	1	3	
10		26	2	2	
—		100	2	5	
160 kild & wounded		20	1	1	
140 more betwixt		00	3	1	
ferry bridge &		11	1	4	
Sherburne		3	2	2	
		11	3	3 July 8th	
		1	1		
		2	1		
		4	62		
		8	5		
		17	8		
		10	1		
		3	2		
		4	1		
		2	4		
		7	4		
		5	1		
		3	4		
		2			
		3	2		
		252	133		

And on the same page, this per contra memorandum of the loss on the side of the besieged : " 18 July" being corrected into "19th," and " in all 98" being altered into " in all 99."

<small>There is dead of men women & children of 'all deseases with those wch was killd within the castle from the 24th December 1644 till the 19 July 1645 in all 99 parsons.</small>

It will be noticed that in the table, as in that on page 24, which he made repeated but unsuccessful effort to correct, Mr Drake's reckoning is somewhat inaccurate.

The list of names which follows was evidently intended to be a complete list of the " Gentlemen Volunteers," to include those who entered the Castle in the interval between the two sieges, and to supersede a list which is found further on. Singularly enough, however, it does not include Mr. Kelham (Cellom) who is found in the early list as an alderman, which could not have been till after the death of Mr. Wilkinson, on 12 April.

For of the thirteen Pontefract Aldermen, ten (including the Mayor) entered the Castle, the only members of the Corporate body who separated themselves from their brethren being Mr Joshua Wakefield, an aged man, Mr. Robert More, and Mr. Robert Frank. There is, however, every reason to believe that Mr. Wakefield's sympathies were with the great majority of his brethren, though those of the other two seceders were with the besiegers.

The names of the members of the four divisions into which the garrison was divided are in four parallel columns, but for the sake of clearness, they have been printed here on two pages. The open volume will, however, represent their position on the manuscript, according to their respective rank. The names in the left hand column are slightly defective, owing to wear and tear in the MS., but that defect is partly supplied by a careful comparison of this list with that which it superseded.

There is moreover a copy of the Diary itself, written carefully on one side of the paper only, with a rather wide margin which has been the receptacle of many very necessary corrections. This which is on paper of the early part of the eighteenth century, may have been made by the author of Eboracum, but it has many inaccuracies, although it sometimes supplies a deficient word. But unfortunately it is not complete, and the first four pages which are missing have been supplied in a considerably later hand, that of a person who could not altogether decipher the original.

A True list of the manner of our watches undertaken by the knightes gentlemen, & wollunters in the First Seege, with the names of them as they were listed in theire squadrones & divisions.

And first by the way you may take notise of the standing officers of the Garrison.

Collonell Lowther, Governor, adjuted by the paines of his Brother Mr Robert Lowther, Lieut. Collonell Wheatlay, Lieut. Collonell Middleton, Major

Collone Grayes list.	Sr Richard Huttons list,
Collonel Gray brother to the Lod Gray of Warke	Knight, High Sherife of Yorkshire
Lieut. Coll. Darcy son to the Lod. Darcy of Hornby	Captin Constable
	Capt Musgraive
Sr Ed. Radcliffe, Baronet, pa.	Capt Standeven
Sr. Frauncis Radcliffe, p.	Capt Laiborne
Leiu. Coll. Portington	Capt Croft
Major Huddlestone	Leiut Smith
Capt. Huddlestone	Leiut Antrobus
Capt. Rodger Portington	Corronet Nailor
Ca. Grimstone	Cor. Bamford
Capt. Vavasor, pa.	Cor. Matthwman
Capt. Best, pa.	Mr Gravener
Capt. Wheatley	Mr Empson
Capt. Lumsdall, } Scots	Mr Atkinson
Capt. Seaton,	Mr Preston
Lieut. Wheatley	Mr Johnstone
Smith	Mr Massey
Lathum	Mr Madockes
Percy	Mr Taytom, ju.
....le	Georg Wentworth
Battley	James Ellison
Hoult	Peeter Swift
Cape, pa.	John Langwith
Mr John Thimbleby	Steeven Scammenden
Mr Charles Jackson	James Kendrick
Mr Tokefeild	Mr Burchell
Mr Hammerton, pa.	Mr Hopgood
Mr Stappleton, pa.	Mathew Sutton
Mr Anne, pa.	Robert Hallyfax
Mr Ratcliffe	Robert Burton
Mr Cutbert Medcaulph	William Watson
Mr Jo. Medcaulph	Thomas Walker
Mr Abbot	Edward Gauthrope
Coronet Spurgion	John Farram
Cor: Harrington	Sargiat Fether
Ensig: Harbert	John Heslam
Mr Stables, Allderman	Robert Moore
Mr Smith, Alld.	Thomas Senior
Mr Taytom, Alld.	Mr Binnes
Mr Higford	Mr Willson
Mr Wilkes	Tho. Pouke
Mr Burton	John Oxley
Mr Hey	Walter Steele
Quartemr French	Clergy to this devision
Clergy to this devision	Mr Buchanan
Mr Key	Mr Mankenhole his peculiar chaplin
Mr Oley	
Mr Buchanan Scotus	
In all 48.	In all 45.

Dinnis, Capt. Cartwright, Capt. Munra, Capt. Gerrard Lowther, Sonne to the Governor & Capt. of horse, as was also Capt. Musggreve, but those horse now turned foot & commanded by Mr Lowther.

The Gentlemen wolunteers were listed into 4 divisions, the First Commanded by Collonell Gray, the 2th. by Sr. Richard Hutton, the 3th. by Sr. Jon Romsden & the 4th by Sr. George Wentworth, who had in theire divisions these Gentlemen Followinge.

Sr. John Romsdens List.	Sr. Georg Wentworthe list.
Sr Gervis Cuttler	Sr. Thomas Bland
Leiutenant collonel Tindall	Collonel Vauhan
Major Warde	Leiutenant Collonell Wentworth
Major Wentworth (*interlined*)	Major Coppley
Captin Pilkinton	Major Beamond
Capt Morrett	Major Mountaine
Capt. Horsfold	Cap Baron Hiltons sonne (*written*
Capt. Swillovant	Captin Harris [*over* "*son*"])
Capt. Standeaven	Capt Romsden
Capt Clough	Capt Benson
Capt Beale	Capt Chadwicke
Capt Shaw	Capt. Washington
Corronet Harrington	Mr Gervise Nevill
Cor Nunnes	Mr Jo. Thimbleby, Sen. pa.
Leiutent Saivill	Mr Anne, Jun., pa.
Leiut Fleeming	Mr. Brian Stapleton
Mr Burton	Mr. Emson, sen., pa.
Mr Baumforth	Mr Hammerton, pa.
Mr Carwike	Mr Rookes
Mr Stringer	Mr Richard Lister
Mr Gascone	Mr Rusby, Allderman
Mr Pearcye, Se., pa.	Mr Oates, Alld
Mr Will. Tindoll, pa.	Mr Austwick, Alld
Mr. Hodgshon	Mr Clithrow
Mr Pearcy, Ju., pa.	Corronet Audeslay
Mr Jackson	Cor Saunderson
Mr Reeser	Leiut Cooke
Mr Georg Tindoll	Leiut Cutbert
Mr Foster	Mr Farmarie
Mr Hitchin	Mr Allott
Mr Scillito, Maior	Mr Fenton
Mr Tho. Wilkinson, All.	Joseph Oxley
Mr Jo. Wilkinson, All.	Rich. Pilckliffe, pa.
Mr Lunne, Ald.	Danyell Feilding
W . . . Strickland (? *Mr. on an*	Tho. Biggleskeike
Nathan Drake [*erasure*]	Tho Motherby
Peeter Heaton	Gilbert Gray
David Morrett	Richard Dobson
Steven Standeven	Rich. Beamond
Georg Scillito	Clergy to this company
John Oxley	Dor. Bradley
Clergy to this devision	Mr Lister
Mr. Pickrin	Mr Massom
Mr Hirst	Mr Burley
Mr Sickes	In all 44.
Mr Corkor	
In all 46.	

These names are all written in the ink which came into use about May 10 : that which was used in the earlier part of the siege being of a much better black.

The diarist's care to distinguish the "Papists" by the affix "p" or "pa" is noticeable, as is the fact that he records the name of no Roman Catholic Priest. It is probable, however, that the Roman Catholics at this time worshipped with the members of the English Church. But there seem to have been two "preachers" of the name of Buchanan ; one of them being a Scotsman, and so distinguished ; that is, apparently, a Presbyterian.

This List—the so called "true list" is evidently later than the superseded, and by implication, inaccurate list, which contained the names of Capt. Waterhouse, of Netherton, killed at the opening of the first siege on 27 December, Capt. Browne killed in the Barbican on 21 January, and Capt. Redman killed 21 March, at the beginning of the second siege. As the name of Capt. Benson, who went to Sandal Castle on May 14 and seems not to have returned to the Castle, is included, it is probable that the date of the compilation of the list is exactly what we have already inferred from the colour of the ink, before the beginning of May. It is singular that the "true list" does not contain the name of Capt. Flood, whose very distinguished conduct on several occasions is narrated during the progress of the narrative ; it gives only two Pearcyes, two Annes, and two Hamertons, while the former list had three of each ; it has a second Lieut. Smith, but omits Lieuts. Gibson and Collinson, Mr. Musten, Mr. Currer, Mr. Seaton, Mr. Foster and one of the Mr. Masseys.

But on the other hand it contains several names which do not appear on the early list: the "Governor's brother" Mr. Robert Lowther,—there were thus three of that family concerned in the defence of Pontefract Castle— Colonel Gray, brother to Lord Gray of Wark ; a second Mr

John Thimbleby, Mr. Metcaulph, and Mr. Stappleton ; Mr. Ratcliffe, Mr. Higford, Mr. Wilkes, Mr. Burton, Mr. Hey, Quartermaster French, a second Capt. Standeven, Mr. Madockes, Mr. Taytom, junr., Mr. Burchell, Mr. Binnes, Mr. Willson, a second Cornet Harrington, Lieut. Fleeming, Mr. Burton, Mr. Baumforth, Mr. Carwike, Mr Hitchin, a second Mr. Empson, Mr. Lister, Mr. Allott and Mr. Fenton; besides 34 volunteers, including the diarist himself, not of sufficient social status to be distinguished by any prefix.

It is moreover remarkable that few of the names of the defenders of the Castle, with the exception of the Aldermen, are those of Pontefract people who appear on the contemporary Church books. But the county gentry, men of mark, men of standing, men of middle age, the pith and pick of the aristocracy, the remains of the former generation, came forward freely. Nathan Drake himself, we might have judged to have been of mature middle age by the style of his handwriting, had not the fact been easily ascertainable from other sources; for he retains many old-fashioned peculiarities then going out of use. His *y* is for instance frequently shaped in the fifteenth and sixteenth century style, like a long *z*—his *th* had not yet assumed the form of *y*, which was general fifty years afterwards, and was even then coming into vogue. Other particularities of his phraseology are also very discernible. The word Ensign of the formal list, becomes Auncient in his narrative, while his use of Dauncaster, Ferry Brigge, West Chaster—for Chester —suffice to indicate the broadness of his speech, as clearly as " green sawse," " the graft," and similar homely expressions show that he was a West Riding man.

Of the clergy to either of the divisions, we recognise only Dr Bradley—rector of Ackworth and Castleford,—in the fourth company, as being connected with this neighbourhood. Mr Mankenhole, "his peculiar chaplin", was of course, chaplain to the high sheriff.

On the other side of the leaf, and still in advance of the narrative of the siege proper, in the inferior ink, and evidently all written at the same time, probably as a compilation from original memoranda, are the following particulars of the number of shot fired by the besiegers, and the progress of the siege. These particulars are thus introduced:—

The enemy begunne to play with theire Cannon against Pontefract Castle upon Fridday morning before Sunrising, being the 17th January 1644 [1644-5].

Theire Cannon was planted upon the west end of the Castle upon Mr. Lumne's back yeard.

Fridday	Saturday	Sunday	Munday	Tewsday		
6 4 5 5	5 5 3 4	4 4 4 4	2 2 2 2	2 5 5	Wedensday	0 3
5 4 5 5	6 5 4 4	4 4 4 4	1 4 2 3	2 5 5	that night	3
5 4 5 5	6 3 4 3	4 4 4 4	1 3 2 5	2 4 5	Thursday	0
5 4 5 4	6 5 4 3	4 3 5 4	2 2 3 2	2 5 4	that night	3
6 3 3 4	6 5 3 4	4 4 4 4	1 2 3 3	3 5 5	Fridday	2
4 4 5 5	5 5 4 3	4 4 5 4	1 2 2 4	2 5 5	Saturday	1 5
5 4 5 4	5 4 4 3	4 4 3 4	2 1 3 1	3 5 5	Munday	1
5 4 5 5	5 5 4 3	4 4 2 3	1 2 2	3 5 5		
5 4 3 5	5 2 4 3	4 4 2 4	1 2 2	3 5		2 7
4 4 4 5	5 4 5 4	3 4 3 4	1 2 2	3 5		1 8 9
5 4 4 5	5 4 4 4	4 4 3 4	2 2 2	3 5		1 4 4
5 4 5 5	5 5 5 4	4 4 3 4	1 2 3	4 4		2 8 2
5 4 5 5	5 5 4 5	4 4 4 5	1 4 3	5 5		3 4 8
5 4 5 4	5 4 4 5	3 4 4 3	2 4 2	5 5		4 0 0
5 4 5 5	5 5 4	4 4 4 5	1 2 2	5 5		
5 4 4 5	5 5 4	4 4 4 4	2 2 2	5 5		1 3 9 0
5 4 4 5	5 5 4	4 4 4	2 2 3	5 6	Feb 4th	0 0 0 3
4 5 5 5	4 5 4	4 4 4	2 2 2	5 5	12th	0 0 0 3
4 5 5 5	5 5 5	3 4 4	4 2 2	—	16th	0 0 0 2
4 5 5 5	5 4 3	—	4 2	1 8 9	Shroove 18	0 0 0 2
3 5 5 5	5 3 3	2 8 2	—		Tewsday	
5 5 5 0	5 5 5		1 4 4		26th	0 0 0 3
					28th	0 0 0 3
4 0 0	3 4 8					
	3 les	2 7 5	1 2 2	1 8 6		1 4 0 6
				4		

After this tabular list follow a series of memorandums, the first of which fills the centre of the page, as follows:—

Sunday, being the 19th January, 1644 (1644-5)
Pip' Tower fell about 9 a Clock in the Morning, ther having beene 78 shott made that morning before it fell.

REMAINS OF NEW HALL. MARCH 31ST 1885.

Then follow other statements of particulars with regard to the employment of artillery, to the record of which the whole of this page is devoted. The doings of "the Enemy" and "the Beseeged" are entered in parallel columns as follows :—

> About the beginning of May, the enemy brought againe a long Drake, belonging to Sr John Saivell, and planted hur upon Baghill upon the Southside of the Castle, and there she played about 8 shott, and then they Conveyed hur away.
> The 20th June the Enemy brought againe a dimiculverin bearing a bullitt of 18 lb. weight. she was brought to New hall that day, and the 21th day at night they brought hur to Munkhill on the Northside of the Castle, where they planted hur that night agt the Church, & the 22th Day being Sunday.
>
> The 22th day they playd .. 13 Cannon
> The 23th day they playd .. 60
> That night they playd 01
> The 24th day they playd .. 01
> The 26th day they playd .. 02
> The 27th day they playd .. 01
> July The 2th day they playd .. 01
> The 5th day 02

Thus its first attack was a deliberate assault on the Church, the Diarist evidently intending to lay special stress upon the use of the demiculverin being inaugurated on Saturday night, and during the Sunday.

And it is remarkable that this, the first mention of the active proceedings of Sir John Savile against the Castle, escaped transcription in the Surtees Copy.

> The beseegeds Cannon
>   playd the First
>   seege
> There was play from the
> Castle to the enemy in the Towne
> and about the towne from
> the 24th December (*erasure*)
> 1644 till the 1th March
> Following, in all .. (not filled in)
>
> The beseeged playd againe
> the Second seege from the
> 21th March, 1644 to the (*blank*)
> July, 1645, in all .. (not filled in)

AND THEN commences the diary proper, every page being written on both sides, and in double columns, each containing from 65 to 70 lines, the details of the doings of either side being generally suitably headed, as in the first paragraph,

Beseeged.

Uppon Christmas day, 25th December, 1644, Pontefract Castle was beseeged & the towne taken that day by the beseegers, and the beseeged playd 3 Cannon against them. the 26th & 27th, 16 Cannon. the 28th, being Saturday, the beseegers tooke the low Church about 7 of the Clock in the morning, wherein was 11 men & boyes : that day the beseeged made 3 Sallyes downe to the low Church wth losse of 3 men being killed in the Church yeard and 11 men more wounded, whereof are dead since Captin Waterhowse of Netherton & 3 other men more. the rest are all recovered againe, & the beseeged playd that day 11 Cannon, but what was killed (by the *erased*) or wounded of the beseegers at that time (is not knowne, but the Constant report is that *erased*) we had an account the same night that (*substituted in a faint ink*) there was (100 *erased*) 40 (*substituted*) wounded men Caryed away, & there was (many *erased*) 60 (*substituted*) kill'd within the Church & church yeard at the same instant by the beseeged.

The 29th day being Sunday, those 11 men & boyes having beene 5 daies in the steeple without meat or drinke (both being left in the Church by the beseegers suddeyne aproach) they Came all down the west end of the Church by a roape. at wch time Joshua Walker (their Captin) was shott into the thigh (but since recovered) and one other of them killed in the Churchyeard. All the rest escaped without any hurt at all. that day & the 30th & 31th, the beseeged shott 15 Cannon.

Pontefract Church has a remarkable double staircase round a single newel, which, entered from the nave,—the outside of the present Church,—admitted to the roof, and gave access to a second staircase opening below, under the tower. From the wording of the diary, it would appear that the 11 men and boys, not being able to descend either of these staircases, made their way across the roof of the nave, and descended at the west end. A small turret at the south-west angle probably helped them in their adventure.

January 1th, 2, 3 & 4th, the beseeged sott 15 Cannon.

Sunday, 5th. Mr. Pattison was killed upon the topp of the round tower, being shott into the head wth a muskitt bullit from the beseegers.

Mr Pattison's name does not appear in either of the lists of the names of the garrison.

the 6, 7, 8th, the beseeged plaid 12 peses of Cannon into sev'rall places of the towne. the 9th being Thursday, the beseeged plaid one Cannon against Newhall, wheare it broke a hoale into the wall & one of the stones hitt genrall Forbus on the face but was but a little hurt. that day the beseeged playd 10 Cannon. the 10th, 11, 12, 13, 14 & 15th, the beseeged plaid 24 Cannon into sev'all places of the towne. the 16th day the beseeged playd 1 cannon into the Closes below the Towne, amongst the Cutters up of Clottes, but what was killed is not knowne, but they Came there no more, & the beseeged plaid 6 Cannon more: and during all this time there was 15 sling peeses shott. There is in all 128 Cannon shott to this day.

These Closes below the town were probably the part called Denwells; then in a very great measure common. The piece was in 1657 leased to Mr William Oates with a special reservation of the right of the Inhabitants of the Town to fetch water from the well, and to bleach clothes there. (See Booke of Entries, pp. 36, 181, 304.)

The 17th day, the beseegers begunne to play wth their Cannon against the Castle. The 17th, 18, 19 & 20th the bese'd playd 16 Cannon. The 21th, Captin Browne was killed in the Barbican with a muskitt bullitt from the beseegers. about that time was one John Spence killed in the barbican by overcharging his owne muskitt wch burst & killed him.

Neither of these names appears in the lists.

From the 22th to the 31th, the beseeged playd 18 Cannon.

Feb 1th. The beseeged plaid 4 Cannon. from the 2th February to the 15th, there was 29 Cannons Drakes and Sling peeses shott. the same day was the howses behind Mr. Wakefeildes set on fire; & there was shott of those from (Constable T *erased*) Swillinton Tower 5 drakes to the hospitall, and 12 Sling peeses was shott from Sevrall places. 16th, 3 peeses of Cannon. the 17th, 3 Sling peeses (from the 2th *erased*).

This slip in writing Constable Tower, instead of Swillington Tower is remarkable, from the fact that Leland did the same. It is quite possible that the advance tower, which we now call Swillington Tower, was at one time really called indifferently Swillington's or Constable's, the then Constable being a Swillington. There is, however, no doubt, that in Drake's time, it was called by the name which he deliberately selected. The remark, moreover, tends to prove that the Tower was of some considerable height, since it must have rather overlooked "The Hospitall," *i.e.*

that of St. Nicholas. Only "Drakes" are here mentioned as having been shot from Swillington Tower.

This entry concludes the first column of the first page of the diary: the second being again headed,
Beseeged.

Feb 18th, being Shrove tewsday, the beseeged shott 2 peeses of Cannon (from *erased*) Into the Sentry howses at the lower end of Northgate wch was then set on fire by the beseegers, & 1 Cannon into the Markit place, & the beseeged killd that day 5 men out of the round tower into their workes from wardes howse along the ditch wth muskitt shott. the 19th day, the beseeged killd a Captin in the said workes. the 20th, one of our men was shott thorough both the Cheekes in the barbican but not kild. that day the beseeged shot one (cannon *erased*) Sling peese.

21th, the beseeged shott 3 Sling peeses & kild 2 men that day. 22th, the beseeged shott 2 Cannon into the markit place & what wth the cannon & muskittes the beseeged killd above 30 men in Sevrall places. 23th, the beseeged killd 3 men. 24th, the beseegers killd one of our men in the barbican being shott thorow the head wth a muskitt bullitt and Captin Smith had his lippe Cut wth a stone wch was broke wth a muskitt bullit, but very little hurt. that day we playd 1 Cannon into the Parke where 3 men was seene to fall of the beseegers. (the 26th *erased*) that day there was 11 Sling peeses shot by the beseeged and divers muskittes, & killd 5 or 6 men of the beseegers. 25th, the beseeged killd many men in divers places. 26th, the beseeged shott 3 Cannon into the markitt place & 1 Cannon to the beseegers gunnes where many of the beseers men was killd, & that day there was killd Captin Maullett upon the top of the round tower, being shott into the head with a muskit bullit. 27th, the beseeged shott many muskitts but what was killd is . . . 28th. the beseegers fired Elizabeth Cattell's howse & the howses below Munkhill, and that day the beseeged shot 4 Cannon into the Markitt place & is thought did great execution. That night the beseegers tooke away all their Cannon & marched over Ferry brigge.

Elizabeth Cattell was the second wife of Thomas Cattell, who had been Mayor of Pontefract in 1603. She had been his widow since 1621, and occupied that part of the Greave Field called Cattle Laith. It was enclosed some thirty years after her death. According to the Fee Farm Book of 1649, her house was a quarter Burgage in Walkergate.

March 1th, Saturday. the beseeged shott 12 Cannon to the beseegers when they was Drawing of their Armye from divers p'tes both into the towne & about the towne, and noate this, that there was not one day that the Castle was beseeged, but that there was summe of the beseegers killd by the beseegedes muskitts besides those was killd wth the beseegedes Cannon. there was shott from the 17th January to the 1th of March, 96 Cannon, & from the 25th December till the 17th January 128 Cannon; in all, to the 1th of March, 224 Cannon.

Here the Diarist allowed a considerable interval before

resuming his narrative, as if the greatness of the coming news deserved to be emphasized with a rhetorical pause. Resuming, he gives a graphic account of the battle in the Chequer field, which was an open common lying between Pontefract and Carleton, and apportioned between those two townships. It had been formerly of much more considerable extent, but at this time was being gradually absorbed and enclosed, sold in fact in allotments, by the respective townships. It lay for the most part between Church Balk Lane, and Darrington Lane, and included the Swanhill flat.

The graphic account of the battle which follows, and little of which could really have been seen from the Castle at that season of the year, though the horror of it can be imagined, continuing as it did on March 1 from " almost 6 " in the evening, about twilight, till 10 or 11 " in the night." There must thus have been at least three or four hours' fighting in the dark.

About 3 of the Clock, Sr Marmaduke's forelorne hope did appeare upon the topp of the hill on this side wentbridge, and so marched, one Company after another, till his whole Army Came all into the Chequor feild, where both the Armyes mett, & faced one another till all most 6 of the Clock, the Parlament Armye allwaies giving ground (when Sir Marmadukes Armye advanced) till they Came to their foot wch they had placed, and lyned the Long hedge from Englandes howse to the hill toppe, where the first encounter begunne (with *erased)* very furiously, the enemyes foot (behind the hedge) giving fire upon the front of our horse very valiantly, wch was soone asswaged, for then our foot (from the Castle—*interlined in faint ink*, as are several additions in the following paragraphs which will be thus (*) distinguished) Coming on & the horse Charging wth the foot 4 or 5 times, recovring the hedge from them, beat them quite away towardes ferry bridge, Continually Charging them all the way, there being left dead and wounded upon the ground about 160 men. And at Ferry bridge the enemy playd 3 times wth one Cannon, viz. 2 Case shottes & 1 Cannon bullitt, killed there 4 of our men, but we bett them from their Cannon, & tooke it (* & brought it away, &) Followed them in Chase betwixt Shearburne & Tadcaster, killd 140 of their men (as is reported) in the Chase, tooke 600 prisoners, Commaunders & officers, 57; doble barrells of powder 47, (* Containing 124 lb. a peece); Armes 1600; Collores both horse & foot above 40; and many wounded men brought & many dead since, & we lost not above 20 men in all the fight, the enemy being allmost 6 for one. there was brought in to the Castle neare upon 20 (originally written 40) Cariages wth all their match, (* muskits, pikes,) bullits, & all other p'vition, & many packes taken in the Chase, and the Plunder of the feild was to the Souldyers & to the Contrey about. Sr Marmaduke Langdale Coming into the Castle betwix 10 & 11 of the Clock in the night, having quartered his horse in the townes about, and he Continued about the towne, refreshing of his men, till the Munday Following, being the 3th March, at wch time he marched away wth the most of all his horse & foot.

That Nathan Drake was personally concerned in this battle, may be deduced from his use of the first person throughout ; and his efforts to arrive at the exact truth, and to overstate nothing, are evident from his many interlineations and corrections.

He concludes this account of the doings of the besieged with the following memorandums, added at some subsequent time.

During this time of the seege there went out of this Garrison to Newarke wth Captin Tulley 140 horse and men (the 8th January *interlined*).

There went also wth Mr Corker at another time to the Prince out of this Garrison during this seege 16 men and horse

the 6th of February : he was the onely man that p'cured Sr. Marmaduke Langdall to Com to releeve us, wch was p'formed the 1th March.

Mr Corker was a Preacher. That the name of Mr Tulley does not appear in the "True List" is another indication of its having been compiled subsequent to his departure on January 8.

Another gap is left in the MS., apparently to afford space for any additional notes of events that might occur to the writer, who then proceeds to give an orderly account of the doings of the Besiegers.

Beseegers.

The 16th January the enemy brought into the Markitt place in Pomfret 6 peese of Cannon the same wch had beene at Hemslay & Knavesbrough before, one Carying a bullitt of 42 li. weight, another 36 li., 2 other 24 li. a pese, & the least 9 li. we hearing they would plant them against Pip' tower & betwixt that & the Round Tower where there was a hallow place all the way downe to the well, the gentlemen & Souldyers fell all upon Carrying of earth & Rubbish & so filled up the place in a little space ; and we rammed up the way that passed through pip' Tower w'th Earth 4 or 5 yeardes thick.

It is surprising that here is no mention of the semicircular erection, the base of which has been recently opened out in front of Piper Tower. The inference is that it must have been levelled and destroyed long before the time of this siege. The well has not yet (June, 1883) been discovered), but in this passage, there are many data that may assist in the search for it. Betwixt Piper Tower and the Round Tower is "a hollow place," hollow "*all the way* DOWN to the well." The well was then evidently much —*all* the way—lower than the upper part of the hollow place. This "hollow place" was filled up by the gentlemen and soldiers with earth and rubbish; after which they "rammed up the way that passed through Piper tower with earth 4 or 5 yeards thick." This last has been cleared out; the rest remains to be done.

Piper Tower, the remains of which are a good example of early wide-jointed Norman, was the only Tower that gave way to the battery brought against it.

Along the margin between the columns of this page of the Diary, the writer appended an addition—always in the faint ink used in May and June,—comprising some illustrative information omitted when he made his daily record.

Beseegers.

1644, Jan. Upon Fridday, the 17th January, the beseegers begun to play wth their Cannon about 7 of the Clock in the morning. that day they playd 400.

18th, they playd 348. the 19th, 286 Cannon. This day, about 9 of the Clock, was piper's tower beaten downe, by wch fall, a breach was to be made into the Castle wall, & which fall 2 Brothers of the Briggses of the haulphpeny howse was killd, and 3 or 4 much hurt, but they are all againe since recovered, and 27 of the beseegers men blowne up wth (their *interlined*) owne powder by a shott from the Castle wch hitt their match & so struck fire into the pouder.

There is here an addendum along the margin:

Our men went out every day into the graft & fecht in theire bullets for 4*d.* a peece.

The diary resumes:

The 20th they shott 144 Cannon. 21th, 189. 22th 3, & 3 in the night. 23th. that night 3. 24th. that night 2. Saturday, 25th. 15 Cannon. 27th. 1 Cannon. In all to this day 1349, (1390 written over in the faint watery ink) and not any (more *interlined*) cannon shott made since till the 1th Feb. nor not any one man killd wth the Cannon bullitt, nor any man hurt wth the Cannon bullitt, but one James Ellyate (the little gunmaker of Yorke,) who had his Arme bruised wth a stone (burst wth the Cannon bullitt,) & so p'sently Cut of, wch is since well againe.

4th day 2 Cannon & 1 in the night. The beseegers playd no more wth their Cannon till the 12th February and then they shott 3 Cannon without any hurt at all to the beseeged. The beseegers have now shott 1400 cannon against (obliterated).

The following is the addendum to the above:—

reeede from this place Feb 1, in the 5th and 6th leafe, and then beginne againe.

The reference is to the correspondence between General Fairfax, General Forbes, and Colonel Lowther, which will be found a few pages forward.

16th day they shott 1 Cannon. Shrove .... 18th, 2 Cannon witho' any hurt.

The copy of the Diary omits this word Tuesday, showing that the injury to the original is of very old date.

Munday, 24. There came marching over Fe..........(evidently Ferrybridge,) 6 Collors, 250 men to the beseegers, (:...? one) haulph marching thorow the Parke to the Towne, and the other haulph throrow the Frealles to the Church, the beseeged giving them a kind salutation from the Castle, and the beseegers gave 2 valley of Shott about 7 of the Clock at night, wch the beseeged thought was at the funrall of Summe great commaunders. the 26th, the beseegers shott 3 cannon without any hurt to the beseeged. the 27th, the beseegers shott 3 Cannon wthout any hurt to the beseeged. the 28th they shott 3 Cannon w'thout any hurt. but the beseeged had one man shott thorow the Caulph of his legg wth a muskitt bullitt in the barbican, but wthout any danger of death. that night the beseegers drew of their Cannon and begunne to march wth it away, having shott 1406 Cannon against the Castle.

A third addendum in the margin is as follows :—

the First night after they begunne to shoote, was Capt Munroe & Capd Laiborne sent out to vew how farre they had Battered in the wall, wch the found to be a yeard & a yeard haulph, whereupou our men was commanded to Carry earth to strengthen the wall within, wch was done wth all speede.

Here again the Diary makes a fresh start :—

One thing was forgott wch is now heare inserted for. After that the Enemy was weary wth bursting their Gunnes wth Battery of the Castle upwardes towardes heaven & see that they Could not p'vailed that way, then they Came to be p'tners wth Guydo Faulkes to dive downewardes to the divell, to undermine us & to blow us up by their sevrall mines, where of one mine was below Wardes howse under the moate of the Castle towardes the Round tower, another within the Hospitall towardes the Kinges Tower ; making their boastes that they would bestow 100 barrells of powder upon us to blow us up, but, we p'ceiving theire intentions, we answered them at theire owne weapones and myned as fast as they, sinkinge in s'verall places wthin the Castle & mining from thence and allso wthout the Castle walles neare to the Castle. We had allso made 2 sev'all Traverses wthin the Castle yeard very strong & to good purpose wch was volentarely p'formed by the volentary Gentlemen within the Castle, and allmost quite finished at the time of our releese when Sir Marmaduke Langdale Came to releeve us.

We sunke 8 (*altered into* 11 or 12) Pittes in sevrall places from whence we mined under the Castle walles that we Could have mined from one place to another round about the Castle if neede had required, and so have prevented all their plottes.

With which innocent bit of braggadocio the original Diary ends. We may add that no trace of these mines has yet been met with, and knowing what we now know of the depth and strength of the Castle walls, especially those towards the Hospital, and that the garth was solid rock, faced with masonry, it is difficult to understand how the besieged could have thought they had undermined it. Such undermining would have been, with their means, an impossibility.

The next column is divided, to receive the original nominal list of the Garrison, afterwards superseded by the more correct " true list" (see pp. 20-21). It is as follows, and is thus headed :—

A list of all the Vollunteres as were in Pontefract Castle, the 25th Decemb'r 1644.

Collonells.
Coll Lowder, gov'nor
Coll Hutton
Coll Romsden
Coll Wintworth
Coll Cuttler
Coll Gray
Coll Vawhan
Coll Middleton
(Called Lieut-Col. in the revised list.)
Knightes.
Sr Thomas Bland
Sr Frauncis Ratcliff
Sr Edward Ratcliffe
Leiutenant-Collonells.
L C Wheatelay
L C Wintworth
L C Darcey
L C Tindall
L C Portington
Maiors.
Ma Beamont
Ma Hudlestone
Ma Mountaine
Ma Wintworth
Ma Copplay
Ma Warde
Ma Dinis
Preachers.
Dor Bradley
Mr Hirste
Mr Lister
Mr Kay
Mr Pickrin
Mr Corkor
Mr Masham
Mr Sikes
Mr Oley
Mr Burley

Mr Manknehole
(Mankenhole in the revised list,—the Sheriff's private Chaplain)
Mr Buckanhanan
(Buchanan in the revised list)
Alldermen.
Mr Maior
Mr Rusby
Mr Stables
Mr Thomas Wilkinson
Mr Austwicke
Mr Taytom
Mr John Wilkinson
Mr Oates
Mr Smith
Mr Cellom
(This name does not appear in the revised list)
Mr Lunne
Captenes.
Ca Constable
Ca Mollett
(Morrett in the revised list)
Ca Hillton
Ca Hudleston
Ca Shaw
Ca Romsden
Ca Harrise
Ca Vaucer
(Vavasor in the revised list)
Ca Grimstone
Ca Washington
Ca Clough
Ca Beale
Ca Chadwicke
Ca Layborne
Ca Croft
Ca Seaton
Ca Wheatley

Ca Waterhouse
(*Killed 27 Dec.*)
Ca Pilkington
Ca Redman
(*interlined :—killed 21 March*)
Ca Horsfold (*Horsfall*)
Ca Swillavant
(*altered from Swillington*)
Ca Porlington
Ca Cartwright
(*also interlined*)
Ca Standeven
Ca Lowther
(*a third interlineation*)
Ca Lounsdale
Ca Best
Ca Cape
Ca Browne
(*Killed 21 January*)
Ca Munroe
Ca Leiu Smith
(*Lieut Smith in the revised list*)
Ca Flood
Ca Musgreve
  Leiutenants.
L Wheatley
L Saivell
L Lathome
L Hoult
L Gibson
(*not in the revised list*)
L Pearecie
L Battley
L Cooke
L Couthburt
L Collinson
(*interlined, and not in the revised list*)
L Cape
L Antropose
(*Antrobus in the revised list*)
  Corronettes
Cor Nunne
(*Nunnes in the revised list*)
Cor Harrington
Cor Audley
Cor Saunderson
Cor Naylor
Cor Baumford
Cor Spurgion
Cor Adcherman
(*Matthewman in the revised list*)
  Phisition
Dor Collinnes
  Chirurgions
Mr Gray
Mr Parker

Mr Norton
Mr Hutchinson
  Gentlemen Vollenteres.
Mr Stringer
Mr Hodgshon
Mr Gaskon
Mr Jackson
Mr Foster
Mr Reaser
Mr Harebread
(*Ensign Harbert in the revised list*)
Mr Rookes
Mr Farmarie
Mr Nevill
Mr Stappleton
Mr Thimbleby
Mr Pearcey, Sen.
Mr Pearcey, Ju.
Mr Pearcey, Frater
(*not in the revised list*)
Mr Tindall
Mr Anne, Sen.
Mr Anne, Jun.
Mr Anne, Frater
(*not in the revised list*)
Mr Tofeld
(*Tokefield in the revised list*)
Mr Emson
Mr Massey
Mr Musten
(*not in the revised list*)
Mr Atckinson
Mr Preston
Mr Johnson
Mr Hopgood
Mr Correr
(*not in the revised list*)
Mr Grauner
Mr Abbott
Mr Strikland
Mr Medcaulph
Mr Hammerton, Sen.
Mr Hammerton, Ju.
Mr Hammerton, Fra.
(*not in the revised list*)
Mr Benson
(*This may be the Capt. Benson of the revised list*)
Mr Clithrow
Mr Tindoll
Mr Seaton
(*not in the revised list*)
Mr Foster
(*not in the revised list*)
Mr Massey
(*not in the revised list*)

The names of these gentlemen volunteers are to be found recorded in every work treating of Yorkshire. We therefore take no particular notice of each individual here, considering it to be our present duty to elucidate only passages connected with Pontefract history. As moreover any worthy attempt to narrate the history of the various county families, the names of whose different members occasionally appear on these pages, would occupy far too much space, we are forced to content ourselves with making these lists as complete as possible in respect to each other and to the interesting narrative in which they occur.

It is singular that Mr Cellom (for Kelham) should have had his name inserted on this list of Aldermen, and senior to Mr Lund. For this is his only appearance on any authentic record—with one exception—that we have been able to discover. Church Books, and Town Books, equally omit to call him Alderman, and as already remarked, the aldermanic number was complete without him. The only other authority for his ever having been Alderman is Dugdale, who so styles him at the Yorkshire Visitation of 1666. As he was still living at the time, the description must have been made with his consent and approbation, which adds to the difficulties.

The page had become full when the list had reached so far as the "Chirurgeons." The "Gentlemen Volunteers," occupy the left hand margin of the dorse, the remainder of each page being filled with the following copies of documents connected with the siege, all written with a pale watery ink which was in use towards the end of the siege, and which seems to have been hardly thick enough to hold its own on the paper, as, indeed, is evinced by the large superfluity of moisture. The injuries, indicated by blanks or suggestions in parentheses, must have been of long standing, for all the copies of the Diary give some indication of its imperfection at this point, and offer conjectural emendations. Some of these are obvious, and have been here adopted; while others are not so satisfactory, for while making sense, they do not accurately fill the space lost from the original MS.

The Diarist connects the letters with a thread of narrative which gives considerable completeness to the whole account.

One thing I forgott wch heare I insert about a summons was sent by the Lord Fairfax the 16th January, the day before they begunne to play wth theire Cannon.

To the Commander in Cheife of Pomfrett Castle.—

In p'formance of the trust reposed upon me by the Parlamemt for the service of the publique and perticuler safety & preservation of this Contrie, I [have marched] p'te of the forces under my Command [to endea] vour the reducing of that Castle, wch hitherto [hath] oposed the p'lament & Infinitely p'judiced [the coun] trie, to obedience of the Kinge & Parliament: [This I] much desire may be effected without the effusion of blood, and to that end now send you this Summons to surrender the Castle to me for the service of the King and Parlament, wch if you p'sently doe, I will engage my (selfe *erased*) power wth the Parliament, for your reception Into mercy & favour therewith; but your refusing, or defarring the same, will compell me to the triall of the successe wch I hope will p'vaile for the publique good. I shall expect your answer to be returned to me by Collonell Forbes to whome I have given further Instructions in that behaulph.—

FER. FAYRFAX.

The Governor upon the recaipt of this Summons gave answer for the p'sent to the Messinger by word of mouth that the matter was of great Consequence, & would require some time to Consider of it, that he would Call the Gentlemen of the Castle being many of good qualitie & Consult wth them about it, & upon Consultation wth them he would send him an answer wch should be somtimes on the morrow at the Fordest:

Collonell Forbes to whom this answer was deliv'ed replyed that it should be wellcome to him, if it Came not too late, & this delay the governor made wth good advise, that in it he might have time to finish a battery wch he had Caused to be planted right against them, & to line the battlements & strengthen the walles on that side, for wch purpose he sett 60 men on worke the same night. Against the morning (according to his p'mise) he shapt this Answer:

According to my (p'mise *erased*) Allegiance to wch I am sworne, and in pursuance of the trust reposed in me by his Ma'tie, I will defend this Castle to the uttermost of my power, and doubt not by Godes assistance, the Justnes of (*turnes over*) The Justnes of his Ma'ties Cause, and the vertue of my Comrades, to quell all those that shall oppose me in the defence thereof for his Ma'ties service. for the blood that is like to be lost in this action, lett it be upon their heades who are the Causers of it. this is my resolution wch I desire you Certefie the Lord Fairfax from

  Pomfret Castelle,   Your affectionate frend,
  16th Jan, 1644. [1644-5.]   RICHARD LOWTHER.

But they p'vented the sending of this letter, for the next morning by that it was light they fell a battring & the same day gave us 400 shott.

The 21th January, about 11 a Clock, there Came a Drumme to the gates from Forbes and Beate a parly. word was brought to the Governor who sent to know his busines. he tould them he had a letter from Coll. Forbes to the Governor. the governor returned answer, he would receive no letters from him unlesse they would sease battering. whereupon Commaund was given that the Cannons should Cease playing. then the drumme was commaunded to go Downe to the lower gates, & then they lett him in, who brought wth him this letter following :

Sr, I desire to have a positive answer of the Summons sent in upon Thursday last, that I may give an accoumpt to my Lord (who is now heare,) of your resolutions. likewise I desire to know whether Mr [Ogales] exchanged for Leiutenant Browne, or for money, and if [for money] for what summe.
Pomfret, this 21th of   Sr, I shall remaine your
January, 1644.   frend, WILL. FORBES.

To the latter demaund in the letter the governor sent no answer at . . . writing I know not, but to that other Concerning the Summons he penned an Answer before, wch he now sent to all the Gentlemen for theire advice & to know how they likt it, & whether they would stand by him to make it good : unto wch they all assented wth (great *interlined*) allacrity, upon wch approbation he dispatcht the drumme away wth it. And supposing that upon our refusal they would have assaulted the breach, and [seeing] theire horse drawne up into a body in the Parke, and many of theire foot wth Roasemary in theire hattes, as soon as the drumme was dispacht, the Governor Commanded all the drummes to be beate and Trumpettes to sound upon the Battlements, all men Commaunded to Armes, every Squadron to theire Sev'all poastes, as they were before sett out, expecting the enemy wth as much Cheerfullnes as if they had beene going to a feast. in this posture we stood all the afternoone, theire Cannon playing all this while vehemently upon the breech & the Kinges Tower : for this day, notwthstanding the Sessation for 2 howers, they gave us 189 great shott, but theire Souldiers had no mind to the busines to enter upon the Castle in any place, seeing themselves so much deceived, for the Commanders p'swaded them that they neede not strike a stroke but that the Castle wonld be delivered upon a Summons, (now, after they had made a breach.) But they p'ceiving the Contrary, & seeing how Confident & resolute the Castle was to defend it sellfe, they were much dismayed, many of them Runnd away for feare they should be putt upon such a desparate service, whom theire horse pursued & Catt, but Could recover but some few of them. this night they gave us 4 great shott, (according to their usuall manner.) On Weddensday the 22th they weare resonable quiet, theire Ordinance Ceast playing, whether they wanted powder or thought it but wasted on us I know not, but this day & the night they gave us but 6 great shott.

and the Lord Fairfax not finding the breach so Cleare as he was Informed, & not able to gett his men to venture on it, returned to yorke againe, wthout possession of the Castle, where upon the Munday before both he & his Son Sr Thomas Fairfax Came to towne to take the honnor of the busines, and possession of the Castle, who were entertained wth great honnor & exalltation, gaurdes of horses & foot ready to receeve them, wth great showting & volly of voyces & vollyes shott ; but went away wthout either beating of drumme or sound of Trumpitt.

The succeeding parts of the Diary bear very many evidences that they were written day by day. Those additions, which are clearly so, we shall take care to point out, so that the document may fairly tell its own tale,

The next portion is headed at the top of a page
The Second Seege against Pontefract Castle,
March, 1644.

From the 1th March to the 10th there was but little done in Pontefract Castle but fetching in of Provision & other necessaryes for the use of the Castle.

upon Tewsday, the 11th March, Captin Layborne & Major Mownteynes man (went *erased*) Rid out towards Wenthill & betwixt that & Ferrybrigg tooke Mr. Ellis of Brampton, (that great Sequestrator,) & one quartermaister & brought them into the Castle.

Mr Ellis, of Brampton, "that great sequestrator" has his name well represented on the Fee Farm Book of 1650, in which a very goodly portion of the town is represented as being "late Ellis land." For several generations, members of that family had flourished in Pontefract as farmers of the lords' rents, and in similar financial capacities.

Wenthill is to the south-east of Pontefract, in Darrington township. The high road connects Wenthill and Ferrybridge.

---

the 13th. 20 or 30 of our Gentlemen went down to Turnebridge, and brought in Leiutenant Collonell Lee, and Leiutenant Collonell Ledger, and 3 gallant horses. the 15th day, there went out a p'ty of horse towardes Dauncaster and in that way they mett wth Collonell Brandlin's regiment and routed them, tooke one Major, one Captin, one Leiutenant, 3 officers, 67 Souldyers, and about 100 horse. that night allso our men went downe to Turnebridge again, and brought away from the enemyes storehowse 40 new paire of bootes wth other p'vision.

Boothroyd,—misleading as usual—interpolates "beyond Ackworth" after Turnebridge, which is in a very different direction to Ackworth. It is "beyond Snaith,"—due E., and not "beyond Ackworth," which is S.W. (See Appendix B.)

Fridday the 21th March. about 2 of the Clock in the after noone the Enemy Came in again and tooke the upp' towne, killd Captin Redma' (about the bridge *interlined*), and a Souldyer upon the toppe of the Round Tower & tooke 3 of our men prisoners. that day we shott 14 Cannon & 2 in the night, but the Lower Towne we had at liberty. they Could not beseege it upon that end, and from thence we fetch in wodde from the burnt howses & other necessaryes, the enemyes forces being not so strong by much as was thought. The truth is thought that this seege was for nothing but to keepe us (wth *interlined*) in the Castle untill they (had *interlined*) areyed men, & plundred the Contrey to p'vent the Prince's victualls at his Coming.

"The Bridge" is in the centre of the present township of Pontefract, close to the Town Hall. It was the division between the three old townships, as they might be called, Pontefract, West Chepe, and Tanshelf, the two former being *cir* 1250 merged into one. At the time of the siege, the division still existed for ratal purposes, the districts being Above Bridge and Below Bridge respectively, and separate Overseers were appointed for each. It seems remarkable that Capt Redman should have been surprised so far from the Castle, for The Bridge is above a quarter of a mile away.

The 22th we shott 15 Cannon to sevrall places & we had a woman shott thorow the hand, and a man shott thorow the thigh wth the same bullitt upon the toppe of the round tower (but neither killd). the enemy fell a trenchinge in divers places about the towne but espetially before Allderman Lunnes howse.

This then was the first day of the real siege, when the besiegers commenced their effective blockade. Ald. Lunn's house was next east to the property of the Trinities Hospital. And it will be remembered that the cannon that brought down Piper Tower were fired from his premises. The house will receive frequent subsequent mention.

The 23th, we playd 5 Cannon all into the Towne.
The 24th, 1 Cannon into the towne.
The 25th, 3 Cannon into the Parke to Will : Boothes & 1 Cannon into the towne.

"Will Booth" occupied a house in the Park, which will be mentioned again presently. But there was another "Mr" Wm. Booth in the Castle at this time. The Booths were very numerous in Pontefract, and we have collected from the Church Books between 1585 and 1660, three-quarters of a century, the names of nearly fifty belonging to above a dozen different families, no two of which can be connected without extraneous aid.

The 26th, 1 Cannon (but uncerteine what execution all these Cannon did— *added subsequently*).

The 27th, 7 Cannon, but how many men was killd wth the Cannon is not knowne, but there was 3 men killd wth muskitt bullitts.

The 28th, 2 Cannon towardes new hall. we had two of our owne men shott that day, the one by the Cock of his peese at unawares shot his next man into the thigh, & the other the barrell of his muskitt burst & so hurt him sellfe. and we killd upon 2 Sallyes forth, 1 of the enemes at Munkhill, & 2 upon Bughill.

The 29th at Night 10 Cannon, all to Mr. Rusbyes, and up that streete, but what execution was done is not knowne to us.

Mr. Rusby's was in Micklegate, (*i.e.* Horse fair), next to Mr. Lund's. Mr. Oates's Leaden Porch was opposite.

The 30th day, 2 Cannon into the towne and we had one Nicolas Baune killd wth muskitt bullitt upon the platforme by Treasurer Tower (by the Cannones mouth—*added subsequently*.)

The "platform by Treasurer's Tower" seems to have been on the upper part of an earthen bulwark, outside the Tower itself, level so as to support ordnance, and overlooking the Butts. It might have been the site of some extramural erections, perhaps of the medieval St. Clement's Chapel, destroyed at the Reformation.

The 31th, 7 Cannon into the towne & Parke and killd 3 men there. and that night Captin Smith wth 30 Souldyers did Sally forth of the Castle & burnt downe the enemyes Sentry lathe, killd them 4 men at least; and there was 3 Cannon more Shott in 2 Sev'all places of another Sentry lathe.

Apr., 1645, 1th, the beseeged killd 1 of the enemyes att Munkhill & 1 more at the low Church.

2th day, 2 horsemen rid forth & killed [and brought *supplied from the Copy*] in 2 Footmen to the Castle.

3th day, we shott 12 Cannon into the towne & 1 in the night but what was killd is not knowne, but one drummer was killd wthin a howse of serteyn.

4th day, the beseeged shott one Cannon into Mrs. Oates howse & 1 Cannon to the Sentry at Skinner lane end; and 2 cannons towardes new hall, but what hurt is not knowne. That night we Sallyed forth in 3 Companyes in all 90 men, & we shott 7 Cannon & burnt downe Allderman Rusbyes lathe (being their sentry) & p'te of his howse; killd there 1 Captin & 3 souldyers more wch was knowne; beat them from all their sentryes in the lower end of the towne. we had one man taken prisoner. They lined divers hedges betwixt the well & the Parke, & sett up their Collors, att Skinner Lane (end *erased*) head, but our Cannon from the Kings Tower beat them Downe. thus were we still Imployed on both sides.

This seems to have been a busy Good Friday. Mrs. Oates's house was in the Market Place, not far to the east of St. Giles's Church. It extended from the Market Place to Church lane, then called Pudding Middens. One side of the back premises is now owned and occupied by Mr Blackburn, tinner. The Well was Denwell, or Clerkwell, as it was sometimes called.

5th day, our horse did Sally foorth under the Commaund of Captin Washiugton & Captin Beale and 40 musquteyers under the Command of Captin Smith. our horsemen behaved themselves valiantly. ; facing a whole troope wth 5 men, made them retreate wthin the Towne & duble their number of horse and fall forth (wth *interlined*) 100 musquetears & lined th.... they gave fire freely on both sides but our men manteyned the feild bravely and took 2 butchers and their horses loaded wth flesh to the towne, before the enemyes faces, wch did very good service to the garison upon Easter day ; but, the said 5th day, we killd one man upon Baghill, & tooke another prisoner, & tooke 2 horses; and we shott 6 Cannon that day both into the Towne & other places, and that night 5 Cannon into the towne, but what hurt was done is not knowne.

This was the Pontefract market day, and thus, notwithstanding the siege operations and the constant firing of cannon, the market was held as usual, and the butchers brought in " their flesh " as if there was no such thing as war. Doubtless the Diarist was right when he reflected on the good service that the beef did to the garrison at the close of their Lenten fast; but by this time he guessed perhaps that they were about to pass through a fast of much more than Lenten austerity.

The enemy basely stayd all wine from coming to the Castle for serving of the Communion upon Easter Day, allthough Forbus (their Governor) had graunted p'tecktion for the same, and one Browne of Wakefeild said if it were for our damnation we should have it, but not for our Solvation. but that day, being Easter day, (the 6th Aprill), wch was prepared for the health of our Soules, was p'pared for the liberties of our bodyes, for, after Sarmond done att 11 of the Clock the Govern'r gave strait command that all men should p'sently be in Armes, which was as willingly done both with horse & foot. then, after a little delibration, (orders being agreed upon,) Captin Washington and Captin Beale Commanded the horse. Capt. Munro wth 50 musquetears did Sally out of Swillinton Tower up into Northgate. Captin Flood wth 50 musqutears Sallyed forth of the Lower gate, & so up by the Haulpeny howse & fell upon their trenches. Then there was 50 Gentlemen (volunteres) whereof one haulph did Second Munroe's musquetears and the other haulph Capt' Flood's. The Gentlemen weare Chosen out from the 4 Collonells wthin the Castle viz. :—Sr Richard Hutton, 12 gent' Commanded by Capt' Croft : Sr George Wintworth 10, Commanded by Leiut. Warde: Sr John Romsden 10, Commanded by Capt Benson: And Sr Jarvis Cuttler 10, Commanded by Capt Oglebie. These resolute spirites, (having received orders) Cherefully passed upon their service, entred their Trenches, gave a long & strong allarum, & returned wth honour. our Cannonears allso plaid their p'te bravelie and did good execution in the Markit place & other places in the towne. we killd in that Sally 26 men or more, tooke one prisoner, and divers muskittes & swordes & drummes, and we had 2 men killd & 2 men wounded and we shott 26 Cannon wherewth is supposed Could be no lesse then 100 men killd. But we lett them not rest thus, for the same night, about 10 of the Clock, Captin Smith, Capt' [Ratclife], & Leiutenant Wheatlay wth 100 musquitears fell upon Northgate & (so *interlined*) into the Midle streat of the towne (above their trenches) gave fearce fire amongst them and did bloody execution (*illegible erasure*) for allmost one hower, where was very many of the beseegers killd, and we had but (2 *erased*) 1 (*substituted*) man killd, (the one *erased*) his name (*substituted*) was quartermr Dawson), and (the other *erased*) one (*substituted*) a Comon Souldyer, was wounded; and we shott of 6 Cannon then, where the enemyes powder was sett on fire at Mr Lunnes, and about 20 men burnt, but few of them likely to live.

Rather a busy Easter Day; more active than contemplative. But the garrison were evidently angry that they had been so "basely" treated.

There seems to have been by this time a considerable re-arrangement of the Companies; since here Col. Gray's is not mentioned by his name, having apparently been put under Sir Gervis Cutler. A Lieut Warde appears in Sir George Wentworth's list, and a Capt Ogleby in that of Sir John Ramsden; while Capt Benson who was formerly in Sir George Wentworth's company, now serves under Sir John Ramsden. Capt Smith, Capt Ratcliffe and Capt Flood did good service on this day, neither being on the nominal lists.

The 7th Aprill, we made a Sally forth to Baghill wth 12 horsemen, killd one man there & brought away his horse, and tooke one Willson, a troop', prisoner, & brought in his horse, and killd 8 or 10 men wth muskittes from the Round tower in their trenches. that day we shott 2 Cannon into the towne but what hurt was done is not knowne.

Thus each day had its employment, and at present each day had its sally, the garrison showing no disposition to allow any aspersion on either their valour or their intention to resist, actively as well as passively.

The 8th day, our horse did Sally forth to Baghill under the Command of Capt Washington and Captin Beale and 40 muskitears Commanded by Leiutenant Moore. our horse faced the enemy a long time, & they retreated and dobled their horse, & brought up (the *erased*) 100 musketers, & lined the hedges, and our men, seeing them bring up such forces, retreated in time without any losse;

onely Leiutenant Moore was shott thorow the Arme but now (allmost *erased*) well againe. that day we shott 2 Cannon and 2 sling peeses into the towne but what hurt was done is not knowne.

Baghill, a fortress at their very door, was thus at this season the chief point to which the garrison directed their attention.

The name of Lieut Moore has not before appeared.

---

the 9th, Leiutenant Perry dismounted one of their scouts on Baghill, runne him twise into the body, but his Comrad faild him, & so he lost both horse & man. that day we shott 3 Cannon into the towne at the releeving of their sentryes, whear was killd 2 men & a woman, & the beseegers carryed away 5 wayne loade of wounded men.

These wounded men, five waggons full to-day and a similar load to-morrow, seem to have been carted off towards York, then the head quarters of their army.

Apr 10th. 10th day, our Cannons made 5 shott, & kild 2 men wch was knowne; & 5 men was killd from the round Tower, & 4 men & a horse at Munkhill. that day they Caryed away 5 waine loade of men over ferry brigges, & the same day the enemy drew their men into a body, it was thought to know what force Sr John Saivell brought of horse & foot, being newly Come from Sandall with little Comforth. that night our Cannon made 2 shott Charged wth Case shott into their trenches where the enemy was heard to Crye O is me, O is me, divers times.

Thus the trenches were so close to the Castle that exclamations in one could be heard in the other.

11th. The enemy Came forth wth a p'ty of 12 horse & 30 musketers. they lined Baghill allong the ould hedge 2 howers & then retreated under a hill for a safegard. that day our Cannon plaid 2 Cannon & 1 in the night, but what hurt is not knowne, onely one man was kild upon Baghill wth a muskitt from the round tower.

The enemy were evidently preparing for the attacks upon Baghill to be continued. But "In vain is the snare set in sight of any bird," as was literally the case in the present instance. The garrison determined that there should be no more such attacks on Baghill as had been made during the first days of this Easter week.

12th. Alderman Thomas Wilkinson (unfortunately *interlined*) was killd with a muskitt Bullitt from Baghill at Barbicon yate : and our men did Sally forth with 7 horse to Munkhill but no execution done with the horse on either side, but one of our footmen killd 2 horses there, but the men got Clere. that day we shott 5 Cannon into the towne, but what hurt was done is not knowne.

There are no present traces of this Barbican Gate, the scene of the death of Mr Alderman Thomas Wilkinson.

13th. The enemy shewed 3 or 4 Troopes of horse as though they did intend to draw into a body, But drew away into severall places. Before noone a troope or 2 Came to . where being drawne into order upon the sand bed below the hall, our Cannoncar made a shott from the kinges tower when we was at the Sarmond, dismounted a whole file, killd 2 dead both man & horse, the other 4 were sore hurt. the enemy showed 5 troopes of horse more then was before that day. that day our Cannons made 6 shett into the towne, and 3 Cannon more that night to the enemyes baricade wch was broke quite downe but what execution was done is not knowne.

There is here a hiatus in the MS. where the name of the place should have been; but the context shows clearly that the gap should be filled with the words "Newhall." "The sandbed below the hall" is on the line where the limestone runs out: for the small area round Pontefract Castle contains within two hundred yards in either direction sandstone, coal measures, sand, and limestone, all which may be sometimes found, as was the case at both the Castle and the Priory of St. John the Evangelist, within one curtilage.—"The enemy" were now steadily increasing their strength, notwithstanding numerous defections, and the loss of so many wain loads of wounded men.

14th, about 10 of the Clock there Came a p'ty of the enemyes foot to drive away Summe Cattell wch was sent out to feede neare to Swillington Tower, but our musketers Caused them to runne away & saved the Cattell. about the same time there Came 3 loade of munition whereupon we Coniectured they doe intend to fight wth the prince hereabouts, because that 3000 Scotts lyes at Leedes & other places quartered to Joyne wth theire forces when they were drawn from Knavesbrough, Skarbrough, Yorke, Cawood, Selby, & Pomphrett, to make a body for a feild. About 20 (of our *interlined*) Souldyers wth muskits and Swordes went to a Corner of a hedge near to New hall where the enemy had a baricado, Came suddenly upon their worke, & beate the enemy from it; & they fled to their horse gaurds, but our men fell a pulling downe theire worke so long as their horsemen were ready to Charge them & then our men retreated. they had not any Command to goe, nor no Commander to Command them but one william Wether (alias Belwether) led then (*sic*) on. 5 of our footmen being ingaged wth 4 of theire horsemen neare Baghill, Leiutenant Perry & Jonathan (Sr Jarvis Cutler's man) mounted upon their horses & rid up to them, quit the men at Perryes coming ; but Jonathan seeing one of the enemyes Coming back, Charged him bravely wth his Sword ; but he turned his horse & run away basely, & so our men retreated wth Creditt. the same night about 6 of the Clock the afforesaid Bellwether wth 6 Firelockes fell on the enemyes trenches below Brodelane end & beat them from theire trenches. there was great shooting on both p'tes, & we killed of the enemies 1 Commander wth a buffe Coate & a black skarfe (is supposed to be Collonell Eden *interlined*) & 3 Souldyers more, besides what was killd wth the Cannon. Our Cannon plaid 5 times into the towne and to Trinitie backside, and that night we playd 4 Cannon into the towne, but what hurt was done is not certeyne.

Apparently there was as yet no scarcity of cattle; and the animals sent out to feed were probably a part of those brought in in February. The pun upon William Wether, Bill Wether, and Belwether (the leader of a flock of sheep that carries the bell) was obvious, and probably inspirited the man himself to do justice to his name. As Broad Lane end was on the Baghill side of the Micklegate or Horsefair, so Trinity backside was on the Northgate side of the same thoroughfare, but further from the Castle. The trenches at Broad Lane end having been disturbed in the summer of 1883, while the drainage operations were in progress, showed in many places a thick black soil ten or twelve feet deep. There were also the remains of bones, and of a more recent fish-pond.

15th. Two of our musketeres went up to Baghill & beate of the enemyes scoutes & so retreated. our Cannon playd 9 times into the towne & to baghill but what hurt was done is uncerteyne, onely at one Cannon was scene 4 men to fall at the least. thankfuly was 2 men killd upon Munkhill, one upon Baghill, and 1 in their trenches. About 12 of the Clock the enemy drue forth 30 musketers & lined the ould dike upon the topp of Baghill & gave fire towardes the Castle all the afternoone till 6 a Clock, about wch time we shott of that Iron gunne into the bottom of the hedge where the enemyes lay, wch Caused them to make a great lamentation, but what was killd is not knowne. There was one of the enemis horsemen Came into the Freales, & there light wth a Foot man of ours (his mame (*sic*) T.G.) was walking late at night in the Closes where they had an encounter and the Enemy runne the Footman 4 times into (& thorow his arme & thigh), but wthout any danger of death ; & he runne the horseman thorow the legg, & into his horse noase, & the horseman himsellfe allmost to the midle of his rap' into his body, & so the horseman gott away, but whether alive or dead is not knowne. that night there was 2 Cannon playd into the towne.

After these fierce hand to hand conflicts and these miraculous escapes, we naturally cease to wonder at the slight damage which resulted from men being shot through an arm or a leg, or along the back, and escaping with life after all. A good deal can be allowed on the score of weak powder; but it can hardly be denied that there may have been some vapouring in such recitals.

These Freales are usually called the Preales (see Booke of Entries, page 21), and the name suggests a very curious remembrance of the Cluniac monks of Pontefract, of whose history so little is known. As a French body — an alien priory—the monks of St. John of Pontefract, had their mother house at Cluny, and doubtless (the French being their native language) they would have used it colloquially more frequently than they did that of the country of their adoption. Very few traces of its use by them have, however, been left in the soil. It is known that Malfay-gate was the fourteenth century name for what is now Southgate, and that "Malfay" was evidently a skit of one set of religious professors upon another; but the name has been so long superseded that we doubt whether any of the last five or six generations have heard it used. "Bouton" survives in "Button Park"; and here we have the "Prealls," the "high meadows" of the Frenchman left stranded as the once common name given by the monks of St. John's to the extreme portion of the East Field of Pontefract, and to the lane by which those meadows are approached. Its appropriateness will be evident to any who, placing themselves on the site of St. John's, the present Grange Field, look to the south, and see the Prealles in a long line filling up the gap between the enclosures behind Baileygate and Bondgate, and the sky line to which they extend, and which they include. The Commonwealth forces, by passing through the southern portion of the Preales, that is the part with a northern aspect, would be just beyond the purview of those in the Castle, unless placed on one of the Towers.

To carry the history of the Prealls further back, we have little doubt that they were part of the original Saxon endowment of the church of Pontefract, which seems to have been granted at the time it was the fashion—and there was a fashion about endowments as about so many other things—to endow the church of a township, not only with the tithes of the produce, but with a definite proportion of the land, the tithes of the remainder being added as the out-lying lands came under cultivation, in other words,— as the population increased, and therefore the labours of the parson; the Church, like other owners, having to reduce the allotments into cultivation. What progress the various priests of Pontefract had made before the Norman Conquest, with the cultivation of their allotment— or glebe—is not clear, but soon after that important event, and as a part of the development of the new relations between the over-lord and the cultivators of the land to which the Conquest led, the Church of All Saints' and its endowments, were appropriated (as the phrase was) to the Priory of St. John.

But the more personal reason for its appropriation to them by Robert de Lacy is not far to seek. For besides the desire to provide a maintenance for the monks, and previous to it, was the wish to bring the land under cultivation; and to accomplish this object was the very reason that the monks had been encouraged to immigrate, and had been located on the spot. How much we are indebted to these religious who made labour a matter of obligation (*ora et labora*—Pray and Work—was their motto) we shall never perhaps know; for these early monks turned the desolate places into a fruitful pasture—the East Field into so many closes—without seeking to identify their own names with their labours; Monkhill, at one end of the township, and Monkroyd (or Monk's clearing) at the other, say somewhat, as these Preale Closes say more;

though by an irony of fate, the monks had for their earthly reward an obloquy which their memory shares with that of their degenerate successors. In their own time, however, all these pioneers of agricultural progress had the proud satisfaction of knowing that whether future ages might recognise it, or might never know it, they had been the benefactors of their adopted land, by having increased its area of cultivation. And among such benefactors, we are convinced that the Cluniac monks of Pontefract were not by any means the least deserving. Their history and that of the great metropolitan priory to which they were attached, remains, however, to be written; and even the materials are yet to seek.

16th. William Ingram plaid 2 Cannon into the towne in the morning & shott thorow Mr Lunnes howse topp, into the Markitt. about 10 of the Clock we made a strong sally forth into their trenches. Captin Himsworth wth 50 musketers went out of (Swillinton Tower *erased*) the Lower gate (*substituted*) to the Trenches at Allderman Lunnes howse : Capt' Munro wth 50 musketers out of Swillinton tower to Northgate, & so through the upp' trenches. There was appoynted 5 gentlemen (musketers *erased*) wollunteres (*substituted*) to second the musketers : Collonell Hutton Commanded 12, by Capt' Croft : Collonell Wintworth 14, Commanded by Leiut' Ward : Collonell Rumsden 12, Commanded by Lieut. Coll. Galbreth : Collonell Cuttler 12, Commanded by Capt' Ogleby.

This is the first mention of William Ingram, of whom we shall hear more presently. As the name does not occur among the "Gentlemen Volunteers", he was probably not a member of that Yorkshire family, a branch of which was at this time settled at Knottingley. Nor is either the name of Capt Himsworth, Lieut Ward, Lieut-Col Galbreth, or Capt Ogleby on the nominal lists.

After these gentlemen followed Leiutenant Fevell (Captin Himsworthes Leiut') wth 10 musketers to a little worke. all the rest Followed Capt' Himsworth who assaulted the great trench. they Cleared the little worke & the great trench wth much vallor, beate the enemy up to another trench nearer the bridge ; there was kild in the great trench 17 men, & many hurt. Our Cannon plaid 20 shott during the time & did much execution. there was one Captin Wade taken prisoner & 4 Souldiers ; it is thought there was killd, hurt, & taken prisoners 50 men (at least *interlined*), 1 Leiutenant killd, taken 60 Armes, 7 drummes. Our horsemen did sally forth wth 38 horse under the Commaund of Captin Beale and Corronett Speght, stayd all the time upon Baghill & there faced the enemy that their horse never Came forth to any rescue. Captin

Washington & Corronet Speght rid out in the affter noone wth 2 horsemen more & mett wth 1 quartermaister Hill, & tooke him & his horse, & brought them to the Castle. that after noone we playd 6 Cannon & 4 sling peses, but what hurt is not knowne.

The name of Lieut Fevell appears here for the first time, unless it is that of the Lieutenant whose name is lost from Col. Gray's list on page 20.

Cornet Speght's name is also a new one: it does not occur in either of the lists, unless it is a corrected spelling of Cornet Spurgion's name.

This entry shows that all the so-called Plans of the Siege Operations are incomplete. For after the "little worke" and the "great trench" had been cleared, the besieged "beat the enemy up to another trench near the Bridge." The first was evidently about Broad Lane, and the second at the Sandhill, (as it was called)—that is, between the Post Office, and the Trinities. None of the plans show both these trenches.

This day there Came newes from Bonevant (the Governor of Sandoll Castle) that at 3 Sev'all Sallyes they had killd 42 men, and taken above 50 prisoners, whereof one was a Captin. The passage of this busines was after this manner. Sr John Saivell wth his hipocriticall & Trecherous Rebells beat their drummes to praiers, & being singing of Psalmes before Sermond, Captin Bonevant Caused his drummes to beat to praiers, so that they thought they was secure, but our men after they had dedicated themselves unto God, wth upright hartes & religious praiers in breefe mannor : (To Armes, & fell upon them.)

It was to this Capt. Bonevant that the exploit of Colonel Morris, of seizing the Castle, in 1648, was at the time attributed. Indeed, the earliest news of the circumstance which reached the Parliament contained Capt Bonevant's name as the leader of the party which effected the capture, and made the Commonwealth garrison prisoners. He was then a Colonel,—Collonel Bonnivent, *(see Post.)*

17th. Our men Sallyed forth to their worke at newhall, but did nothing wo'th the noting. the enemy Carryed away this day 7 wayne loade of hurt men, was hurt the day before at the Sally forth of our men. that day our Cannon playd 5 times & 3 Sling peeses into Sev'all places from the Castle, but what execution was done is not knowne.

Seven wains load of wounded! No wonder the Diarist interlined the 50 of the previous day, with a subsequent "at least"; and no wonder the besieged rested this day to recover breath as it were, for the raid they were about to make upon the live stock "in the Feilds",—probably the Chequers, the scene of the night victory of the Royalists seven weeks before.

18th. This day there was 44 Oxen & milchkine grasing in the Feildes, wch we espying from the Castle, Sent out 30 horse Commanded by Captin Speght & Captin Beale, and 50 Foot Commanded by Maior Bland and Maior Dinnis, and brought them into the Castle. at that same time was Sargiant Munkes (one of our Sergiants) shott in to the thigh & there is great hopes he (will *erased*) is (*substituted*) recover againe. wthin one houre there Came to Newhall 600 horse and foot (of Scottes) Commaunded by Collonell Mountgommorey; they are all Commanded men w'thout Collores. So as now we are belegured round about againe. but thou, our good God, be our Comforthes, & deliver us from these Rebellious Tra)tors. That day we playd 21 Cannon & 3 Sling peses, and at theire Coming in was killd Summe say 4 of theire Commanders (Collonell hamelton was thought to be one *interlined*) and 6 Souldyers, & others say 2 Commaunders & 8 Souldyers; whereupon the enemy drew forth a great body of horse & 50 muskters to Baghill to p'vent our men from Sallying forth least thay should take up markitt folkes who should have brought fresh meate to the Markitt, but our Cannon plaid once amongst them, killed one man, hurt divers, and made them all to runne away, and we had a gunner's mate killed wth a Muskitt bullitt thorow the Portehoale, as he was about to give fire to the Gunne. This day allso we sent out about 20 bease from the Castle to grase in the Closes about the Castle walls and 30 musketeres to gaurd (them *interlined*), and the Scottes Came forth & lined the hedges & gave fire upon our men. but 2 other of our men Came forth behind them, & gave fire upon them & beat them into their gaurd, & killd one of them & hurt another. (this day we fired the lower end of the towne & the lower end of Munkhill *interlined*).

Note that Cornet Speght is now Capt Speght, and that the garrison had hardly secured the "44 oxen and Milchkine" before a fresh body of Six Hundred came to the aid of the besiegers, surrounded the hapless few within, and did what in them lay, to prevent any more such sallying, especially as the next day was Market Day, when a sally might be more than ordinarily profitable in the way of provision for the besieged garrison. But with what a picture are we provided here, of Civil War with its rival arrays, on the one side, and the quiet country people coming in to Market as usual, disregarding the cannon balls, to the ravages of which they were momentarily liable.

This use of "bease" as the plural for beast is notable. It is not a mis-spelling: it was at one time a common use, and even spelt "beese" and "bees"; so that "Marchand de Bees",—a "cattle-dealer"—has been misunderstood as being a bee-keeper!

19th. A Few of our foot went out to Munkhill, and beate the Scottes 3 times from their workes, and killd 2 at one time, and there was seene divers to faule at other times. and, in the after noone, 3 of our men went up Grange lane and beat the Scotts from the upp' end of the Lane where was seene 1 or 2 to fall at that time. that day we shott 3 Cannon, one of them to Baghill (loaded wth Case shott), and shott thorow the hedge where lay many of the enemyes foot, and there was seene diveres hattes to fly of and is supposed many men killd.

Apparently this day's sallies were directed to the Monkhill side, that "the Scotts" might have a taste of the quality of those whom they hoped to subdue.

20th. Sunday morning, the Scottes fired the upp' end of Munkhill about 4 of the Cloke, & fell a trenching from the upp' end of Bonegate Millne dame to (Wardes *interlined*), theire baricade at Cherry orchard head neare Newhall, & from thence made bulwarkes in divers places to munkhill topp. This day we playd 5 Cannon, whereof one was to theire Baricade upon the back of the Schoolehowse, and shott it thorow, where there was many of their men, & is supposed did great execution. the rest was shott into the Towne, & one of them to newhall. this day the Scottes made a strong allarum among themsellves; & a musketer of theirs killd a maior of theires for a Cavelear.

The communication between besiegers and garrison seems to have been tolerably complete. The garrison at least, had frequent information of what had happened outside their walls, though hint is seldom given of the way in which the communication was effected.

21th. The Iron Gunne wch lay in the outworke above the upp' gate was fecht in to be planted upon the mount before the Castle gate wch was then making ready for hur being there, but was not finished fitt to play till the 24th day. at night the beseegers in the upp' towne brought about 40 or 50 musketeres to Baghill, and there lined all allonge the hedge and the dike wth them, wch gave fire (for (an *erased*) two (*substituted*) howers & a haulph or more upon our men wch were making the pltforme for the gunne) very vehemently but did no hurt there. this after noone the Scotts sent a drumme to the Castle, & Captin flood & a Souldyer was sent to fetch him in from the lower gate: but the Scotts shott from Munkhill at them, & shott the Souldyer throug the legge, and after the bullitt grased upon Captin Fluddes legg, & nummed it a little, but no hurt. the Souldyer's name that was shott was Anthony Foxkroft. that day we shott one Cannon into the towne. Captin Grimstones man, being taken wth the enemy as he was Coming to seeke his Mr, wch was gone away wth Sr Marmaduke Langdale 6 weekes before, was soare burned wth match because he would not (tell *erased*) Confesse (*substituted*) where his Mr was, wch he Came to seeke & did not know where to find him.

The "Mount before the Castle Gate" is called in the Bill of Demolition, Neville's Mount; but although then professedly demolished, it is of very considerable size, and towards Baghill still prominent.—This seems to have been a traiterous action of "the Scotts"; but it will be seen, as we proceed, that the Garrison had on many accounts, and not altogether without reason, a very great prejudice against soldiers of that nationality.—Nor was the use of Torture on Capt Grimstone's man a pleasing feature, or likely to cause the garrison to look with favour upon those who employed it. The mention of the circumstance incidentally shows that Capt Grimstone, and probably others besides, went away in March with Sir Marmaduke Langdale, who thus at the same time relieved the Garrison, and recruited his own strength.

The substitution here, of "Confess" for "Tell" as the descriptive word, implies the corresponding word Torture. It was by "Torture" that criminals were forced to "Confess".

22th. The Scotts Continued making their trenches stronger, but runne them no Further on, and the English in the upp' towne brought up theire men to baghill, where they playd very hard upon our men wch were working at the platforme upon the mount. (*An erasure of four lines occurs here, apparently narrating, under the wrong date, the accident to the young maid, which occurred on the 23rd.*) that day we shott 1 Cannon & 3 Sling peeses, but what execution was done either by them or by the muskittes is not knowne. that night the Scottes marcht all away from Newhall thorough the parke that same way they Came.

Thus the Scots stayed at Monkhill for five days only. The phrase "They marched back through the Park *the way they came*" throws a light on the narrative of their coming, which the former account did not afford. Hitherto the soldiers had come from the direction of York, over Ferry-bridge; these Scots came through the Park, probably from the direction of Tadcaster, and over Castleford Bridge.

The 23th, being Weddensday morning, Came Sr John Saivell wth his Company to newhall, & possest the place wch the Scottes had left, (not wthout great stores of Company *interlined*). this morning Came the beseegers from the upp' towne to baghill wth 50 musketeres, & lined the hedge & the dike wth them; they playd very soare against the Castle but did no harme, onely a (maid *erased*) young maid was Drying of Clothes in Mr. Taytons Orchard (Close by the lower Castle gate) She was shott into the head whereof she dyed that night. that Day we shott 5 Cannon, but what hurt was done is not knowne. (there was 2 killd that day, 1 in trinetyes, & the other on Mr Lunne's back side, *interlined*).

The Scots were notorious for their dirty habits and the Diarist probably knew—he was at the time eighteen years of age—how those who accompanied King James, when in 1603 he came to take possession of the Crown, had rested at, and passed through Pontefract, to leave the Plague behind them, as they did in so many other places. His subsequent discovery that they left at Newhall "Stores of Company" in the shape of vermin, he seems to have considered to have been sufficiently characteristic to deserve an interlineation. As elsewhere, this supplementary portion of his Diary is not the least interesting.—And amid the harsh sounds and scenes of war, a maid—a "young" maid, as Mr Drake emphasises it, as an afterthought, comes out innocently, thinking to dry the clothes in Mr Tatham's orchard; but only to receive a death wound. The musketeres "playd very soare against the Castle, but did no harm" to it, while the young maid out of the line of fire was shot. As for the Orchard, it is there still, very near the site of the Lower gate, in the Booths. The name of the owner was Tatham, misspelt "Tayton" and in the nominal list "Taytom". He was an alderman of some standing, had been mayor in 1641, and was one of the largest property-owners in the town. We have in the Fee-Farm Book of 1650, a list of his properties extending over nearly two pages ; and this orchard is named next after his house in the New Market. It is described as "an Orchard in the Boothes, Escheat land" and he is assessed at 3s. 2d. rent for it.

It will be noticed that the "young maid" was interred next day at the Church, with military honours, and probably Mr Tatham himself was with the musketers who attended her funeral.

24th. The beseegers Came up to Baghill with 40 musketers in the morning, and they shott at Cattell wch was grasinge in the Closes under the Castle, & likewise they shott at the Castle ; and our musketeres from the Castle shott at them, & kill'd one of them there, and beate them away from thence. p'sently after a few of our men went to Munkhill, & killd one of Sir John Saivelles men there, and in the afternoone, at the buriall of the maid, a few of our musketers attended the Corpes to the Church, & gave a valley of Shott,wch gave the beseegers in the upp towne an Allarum, whereupon they Came to baghill both wth horse & foot, & playd very hard for a little time against the Castle : & likewise our (men *erased*) musketeres (*substituted*) shott at them from the Round Tower & beate them from thence & we killd 50 of the enemyes in their Trenches : from the Round Tower that time we shott 4 Sling peeses to Bagghill, & 3 Cannon,or 2, at night into Mr Lunnes howse, where it was spoken that the Officers & Commanderes were met upon a Consultation ; but what execution they did is not knowne. this day the aforesaid Bellwether tooke a woman, (a Suttler wch Came from Barwick), as she was Carying a stand of Ale to the Souldyers at Newhall, and brought hur wth the Ale into the Castle, (but eased hur of hur money she had about hur before). she Confessed the battell wch was made about Westchaster, & that the Kinge had there gott the better, & that the beseegers in Pomfrett were not to stay above 2 or 3 daies at the furthest.

Here we have one instance of the way in which gossip was received as reliable information. Barwick-in-Elmet is a hamlet, some ten miles from Pontefract, in the direction of York ; the woman had probably followed the soldiers from their first coming, and drove her trade with them. But it does not seem to have occurred to the besieged that she was hardly a likely person to have been entrusted with the plans of their enemies.

25th. The beseegers from the upp' Towne Came up to Baghill in the forenoone wth about 50 musketers & about a Troope of horse 'in Sevrall Companyes. the foot lined the hedge & the dike all a long Baghill, & shott very Furiously for about 4 howers together, but did no hurt at all to the Beseeged. During that time we playd 6 cannon & 4 Sling peeses, but what execution was done by the Cannon is not knowne, but we saw eaither hattes or heades flye up at the fall of the Bullitts, & the Bullittes grased amongst them 3 times, from whence was heard great exclamations at one time. in the affternoone 3 (or 4 *interlined*) of our Souldyers did Sally forth to Munkhill, & beat 16 of Sr. John Saivell men 3 times from the howses at Monkhill to theire workes; and after tooke a Souldyer in Munkhill Closes & brought him into the Castle. that day we killd one man from the Round Tower in the morning, and 4 men more in theire Trenches at night, at the releevig of their Sentryes, from the Round Tower.

This rehearsal of the valiant doings of the besieged shows the implicit faith the Diarist had, not only in the justice of his cause, and in the bravery with which that justice inspired those who adopted it, but in the pusillanimity, weakness and imbecility of its opponents. "Fifty musketers" accompanied by a troop of horse—more or less and in several companies—shot for four hours at the besieged, but "did no hurt at all"; while on the other hand three,—he unwillingly concedes a fourth,—sallied forth, beat 16 of the enemy three times over, and then got back safe, bringing with them one whom they had bagged by the way.

26th. The Beseegers from the upp' towne Came to Baghill about 8 a Clock wth about 40 or 50 musketers, & lined the hedge & dike all alonge the hill side, and shott very hard for 5 or 6 howers, but wthout any hurt to the beseeged. at that time was 1 Cannon shott full amongst the throngest p'te of them but what execution it did unknowne to us. there was once Cannon playd more into the Graunge Lathe where there was many officeres & Souldyers, & 1 Cannon more up into the town into the Markitt place. (but what execution was done is not known. the First *erased*) that Cannon killd one man against Mrs Jackson doore, & so grased up the Markitt place (& the other Cannon bullitt grased all along the Markit place were there was many people, but as yett what execution was done, was uncerteyne to us *erased*).

This day, the "musketers" shott for five or six hours "without any hurt to the besieged", who replied by cannon. The careful way in which the effects of the cannon that were fired into the Market Place are recorded, deserves particular notice. The Diarist receives one tale, amends it, and finally adopts another. But the whole narrative bears upon its face an evident desire and intention to get at the truth, that makes the method by which he arrives at that result, exceedingly picturesque. For every word, though half-written, and wholly erased, is a negative detail, perhaps more full of information, than if it had been left in its original state; recording as it does explicitly "That such and such a tale was current, that I at first received it as true, but that I received subsequent information which showed that it was untrue, and that what I now leave on record, as the ultimate result of my careful enquiries, was the true state of the case."

About noone, 7 or 8 of our Souldyers sallyed forth to Munkhill, & there fought wth a p'ty of Sr John Saivell's Souldyers, killd one, laymed another, and beat them into theire trenches. there Came allso about 40 horse into the Closes hard by Munkhill to have taken our men but they retreated a little back wthin Muskitt shott of the Castle, but the horsemen durst not Come wthin that Compase. about 2 a Clock allso there went up againe to Munkhill 5 of our Souldyers, & gave them a Larum, & beate them back, & killed another man, and brought him away wth them downe to Denwell, & went up againe & killd another horseman wch Came braving up towards them, but that horse & man was both fetch of, & that man was Caryed behind another man to Pomfrett where he dyed p'sently after he Came thither.

This day's doings are narrated in batches. The former paragraph gives the morning's work; now we have the occurrences of the middle day. The Closes hard by Monkhill, must have been the Grange Field—the site of St. John's Monastery,—and the Closes on the opposite side of the Grange Lane. The Diarist seems to consider it somewhat of a personal grievance that "the Enemy" would not come within musket range.

about 4 a Clock allso 7 or 8 of our Souldyers Sallyed forth to Munkhill toppe & a little farther, & made show as though they weare l"lamenteres, Call'd to a horseman (was supposed to be an officer) who Came allmost Close to them, & then saw he was mistaken, & Cockt his pistoll at them, but they discharged 2 muskits upon him, & shott him thorow his side but his horse Carryed him off to New hall, there being little hopes of any life of him; and then they wheeled about to the toppe of the Abbey Close, Calling to the Souldyers upon the toppe of the Castle, bidding them Come forth out of their houlds if they durst, & Calld them Papistes, & so went downe to the bottom of the Close into the lower Abbeye Close where, upon the other side of the hedge, were many musketeres lined, & they Called to them, & wished them to goe nearer wth them & shoot at the Castle, & then one of them Came forth to them, & Came forwardes wth them towardes the Castle, but, having got him at a little distance from the rest of his Companions, they tooke his muskitt from him, & brought him along wth them into the Castle. This day Came 150 Foot Souldyers over Ferry brigges to Newhall. about 6 a Clock at the releeving of the Sentryes, we killd 2 of theire men from the round tower, & shott other 2, and then we shott 1 Cannon into the Markitt place, where there was many people, & the bull' grased all along the Markit place, but what execution it did is uncerteine to us. that night the beseegers sent foot, at least 100 men, to baghill, & threw up a trench haulph the way in the ould dike, and about 12 a Clock in the night, we Sallyed forth of Swillinton Tower, wth 60 men Commanded by Captin Smith and Leiutenant Faivell, into Northgate, and gave them a strong Allarme, wch Caused them to beate their drummes and faule to theire Armes, both in the Towne & throughout all theire trenches, & the shott very Furiously in all those places, our men shooting at them very hard w'th their muskitts for the space of haulph an hower, & so retreated wthout any hurt at all. At the Same time allso there Sallyed Forth, wth the other, 16 men Commanded by Leiutenant Smith (Leiut' to Capt' Munroe) : he led them downe to one of theire Sentryes at the lower end of the towne, beate them from theire workes, & Caused them to Runne towardes New hall to the other trenches. during that time we shott of 2 Cannon to Baghill, but what execntion was done is unserteyne.

Taking it altogether, a tolerably sharp day's work with which to conclude the week. The object of the besiegers evidently was to make a trench on the top of Baghill. And as this generation knows, having seen the hill cut up in all directions, and much of it within the last three years carried bodily away, they could hardly have had a more unpromising occupation. For the cap of almost every one of the isolated hills which surround Pontefract on every side, is a yellow kind of limestone locally called marl, to distinguish it from neighbouring lime-stones in which the lime is present in greater quantity, and into this marl the pick can be induced to penetrate only with great difficulty. It is ten or twelve feet thick, and beneath it lies either a soft sandstone, or sand itself, each easily worked. The "upper trenches" "just below the Bridge" were exactly where this sandstone was most favourably placed for working, as its then name — The Sandhill, now forgotten —shows. The site of Pontefract seems to have been in pre-historic times, a large fresh water lake of transmission, through which a considerable river flowed. The old town of Pontefract was built in the bed of this river, that is in the deepest part of the "lake", Bond-gate indicating its direction.

27th. Sunday the beseegers Came againe from the upp' towne to Baghill about 8 a Clocke, & there Continued all the day, shooting very hard at any they Could see either wthn or about the Castle wth about 100 musketeres, so that we Could not put forth our Cattell to grasse. in the fore noone there Came downe 3 very good hoggs downe at brode lane end, towardes the Castle, and our Souldyers seeing them (out of Barbican), went out & fetcht then (*sic*) in, wch was a good booty for the Souldyers. About 12 of the Clock, A killnehowse of Mrs Oatsees, (neare to the upp' Church), was sett on fire, but by what meanes is unknowne to us. During the time of the burning our Cannon made 7 Shott to that place, & to the places thereaboutes, but what execution was done is uncerteine to us. our men shott very hard all the Day into theire workes, as well as they to us, where there was seene one man of theires killd & diveres shott & Carryed of, but we had not any man hurt (praised be God). that night, about 11 a Clock, 6 of our Souldyers, Commanded by one Lowder, Sallyed forth Downe to their worke below the low church, gave them a Larum, beate them from their workes to New hall, wch Caused them to give Fire throughout all theire workes round about the Castle. and that night was 100 men working in their trenches at baghill, but went not fare forwardes by reason of the stones there.

Now that they were so closed up that they could not even put forth their Cattle to grass, how the hearts of the soldiers must have leaped at the sight of the coming roast pork, sedately wandering from Broad Lane End into the very mouths of the longing watchers. Truly, " a good booty for the Souldyers " ; and perhaps even some of the " gentlemen volunteers " may have condescended to it.

Aprill 28th. The Beseegers from the upp' towne about 6 a Clock Came wth above 150 men to releeve those wch were on Baghill all night, and wrought still forwardes in their trench all the day, and shott very Furiously upon the least occation, but did no hurt to the beseeged (*altered from* beseegers), and we drive out our Cattell to grase neare the Castle, & brought them in againe in safety after they had beene feeding most p'te of the day. about 9 or 10 of the Clock, 3 or 4 of our men went to (bag *erased*) Munkhill, & there met w'th Summe p'te of S'r John Saivells men, & killd one of them, & Came back againe. About 11 of the Clock there went 200 horse from Pomfrett (or the townes thereaboutes) thoroug the Parke to Ferry brigges, and about 3 a Clock 12 of our Souldyers went forth to Munkhill wthout any order or knowledg of the Governor, being led up by one Lowder a Souldyer, a good stout man, gave (them *erased*) an Allarum to Sr John Saivells quarters about Newhall, from whence Issued foorth neare 100 Souldyers. our men Charged them bravely till they Came allmost Close to one another, where onr men killed 2 of theires, & wounded as many men (as is thought) of theirs as went up of oures, & then they basely runne away, & tooke one of the killd men along wth them, but the other our men brought downe wth them to Denwell, & buryed him by the other was killd 2 daies before ; though they suffred our men wch were killd at the Low Church to lye there 10 dayes unburyed, having beene often sent to & requested to doe it.

From this and the circumstance recorded " 2 daies before ", it would appear that the besieged had command of Denwell. Lowder, the good stout man, seems to have been a born leader ! We shall meet with him again presently. Like Ingram, his having a name similar to that so ancient and eminent a family as the Lowthers, could not have been without an inspiriting effect upon him.

This Day we shott 2 Cannon & one Sling peese to Baghill, but what execution was done is uncerteyne. that night allso about 12 of the Clock we shott one Cannon to Bagghill amongst 100 men at least standing together, wch grased through them, & made a lane, but what execution was done is not knowne. that night there was at least 300 men lay in that trench working, & shott very Furiously all the night.

The way in which the numbers of the enemy, working at Baghill were increased, is exceedingly suggestive of the difficulty of their undertaking. 100, 150, and now 300 were at work at the marl, or taking it by turns to shoot "very Furiously"; and from an expression used on the next day, they seem to have made some progress, as well they might do from their very numbers.

29th. This morning we put out summe horse & cattell to grase about the Castle, but the enemy shott 1 Cow & 2 horseyes that they dyed that day. the enemy shott still very hard all that Day from Baghill, & from other workes wch they had made under the hill (betwixt it & the Castle) and they Continued still making their trench all along the hill (wch they had allmost finished.) we shott 4 Cannon that day to Baghill, and our men shott very hard that day wth muskits from the Round Tower to Baghill, where was 2 killd, the one was supposed to be an officer, the other a Souldyer. and that day 9 of our men went out to Munkhill, & beate Sr John Saivell's men from their first Trench there, and so Came back to the Castle wthout any hurt to either side. That night 4 of our Commanders, wth theire Servantes (being as many) rid forth of the Castle towardes Sandall, & so to Newarke. they weare accommodated w'th the Leiutenant Collonell & 20 musketeres & firelockes (into the Parke *interlined*,) where Just after their parting the Commaunderes mett wth one of the enemyes Scoutes, gave fire upon him once, & is supposed either killd him or tooke him along wth them. and after theire departure the musketeres & firelockes Came throug Norgate back againe to the Castle, and they went up to (theire *erased*) the enemyes (*substituted*) lowest trench nere Mr Russbyes, and gave fire twise (over *interlined*) upon them very bravely, & so retired into the Castle wthout any hurt at all.

Through Northgate into the Castle must mean by way of Swillington Tower, which thus evidently afforded an easy means of egress and ingress.

Note the peculiar but quite correct use of the word "accommodated".

---

30. The enemy Came very yearely in the morning, wth 160 men at least, to Baghill to releeve the Sentries there, and gave fire very furiously upon any

occation all that day, where they killd one horse in the Barbican. And our men from the Round Tower did not let slip the least Ocation, but gave fire upon them, where we killd 2 there, one was supposed to be an Oicer, the other a Souldyer & shott 2 or 3 men more there. we shott allso very hard upon any sight of any man into all the Trenches above the Castle towards the towne, where we saw one or 2 men killd, & at least 4 or 5 men more shott. that day the enemy burnt poore Cate Lillhole howse on Munkhill & allso that night they burnt a little howse under the Castle wall, betwixt the haulpeny howse & the wall.

This mention of Haulpeny House has been a source of some little difficulty. It occurs four times; and as on the first occasion (19 January), it was quite independent of the context, Boothroyd supposed it must have been on the road to Wakefield, by some confusion, on the one hand with Halfpenny Lane (Causey Lane or Featherston Lane, as it was also called), and on the other with Penny Lane which was another name for the Wakefield (and Sandall) Road. But from this context, it is evident that the Halfpenny house which is at the termination of Halfpenny Lane in Tanshelf, cannot be meant, for the Halfpenny house of the text was close to the Castle. We suggest that the Diarist's Halfpeny house, was a contraction or a corruption of Hope and Anchor, the present name of the house at the corner of the road to Monkhill from the Castle. The religious origin of that sign is evident, and the sign itself was probably derived from the immediate neighbourhood of the house to St. Nicholas Hospital of which it must have been at one time an appurtenance.

There is now shott in the Second seege from the 21th March to the 1th of My (ay *interlined above in faint ink*) 315 Cannon of by the beseeged.

This memorandum is squeezed in at the bottom of a page. The next page (13 of the original) begins (as usual at the commencement of a page) with not only the day of the month, but with that of the year.

May 1th, 1645. This morning the enemy releeved their trenches on Baghill very yearely, w'th (as we supposed) 150 men, where they had made a Triangle worke, & walled it wth stone, and Filled it wth earth, and as we Conceived, there was a little worke wthin it for officers to sitt in, & to shelter them from Rayne. we playd one Cannon to it that morninge, wch burst the stone wall wthout, & we supposed shott through the Inworke allso, where they was drinking (for they had greate store of Ale brought them that morning) and very many of them runne out of that worke very fast. So that we supposed the Cannon did good execution. That day they shott very Slowly both from Baghill & from their lower worke in the Round Close under Baghill. In the After noone 8 of our men went out to Munkhill, where Sr John Saivell's Company had lined a long hedge & a deepe ditch wth about 60 or 70 men. we shott at them from the Castle wth our Muskitts, as well as those 8 of our men wch went up the hill into the ditch, and at that time we killd 2 officers, and our men runne hastely into the ditch, & beate them all away where they runne all away very basely. Our men (then *in,'erlined*) retreated downe the hill, and had summe more Ammunition sent to them. After that the enemy drue up a groat p'te of their horse wch they had both in the Towne & at new hall, & they drue up the foot all so from both places, but the horse staid not w'thin muskitt shott of the Castle. Our men Fell up twise more to Munkhill, & beate them from the hedges into theire workes, & killd them 2 men more at that time, & shott many more. after that went up 3 men more from the Castle, & beate them from theire workes. our men then retreated back, and in theire retreate one of those 3, (his name was Nathanyell Sutton,) (a barber), was shott into the Shoulder & so into the body, whereof he dyed Instantly, but our men brought him offe. there was another of those 3 allso (was *interlined*) shott on his brow (that *erased*) & (*substituted*) it entred (not *erased*) the Skull (a little *interlined*) so that (we hope in a short time he will recover *erased*) he is well againe (*interlined in the faintest ink*) (his name was Captin Dent). The 3th of those men was allso shott through his Dublitt as he stooped, & so it went up to his neck, but never bruised the flesh, so that he was not hurt. (he was a drummer,) but had no drumme at that time. Our men had done very good service that day, if those 3 men had not gone up wthout either order or Commaund. That night the enemyes Cutt bowes under Baghill, and made blindes at either end of theire Triangle worke, and planted a drake (as we supposed).

There is no appearance on the old Siege Plans of any Triangle Work such as the Diarist mentions; but it is probable that Major Lambert's Fort Royal is meant.

The Round Close under Baghill—its proper name was Primrose Close—has now almost entirely disappeared. The Midland Railway passes through its site, at a level some yards below the original surface. Primrose Cottage, also, has vanished with Primrose Close.

May 2th. This morning they shott theire drake (as we supposed). they releeved theire Sentryes before 8 a Clock, (& went of as we Could pretty well tell) about 120 men. they shott very little all that day, but they killd one oxe of oures from Munkhill nere Swillinto' Tower, but we fetcht him offe. we killd that day wth our muskitts, from the Round tower, at least 14 men, & shott many more. At the Releeiving of our gardes, betwixt the Lower gates and the Mound, one of our Souldyers, as he was Coming of, was shott into the head wth a muskitt bullitt, (we knew not whether the Bullitt Came from Baghill or Munkhill), whereof he dyed Instantly. This night we gave an Allarum to the enemy in the North Street at their sentryes, upon the backside of Mr Lunnes at wch time we sent away Mr William Booth & Mr Thomas Baumforth to Newarke.

As we pointed out on p. 39, "Mr William Booth" was a very different person from plain William Booth. He is returned at Dugdale's Visitation in 1666, as being Keeper of Pontefract Park, and an elder brother of Mr Alderman Edward Booth, of Pontefract.

The Mound was Neville's Mount in the Barbican.

May 3th. This day the enemy releeved their (sen *erased*) gaurdes, as formerly they did, both at Baghill and at other places, and they shott very slowly, every day lesse (then *interlined*) other, but the enemy shott a ould meare of oures was turned forth to grasse, and allso they shott 2 oxen more of oures wch weare at grasse, but we fetcht them of & made very good use of them, & they likewise shott a boy of (Munkhill *erased*) a poore mans of Munkhill (wch was keeping of the Cattell) into the Thigh, & so glented of, but little hurt. but, at the releeiving of their gaurdes towardes night, we killd 4 of their men from the round tower about Trinities, & at the lathe end, behind Mr Lunnes, and shott many more of them, and that night we had 2 letters sent from newarke wth very good newes from the South, and allso of the good Condition that all the Kinges forces were in, wch did not a little Comforth us to here of theire good p'ceedinges & our freindes wellfare.

There was evidently a distinction (perhaps of number) between sentries and guards.

And thus the hopes of the besieged still maintained their high pitch, while the grip of the besiegers was getting tighter.

4th. This day, being Sunday, the enemy releived their gaurdes, as at other times, but shott very slowly on both sides all that day. and in the afternoone there Came a Souldyer into the Castle wch Runne away from the Enemy, and tould us (as neare as he Could) how all thinges stood wth the enemy ; and we exchanged summe prisoners wch were taken from about newarke, or on this side, & brought to Pomfrett, & so they was sent into the Castle.

5th. This day they releeved their gaurdes as at other times, but wth farre lesser numbers, for whereas at sumtimes before there Came up 150 to theire releefe, theire Came up this (day *interlined*) 34 & 2 officeres, & they shott very little all the day, but at Munkhill they had made waye through all the (burnt *interlined*) howses along the toppe of the hill till they Came to widow Tupman's howse (wch they had burnt,) and in it they Cept their Sentry howse, and shott out of it when they Could see any occation, but they did no harme all the day. There was great shooting from their trenches about paradise Orchard, Trinities, & Mr Lunnes, & Mr Rusbyes against the Round tower & the north side of the Castle, but they did no harme to the beseeged, but we shott from the Round tower very hard, & at the releefe of their gards we killd one man, & shott many more of them.

This commences a fresh page—page 14 of the Diary,—and again occurs the date of the year. Part of the last page is worn away, *tower* in the last line but two, and *ard* in the last line but one, have quite gone.

1645, May 6th. The enemy releeved theire gaurdes this day at Baghill as at other times, but shott very little from thence all the day, nor from their gaurdes at Munkhill, but in all theire workes up the towne they shott very hard, (& we likewise att them *interlined*), where we killd one of them in Paradise orchard, & allso another in theire trenches on Mr Lunnes backside, & shott 3 or 4 more of them. There Came in this Day a horselitter from Ferrybrigges into the towne, wch went away next morning (the same way it Came *interlined*) We supposed did Carrye away summe wounded officer in it. That Day we playd 2 Cannon to Baghill. a little before the shooting of the First was 2 women seene to bring 2 standes of Ale into their Triangle worke, at wch time the first Cannon plaid full into that work, & made a breach into it, & we supposed did summe execution for they runne very fast out of the worke: and the other Cannon drive away 3 or 4 stones from the toppe of the worke amongst them wch was wthin, but whether any execution was done or not is not knowne. This night there Came into the Castle a Sargient from the enemy, wch tould us summe newes of the enemyes p'ceedinges in the towne.

How interesting "summe newes of the enemye's p'ceedinges" would have been to us, had it only been set down with as much particularity as was usual with the Diarist when recording what he saw with his own eyes.

The above paragraph contains a very singular division of a word which we note as an illustration of the Diarist's total disregard of the necessity that the division of a word should be according to its syllables. He divides one of his words with "horsel" in one line, and "itter" in the next. But this is only an outrageous instance of the way in which he crowds his matter at the end of a line. "Dra" finished off with "ke" interlined, is an example of a very ordinary method, from which his page is hardly free for a dozen lines together. This makes the end of his second column frequently almost illegible.

7th. This morning the enemy shott of theire drake from Baghill to the Castle (it was loaded wth Case shott), & scarce hitt the Castle, for summe p'te of it hitt the Stable, & summe the Battlementes of the Castle, & the rest flew over the Castle, but did no hurt at all. the enemy shott one of our (men *interlined*) from Baghill as he was working in a trench in the Barbican. they shott very little all this Day from all theire workes. in the after noone there Came 10 of the enemyes Souldyers vaporing wth theire Swordes into the lower Church, but 8 of our men, seeing them, went downe wth theire muskitts, gave fire upon them, & they runne away as fast as they Could. this afternoone at the releeving of theire gaurdes we kill'd one man in the trench before Mr Lunnes, & one more in the trench behind Mr Rusbyes, & there was 2 or 3 more laymed in the out workes.

This shows that the Main Guard was then still called the Stable; and perhaps it was still used for the purpose. The mediæval Stable recently opened out is not referred to throughout the Diary.

8th. This Day was but little shooting on all sides till the afternoone at the releeving of their gaurdes, at wch time we killd one in their trenches behind Mr Rusbyes, and divers was hurt but no more seene to fall. there was but 34 went up to Baghill to releeve theire gaurdes at releeving time, but there went up 20 more was seene to goe up against night. this night Captin Horsfold (wth his man) went forth to Sandoll Castle, and allso Bellwether was sent againe towardes newarke. they had a Few musketers went forth wth them to Baghill, but they saw not any was stiring there, so they returned back againe into the Castle.

It would appear as if the passing of men into and from the works was a mere blind, and that they were actually employed on other service, but though the musketers may have been suspicious of the ominous silence, they refrained from an attack, lest there might have been an ambush.

9th. This Day we shott 2 Cannon from the Kinges Tower towardes the Markitt place about 10 of the Clock, and allso 1 Cannon more thither in the Afternoone, but what execution they did is uncertein. we shott little on both sides all the forenoone, but, at the releeving of their gaurdes, there was hard shooting on all sides where we saw one man to Fall in the Porte hole upon Baghill, & we killd 2 more by their workes below Brodelane end, whereof one was an Officer (all in Redd) wth a staffe in his hand (his name was . . . . . *interlined*) the other was a Souldyer. About 4 of the Clock the enemy sett on Fire and burnt divers Barnes & howses in Sevrall places (of the Towne *interlined*) as namely, from the North Street 2 Barnes of Mr Maiores & Mr Robt. Battleyes, (Joyned together) and allso all along those howses from that place in to the high streete (Call'd Miccklegate) where there was many good howses & killnes burnt, & Mr Robt. Battleyes new howse. the fire burnt all the night (in the barnes *interlined*). they allso sett on fire another howse below Mr John Wilkinsonnes (but was put out *interlined*) on the other side of the streete. that night, about (8 *erased*) 9 (*substituted*) of the Clock, the enemy gave a valley of Shott in the Markitt place. we heard it reported at the buriall of a Leeuetenant (*erased, but the substituted word is illegible; though it is probably* Lieutenant Colonel.) we shott 1 Cannon more from the side of the Treasurers Tower upon that platforme. that Cannon playd full into the Middle of the Fire, & brought downe a pte of the howse wth it, but whether it did any execution more or not is not knowne.

This Entry is the last in the original ink; which afterwards assumes the brown tint so much more difficult to read, in which those memorandums as to particulars that we encountered at the commencement of the volume were written, and which was the medium of most of the interlineations.

For instance, those under this date are exceedingly difficult to decipher. In one case,—the name of the "Officer all in redd, with a staffe in his hand"—the Diarist seems to have considered that any attempt at completing the Entry would be futile. But he made a supplementary memorandum up the margin

his name was Capt. Cowbeck.

Similarly along the margin of the lower part of this day's Entry, he has attempted an explanation of what he had already failed with in the text. His more successful though still doubtful Entry seems to be

Leiwtenant Collonell Eden,

But the first syllable of the name is far from certain.

In this Entry and once or twice in other places, the Diarist writes North Street for North-gate, showing that although he had a Pontefract wife, he was not quite at home with Pontefract speech; and that with him Street was colloquially, as it is really, equivalent to Gate.

10th. This day the enemy made a new worke, on (bag *erased*) Munk (*interlined as a substitution*) hill in manner of a haulph moone, to p'vent us from (Swillington Tower *erased*) Sallying forth out of Swillinton Tower. the same day there was one man killd from the Round Tower in the Bearne or behind Mr Lunnes, & Somme hurt, but we know not how many. this night there went out of the Castle 2 men to S(willing *erased*)andoll (*substituted*.)

This haulph moon was another decided step towards completing the environment of the fortress. Hitherto, the beleagurement had been far from complete, as even the departure of the two men for Sandall shows. But their return, or the return of a similar party on the 27th, with above a hundred head of cattle, and the bold way in which the party drove 97 of the herd into the Castle in the face of the enemy, was one of the most striking adventures of the siege.

11th. This day being Sunday, we had 2 learned Sermonds, the one by Docter Bradlay, the other by Mr Oley (as we have every Sonday 2) the Lord give us grace to Follow them. this day we killd 2 of the enemyes from the Round Tower. this day allso we had one of our men was looking out of a Port hole on the Round Tower (A wright by trade), & seldome using to Come thether, but he was shott thorow the Arme, and though at a weekes end full of payne yet there is no signe of his death.

We had allso a boy about 9 yeares of age (as he was getting of greene sawse wthout Swillington Tower) was dangerously shott in the Belly from their workes at Munkhill.

This night, also a Gentleman of ours was talking wth one of the Ennemyes Officers (Conditioning *erased*) upon the Round Tower (Conditioning that neither side should shoot,) but yett one of the Enemies Souldyers, (Contrary to Conditions, shott in at the poarthoale side, where the bullitt grased upon the side, & so hitt the Gentleman upon the Buckle of his Gerdle & burst it, but (praised be God) did not so much appeare as the very show of a hurt.

The way in which the members of the garrison thus received flesh wounds, terrible enough in their character, and yet not fatal, is surprising. The gunpowder used must have been very feeble.

At this time of the year—the middle of May—" green sawse ", as the children still call it round Pontefract, is very plentiful. It is a species of sorrel, and is not only chewed by the little ones, but is used as a medicinal vegetable. Some may be found even now, in the season, within a few yards of Swillington Tower.

Note, on the side of the Garrison all was openness and confidence, and trust; on the side of the besiegers there was treachery, unexampled, and base, and contrary even to conditions; but a protecting Providence guarded the innocent victims of the baseness, and there "did not so much as appeare as the very show of a hurt." The freshness and transparent simplicity of the Diarist's remarks are continual illustration of the strength of the confidence he felt in the justice of his cause.

12th. This day there wase (given *erased in the original ink*) fire (given *interlined*) very Freely on both sides, but not any hurt to 'ur knowledg on either side. About 8 a Clock our Irou gunne plaid to Baghill, but what execution it did is not knowne. this night, about 9 a Clock, our Gentlemen & Souldyers being merily disposed, did drinke (whole *interlined*) heallthes (of the New well water) to the King & all his good freindes, pledging one another wth such hallowes and Showtes, as the e'emy, wondring what should be the Cause of such sudden Joy, Tooke an allarum, drew out all theire horse into the feild and dobled all theire gaurdes (wch pleased us well) and then, our Taptoo being beat, every man to his gaurdes or to his bed.

The Garrison seem to have been very proud of their iron gun, and to have watched its performances and those of its gunner, with much of a personal interest. Of which we shall see repeated instances as the Diary proceeds.

This "new well water" is one of those mysteries upon which we may wish that the Diary had given more enlightenment. The only suggestion we can offer is, that it was water from a tank that they had constructed, and that the tank was in "the King's Chamber." For when this Chamber came to be cleared out in 1881, it was found that there had been constructed in it, a tank with floor of good sound bricks, under which was a mass of well-worked puddle, six inches thick, though even when this was removed the actual floor was reached only through a bed of sand and small coal. All this has now been cleared out in order to restore the original height of the Chamber from arched roof to rock-floor.

The Garrison seem to have been much tickled at this notion of giving the enemy an unwarranted alarm.

13th. This day we kill one of the Enemyes upon Baghill, and 2 from the Round Tower, and divers more were hurt. They grow now so fearfull that they will scarcely looke out of their Trenches, but when they are forced to releeve their gaurdes. this day were Carryed away 3 or 4 lodes of goodes towardes Ferry Bridege, wch makes us thinke they will not stay long.

All this was, however, preparation for the coming storm ; and not of such good augury as the Garrison supposed.

14th. This morning the enemy drive both sheepe & Cattell towardes Ferry Brigge. Somme thought it was to victuall Yorke, others thought it was to p'vent our Army from having any victual, for they fecht them from the townes nere about Pomphrett. In the Afternoone Corronett Thurley was Shott (above *an illegible erasure*) in the Arme in Barbican. there was this day one of the Enemies killd and devers shot from the Round Tower. About 5 a Clock there Came a troope of horse Riding fast from Dauncaster, fower of them Rid into the Towne, and the rest to (Ferry Brigges *erased*) New hall (*substituted*). in the eevning (*sic*) all their horse was drawne up in a body into the Parke, to what end is not knowne. This night, Captin Benson, wth his man & two more, went to Sandall Castle, and we see divers Fires abroade this night, but we know not the Occation thereof.

Which shows that the force of the enemy was not yet sufficiently strong to complete the blockade.

"The Park" at this time covered about 900 acres of ground, that is some three times its present extent. Of these the Vicar's Closes, comprising 160 acres, and Ellen Carr and Ben Carr containing 140 acres, made a total of 300 acres between the Upper Park House, at present the residence of Colonel Muscroft, the Low Park House, at the end of Skinner Lane, and the Castleford Road. The other 600 acres included southwards to the Nursery, and the rest of the cultivated land now called the Pontefract Park District. The present extent of the Park is only 325 acres.

15th. This day was the Souldyers set on worke to fill up a Filthy pond wch was in the Castle yeard, and made a place to draw the water away under Ground, & (caried *erased*) sett it, and Covered it wth stones & earth againe, and Clensed all the Castle yeard, wch was a very good worke to Clense the Castle from many noysome smelles. About 2 a Clock in the after noone, Thomas Lowther (a Souldyer), wth 2 Souldyers more, espyed Two of the Enemyes to Come out of their workes (being both of them Leiutenants) to watch our men wch was fetching (in *interlined*) of wodde from the lower end of the Towne, Fell upon them Suddenly, and one of them struck at Lowther wth his partisan, but he awaded the dangerous blow, and Runne him quite thorow wth his Raper ; and another of his fellow Souldyers shott him thorow the thigh, but was not slain, but brought into the Castle. the other Leiutenant Runne away. The name of him that was brought into the Castle was Thomson ; his woundes was p'sently drest by a Chirurgion of ours in the Castle, and w'thin Two howers there Came a drumme for him upon exchange out of the Towne, and he was exchanged for a Leiutenant of ours that was prisoner at Cawodd. About 12 a Clock in the night Came in Bellwether that was sent to Newarke 7 daies before, and another Souldyer of ours wth him wch was there. And all so Tho. Hanson, wch was sent to Sandall Castle 3 daies before. they mett both together at Swillinton Tower and brought letters from his ma'tie wth very Joyfull newes. GLORIA DEO.

Well done, Thomas Lowther, once more. We shall meet with you again, when you will not be quite so fortunate.

There is no present trace of the position of this " filthy pond" thus filled up. The Diarist locates it in the Castle Yard, but it is very doubtful whether he does not mean the Outer Barbican.

16th. This day we gave the (Enemye *erased*) Enemies (*substituted*) 2 Allarumes ; the one at Munkhill, about 1 a Clock, where we fell upon the new worke, and Charged their sentryes before they tooke the Allarum, and then they fled from thence Into the New hall, and dobled their gaurdes and Charged again upon them, So our men retreated, and Came into the Castle. About 5 a Clock a Few of our men went forth to their worke below the low Church, and gave fire upon them, then they drew out about 30 men into the Graunge barne, right opposite againt (*sic*) our men. Then our men fell into a thick Orchard of trees, and so they gave fire one against another for haulph an hower, and then our men retreated againe into the Castle wthout any hurt to our knowledg. About 10 (the *second* figure is so curved as to give the appearance of a cipher, imperfectly formed, which is probably the exact state of the case, but it has been read as 1) a Clock in the night we made out a (strong *erased*) p'ty, mere (*sic*) about 40 men, to a new worke the enemy had made at the Bottom of the Abbey Cloase, where we Itended to have fallen on to some good purpose, and we shot of one Cannon from the Kinges Tower against our falling on. but by report a woman got out of the Castle, & gave them Intelligence, but is sure they had Intelligence, for they had lined all the hedges there abouts, and Call'd to Captin Smith, & tould him they were p'vided for him. Neverthelesse we gave fire upon them for all most haulph an hower, and so retreated into the Castle, having had 2 men hurt in that service. and during this time we sent out Thomas Hanson & another man to go to Sandoll Castle.

The new work at Monkhill, and that at the bottom of the Abbey Close were evident parts of a connected operation to prevent the continued egress from Swillington Tower. But once more Thomas Hanson is sent out on his perilous expedition, the exact object of which the Diarist does not even hint at, though subsequent events told it pretty clearly.

17th. This morning there was one of the enemyes killd in the Markitt place from the Round Tower, and we had one man shott going out of Swillinton Tower. there was this day a drummer from the Towne, & all so a Trumpiter from the Lord Mountgommreyes Brother ; both Came to the Castle together. the Trumpiter was fecht up into the governer's Chamber, & stayd there for about haulph an hower, & so they went away both together. This day there (Came, *erased*) went a Cariage from the Towne loded, & Covred wth Red, and drawne away wth 14 oxen & a horse, & went towards Knottinglay, but was gone the next morning very yearly, we heard not whither. The Trumpiter tould us that (they *erased*) the (*substituted*) enemy, was not above 8000 both horse & Foote in all the Contrey.

All so many indications of the activity of the preparations of the besiegers, whatever the "Trumpiter" might say.

This slight glimpse of the travelling state of the seventeenth century is very interesting. It shows us a carriage—or superior waggon—drawn by 14 oxen and a horse, and therefore travelling slowly, and with some stateliness. The roads of the period must, at that time, have been mere quagmires, except in summer, and calculated for horse-traffic only, and not carriage-traffic.

18th. Being Sunday, after praiers was done in the morning, the Governor staid the Sarmon, and gave order that all should to Armes, wch was wth all willingnes p'formed. Ould Maior Warde was Commanded to the New mount w'thin Barbican to observe, to observe (*sic*) all the Towers in the Castle towardes Baghill that no man nor woman should make any Signes either wth hatt, hand, or handkircher, or any thing ellse that might be p'ceived to be a signe to give notice. In the Intrim, Captin Smith & Captin Flood, Ensigne Killingbeck & Sargiant Barton went out first over the Bridge to wardes Munkhill. Capt Smith wth 30 Souldyers went up by Denwell lane to the outworks upon the back of of (*sic*) Munkill, & beat them from those workes, & so went along therie trenches, & Cleared them as he went to theire first low (er *interlined*) worke. Captin Flood wth Anchient Killingbeck & 50 Souldyers Charged up the high street to Munkhill toppe, Fired the howses there, & so fell upon their first workes in the high streete by Scottes and entred (that, enemyes, Fir, *each erased*) that worke where he met wth Captin Smith. Close wth him Capt' Munroe wth Ensigne Ottoway & Sargiant Copland wth 70 men Issued out Close after the other & went downe Close by the low Church, Charged upon theire lowest worke, beate them from it, killd so many as they Could overtake, Fired the howse neare to it, Runne up the Lane to the Graunge Bearne, and killd all that was wthin it who was drinking heallthes (affter their dinner) to the higher howse of Parlament. from thence went up to Munkhill to the workes there, and over tooke the other Companyes at Cherry Orchard head neare Newhall. Leiutenant Collonell Gilbreth (Cap *erased*) Leiutenant Willowby and Leiuten't Warde wth 60 (men *erased*) musketeres stayd at the low Church. and ould Maior Warde & Leiut Fevell wth 40 musketeers lined all the walles in the low Barbican. for these men, at the low Church & heare, weare reserves upon purpose that, if either the Towen (had *erased*) or Baghill had Faullen out to have seconded the Enemy at Newhall, then upon the first notise they would have rescued our men. we had allso about 20 horse Commanded by Captin Beale Came up to Munkhill upon that service, but they Could not passe the Trenches (an illegible *erasure*) was made there.

It will be remembered that two days before, an attack upon the besiegers had been almost frustrated by the speedy intelligence which enabled them to prepare for it. In that case, some woman was suspected to have got out of the Castle, and given the information, and accordingly every precaution was taken on this occasion to make such a circumstance impossible ; the care of watching for the waving of hat, hand or handkerchief—the Diarist by no means scorns " alliteration's apt and artful aid"—was entrusted to Ould Major Warde himself, while the Governor kept the design within his own breast until the appointed moment, when he stopped the sermon, and commanded the attack.

"The trenches was made there" is an instance of the Diarist's frequent omission of the relative pronoun. He means "which was made there," and his omission of the relative seems to be so habitual, as to be a part of his grammar.

The transaction thus graphically narrated seems to have been a very successful operation, and its circumstances tend to show both how lax were the notions of military discipline among the besiegers, and how very weak was the attacking force. Here were three considerable works attacked by the besieged, who traversed them in every direction at their own sweet will, and even advanced to the "Grange Barn" and killed all those at dinner there, without alarm being given by sentry or guard, or the main body of the enemy being warned in any way of what was going on: at least 250 of the Garrison (30, 40, 50, 60 and 70) and about 20 horse were concerned in the affair, or took part in the proceedings, so that with officers, and those left behind, considering the "lads" or "wenches" of whose presence, in addition, we have constant intimation, and the women to guard against whose possible treachery Major Warde was put upon special duty, there must at this time have been at least 400 souls within the Castle gates. A question may naturally arise, How could sleeping accommodation be found for this large company, winter and summer, not a tithe of whom could have been received into the Towers. Unfortunately, we get not the slightest hint of the way in which this difficulty was met. The accommodation must have been meagre, to say the least of it; but such as it was it was borne without a murmur for seven long months, as so much of a most ordinary matter of course, that the Diary may be perused from beginning to end in search of an answer to the question, without the discovery of a single ray of light to enlighten the obscurity.

The "Grange Barn," as it was called, was probably an adaptation of the chancel of the Church of St. John the Evangelist, the place of worship of the Cluniac Monks of Pontefract, demolished at the Reformation. The Grange Field, as the enclosure is called even now, was the piece of ground, containing but nine acres, within which stood the monastic buildings, the type and model which Archbishop Thurstin took for Fountains Abbey. Not a trace of all now remains above ground, except that in the boundary wall an occasional moulded stone may be traced. A considerable part of the common burial ground is still however in position to the north of the Church, its eastern end having been carted away bodily, some ten years ago, while the ground was being levelled to receive a malt house; but the cloisters, the burying place of the Priors, can easily be discovered, as can the foundations of the Church, of the Guest House, and of many of the monastic offices. Part of the

Porter's Lodge, also, was remaining in living memory, and the sides of the gateway through which the mob flocked to pay devotion at the tomb of St. Thomas, and which the burly Gascons in the time of Hugh le Despencer were specially set to guard, exists to this day, built up in the wall. That not a trace of the honoured dead buried within those walls should now appear, is sufficiently remarkable. For it is claimed that the great Ilbert himself, and his wife, that their son Robert, and his wife, and that Ilbert, the son of these latter, were all buried in the Church of St. John. It is moreover, known, that it received the remains of Archbishop Thurstin, that within these precincts was laid the body of Thomas, Earl of Lancaster, executed on the neighbouring hill, in 1322, and that here for many generations his tomb was the object of as devout reverence, as was his picture in St. Paul's Cathedral. Here also was temporarily buried Richard, duke of York, beheaded at York, till his son Edward, having by the battle of Towton made himself King of England, had it removed to Fotheringay. This field, now so bare, is thus full of historic memories, while its pastures hide the remains of those who were in their day and generation leaders of men, both in things Ecclesiastical and in things Civil.

The Commanders affore-named Charged very Bravely to the very Newhall (gate *erased*) of wch they left sufficient (wittnes *erased*) evidence (*substituted*) in 2 men wch they there killd.

It hardly required this additional memorandum to show that it was a very brave sally, gallantly executed in every detail. All concerned were doubtless proud of it, in its conception, execution, and result. (See also 15 July *Post.*)

The enemy Runne away Basely by 40 at a time over St Thomas Hill towardes Ferry bridge, & what way they Could soonest take. our men did greate execution. both breefely & gallantly, having not left one man in all theire trenches but dead, and retreated Honorably the same waies they went out, and in theire retreate looked over the slaine men, and, though they staid not to strippe them, yett they tooke offe somme of theire best loose garments as hattes & shoowes; not forgetting their pockittes, where they found in Somme 10 groates, some 5sh, some 10sh., some moie, wch gave them some encoragement (for *erased*) in want of pay. having left dead upon the ground about 50 or 60 men and mauked (we beleeve) as many more, and brought in to the Castle 2 prisoners, & 2 leguer ladyes (wch Ladyes we p'sently dismist), we having had onely one man killd, a gallant gentleman & a brave Souldyer, (his name was (Corronet Blockley) who was shott neare Cherry orchard side, but Came to Munkhill of him sellfe & from thence brought into the Castle, where he dyed that night, and allso a Common Souldyer soare wounded & taken prisoner. during wch time our Cannon plaid twise from the Kinges Tower where the enemy had a troope of horse, & the Bullitt grased full amongst them (& killd one man wch we saw *interlined*). Two Cannon more was shott to Baghill: the first was loaded wth Case shott, havinge 16 dozon of muskitt Bullites in hur, wch tooke at least 10 yeardes Compasse Just upon the toppe of theire worke at Bagghill, from whence the enemy shott not one shutt (*sic*) of 2 howers after ; & the other Cannon was playd at a Company of horsemen wch was behind the hedge at Baghill, wch grased amongst them, but what execution the both did is unknowne to us. (One thinge I had forgott,) for, besides the light pillage our men brought away, yet they tooke time to take up theire Armes too, as Swordes, muskuites, haulbordes, drummes, Saddles, spades, and in every trench a bagge of powder & somme match, wch for hast they had left behind them.   That night, about 9 a Clock, there was 2 waggons loded at new hall, & went towardes Ferrybridgg. we supposed they was loaded wth wounded men. and about 11 a Clock there was a great fire seene upon the toppe of Sandall Castle, wch Continued for the space of 2 howers.

The hint here concerning want of pay, reminds us that throughout the Diary, there is no mention of any coining operations, though it has been circumstantially asserted, and possibly with truth, that Sir Jarvis Cutler took all his family plate into the Castle, in order that it might be turned into money to pay the King's Troops. But as what are known as the Pontefract siege coins belong to the third siege, and bear its date, they could not have been the produce of Sir Jarvis Cutler's silver. There are, however, certain undated coins which may possibly have been made in the Castle at this time; though it is singular that the Diary has not even the remotest hint, of any coining work having been in progress, at the time of its composition.

With regard to the "Company of horsemen which was behind the hedge," a reference to the configuration of the ground at Baghill may tend to make the allusion clearer. Behind the ridge of the hill, as seen from the Castle, is a rather extensive plateau, which could indeed be overlooked from the Tower, but was hardly, if at all discernible from the Castle Yard. Its slope was slightly in a southern direction, that is away from the Castle, so that it was the obvious position from which the fortress could have been bombarded, now that gunpowder was coming into use. Dividing this arable plateau from the pasture of the hill was a long hedge, as it is called page 29, nearly parallel with the Castle buildings; while about a hundred and fifty yards away on the other side of a ten acre field, was a second hedge which slightly converged towards the first in the direction of the Darrington Road, that by which the Castle was approached from the south. Behind this second hedge was an accommodation road, about eight feet wide, and this is partly sunk below the natural level in order to meet the main road which approaches the Castle through a deep gorge. It was in the trench thus formed that the horsemen seem to have been posted.

Beyond these Baghill Closes, lay the Willow Tree Closes, (now sometimes called Willow Park), and still further beyond were the Chequer Fields, now also enclosed, the scene of Sir Marmaduke's exploit which terminated the first siege, as related on page 29.

19th. This (day *erased*) morning, in the Fore aoone, the enemy Cept theire workes so Close that we Could scarce gett any shott betwixt the Round tower & the Kinges Tower, yett we killd one man at theire worke side in the bottom of the Abbay Close. our Souldyers, seeing the Could not gett any shott, fell a Showting upon the leades & Cryed a prince, a prince, so Lowd and so strongly as that the enemy tooke (an *erased*) strong (*interlined*) Allarum, Fetcht all theire horses from grasse soddenly, saddled them, & drew them into the graunge lane. there went downe from the towne 42 men to New hall, & as many to Baghill to strengthen theire gaurdes.
In theire running to & from we killd 3 or 4 more of the enemeys, & wounded as many.

It might hardly have been thought that so simple a device to obtain a living target could have succeeded so well as it evidently did. But "3 or 4 of the enemyes", if not twice as many, were victims to it. And not the least remarkable circumstance recorded is, that the besieged were able to count precisely how many men passed from one part of the works to another—42 to relieve one battery, and "as many" to strengthen another.

20th. this day we had a report that the enemy had (a report *erased*) Footmen at Ferrybrigge, but at noone this great number appeard and p'ved but 22. thus they Feed their Souldyers wth bragges. afterwardes there appeard about 200 horse from Ferrybridge, marching under the hill from darington to the westfeeld, & so into the Parke, & then turned into the Lane at tansill, & so into the Parke againe. then our Cannon from Treasurers tower plaid upon them & killd 2 men. and then they made haste behind the Ridge of the hill in the parke, out of sight; and that night there Came 6 or 7. more troopes to them, & marched from thence to wakefeild or thereabouts. there was this day 5 or 6 men killd from the Round Tower at Baghill, and at the other workes under the shott of the Round tower. our Cannons playd twise more that day up the towne, & to newhall, but what execution was don by them is not knowen to us.. the enemyes little Cannon (or bable) at Baghill plaid 3 times this day towardes the Castle, but we naither know nor Can learne where it hitt or gave any Impression.

This would be hardly intelligible without the knowledge—see page 68,—that "the Park" then extended on both sides of "the lane at Tansill"—Causeway lane, as it was then called, Featherstone lane, as is its present name. That lane now bounds the Park to the west.

21th. This day, being a very Rayney day for the most p'te, there was little done worth the noting till about 2 a Clock 5 or 6 of our men went down to the lower towne to fetch wodde, whereupon the enemy, both from Baghill & all theire workes about Munkhill, shott as if they had beene madd, and in the middle of that Allarum there Came out of the Towne & marched in single file thorough the lower end of the Parke to Newhall about 500 men wth theire drummes & Collors to releeve theire gaurdes there. we shott two Cannon towardes them, but what execution was done we know not, but onely one man & his horse was killd. and towardes night & in the night there went about 300 men from new hall up into the Towne to refresh themsellves, for Sr. John Saivells men had scarce ever beene in bed since they Came to newhall. this night will wether Alias Bellwether went to Newarke againe, (and allso Capin weshington & Leiutenant Wheatelay went towardes Newarke, and there was a bonefire made upon Sandoll Castle, wch was some signe of good newes, *erased*.)

The rain of this 21st May, has left an evident impression upon the MS.: which here becomes suddenly very indistinct and worn. This appearance was, probably, owing to the removal of the size from the paper, or to injury received by it from hands damp with rain; the injury causing the ink to run more freely upon the paper than it should have done, and to penetrate it more thoroughly than was intended. The consequence is that the material has here become almost as brittle as if it had been scorched, requiring the most careful handling to prevent its breaking to pieces. In a few places where something similar to this has occurred, the MS. copy supplies the hiatus; but once or twice even this resource fails, showing that the completion of the injury was very early in the history of the MS.

These repeated bonfires and signals between the two Castles, whose significance was kept within the breast of the Governor, or at least was not so generally known as to have been understood by the Diarist, probably referred to the projects of relief, now in contemplation.

22th. This morning one Kerbyes Sonne, Going to gett grasse for his Fathers horse, was shott wth a muskitt bullitt. This day the enemy made two Shottes wth theire bable from Baghill, but we know not what became of the Bullittes. this day allso our Governor had letters from his Matie & Sr Marmaduke Langdall that a Royall Armey was advancing towardes us for our releefe, (a Comforth long expected & as Joyfully accepted), w'th harty desires & Earnest prayers for a (p'sperous *interlined*) blessing upon theire endevours. this night allso Came Hanson wth letters from Sandall Confirming the former repoart. In the Intrim we yett (have *interlind*) no want of victualls, but are fully resolved to mantane the Castle against all REBELLS whatsoever.

The reason for the Diarist's use of the term "Bable" is not altogether evident, unless Bable is a form of the word Babble, applied metaphorically to the gun, as talking much, but effecting little.

The emphasis with which he wrote REBELS must be seen to be understood. Type cannot do it adequate justice.

Here is the first hint of the possibility of the garrison being shortly at a strait for victuals.

23th. This morning the Enemy shett theire little Bable from Baghill againe, but did no execution, not so much as made any signe of Impression in the (Castle *i-terlined*) wall. we had allso letters this day that, from Skipton Castle & Lathom Hall, they sent ayd and releeved Grinoway Castle in Lankeshire wth 60 Beastes & other necessaryes when it was at the very poynt of yeilding to the Enemy for want of victualls, & being a very Considerable place. there Came also Michaell Blagburne (a Clothier) (& Tenant to Sr. John Romsden *rased*) & a

Tennant allso of Maior Beamondes, who tould us that the Scottes was marching northwardes, & reioyced much at the wellfare of theire Landslordes. wch this theire Creeping into Favour wth theire Landslordes we tooke as a good signe that we weare in a good Condition & that we should shortly regaine our liberties so long desired. this day allso there Came a Captin from the Enemy (wth A drumme) to speake wth Captin Spaght, who said he would tell us the Truth, that the kinge was advancing to releeve us wth all speede.

23th. This night allso went Captin Washington & Leiutenant Wheatelay to (Newarke *erased*) Sandall (*substituted*) and there was a great bonefire made at Sandoll Castle, & we answered it wth another in that night, wch wee tooke for a signe of good newes. we had allso newes that they from wthin Skarbrough Castle Issued forth from thence & killed & tooke 300 of the Enemyes, & nayled up theire Cannon & burnt theire Cariages & so retreated into the Castle. the Tennants allso before meutioned tould us that Collonell Bruerton had drawne offe his Forces from the seege of Westchaster, upon the report that the King was advanceing.

It is evident that here again, the garrison were allowed to think that Captain Washington and Lieut. Wheatley had gone to Newark. While on better information the Diarist subsequently substituted Sandal for Newark.

---

24. This morning about 3 a Clock the enemy gave fire as though they would have entred the Castle p'sently, upon what reasons we know not, unlesse (they *interlined*) weare greeved at the bonefires upon the Round Tower that night, for they shott most at that place. about 10 a Clock, a woman wch was gathring of pott hearbes was shott by the enemy into the thigh, but not dangerous of death. about that time our Iron gunne shott once into the Towne but what execution it did is not knowne. about 4 or 5 a Clock in the after noone, 4 of our men went downe to the low Church (where the Enemy was) and as soone as the Enemy espied, they fled all away but one (who was supposed to be a Leiutenant). he stayd behind, & threw stones so fast that our men Could not enter in of a good time, but at length One Thom. Lowther, a man who, if his Judgement had beene according to his vallor, was as sufficient as most men, he bouldly entered upon the Leiutenant, and wthout all question had brought him along wth him, had he not beene unfortunately shot by the enemy at that instant thorough the boane of his legg, wch the enemy espying runne in all hast to Catch him, but our men (with much labour) brought him offe into the Castle, where he had his legg p'sently Cutt of. and now recovers very fast againe. this day we had letters that his Maties Armyes was devided, & the king wth one haulph Came to releeve us, and that PRINCE MORIS went wth the other haulph towardes the releefe of Carleell; the Army Consisting of 15000. this night the enemy shott very Freely, but towardes morning they exceeded, giving whole vollyes of shott round about the Castle & Crying a Cromwell, a Cromwell, the officers having possessed the Souldyers that Cromwell was marching (in his Maties REARE) wth a strong Army. and towardes morning the enemy burnt 2 or 3 howses in the Northgate, as allso the sett fire in the Water mill below the Castle, & burnt downe 2 or 3 little howses there abouts, & tooke a poore Tailor & his wife (who dwelt in those howses) prisoners; the rest of the people wch was within them escaped towardes the Castle, wch when our men espied gave fire upon them from the Castle, kill'd one (was an officer of Certain) at the Millne doore, & shott another into the (Castle *erased*) Shoulder. the one (they *interlined*) fetcht of dead & the other quick. we know no reasones

of this burning of howses in the Northgate, unlesse it were to draw on the Townesmen to pay theire assessments freely (wch about 2 daies before they had assessed) or ellse they would burne the towne.

The description of Thomas Lowder, as one who "*If his judgment had been according to his valour*, was as sufficient as most men," seems to have been very suitable to the circumstances of the case.

This is the first mention of Cromwell in the Diary. His name occurs twice subsequently 20 June and 15 July; but he took no part in the siege.

25th May, 1645. This day, beeing whit sonday, there was little shooting from either side, nor not any one hurt that we heare of. we had 2 very good sermondes that day, & so went quietly to our rest, we hearing that the enemyes made theire gaurdes very strong & Cept strickt watch least we should sally forth upon them, as we had done the Sunday before.

How careful was the garrison not to sally when they were expected to do so. But they would not risk the memory of their brave exploit of the previous Sunday, by an injudicious venture. The fate of Lowder and his amputated leg, must also have been not without its effect as a warning to the more adventurous.

To this Entry, commencing a fresh page, is prefixed the day of the month, the month, and the year.

26th. This day, being whitson Munday, we had our great Iron gunne removed from the mont before the gates & planted (of *altered to*) on the platforme withou the upp' gates where she was before, and we plaid one shott wth hur into theire sentry howse over against Mr Rusbyes, where it gave such a blow as they runne out of it by 40 or 60 at (a ti' *altered to*) altogether & was thought did great execution. This day allso was the little drake planted upon the toppe of Swillington Tower, and was twise shott towardes Paradise Orchard, where there was a strong gaurd Cept in that worke all along the hedge, but what execution they did is not knowne. There was one Will: Jubbe & a boy went out of the Castle to fetch in some grasse for the horses & Cattell (as there went out many more besides them) but, they being too negligent to looke well about them, the boy was shott in at the mouth side, & thorow the Cheeke, but not any mortall wound, and Jubbe was taken prisoner & Caryed up into the towne, where, they finding him to be but a simple man, many Came about him & gave him good store of stronge (Ale *interlined*) till the had soundly foxt him, thinking then to have gott good Intelligence out of him. and in the night brought him towardes Newhall (there to be examoned,) but in the way (the souldyers beeing not too vigilant over him) he tooke his opportunety & slipt away from them, & Came into the Castle againe before 11 aClock. This night allso Came in Captin Washington from Sandall, who went thither the Fridday night before, and brought good newes of the Princes good p'ceedinges, that he had summons to Manchaster to turne out the women & Children out of the towne, or ellse he would Come before it, that Westchaster (seege *interlined*) was (releeved *erased*) reised, that Darby was (beseeged *erased*) (sumoned *interlined*) (that Carlell seege was reised *erased*) and that Skerbrough had releeved themsellves, killd all theire officers expeting 2 or 3, and had killd & taken 300 men, dismounted theire great Iron Gunne & the 2 pockitt pistoles, wth all the rest of theire Cannon theare, & that they had nailed theire Gunnes and burnt theire Cariuges there, & had taken Skarbrough Towne. whereupon for Joy was a boanefire made upon the toppe of the Round tower (and Hanson was, *erased*). this day allso the enemy sett on fire theire owne worke in the northgate. we suppose it was by some mischance, but it was quench again that night. there was allso a p'ly this night betwix 3 of our Capteines & 3 of theires, but the enemy gave fire upon our men, & then our Souldyers gave fire towerdes theires (*appa·ently erased, but the apparent erasure here is caused by the erasure of the word Castle on the previous page*) & so the p'ted.

Altogether a singular exhibition of recklessness and want of watchfulness on both sides. Jubbe and the boy, too negligent to look well about them; the guards not too vigilant over the prisoners; and to crown all, the "simple man" being so easily " foxt " with the strong ale, but yet able to seize the opportunity offered him by the lack of care displayed by his guards.

This day, Whitmonday, occurred the earliest indications of a disposition on the part of the garrison, to consider the possibility of being reduced to treat.

The use of " the " for "they," as in the close of this day's entry, is frequent in the Diary; but although it appears to be quite in accordance with the Diarist's grammatical system, there are one or two instances in which he has subsequently added the " y," as a correction.

27th. This day we plaid two Cannon in the morning, the first thorow their Trenches against Mr Rusby, & the other thorough Mrs Oates howse, in the markitt place, but what execution they did is not knowen to us. there was little shooting all that day, but Joshua Walker killed one of the enemyes who was taking a pipe of Tobackoe in the lane by the primrose Cloase, under Bagghill. there was a little poore wench was keeping of a Cow under Swillington Tower was shott into the thigh by the enemy, but not killd. This night, a little after 12 a Clock, Came in Leiutenant wheatelay, who was sent wth Capt' Washington the Friddy night last, who brought along wth him betwixt 40 and 50 horse, and as they Came by the way they light wth 2 of the enemies Skoutes & toke them & theire horses. the allso (tooke *interlined*) about 120 or 130 Cattell wch (the *altered to*) they brought along wth them and Came to Bagghill toppe. an hower before wch time, our men was all in readines. p'te of them was in Barbican neare to the Sally poart, and the rest was betwixt the lower gate & the mount at the Castle gate, expeckting a signe when they shoud salley foarth (wch Fell out thus). the Cattell being many together, & making great loowing in the Checquer Feeld, before baghill, Leiutenant Wheatelay Came riding before them as fast as he Could downe the Closes by Baghill, Crying Armes, Armes, to your Armes, a prince, a prince, wch was a signe to us. Whereupon was all the 3 Great Gunnes discharged p'sently, wch was a signe for us to sally foorth, wch we did p'sently wth all speede. Capt Flood, wth Captin Ogleby, & Leiutenant Killingbeck wth 50 musketeares, was Commanded to Baghill, and was not to enter the enemyes worke, but to stay under the hill side Close to theire worke, & to give fire upon them if they should sally foorth, wch they p'formed very bravely wthout daunger of Shott. Leiutenant Collonell Gilbreth wth Leiutenant Smith & Leiutenant Warde followed next after them up the hill wth 40 musketeares to theire worke at the little round Close Called primroase Close under Baghill, from whence they p'sently beat the enemy into theire great worke at Baghill. next after him followed Captin Smith & Leiutenant Ogleby wth 30 musketeares who went up to Elizabeth Cattell's howse & to the Burnt howses thereaboutes, who shott from thence to theire lowest workes under broade lane end, for going to releeve them on Baghill where they gave fire very bravely, & Cept them from releeving them. During wch time Capt' Munroae, wth Capt' Barthrome & Sargiant Barton, Issued out at the lower gates to the enemyes (quarters *erased*) workes below the (workes *erased*) Church, where he Cept them from Issuing forth, or from thence or from Newhall. And Capt' Joshua Walker wth his about 20 Snaphanches went out through the howses on the Southside of the Church, & so up the Closes to the toppe of Baghill, where they mett all the Cattell wthe the Sandall brave Souldyers, who delivered them to him, and then went all back againe excepting some 10. or 12. wch helped to bring downe the Cattell to the Castle, but, they driving them downe the hill too fast, they lost many of them. but they brought in 97 into the Castle, and a foale above a yeare ould wch runne in wth the Cattell. And then our drummes beate a retreate for all our men to fall of & retire to the Castle, wch they very orderly did, and during wch time our Iron gunne plaid 3 times to theire workes in the towne and about the towne. thus having (by Godes assistance) releived the Castle to our great Comforth, we made boane fires upon the Towers of the Castle, and played wth our Cannon from the Kinges tower into Mrs Oates howse in the Markit place in signe of this great releife wch God had bestowed upon us, not having so much as one man hurt during this time, but onely one William Dickson whe was firing the great gunne was shott from Baghill on the side of his Cheeke, but (never *erased*) touched the boane, & was almest Cleane well wthin 4 daies after. Our Commanders had very much to doe to kepe theire men from falling upon theire men from falling upon theire workes both at Baghill, and allso they would needes goe up to New hall, though they had Commaund to the Contrarye.

The lane by Primrose Close has lately been widened to form the approach to the Midland Railway (Baghill Station). The present northern boundary is the original hedge, but that which separated the lane from Primrose Close has gone, and the greater part of Primrose Close itself has been cut away to make room for the main road.—But see page 61.

"Tobackoe" was at this time in common use among soldiers of both armies, notwithstanding the late King's "Counterblaste;" and remains of the short pipes then in vogue are frequently met with in the neighbourhood of Pontefract, though always broken at the foot of the bowl ; for, as the part of the tube where the bowl joins the stem seems to have been a peculiarly weak place, perfect pipes are exceedingly rare.

The way in which this exploit was performed, was particularly neat. It is evident that all the details had been most carefully and secretly planned to prevent information from leaking out to the enemy. Intelligence between the two Castles being established by means of answering bonfires, Capt. Washington and Lieut. Wheatley went to Sandal on the Friday, but allowed it to be understood that they were bound for Newark. During the two or three days between their departure and their return, all was hushed preparation ; and on the Monday, Capt. Washington came in with particulars of the way in which the projected undertaking was to be executed. His safe arrival having been signalled by a bonfire on the Round Tower, Lieut. Wheatley started from Sandall the next day with a herd of 120 or 130 cattle, escorted by 40 or 50 horse. He timed his arrival, a little after midnight on Tuesday, when the garrison, themselves unaware of the details of the project they were about to assist in, were ready posted in the Barbican, near the sally port, the very site of which is now unknown, and the rest under their different Commanders in other parts of the Outer Garth. Meanwhile the Cattle, being brought from the Wakefield Road across the fields to the Chequers, were about 300 yards from the Castle, when Lieutenant Wheatley galloped across the intervening closes making an alarm which, while startling the besiegers, should inform the garrison of his arrival. Three guns were then fired from the Round Tower, as the signal for the sally under cover of which the cattle were to be got in. This movement was made in three divisions in the following concerted order. Capt. Flood, with a detachment of 50, went into the Baghill road to confine the enemy to their works; Col. Gilbraith followed with a party of 40 attacking the lower work, and was himself followed by Capt. Smith with 30, who turned off to the right to prevent the Broad Lane party from strengthening those at Baghill. Meanwhile Capt. Munroe went out at the Lower Gate, through the Booths, and past the Church, to keep the Newhall party back, thus still further isolating those on Baghill, while Capt. Walker, with his 20, broke through the houses to the south of the Church, and reaching the top of Baghill through the Closes to the right, met the cattle on the plateau. There taking charge of them, they drove them straight down the road towards the Castle, and the way being kept by the different parties of musketeers, they were able to get as many as 97 beasts in at the sally port, about a quarter of the whole herd escaping during the hurry and confusion. The triumphant bonfires which were at once lighted must have been looked for eagerly at Sandal.

The perverseness of the undisciplined men who did not understand the importance of what was being done, but " would go up to Newhall" might have done serious disservice, had the besiegers been better handled.

We pause to note the expression "or from thence, or from Newhall," so exactly corresponding to the modern French *ou* . . . . *ou*. It is noteworthy to find that form of expression lingering in Yorkshire speech in the middle of the seventeenth century. The phrase would now be "*either* from thence, or from Newhall."

Mrs Oates's house seems to have been a prominent mark. We have it mentioned twice in this paragraph, as we had it on April 4, and as we had her adjoining kilnhouse, on April 27th. The property was extensive, and self-contained, forming four sides of a quadrangle, the usual style of a mediæval mansion house, the quadrangle being entered both from the Market Place and from Ratten Row, as it was then called, which included both Salter Row and Middle Row. The house is now subdivided, and part of the quad built upon. Mrs Oates was Isabel, daughter of Mr Alderman John Frank. She was the widow of Mr Alderman Wm. Oates, and mother of Alderman Richard Oates, and Alderman Wm. Oates.—See Appendix B.

---

28. This day the enemy would scarce speake to us of all the day long, being so asshamed that they, having so many men in all theire workes, should suffer us to be thus releeved, and tould Collonell Ourton (theire Governor) that there Came 500 men wth the Cattell, where we had not above 50 horse in all. the enemy shott very hard to the Castle all the day, but did no hurt at all (praised be God). Theire Governor allso sent a letter wth a drumme & 3 women (owners of p'te of those Cattell, *interlined*) as it weare in a Commaunding manner to our GOVERNOR, either to deliver back the Cattell, or to take Composition for them in money, wch our GOVERNOR p'sently answered that if he Could take the Castle, he should have the Cattell, otherwise he should not have the worst beast was brought in under 40*li*. we killed one of the enemyes horse this day under the P'adise orchard this day *(sic)* in Mr Rusby Closes. this night those 10 or 12 men wch Came from Sandoll intendid, to have gone thother againe, but, as they went downe by the Castle side towardes Munkhill, our musketeres wch should have gone wth them to the workes at Munkhill having theire matches all lighted, the enemy espyed & shott at them, &, at the hospitall doore, hitt one of the Sandall men upon the side of his Cheeke, so that that they turned back againe into the Castle. during wch time we shott the Iron Gunne into the hedge by theiro workes at Baghill, where there was many horse, but what execution it did it is not knowne. this night allso the enemy sett on Fire a howse on the lower end of northgate, wch burnt above 2 daies & 2 nightes. they all so made a Barricado in the lane going up to (M *erased*) Baghill, to stoppe us from sallying forth.

The report among the besiegers that only 50 beasts had been got into the Castle, and that 30 had been prevented from entering, is a partial corroboration of the Diary, which acknowledging that about 30 escaped, names 97 as the number that entered. Naturally the "enemy" were inclined to depreciate the relief that had been obtained by the invested garrison. But their report that 30 escaped being thus corroborated by the Diarist, inclines us to put implicit confidence in the accuracy of his other details.

It would seem that the amateur cattle drivers had added "cattle lifting" to their other accomplishments, and on their road to Pontefract had picked up a few additional beasts, which they included among their herd, to the natural indignation of the rightful owners. "Their governor" as naturally seized the opportunity of making capital out of the transaction, and of posing as the friend of the oppressed.

In this and all the transactions which "the GOVERNOR" had with the REBELS, one cannot but admire the spirit of the old Cavalier, who, as he put it with a neat antithesis, would give them the Cattle, if they could take the Castle.— The Diarist's use here of the word "presently", as it frequently occurs, is in its original meaning—at the *present* moment. Now the word "presently" has come to mean "at a future time."

There is thus no doubt of the number of the Sandal men that shared in the episode of the adventure with the cattle. The Diarist's repetition of the expression "10 or 12" shows that he at least had no doubt that there were not more than a dozen.

They started for home " by the Castle side ;" that is out of the Lower Gate, but not through the Booths, for they kept close to the Castle towards " haulpeny howse," that is the " Hope and Anchor,"—see page 60. As one was wounded " at the Hospitall doore,"—that is St Nicholas hospital—a few yards past the Hope and Anchor, it is evident that the shot had come straight down the road from Monkhill ; which must have shown them that it was against all hope to expect to evade the vigilance of the besiegers, and that their persistance would have been literally and actually an advance to the cannon's mouth. The well-planned diversion on the part of the garrison, in shooting towards Baghill in order to distract attention from Monkhill, was therefore a failure.

The construction of a barricade at Baghill lane the day after so many cattle had been smuggled into the Castle was vastly like an impotent attempt to lock the stable door when the steed had already been stolen.

29th. This day Some of our Souldyers went forth to Gett grasse for the Cattell & horses, and one Covetous man, having beene 6 times before (and had 4d. for every burthen,) went out the 7th time, and would not Come away wth the rest of his Fellowes, and so was shott by the enemy. and after they had taken him & (runne hime thorough *erased*) & (giving *altered to*) given him quarter, another of the enemyes runne him thorough & so killd him quite out, but Could not take him away, so we fetcht him offe. this day we killd all so another of the enemyes horse, in the same ground where the other was killd before, under p'adise Orchard. in the afternoone the enemy sent downe about 300 men to Newhall (being the Tenth day,) to releeve theire gaurdes there, and at that time, when they was all about newhall yeard, we plaid one Cannen from the Kinges Tower into Newhall yeard, where we supposed they all was, but what execution it did was not knowen. there Came back from newhall, about 7 a clo', in single file through the Abbay Close, about 480 men, & so marched up into the Towne. this night the enemy made a triangle werke in the Closes above Denwell, neare to the upp' side of Swillinton Tower, to p'vent our sallying forth from thence. abou 3 a Cloc in the morning there went about 30 Souldiers more from Newhall up into the towne. they marched (as before) in single fille through the Abbey Close.

Where the members of the garrison could go to get grass might be a reasonable subject for wonder. With their fortress professedly invested, themselves virtually prisoners, they yet went out to get grass for their 97 cattle and their still numerous horses ; and went out with so much impunity that one particular man went as many as seven times for the stipulated remuneration of fourpence a journey. Naturally he came to grief presently: his seventh journey being one too many. It will be remembered that fourpenny journeys were made weeks before to fetch in the bullets that fell on the graft (see 17th January.)

The shortening of "about" into "abou" can have proceeded from accident only; for within but a dozen words occur "abou 3" and "about 30."

The Abbey Close, or Abbot's Close, as it is generally called in Pontefract, is now cut up for the Railway and the Workhouse. At the time of the siege it adjoined the Park, from which it was then separated by Skinner Lane only. Now, so much of the Park has been enclosed that the boundary of that enclosure is removed at least a third of a mile from the Abbey Close.

From Denwell to Swillington Tower is about two hundred yards: and yet between those two near points, there were this triangle work, and the works connected with Swillington Tower itself; so that only a very small space separated the two opposing forces.

The party evidently marched in single file, as affording a smaller mark for a stray shot.

30th. This day the enemy shott very hard from all their workes, but did no hurt at all, (praised be God) and we shott our little drake, wch was planted upon Swillinton Tower, 6 times to theire new worke over against it, where we beate them out of the worke behind the out side of it, but what execution was done we know not. about 8 a Clock towardes night we shott of the great Iron Gunne into theire workes behind Mr Rusbyes & Mr Lunnes, where it shott thorough theire workes amongst them, but we know not what hurt was done. this night the enemy repaird theire new worke against Swillington Tower.

The second siege had now been in progress for above two months; and with all this interchange of shot, the besiegers knew not that any "execution" had been done against them; while they themselves could not assert that by all their own efforts any "hurt was done," except that the "great Iron Gunne" was shot "through theire workes amongst them."

31th. This morning one of our Souldiers killd a woman in the Markit place wth a muskit from the Round Tower. the enemy shott very hard all the day from all theire workes round about the Castle, but did no hurt at all (praised be God). In the Intrim we sent some shottes amongst them wth our muskitts when we saw the least opportunitie to keepe them in play, and likewise we mixed amongst them some Cannon shott. we shott in all 6 Cannon & most of them to the markitt place, where we saw 3 draughtes (wch Came empty in the morning) was loading about Bonny Coup's (shoppe *interlined*) & there abouts, but 2 of those Cannon was plaid from the Kinges Tower, wch made them soone remove their standing quite away & went towardes Ferry bridge. we supposed they was loaded wth goodes out of the shoppes and at the other Cannons playing there was supposed divers to be shott, for we saw them carrye away 3 men at one time, but what execution more is not knowne to us. The Governor of the towne sent a Complamentall letter to our Governor about exchange of men & other matters, but in the Conclution he writt, beeing too weake an enemy (*a space never filled in wa. left for 25 or 30 words, probably the length of the intended quotation from the Governor's letter*). this night there Came in letters to the Governor of very good newes, wch was Imparted to the gentlemen the next morning.

The musket shot which (fired from the Round Tower to the Market Place) killed a woman, must have been better than usual. The distance is at least a third of a mile.

"Bonny Cowper" was a grocer in the Market Place, who (or his namesake) afterwards, for the convenience of his customers, issued one of the farthing tokens of which thirteen were coined between 1649 and 1669, for different Pontefract tradesmen.

It is a matter of regret that the subject of this message cannot be recovered. It would be interesting to know what it was that so excited the Diarist's contempt as to strengthen in him the opinion that the governor of the town was but a "weak enemy." Doubtless such was the case; but still the evidence of this particular weakness would have been very acceptable.

This "good news" was mostly unauthentic and inaccurate, as we learn from the account of the next day's proceedings, the principal items in which were afterwards, apparently on better information, so totally erased as to be now illegible.

June 1th. This morning being Sunday (the governor .... was the newes........ was both taken *erased*) and allso that upon Tewsday last was Durby Summoned by Sr. Marmaduke Langdall, and allso greater Confirmation of Raising of the seege at Skarbrough, & the taking of many Collonells & officers and the killing of Melldrome there. this day we had 2 good Sermondes; and in the afternoone, whilst we was at the Church, there beeing many Souldyers upon the Round Tower, upon theire watch there, & many of them sleeping there, one of them as he lay upon his belly sleeping, there Came a bullitt wch shott him thorough the thigh, but touched no boane, so that we hope he will quickly recover againe.

While thankful that so much of this remarkable Diary has been preserved to us as an illustration of seventeenth century life, it is provoking to find how silent it sometimes becomes just where another few words would have revealed most interesting matter. In such cases we can deal but in inferences, though, as in this instance, our inference is probably well-founded.

Thus, "Whilst we was at *the* Church," mentioned in this casual way must clearly mean that the main body of the Gurrison were actually out of the Castle, and had gone for worship, through the trenches, to the Parish Church, which had not yet passed out of their hands. This is the only passage in the whole Diary in which the *locale* of the usual Sunday Service is mentioned, while it may be that this occasion of visiting the Church was special, as being the first Sunday in the month (compare June 3rd, *Post*.) It was three weeks later, before they lost the Church entirely.

It should, moreover be borne in mind that at this time by the word Chapel was meant a place of worship belonging to the Church of England, other than a Parish Church, and that it was long afterwards that the meaning of the word was extended in common use, to include buildings not belonging to the Church. When the Diarist said that the Garrison, or some of them, were at the Church, had he meant at St.

Clement's, he would have called it "The Chapel" as he did on June 26, on the occasion of the burial of Sir Jarvis Cuttler; but he could not have used the word Church in this case by mistake for Chapel. His use of the definite article makes the case even still stronger.

We consider therefore that we are quite warranted in drawing the deduction that habitually the Garrison attended the services of the Parish Church during the sieges of the Castle.

2th. This morning we shott the great Iron gunne loaded wth Case shott, having 14 dozon of (large *interlined*) Muskitt bullites in hur. she was shott into the enemies works behind Mr Rusbyes & Mr Lunnes, where there was many officers mett, and flew full amongst them, but we know not what execution was done. this day allso was Mr Massey sent into the Towne about exchange of prisoners from Hull & other places (wch the (*sic*) Ourton theire Governor) graunted as much (as *interlined*) he demanded, & sent away for them p'sently where before he had fallsefied his word. the officers in the towne p'swaded the Common Souldyers that we sent Mr Massey to parley wth theire Governor about deliv'ing up the Castle to them, (thus they feede the Common Souldyers up wth lyes). During Mr Masseye's stay wth Ourton (theire Governor) there Came in a Commander wch told the governor that he Could not keepe the Souldyers from mutaning, whereupon theire governor was not well pleased that he should speake it before Mr Masey. this night the enemy made a new worke like unto a haulph moone in the Closes below Baghill over against the Church, having now 26 (*altered from* 24) workes & trenches round about the Castle, wch puttes them to extraordenary hard duty to mantaine all theire workes, wch makes them wondrous leane & in bad liking.

It seems to have been quite an undertaking to fire this "great Iron gunne." Mr. Rusbye's and Mr. Lunne's were evidently adjacent properties in Northgate, but their exact position cannot be defined.

As an illustration of the Diarist's arbitrary method of spelling, and indeed of the absolute want of rule in that behalf at the time, it may be noted that Mr. Massey's name occurs here thrice in six lines, without being spelt alike twice.

The "New worke like unto a halph moone, in the Closes below Baghill over against the Church," which completed "26 workes and trenches" was evidently a continuation of the effort to prevent a second sally, such as that of the preceding Tuesday, when 97 beasts were added to the stores of the Castle.

3th. This morning (*altered from* day) we had good newes Came from newarke, that upon Saturday morning last, about (4 *erased*) 6 (*substituted*) of the Clock, the king tooke Laister by an assault (in 2 howers, *interlined*) tooke 1000 horse, tooke 1000 men prisoners besides the Governor of the towne wth many great officers (besides all wch was killd in the assault), tooke a Countis was in it wth hur 3 Coatches, tooke allso 8 peses of Cannon wth all theire ammuniton & powder (wch is said to be very great), hath allso sent to Newarke from Leistershire, Darbishire, Nottingamshire & other places 4000 horse least the enemy should follow after them wth any Carriages, & from thence marchth to Darby, after wch (God willing) he will visitt & releeve these north p'tes. this daye we had a man went forth to gett some grasse for the Cattell & horses, (as went many more besides him), but, as he was Coming In at the lower drawbridge, was shott in the legg, but hit not the boane, for he brought in his burthin. we had another man allso shott going from praiers to the watch, wheare, leaning upon the great gun above the upp' gate, was hitt wth a Bullitt Came therough a Clift of the worke was made befor it, & so shott him thorow the arme, & then overquart his back Cleare wthout the boanes, & stuck in the outside of his back, & Cutt out, and yett there is very good hopes of his recovery (is now well againe *interlined*) for his arme is the wo't. after this there was one Cannon shott of from the Kinges Tower into the Markitt place where there was great store of Company (but what *erased*) and did great (*substituted*) execution (there *interlined*) was (done we know not *erased*) sene 3 or 4 taken up (*substituted*.) This night the enemy repaired a little the new worke they had made the night before.

The expression " From praiers to the watch"—seems to imply that a daily Service was held in the Chapel, as perhaps was indeed the case; the more formal Sunday Service being held in the Parish Church.

At first reading it might be doubted whether " Overquart" meant " athwart," that is " across" the back, or " over quarried," *i.e.* quarried over the back in a shallow unpenetrating manner. But although we have met with no use of this word exactly parallel, we have seen one so near that we have little doubt that the Diarist meant "overthwart." In Leland's Collectanea III. (IV.) 190, recounting the visit of King Henry VII. to York in 1486, the writer says " In divers Places of the Citie was hanging oute of Tapestry, and other Clothes, and making of Galaries from on Side of the Strete *over thwarte* to that other."—This use of the word as meaning " across" is identical with that of the Diarist.

There is now shott of our great Cannon from the 1th May till the 4th June 37 Cannon & 8 drakes, & the enemy shot during that time 7 drakes.

This summary exactly fills the column, and seems to have been prepared for the purpose of doing so.

June 4th, 1645. This day the enemy shott very little of all the day till towardes night, and we killd one of theire men in theire workes at monkhill from the Queenes tower. they likewise shott one of our men wch was sleeping in the low Barbican. the bullitt first grased upon the wall, & then it turned the bullitt so that it light upon the outside of his Arme, and runne up at least 4 Inches through the flesh, but touched not the beane & So he growes allmost sound againe. we shott one Cannon from the Kinges Tower to the new worke in the Closes under Bagghill (against the Church) but the gunne lying too hie for the place did no execution. this night they begunne a new worke againe, neare to Zachreye Stables Orchard head, about 120 yeardes from the other, and this night allso they made a boanefire upon Sandall Castle, wch so soone as we p'ceived we se(c *interlined*)onded wth another upon the Round Tower. (one thing I had forgott, that at the releeving of theire watch, about 7 a Clock, the enemy gave fire from all theire workes round about the Castle as if they Intended p'sently to take the Castle wth theire muskitts, but theire fury lasted but a little, & not any hurt done at all, (praysed be God.)

The mention of the new work as being "by Zachreye Stables Orchard head," about "120 yeardes from the other" new work, does somewhat to fix the position of Zachary Stable's Orchard as behind the houses to the south of the Church.

This was the 27th work of the besiegers.

The Diarist being more intent upon his matter than upon his manner, we must not suppose that the enemy made the fire upon Sandal Castle. The rather let us imagine that he used "they" in this instance in the sense of the French *On*.

5th. This morning there was a boy, who was prentise wth Mr Richard Stables, but now in the Castle, he went forth to gett some grasse for the Castle's use, (for the horseyes & cattell,) but was shott thorow the arme & p'te of the shoulder, but recovers prett well againe, & walkes up & downe the Castle yeardes : and this day we killd an ensine of the enemies, & shott another man of theires, but they gott him into the worke. there was great shooting all this day, and towardes night Will. Ingrame shott the great Iron gunne 3 times into one of the enemies new workes under baghill, & was thought did very great execution. At the releeving of the watch the muskittes & firelockes on both sides spared not any powder, where we killd 1 of the enemyes men at the primrose Close under Bagghill, & shot another upon the topp of Baghill. this night the enemy stole some hides againe out of Peeter Redman tanpittes.

This is the third day in succession on which one of the besieged received a flesh wound, deep enough to frighten him, but not deep enough to do him real harm : the escape being in each case regarded as providential and ominous of good.

"Stole some hides *again.*" The former "theft" is no recorded. Note, the "enemy" steal; "we" bring in. But this "stealing" by the enemy, is another indication that they were drawing nearer, and covering ground which had hitherto been well defended.

It is difficult to realise that the conditions of every-day life were so little changed during the siege. On April 23, we found a "poor little maid" shot while composedly hanging out clothes within musket range: and here, at this late time, when active war had been proceeding for nearly six months, tanners pursued their daily occupation, their hides being exposed to the predatory attacks of the besiegers. It is astonishing that impunity should have lasted so long.

Peter Redman's tanpits and some of Peter Redman's buildings have been in use to the present day. They are now owned and occupied by Revis Waddington, whose property escaped the almost total destruction which befell the property of his neighbours to the west.

6th. This morning the enemy showed divers troopes of horse round about the towne, wch made us thinke that they would draw into a body, but there was 4 of the enemyes in the mill under the Castle (and one of ours w *erased*) stealing the Iron from about the mill, & one of our men espiinge runne downe & Cryed Come on, we shall take them all, & 3 of them runne away & then our Souldyer tooke the 4th man & brought him into the Castle. and then that man tould us that those horse Came from Dauncastar, & that they were still about the towne: he said allso that a p'te of the king's Forces were Come as Farre as Tuxford, but theire officers did Conceile it from them till that morning. he tould us likewise tht our Iron gunne had killd the night before a muster maister & a Common souldyer in theire workes: he likewise tould us that the enemy tooke all the men the(y *added*) Could wthin 4 miles of the towne in theire beddes & brought them to towne, & said that they had taken about 140. he allso tould us that the souldyers runne away every day Summe. this eevning our men killd one of the enemy near primrose Close, by theire workes, & shott another upon Baghill, but they drew him into theire workes. this evning Will. Ingrom shott the Iron Gunne to the upp' worke above Zacherey Stables, & hitt the toppe of it, & the hedge where under it many of the Souldyers lay: & after that he shott another into the Markitt place where there was many men standing there, but what execution they did is not knowne to us. about 12 a Clock on the night the ennemy Came out of Newhall wth 5 drummes, one of them a good distance from another. one of them stood at Newhall Cherry orchard & 2 in the Abbay Close, the one at one end, the other at the other, &, so beate along towardes the towne, in manner of Scotch march answering one another, & there was one or 2 beating in the towne. there was allso a Trumpitt Sounding in the Parke, to make us beleeve (or ellse theire owne Souldiers) that the Scotch was Coming, or ellse for feare we [should sally forth,] but we never regarded it, [but the enemy stood] on theire gard all this night & had done so the night before.

The " Mill under the Castle" was evidently that below St. Nicholas Hospital. The glee with which the Diarist narrates the feat of the "one of ours" who frightened three out of four and captured the fourth, was natural; and shows how much of human nature entered into his composition. But, on the other hand, the manner in which the captured man fooled his captors to the top of their bent, and the way in which they greedily swallowed his tales are equally amusing. He probably was willing to tell them anything they wished to know.

Meanwhile, step by step, the besieging army was approaching, however slowly; and week by week they were drawing the toils closer and closer.

From what afterwards occurred, it is quite possible that the midnight trumpet-blowing was not altogether a false alarm; but that the Scotch were really coming to reinforce the besiegers.

7th. This day was there little shooting till towardes night at the releeving of their gaurdes, but about 10 a Clock our men espied a souldier of the enemies Coming downe from Munkhill to the mill, where[upon] 2 of our men went out: one was Jonathan (Sir Jarvis Cuttler's man,) the other was Rich. Laipidge. Jonathan tooke him and brought him into the Castle & eased him of his money, but he Confessed little for he was then drunke. At the releeving of the gaurdes (as before) there was very hard shooting on both sides, & we shott from all places of the Castle because we had about 20 men was getting gras for the Cattell in divers places about the Castle: and we shouted so very hard, as we gave the enemy 2 allarumes, wch Caused them to draw out some of theire men from theire lowest worke under broade lane end, and we beate them twise back into theire workes, & killd one of them & shott another, but what ellse more was hurt We know not, and the enemy shott one of our men was Cutting of gras Into the (back *erased*) side (*substituted*) but he is little worse for it praised be God.

Jonathan (why could not we have been told his other name?) was as daring as many men ; but more prudent than most. Note that Jonathan took a companion with him to capture the drunken man ; but he seems to have taken care of the booty for himself.

The contrast between these proceedings and those of modern warfare is considerable. We seem to be perusing the account of a Chinese war. " We shouted so very hard, as we gave the enemy 2 allarums" is inimitable.

8th. This day, beeing Sunday, we had 2 exceeding good Sarmondes by Mr. Key & Mr. Hirst. the enemy sent away 9 prisoners towardes Yorke, but there was not any of them was taken from the Castle. there was little shooting all day till about 6 a Clock, but none hurt then of either side. about that time (came *erased*) we espied a great body of horse from the towers of the Castle Coming from Wenthill, & there they devided themsellves, Some to Cridlin stoopes & 5 troopes Came all most within Cannon shott of the Castle, & so went towardes Knottinglay. these horses, wth divers more wch went over at Medlay bridge, was reported to be quartred about Tekhill, Rosinton & other places beond Dauncaster, to the nombr of 400, and, hearing of our Army advancing towardes these p'tes, removed theire quarters. they brought 2 Cariages along wth them. the enemy releeved not theire gardes at Baghill till towardes 9 a Clock at wch time there was very hard shooting & we killd one of them Coming to theire low workes under Baghill & shott another man ; but in the night the Leiutenant Collonell put out his meare & foale, tyed hur in a Cloase neare to Swillington Tower, but the enemy espied hur, Came & cutt the roape, gott upon hur back & rid away, Calling to our men wch stood neare by that place (but saw him not) wishing them to take up the foale. he had 9 or 10 firelockes wth him, but our men never saw them.

"Hurt" is a common equivalent in the Diary for "wounded"; Cridlin Stoopes is Cridling Stubbs, to distinguish it from the neighbouring Walden Stubbs ; Medlay is Methley, the bridge over the Calder into that township. For Methley, the mid-meadow, occupies the triangle formed by the approaching confluence of the Aire and Calder, which bound Methley respectively to the north-east and south-east.

The question naturally occurs,—How did the Garrison know that there were "9 or 10 firelockes" if they did not see them? Was the remark a mere gasconade?

> 9th. This morning one of our Souldiers, standing upon the toppe of the lower gatehowse wth his back towardes Munkhill, was shott from thence sidlinges upon his back daungerously hurt, & the bullitt not taken out of 4 daies after, hath beene in great paine since, but no feare but he will recover againe. (he is well againe *inserted above in the very pale ink, and almost illegible*) they had a strong gaurd of horse releived Newhall the last night, about weh time ridd 2 men galloping into the towne in great hast, we supposed to bringe some newes from Yorke. the enemies drumme reported it openly at the lower Barbican wall that the king had taken Darbye. we heard the Cannon play divers times that day, some supposed to be at Welbeck, others about Sheffield. there was hard shooting this Afternoone about 8 a Clock from all p'tes round about the Castle, but we heare not of any hurt wth the muskitts at wch time Will. Ingrome shott his Iron gun into the Markit place, where there was many Souldiers Coming from theire gaurdes, & was there gathred together. the bullitt grased twise in the streete Amongst them, where there was great running away, but what execution it did is not knowne to us. this night one of the Sandall Souldiers went forth of the Castle about 11 a Clock, and about 12 we saw a fire upon the toppe of Sandall Castle and we answered it again by another from the round Tower, we hope p'sageing some good newes. there was 2 killd & one hurt from the Round Tower.

"Sidlinges," for "sidelong."

Evidently "our Governor" allowed no one to know his plans. The meaning of the answering fires between Sandall and Pontefract was unknown to the Garrison, or it would have been recorded here.

> 10th. This morning the enemy was hard at worke in a Cloase neare Baghill Called moodeies close to p'vent any p'vision for Coming to us. they likewise begunne a worke neare to Swillington Tower, but beeing espied by our gaurdes from thence, we made them to leave worke in hast. this day the enemy shott a boy of ours was houlding of a Cow at gras, and we had a man likewise (killd *erased*) shott in the neck but little hurt. this night there Came 8 troopes of horse from Dauncaster & drew up into a body neare Carleton, & so marched under the hill out of our sight towardes hardwicke. there Came another troope from Darington and marched into the towne, & another troope from Ferrybridge to Will. Boothes in the Parke, & stood still there till they sent 6 men into the towne. there Came 8 troopers galloping back & spoke with them. then they departed 4 waies, all galloping away.

Hardwicke was the outlying hamlet now called East Hardwick, to distinguish it from its neighbour, West Hardwick, the two being respectively east and west of Ackworth. There is another Hardwick better known in Pontefract, of which township it now forms a part, although, even as late as Hepworth's Map (1777), it had well-defined township boundaries of its own. This is sometimes called Blind Hardwick, but more generally Spital, or Spittle, Hardwick, as belonging to the Hospital of St. Nicholas.

11th. This day we had little shooting all the forenoone, but about 2 a Clock the Governor Commanded all men to theire Armes. wch was p'sently p'formed, but there fell a shower of Raine for a good time, so as all men gott under shadow till the Rayne was over about 4 a Clock when it was Cleare agane, & then having (had *interlined*) orders what to doe, they Sallyed foorth. Captin Munroe led out the First Company & wth him went Leiut. Moor & Sar. Barton wth 30 musketeers; these went down to the Church, & so, vewing it whether there was any enemyes or no & finding none, went through it, & so to Mr Kellomes howse, from whence found out some of the enemies was there; & there he stayd wth his Company to defend that place, least the enemy should sally forth from the lowest worke below the Church, but they all runne away at his first Charge.

The Diarist was one whose religious emotions and principles were lively, but not necessarily always on the surface; they were deep rather than superficial, part of his own inner self rather than producible for parade before others. He appears to have taken religion as a matter of course, and not as a subject to be continually in his mouth, as if it were a novelty to him. And, therefore, this being St. Barnabas day, and moreover a Wednesday, that is Litany day, it is not unlikely that, although he gives no hint of it, some part of the morning was spent in devotion either in the Church or in the Castle Chapel; and that, in that manner, without his mentioning the real occasion of the slackness, the "little shooting in the forenoone" was partly accounted for. In the afternoon, however, of "Barnaby bright, all day, no night," as says the old adage, there was, notwithstanding two hours of rain, full compensation for the quietude of the forenoon.

And firstly Captain Munroe, with his party of 30 took possession of the house then, as now, the last on the south-east of the Church—Mr Kelham's (the alderman, and yet not alderman, see page 35), which remained in the ownership of his family and name, for at least a hundred years after this time.

The enemy seem not to have had much spirit, in thus running "away at his first charge." But they were evidently badly handled.

Next after him Sallyed forth Captin Smith & Captin Flood, & wth them Aunchient Killingbec, & Anchient Ottoway, wth 80 musketeers; they followed after Capt' Munroe, through the Church, & so through Zachrey Stables howse up to the lowest worke the enemy had, neare to his Orchard head, where Capt' Smith wth his Company led up first to the worke, and so past by it a little further along the hedge (above the worke *interlined*) to p'vent the enemy from sallying forth of theire upper workes to the releefe of those who was in the lowest worke, wch place he bravely mantaynd. during that time Capt' Flood wth his Company fell upon the workes, wch were very hard to enter, because but one little place for entrance, & that so narrow & low that one man Could scarce enter but (must *interlined*) stoope ; there he playd upon the worke & shott in at most of the porthoales where the enemies wthin mantayned the worke very stoutly, & shot very hard at our men so long as a forst entrance was made, but during that time 8 or 9 got out over the worke, but one or two of them was shott & taken, the rest got away. Capt' Flood entred the worke & tooke the Captin, the Sargiant, the Corporall and 8 more soure wounded, and killd all the rest wthin & about the worke & so retreated, bringing the prisoners along wth them to the Castle.

The scene of this was evidently the next house to the west, that of Zachary Stable. This is now rebuilt into cottages. The locality has been already mentioned, on June 4, in connection with Zachary Stable's Orchard head.

Collonell Gilbreth, wth Leiutenant Wheatley & Leiutenant Warde, wth 40 volunteers and Souldiers, both Clubbes & Muskitts, were a reserve in the Orchard hard by the worke, in case the enemye should sally from any place to p'vent them.

The group in Zachary Stable's orchard, nearly behind his house, completed the disposition of the parties to the south of the Church, in this offensive operation upon the "new work."

It is remarkable that a brook which bounds or intersects all these properties is not mentioned ; though its presence must have had an influence upon the arrangements, it being necessarily in the lowest part of the valley, while the ground commenced an ascent directly the brook was passed; an ascent which was continued till the Preale Closes were reached, and the table land beyond.

Leiutenant Willowby & Leiutenant Midelton & Sargiant Parker, wth 40 musketeers, mantained the howses on the north side of the Church about the Starre, and there p'vented the enemy from Coming from the Graunge lathe & that p'te of Munkhill, & those workes to our Annoyance, wch he well p'formed.

On the north side of the Church, there was thus a "Starre". The Star Inn, kept by Jo. Withers in 1666, and by James Owthwaite in 1657, was in the Market Place, and the identification of its site is preserved by the name of Star Yard. But we have nowhere else met with the mention of a "Starre", either as an inn or as a dwelling house, on the north side of the Church. It was probably to the west of the Old Vicarage, and that it commanded the Grange, fixes its position very nearly; but there is no present trace of it, or its belongings.

Leiutenant Monkes, wth Sargiant Barton & 3 files of musketers, being in all 20 men, was Commaunded towardes Munkhill to stoppe the passage, least they should Issue forth; where they playd theire p'tes bravely, the enemy & they striving both for one wall & a hedge, wth that little Company our men both got the wall, & mantaynd it, bringing up one file at once to the most Convenient place, where they gave fire freely, & fell offe again, & another Company Came up. So that the enemy suppos'd to be theare a great Company, & so our men beat them back to Munkhill againe, and killd one man all in Redd, & supposed to be an officer, & shott 2 or 3 more, and so at the beating of our drummes for a retreate (according to order) they Came offe wth honor.

There was a Sar. Barton went with Captain Munroe in the first company. If there is no mistake in the name, this "Sargiant" is a namesake of the first. But as neither is on the nominal roll of Volunteers, it is to be presumed they belonged to the reinforcements which had come into the Castle during the siege, and which had very nearly supplanted the early defenders of the Castle.

Red or scarlet has always been the livery colour of the royal family of England, the ground of the royal shield and the royal flag, the field for the three golden leopards, now represented as lions. And thus it came to be the colour of the foot soldier, of the mail coach and its guard, and of the post-men ; all being originally attached to the private service of the King. In this case, and as we shall see in the next paragraph, the Parliamentary Army had adopted the colour as an emblem, in some measure, of the authority which was traditionally assigned to it.

Evidently the Garrison and the Diarist were equally proud of this piece of good and brave service, though nothing practical resulted from it, except harassing the enemy.

It may be noted that " 3 files" made " 20 men in all", now with the musketeers, as on the following day with the snaphanches and firelocks.

<small>Captin Joshua Walker, wth his 3 Files of Snaphanches & Firelockes, beeing 19 or 20 men, Sallyed forth of the Castle wth the first Company Into the Church, & so into the Steeple, where he was Commanded to stay 24 howres, tooke wth him both victuales & drink, match, powder, & other amunition, and mad all his men in a readines against the enemy should Come forth of theire workes to the rescue of any of theire men, & allso to anoy them at the releeving of theire watch, wch he bravely p'formed : for, after our men had taken the First worke & left it againe, the enemy coming downe to recrute it a new, he gave fire freely upon them, & killd 12 of the enemyes before night, whereof 3 weare officers, one of them was supposed to be a Leiutenant collonell or a Captin at least, in a gallant shuyt of apparell wth a great redd skarfe. There was also divers more was wounded & mantayned the Church and steeple, the time of his Command, to the great anoyance of the enemy.</small>

Having explained the position to the south and north of the Church, the Diarist returns to the Church itself, which with its steeple was " mantayned" by Captain Joshua Walker, with whom we made a specially gratifying acquaintance on May 27, (see page 81), but who had also a very early knowledge of the capabilities of the Church as a military post (see Dec. 31, page 26). We shall meet him again in the Church, and always with his snaphanches, the precursors of the trigger gun now going out of use.

The musketeers of the time ordinarily used matchlocks, fired by manual application : the snaphanche was an improvement on their system as saving the match, and firing the piece by percussion.

> The Firelockes & snaphanches of volunteares remayning wthin the Castle was [commanded] to the toppe of the tower & Battlements [round] about the Castle to p'vent [the enemy] from sallying forth of [theire workes to the] rescue of theire men, wch was a very god (*sic*) service, for we saw one officer fall upon Bagghill was shott from the Round tower besides what was shot in other places.
>
> All the rest of the Commanders officers & volonteares was left in the Castle was Commaunded downe into the Barbican, wth haulberdes, Clubbes, pikes & some muskits & firelockes to p'vent the enemies aproach neare to our men.

The Volunteers thus served as a cover to the expeditionary forces, and it would appear as if the Diarist who says, " we saw" *i.e* from the top of the Tower, was one of that party, and not one of those in the Barbican. But the dignified modesty of the man is so great that it is difficult to learn what were his personal movements. He seems to have been always willing to divest himself of his individuality, and in the spirit of a true soldier, and not of a gasconade, to consider himself as only a member of the body to which he belonged, and which had absorbed his personality. We might well wish he had been less modest.

> During this time & in all this daies worke there was killd of the enemy above 40 men, and 11 men brought prisoners (as before said) into the Castle, besides divers men was wounded ; and our men brought wth them all theire muskits, pikes, powther, shott, match, wth all other amunition was wthin the worke, and the pillage of all the Souldiers wch did not a little re(fresh *erased*) joyce (*substituted*) our men. and in all this time we had bu (*sic*) 2 men wounded whereof the one is dead since. the other is but little hurt, & those was shott behind the howses on the northside of the Church.
>
> during the time of this sallying forth we plaid 4 Cannon. 3 of them was shott out of the Iron gunne by Will. Ingrom to the upp' worke about 80 yeardes from that worke was taken, & shott twise through that worke wth Cannon Bullitts & once wth Case Shott wth into & round about it. the other Cannon was plaid from the Kinges Tower to (Newhall & that waie, *written in two small lines in a space left for but one word*) but what execution was done by the Cannon is not knowne to us.
>
> After all this, divers of our men went forth into the Church yeard to gett gras for the Cattell & horseyes, where we had one man kild & another man shott.

Having in so orderly and methodical a manner recounted the doings of the various parties, sallying and covering, the Diarist sums up the results of the day's operations; the work—the "new" work—taken and pillaged, 40 killed of the enemy, and 11 brought in wounded and prisoners. On their own side but 2 men wounded, one of whom died of his wounds.

Meanwhile 4 cannon had been fired by Will Ingram with not much ascertainable result, and after all was over, "divers of our men" went to the Churchyard in the cool of the evening to get grass.

A small blank here closes one of the columns of the Diary, and the fresh column (and page) commences with full date, day, month, and year; perhaps with an underlying intention to emphasise the change in the command, and to show that the besieged were quite aware that they were approaching the crisis of their fate.

1645, June 12th. This morning Came the Lord Fairfax and the new Generall (Pines *altered by interlineation to*) Pointes from Yorke to Pomfret (wth 4 troop of horse to gaurd them *interlined*). it is said that Poynts (es *interlined*) Came to take an accountes (of *interlined*) what Souldyers the ould genrall did deliver to him. there was little shooting this day till towardes night at the releeving of the senteryes, at wch time the enemy shott very hard from all theire workes round about the Castle, at least a whole volly of shott from every place, where unto we gave them answer from the Castle, and what wth shooting & showting we gave the enemy a strong allarum, wch Caused the enemy to bring up theire horse in small Companies to the further side of Baghill but staid not theare any while. this day we killd 4 men of the enemies from the Church, and about 6 a Clock we had a man shott (was shott at of first for the Cattell *erased*) Leiut. Warde in the left arme was going downe to the Church (*interlined*) but no danger of death.

The Lord Fairfax & the new Generall Poyntes went towardes Yorke againe. Captin Munroe mantained the Church that night till the next releeving.

"Shooting and Showting" is one of the Diarist's characteristic phrases. We have before noticed his fondness for alliteration.

This is another instance of the coolness of the besieged in presence of the enemy. In the face of the beleaguring army, it appears that the garrison had treated the Church and the houses in its neighbourhood as an advanced guard, and Lieut Warde was thus shot while passing between the Church and the Castle. He was in Sir George Wentworth's company, as we already know (see pp. 41, 48), and was a junior lieutenant, as he is mentioned after Lieutenants Willoughby (page 70), Smith (page 81), and Wheatley (page 98). Probably he did not recover from his wound in time to take any further active part in the defence, for this is the last we hear of him. It is at least unfortunate that in this passage the Surtees copy by some accident omits this distinguished name, especially as Lieut Warde's collateral, if not direct, descendants are still among us (see BOOKE OF ENTRIES, page 58). Lieut. Warde's name does not occur in either of the nominal lists, and as his Christian name is not mentioned in the Diary we cannot assign him his place in the Warde pedigree.

"We had a man shot was going down" is an example of the Diarist's most common ellipsis. He omits, as frequently as not, the relative pronoun between two such dependent clauses.

Capt. Walker took 24 hours' provisions with him on the 11th. Now we find him relieved by Capt. Munroe on the 12th. Henceforth for some days there was a distinct command in the Church, of a Captain and twenty or thirty men relieved daily.

The name of General Poyntz, afterwards so distinguished, was at this time quite new to the Diarist, who made amusing struggles to get it on his MS.

13th. This day the new generall Poyn(t *interlined*)es Came from Yorke poast againe, we supposed it was to draw up all theire horse to be neare together. this day we drue down a trench from the lower Castle gate, through Mr Taytomes Orchard, to the Church, for the safeguard of our men thither, wch we allmost finished; & made blindes of bowes & soddes, wch the enemy had gott, from the Church to Mr Kellomes, for our men to gett gras that way. Wheare they brought in neare 100 burdin, wch they got neare to the enemyes workes; for our men did so ply them wth shott from the steeple that they durst not looke out of theire workes, & from the Steeple they killd one of the enemyes Coming from baghill to the worke & shott 4 or 5 more. (Captin Munroe *erased*) Leut Willoby (*substituted*) Releevid the Church, & mantaned it wth 24 men till the next night, at wch time there was great shooting on both ptes, but we heare not of any man hurt.

How the Royalists must have enjoyed the humour of so plying "them with shott from the Steeple that they durst not look out of theire workes," while "our men" passed through Mr Kelham's house with near 100 burdens of grass. But it was their very last piece of liberty.

Hitherto, the communication with the Church had been through the Booths, the "high street"; now the Garrison made a trench through the orchard, Mr Tatham's Orchard in which the "little maid" had been killed. On the 22nd, their enemies attacked them by means of both these trenches.

The day finished "with great shooting on both parts, but we hear not of any man hurt." Hurt=wounded, as before.

14th. The morning there went out a young man from the Castle himselfe alone to the workes at Mr (James *erased*) Rusbyes backside, &, fynding but 2 men there, he entred the toppe of the worke & shott one of them, & the other fled away, & so he returned to the Castle. Our men in the Church plaid theire p'tes well, & shott into the (*sic*) theire workes, in at the poart hoales, and killd a woman was bringing a stand of Ale from (the *erased*) Munkhill by the Grange lath side, & shott 2 or 3 men more thereabouths & at other workes.

This young man who went alone to the works behind Mr. Rusby's, in Northgate, perhaps considered that confining the operations to the lower part of the town rendered things in general rather monotonous. But he certainly discovered a very weak place in the arrangements of the enemy.

"A woman bringing a stand of ale from Monkhill by the Grange lathe side," in the midst of all this murderous work !

This day, beeing the 10th day for theire releefe at new hall, there went downe from the towne about 320 men, and the other wch was there returned back, and in theire going back the Dutchman playd his Cannon from the leades by the treasurer Tower & killd 3 men in one file in the Closes under the headlandes, what more was killd or hurt is not knowne. The Iron Gunne allso playd once up into the towne into the howses neare to Allderman John Wilkinsonnes, & through those howses, but what hurt was done we know not, but they runne out fast out of theire howses. Captin (Munroe *erased*) Himsworth (*substituted*) releevid & mantayned the Church wth 26 men till the next releefe.

This is the first we hear of the Dutchman, un-named. Henceforward we shall meet with him frequently.

There were at this time many of his nationality in the town and neighbourhood, especially towards Goole and Hatfield, where extensive draining operations had been going on for some years under the patronage of Charles I. Sir Cornelius Vermuyden, the "undertaker," and his assistant Dutchmen were therefore naturally supporters of the royal authority, especially as the people of the neighbourhood, with whom they had much altercation and litigation, were rather inclined to take side with the growing resistance of Parliament.

It is exceedingly interesting thus to find this Dutchman among the defenders of Pontefract Castle.

There seems to have been a platform by the Treasurer's Tower on which the Dutchman's gun was placed, so that his range extended to the Headlands in the one direction and to the Market Place in the other.

The fatal battle of Naseby was fought this day.

June 15th. This day, being Sunday, at afternoone the enemy went downe boanegate wth a troope of horse, wch we espying from the Kinges tower, we plaied the Cannon from thence, wch light amongest them, where we see 3 horses & men lay killd; what others more was hurt or killd we know not, (but horses was seene to runne away without men *interlined*). we playd allso another Cannon up the towne, wch went through the howses against Mr Rusbyes, but what hurt was done we know not. this day there went 2 loaded waynes wth (goodes *erased*) wounded men, as we supposed, (*interlined*) from the towne through the Parke to Ferry brigges, & allso 2 wagons loaded wch went through Chequer feeld to Ferry brigges. towardes night, at releeving of the gaurdes, there was great shooting on boath, but we heare not of any man hurt. Captin Cartwright releeved the Church wth 26 men till the next releefe; but this night the enemy dune a trench on the south side of Mr Kellomes, to p¹vent our men for getting of grass where they gott before.

The troops going *down*, must have been going towards Ferrybridge or Knottingley.

The expression "Through the Parke to Ferrybridge" cannot be understood without remembering that the Park extended, at that time, much more towards the east than it does now. The "waynes" would have gone, by a northern route, through the eastern part of the Park, past Fairy (or Ferry) Hill to Ferrybridge ; the "wagons"—whatever subtle distinction might be involved in the difference in spelling—by a southern route across and along the Carleton boundary.

Boanegate—the present Bondgate—signified the way to the boundary which separated the township from Knottingley and Ferrybridge. This was Bubwith bridge, the bridge which having only one side, looked as if "Broken," and gave its name to the town.

Capt. Cartwright "releeved the Church" ; but the "2 exceeding good Sarmonds" preached the previous Sunday— which were in all probability preached from its pulpit, were the last which were to be delivered within those walls for many a year. The unroofed building, exposed to all the fury of the elements, is still a monument of the ravages of war, while those few pregnant words of criticism, written from the fulness of his heart by Nathan Drake, have remained a silent memento of the stirring exhortations delivered that day by Mr. Key (Kay, on the nominal list, p. 33), and Mr. Hirst.

Thus the bonds were being drawn tighter and tighter round the beleagured garrison. But still the besiegers had not at this point taken possession of any building belonging to the town. Their efforts in that direction were confined to excluding the garrison from the pasture of the fields.

16th. This morning we had a boy & a man shott as they was getting of apples. the same boy was shott through the side of the Cheeke about a weeke before, & growne well againe, but now playing the Foole & Calling to the enemy saying why durst they not shoot, & they so neare them. but they p'sently shott the boye through the body & the man into the thigh wth the same bullitt. the boy is not likely to recover, but the man will soone be well againe, (as the Chirurgions report.) There was great shooting, showting & rejoyceing this day by the enemy; & bragging that theyre forces had beaten & routed the Kinges forses, & that the King was fled & Could not be found, and sent to us a letter of it into the Castle; and likewise Genrall Poynts sent downe a Gallant man in apparell wth a drumme and a letter like to a Sumons to our Governer, to deliver up the Castle, for they had great forces Coming towardes us, (but yet there was mercy if he would yeeld, *interlined*) wch our Governor no sooner heard, but by word of mouth made p'sent answer, that he neither feared his forces nor vallued his mercy, & bid him p'sently be gone & tell his Mr' soe, & then he was sent p'sently away. but we had a letter that day from Collonell Washington (that the *erased*) dated 14th June at Newark, that the King was that night at Melton Mowberey, & intended, God willing, to be wth us wthin 10 daies, & this battell wch the enemy speakes of sheuld have beene the day before, wch we Conceive (Can *erased*) not be true. there was this day 4 or 5 waynes loaded in the towne & went through the Parke towardes Ferry bridge. we playd allso 3 Cannon this day from the Kinges Tower, 2 of them to Baghill to 2 troopes of horse was theare, & one to the Markitt place to some horse was there, (what hurt *erased*) but what hurt was done is not knowne. there Came many troopes this day to towne, & quartered about the towne. Captin Smith wth 20 musketers (and 6 volenteares snaphanches *erased*) releeved & mantayned the Church till the next releefe. this night the enemy runne a trench throu 2 little Closes neare to the worke to p'vent our men from getting of gras.

This apple-getting seems to have been a great temptation, and in reading the story the first reflection naturally is that the apples could not have been worth so much risk as early as the 16th June. But it must be borne in mind that the then reckoning was by "Old Style," which was at this time, earlier by ten days than the modern reckoning. For 16th June must therefore be read 26th, when any attempt is made to compare the seasons of the seventeenth century with those of the nineteenth.

This same sort of "Foole"-hardiness was exhibited by some of the townspeople at the siege of Worcester, when grimaces were made at "the enemy" in a spirit of bravado with a similar taunt that they "dare not shoot"; a taunt answered in a similar way by a successful shot at the "foole"-hardy target, so daringly offered.

We thus learn that the news of the result of the battle of Naseby, fought on Saturday, had reached the besiegers by Monday, comparatively early in the day. For the Diarist seems to have adopted a regular method in making his entries three or four times a day, if only a few lines at a time. Thus the subsequent summons would have been about noon.

"Present answer," "presently be gone"—in these cases mean as we should say "instant" and "instantly."

The pert apt answers of the Governor are eminently epigrammatic and characteristic. "He neither feared his forces, nor valued his mercy," was the answer of a truly gallant soldier, who would not recognise that he was beaten, until there was no possible scrap of hope left to feed upon.

But the garrison had still real substantial reason for hope, when they received Colonel Washington's letter—who must have been Lieut-Col. Washington of the 13th Regiment, and possibly was the Capt. Washington of 1640. If so he was not one of the Washingtons of Pontefract and Adwick, but was the surviving son of Sir Wm. Washington, Knight, who married Elizabeth, daughter of Sir John Pakington, the Worcestershire Baronet, survived the Commonwealth, and died in 1663 without male heirs.

The chivalry of General Poyntz, and his resolve to give good terms to the garrison, while yet the power was in his own hands should not miss recognition. He evidently respected and admired the bravery and tenacity of the Royalists; while knowing well that time being in his own favour they were playing a losing game, and that presently the odds would be so much against them, that they would be helpless, he desired that they should surrender before that extremity was reached. Hence his well-meant persuasion.

The "Troops that came towards night" were another indication of the approaching severity of the siege, and perhaps General Poyntz was aware of their approach when he made the advances to the garrison just recorded.

The "Trench through two little Closes," which was made this night, was probably a continuation of the trench made the previous night on the south side of Mr Kellom's. It would have intersected the two closes that lie west of Parsnip garth. Few of the properties at this end of the town have been much sub-divided since the date of the siege ; except that some of the houses have been rebuilt and perhaps a couple more sites occupied with buildings, all is nearly as it was two hundred, and probably four hundred, years ago, an illustration of the proverbial unwillingness of an English town to extend its boundaries to the east.

17 June 1645. This day there hath goane many loaded waines from the towne towardes Ferrybridge. the enemy would gladly have enlarged theire lowest worke where (we *interlined*) tooke so many of theire men in it, but our men plyed them so wth shott from the Church, that they durst not looke out whilst it was light. In the afternoone there was very hard shooting on either side but we heare not of any man hurt. Leiutenant Wheatelay, wth about 20 musketeers & firelockes, mantayned the Church till the next releefe. This eevning about 8 a Clocke our Souldiers were disposed to be very merry, hearing that the enemies letters wch they had sent into the Castle the day before was nothing but lyes (as indeede it is theire usuall trade), & the day Following Capt' John warde mantained it upon his solvation to Sr George wintworth that the king was routed at the battell). Our men made many spoartes, playes, & showtes in the Castle. yeard, and they likewise went up to the toppe of the Round tower where they made 3 or 4 great Showtes, and allso those in the Church did the like, wch Caused the enemy to take theire Armes & goe into the markitt place, at wch time we had made ready the Iron Cannon & playd one shott through a howse upon the bridge, & so grased in the Markitt place full amongest them but what execution was done we know not. this night the enemy went for ward wth running of theire trench, keeping theire men mostly at worke to make them bele [*probably for* believe] we would p'sently yeild up the Castle.

This allusion to the "taking of so many men" appears

to refer to the exploit of Capt. Flood on St. Barnabas day (see page 98).

Capt. John Warde was afterwards a Commonwealth justice of the peace for the West Riding. His signature, as the presiding officer at civil marriages, is to be found in every parish register in the neighbourhood now extant.

Sir George Wentworth, who received his assurance, was the commander of the fourth division of the besieged (see page 21).

As was to be expected, the common soldiers had no ordinary access to the interior of the various Towers of the Castle. Their place was the Castle Yard, and the roofs. The question accordingly arises, how did these communicate, independently of the Towers themselves. So far as the Round Tower is concerned the entrance by the Postern seems to have been private, from the private garden. It communicated with the Dungeon, and with the Governor's apartments. The way of access from the Castle Yard to the roof of the Round Tower, which the soldiers must have reached readily, where they lay and basked, and where they occasionally were struck with stray shot, was probably by means of the short exterior staircase, just beyond the Castle walls. Passing up this staircase, crossing the Bowling Green, skirting the mound, and passing up the stairs at the splay between the Round Tower and Piper's Tower, which admitted to a circular turret staircase, they would reach the roof without disturbing or interfering with the retirement of those in the inner and private rooms.

"Bele" in the latter part of this entry, is another instance of a peculiar omission, in which the Diarist frequently indulged.

18th. This day we had 2 letters from Newarke dated upon Sunday last, wherein was specified that upon Sunday the y (sic) Kinge was at Melton Mowberey and that (god willing) he intended to be at Newarke upon Tewsday & so march for our ayde. there was allso newes in them of the great dissentions in the parlament & in the Citty of London about many matters. this day the enemy shott a Cowe of ours was Feeding in the Church yeard, wch we drivd up into the Castle & kill'd hur p'sently. The new Generall POYNTES, and Overton the Governor of Pomphrett, wth other officers & Commanders, met this day about Dauncaster, to Consult upon a Counsell of warre: and this after noone there passed by through Ferrybridge towardes Dauncaster 13 or 15 loaded waines, we supposed they was all loaded wth Amunition, because they was gaurded wth 4 troopes of horse & some foote, but we Could not well diserne the foot because it was a darke day & they passed Close by the Cariages. This night Captin (C *erased*) K(*substituted*)itchen wth 20 musketeers & firelockes manteined the Church till the next watch. and there was not much shooting nor any man hurt this day that we heare of, of either side. Abou 11 a Clock in the night there was boanefires sett both upon the toppe of our Castle & allso upon the toppe of Sandall Castle, both about one time, wch we held for a token that they had heard the good newes as well as we.

This concludes one of the columns of the Diary. The "good newes" was but a misleading gleam.

19th June, 1645. The enemy mustred theire men this day, so that there was little shooting, & drew up theire men into the Markitt place about 2 a clock, (about *altered to*) at wch time Will Ingrom made ready his Iron gunne & playd to them, where it grased but a little before them, & so went through them, but what execution it did is unknowne to us. this day Came draughtes back againe wch went the day before towardes Dauncaster, and the Governor of Poumphrett Came back to the towne wthe the Genrall Poynts wth him from Dauncaster. this day the enemy made great poasting up & downe, never resting. at the releeving of the watch Capt^r Joshua Walker went downe to releeve the Church wth his 20 snaphanches where p'sently they killd 2 of the enemy. this night, about 11 a Clock, was sent out from the Castle Captin Washington & Lieutenant Emson towardes Newarke. they went through Denwell lane, & so up the Closes, & gott Clear of all the enemies workes wthout hearing of either muskitt or pistoll going of whilst they was w'thin the hearing of the Castle. this night allso (was a *erased*) there was a great Boane fire made upon the toppe of Sandall Castle, & we answered it wth an other from this Castle.

These two days seem to have been occupied by the besiegers in consultation. Hence the cessation of offensive operations. The Diarist has omitted "our" before "hearing." He evidently means that the garrison heard no shot while Capt. Washington and Lieutenant Emson were commencing their perilous journey.

20th. This morning Genrall Poyntes, (being Come from Dauncaster the night before,) Called a councell of warre, & he and his officers sate upon it (as the Lady Cuttler tould us, who Came from them at noone. This (new *erased*) day we had newes brought us of the Battell wch the enemy gott against the Kinges forces (com *erased*) neare to Harborow as they was Coming from Oxford, upon Fridday night & Saturday the 13th & 14th of this Instant. But, upon

Sunday morning, Genrall Goring wth Genrall Jarett Came in the Rescue, & plaid theire p'tes bravely, both that Day & the day following, and recovered all the 12 peeses of Cannon was lost before, & all the forces the enemy had taken, wth all theire ammunition, wheare (it is said) that Gen. Cromwell was slayne, & we gave them Chase to Norhampton from whence the enemy had drawen allmost all the Forces was in the Towne to the Battell. Thus the newes Came to us. This Afternoone the enemy Came to Newhall wth a wagon & a Cannon in it, & 4 other loaded waynes. the Cannon was brought up to Munkhill to a place wch they had beene making ready 2 nightes before to plant hur in, and towardes night there was a wayne loade of Planke brought from the Towne through the Parke to Munkhill, where they unloaded them, & wrought all that night (& the next *interlined*) Day (& finished *erased*) and at (*substituted*) both the worke and the platforme to plante the cannon against the Church. There Came wth the Cannon about 90 Footmen, wch marched in a single file by Newhall Orchard head through the Parke, & so in to the Towne; they was all new Arreyd men. The enemyes wagon, wch brought the Cannon & the Fower waines, Came all downe the back lane on the northside of St. Thomas hill: at wch time our Cannon plaid 3 times from the Kinges Tower, whereof 1 Cannon plaid full amongest 3 of the Cariages being alltogether, & the other 2 Cannon playd to the men, but what execution was Done we know not. Leiutenant Smith wth 20 musketeers mantained the Church till the next watch. This night there was a fire (at *erased*) upon (*substituted*) Sandoll Castle, & we answerd it wth another from this Castle.

"Up the Closes" is evidently up "Abbot's" Closes.

The Garrison seem not to have understood that the preparations to bombard the Church were made with that intention. But their eyes were soon to be opened.

1645, June 21th. This (*sic*) we had a poore man who before this Seege dwelt at Munkhill and having his howse burnt by the enemy Came into the Castle for suckor, & going forthis (*sic*) morning to gett grasse for the Cattell by Munkhill mill, was there shott dead upon the place where he was getting of it & fetcht in at night & buryd.

Monkhill Mill was the Mill which was otherwise called Mill Dam. The Sandall party were fired at on May 28th (see page 84,) before they reached it. It was only a few yards beyond the Hospital.

The Diarist does not say where this "poore man" was buried; but doubtless it would have been in St. Clement's Chapel.

Our Cannon from the Kinges Tower playd once to them was makeing the platforme for theire Cannon at Munkhill. there was little shooting all this day by the enemy. our Snaphanches shot often at those was making the worke for the Cannon. This day Came downe Owerton (the Governor) wth divers more officers wth him to see the worke, and the enemyes wrought very hard all day in the platforme, and finished the worke. We had newes this day that the Forces fro' Newarke went into the Isle of Arkesam and there met wth a strong p'ty of the enemyes horse, & there tooke & kill 500 both of theire horse & foot about Arksey. Leiutenant Willowby wth 20 musketiers mantained the Church this night till the next watch. This night there Came in a Souldyer from the enemy, who brought with him his muskett & his Sword. he tould us that he Arreyed but a little before, & said that they scarce left any man in the Contrey, but arreyed (him *ı ased*) them (*substituted*) and brought them thither. he likewise tould us that the enemy Gott the better of the Kinges forces at the battell the 2 First daies, but at after the king recovered all was lost before, & routed the enemy. this night the enemy brought up the Cannon from newhall, & planted hur against the Church. this night allso we begunne to make a new worke before the lower Castle gate to p'vent the enemyes Cannon from anoying us there.

Evidently the Diarist considers the Isle of Arkesam (Axholme), and the township of Arksey, to have had names of a common derivation, which he does his best to exemplify by his phonetics.

"At after"=that after. "All was lost"=all that was lost.

22th. This morning about 2 a Clock, the enemy fell upon the Church on every side, entred into the Church wth about 100 men, and allso Came up our trench, haulph way to the Castle, & allso up the high streete towardes the Castle, but our men wthin the steeple & the Church topp plaid theire p'te very bravely, and beat them both out of the Trench & highway, out of the Church, and out of the Church yeard, for they shott wth theire muskitts & likewise threw downe stones amongst them both into the Church & Churchyeard : and likewise our men shot from all p'tes on that side of the Castle, (and we shott 2 sling peeses *added in the margin*) so that they gave them small Comforth to tarry there. we killed 4 or 5 of the enemyes men, wch we say (*sic*) them dragg away into Mr Kellomes howse, besides many was shott & wounded, & Caryed away ; for, after our men in the Church by Ringing the bell theare had given us an allarum into the Castle, we made them too hott service to tarrye there, and then every man fled to theire workes Carying theire dead & wounded men along wth them. this fight Continued for haulph an hower, for, after our men begunne to sally forth of the Castle, they p'sently tooke to theire heeles.

Up the Trench, *i.e.* in the Booths. So that " the enemy " attacked the Lower Gate by two converging trenches.

If we could emphasise the personal pronoun in the marginal addition, and believe that the " we " included the Diarist himself, we should have an almost solitary gleam of light upon his personal performances. But it must be confessed that the *we* might quite as readily refer to the

Garrison in general, as to the small party which included the Diarist. (See also page 101).

"Comforth," for comfort, as on pp. 50, 77, and 81.

"Ringing *the* bell there" rather implies that there was but one. If so, it was the very "sweet gallant bell," which being cracked, was melted down about twenty years ago. The current story—repeated by Boothroyd, and copied by Fox—is that "there is a tradition that Col. Bright, who was a distinguished officer in Lambert's army, and was deputed to treat for the surrender of the Castle, availed himself of his interest with the General to obtain some of these bells for his own Parish Church of Badsworth, where they now remain."

Boothroyd adds, and Fox repeats the statement:—
"Having examined these bells, it does not appear from the dates that more than one bell could have been removed, unless they have been re-cast. The tenor is dated 1582, and the three others date after the Restoration."

But the expression "ringing the bell," when read with the remark under June 23rd, page 116, leads to no conclusion except that at this time, the bell was solitary, as it remained during the next two hundred years; and that the story of Col. Bright's having removed the rest of the bells, at some date subsequent to the catastrophe of 1648-9 is a pure myth.

P'sently after this was doone, the enemyes Cannon (bearing a bullitt of 18 weight) begunne from munkhill to play at the lantirne of the Church steeple & playd 13 times wthin little more then an hower & a haulph. during that time, our Cannon from the kinges Tower begunne to play at theire worke wher the Cannon was planted, and in 5 times Shooting dismounted their Cannon, so that they plaied no more that day. all this day, (beeing Sunday), the enemy Cept men at worke making ready theire Cariages againest the next morning, wch they finished. all this day, after this morninges worke was done, was little shooting on either side; but, in the afternoone, the enemy releeved all their gaurdes, & brought downe 400 men to newhall, & likewise there went as many back from thence into the Towne. Leiutenant Faivell (Leiut. to Capt. Himsworth) releeved the Church and mantained it till the next releefe. This night the enemies Officers from all theire workes neare to the Castle tould us so many abominable & apparent lyes as is a shame to heare them related, (but indeed such hath been theire practise from the beginning,) and p'suading us now by Faire meanes to yeeld up the Castle.

This gives us clearly the speed in Artillery practice attained by the best practitioners in these early days. Thirteen times in little more than an hour and a half is once in about twelve minutes.

The besieged themselves seem not to have been so expert as those outside, since, although with ample time for preparation, they were able to fire their piece only five times to the thirteen shots of the enemy; while it is reasonable to suppose that they would have commenced very soon after the Monkhill battery opened.

Note the emphasis with which the Diarist records the circumstance that all through Sunday, the besiegers were making active preparations to commence a bombardment in the morning. And perhaps their exertions were so to say ostentatious and obtrusive, in the hope that the sight of such determination might the rather induce the besieged to surrrender quietly.

The Diarist makes constant complaint of the inaccuracy of the news which reached the besiegers, and which these latter were only too ready to impart. It is unfortunate, however, that he does not give voice to the rumours, and inform us what the statements actually were. For by this time the besiegers must have had the truth of the result of Naseby, which had been fought a full week before.

23th. This morning, about 2 a Clock, the enemy begunne againe to play theire Cannon, & playd but one, & that we Could not p'ceive did hit the Church, & rested till it was lighter and then begunne againe to play, and at the 16th shott there was an open place made in one side of the Lantirne of the steeple. and after that they playd 8 shottes to the steeple below the bell & 1 to the lower gatehouse of the Castle. all this was done before 6 a Clock, & then rested till after 12 a Clock, & then begunne againe to play and playd that afternoone to the Steeple & the Church 34 shott. they shott in all this day to the Church, wth that one to the Castele gate, 60 shott. during all this time since morning there was little shooting wth muskitts on either side, yett we had a souldyer was lying a sleepe in the lower Barbican was shott into the arme wth a bullit from baghill, he supposed he lay wthout any hurt of shott. There Came this day wth the Cannon from Ferry brigges 74 Foot Souldyers all newly Arreyed men, they Came all in a single file marching through the Parke to the Towne. Towardes night, Leiut Moore wth 20 musketeers was sent downe to the Church, but not to stay there, but leave 2 there for a sentrye, (because there was likelyhood of keeping it,) and the rest of his Company to stay in the open howses above the uper side of the Churchyeard there, to anoy the enemy if they Came, & to give us warning of theire approach, (wch we expected they would doe,) because they drew many of theire forces downe to theire lowest workes neare the Church. Against night we drew our Iron gunne from above the upp' gatehowse, into the Gardin wthin the gatehowse where we had made a platforme, & sette up a sconce for saufgaurd, & made hur ready to play against the Church, and about one A clock, (as we expected,) the enemy shott of 1 warning peese to the Church, for theire men to fall on, wch they did & Came into the howses round about the Church but entred not the Church but wth 2 men. and then Leiutenant Moore wth his musketeers gave fire Into the Church, & likewise the Iron gunne, being soundly Charged before, gave fire allso upon the Church, wch Caused them all to quitt those places, & runne away to theire workes, but what execution was done we know not.

The rapidity of the artillery fire this day agrees curiously with that of the 22nd, allowing for the rest in the early morning, until the day was more advanced.

"Below *the* Bell" evidently implies that there was but one bell in the Tower. (See Appendix D.)

But this repeated mention of *the* Bell makes it quite clear that if even there ever had been more, they had been removed long before Colonel Bright had much to do with the Castle. In the siege with which we are now concerned, he is not mentioned at all until the question was on the carpet, of a surrender. And it may be remarked that few Yorkshire Churches have more than one Pre-Reformation Bell: they probably underwent the penalty of losing the rest on account of their having been rung to call up the people at the time of one of the Tudor risings shortly after the Reformation.

"Because there was likelyhood of keeping it."—The pluck and resolute firmness of this Garrison are extraordinary. With the enemy closing around them, whose preparations were almost in full view, and with adverse news reaching them day by day, their reliance on the goodness of their cause, the impregnability of their fortification, and the strength of their own right arms was such that they would give up but inch by inch. And thus the moment they lost the Church as a post of offence, they turned their own fire upon it to render it untenable by the besiegers.

The platform in the "Garden within the Gatehouse", to which the Iron Gun was next removed, was the small plot of ground behind the Main Guard; and the need for a platform is evident so that the discharge might be from above a low curtain wall, which is but breast high, and that it might pass well over Neville's Mount, (so called for some inscrutable reason, perhaps as being the site of the King-maker's address to his soldiers before Towton), where the Gun had previously been when directed against Baghill. The "Garden within the Gatehouse" commanded the Church, and so long as the besieged hoped to retain that sacred edifice as an advanced post, so long did they keep their Gun in the position to which it was now removed. When surrender was imminent, it will be found that the Iron Gun, of which they were so proud, and whose doings they had watched so often, so closely, and with such almost affectionate interest, was returned to its former position of defiance, above the "Upper Gate House."

William Ingram seems to have been its permanent gunner.

from the 4th June till 24, 29 Cannon.

These few words are added at the bottom of a column, in poor ink, and with a feeble hand. They are probably the work of the Diarist in those anxious moments which preceded the surrender, when he wished to utilise every vacant space in the margin of his volume.

24th. All this day, till about 5 a Clock in the afternoone, there was little shooting on either side, at wch time we playd 1 shott wth our Iron Gunne into theire lowest workes against the Church, wch playd through the werke, but what execution was done is not knowne. after wch was done, the enemy playd 1

Cannon to the Church steeple & no more; and, after that was done, there was hard shooting on both sides wth muskittes at the releefe of theire gaurdes, but we heare not of any hurt, excepting one of our Souldyers was getting of Apples was shott in the legge.

This evning was Aunchient Autteway Commanded downe to the Church wth 2 files of musketeers, but not to stay there any longer but till Tapptoo beate, wch was about 10 a Clock, & then to retire back into the Castle, for we expected the enemyes falling on that night into the Church.

This night they did not hope even to leave sentry in the Church all night through, but at Tapptoo beat, "about" 10 o'clock, they were to retire. It was Midsummer day, and the hour of "Tapptoo" varied with the seasons.

Thus from June 11th to June 24th, from St. Barnabas day to St. John Baptist, a space of 14 days, there was the following constant night guard kept in the Church :—

June 11.—Capt. Joshua Walker with 19 or 20 men.
June 12.—Capt. Munroe (Smith being his lieutenant.)
June 13.—Lieut. Willoughby with 24.
June 14.—Capt. Himsworth (Favell being his lieut) with 26.
June 15.—Capt. Cartwright (Moore being his lieut) with 26.
June 16.—Capt. Smith (Ottoway being his lieut) with 20.
June 17.—Lieut. Wheatley with about 20.
June 18.—Capt. Kitchen with 20.
June 19.—Capt. Joshua Walker with 20.
June 20.—Lieut. Smith (Capt. Munroe's lieut) with 20.
June 21.—Lieut. Willoughby with 20.
June 22.—Lieut. Faivell (Capt. Himsworth's lieut)
June 23.—Lieut. Moore (Capt. Cartwright's lieut) with 20 (not to stay.)
June 24.—Ensign Ottoway (Capt. Smith's lieut) with 2 files.

This constitutes a system of eight reliefs :—Capt. Joshua Walker, whose were the Snaphances, the precursors of the triggered muskets ; Capt. Monroe with Lieut Smith ; Lieut Willoughby ; Capt. Himsworth with Lieut Favell ; Capt. Cartwright with Lieut Moore ; Capt. Smith with Ensign Ottoway ; Lieut Wheatley ; and Capt. Kitchen ; which (if the men were different in each party, as well as the officers,—as it is probable was the case) would imply a garrison of not much short of 200 fighting men.

———

25th. This morning about 1 a Clock the enemy entred the Church, & the lower end of the towre, there beeing none to resist them, at wch time our musketeers from the Castle (playd *erased*) shott (*substituted*) very hard at them, and likewise we playd 5 peeses of Cannon from the Kinges tower to the Church steeple, and allso the Iron gun from the Guarding playd 5 shott into the Church so that they durst not appeare in the steeple, but what execution was done is not knowne. There hath beene little shooting all this day, but the enemy keepes digging up dead men's Corpes, & making a worke in the Church. This day morning, that worthy knight Sr Gervis Cuttler dep'ted this life, the enemy not suffring any fresh meate ever to be brought to him since he fell sick, onely one Chickin & one poore Joynt of meate his lady brought wth hur 2 daies before he dep'ted, neither will the ennemy suffer him either to be buryed [in the Church, or Conveyed to his owne habitation to take place wth his Auncetors. This night we playd our Iron Gunne to the Church but it was not answered againe by the enemy.

A careful distinction seems to be made here between the modes of using Cannon and Muskets. Cannon are "played," Muskets are "Shot."

The Diarist makes a mistake as to the day when Lady Cutler came, unless indeed, which is unlikely, she went out into the town, and returned. She came in on the 20th at noon.

Incidentally we thus learn that there was no fresh meat in the Castle at this time; so that we have here a slight indication of the privations to which these brave men were ultimately subjected.

Lady Cutler was Sir Jarvis's second wife. She was Magdalene Egerton, daughter of John, Earl Bridgewater, for Sir Jarvis Cutler (baptised at Barnsley, 20 April, 1593) had married twice. His first wife, Elizabeth, daughter and co-heiress of Sir John Bentley, of Bredsall Priory, Derbyshire, died childless, and was buried at Silkstone, on January 22, 1623-4. He re-married ten years afterwards, with the Lady Magdalene Egerton, whose father was some time Lord President of Wales, and had been Lord Lieutenant of each of the sixteen counties of Shropshire, Worcestershire, Herefordshire, Monmouthshire, Anglesey, Carnarvon, Merioneth, Flint, Denbigh, Montgomery, Pembroke, Cardigan, Carmarthen, Glamorgan, Brecknock, and Radnor. Lady Cutler's mother, née Stanley, was herself co-heiress of her father, Ferdinando Earl Derby. Only twenty-eight when she lost her husband, this devoted woman, who was afterwards treated with such indignity by the besiegers, had for her mother a Stanley, whose mother was a Clifford, whose mother was a Brandon, whose mother was a Plantagenet, eldest daughter of Edward IV. Lady Cutler had nine children in her short wedded life, two of whom died infants, while her eldest son, the heir of his father, was but four years old when he was thus left an orphan.

By his will, made in 1633, Sir Jarvis had directed that he should be buried in his St. James's quire in Silkstone Church, but his removal thither was thus prohibited. Evidently the good will of General Poyntz was being overruled, or there would have been no such arbitrary prohibition.

26th. This day we had newes brought to us that Tanton was taken by an assault by Sr Richard Grinfeild & that there was 1500 men killd & taken prisoners & (16000 *altered to*) 10000 armes taken besides their gunnes (60, *interlined*) & Amunition, but of this we are not Certeyn, yett the enemy did Confesso this night that it was taken. This day we allso buryed that worthy knight, Sr. Jarvis Cuttler who was first Cophined & then the Cophin & all wraped up in lead, and after a Funrall Sarmond he was buryed in the Chapeell wthin the Castle, wth 3 gallont vollyes of shott according to the honnor of such a brave Souldyer as he was. from whence his Corpes may be Conveyed to the place of his Auncesstors (after the seege) when his freindes please. the enemy yett keepes the Lady wthin the Castle & will not suffer hur to goe to hur Children, though often sent to about it. this night there went out 2 of the Sandoll men from the Castle & they tould us they would goe to Sandoll. This night allso there runne a Rouge out of the Castle to the enemy, his name was Medcaulph, who tended of Allexander Medcaulph being sick of the gout. he stole of the Chamber a Riding Coate, a doblitt, a paire of britches, a paire of stockinges, a paire of shoowes, a hatt & 3 bandes (and a rapire *interlined*) & got over the barbican wall, his Company being that night upon the watch there : &, Coming to the enemy, he Caused the Chirurgion & the drumme (wch used to dresse the prisoners woundes & to bring victualls to the prisoners in the Castle) to be Committed to prison ; Informing to theire Governor against them that they brought newes into the Castle, & likewise that they brought us Tobackoe.

In "confessing" that Taunton was taken by the Royalists, it seems that the besiegers were not such determined falsifiers as the Diarist sometimes thought them to be. The incorrect news reached them as well as the Garrison; and in this case they believed it, although their chance of obtaining accurate information was, of course, much greater than that possessed by those within the Castle. It is very curious to notice this constant alternation from artillery practice to gossip. Those engaged in the siege, whether as besiegers or as besieged, were ready at any moment, to exchange shot or exchange news.

In thus burying Sir Jarvis in the Castle Chapel, it is quite clear that the Garrison intended to give him there a temporary grave only.

This " rouge" going over to the enemy was acting the part of the proverbial rat. The provisions were now failing, and for the remaining three weeks of the siege, the hardships so patiently endured by the Garrison must have been very considerable.

The clothes stolen by the " rouge" seem to have been almost a complete outfit. Perhaps, indeed, he vested himself in those belonging to his master. But the " 3 bandes" were surely more than he could have worn at once.

The description of the Chirurgion and the Drumme is characteristically concise. The Chirurgion to dress the prisoners' wounds ; the Drumme to bring victuals to the prisoners. But a similar description of Dr Samuel, and his father, the Diarist, as engaged in the sieges of Newark and Pontefract, that is the son at Newark, the father at Pontefract, is constantly misinterpreted as if each had been at both sieges. The expression is parallel to that in the text.

27th. This day there was divers troopes of horse round about the Towne, & they weare still Cept Sadled in the Closes till about 4 a Clock, at wch time those towardes the upp' end of the Towne went on the high way towardes Carleton in vew of the Castle, those allso wch was about newhall & the lower end of the Towne went on by Baghill faceing the Castle till they Came to Carleton way, & then they all passed through Carleton, & round about the hill, & some of them went downe towardes the high Road & so Came In againe, & others Came back through Carleton againe to make a show as though they was so many fresh troopes to releeve them, wch we little respected.

It appears as if the common stage trick to multiply a

small force was well known in the seventeenth century. These apparently meaningless circuitings of the town, occurred frequently, to the great delight of the Garrison.

> The enemy had this day a Thanksgiving both in the Towne & allso at newhall for some great victory obtained agt the King & had 2 Sarmondes at least. And for Joy whereof they shott 2 valley of shott throughout all theire workes, (one after another *interlined*) round about the Castle, and allso playd 2 Cannon, wth one whereof they play throwgh the drawbridge & allso through the lower Castle gate, the other plaide short of the drawbridge & litt upon a peese of Timber & rive it in peeses. the enemy allso shott 2 of our men wth one bullitt in the Barbican from baghill, but did them very little hurt. and we killd one of the enemyes from the Round Tower on Mr Rusbuyes back side. this night was a boane fire at Sandoll Castle, and we answered it wth another from the Round Tower.

The victory, which caused these rejoicings, would have been the battle of Naseby, of which some official news must now have reached the General.

It must have been a better aimed shot than usual, and fired point blank, that traversed the Castle area in this manner.

In at one gate, along the Castle Chain, and out at the other gate, is a distance of some two hundred yards.

Mr Rusby's property was a prominent mark, owing to its being bounded by an important trench, which divided it from the property of Mr Lund, from whence the first bullet was fired in the first siege, at the commencement of the attack which brought down Piper Tower. When the second siege commenced, and the enemy fell a trenching on Saturday, March 22nd, their work was "especially before Allderman Lunne's house." A week after, on the following Saturday, the besieged fired 10 cannon, "all to Mr Rusbye's, and up that street." On April 4th, they shot seven cannon, and burnt down Alderman Rusbye's lathe (being their sentry) and parte of his house. This seems to have exposed Mr Lund's, for "they set on fire the enemy's powder at Mr Lunne's, and burnt about 20 men." On April 16th, they shot through "Mr Lunne's house topp," and constant mention is afterwards made of the work connected with these two properties till the very close of the siege. It appears by comparing the various passages, that the besiegers entrenched themselves behind the dividing wall between the properties, and that they there made a series of square pits in the sandstone, traces of which now remain. Thus the wall would have been a curtain, behind which they could have passed from pit to pit.

The signals now recommenced between Sandal and Pontefract, would appear from what follows to have been a request for aid.

28th. This day we had newes that the Scottes begunne to stoppe up the passages about newarke & to bessege it. But the newarke forces p'sently sallyed forth of the Towne & fell upon them, killd 500 of theire horse & foote, and beate all the rest quite away & tooke theire Cannon along wth them. and this we imagine to be true, because that it is genrally reported that this day there went by 5 or 600 horse & Cariages towardes Ferry bridge, & is supposed that the Cannon went along wth them, & we heare that the most of the Scotch army lyes betwixt Dauncaster & Rothrom or thereabouts. This evning the Lady went forth of the Castle, being sent for by a drumme from Ourton (theire Governor) to goe home if she pleased. but when she Came to the enemyes first gaurd, they stript both hur & hur wayting maid to hur very smock, & likewise hur Chaplin & a tenant of hurs wch Came downe wth the Chaplin to the Sally poart, to search for letters but they had none. they Cept the Lady & hur mayd at theire gaurd all night till the next day at noone, & would not suffer hur to goe up towne, (for it seemes the Genrall Came in after, & denied hur Coming from the Castle.) this day we had a horse turned forth into the Castle dikes to feede there, but, the gras beeing bad, he strayd a little forther to the sight of the enemy where they shott very hard at him. our men ventured to fetch him back, & they shott very hard at our men, but yett they fecht him of, & our men kild one of theire men wth great hazard of theire owne lives.

Naturally, the connection between the Nathan Drake at Pontefract, and the Samuel Drake at Newark would cause the one to take considerable interest in the doings at the temporary dwelling place of the other. Hence, to a great extent, the continual receipt and chronicling of intelligence from Newark.

All may be fair in war, but this poor widow lady, her maid,

and her chaplain, seem to have had hard usage. We learn incidentally that the Chaplain, whose name is not given, was an aged man, for Capt. John Hodgson in his Memoirs says : " After this (the events of May 27) they grew quiet, and made no sallies. They then began to turn out women and children, and one old man ; and our Governor Colonel Overton, examining them, sent them in again."—This account is, however, in many respects manifestly incorrect. For it was nearly five weeks after May 27th, when Lady Cuttler left the Castle ; and she had no children with her, the very reason that she was allowed to leave having been that she might " go home to her children." See next Entry.

June 29th. This day being sunday, (*an illegible erasure*) there was little shooting all this day & the enemy did not releeve theire gaurdes till about 9 a Clock.

a little after noone, the Enemyes Genrall (Poyntes) sent downe the Lady Cuttler wth hur waytingmaid to the Barbican gates againe, she having not had any meate of 24 howers. Our Governor of the Castle would not suffer hur to Come into the Castle againe, because they had sent for hur out & given hur free liberty to goe home to hur Children, therefore he thought it stood not wth his honor to be so Fooled by them, and by that meanes the poore Lady wth hur maid & hur Chaplin staid starving in the streetes till about 10 a Clock in the night, at wch time the Enemy sent for hur up into the Towne, & for any thing we heare, she sent for 2 horseyes that night, & so went away the next day. There was this night 2 Boane fires this night (*sic*) made upon Sandoll Castle and we answered it (*sic*) wth one heare upon the Round Tower. we supposed to be good newes because of 2 Fires.

The two "boane fires" probably meant that relief should come in two days ; but the secret, as in the former case of relief, was well kept, and none of the Garrison knew what was proceeding. Even the Diarist and his intimates only " supposed" that such a signal meant good news. But the concurrence of this signal with the events of the evening of July 1st, and the midnight preparations for something which did not come off, must be more than a mere coincidence.

30th. This day the enemy drew all theire horse from all p'tes heareabouts, and brought along from Dauncaster some Cariages wth them. they allso drew downe theire horse from about the Towne to Brotherton marsh, there to make theire genrall Randisvowes (at wch time, as one troope of horse marched over

St. Thomas hill, our Cannon playd once at them from the Kinges Tower, but it did no execution). We supposed there was 1000 (horse *interlined*) at least. after they had done there, there Came up about 400 horse faceing the Castle over Baghill [and they went down, *utterly perished*] behind the hill & there stayd feed [ing theire hor]ses in the back Closes and in the Corne in the townefeild behind the hill. other Companyes went thorough the Parke & so went p'te to Fetherstone, & p'te into the Closes upon the west end of the Towne neare Clay dicke, where they stood the last time when Sr. marmaduke Lungdale Came to releeve us (& we well hope he will Come againe). other Companyes went to Carleton & Townes thereaboutes, & many stayd at Ferry bridges and Knottinglay. So that we Conceive that the most of theire forces lyes now heareabouts (and we allso heare that the (*qy* Generall) is about westfeild *erased*) wch makes us thinke that we have some forces Coming to our releefe, & that these either intend to give battell heareabouts to the King or ellse to draw northward very shortly.

Brotherton Marsh is opposite the Castle, but separated from it by the river Aire ; and the Castle can be reached from the Marsh only by a *detour* over Ferrybridge Bridge, or by boating across the stream.

At this point the MS. has suffered much, through damp, by cross folding, and owing to the quality of the ink. All these causes have combined to make the paper as brittle as if it had been scorched, and to destroy its fibre utterly ; so that a smart blow, or an awkward fall, would knock off splinters as if the whole was a piece of glass. Some of the present injuries have happened since the copy was made, which here comes in very usefully to help to a restoration of the text.

But about forty or fifty words in this column are so thoroughly erased as to be irrecoverable.

This (night *erased*) afternoone (*substituted*) the enemy drew downe about 600 Foot from the Towne to releeve theire gaurdes about Newhall & Monkhill, and there Came as many back from thence into the Towne. Now for Certeyne (they *erased*) there (*substituted*) stayd not above 300 men about New hall, but onely to make a show to us that they was so many (wch we little respeckted). this eevning there went 7 or 8 empty waynes into the towne but to what end we know not. we expeckted this night that the enemy, (being so many *interlined*) would have made an assault upon the Castle in all places where the Could, wch made us duble our gaurdes & keepe strong watch, but in stead of assaulting us, they Cutt downe a great Company of boughes from the trees. they had neare upon 20 Axses hewing, but in stead of fauling upon us they made a baricado at Farrow doore, least we should sally forth against them.

The construction of a barricade at this time, seems to have been quite a surprise to the garrison. Its real meaning was explained by the operations of the following day.

1645. July 1th. Of all the wodde the enemy Cutt downe the last [night, *supplied by the copy*] this day the made up gappes to turne our men from going forth to gett gras, & wth the rest of it they [made, *supplied by the copy*] Figates of wch they made a baricado, & wth wodde allso Crosse over the lane going up to Baghill, & from the end of it runne a trench all along the hedge against Alderman Stables backsid, o[ut] of wch they have shott since very hard, making [it] full of poart hoales to shoot out at. this day the[re] was very hard shooting wth muskittes on both sid[es], & we Cannot Conceive but that we killd very many of them, for we shott full amongst them into the[ir] worke, where was seene divers to faule, so that there is many wounded or killd. we playd 1 Can-[non] from the Kinges Tower up into the Towne, but what execution was done is not knowne.

Alderman Stable's house seems to have been the corner house of Baghill lane. It would have been nearly opposite the gate into the Barbican, through which the cattle were driven on May 27th. The area behind the house is not so extended as that behind the parallel properties, for Baghill lane makes a curve to bound it to the south, almost opposite Primrose Close. The Barbican gate has been quite destroyed, and there is now no evidence of the former existence of a road by it into the Castle.

This eevning the enemy was seene to bring downe some ladders to the lower end of the towne & figates all so, wch mad us to doble our gaurdes; and, about 12 a Clock in the night, the most p'te of the men in the Castle was commanded downe into the Castele yeard to theire armes, to be ready if the enemy should make any assault, (wch was willingly done.)

This commanding down into the Castle yard seems so very much like the preliminaries to the relief of May 27th, that we cannot resist the conclusion that such an another relief was on this occasion frustrated only by the increased vigilance of the besieging army.

2th. This morning one of our souldiers was talking above the upp' Castle gate wth one of the enemyes in theire trenches, wch another of the enemyes espying & shott him through the head whereof he dyed Instantly. p'sently after the enemy playd theire Canon to the lower Castle gate, but miste his marke & hitt the wall end, & so did no harme at all, but the bullitt fell under the draw bridge. in the Afternoone our dutchman playd his Cannon from the platforme by Treasurers Tower into the Markitt place, where we saw 2 or 3 kild dead before the bullitt (hit, & *erased*) g[ra]sed, (*substituted*) but the enemy runne in so fast after the (shott *supplied from the copy*] that we Could not see how many was killd, but supposed there was many. after that we shott 1 Cannon from the Kinges Tower to baghill lane, amongst a troope of horse, where we saw one horse runne away wthout his rider: what more hurt was done we know not. he allso shott another Cannon from the Kinges t[ower *supplied from the copy*] to into the frealles to a troope of horse, but what execution was done we know not. tow[ardes *supplied from the copy*] night we Could see (10 *erased*) 15 (*substituted*) troopes of horse at lest about the Towne, wherof 5 went downe to Ferrybridge, and about 200 horse went out of Rop'gate end, & so through the Chequor feeld, facing the Castle, in a single file over Baghill whereof 2 troopes went out baghill lane, towards Darington, and the rest went downe by Newhall, & so up thr(ough *interlined*) the parke to Tansill, & to the Kinges Close, & the west feild, where they stayd all night till about 4 a Clock of the next morning, then they went to theire quarters. this night allso we sett a doble (watch *interlined*) of the Vollontears as well as of the Souldyers, to be ready against any occation, because the bring so many horse about us; but we thinke it is rather to keepe the Foot Souldyers from running away.

"To into." Evidently the second word was to have supplied the place of the first which, however, escaped erasure. The first work was originally "too," but the second "o" has been taken off, as with a penknife, leaving its stain on the paper. This is the only instance in which we have suspected such an erasure in the Diary; and here we are not certain of the fact. It is however clear that there is a stain of the second "o", and that there is space for it, before "into."

Of the Frealles (for Prealls) we have already said somewhat.—See page 46.

Tansill=Tanshelf. These 200 horse thus made a complete circuit of the town, settling at King's Closes, not very far from Ropergate end, whence they started.

The King's Closes, it may be noted, are still Crown, or at least Duchy, lands. It is curious that these Closes thus hold the name of "King's": which points to their having been enclosed,—probably as the Duchy share of West Field, when it was made common,—sometime after the Duchy estates had merged in the Crown, upon the accession of Henry IV.

3th. This morning many troopes of horse went out of towne very yearely; and, about noone there Came In above 20 troopes of horse, & stayd there till towardes night, about wch time they was all disparsed, we know not wch way, to theire sev[erall] quarters, so that there was but very few left about the Towne at night. This day Came in the enemyes Generalls Trumpitt desiring that Captin Clarke's mother might Come to see hur Sonne, and allso that they might bring in doctor Oyston (*called Gybson in the copy*) to see him, and that they might bring victualls to the prisoners themsellves, and deliver it to them, wch was all graunted, & they Came into the Castle. there was great shooting this day wth muskitts on both sides, but we had [not] one man hurt, praised be god.

Yearley = early. — See also July 4.

This is the only mention of Capt. Clarke in the whole of the Diary.

Our men from about the kinges Tower shott (shott *erased*) some of the enemyes about theire workes nare to the Church, & see them fall, but whether wounded or killd we know not. This night we sent 2 men out to Sandoll & so to Newearke, and one of Captin Cartwrightes Souldyers runne away this night to the enemy.

Another message for that relief which was so long a-coming, which was never to come; and another ratting "rouge."

4th. This morning the enemy had an allarum, but we knew not where, but all the horse that went out last night Came in againe very yearely to the Towne, & the drew up about 400 foot into the (upper *interlined*) Markitt place & stood to theire armes wth theire knapsackes on theire backes: and about 12 a Clock all the horse wch was about towne drew towardes wentbridge and appeared in 2 bodyes upon the hill topp on this side wentbridge, and stood there for the space of haulph an hower or better, & so Came back againe into the west feeild neare to Pomphret stone wind(*e* or *d*) millne where we suppose(*e* or *d*) the most of the Yorkshire horse belonging to the p'lament met wth them, & there drew into Sev'all bodyes where we Could not see them under the hill, but we supposed there Could not bee so few as 2000 horse. they stood there for the most p'te from 12 till 6 a Clock, about wch time they begunne to draw offe by troopes till a great p'te of them was gone, & the rest stayd there all night keekeing (*sic*) great fires amongest them.

About 8 a Clock there went about 100 men downe from the Towne to Ferry-brigges, and allso about 50 more from Newhall. we supposed they went to gaurd the bridge, & to stop theire souldyers from running away. this night we sent 2 men out towardes Sandoll.

Troops were now assembling fast. There were 1000 horse, on the 30th June. Now there are 2000; or rather, "there could not be so few as 2000."

Note: The Pomphret stone wind mill was in Tanshelf

locally, although belonging to the municipal corporation of Pontefract. When the division of West field was made between the two townships, at the time that the original Manor of Tateshall was broken up, the part of the common-land adjacent to the mill, with the ground on which the mill itself stood, became civilly part of Tanshelf, while the property in the mill remained in the bailiffs or other governing officers of Pontefract.

The idea that 150 horse were sent to guard the bridge, and prevent the foot soldiers from deserting is good. *Quis custodes custodient ?* Who would have taken care that the horsemen did not desert ?

"Two more sent out towards Sandoll:" evidently the prospect was becoming desperate. All pretences of going to Newark had now ceased. Two went on the 3rd to Sandal, and so to Newark: two on the 4th, only *towards* Sandal, probably to hasten in some of the former messengers. The difference in expression is ominous.

5th. This morning the enemy playd 1 Cannon to the lower Castle gate, but shott short of the gate above 20 yeardes, & did no harme at all. The enemy allso brought into the Towne this morning a Small dimiculvarin or some other smaule feeild peese wch was said thay Caryed up into the west feild. and about 3 a Clock the enemy shott of theire Cannon againe to the lower Castle gate & shott thorough the draw bridge, & so fell betwixt the bridge & the gate. The enemy drew all theire horse into the west feild from all theire quarters about the towne, & drew up in to sevrall bodyes, & there staid a great p'te of the Day ; and towardes night there Came 3 or 4 troops into the parke, & so went downe the forther side of the parke, and so Came downe to Newhall, & from thence went up to the west feild againe, where we supposed the most p'te of them stayd all night.

The course of this shot shows that there was at the Lower Castle Gate, a drawbridge in advance of the gate. But there are no present remains of any such structure.

This afternoone we killd 2 of the enemyes, the one from the round tower, wthin Mr Rusbyes Baricado, the other from the Kinges tower neare to william Farrowes under Munkhill.

It has already been pointed out that Mr Rusby's and

Mr Lund's were adjacent properties, Mr Rusby's being the nearer to the Castle.—William Farrowe's (Farrer would have been the correct spelling) was mentioned a few pages back.—(See page 125.)

This night we Cept doble watch as we had done all the weeke before, and this night (there *interlined*) was 2 boane fires made upon the toppe of Sandall Castle, and we answered it (*sic*) againe wth 2 more upon the Toppe of the Round Tower.. we did suppose that by those 2 boanefires at Sandall we was to have Ayd within 2 daies.

Now at last, they understand the meaning of the varying number of the bonfires.

6th.. This day, beeing Sunday, we had 2 exceeding good Sarmondes by Mr Key in the forenoone & Mr Hirst in the after noone. there was little shooting on either side of all this day, and the enemy drew up the most of all theire horse into the west feild, where they Continued for the most p'te of all the day, and towardes night they drew of some troopes into Sev'all places about the Towne, but about 9 a Clock at night there was 6 Trumpitts of the enemyes sounding, wch Calld them all up to the west feild againe and the had an allarum given, & the Souldyers wthin the Towne stood all wth theire ligted match: and a Wellshman (one of theire owne souldyers) tould one of our owne souldyers (a Wellshma' allso) that all theire horse was gone towardes dauncaster to meete the prince, but they was returned againe before morning. This night we saw 2 boanefires betwixt wentbridge & dauncaster, we supposed they was for horse gaurdes. This night allso we had a letter Came into the Castle from the 2 went out 4 daies since to the Kinges Army, wth very good newes.

These sermons would have been, presumably, at the Castle Chapel, for the Parish Church was in the possession of the besiegers; but a few days afterwards, prayers were read in the Hall.

"the had an allarum"—one of the many instances in which the Diarist drops the final letter of "they."

"Four daies since" should be three days since. They were sent on the 3rd.

7th. This morning about 8 a Clock there Came in 200 horse Thorough the Parke and they drew up into the west feild.. we supposed they Came from Sandoll, for the seege is [*hiatus*, raised *supplied from the copy*] from thence.. This day allso Came in [*hiatus*,] the Scottes both horse & foot, for so [the] enemyes Souldyers out of theire qua[rters] tould us.. we supposed that all the 'ho[rse] they now had in all places & from all [garr]isonnes was drawne all hither to sett [down] heare for a pitcht feild. They stood to theire Armes the greatest p'te of this [day] in the west feild, and Tewardes night [they *supplied in the copy, unnecessarily*] drew of about 7 or 8 troopes towardes Carleton (we kild 3 men this day in theire workes *interlined*) & went bridg & there abouts, an[d] other troopes they drew of to Sev'all (of the *supplied in the copy, again unnecessarily*) medow Closes round about the Towne. (theire went 140 Scottes downe to new hall, *interlined*). This night about 10 a[Clock the enemy] sounded theire trump[ittes for theire horse to come] into the west feild, & then the foot lighted theire matche & stood to theire Armes, haveing taken an allarum from Some place.

We have already noted that Oyston in the original is misread Gibson in the copy. That misreading, and these unnecessary alterations, illustrate the rapid changes that had taken place in the seventeenth and eighteenth centuries, both in the character of the handwriting and in the habits of thought, between the members of the Garrison and of their great grand children. These latter could hardly read the handwriting of their great grandfather, while they could not understand his idiom at all.

This part of the M.S. is again much injured. The few words placed in brackets, are wanting in the Diary; but have been supplied from the Copy.

The " allarum" might have been another attempted relief. This was the second day that the Garrison did, so to say, nothing; nothing more than watch.

8th. This morning, about 4 a Clock, the enemy drew out of that worke against Swillinto' Tower about 70 men who we supposed marched into the west feild. about 6 a Clock there Came above 1000 foot out of the west feild marching into the towne to theire quarters for a little time (as we supposed, & we heard the went back againe, but they drew them out of all theire workes round about the Towne as we supposed. The horse Cept the most p'te of the day out of sight behind the hill towardes the bottom of the west feild, and towardes night there Came some troopes wch quartred about the towne. Some stayd in the west feild where they Cept 2 great fires, & the rest went away we know not whither, but we supposed to wardes went bridg, for there they keepe a strong gaurd & had a strong allarum the last night. This evning, being the 10 for releefe of newhall, about 9 a Clock or after, there was sent downe from the Towne very many (from *erased*) to new hall, and they likewise sent the other back to the Towne. the enemy releeved all theire gaurdes very late this evning. This night Came downe Genrall Poyntes to the worke against Barbican gate, & asked to speake wth our Governor, but the Governors sonne being there made him answer that his Father was not there, wch if he had beene he would not refuse to speake to him. Then the Genrall begunne to demaund the Castle to him, wch if we did wthin 3 daies or there abouts we should have honorable tearmes, but if we stayd 10 daies or 14 daies we should then looke for nothing but to walke wth a white rod in our handes, as Souldyers doe in the low Contreyes when they march away upon a forced Composition. But Captin Lowder made him this Answer, that the Castle was Cept for the King, & if they stayd 14 daies, & 14 daies more after that, there was as many Gentlemen wthin the Castle as would make many a bloody heade before they p'ted from it (or wordes to the like effeckte). Then the Genrall begunne to give some harsh Language, & say that our Souldyers did abuse him in base wordes. but Capt' Lowder answered him that neither he nor his Father Could rule the Souldyers Tounges, but they would speake what they pleased. And [then] the Genrall (tooke *erased*) bid Good night & went away. There was of the enemyes souldyers this night that tould to some of our Souldyers (theire frendes) that we (had *interlined*) helpe Coming neare to us, & that they intended to be wth us as soone as wth Convenience they Could, before our Armye Came to releeve us.

To wardes went brig=Towards Wentbridge.

Another day of absolute inaction; but the episode at its close was worthy of all that had gone before. Capt. Lowther continued to show himself an intrepid soldier, and as ready with his tongue as with his sword. But the noble conduct of General Poyntz is beyond praise. Knowing well that the surrender of the Castle was but a matter of days, he seems to have striven with all his might to gain possession without unnecessary effusion of blood. Admiration for the endurance of the besieged would also have had its due place. But meanwhile, the Garrison were buoyed up with the false hopes engendered by the gossip which passed between the men on each side.

9: This day the enemy hath made very little show, but we suppose they are behind the hill in the west feild or there abouts where we cannot see them. there hath beene very hard shooting this day both to the Castle & from the Castle, and the ememy (*sic*) makes great riding both from the Towne to New hall, & likewise back againe on both sides of the Castle, but we heare not of any [was] killed of the enemyes, but all this shooting could not be but that there is Some killed of the enemy, but there is not one hurt wch belonges to the Castle, & yett we fetch in gras & parsneppes all day long as we have done for the most p'te this 3 weekes. [The enemy beguane a] fence all along the he[dge side] from theire worke against Swillinton Tower into denwell lane out of wch they shoote at our men wch Come to gett gras Continually, but of late there is but few hurt (praised be God). This night we sent out 5 men, Somme went to Sandoll, & others went to the Kinges Armye wch should Come to releeve us, or ellse to goe on to Newarke to bringe us some Intelligence.

The refusal of terms by the besieged was evidently the inciting cause of the increased energy of the fighting men: the besieged to show their energy and resolution in defence, the besiegers to manifest their determination to compel a surrender.

One of the singular moral phenomena illustrated by this naive history is the one-sided way in which people look at circumstances as they affect themselves, and as they affect others. This day's record is a striking example. Shots were confessedly exchanged with great vehemence, possibly with equal effect. The besieged proclaim that none of themselves were injured, and yet they could not believe it to be possible that their own shot should be equally ineffective.

The sending out of 5 men, is an indication of the straits to which the Garrison were now becoming reduced.

10. This day there hath beene hard shooting, the enemy having runne so many trenches so neare the Castle, where they lye lurking to shoote at our men to p'vent them from getting of gras, wch they Cannot doe, for they gett grass still as much as will suffice, thoug it be at deare rates. we had a man shott by the enemy in an appletre. as he was getting of Apples he was shott thorow the arme, but no mortall wound. we allso kild one of the enemyes from of the lower Castle gatehowse toppe along theire trenches below. and about 6 a Clock, at the releeving of our gaurdes, one of our First sentry men wch went up to the toppe of the Round tower & stood upon a stone & looked over a poartehoale, wch being soone espied by the enemy, was shott thorow the head wherof he dyed instantly. this (eevning we sent *erased*) day we had (*interlined*) letters brought in (that *erased*) of Certeyne intelligence that Genrall Goring had given Sr Thomas Fairfax a great overthrow neare unto Tanton, & allso more p'feckt newes of the taking of Tanton. There allso Came in a drumme last night from newarke to us to know whether we had yeilded up the Castle or not, for that the enemy had bruited it all abroad that we had yeilded up the Castle unto them: but the enemy stayd the drumme in the Towne all night & would nott suffer him to Come to us, (but keepes him still *interlined*). but at Mr Washington's, where he stayd all night, he tould Mrs Washington to Come downe & speake wth hur husband, & to (lett *erased*) bid us be of good Cheare, for that we had forces Comming to releeve us wthin 4 or 5 daies, whereupon she gott a drumme to Come downe wth hur to speake wth hur husband at Barbican Sallypoarte & there he mett hur, & she tould him this newes whilst another taulked wth the drumme, and she shaked handes wth another man was one of hur accquaintance, & then thrust him in 2 letters into his hand. This eevning we sent out 2 men & a boy

to goe either to Sandoll or to the Kinges Army wch they Could most Con-
veniently, & they gott Cleare away for any thing we heard. this night there
was made 4 boanefires upon Sandoll Castle where by we know that all our men
gott Cleare away the last night, & allso by them we had notise how neare our
helpe was Coming to us. We allso answered them againe wth 1 from the
Round Tower.

Note, the "poartholes" were so high that a man could not look through them without standing on a stone. Or was it that the enemy were so near that they could not be seen, except from an almost perpendicular point of view.

From the fact of this "drumme" coming in from Newark, it seems that the Newark people were in quite as much uncertainty as to what we might call the news of the day, as were those thus besieged in Pontefract.

The Diarist is consistent in spelling the possessive pronoun "hur." Lady Cutler was always spoken of as "hur," as is now Mrs Washington. On the other hand "the," "thay," and "they" are variations in the mode of spelling the nominative plural.

---

11. This morning, about 8 a Clock, the enemy appeared in the west
Feild againe [in] 4 great Bodyes, wth a smaule reserve a good distance from the
other. they appeared to us as though they were at exercisinge of theire Souldyers, and they [co]ntinued there for the space of 3 hewers, & then went out of
our sight, Some p'te behind the hill, and others went as we suppose to Sandoll,
for Some of our men wch we sent out to Sandoll (2 daies since *interlined*) are
Come in againe this night, & they tell us that about 2 Regiments of horse goe
every day to Sandoll. about 9 a Clock there Came 4 Cariages loaden wth
8 Oxen in a draught thorow the Parke, & so went by the west end of the Towne
into the west Feeild to the Company wch was there, but whether [they] was loaded
wth Amunition or Provitions we know not, but we Conceive they was the one of
these two. this day the en[emy] held a Counsell of warre to what effeckt we
know not, but we suppose it was wh[ether] to give the King battell heare or not.
 there was little shooting by us this day (it beeing fast day,) nor by the enemy,
neither doe we heare of any man hu[rt] of either side. This evninge there was
2 Boanefires made upon Sandoll Castle, wch we answered wth one from the
Round Tower. This day the 2 men wch we sent out 10 daies since to Newarke
Came againe to towne, & though they Could not gett into the Castle to us yett
they Showed forth such signes as we knew we had good newes towardes us. This
might 2 of those m[en] we sent out 2 nightes before to ¦Sa[ndoll] came in againe.

The eager anxiety with which every motion of the enemy is thus noted, and commented upon, is not to be wondered at ; while the straightforward honest simplicity with which the Diarist records the deductions, favourable and unfavourable, made by the Garrison, is instructive.

This is the only mention of a "fast day" on Friday during the siege.

For a second time, these messengers could reach the town, could let it be known that they had done so, but were not able to get into the Castle.

This might signify either that the guard had become too strict, or that the Garrison had no wish to place themselves voluntarily in a situation of so much privation, as they must have known ruled within. Two of the Sandal messengers managed to effect an entrance; which shows what might have been done by those who were in earnest.

12th. This morning the enemy made little appearance in sight wth theire horse but such as was wthin the Closes round about the Towne. The rest was at theire quarters except such as was sent out to Sandoll. this Day the letters wch. Came in from Sandoll the last night was p'used and In them was notifd that we are to expeckt helpe very Shortly. the other letters allso wch Came into towne yesterday was sent in this day, but the key to open those newarke letters was not (yett *erased*) att first (*substituted*) found, but is now found wth good newes, and both the day & time of the day sett downe when Sr Marmaduke Langdall intendes to be wth us, (if God p'mitt) & succors appoynted to meet him heare. the Lord Come along wth him & give him victory over his & all our enemies. There was allso newes in them of the great victory wch Gen. Goring had agt Sr Tho: Fairfax, that he had quite Routed his forces, & that Sr Thomas was not to be found. there was little shooting this day betwixt the enemy & us, neither doe we heare of any one that was hurt. This day likewise the enemy begunne to fortyfie Ferry brigges, & to make workes about the bridge (& made a mound *interlined*). we suppose they Intend to plant theire Cannon there agt the day of Battell. This night The enemy had an allarum in the Towne, Sounded theire Trumpitts, lighted theire matches and Calld to horse, horse, where they stood upon theire gaurdes all night.

What a truthful natural touch there is in the erasure. Evidently the garrison were for some time before they could understand the message of these fateful letters. But at last even after their failure is recorded in this truthful diary, the key to the hidden writing is discovered, and all is plain.

With lighted match in the hand of every man on guard, the appearance of the besiegers in the Closes must have been very picturesque, if the spectator could have forgotten the bloody work on which they were all engaged.

> This night allso There was a boane fire made upon Sandoll Castle, wch we Answered wth another from the Round Tower.

This was the last bon-fire made from Sandal and descried with certainty. There was one on the following Monday, but the Diarist speaks of it with uncertainty; but it must not be supposed that the Sandal seige had yet closed. The garrison there held out till October.

> 13. This morning, being Sunday, about 4 a Clock, the enemy stood in great bodyes on horseback in the west feild as many as ever formerly they had done.
> The enemy hath now sett up theire Tentes and Intrenched them sellves in the west feild, and there the Generall lyeth every night, and they draw of many of theire foote out of all theire workes every night into the west feild. there Came this day about 60 Foot from Ferry bridge. some said they was new a Rayed men brought to the Garison.
> They have planted a drake in the Market place out of sight of the Castle.
> It is reported to us that Skipton horse went by Sandoll last night, & gave the enemy an Allarum; if they bee, they are gone to Sr Marmaduke. This night the Enemy had an Allarum, & sounded theire Trumpitts for Horse. This evning our Souldyers, being very Joyfull & merry, gave a great Showte wthin the Castle yeard, & after that was done they went up to the Round Tower & gave 3 more showtes.

These fragmentary records, evidently jotted down at various times during the day, open ominously the events of the last week of the siege.

The West Field was now evidently becoming the active head quarters of the besiegers, they being driven out of the town by the plague which was beginning to make its appearance, although the intelligence of its advent had not yet reached the Garrison.

> July 14th. This day the enemy Cept still making their Trenches (this erased) in the west Feild, & setting' up their Tentes, and allso sending out stronge p'ties of horse both towardes Dauncaster & to Sandoll. they allso made up theire workes betwixt the 2 Triangle workes they had on the north side of

Swillington Tower, & made many poartholaes to shoot out at. the enemy allso made greate shootinge at the Castle this day, but we heare not of any one hurt of either side. It was tould us allso this evning by the enemyes owne Souldyers that there was 5 Souldyers buryed this day of the Plague: they dyed in the howses in the Barly markit place; and that they intend to morow to remove the Souldyers all out of the Towne into the west Feild & make that theire Le[agure *supplied from the copy*.]

The "great showte" of the previous night in the Castle yard, and the "three more showtes" on the Round Tower, appear not to have affected the besiegers so much as was expected by the "Souldyers"—"joyfull and merry" as they were. And accordingly, Monday morning found them busy with their entrenchment and encampment in the West Field, where they intended to await events, and escape, if possible, the plague.

The Barley Market place is now called the Wool market, having, in the eighteenth century, had the intermediate name of the Hemp Market.

This night theare was either one [or two] (lowe *interlined*) Boanefires made upon the toppe [of San]doll Castle or ellse 2 little ones, a[nd] we made one upon the toppe of the [Round *supplied from the copy*] Tower. (There was allso a boanefire seene towardes [daunca *supplied from the copy*]ster (*interlined*.) we had sent out 2 men [this *supplied from the copy*] night to goe to the Kinges Armey, but [one *supplied from the copy*] of them was taken, being miscryed [by the *supplied from the copy*] boy wch went out the night before, [and was *supplied by the copy*] taken at Knottinglay, & so tould the e[nemy *supplied from the copy*] wch way he went out. the other gott [backe *supplied from the copy*] againe into the Castle, but he was [pur *supplied from the copy*] sued by 5 men.

This entry is very imperfect, the MS. being again defective.

"Miscryed"=betrayed: or, perhaps the reverse of "discried."

15th. This morninge about 5 a Clocke went (out *erased*) 12 Souldyers out of the [Castle *supplied by the copy*] to gett apples in the Northgate where they weare all espied upon the Toppes [of *supplied from the copy*] the trees (Close by theire workes) and [on that the enemyes *supplied from the copy*] Souldyers Called & said [Come *supplied from the copy*] alonge, they are all [ours, when our *supplied from the copy*] Souldyers leapt all downe, [amongst them *supplied from the copy*] but the enemy either killd [or *supplied from the copy*] tooke 2 of them, the rest gott all away wthout (any *erased*) any hurtt, excepting one man wch gott 3 or 4 blowes; and since that time they Call to us & bid us fettch of our dead men, (*and then is added in a perceptibly different style, evidently later on in the day*) but we heare since they are not killd. after wch time we had another man went out to gett p[eares *supplied from the copy*] and was shott in the tree into the side of the Cheeke boane. So greedy are our souldyers of getting of Apples & peares wch they sell amonst women for 4. 5. or 6 a penny or sometimes more if they be little ones. there was another man of ours allso shott yesterday upon the Dutchman's platforme of his gunne; the bullitt went through his britches & rippled of the Skinne but did no more hurt.

The erased "any" is a peculiarly good example of the difficulties of the MS. As there was not room for the whole of the word at the end of the line, the Diarist wrote "an" in the line, and above the line a character which being intended for *y* is frequently mistaken for long *z*, in fifteenth and sixteenth century MSS.: then apparently changing his mind, he erased what he had written, and re-wrote the full word at the commencement of the next line, in this case using the ordinary seventeenth century "y."

Evidently the female pear-purchasers must have been among the Garrison. For the soldiers could not have gone outside to sell their pears.

But whence was the store of money? For, be it remembered, that the Pontefract siege coins belonged to the siege of 1648. Throughout the Diary we have met with not a single expression referring to coining operations; and yet it is asserted that Sir Gervas Cutler, among others, brought into the Castle his family plate, that it might be coined into money for the King's use. That contribution of Sir Gervas has been valued at £1000.

The Dutchman was allso shott through the stockinge of his legge in the Barbican, but toucht not the flesh, and after that he Came up to his gunne and there standing by his gunne was (shot *erased*) hitt againe by a splinter of wodd wch a bullitt rive out; it hitt his legge, but did scarce strike of the Skinne, onely brused it a little, but in requitall of this there was about 4 troopes of horse went downe from the Towne through the parke to newhall & soe faced about and Came back againe, and he seeing them made ready his gunne agt they Came backe, & gave them a shott into the parke where we saw both one man & a horse to fall. Some say there was 4 horse & men fell but that we know not Certeyn, but these lay there. they (rid *interlined*) 3 or 4 a brest.

The "Dutchman's platforme" was outside Treasurer's Tower, and there are still considerable remains of it.

This substitution of "hit" for "shot" shows a very nice discrimination. On page 73, we noticed similarly; "evidence" being expunged to make room for "witness," a word better suited to the sense, in the opinion of the Diarist. In this instance the Dutchman was "hit" by the splinter. He would have been "shot," had the blow been delivered by a missile.

Note the addition to the paragraph that "they rid 3 or 4 a brest," inferentially admitting the possibility that the four horses might have been struck at one shot.

15th. This afternoone the enemy sent in a drumme wth a noate in his hand wch he red by the way to their owne (gaurdes *ernsed*) Souldyers (*substituted*) at theire workes neare to Barbican gates, & he bid the Souldyers be of good Cheare for that they had ayd Coming to them both Fairfax, Cromwell, & Rosseter, & that they had rooted both Genrall Goring & Sr Marmaduke Langdall; and this noate he after brought into the Castle. And p'sently after that, Genrall Poyntes sent a Trumpiter into the Castle wth a letter from himsellfe & the Committy at Yorke. the letter was wordes to this effeckt :—
That whereas they had heretofore sent to sommone the Castle wch was still reiected, but now takinge into Consideration the great Care & love to soe many Gentlemen and Souldyers wch weare wthin the Castle, and [the *supplied from the copy*] miserye we lived in, and the effusion of so much Innocent blood, wch there was likely to be made, and many a sackles man [in *from the copy*] it, they thought good once more to Sommond us and to give us to understand that if we pleased to Come to a treatye abou the surrendringe of the same, they would Treate wth us upon honorable tearmes, and wth Conditions fitting for such a garison, & give hostages for the same. whereupon Answer was given by the Governor, that it was a matter of too great a Consequence to treate or give answer at the First, but he [would *from the copy*] Conferre wth the knights & Gentlemen [of *from the copy*] the Castle, & returne answer as speedely [as *from the copy*] he Could (or wordes to that effeckt), whereupon the Trumpitt was sent away.

Here is now the first sign of a willingness to treat, on the part of the Garrison. The way was well prepared. The "noate" in the hand of the Drumme, which he afterwards brought into the Castle, was probably one of the printed news-sheets, of which there were so many at this time. The communication was hardly a letter, in the later sense of the word, or the name of its writer would have been added to it to strengthen its authority; while at the same time it was open news, and easily read, for the drumme read the contents to the besieging soldiers who were at the workes near Barbican gate.

Following the note, came the Trumpeter with a formal demand for the surrender of the Castle, this time accompanied by no threat, but couched in as conciliatory terms as it was possible to use, with a summary of the arguments that were likely to prevail. The whole was well calculated to influence the Garrison, who were gradually becoming convinced that it was now a mere matter of hours before fell famine would compel what they had so long refused.

But although thus evidently yielding—for a willingness to treat is a confession that surrender is a possibility, which had been hitherto denied—the Governor maintained the worthy dignity of a gallant soldier. He would make no answer but after conference; though he was willing to confer, and listen to the opinions and advice of those who had hitherto supported him so loyally.

The two Commanders were worthy of each other; each was a brave considerate enemy.

" Sackless=without baggage; with no real stake in the matter; mere hired soldiers; seems to be the sense of this word, now quite obsolete.

16th. This morning we had a man was get[ting *from the copy*] of Apples and was shott through the Skull of his brow all along the brow, & he fell downe, and in the afternoone did both speake & eate meate, so that it is thought it is not unpossible but that he may live. after that we kill'd one of the enemyes Souldyers from the Round Tower on Mr Rusbyes backside. This after noone was appoynted Sir Richard Hutton, Sr. Tho. Bland, Maior Copplay, & Mr Willia' Tindoll to goe forth & meete wth 4 of theire officers about the Castle walls (but had no authoritie to treate of any thing) onely to drinke & be merry, wheare they stayd wthin the Burnt haulpay howse (it beeing to hott wether to stay out of doores,) where they stayd for the space of 2 howers, & drunke both Sack & Ale together, wch was sent out of the Towne. during this time the Governor sent for (all *interlined*) the Gentlemen & Captins, & Volunteires into the Hall, to Consult what was best to be done; out of wch was Chosen forth to treate of the Business for the Gentry, Sr. Rich. Hutton, Sr. John Romsden, & Sr. George Wintworth; for the Clargie Mr Hirst & Mr Key; For the volunteers & reformadoes, Mr Hodgshon & Mr Harebread; for the Townesmen, Mr Austicke & Mr Luune; and for the Souldyers, Leiutenant Collonell Wheatelay,

Captin Himseworth & Capt' Munroe. During this time there was a parley round about the Castle of men & women of all soartes; and, during this time allso, the Souldyers on both sides agreed to Robbe an Orchard and agreed well to bee in the trees together at least 20 of a side or more.

"Unpossible" seems to have been a good classical word at this time; and it is found in the early editions of the authorised version, though the Queen's Printers have arbitrarily substituted "impossible".

Burnt "haulpny howse," we have already suggested to have been the "Hope and Anchor" in ruins.

"Beeing to hott wether" is perhaps unique, in respect that each of the four words has an orthography varying from that now in use.

Clearly the surrender of the Castle was now understood on all sides to have been practically determined upon, and but for the foolish talk of "a Captin of the Castle," the "Souldyer killed upon Mr Rusbye's back side,"—a slip of garden ground between the Horsefair and Northgate, —would have been the last killed during this wearisome siege.

17th. This Fore noone the Governor sent out a drumme wth a letter to Genrall Poyntes that they was ready to Treate when the Time and place was appoynted, and the drumme Came back wthout any answer, so that, till about 4 å Clock, there was little shooting of either side (& the enemyes walked openly; & we taulked wth them & they wth us wthout any shootinge). about wch time, Ouerton the Governor of the Towne sent in a druome wth a letter about 3 or 4 lines to this effeckt, that they would take time to treate, & not bee so hasty as they was. It seemes a Captin of the Castle wch went out the day before after the Gentlemen, (unknowne to the Governor & wthout order,) tould one of theire (of theire *erased*) officers that we had but victualls for 5 daies, wch Caused them then to refuse to treate, & moreover the enemies Souldiers reported that they Intended to sterve us, & to strippe the Souldiers at theire going out, & likewise that they would have all the pillage of the Castle. butt in the Intrim we had a letter Came from Newarke that the 12th of this month Sr Marmaduke Langdall wth all his owne forces & 4000 Irish begunne theire March towardes our releefe, & likewise that Mr. Garvis Nevell was sent from Newarke to him to hasten his Cominge to us. (w *erased*) there was allso other good newes in the letter, that Genrall Goringe had given Sr Tho. Fairfax an overthrow, and likewise that the Lord Muntrosse had beaten the Scotch forces, routed them, and killd Genrall Bely (the Scottes great Genrall). all this was not a little Incoragement unto us amongst all [the *from the copy*] miseryes wch at that time we was affrighted wthall, and to adde a remedy to this the Governor sent into all the Gentlemen's Chambers wthin the Castle to see what p'vition they Could (find, *interlined*) allowing to themselves no more then a common Souldyer, that soe wee might all live or want together; wch beeing done, there was p'vition found to keepe us all at a reasonable rate of dyate about (*an unfilled blank*) daies. After wch time, about 6 a Clock, when praiers was ended, (the Governor himsellfe being not able to Come forth of his Chamber) desired Sr Richard Hutton & Sr George Wintworth in the Castle yeard to reede (before the Gentlemen & the Souldyers) both the letter was sent from theire Governor, (out of towne *interlined*) & allso the letter was from Newarke, and wthall tould the Souldyers that the Gentlemen were all Content wth that dyate, & was willing to Sacrifise theire lives (rather *interlined*) then yeild to such Conditions, & if the worst Came to it (if releefe Came not in the meane while) to burne all the goodes wth the Castle & to make out our waies through (the enemy *interlined*) by the Swoard. at wch wordes the Souldyers all wth one Consent said they was ready to runne the same hazard that the Gentlemen did, & was Content wth the like dyate, and wthall Thrw up theire hattes and made 3 great & Lowd Shoutes wthin the Castle yeard, and then the Governor sent out 2 flagges of defiance, the one to be sett upon the Kinges Tower & the other upon the Round Tower wch was Instantly done and displayed, & the flagge left standing upon the Round tower. a presently Gave Commaund for our Cannon to play. the dutchman begunne first, & playd his Cannon into the markit place, where (they *altered to*) there was many standing together, and the bullitt grased full amongst them, but what execution it did is not knowne to us. after that the Cannon was playd from the Kinges Tower Into the new hall, but what execution was done is not knowne. during this time the Iron gunne was Carryed out from wthin the Castle to the platforme wthout the Upp' Castle gate, and Will: Ingram playd one Cannon Into theire first Sentry howse nearest to the upp' Castle gate where (we *altered to*) it beate downe the wall, Shot one man of by the middle, wch we saw; one or 2 more we saw them Carye away, and we Conceive there was many more kild wth the stones was burst out of the wall (beinge many in the howse). and then he playd againe another Shott into the enemyes workes (Just against Barbican gates) where we saw (lighted *interlined*) matches struck downe, but what hurt was done was not knowne to us. after this our muskittes shott from the walles wheresoever they Could see any opportunitie. The enemy Seeing and hearing all this, sent downe a drumme wth victualls for the prisoners to the Castle wch we refused at first to take in. and about 9 a Clock, Ouerton theire Governor sent downe a drumme wth a letter being sory that we refused to take in his first drumme wth victualls, and allso desiring that we would maintaine the Treaty, excusing themselves that theire Genrall was at yorke, & therefore they delayd to goe about the Treaty, or wordes to the like effecte. this night we made a boanefire upon the Toppe of The Round Tower.

This final scene of the long tale of bloodshed was a display of vigour of which the Diarist seems to have been proud. The thirty or forty hours' truce having come to a sudden end by the re-call on the part of the Governor of his offer to treat, the Garrison having spent the afternoon in deliberation and in fairly looking their position in the face, and in ascertaining their power of endurance, resumed hostilities with an energy which compelled the besiegers to reconsider their hasty and ill-considered determination to continue the active warfare.

The incidental " about 6 o'clock, *when prayers were ended,*" implies that that was their ordinary hour of daily service—which would thus be some time before 10 in the forenoon, and before 6 in the evening.

<blockquote>
18th. This day, before 10 a Clock, Genrall Poynte Sent in a letter wth a Trumpitt to our Governor to give notise at what time and place the Treatye should beginne, and allso to lett them know that there (they was *interlined*) ready for them, wch Trumpitt staid whilst servise was done in the hall, & then tooke his answer backe, and after that was done they sett up a Tent in the Bottom Cloase under Baghill a little above Brode lane end wch they made Ready; and about (4 a Clock *interlined*) Theire Genrall wth Collonell Ouerton & 9 offcers more Came wth him to the Barbican Gates where they met wth our Committies, and from thence they walked all together to the Tent wch they had sett about wth Gaurdes of Musketeers, about 100 yeardes distant from the Tent on every side. The Committeyes for (us *erased*) our p'ty was Sr. Richard Hutton, Sr. John Romsden, Sr George Wentworth, Leiutenant Collonell Gilbreth, and Mr Hirst, (Clarke, for us *interlined*). And the Committies for them was Mr [aL *filled into a blank as if the first letter of the word Lawyer*] Wasthill (a lawyer *interlined*) Collonell Bright, Leiutenant Collonell Fairfax, and Leiutenant Collonell Copplay. They Treated there in that place as long as light of day did appeare, till about 9 a Clock, but Concluded upon Nothinge, but deferred it of till about 9 a Clock of the next day, at wch time they appoynted to meete againe. during that time Genrall Poyntes & Collonell Overton Came into the Tent & drunke wth them, & soe went away. That night, wthout any matter of Shooting on either side.
</blockquote>

The game of Brag on each side was now drawing to a close; but the Garrison still kept it up bravely. When the Trumpeter arrived, before ten o'clock, which presumably would be after half-past nine, he was kept waiting because divine service was proceeding in the Hall. This gives us approximately the hour of prayer as being between nine and ten in the forenoon. And (on this occasion only,) the service is said to have been held in the Hall.

The Committee for making the Treaty was constituted somewhat differently to that originally appointed. On the 16th it comprised twelve members: now, but half that number. To Sir Richard Hutton, Sir John Ramsden, and

Sir George Wentworth, were added Lieut.-Col. Gilbraith; and Mr Hirst completed the number. But even with so reduced a roll of members, the conference extended over five hours without concluding anything. Evidently impossible conditions were still demanded on each side. Meanwhile the Garrison knew how greatly events without were telling against them, but the besiegers suspected only how hard they within were being driven, and how very small a margin remained to them.

19th. This Morning about 8 a Clock (the Dutchman *interlined*) having his Gunne Charged, gave Fire, & she plaid into the Markitt place, but whether he had any orders for it or not I Cannot heare, but there was no more shott that day wth any Cannon, neither scarce any shootinge at all wth muskitts on either side; and, at the Time appoyned, Genrall Poyntz sent downe his Trumpitt to Fetch our Committies to meete at the Tent where they mett the day before, wch they had gaurded (as *interlined*) they day before they had done, wth musketears; and betwixt 9 & 10 a Clock they mett, and fell upon Treating, and so Continued all the Day, (excepting Dinner Time,) till about 6 a Clock, and Concluded upon nothing; and Soe our Committies Came away, Declaring to them our full Intente that they did not vallue theire lives but theire honnors, and that they would fight it out to the last man; and soe, wth that resolution, Came away, and Sir John Romsden, (being in the gout,) Ridd Cleare into the Castle attended wth Captin Samond on horse back to the Castle gate, and 5 or 6 more Officers came [along *from the copy*] with him. But the Other Committies followed [after *from the copy*] our Committies, and desired them to [meete them *from the copy*] again the next day at the same place, [& they *from the copy*] would then made an end of their[e treaty *from the copy*] if possible they Could, wch our C[ommitties did *from the copy*] Condescend unto.

"The Dutchman" seems to have been determined that his powder should not be wasted. Having his gun charged, the absolute necessary consequence, as it appeared to his mind, was that it should be discharged, whether to kill or to maim, whether with orders or against orders, he seems not to have stayed to consider: his gun should be fired. And almost with the sound of the report echoing in his ears, General Poyntz, with supreme, if not contemptuous, disregard of this virtual breach of truce, came down to continue the Treaty.

And then terminated, not ingloriously, the Second Siege of Pontefract Castle, in which according to the Diarist's caloulation (see page 18), completed from his subsequent entries, the besiegers lost in killed and wounded about 463 men, and the besieged as many as 99.

By his Entry of the number of killed and wounded (see *Ante* page 18) it appears that the Diarist calculated that the siege would have closed on the 18th, for he altered his numbers, already made up, from 98 of the besieged on the 18th, to 99 on the 19th. With regard to his calculation of numbers killed and wounded of the enemy, he ceased his reckoning on July 7th, marking "July 8th" against the place where the casualties of the next day were to be entered. His last two figures are 2 on July 5, and 3 on July 7th; after which there are mentioned in the Diary, 1 each on July 10, 15, 16, and 17, making a total of 463, most of whom are distinctly accounted for, with the occasion of their death. His calculation on April 6 (Easter Sunday) is perhaps a little hazy—on which day he reckons for the loss of 26, 100 and 20—see his first column of the killed and wounded in the second siege, page 18—but on the whole his figures seem to be conscientiously trustworthy.

The last few lines of the MS. are much injured. It may be a good illustration to produce them here for comparison with the full text on the opposite page. They read thus, the hiatus being produced by a hole in the paper:—

```
and 5 or 6 more Officers came......with him.
But the Other Committies followed........our
Committies, and desired them to..........again
the next day at the same place................
would then make an end of their..............
if possible they Could, wch our C............
Condescend unto.
```

And thus this remarkable Diary concludes, leaving us to ascertain from other sources the particulars of the result, for unfortunately the Diarist does not even give the number of those who marched out, as was done by the survivors of the third siege (See page 150).

It is clear that both parties had been anxious to terminate the long investment; the besiegers because they had the plague among them, the besieged because their provisions were almost absolutely at an end, while the desire to obtain possession of the Castle and its stores, in good condition, would have had much influence on General Poyntz. At present there was no intention to destroy it; and there need be little doubt that had the besieged carried out their threat (see page 142) those who so long invested the place would have felt a bitter mortification. The agreement at length arrived at on the following day Sunday, July 20th, four weeks from the day on which the demiculverin had opened on the Church (see page 25), was that the Castle should be delivered up at 8 o'clock on Monday morning, with every thing therein; including 8 pieces of ordnance, a store of arms, and their ammunition; that the officers should each be allowed to have a "cloak bag" full of his own personal property, and no more; and that the garrison should march to Newark, as one account says "with drums beating and colours flying, and bullit in mouth, with six shot of powder, and bullet in proportion".

Of what afterwards befel them, we have no knowledge. The Diarist, as we have already said, subsequently took up his residence in Pontefract, but seems not to have resumed his military life.

Meanwhile the Castle was in possession of the Presbyterians, Sir Gervis Cutler lay in his tomb in the Castle Chapel, and an interval of nearly three years preceded the third siege; which interval we now proceed shortly to consider.

WHEN THE SURRENDER of the Castle by "Our Governor" was notified to the House of Commons on the following Thursday, Col, Poyntz's letter announcing its capture having been read, a debate followed, as we learn from the Journals, which terminated in the appointment by the House of Sir Thomas Fairfax as Military Governor. Which had no sooner been done than a message came from the Lords, requesting that Poyntz have the governorship of Poyntfract Castle (as the message styled it) apparently in consideration of the reduction of the stronghold having been his first considerable martial undertaking.

The Commons answered the Lords that they had already made the appointment, but that Poyntz should have the earliest similar office that came into their hands Upon receiving which conciliatory reply, the Lords appear to have withdrawn their request.

The next mention of the town in Parliament was on Monday, July 28, when the papers and letters taken at the Castle were referred to "The Committee for the King's Cabinet letters." On the following 20th August, they were ordered to be read on Saturday "The first business," and the House made special order that no other business should intervene; but no record exists, so far as we can learn, of what transpired when the subject was brought forward, according to this unequivocal order.

The House was yet, however, to have trouble from the place, for on Nov. 30, 1646, a letter was read (dated 27 Sept.) relating an attempt alleged to have been made to surprise the Castle; and the names of those concerned were said to have been "the Lady Savile, Phillip Ann, Esquire,

Mr Michael Ann, Lieut-Col. Morris, and Mr Samuelle Savile." (See Appendix E.)

The alleged conspirators were at once ordered to be seized by the Sergeant-at-Arms, and letters were addressed to various persons, requesting them to assist him. The result was that several prisoners having been sent to London on the charge, an order was made on Jan. 12, 1646-7 "That those persons that are sent up as having an hand in betraying Pontefract Castle be referred to the examination of the Council of the Northern Association"; but on Jan. 21, Lieut-Col. Marries (as he is called during the proceedings) managed to convince the House that he was innocent, and he was accordingly "discharged, and to pay no Fees," £60 being given to the Sergeant-at-Arms to pay the necessary charges in apprehending and bringing up the various accused persons.

Alarmed at the reports of this attempt to take the Castle for the King, the House on 17 Feb., entered into a a serious consideration of what should be done with it. A large majority, 125 to 87, decided that it should not be garrisoned, while a very unanimous decision was come to, that it should not be demolihed. A middle course was adopted in a resolution that the fortification should be made untenable.

Fifteen months afterwards, however, the Castle again fell into the hands of the persevering Royalists. The story of its capture reads like a chapter of romance, and fortunately we have on record a very full account of the daring transaction, for one of those engaged tells the story in the following letter, which was originally published in 1702 by a printer in the Savoy. The volume is a quarto of 23 pp., but it is uncertain to whom it was addressed. It was "Reprinted for the Widow," in 1719, and as an octavo at Oxford, in 1747. It is from the 1719 Edition we have reproduced it.

PONTEFRACT CASTLE: An account how it was Taken; and how General Rainsborugh was Surprised in his Quarters at Doncaster, Anno 1648.

SIR,—I Received your Letter, wherein you tell me, That the late News of Prince Eugene's surprising the Marshall Villeroy, in his Quarters at Cremona, put your self, and some of my Friends, in mind of the Surprise of General Rainsborough, at the Siege of Pontefract Castle, in the late Civil Wars of England. And I being the only Person now living, that was an Actor in it, you are pleased to desire a particular Account of it; which, as far as I know, was never yet fully published.

I appeal to you, and all that know me, if ever I had the Vanity to boast of it, or so much as mention it, but sometimes at the Request of a Friend, as I do now at yours; tho' I had rather refuse to comply even with your Desire, at this time, than be thought so vain as to make any Comparison (other than of small Things with great) between such a particular Action in our own Country, and so publick and glorious an One, as that of Prince Eugene, on the Stage of Europe; which failed but by one accident, of having been yet much more glorious.

But this I may say without Vanity, that our Design was Honourable, not to kill a General in the midst of his Army, but to take him Prisoner, and thereby to save the Life of our own General, Sir Marmaduke Langdale, then a Prisoner, and condemned to die, under whose Command we had served in the precedent War.

It may not be unacceptible to you, being a Yorkshire Man, to know the most minute Particulars of this Enterprize, we being all Yorkshire Men, who had a Share in it.

And first let me tell you how we took the Castle, which was a Garrison for the Parliament, as they call'd the Government, then Established in a small Part of the House of Commons, and a very small Number of the Lords, sitting at Westminster.

Pontefract, commonly called Pomfret-Castle, was thought the Greatest and Strongest Castle in England. It was the ancient Inheritance of the Dukes of Lancaster, called The Honour of Pomfret : And it had the Honour to be the last Garison in the War begun in 42, that held out for the King.

In the Year 1648, the first War being over, we, that had served the King in it, submitting to our common Fate, lived quietly in the Countrey, till we heard of an intended Invasion by Duke Hamilton : Then we met frequently, and resolved to attempt the Surprising this Castle, of which Colonel Cotterel was Governor for the Parliament, having under him a Garrison of an hundred Men, most of them Quartered in the Town of Pomfret, and in no Apprehension of an Enemy.

The Design was laid by Colonel Morice (who in his Youth had been Page to the Earl of Strafford,) my two Brothers, who were Captains of Horse, and my self Captain of Foot, and some others. We had then about Three hundred Foot, and Fifty Horse, of our old Comrades privately Listed.

We had secret Correspondence with some in the Castle ; among the rest with a Corporal, who promised, on a certain Night, to be upon the Guard, and to set a Centinel, that would assist us, in Scaling the Walls by a Ladder, which we had provided, and brought with us. But the Corporal happened to be drunk at the Hour appointed, and another Centinel was placed, where we intended to set our Ladder, who fired upon us, and gave the Alarm to the Garison. They appearing upon the Walls, our Men retired in haste, leaving the Ladder in the Ditch ; whereby the next Day they within knew that it was no false Alarm, but that there had been a real Attempt to surprise the Castle.

They took not a Man of us ; our Foot dispersed themselves in the Country ; and half of our Horse marched to Sir Marmaduke Langdale, who had then taken Berwick and Carlisle. The rest being twenty or thirty Horse, kept in the

Woods, while we sent Spies into the Castle, and found that our Confederates within were not discovered, nor our Design betrayed, but only failed by the Corporal's being Drunk.

The Ladder being found the next Morning, made the Governor call the Souldiers out of the Town, to lodge in the Castle: in order to which, he sent his Warrants into the Country for Beds to be brought in by a Day appointed.

We had Notice of it, and made Use of the Occasion. With the Beds came Colonel Morice, and Captain William Paulden, like Country Gentlemen, with Swords by their sides; and about Nine Persons more, dressed like plain Countrymen, and Constables, to guard the Beds, but arm'd privately with Pocket-Pistols and Daggers.

Upon their Approach, the Draw-bridge was let down, and the Gates opened by our Confederates within, Colonel Morice, and those who were with him, entered the Castle. The Main-Guard was just within the Gate, where our company threw down the Beds, and gave a crown to some Soldiers, bidding them fetch Ale, to make the rest of the Guard drink: and as soon as they were gone out of the Gate they drew up the Draw-bridge, and secured the rest of the Guards, forcing them into a Dungeon hard by, to which they went down by about thirty Stairs; and it was a Place that would hold two or three hundred Men.

Then Captain William Paulden made one of the Prisoners show him the Way to the Governour's Lodging, where he found him newly laid down upon his Bed, with his Cloaths on, and his Sword, being a long Tuck, lying by him. The Captain told him, the Castle was the King's, and he was his Prisoner; but he, without answering any thing, started up, and made a Thrust at the Captain, and defended himself very bravely, till being sore wounded, his Head and Arm cut in several Places, he made another full and desperate Push at the Captain, and broke his Tuck against the Bed-post; and then asked Quarter, which my Brother granted; and he, for the present, was put down, among his own Soldiers, into the Dungeon.

Notice was immediately sent to me, lying hard by, of the Taking of the Castle; upon which I marched thither with about Thirty Horse, and it being Market-day, we furnished our selves with all manner of Provisions from the Town.

There came speedily to us, in small Parties, so many of our old Fellow-soldiers, that our Garison was at last increased to Five hundred Men, which at the rendering of the Castle afterwards, were reduced to one hundred and forty.

We found in the Castle a good Quantity of Salt and Malt, with Four thousand Arms, and a good Store of Ammunition, some Cannon, and two Mortar-pieces. We expected a Siege very suddenly, and got what Provisions of Corn, and Cattle, we could, out of the Country.

Particularly in one Sally, having Notice that there were at Knotingly, 3 Miles from the Castle, three hundred Head of Cattle, bought up in the North, going into the South, under a Guard of two Troops of Horse, we marched out at Night with thirty Horse, and Half a Dozen Foot, with Half-pikes to drive the Cattle. We faced the Troops that guarded them, while our Foot drove the Herd towards the Castle; then we followed, and kept betwixt them and Danger, the Enemy not daring to charge us, and so we came all safe with our Purchase into the Castle. This, and other Provision, we got in by several Parties almost every Night, enabled us to keep the Castle above nine Months, though we had not one Month's Provision when we were first Beleaguer'd.

For in a very short time after, we were besieged by Sir Edward Rhodes and Sir Henry Choldmondly, and five thousand Men of regular Troops: But we kept a Gate open on the South-side of the Castle, which was covered by a small Garison, we placed in an House called New Hall, belonging to the Family of Pierrepoint, being about a Musquet-shot or two from the Castle.

Some time after, we heard Duke Hamilton was beaten at Preston in Lancashire, and Sir Marmaduke Langdale, taken Prisoner, and brought to Nottingham Castle. He was General of the English at Preston, who behaved themselves bravely; and, in truth, did all that was done there. • He had, also, as I said, been our General; we had his Commission for taking the Castle, as he had the Prince of Wales's, and we were resolved to run any Hazard to release him: For it was commonly given out, that they intended to bring him before Pomfret-Castle, and to execute him in our Sight, if we would not immediately surrender.

It being like to prove a tedious Siege, General Rainsborow was sent from London by the Parliament, to put a speedy end to it. He was esteemed a Person of great courage and conduct, exceeding zealous and fierce in their cause, and had done them great Service by Land, and also at Sea, where he was for a time one of their Admirals. His head Quarters were for the present at Doncaster, being twelve Miles from Pomfret, with twelve hundred Foot: a Regiment of his Horse lay three or four Miles on the East of Doncaster, and another at the like Distance on the West.

Captain William Paulden, who commanded all the few Horse in the Castle, laid a Design to surprise him in his Quarters at Doncaster; not to kill him, but to take him Prisoner, and exchange him for our own General, Sir Marmaduke Langdale; and it was only his own fault that he was killed, and not brought Prisoner to the Castle.

The Design seemed the more feasible, because the General and his Men were in no Apprehension of any Surprise; the Castle being twelve Miles off, closely besieged, and the only Garrison for the King in England.

In order to execeute this our purpose, Captain William Paulden made choice of two and twenty Men, such as he most confided in. At Midnight being well horsed, we marched through the Gate, that was kept open, over the Meadows, between two of the Enemies Horse-Guards, whom, by the favour of the Night we passed undiscovered. Early the next Morning we came to Mexborough, a Village four Miles West above Doncaster, upon the River Don, where there was a Ferry-boat. There we rested, to refresh our selves and our Horses, till about noon.

In the mean time we sent a Spy into Doncaster, to know if there was any Discovery of a Party being out, and to meet us, as soon as it was dark, at Cunsborough, a Mile from Doncaster; which he did, and assured us, there was no Alarm taken by the town, and that a Man would meet us at Sun-rise, it being then the beginning of March, who would give us Notice if all was quiet. Thither the Man came accordingly; the Sign he was to bring with him, to be known by, was a Bible in his hand.

Captain William Paulden then divided his Two and twenty Men into four Parties; Six were to attack the Main-Guard, Six the Guard upon the Bridge; Four were ordered to General Rainsborow's Quarters; and the Captain, with the remaining Six, after he had seen the Four enter the General's Lodgings, was to beat the Streets and keep the Enemy from assembling.

We presently forcing the first Barricades, and the Guards there dispersing into the Country, all the rest succeeded as we wish'd; the Main-Guard was surprised, we entring the Guard-Chamber, and getting between them and their Arms, bid them shift for their Lives; the same was done to the Guard upon the Bridge, their Arms being thrown into the River.

The Four that went to General Rainsborow's Lodging, pretended to bring Letters to him from Cromwel, who had then beaten the Scots; they met at the door the General's Lieutenant, who conducted them up to his Chamber, and told him, being in Bed, that there were some Gentlemen had brought him Letters from General Cromwel. Upon which, they delivered Rainsborow a Packet, wherein was nothing but blank Paper. Whilst he was opening it, they told him he was their Prisoner, but that not a Hair of his Head should be touched, if he would go quietly with them. Then they disarm'd his Lieutenant, who had innocently conducted them to his Chamber, and brought them both down Stairs. They had brought a Horse ready for General Rainsborow, upon which they bid him mount; he seem'd at first willing to do it, and put his Foot in the Stirrup; but looking about him, and seeing none but four of his Enemies, and his Lieutenant and Centinel (whom they had not disarm'd) stand by him; he pull'd his Foot out of the Stirrup, and cry'd *Arms, Arms.* Upon this, one of our Men, letting his Pistol and Sword fall, because he would not kill him, catch'd hold of him, and they grappling together, both fell down in the Street. Then General Rainsborow's Lieutenant catching our Man's Pistol that was fallen, Captain Paulden's Lieutenant, who was on Horseback, dismounts and runs him through the Body, as he was cocking the Pistol. Another of our Men run General Rainsborow into the Neck, as he was struggling with him that had caught hold of him; yet the General got upon his Legs with our Man's Sword in his Hand; but Captain Paulden's Lieutenant ran him through the body, upon which he fell down dead.

Then all our Parties met, and made a Noise in the Streets, where we saw hundreds of their Soldiers in their Shirts, running in the Fields to save themselves, not imagining how small our Number was. We presently marched over the Bridge, the direct Way to Pomfret Castle, and all safely arrived there; carrying with us forty or fifty Prisoners, whom we met by eight or ten in a Company. We took no Prisoners at Doncaster; nor were any kill'd, or so much as hurt there, but General Rainsborow and his Lieutenant, and they too very much against our Will, because our main Intention was defeated thereby, which, I told you, was to exchange and redeem our own General Langdale; who, however, the very Night before had fortunately made his own Escape, and lived to see King Charles the Second's Restoration, and to be made a Peer of England for his eminent Services in the War.

But to go on with our Affairs at Pomfret, seeing you have also the Curiosity to know what became of us at last. After the Defeat of the Scots Army by Cromwel at Preston and Wiggan in Lancashire, Major General Lambert came against us; and then we were close shut up, without hope of Relief, and our Provisions very nigh spent, which put us upon Capitulating, and they threw Papers over the Walls, offering honourable Conditions, saving that six Persons were to be excepted from any Benefit of the Articles, who were not to be named till after the Articles were signed by the Governour.

The Governour, Colonel Morice, hereupon call'd the Officers of the Castle together; and we unanimously promised, we would never agree to deliver any Person up, without his Consent.

Upon this promise, our Governour sent six Officers out of the Castle, to treat with the same Number named by Major General Lambert. Of our Number I was one. When we met, we told them, That we came to Capitulate about the Surrender of the Castle, but they could not expect that we would deliver our selves up to Execution.

Upon which, Colonel Bright, the first of their Commissioners told us, That he had Authority, from Major General Lambert, to engage, That none of us that treated should be any of the excepted Persons: We told him, That perhaps the Governour might be one of them: He answered, That he did believe the Major General did not so much look upon the Governour, as some that had betray'd the Castle to us, when it was taken. So we parted for that time, without concluding any thing.

At our return to the Castle, we acquainted the Governour with all had passed; some of our Commissioners telling him, that Colonel Bright had engaged he should not be excepted. The Governour asked me, what I thought of it. I plainly told him, I thought he was intended to be one, and repeated to him the very Words that Colonel Bright had spoke, which made me suspect he would be excepted, because he had not engaged that the Governour should not be, as he

MAJOR-GENERAL LAMBERT,

Commander-in-Chief in the North. Entered on the siege of Pontefract Castle, December 4th, 1648. Took Possession March 24th, 1648-9. M.P. for Pontefract, as Lord Lambert, 1658. Unsuccessful Candidate for the Protectorship after the death of Cromwell, 1659-60.

Born at Calton Hall, Kirkby Malhamdale, September 7th, 1619. Died in Confinement on Plymouth Island, 1683.

had, that we that treated should not, but left it ambiguous. Then one of our Commissioners told him, that Lieutenant-Colonel Crooke had assured him, that our Governour was none of the Excepted; upon which, he resolved we should go out, and conclude, saying generously, that if he was excepted, he would take his Fortune, and would not have so many worthy Gentlemen perish for his sake.

Upon this, I desired the Governour to send some body else in my place, for I had promised solemnly, I would never consent to deliver him up; (which he would have had me sworn to before, but I told him my Word should be as good as my Oath.) So they went out, and concluded, and signed the Articles; and after signing of them, they brought to us, in the Castle, the names of the excepted Persons, whereof the Governour was the First:

Their Names were,

Colonel Morice, our Governour.

Allen Austwick, Captain W. Paulden's Lieutenant, as one of those that kill'd Rainsborow.

Blackborne, Captain Paulden's Coronet, for the same Reason.

Major Ashby, }
Ensign Smith, } These three had been our Correspondents in the Castle, when
Sergeant Floyd, } we Surprised it.

We were not obliged to deliver up any of these excepted Persons, but they had liberty to make their Escape if they could, which they attempted on Horseback, the next Evening, by charging through the Enemies Army. At that very time their Guard unluckily happened to be relieving, so that the Number was doubled they were to break through.

The Governour, and Blackborne charged thro', and escaped; but were taken in Lancashire about ten Days after, (seeking for a Ship to pass beyond Sea) and brought to York, where they were both executed.

Smyth was kill'd in the attempt. Austwick, Ashby, and Floyd, were forced back into the Castle, where they hid themselves in a private Sally-port (which we had covered, designing to take the Castle again by it, when there should happen a fair Opportunity.) Thence they made their Escape the next Night, after the Castle was surrendered, and all lived till after the King's Return.

Thus ended the Siege of Pomfret-Castle, which was soon after demolished; so that now there remains nothing of that magnificent Structure, but some Ruines of the great Tower, where the Tradition is, King Richard the Second was murthered.

I crave your Leave to add, what I had forgot to mention before, that we kept the Castle, till after King Charles the First was Martyr'd: When we solemnly proclaim'd King Charles the Second in it; and did not deliver it up till almost two Months after.

Be pleased that I inform you farther, that my Brother Captain William Paulden died of a Fever in the Castle, a Month before it was surrender'd; my other Brother, Captain Timothy Paulden, was killed in the Fight at Wiggan, being then Major of Horse to Colonel Matthew Boynton, under the Command of the Earl of Derby. I my self followed the Fortune of King Charles in his Exile, and was sent into England, on several Occasions for his Majesty's Service. I was once betray'd, and brought before Cromwel; but I denied my Name, and nothing could be proved against me: However he sent me to the Gatehouse in Westminster, from whence I made my escape, with our old Friend Jack Cowper, by throwing Salt and Pepper into the Keeper's Eyes; which I think, has made me love Salt the better ever since; as you, and all my Friends, know I do, with whom I have eaten many a Bushel.

I went again beyond Sea; and, upon King Charles the Second's Restauration, returned into England, accompanied with my old Companion, Loyalty, and with the usual Companion of that, Poverty. The first never quitted me; the other by the Favour and Bounty of the Duke of Buckingham, was made tolerable.

And having now survived most of my old Acquaintance, and, as I verily believe, All, who had any Part in the foregoing Story, being in the 78th Year of my Age, I am glad I have had this Occasion of shewing my ancient Respects and Friendship for you, by obeying your Commands in this Particular; tho' you will not let me have the Honour to mention your name, otherwise, than as a Yorkshire Man, and a Lover of them, who had faithfully served King Charles the Second, as you your self, had done.

After all, perhaps, it will not be thought amiss, by your Countrymen of Yorkshire at least, that I have lived on to this time; if for nothing else, yet for this, that when the Memorable Action at Cremona shall hereafter be spoken of, with the Honour it deserves, this Attempt at Doncaster may not be altogether forgotten by Posterity.

Sir, I am your most Faithful
Humble Servant,
Thomas Paulden.

London March
31. 1702.

As a matter of mere English composition, the difference between Drake's Diary and this letter is very much more considerable than that between the ages of the respective writers. The Diary, as we have had sufficient occasion to point out was archaic to a degree; while there is scarcely a word in this letter that would require to be altered to fit it for the middle of the nineteenth century. Governour, entred, garison, publick, unacceptible, beleaguer'd, and a very few other words show that the composition is 180 years old, but there is no use of such obsolete words as overthwart, of which Drake supplies us with so copious a vocabulary. Of course the eighteenth-century corruption Pomfret makes its appearance—and equally of course with the proviso "Commonly called"; introducing the corrupted name, as it were with an apology.

In other respects, the diction is rather inflated] and formal; and as it consists of hardly the sort of phraseology we should expect in the mouth of an aged soldier used rather to camp than court, the conclusion is irresistible that a more scholarly pen than his own was employed to turn the campaigner's narrative into good readable prose.

Born in 1624, he would have been scarce old enough to

have been in Drake's siege in 1644-5, and but 24 years of age when he had part in the gallant exploit at Doncaster; for notwithstanding his not being one of the excepted persons the continual use of the first pronoun in the narrative, forces upon the reader the conclusion that if not one of the four who attacked Rainsborough, he was certainly one of the twenty-two chosen by his brother Captain William, doubtless his elder brother. His share in the adventure was probably that of one of the six who surprised the Main Guard.

His tale is singularly clear and lucid; he lays great stress upon the intentions of the party in the surprise of General Rainsborough; and repeatedly shows that taking his life was no part of their project, while his death destroyed all their hopes of having a live General in their hands whom they might exchange for Sir Marmaduke Langdale, then a prisoner to the Parliament.

He was not one of those who had seized the Castle, under Morris; though he was evidently one of the thirty who made an excursion to Knottingley, and provisioned it with 300 cattle; and he was one of the six appointed to treat of the final surrender.

His quite incidental mention that it had been the tradition that King Richard was murdered in the Round Tower is an additional evidence, if any were needed, that such was indeed the tradition; notwithstanding that after the disappearance of the hacked pillar—probably a wooden one, for there is not the slightest trace that there ever was on the site of the Round Tower, such a pillar of stone—the scene of the murder became shifted to that stone-roofed apartment in the Gascoigne or Red Tower, which later ages have accordingly called King Richard's Chamber.

But the very mistakes in Capt. Paulden's narrative confirm its truth. He says for instance—when endeavouring to indicate the time at which the messenger from Doncaster was to meet the party—at sunrise—that it was then the beginning of March ; which was a singular mistake, as Rainsborough was seized on 29th October, 1648. But the time of sunrise was the same at the beginning of March (old style) as at the end of October, and thus Capt. Thomas Paulden's very slip itself, tends to confirm the truth of his narrative.

Capt. Paulden informs us that Colonel Morris had in his youth been page to the Earl of Strafford, whose seat was at Ledstone Hall ; and it was in that capacity probably that he made the intimate acquaintance with Lady Savile, the two Mr. Anne's and Mr. Samuel Savile, which brought him in their company into the custody of the Sergeant-at-arms. The Colonel himself was a South Elmsall man, though unfortunately the South Kirkby registers are deficient at just the time when his personal records would have appeared on their pages.

We make every effort to prevent these pages from being crowded by extraneous matter that may be obtained from other sources, and to confine what we have to say to remarks bearing strictly upon local subjects; but a few lines of explanation seem required here.

Lady Savile was daughter of Thomas, Lord Coventry, keeper of the Greal Seal, and to her the escape of Sir Marmaduke Langdale from Nottingham Castle was in a great measure, if not altogether, owing. She was then widow of Wm. Savile, the 3rd baronet of Thornhill. Her son, the 4th baronet, was subsequently created Baron Savile, of Elland, and afterwards Earl of Halifax. Sir William's grandfather, the 1st baronet, Sir George, (created 1611), was in his time the principal cultivator of liquorice here, and his argent owl on an armorial torce, is the original of the nondescript bird on a gate, which is the present trade-mark of Pontefract liquorice. Mr Samuel Savile was of another branch of the family.

Phillip Anne, and his son, were of Burghwallis, where the name has continued till now.

Col. Morris was brought up in the household of the Earl of Strafford, and in the list given by Hunter (South Yorkshire, II.84) his father's name appears as twelfth in rank out of sixty four, My Lord, My Lady, and My Lady Savile being the first three. Mr Richard Marris was "steward and antient" to the earl, and was buried at Wentworth near him (Hunter II. 99), as also was Colonel Morris himself, at his own earnest desire that he might be laid near his dear master, as he loved to call the Earl. The monumental inscriptions remain in a south chapel, but the church is in ruins.

The party that surprised the Castle appears to have entered by the Upper Gate towards the town, at the end of what is now called Spink Lane, where there was a Drawbridge, and then to have taken possession of the building which Capt. Paulden calls the Main Guard, but which had been for a century previously, and was for nearly a century afterwards, used as a prison. In recent times it has been converted into dwelling-houses, of which that farthest from the site of the gate is now a Museum of Antiquities connected with the town and neighbourhood under the charge of Mr. Edwin Foster. The dungeon into which they forced the Garrison was evidently the excavated cellar which belonged to the more ancient Hall, and which was for many years used as a storehouse for Liquorice, at the time the Castle Garth was devoted to the cultivation of that succulent plant. Capt. Paulden says they went down to this Cellar by about thirty steps. The number is really rather more than forty.

He makes another slight error when he says that they

kept open a gate on the South side of the Castle. He must, in that place, mean the East Gate at the top of the Booths, which communicated with New Hall, All Saints' Church, and St. Nicholas Hospital. But on the whole, the result of the most critical examination will confirm the opinion that Capt. Paulden's narrative is that of a trustworthy witness. It is remarkable that Mr. Clement Markham, in his Life of Fairfax, similarly describes Pontefract Castle as standing on an elevated rock, *south* of the town. It is really nearly due east, inclining northwards.

The private Sally Port in which Austwick, Ashby and Floyd were hidden, which remained so long blocked up as they left it, is now, to a considerable extent, cleared out, after the lapse of above 230 years.

In his seventy-eighth year in 1702, when he published this letter, Capt. Paulden was dead in 1719, when it was " Reprinted for the Widow," but the actual date of his decease is unknown.

Having thus perused the account of the taking of Pontefract Castle by one who was an actor in that exploit, we turn to other sources to ascertain what report out-siders made. And firstly in the Church Books we find the following :—

Md that upon the 3d of June, 1648, the castle of Pontefract, was surprised by Major Morris & his confederates which occasioned a long siege & great trouble : in which time there was no setled mi'stry in this parish, & none order observed therein, till it pleased gd to returne the minister on the 2d of Aprill, 1649.

Morris and an other ringleader in yt *rebellion** being not long after executed for their treachery, & ye castle ordered to be dimolished.

Jos : Ferrett, mi'ster.

(*A subsequent hand has added in a foot note " alias Loyalty").

This is, however, a record of a date long posterior to the event. To obtain the news of the day, we turn to the King's Library in the British Museum, a collection of MSS, printed Books and Pamphlets, which King George III.

accumulated during his long reign, and which contains many works of which no other copy is known to exist. In a scarce Tract in that collection (E. 446) occurs the earliest rumour of the astounding news as it reached London. The Title is " Num 12. Packets of Letters from * * York * * to Members of the House of Commons * * *. Brought by the Post on Monday, June 5th, 1648"—the Castle having been taken on the previous Saturday—" and the taking of Pontefract Castle for the King by Collonel Bonivent with 100. prisoners, 80. Barrells of Gunpowder, 4 Piece of Ordnance, 3 Coullours, and 3000 Armes."

The following is the text of the particular letter which refers to the taking of the Castle, but the Pamphlet states neither the name of the writer nor of the person to whom the epistle was addressed :—

Honoured Sir,

Wee are in these parts preparing what we can for our defence, But Pontefract Castle is unhappily surprised, by a party of about a 100 from about Sandall, who passed the Country severall ways, on Horse backes, some with sacks of Corn, others with bagges, cheeses, baskets, &c., as if they had beene Country men, and had businesse at some Market, or else were in order to private affaires. The cheife of them is said to be one Bonivent. It seemes they corrupted some of the Souldiers of Pontefract Castle to joyn with them for betraying it, which they have unhapply accomplished, whilst the Governour, Master Cotterell, had sent an Officer for a supply of Horse, when the Governour saw the enemy had surprised him he drew upon them, and with some others opposed, but they being entered he could not withstand them, he is wounded and taken Prisoner.

Yorke, 3 *June* 1648.

A List of the particulars taken in Pontefret Castle by the Enemy ;

3000 *Arms*, 80 *Barrels of Gunpowder, match and bullit proportionable*. 2 *Culverins*, 1 *demi culverin*, 1 *Morterpeece*, 2 *Coulors, Victuals and Ammunition plenty.*

Thus the news of the taking of Pontefract Castle reached York in very distorted style, the day of the occurrence ; and the intelligence was at once despatched to headquarters, as we have seen ; being received in London on Monday morning.

This seems a favourable opportunity to explain that a Culverin was the heaviest field-gun then generally used.

It carried a ball of 17lbs., and required ten horses to transport it. The Demi-culverin was a nine-pounder. The Drake, frequently mentioned in the Diary, was generally a three-pounder.

Colonel Bonivent, the Governor of Sandal in 1644-5, had at first the credit of the exploit, and it appears to have been sometime before its true author became known ; for in the same collection of Pamphlets (King's Library E. 446. 29) we have found the following, unfortunately undated, but evidently old news.

The Declaration and Proclamation of Colonell Bonivent, and the rest of his Majesties Commanders in the North, wherein is declared their Resolutions and Protestation concerning their present Engagement for the King.

Honoured Sir,

Divers great Commanders (in these parts) begins to appear visible and active for the King, and have declared the grounds and reasons of their taking up Armes in this second Engagement, having taken an Oath and Protestation for the prosecuting of this their present design to the utmost, and to take all opportunities whatsoever for the promoting thereof ; in pursuance whereof Colonell Bonivent (formerly Groum of the Stable to Sir Marmaduke Langdale) with a party of Officers and Souldiers, to the number of one hundred, consulted together for the surprizall of Pontefract Castle, and at the last resolved to put themselves into a disguised posture, and to act their design in the habit of Country-men, which they did, and upon Thursday last, being Market day, they came from severall parts, and met at the lower town, and the plot being laid, and the time and hour apoined (*sic*) about 20 of them came up to the Castle gate on horseback, with sackes under them, and their armes unseen, and discoursed with the Centinels, and immediately their confederates in the castle, and their associates at the lower town made their appearance neer them, who upon a sudden cast down their sacks, and rushed in at the gates, Major Cotterell, the Governour, receiving this allarm with about 30. men charged them in the Castle yard, but could not regain what was lost, the rest comming up so violently insomuch that the enemy hath unhappily become Masters of this impregnable Castle, and hath taken about 60. Prisoners, 3000. Armes, 80. Barrels of Gunpowder, Match and Bullet proportionable, two Culverins, one Demi-Culverin, one Morter-piece, two Cullers, 600. weight of cheese, and great store of other victualling.

But before they became sole masters thereof, they lost at the least 8 of their men, for Major Cotterel fought gallantly, beating them back as far as the outmost gate, but it was his hard chance there to receive a wound, which gave a great advantage to the enemy, and his body was there seized on, the rest of his men retreated to the Queen's Tower, and held the enemy in dispute for the space of one hour, Killing some of them, but at the last were forced to yeeld upon quarter.

In this narrative, to put aside the inaccuracy of Thursday for Saturday, and the substitution of Colonel Bonivent for Colonel Morris, we have an elaborate and circumstantial, however imaginary account of the great resistance of Major Cotterel, his fight in the Castle Yard, his driving "Colonel Bonivent" "as far as the utmost gate"; and the retreat of Major Cotterel's followers to the Queen's Tower. The whole shows that although the writer knew nothing accurate of the circumstances of the seizure, he knew sufficient of the arrangement of the different buildings, to give considerable colour to his account, especially in the eyes of those who knew nothing at all about it; and that he was totally unscrupulous in the use he made of his knowledge, caring little for strict truth, if only he could please the powers that were by putting those who had seized the Castle in an unfavourable light.

But a previous tract (E. 446.26) in the same volume, which is arranged chronologically as far as it was possible, had said :—

> Langdale's men, do melt from him daily. I do not fear before many days, but you will hear of the dissipating of that Enemy; but notwithstanding, wee have some ill newes, which may prove to the best.
>
> Many of the North being ill-affected they did so connive at a party of Langdales that marched obscurely in the night, upon the moors out of Cumberland into Yorkshire, having some private engagements from some perfidious men that were in trust in Pomfret Castle. One morning there were a certain number of carts, pretending to lay in provision for the Castle, there were some 20 men came in Frocks, with daggers and Pistols under their frocks, who surprised the Guard; then they had a party of horse with muskateers behinde them, which alighted presently, and flanked the horse, and so surprized the Castle.

This again is a still further instance of circumstantial inaccuracy, interesting enough as showing how difficult it was, at the time, to get at the truth. But all this talk of "marching obscurely in the night, upon the moors out of Cumberland" &c., vanishes into thin air in face of Paulden's narrative of the two successive attempts, and of the conspirators keeping in the neighbouring woods, between their first and second more successful venture; to say nothing of the multiplication of the 8 or 10 men who seized the Castle, into 20, with the addition of "a party of horse with musketeers behind them," all taking part in the surprise : the simple truth being that the horsemen (of whom Capt.

Thomas Paulden was leader) did not receive orders to advance till after the Garrison were driven into the Dungeon. (See page 150.)

It is too frequently the case with partisans that where they can do no more, they abuse and defame their opponents. And thus we find the writers of these letters, in order to degrade and make him a person of mean account, bringing forward the statement that Colonel Bonivent was "formerly groom of the stable to Sir Marmaduke Langdale," while we have already seen that even four years previously he had been governor of Sandal; and while, whatever had been his real origin, the forward steps which he had made,—even in the eyes of professed levellers, who indeed are generally the most inconsistent in this respect,—ought to have obliterated the remembrance of his early disadvantages, or have caused them to be remembered only to his credit.

The infamy which his opponents attempted to attach to Colonel Bonivent, they attributed to Colonel Morris also. And in the case of Colonel Morris, it is continued to the present day. For in a work, published within the last few years, we find the remark repeated that "Clarendon says that Morrice 'was a gentlemen of competent estate,' in the neighbourhood of the Castle; but as nobody seems to be able to tell where he lived or where his lands were situated, one would have supposed that he cannot have held a very high social position in the Country."

Naturally, it might be thought that anyone who hazarded such a remark, in defiance of the clear statement of Clarendon, and that anyone who repeated it, would in either case, feel a sort of obligation to make some, ever so slight, attempt on their own part to approach the truth more nearly. But, no; in each case the promulgator contents himself with propagating the innuendo. It therefore remains for us to make a few remarks as to the social position of the Colonel.

As we have intimated, the registers of South Kirkby are deficient just when Col. Morris's baptism should have been entered, for they commence only in 1621, when he was about two years old. But we are able to gather the following particulars, most of which are from the existing registers of that parish.

Col. Morris, or Marris, or Marries, or Morrice, for his name is spelt with at least these four variations, was the son of Mathias Morris, of South Elmsall, whose younger children, registered at South Kirkby, by his first wife—the mother of Colonel Morris—were :

>Dorothy, bapt Oct. 12, 1626, buried April 13, 1646.
>Anne, bapt March 24, 1627.
>Edward, bapt May 22, 1631.

She was buried Feb. 6, 1637-8, as "The wife of Mathias Morris of S. Elmsall", her Christian name not being mentioned; and the widower re-married with Jane, the daughter of George Holgate, of Grimethorpe, by whom he had Matthew, Mary, Wentworth and Sarah ; to which Thoresby (acting on the authentic information to which we shall presently refer) adds Richard, while (no impeachment to his accuracy) he does not name the Mary, who died in infancy.

The arms of Morris of South Elmsall, as used by Col. Morris's eldest son Robert in 1666, are given by Dugdale as AZURE : three eagles displayed OR; on a canton ARGENT, a Castle GULES ; though Thoresby in the following generation, reverses the tinctures of the Canton and the Castle, possibly as a mark of difference for the family of the second son. The Castle itself, on the Canton, has probable reference to Col. Morris's exploit, and Dugdale says he had a son born during the siege, and named Castilian on that account. But if so, the register of his baptism has not been preserved, though the occurrence in the Pontefract Books of the marriage on Aug. 3, 1671, of Mr Castilia Morris and Mrs. Anabella Ashingdon " lends colour to the assertion. For the children of "John Morris, of East Hague," (in whom we recognize the successful leader of 3 June, 1648,) registered at South Kirkby, are Jane, his daughter, baptised August 2, 1646; and John, his son, baptised November 15, 1647, buried May 20, 1648, only a fortnight before the seizure of the Castle. These dates allow for Castilian being born during the siege, even if near its close; in which case he would have been about 22 at his marriage with Mrs. Ashingdon.

Having hitherto made extracts and given dates which are to be found in original sources of information, open however to those who choose to take the pains to investigate, we may now state that Dugdale gives a pedigree which shows that Morris's ancestors, for at least five degrees, that is to his father's grandfather's grandfather, had been at North Elmsall. This is repeated with additions by Thoresby in his Ducatus Leodiensis; and since Castilian or Castilion Morris, that son of Colonel Morris, who had married at Pontefract, Anabella, daughter of William Ashenden, was Town Clerk of Leeds, Thoresby had every opportunity of making himself well acquainted with the exact truth, and of ascertaining the purest sources of information.

From Thoresby we learn that Edward Morris, of Elmsall, had a son Robert, whose son Nicholas, married Lucy, daughter and heir of John Latham, of Carlton Hall, Pontefract, a family extinct before the first Pontefract Register commences in 1585. Their eldest son, Thomas, married Barbara, daughter of John Wentworth, of North Elmsall, and their third son, Richard, was Richard Marris, the confidential friend and steward to the Earl of Strafford, who was the principal person in managing the Earl's affairs in Yorkshire, while he was absent in Ireland, and whose sudden death in 1645 occasioned the Earl considerable inconvenience.

Thomas's eldest son, Matthias, was the father of Col. Morris, the heir of the family, whose paternal grandmother was thus of the blood of Wentworth, Lord Strafford. Reckoning thirty years to a generation, this shows the settlement of the family at South Elmsall to have been continuous from the time of the War of the Roses.

According to Thoresby—informed, or at least put on the track of correct information by the Town Clerk of Leeds— Col. Morris had beside those children we have named, Robert, who died in 1676, and Mary, who is recorded at South Kirkby to have married on May 27th, 1672, Mr Taylor, of Pontefract.

This "Mr Taylor" was a John Taylor, buried at Pontefract on Feb. 7th, 1681-2, after which his widow re-married, still according to Thoresby, with John Jubb, having no surviving issue by either marriage.

So far for the blood relations of Col. Morris who, it was said by those who did not choose to enquire, could not have held a very high position in the County. Now, let us trace his wife. She was Margaret, daughter of Dr. Dawson, Bishop of Clonfert, and she re-married with Mr. Jonas Buckley, of South Elmsall, to whom she bore Thomas, Margery, and Elizabeth, besides a son christened Morris, after the hero of the family, who died in infancy. Her second husband, Mr Buckley, had given his name as prenomen to Buckley Wilsford, whose descendants remained property-owners in Pontefract till well within living memory. Dugdale's Visitation of 1666 reports her as having died on the previous 28th October, in the 38th year of her age. Such marriages and re-marriages all tend to show the rank of society to which Morris belonged, and the facts being on record, and easily verified, reduce to a condition without excuse, those who attempt to impute lowness of birth, and obscurity of origin to the brave Royalist, Colonel John Morris.

In connection with Buckley Wilsford a singular circumstance has recently come to our knowledge. He owned and occupied the house in the Horsefair lately belonging to Mrs. Leak, and now owned and occupied by Mr. Thornton. The house was new-fronted about sixty years ago, but its interior is still a good example of an old-fashioned style, and on the ceiling of the substantial seventeenth-century staircase is a large coat of arms, very much resembling that of the Wentworth family. It is, Three leopard's faces, two and one, between a chevron engrailed, the engrailing of the chevron being all that distinguishes it from the Wentworth achievement. This was the Wilsford arms, as shown on the plate of Pontefract Castle, engraved at the expense of Buckley Wilsford in 1706. It is not a little remarkable that this coat of arms should have remained in position to the present day, as a ceiling ornament, of course whitewashed, while its similarity to that of the Wentworth family may perhaps imply an assertion of some sort of affinity, in which case his wife might have boasted that each of her husbands was a connection of that noble family, one branch of which obtained the Earldom of Strafford, and another the Earldom of Cleveland.

Now with regard to this shield, we have seen in Add. MS Brit. Mus. 12,482, fo. 5, an entry of the arms of Buckley Wilsford, of Barnsley :—GULES, a chevron, engrailed, OR ; between 3 leopard's faces ARGENT. (The Wentworth arms are SABLE, a chevron between 3 leopard's faces OR.) The volume in question contains the original entries for the 1666 Visitation, but as these particular arms of the Wilsfords, of Barnsley, were not finally enrolled, they do not appear in the volume ultimately compiled. Their entry, however, helps to establish a connection between Morris and the local gentry, and to show that it is only by distortion of facts that certain writers have succeeded, to a large extent, in throwing undeserved discredit upon that brave but unfortunate man; most unfortunate, perhaps, in having ungenerous opponents.

The following was Clarendon's account of the events preceding the seizure. It tallies with the fact of Morris's marriage about the time that the army was "new modelled"; for in 1648 he had had four children by his wife, then aged only twenty years. But we print Clarendon's account in full, as we have printed that of Paulden; reserving our remarks till its conclusion.

Having narrated the difficulties which the Independents had in London, during the absence in the North of their ruling spirit, Cromwell, Clarendon continues,

ALL these occurrences were very well known to *Cromwell*, and were the motives which perswaded him to believe, that his presence at the Parliament was so necessary to suppress the Presbyterians, who ceased not to vex him at any distance, that he would not be prevailed with to stay and finish that only work of difficulty that remain'd to be done, which was the reducing *Pontfret* Castle; but left *Lambert* to make an end of it, and to revenge the death of *Rainsborough*, who had lost his Life by that Garrison, with some circumstances which deserve to be remember'd; as in truth all that Adventure in the taking, and defending that place, should be preserv'd by a very particular relation, for the honour of all the Persons who were engaged in it.

WHEN the first War had been brought to an end by the Reduction of all Places, and Persons, which had held for the King, and all Men's hopes had been render'd desperate, by the Imprisonment of his Majesty in the Isle of *Wight*, those Officers and Gentlemen who had serv'd, whilst there was any Service, betook themselves generally to the habitations they had in the several Counties; where they liv'd quietly and privately, under the Insolence of those neighbours who had formerly, by the inferiority of their Conditions, submitted to them. When the Parliament had finish'd the War, they reduced and slighted most of the Inland Garrisons, the Maintenance whereof was very chargeable: yet by the Interest of some Person who Commanded it, or out of the consideration of the strength and importance of the place, they kept still a Garrison in *Pontfret* Castle; a Noble Royalty and Palace belonging to the Crown, and then part of the Queen's Joynture. The Situation in it self was very strong; no part whereof was commanded by any other ground: the House very large, with all Offices suitable to a Princely Seat, and though built very near the top of a Hill, so that it had the prospect of a great part of the West Riding of *York-shire*, and of *Lincoln-shire* and *Nottingham-shire*, yet it was plentifully supplied with Water. Colonel *Cotterell*, the Governour of this Castle, exercised a very severe Jurisdiction over his Neighbours of those parts; which were inhabited by many Gentlemen, and Soldiers, who had serv'd the King throughout the War, and who were known to retain their old Affections, though they liv'd quietly under the present Government. Upon the least Jealousy or Humour, these Men were frequently sent for, reproached, and sometimes Imprison'd by the Governour in this Garrison; which did not render them the more devoted to him. When there appear'd some hopes the *Scots* would raise an Army for the Relief and Release of the King Sr *Marmaduke Langdale*, in his way for *Scotland*, had visited and conferr'd with some of his old Friends and Country-men, who now liv'd quietly within some distance of *Pontfret*, who inform'd him of that Garrison, the place whereof was well known to him. And he acquainting them with the Assurance he had of the Resolution of the Principal Persons of the Kingdom of *Scotland*, and that they had invited him to joyn with them, in order to which he was then going thither, they agreed, 'That, when it should appear that an Army was raised in *Scotland* upon that account, which must draw down the Parliament's Army into the other Northern Counties, and that there should be Risings in other parts of the Kingdom (which the general indisposition and discontent, besides some particular designs, made like to fall out) that then those Gentlemen should endeavour the surprise of that Castle, and after they had made themselves strong in it, and furnish'd it with Provisions to endure some restraint, they should draw as good a Body to them as those Countries would yield:' And having thus adjusted that design, they settled such a way of Correspondence with Sr *Marmaduke*, that they frequently gave him an account, and receiv'd his directions for their proceeding. In this disposition they continued quiet, as they had always been, and the Governour of the Castle liv'd towards them with less Jealousy, and more Humanity, than he had been accustom'd to.

THERE was one Colonel *Morrice*, who being a very young Man, had, in the beginning of the War, been an Officer in some Regiments of the King's; and out of the folly and impatience of his Youth, had quitted that Service, and engaged himself in the Parliament Army with some circumstances not very commendable; and by the clearness of his Courage, and pleasantness of his Humour, made himself not only very acceptable, but was preferred to the Command of a Colonel, and performed many notable Services for them, being a stout and bold Undertaker in Attempts of the greatest danger; wherein he had usually Success. After the new Modelling of the Army, and the introducing of a stricter discipline, his Life of great Licence kept not his Reputation with the new Officers; and being a free Speaker and Censurer of their affected behaviour, they left him out in their compounding their new Army, but with many professions of kindness, and respect to his eminent Courage, which they would find some occasion to Imploy, and Reward. He was a gentleman of a competent Estate in those parts in *Yorkshire*; and as he had grown Elder, he had heartily detested himself for having quitted the King's Service, and had resolved to take some seasonable opportunity to wipe off that blemish by a Service that would redeem him; and so was not troubled to be set aside by the new General, but betook himself to his Estate; enjoy'd his old Humour, which was chearful and pleasant; and made himself most acceptable to those who were most trusted by the Parliament; who thought that they had dismissed one of the best Officers they had, and were sorry for it.

HE now, as a Country Gentleman, frequented the Fairs and Markets, and conversed with equal freedom with all his Neighbours, of what Party soever they had been, and renew'd the Friendship he had formerly held with some of those Gentlemen who had served the King. But no Friendship was so dear to him, as that of the Governour of *Pontfret* Castle, who lov'd him above all Men, and delighted so much in his Company, that he got him to be with him sometimes a week and more at a time in the Castle, when they always lay together in one Bed. He declar'd to one of those Gentlemen, who were united together to make that Attempt, 'that he would surprise that Castle, whenever they should think the Season ripe for it ;' and that Gentleman, who knew him very well, believ'd him so entirely, that he told his Companions, ' That they should not trouble themselves with contriving the means to surprise the place ; which, by trusting too many, would be lyable to discovery ; but that he would take that Charge upon himself, by a way they need not enquire into ; which he assured them should not fail :' And they all very willingly acquiesced in his undertaking ; to which they knew well he was not inclined without good grounds. *Morrice* was more frequently with the Governour, who never thought himself well without him ; and always told him ' He must have a great care of his Garrison, that he had none but faithful Men in the Castle ; for that he was confident there were some Men who liv'd not far off, and who many times came to visit him, had some design upon the place ;' and would then in confidence name many Persons to him, some whereof were those very Men with whom he communicated, and others were Men of another Temper, and were most devoted to the Parliament, all his particular Friends and Companions ; ' But that he should not be troubled ; for he had a false Brother amongst them, from whom he was sure to have seasonable Advertisement ;' and promised him, ' That he would, within few hours' notice, bring him at any time forty or fifty good Men into the Castle to reinforce his Garrison, when there should be occasion ;' and he would shew him a list of such Men, as would be always ready, and would sometimes bring some of those Men with him, and tell the Governour before them, ' That those were in the list he had given him of the honest fellows, who would stick to him when there should be need ;' and others would accidentally tell the Governour, ' That they had listed themselves with Colonel *Morrice* to come to the Castle, whenever he should call or send to them.' And all these Men thus listed, were fellows very notorious for the bitterness and malice which they had always against the King, not one of which he ever intended to make use of.

He made himself very familiar with all the Soldiers in the Castle, and used to play and drink with them ; and when he lay there, would often rise in the Night, and visit the Guards ; and by that means would sometimes make the Governour dismiss, and discharge a Soldier whom he did not like, under pretence ' That he found him always asleep,' or some other fault which was not to be examin'd ; and then he would commend some other to him as very fit to be trusted and relied upon ; and by this means he had very much power in the Garrison. The Governour receiv'd several Letters from his Friends in the Parliament, and in the Country, ' That he should take care of Colonel *Morrice*, who resolv'd to betray him ;' and informed him, ' That he had been in such and such Company of Men, who were generally esteemed most Malignant, and had great Intrigues with them ;' all which was well known to the Governour ; for the other was never in any of that Company, though with all the shew of secrecy, in the Night, or in places remote from any House, but he always told the Governour of it, and of many particular passages in those Meetings ; so that when these Letters came to him, he shewed them still to the other : and then both of them laugh't at the Intelligence ; after which *Morrice* frequently called for his Horse, and went home to his House, telling his Friend ' That though he had, he knew, no mistrust of his Friendship, and knew him too well to think him capable of such baseness, yet he ought not for his own sake be thought to slight the information ; which would make his Friends the less careful of him : that they had reason to give him warning of those meetings, which, if he had not known himself, had been very worthy of his suspicion ; therefore he would forbear coming to the Castle again, till the jealousy of his Friends should be over ; who would know of this, and be satisfied with it ;' and no power of the Governour could prevail with him, at such times, to stay ; but he would be gone, and stay away till he was, after some time, sent for again with great importunity, the Governour desiring his Counsel and Assistance as much as his Company.

It fell out, as it usually doth in Affairs of that nature, when many Men are engaged, that there is an impatience to execute what is projected before the time be throughly ripe. The business of the Fleet, and in *Kent*, and other places, and the daily Alarms from *Scotland*, as if that Army had been entring the Kingdom, made the Gentlemen who were engaged for this Enterprise imagine that they deferr'd it too long, and that though they had receiv'd no orders from Sr *Marmaduke Langdale*, which they were to expect, yet they had been sent, and miscarried. Hereupon they called upon the Gentleman who had undertaken, and He upon *Morrice*, for the Execution of the design. The time agreed upon was such a Night, when the surprisers were to be ready upon such a part of the Wall, and to have Ladders to mount in two places, where two Soldiers were to be appointed for Sentinels who were privy to the attempt. *Morrice* was in the Castle, and in Bed with the Governour, and, according to his custom, rose about the hour he thought all would be ready. They without made the Sign agreed upon, and were Answer'd by one of the Sentinels from the Wall; upon which they run to both places where they were to mount their Ladders. By some Accident, the other Sentinel who was design'd, was not upon the other part of the Wall; but when the Ladder was mounted there, the Sentinel called out; and, finding that there were Men under the Wall, run towards the Court of Guard to call for help; which gave an Alarm to the Garrison; so that, for that time, the design was disappointed. But shortly after, *Morrice*, and some of the same Gentlemen surprised the Castle, under the disguise of Country-men coming in with Carts of Provision: and presently seised on and master'd the main Guard, and made way for their Friends, Horse and Foot, to enter. Then two or three of them went to the Governour's Chamber, whom they found in his Bed, and told him ' The Castle was surprised, and himself a Prisoner.' He betook himself to his Arms for his defence, but quickly found that his Friend had betray'd it, and the other Gentlemen appearing, of whom he had been before warn'd, his defence was to no purpose, yet he receiv'd some wounds. *Morrice* afterward comforted him with assurance ' Of good usage, and that he would procure his Pardon from the King for his Rebellion.'

THEY put the Garrison in good order, and so many came to them from *Yorkshire*, *Nottingham*, and *Lincoln*, that they could not in a short time be restrain'd, and had leisure to fetch in all sorts of Provisions, for their support, and to make and renew such Fortifications as might be necessary for their defence. From *Nottingham*, there came Sr *John Digby*, Sr *Hugh Cartwright*, and a Son and Nephew of his, who had been good Officers in the Army, with many Soldiers who had been under their Command; many other Gentlemen of the three Counties were present, and deserve to have their Names recorded, since it was an Action throughout of great Courage and Conduct.

CROMWELL's marching towards the *Scots* with the neglect of these Men after the first appearance, and only appointing some County Troops to inclose them from increasing their strength, gave them great opportunity to grow; so that driving those Troops to a greater distance, they drew Contribution from all the parts about them, and made Incursions much farther, and render'd themselves so terrible, that as was said before, after the *Scotish* defeat, those of *York-shire* sent very earnestly to *Cromwell*, ' That he would make it the business of his Army to reduce *Pontfret*.' But he, resolving upon his *Scotish* Expedition, thought it enough to send *Rainsborough* to perform that Service, with a Regiment of Horse, and one or two of Foot, belonging to the Army; which, with a conjunction of the Country Forces under the same Command, he doubted not would be sufficient to perform a greater work. Assoon as the Castle had been reduced, they who were possessed of it were very willing to be under the Command of *Morrice*; who declar'd he would not accept the Charge, nor be Governour of the place, knowing well what jealousies he might be liable to, at least upon any change of Fortune, but under the direction of Sr *John Digby*; who was Colonel General of those parts, and was a Man rather cordial in the Service, than equal to the Command: which made him refer all things still to the Counsel, and Conduct of those Officers who were under him ; by whose activity, as much was done as could be expected from such a knot of resolute Persons.

THE total defeat of the *Scotish* Army being now generally known, and that their Friends in all other places, were defeated, they in the Castle well knew what they were presently to expect, and that they should be shortly shut up from making farther excursions. They heard that *Rainsborough* was upon his march towards them, and had already sent some Troops to be Quarter'd near them, himself yet keeping his Head Quarters at *Doncaster*, Ten Miles from the Castle. They resolv'd, whilst they yet enioy'd this liberty, to make a noble attempt. They had been inform'd, that Sr *Marmaduke Langdale* (whom they still called their General) after the overthrow of the *Scotish* Army, had been taken Prisoner, and remained in *Nottingham* Castle under a most strict custody, as a Man the Parliament declared, ' They would make an example of their Justice.' A party of about twenty Horse, but picked and choice Men, went out of the Castle, in the beginning of the Night, with a resolution to take *Rainsborough* Prisoner, and thereby to ransom their General. They were all good Guides, and understood the ways, private and publick, very exactly ; and went so far, that about the break of day or little after, in the end of *August*, they put themselves into the Common Road that led from *York* ; by which ways the Guards expected no Enemy ; and so slightly asked them, ' Whence they came ?' who negligently answer'd ; and asked again, ' Where their General was ?' saying, ' They had a Letter for him from *Cromwell*.' They sent one to shew them where the General was ; which they knew well enough ; and that he lay at the best Inn of the Town. And when the Gate of the Inn was opened to them, three of them only enter'd into the Inn, the other rode to the other end of the Town to the Bridge, over which they were to pass towards *Pontfrct* ; where they expected, and did find a Guard of Horse and Foot, with whom they entertain'd themselves in discourse, saying, ' That they stayed for their Officer, who went only in to speak with the General ;' and called for some drink. The Guards making no question of their being Friends, sent for drink, and talked negligently with them of News ; and it being broad day, some of the Horse alighted, and the Foot went to the Court of Guard, conceiving that Morning's work to be over. They who went into the Inn, where no body was awake but the Fellow who opened the Gate, asked in which Chamber the General (for so all the Soldiers called *Rainsborough*) lay ; and the Fellow shewing them from below the Chamber door, two of them went up, and the other stay'd below, and held the Horses, and talked with the Soldier who had walked with them from the Guard. The two who went up, open'd the Chamber door, found *Rainsborough* in his Bed, but awaked with the little noise they had made. They told him in short ' that he was their Prisoner, and that it was in his power to choose whether he would be presently killed (for which work he saw they were very well prepar'd) or quietly, without making resistance, or delay, to put on his Cloaths and be mounted upon a Horse, that was ready below for him, and accompany them to *Pontfret*.' The present danger awaken'd him out of the amazement he was in, so that he told them he would wait upon them, and made the haste that was necessary to put on his Cloaths. One of them took his Sword, and so they led him down stairs. He that held the Horses, had sent the Soldier away to those who were gone before, to speak to them to get some drink, and any thing else, that could be made ready in the House, against they came. When *Rainsborough* came into the Street, which he expected to find full of Horse, and saw only one Man, who held the others Horses, and presently mounted that he might be bound behind him, he begun to struggle, and to cry out. Whereupon, when they saw no hope of carrying him away, they immediately run him through with their Swords, and leaving him dead upon the ground, they got upon their Horses, and rode towards their Fellows, before any in the Inn could be ready to follow them. When those at the Bridge saw their

Companions coming, which was their sign, being well prepared, and knowing what they were to do, they turn'd upon the Guard, and made him fly in distraction; so that the way was clear and free; and though they missed carrying home the prize for which they had made so lusty an adventure, they joyn'd together, and marched, with the Expedition that was necessary, a shorter way than they had come, to their Garrison; leaving the Town and Soldiers behind in such a consternation, that, not being able to receive any information from their General, whom they found dead upon the ground without any Body in view, they thought the Devil had been there; and could not recollect themselves, which way they were to pursue an Enemy they had not seen. The Gallant Party came safe home without the least damage to Horse or Man, hoping to make some other attempt more successfully, by which they might redeem Sr *Marmaduke Langdale*. There was not an Officer in the Army whom *Cromwell* would not as willingly have lost as this Man; who was bold and barbarous to his wish, and fit to be entrusted in the most desperate Interest, and was the Man whom that Party always intended to commit the Maritime Affairs to, when it should be time to dismiss the Earl of *Warwick*; he having been bred in that Element, and knowing the duty of it very well, though he had that misfortune spoken of in the beginning of the Summer.

AND now to finish this business of *Pontfret* altogether, which lasted near to the end of this year, when *Lambert* came to this Charge (instructed by *Cromwell* to take full Vengeance for the loss of *Rainsborough*, to whose Ghost he design'd an ample Sacrifice) and kept what Body of Men he thought fit for that purpose, he reduced them in short time within their own Circuit, making good Works round about the Castle, that they might at last yield to Hunger, if nothing else would reclaim them. Nor did they quietly suffer themselves to be cooped up without bold and frequent Sallies, in which many of the Besiegers, as well as the others, lost their lives. They discover'd many of the Country who held correspondence with, and gave Intelligence to the Castle, whom they apprehended, whereof there were two Divines, and some women of Note, Friends and Allies to the besieged. After frequent Mortifications of this kind, and no human hope of Relief, they were content to offer to Treat for the Delivery of the Castle, if they might have honourable Conditions; if not, they sent word 'That they had Provisions yet for a good time; that they durst die, and would sell their Lives at as dear a price as they could.' *Lambert* Answer'd, that he knew 'they were gallant Men, and that he desir'd to preserve as many of them, as was in his power to do, but he must require six of them to be given up to him, whose Lives he could not save; which he was sorry for, since they were brave men; but his hands were bound.' The six excepted by him were Colonel *Morrice*, and five more whose Names he found to have been amongst those who were in the Party that had destroy'd *Rainsborough*; which was an Enterprise no brave Enemy would have revenged in that manner: nor did *Lambert* desire it, but *Cromwell* had enjoyn'd it him: all the rest he 'Was content to release, that they might return to their Houses, and apply themselves to the Parliament for their Compositions, towards which he would do them all good Offices he could.' They from within acknowledg'd his Civility in that particular, and would be glad to embrace it, but they would never be guilty of so base a thing, as to deliver up any of their Companions; and therefore they desir'd 'They might have six days allow'd them, that those six might do the best they could to deliver themselves; in which it should be lawful for the rest to assist them;' to which *Lambert* generously consented, 'So that the rest would Surrender at the end of that time;' which was agreed to. Upon the first day the Garrison appear'd twice or thrice, as if they were resolv'd to make a Sally, but retired every time without Charging; but the second day they made a very strong and brisk Sally upon another place than where they had appear'd the day before, and beat the Enemy from their Post, with the loss of Men on both sides;

and though the Party of the Castle was beaten back, two of the six (whereof *Morrice* was one) made their escape, the other four being forced to retire with the rest. And all was quiet for two whole days; but in the beginning of the Night of the fourth day, they made another attempt so prosperously, that two of the other four likewise escaped: and the next day they made great shews of joy, and sent *Lambert* word, ' That their six Friends were gone (though there were two still remaining) and therefore they would be ready the next day to Surrender.'

THE other two thought it to no purpose to make another attempt, but devised another way to secure themselves, with a less dangerous Assistance from their Friends who had lost some of their own lives in the two former Sallies to save theirs. The buildings of the Castle were very large and spacious, and there were great store of waste Stones from some Walls, which were fallen down. They found a convenient place, which was like to be least visited, where they walled up their two Friends in such a manner that they had Air to sustain them, and Victual enough to feed them a Month, in which time they hoped they might be able to escape. And this being done, at the hour appointed they open'd their Ports, and after *Lambert* had caused a strict inquisition to be made for those six, none of which he did believe had in truth escaped, and was satisfied that none of them were amongst those who were come out, he receiv'd the rest very civilly, and observ'd his promise made to them very punctually, and did not seem sorry that the six Gallant Men (as he called them) were escaped.

AND now they heard, which very much reliev'd their broken Spirits, that Sr *Marmaduke Langdale* had made an escape out of the Castle of *Nottingham*; who shortly after transported himself beyond the Seas. *Lambert* presently took care so to dismantle the Castle, that there should be no more use of it for a Garrison, leaving the vast ruins still standing: and then drew off all his Troops to new Quarters; so that, within ten days after the Surrender, the two who were left walled up, threw down their enclosure, and securely provided for themselves. Sr *John Digby* liv'd many years after the King's Return, and was often with his Majesty. Poor *Morrice* was afterwards taken in *Lancashire*, and happen'd to be put to death in the same place where he had committed a fault against the King, and where he first perform'd a great Service to the Parliament.

This account of Clarendon, it will be seen, is an amplification of that of Capt. Paulden, who confined himself to the bare local history, while the historian not only wove in with it, the general history with which he was dealing, but embellished it considerably with the graces of his own composition. Though, having all the evidences before him, he clearly accepted Paulden's letter as containing an accurate summary of the succession of events.

But Clarendon is the only original writer who alleges that Colonel Morris ever "served the Parliament," and notwithstanding his circumstantial narration, we must candidly say that we can find no corroboration whatever of the allegation of intimacy between Colonel Morris and Colonel

Cotterel, made by the historian, nor even of his receiving his rank of Colonel from the Parliamentarians, though we find much that tells against either statement. For Captain Paulden has not a hint of anything of the sort, while as we have already seen, Lieut.-Col. Morris was actually in custody in the winter of 1647 (see page 147-8) as an open enemy, for an attempt to surprise the Castle. This we have gathered from the Journals of the House of Commons, and so far as we are aware, the fact has been mentioned by no writer on the subject, while it seems to have escaped even Clarendon.

Hunter is very precise and definite, and his dates hardly leave time for any service at all for the Parliament. He says (South Yorkshire II. 98 note) :—

I add from the notices of a contemporary that he was born at South Elmsal, where the family had a small estate; that at sixteen years of age he was made ensign to his own company of foot by the earl of Strafford, and soon after lieutenant of his guard. The earl observing his genius for military affairs, said of him, 'that youth will outdo many of our old commanders.' After the earl's death, Morris was made captain in sir Henry Tichburn's regiment. He served in Ireland, and there performed some important services. At Dublin he was made senior captain in the regiment commanded by Sir Francis Willoughby, and major by commission from the earl of Ormond dated June 2, 1642. In England he served in the department of the royal army which was under the command of lord Byron; and when the war was over he retired to his own estate of Elmsal, carefully watching for opportunities of serving the royal cause, and finally gaining possession of the castle of Pontefract in a manner which has been often related.

There were at least three attempts made upon the Castle by the Royalists, who doubtless bore in mind that the body of Sir Gervas Cutler still lay in the Castle Chapel. The first took place in the autumn of 1647, of which we have no particulars. But the two attempts of which we have such graphic accounts were made in the following May and June; the first being thus described in a letter from Lancaster, dated May 19:—

A late attempt was made for the taking of Pontefract Castle. They came in the night with about 80 horse; each horseman brought his footman behind him and ladders, and had placed their ladders, and were ready to mount them, before they were discovered; and as soon as the alarm came to the two companies of foot that were in it, they were in readiness and appeared to oppose. The sentinels fired, and then they withdrew; and there being no horse in the castle, they could not pursue, so that the enemy got clear away.

The date of the letter shows that at least a fortnight elapsed between the attempt to scale, and the successful seizure of the Castle on June 3rd.

The following note is appended to the name of John Morris in the genealogy recorded by Dugdale in 1666. It represents the history as from a "family" point of view :—

"This John Morris being bred up under the right Hoble. Thomas, late Earle of Strafford, was first an Ensigne to his guards, after the said Earle became Lord Lieutenant of Ireld, and when the Rebellion brake forth in that Kingdome was made Serjeant Major to Sr Francis Willoughby, Knt., Major Generall of his late Maties Army there : Where amongst many other his valiant exploits, this one is nor a little remarkable, viz., that after he had received some dangerous wounds in the storming of Rosse Castle, whence he was brought of in a Litter, the English Forces in another encounter against Generall Preston being routed and flying by him, when by perswasions he could not prevaile with them to stand, he got up his led horse (though with much difficulty) and by his couragious example rallyed the disorded troops, and, charging the enemy in the very head of them, obtained an absolute and honourable victory.

"After that he surprised the strong Castle of Pontfract, for King Charles the first, with the helpe of eight men besides himselfe, upon the 3d of June, Ao 1648, and valiently defending it, during a long seige, untill after the murther of that King ; and then being excluded the benefit of the articles, upon delivery thereof to those inhumane Regicides, it being the last in England that had held out against their usurped power, himselfe with two more excepted persons (whereof Michaell Blackburne his Cornet was one) and two servants, with great courage and resolution, made their way through two workes, guarded by about five hundred foot and horse, and got clere from them into Lancashire, having had a promise from General Lambert (who besieged him) that if he could escape but 5 miles from that Castle, he should not be lyable to any farther question : notwithstanding which assurance, they most perfidiously tooke him at Oreton in Furnesse Fells, one Bell, a presbiterean minister, and Wrench a parliament Captaine first discovering him, and Sawrey, a Justice of Peace, with Fell, a Colonell, committing him to the castle of Lancaster : whence he was conveyed to Yorke, where being brought before Thorpe and Pulisdon, two of their then bloudy judges, and indicted upon the Statute of 25 E. 3, for levying war against the King, though he produced his late Maties Commissions for all his most valiant and loyall actings for him, the Jury being then packt, finding him guilty, they condemned him to death, which with much christian magnanimity he accordingly suffred upon the . day of August, Ao. 1649, his body being afterwards buried according to his desire at Wentworth in this county of Yorke, neer unto the grave of his worthy Ld and master' the late famous Earle of Strafford.

Margery, wife of the aforesaid John Morris, was afterwards married to Jonas Buckley, 4th son of Abell Buckley, of Buckley, in com. Lanc., Esq., by whom he had issue 4 children, vizt., Thomas, Morris, Margery, Elizabeth.

How small therefore was the justification for Carlyle to

write thus of Col. Morris : " The Governor of Pontefract Castle is one Morris, once the Earl of Strafford's servant, a desperate man." Yet he did not scruple to do so, in one of his so-called " Elucidations" of Oliver Cromwell's Letters and Speeches. The particular which forms the pretext for this spiteful remark is the summons to Col. Morris, to which we shall come in due course ; and the remark itself shows that Carlyle had but a very superficial knowledge of the history of this Pontefract siege.

Paulden's letter sufficiently explains what passed within the Castle, after Morris and his small party seized it ; how they were quickly reinforced, firstly by those in the immediate neighbourhood of the place, and then by others from a distance, who flocked in as to a centre ; but still the credit of the whole enterprise is evidently due to the Colonel and his handful of associates, for they alone seized the place ; they alone imprisoned the garrison ; and they held it with no help. Reinforcements, doubtless, were soon to hand, but when these reinforcements came, and before even they were sent for, the work had been done, the Castle was in the hands of the King's partizans.

In fine, to Morris and his nine companions, belonged the credit of the design, and of its execution : had it miscarried no one else would have had to bear the responsibility, or to undergo the punishment of failure.

Having seized the Castle, and garisoned it with five hundred men, the next thought of the Royalists was for provisions.

It must be borne in mind that war was actually going on at this time in Lancashire, that a Scottish Army of Royalists under Duke Hamilton was then marching across country, and that Cromwell was on the road to meet them.

COL.ᴸ JOHN MORRIS.

Son & Heir of Matthias Morris of North Elmsall, in the County of York, Esq.ʳ bred to the Military Profession in Ireland, under Thomas Wentworth, the great Earl of Strafford, and distinguished there for his eminent bravery. He was prevailed on, while very young, to enter into the Rebel Army, but repented of his error, retired to his estate, and on the 3.ᵈ of June, 1648, redeemed his reputation for loyalty, by the almost romantic surprisal of the strong Castle of Pontefract, aided only by eight persons.* He held that Fortress against the usurpers till after the Murder of the King; was promised his life at the surrender, in respect to his gallantry in its defence; but was afterwards seized, tryed, and condemned at York; and having been put to death there, in August, 1649, was buried, at his own request, at Wentworth, near the grave of the noble Patron and instructor of his youth. Colonel Morris married Margery, eldest daughter of D.ʳ Robert Dawson, Bishop of Clonfert & Kilmacduagh, in Ireland, by whom he had two sons, Robert, who died without issue, and Castilion, who left a numerous progeny, many of whom settled in, or about Leeds, but the family is believed to be now extinct.

* One of whom, Cap.ᵗ Thomas Paulden published in 1702, a narrative of that Enterprize, which was reprinted in 1719, for the benefit of Col. Morris's widow.

Engraved from an Original Picture, in the Possession of Sir Mark Masterman Sykes, of Sledmire in the County of York, Bar.ᵗ

London Published by Robert Wilkinson, N.º 58, Cornhill.

Hear Carlyle. When it suits the purpose of that partisan writer, he does not hesitate to say :—

> It all depends on Hamilton and Cromwell now. His Majesty from Carisbrook Castle, the revolted Mariners, the London Presbyterians, the Besieged in Colchester, and all men, are waiting anxiously what they Two will make of it when they meet.

There is no question here that war was the then condition; and consequently when three hundred cattle were being brought along the Great North Road from Scotland to London, through Ferrybridge, they came under a military guard, which in their case was two troops of Horse.

These cattle, so convoyed, were seized by a sallying party from the Castle of thirty horse—probably all they had, for the "thirty horse" are mentioned by Capt. Paulden twice—with half a dozen foot to drive the cattle; and this small band brought the beasts safely across country into the fortress, in the very face of the two troops of horse that dared not attack them. We wonder if the archives of the Record office, or any archives elsewhere, will ever disgorge more particulars concerning these two troops, and their brave achievement, or failure to achieve. It is not at all unlikely; certainly not impossible.

The deed was much to be proud of, since there were but 30 horse to two troops; the six pikemen were numerically next to nothing. This act of marvellous daring, Carlyle calls "highway robbery," with no word of explanation; "highway robbery," pure and simple: calls this seizure by this handful of men, of three hundred head of cattle, guarded by two full troops of horse, "Highway Robbery"! Could there be a baser misrepresentation of an awkward fact, the truthful recital of which must have told to the advantage of a man who was to be run down.

But the act was of a piece with Colonel Morris's whole life; his conduct, when wounded before Rosse Castle, was of a piece with his seizure of Pontefract; the seizure of Pontefract was paralleled with the seizure of Rainsborough: while his gallant attempt against General Preston was matched only by his great bravery in cutting through the beleaguring forces at the close of the third siege of Pontefract. Of his self-sacrificing generosity to his cornet and comrade, Michael Blackburn, we shall learn somewhat presently. Yet this well-born man, this descendant of the Wentworths, to whom all fear was a stranger, and gallant deeds but a matter of course, is quietly put down by Carlyle as a " servant," a " desperate man," a " highway robber:" words which call up ideas very, very different from the truth.

Indeed, throughout Carlyle's laboured diatribe, we trace not a solitary expression that shows he ever once looked, otherwise than with the hardest judgment of a narrow-minded opponent, upon any one act of these Royalists: whose loyalty was in his eye " flunky"-ism, and whose devotion to their cause was to him only that of " Yorkshire pudding-heads," or " Confused Welshmen " as he scruples not repeatedly to style those to whom his hero had opposed himself.

But in the earlier times of their possession of the Castle, the Garrison had made excursions of much wider extent. One is recorded under the date of June 28th, as extending even beyond the borders of the county, and to the island of Axholme, near Trent. Even that, however, was not the extreme to which their raids were confined; for two days afterwards (June 30) the report came up to the House,

<small>The enemy at Pontefract Castle still go on at pleasure, taking and plundering whom they please, and yet please to deal so with none but those who have been most active for the Parliament. Having quitted the Isle of Axholme, they came towards Lincoln, and yesterday entered the city, plundered the house of Capt. Pert, who is now in arms in Northumberland for the Parliament, and may do as much for them and many others, to the great damage if not ruin of them. They have prisoners Capt. Bees, Capt. Fines, and others ; Col. Rossiter was at a distance. They went further on, and took prisoner Mr Ellis; they brag they have 3000 listed in Lincolnshire; but there are divers thousands in Leicester, Derby, Rutland, and Lincolnshire, who are ready to join against these</small>

This, however, did not continue long, for under date July 5th, we learn :—

Colonel Rossiter met with the Pontefract forces upon their return after their plundering voyage, and engaged them at a place called Willoughby Field, routed their whole party, consisting of about 1000, took the commander-in-chief and all his officers—the rest routed, but not many slain. Col. Rossiter unhappily wounded in the thigh. List of the prisoners :—Sir Philip Mouncton, General ; Sir Gilbert Byron, Major General ; Robert Portington, Ralph Ashton, Lieutenant Colonels ; Majors Walter Saltingstall, Thomas Scot, John Scot, George Roberts, Edward Fitz-Randall ; Captains John Elvidge, William Bates, John Risby, John Munson, Thomas Byard, Anthony Wright (Pitket), John Rich, Arthur Lee (Downes), John Cooper, one of the sons of Sir Roger Cooper, William Saltmarsh, Edmond Monkton ; Lieutenants John Grimditch, Robert White, Edward Blundevell, Henry Lassell (Bradwell), Marmaduke Dolman ; 4 cornets, 2 ensigns, 24 gentlemen of quality, who have many of them been officers formerly, about 500 prisoners taken, who were all horse, except 100 dragoons, amongst which, many gentlemen who will not yet discover themselves. * *

8 carriages taken with arms and ammunition : Colonel Pocklington and Colonel Cholmeley slain, with many others not yet found, because the fight was in the corn-fields ; all their colours, bag and baggage taken.

And this success was considered so satisfactory that Capt. Harwood, who brought the news to the House, received £100 by their Order. The vote is dated July 8th.

Throughout the rest of that month little is recorded, and it is to October that Cromwell afterwards referred the seizure of the Knottingley convoy. But in the second week of August, the Lieutenant-General himself took a view of Pontefract on his way to the north to meet the Scots. Nothing, however, is on record of his doings here ; though he seems to have left the rawer levies, the militia, under Sir Henry Cholmley and Sir Edward Rhodes to carry on the siege, while he himself took the older and more seasoned soldiers to Lancashire.

Thus in possession of the Castle, and provisioned with the Knottingley beef—probably salted for store, by means of the Republican salt found in the Castle at its seizure—it was not long before the Royalists found themselves invested ; since affairs in Lancashire went otherwise than as they would have had them. As Paulden hints, the generalship shown at Preston was that of Sir Marmaduke

Langdale only, the other leaders were but incapables. The Scottish host—some twenty-four thousand, horse and foot — were defeated, and fleeing before the sword, broken in two. The division of the beaten troops which found itself in a strange country made towards Pontefract, as the last remaining strong-hold in the North—(for Colchester still held out)—soon to be the one strong-hold that continued to defy those upon whom they looked as Rebels.

Cromwell was meanwhile steadily advancing on his course, conceiving and maturing the design which culminated in his assumption of supreme power. It was his part to follow the northern wing of the defeated, those who were making homewards, and in a letter to the Committee at York, under date 23 Aug, 1648, we find him saying of the other division of the Scottish army :—

I have intelligence even now come to my hands, That Duke Hamilton, with a wearied Body of Horse, is drawing towards Pontefract, where probably he may lodge himself and rest his Horse. * * *
Major-General Lambert, with a considerable force, pursues him at the heels. I desire you that you would get together what force you can, to put a stop to any farther designs they may have ; and so be ready to join with Major-General Lambert, if there shall be need. I am marching Northward with the greatest part of the Army, where I shall be glad to hear from you.

But the Lieutenant General was not quite correctly informed. For, two days afterwards, Duke Hamilton in Staffordshire, ill and unable to march, surrendered. Would it be believed that he, Privy Councillor of the Realm, obeying the orders of his own Scottish Parliament, was beheaded for his fidelity to his King. Scarcely, were it not the fact.

His case was indeed peculiarly hard, and his fate long trembled in the balance, before it was decided that he should die. A vote was even passed that as the Earl of Cambridge—an English peerage—he should be fined £100,000, but it was rescinded after being for nearly five weeks on the Statute Book. Passed 10th November, it was repealed on December 13th by the House, when suffering under what was known as Pride's Purge.

The Duke's trial and execution were postponed till March, when following his Royal Master, his dying declaration was that what he did, he did under the orders of the Parliament of Scotland, " whose command, I could not disobey without running into the same hazard there, of that condition that I am now in." In other words, he was put to death by the English Independents for obeying orders; and might have been in the same peril from the Scottish Presbyterians, had he not done so.

Sir Marmaduke Langdale, was at this time recognised by both sides, as the Royalist Commander-in-chief; and in the early days of September, Sir Hugh Carteret and Sir John Digby were allowed to go on parole to Sir Marmaduke, then a prisoner at Nottingham, there to confer with him as to the surrender of Pontefract Castle, the result of the conference being that it should be held. The surrender of the Castle—which held out for six months afterwards—would have been the virtual close of the war, and its surrender being refused, there was nothing for it but to storm. For this, however, the Northern Committee were not prepared : but they sent letters to the House recounting the failure of the negotiations, and asking for £20,000 for the supply of the soldiers. This application was read on the 13th, and in reply to it the House granted £12,000, with which the Committee were forced to remain content for the present.

When Cromwell had followed into Scotland the main party of the defeated Presbyterians—for the contest was now between the Independents and Presbyterians, the latter joining the Royalists—and thus completed the ruin which had been commenced at Wigan and Preston, he turned his attention to Pontefract, which had all this time been weakly invested by Sir H. Cholmondley : so weakly as to invite, and make possible, the attempt to seize Rainsborough, which Paulden has recorded, and which had been preceded by two similar but more successful attempts. One of these was upon Sir Arthur Ingram, who was surprised in his own house, brought into the Castle, and set at liberty only after a ransom of £1500 had been paid. The other was upon Mr. Clayton, Lord Fairfax's steward, who was fetched from his Manor house at Denton, near Leeds. Emboldened by these successes, the Royalists made the attempt upon Rainsborough.

The position was thus:—The steady policy of the Parliamentarians was to destroy the leaders, of whatever rank, and to give liberty, on conditions, to all who were of no account. So they did after Preston; so they did after Colchester; so they did when Pontefract months afterwards succumbed.

Sir Marmaduke Langdale, when compelled to surrender, had been taken to Nottingham, and was in real danger of being tried for his life; while threats had even been made that he should be brought before Pontefract Castle—there has always been a remarkable parallelism between Pontefract and Nottingham, the extreme north and extreme south of the New Red Sandstone—there to be hanged in sight of the Garrison, if they still refused to surrender. All the country was in a ferment: not only had the Scots taken arms, but a large portion of the fleet had revolted, and the sailors had put their Admiral, Rainsborough, on shore. Rainsborough, judged to be as efficient on land as at sea, had been commissioned to come to Pontefract, and supersede Sir H. Cholmondley. The latter, however, was indignant, and appealed to Parliament; while Rainsborough, on his way to take command, yet unwilling to wound the susceptibility of Cholmondeley, had halted at Doncaster. Aware of this, Colonel Morris conceived the daring scheme of seizing

Rainsborough in the midst of his troops, and bringing him to Pontefract, to hold him as a hostage for Sir Marmaduke, to threaten reprisals on Rainsborough if the Royalist General were injured, and to offer him in exchange. Truly a daring scheme; which only failed by a hair's breadth. The Royalist band seized the post at Doncaster, as they had seized Pontefract Castle, threw the soldiers' arms into the water—they had not come to fight—and then the accidental dropping of a pistol by one of the band gave Rainsborough the opportunity to resist, of which he had before been deprived. None evidently could have regretted his death more than those who were its unwilling instruments. For apart from the fact itself, his death actually prevented and hindered their design. The dead General was no fit exchange for a still living leader; his life alone could have been of avail to his captors. And yet Carlyle called the act of these Pontefract men "An assassination"; committed in spite of their earnest effort to the contrary, "Murder; or a very questionable kind of homicide." It is little to the purpose that that atrabilious writer is wrong, somewhere in each of his matters of fact, when he comes to speak of Pontefract: that he states it to have been surprised in the beginning of the year, we know it to have been taken on the 3rd of June: that the attack on Rainsborough was " about five in the afternoon," we know it to have been ten hours earlier in the day, for we have seen the men running about in the streets in their shirts only (see page 151)·: and adds that the "Desperate man," the "Earl of Strafford's servant," ultimately "Lost his head" at York Assizes: but the obvious deduction from all these many inaccuracies is that Carlyle never enquired in the least into the Pontefract facts, but accepted what was on the surface, and to his hand, without taking the trouble to investigate; accepted it moreover with the greater readiness insomuch as it helped the rather to colour a partisan statement of events.

Rainsborough was hardly dead, not buried, when the Lieutenant-General on his journey southwards reached Pontefract. But meanwhile, we may pause a moment to point out that without Paulden's circumstantial narrative, we should have but a hazy account of the circumstances connected with that daring invasion of an enemy's quarters. Most of the versions of the story would lead a reader to suppose that the sally was the work of a few hours only. Carlyle puts it in very few words :—

Sunday, 29th October, a Party Sallied from this very Castle of Pontefract; rode into Doncaster in disguise, and there, about five in the afternoon, getting into Colonel Rainsborough's lodging, stabbed him dead.

Now except the assertion that " A Party Sallied from Pontefract Castle" hardly four consecutive words in this statement is without an inaccuracy. Let us follow out the circumstances of the daring action in order.

1. At midnight on Friday, the party being well horsed, sallied through the Eastgate, over the meadows, between two of the enemy's horse guards.
2. Early on Saturday morning, they reached Mexborough and rested till noon, sending a spy into Doncaster for intelligence, who brought it to them at Conisborough, between Mexborough and Doncaster. His message was that if all were well, a man would come out of the town, and meet them early next day.
3. Sunrise on Sunday morning, the appointed hour, the promised man came with the fore-known sign, a Bible in his hand; on which Capt. Paulden dividing his men, entered Doncaster.

Thus the events of each day are easily ascertained, and there is no reason why later writers should accept as circumstantially accurate the first hurried rumours that were spread abroad of the occurrence.

But even without very particular care, such gross mistakes need not have been made as Carlyle committed; for one of the " Extraordinary posts" that brought the intelligence to London brought also the complaint of Sir Henry Cholmondeley's ill management, and especially that he had allowed the Royalists after their visit to Doncaster "to return back again at *noon-time* of the day, and not a pistol fired at them."

There were thus, on the very surface, alternative versions of the facts; in which case the duty of the historian to sift, is manifest. That Carlyle made no such attempt, but selected the story by means of which he could most discredit the Royalists, sufficiently shows the partizan character of his work.

During the latter part of October, there had been continual complaints of the inefficient way in which Colonel Cholmondeley pushed the siege, and little consideration seems to have been had of the fact that his levies were mostly raw, the militia in fact of the county. Colonel White's, Colonel Briggs's, and Colonel Hacker's regiments having been taken to assist Cromwell and Lambert in Lancashire, only the militia remained under Sir Henry Cholmondeley, and these seem to have looked to the Committee at York, for orders, rather than to the officers of the regular army: for their existed some sort of divided command, which enabled Colonel Morris to intimate an unwillingness to treat till he knew with whom the command rested. Colonel Rainsborough had been sent, but he being strictly a naval commander, and of no higher rank than himself, Colonel Cholmondeley, naturally took umbrage, and his complaints were so loud that on October 20th, a letter from him was read in the House, complaining that the Lord General had given Rainsborough a commission to command-in-chief before the Castle, alleging that the disparagement was great to him inasmuch as he had received his own orders from the Committee of the Militia of Yorkshire, and desiring the

House to give some speedy Order therein: in fact he appealed from the General Fairfax to the House of Commons, as to a superior authority. The House, evidently moved, at once ordered that Sir Henry Cholmondeley's letter should be forwarded to the Lord General, with a desire that he might be pleased to settle the dispute, so as to preserve the honour and clear the fidelity of the complaining commander, and "that the whole business may be carried on against the enemy with all the advantage that may be."

To this the Lord General replied in due course that he would be very tender of Sir Henry Cholmondeley's honour, and would answer the House's expectation therein.

But, meanwhile, the York Committee had found a suitable way out of the difficulty, by writing to Lieut-General Cromwell, then at Durham, urging him to march southwards to take charge of the reduction of the Castle; who replied that there were already upon their march two regiments of horse, and two of foot, which would be there in four or five days, and that he himself would come with all possible speed. He applied for a thousand "working tools, and " what carts they could send" to be ready at his coming, besides ordering three troops of dragoons from Derbyshire to meet him there. He seems also to have looked on the Yorkshire Militia with the contempt of a regular soldier, to have resolved that they should be disbanded with all speed, and to have considered that his own presence and his own soldiers would be able to reduce Pontefract, as they had reduced Pembroke. Nor was it till he had been before the fortress for a fortnight that he found words to write his disappointment and discomfiture.

But although Colonel Rainsborough's death had removed one cause of disagreement, yet as it was very evident that a stronger commander than Cholmondeley was necessary, that event did not cause any alteration of the dispositions which Cromwell had made. It still remained necessary that, whether tenderly or not, Cholmondeley should be superseded. He had been already nearly four months, at a siege which he had reported (see Cromwell's letter of Nov. 13th) to be a matter of no difficulty, or of no difficulty which could not be easily surmounted: while according to all accounts, the Garrison did as they would, in utter disregard of any beleaguring force.

The appearance on the scene of a superior officer, such as Cromwell, even if his presence should be but temporary, was thus necessary to restore united action.

A letter from York, dated Oct 28th, the very day that Capt. Paulden's sallying party halted at Mexborough, on the road to Doncaster gives another graphic account of the doings of the Pontefract Garrison.

The 30 "armed *cap-a-pe*" seem very like our old friends, Capt. Paulden's horse,—a troop of that number, and we may mention that the Capt. Clayton "wounded," was the commander of one of the two brave Knottingley troops that had charge of the cattle that became Pontefract beef. The letter, as a whole, is too good to be lost. It is not accurate in minute details; but its general character is that of a trustworthy informant.

On Sherwood Forest I was set on by some troopers who disarmed me. By all circumstances they were Pontefract men, I then left Pontefract road, and went by Wenbridge, thinking to avoid them. I baited at Hatfield in the room where the Pomfret Castle soldiers were that took Sir Arthur Ingram, who is now at liberty, paying £1500 for his ransom. They are very strong in Pontefract Castle, and go where they list; they are some 500 foot, and 140 horse; some 30 of them ride. armed *cap-a-pe*. They are desperate men, and fall often upon our guards; they have wounded Capt. Clayton, and taken him and most of his troop the last week: they have fallen on Major Ivers, wounded his lieutenant dangerously, killed ten on the place, took both horse and men, fell upon Capt. Greatheads, wounded his lieutenant dangerously.

They have since I came from London taken at least 200 head of cattle, above 100 oxen from grasiers. They sound a parley for a cessation, and make a fair of their horses near the castle, sell them to Sir Henry Cholmley's troopers. and in the cessation they drink to one another, ' Here is to thee, Brother Roundhead' and '*I thank thee, Brother Cavalier.*' They have and do take much salt, corn, beasts, and horses from the country; they prepare for a better siege; 'or this day Lieut.-General Cromwel is expected to come with forces to b.ock them up.

The reason they go thus where they list is, first, all the forces that are against Pontefract, are under the command of Sir Henry Cholmley; and Col. Rainsborough being come to Doncaster, having a commission to command in chief from the Lord Fairfax, Sir Henry Cholmley, having commission from the Northern Committee, takes it a disparagement, and refuseth to let him have the command; so that Col. Rainsborough is come no nearer than Doncaster, and the poor country suffereth.

Here is news, that when Lieut.-Gen. Cromwel cometh up with his forces, all the northern new militia shall be disbanded.

Pontefract men have lately fetched off Mr Clayton, steward to his Excellency the Lord Fairfax, ten miles of Leeds, at his manor at Denton, near Otley.

There is no difference amongst the Pontefract blades as is printed, they agree too well.

Here, once more, we obtain the contemporary testimony of one, who, if not an eye-witness, was at least as active a collector of the flying news as his own instinct of safety would allow him to be. Cromwell, he says, is expected this day, Saturday; and when he "cometh up with his forces, all the northern new militia shall be disbanded." He did not come till the following week, and there is little doubt but that when he did come, and learnt what had been done on the intervening Sunday at Doncaster, he was made none the less determined to carry out his previous resolution to disband the forces that had been so ineffectually besieging Pontefract.

The way in which the two sets of troopers drank to each other was the result of their being so many friends and neighbours, and probably, as far as the besiegers were concerned, with not too much liking for the cause that owned them. No wonder that Cromwell had determined that they should be disbanded. Such forced levies seldom give good service.

There is no suggestion whether this Capt. Clayton, the commander of the troops that convoyed the cattle seized at Knottingley, was a relative of the second Mr Clayton,

LIEUT.-GEN. CROMWELL.

Visits Pontefract, on his way to the North, August, 1648   Returns on November 1st, and summons the Castle, November 9th.   Left for London, December 4th.

steward to Lord Fairfax, of Denton. It is not unlikely; and there is a pedigree of the Claytons, of Oakenshaw, given in Dugdale's Visitation of 1665; but in the absence of Christian names, in each of the two cases, it is difficult to establish identity.

Two days afterwards, on October 30th, the Parliamentarians held a grand day of thanksgiving for the success of their arms in Scotland, and the month concluded with a retaliatory sortie on the part of the Garrison, who managed to kill many of the besiegers, and took a number prisoners.

But to return to Cromwell, and his part in the siege. His visit to the neighbourhood on his way north had been but hasty. Now he had time to stay, and himself take the direction of the proceedings, which had already lasted above four months, and were to spread over more than four months longer. He seems to have thought that four days would have been sufficient, but he had to reckon with men as brave as himself, and with a fortress now well-provisioned and strongly fortified.

It is not clear when Cromwell reached Pontefract; but it is certain that he was here before the Saturday following the attempt to seize Rainsborough; for on that day, news came to the Parliament that

Lieut-General Cromwel is at Biron House, near Pontefract, and there continues till he hath so settled the several posts as that the enemy may not, as they have done, break forth, plunder, and undo the country.

Plainly then, Cromwell was here at least as early as November 2nd; but his arrangements were not made for a week. By that time, he had crossed the river, and settled himself at Knottingley, where he probably occupied the Wildbore seat—now demolished, its very site having been quarried away—close to St. Botolph's Church.

From his quarters at Knottingley, Cromwell despatched the following letter:—

For the Governor of Pontefract Castle.
9th Nov., 1648.

Sir,—Being come hither for the reduction of this place, I thought fit to summon you to deliver your Garrison to me, for the use of the Parliament. Those gentlemen and soldiers with you may have better terms than if you should hold it to extremity. I expect your answer this day, and rest,

Your servant,
OLIVER CROMWELL.

To this open letter, Morris replied; thus accepting the position and responsibility of the Governorship. His reply is not by any means out of character: Carlyle calls it a stiff refusal, but he does not explain how, or specify in what. Nor does he print the letter. It was as follows, on the same day, as "expect"ed.

Sir,—I am confident you do not expect that I should pass my answer before I be satisfied that the summoner has power to perform my conditions, which must be confirmed by Parliament. Besides, the dispute betwixt youself and Sir Henry Cholmley, commander in chief by commission of the committee of the militia of Yorkshire, who, as I am informed, denies all subordination to your authority. When my understanding is cleared in this concerning scruple, I shall endeavour to be as modest in my reply, as I have read you in your summons.

Sir, your servant,
JOHN MORRIS.

Pontefract Castle, Nov. 9, 1648.
For Lieutenant-General Cromwel.

This was on Thursday. On Friday, as we learn, the garrison abandoned and fired the New-hall, but not so effectually as to prevent the besiegers making use of it. This information we get from the following letter written from "Near Pontefract," on Saturday, Nov. 11th. It has been preserved, like many others we have quoted, in Rushworth's Historical Collections:—

We are going on with the siege or blocking up of Pomfret to admiration, considering our wants, compared with the season and discouragements from your parts. Upon our approach in order to a close siege, the enemy the last night quit the New-hall which they had fortified, and set it on fire. Our men suddenly quenched it, it became a very advantageous place and quarter, in reference to a close siege. We have possessed also a strong house near the Old Church, so that there comes not out a man: the case is altered with them. We go on apace with our Line; my Lord General and Col. Bright's foot are upon duty; also Col. Fairfax's and Col. Maleverye's in the town. * *

Col. Cholmley's horse will be disbanded by the Committee, we like well Col. Bethel's. Langdale is escaped out of prison at Nottingham.

It is perhaps impossible to fix the site of this "strong house, near the Old Church", but it would necessarily have overlooked The Booths, which in each of the sieges had been for the Garrison a protected way out from the East Gate.

This letter contains the first news of the fortunate escape of Langdale, for whose sake the Garrison had ventured so much. "Langdale is escaped out of prison":— " I presume you have heard what has become of *him*" says Cromwell on the 20th. In other words, "He has been spared, and he has escaped: so much for the policy of Mercy!"

We trace nothing of Sunday's proceedings. But the following letter from Cromwell, on Monday, tells its own tale. Carlyle published it with the date of November 15th, but as it was read in the House that day, and Parliament then sat in the forenoon, the probability is that it was written on Monday, the 13th. It gives a clear distinct summary of the position: in the nervous graphic words of the Lieutenant General himself.

It may be noted by the way that Cromwell had received commands from his superior, the Lord General Fairfax, to reduce the Garrison. But the nut was too hard to be so easily cracked, and within three weeks of this date, with or without commands, he left his post under charge of the Major-General Lambert while he went to London on other important business which was becoming imminent. We do not find that he ever returned, or that he himself bombarded the Castle, as local tradition sometimes asserts that he did. But we have painful evidence of what occupied his mind during his stay here. To that we shall shortly come. Meanwhile, the following contains the description of Pontefract Castle, as drawn by the pen of Oliver Cromwell himself.

For the Right Honourable the Committee of Lords and Commons sitting at Derby House : These present.

Knottingley, near Pontefract,
[13th] November, 1648.

MY LORDS AND GENTLEMEN,

So soon as I came into these parts, I met with an earnest desire from the Committee of this County to take upon me the charge here, for the reducing of the Garrison of Pontefract. I received also commands from my Lord General, to the same effect. I have had sight of a Letter to the House of Commons; wherein things are so represented, as if the Siege were at such a pass that the prize were already gained. In consideration whereof, I thought fit to let you know what the true state of this Garrison is ; as also the condition of the country, that so you may not think demands for such things as would be necessary, unreasonable.

My Lords, the Castle hath been victualled with Two hundred and twenty or forty fat cattle, within these three weeks ; and they have also gotten in, as I am credibly informed, salt enough for them and more. So that I apprehend they are victualled for a twelvemonth. The men within are resolved to endure to the utmost extremity ; expecting no mercy, as indeed they deserve none. The place is very well known to be one of the strongest inland Garrisons in the Kingdom ; well-watered ; situated upon a rock in every part of it, and therefore difficult to mine. The walls very thick and high, with strong towers ; and if battered, very difficult of access, by reason of the depth and steepness of the graft. The County is exceedingly impoverished ; not able to bear free-quarter ; nor well able to furnish provisions, if we had moneys. The work is like to be long, if materials be not furnished answerable. I therefore think it my duty to represent unto you as followeth : viz.—

That moneys be provided for Three complete regiments of Foot, and Two of Horse ; that money be provided for all contingencies which are in view, too many to enumerate. That Five-hundred Barrels of powder, Six good Battering-guns, with Three-hundred shot to each Gun, be speedily sent down to Hull :—we desire none may be sent less than demi-cannons. We desire also some match and bullet. And if it may be, we should be glad that two or three of the biggest Mortar-pieces with shells may likewise be sent.

And although the desires of such proportions may seem costly, yet I hope you will judge it good thrift; especially if you consider that this place hath cost the Kingdom some hundred thousands of pounds already. And for aught I know, it may cost you one more, if it be trifled withal; besides the dishonour of it, and what other danger may be emergent, by its being in such hands. It's true, here are some two or three great Guns in Hull, and hereabouts ; but they are unserviceable : and your Garrisons in Yorkshire are very much unsupplied at this time.

I have not as yet drawn any of our Foot to this place ; only I make use of Colonel Fairfax's and Colonel Malevrier's Foot regiments ; and keep the rest of the guards with the Horse ; purposing to bring on some of our Foot to-morrow. The rest,—these parts being not well able to bear them,—are a little dispersed in Lincoln and Nottingham Shires, for some refreshment ; which after so much duty they need, and a little expect.

And indeed I would not satisfy myself nor my duty to you and them, To put the poor men, at this season of the year, to lie in the field : before we be furnished with shoes, stockings and clothes for them to cover their nakedness—which we hear are in preparation, and would be speeded : and until we have deal-boards to make them courts-of-guard, and tools to cast up works to secure them.

These things I have humbly represented to you ; and waiting for your resolution and command, I rest,

Your most humble servant,
OLIVER CROMWELL.

The tone of this letter might lead us to suppose that from the 9th to the 13th, more had passed between the Lieut-General and Col. Morris than has been recorded. For Morris's communication hardly bears the tone of finality about it : is hardly the stiff refusal Carlyle represents it to have been. But if there were any such further communications, none have been preserved.

The answer of the House to this urgent appeal was a supply of half the quantity of Powder asked for. But the Guns did not come till the winter had nearly gone; and the tradition that Cromwell battered the place seems to be without foundation.

And now from his quarters at Knottingley during these November days, Cromwell begins to make those urgent appeals for " Justice," which resulted in the King's execution. But firstly there were the smaller leaders to be dealt with. With them Parliament wished to adopt the old policy, of causing them to compound for their estates, of fining them perhaps two years' revenue. But that does not suit the Lieutenant-General : his demand is that they should be treated as Traitors. Concerning the admission to composition of Colonel Sir John Owen, taken with Sir Marmaduke Langdale, he is particularly severe. The latter had been on the 6th November voted as one that should be particularly excepted from pardon; as one " whom the King himself, if he bargain with us, shall never forgive." But Sir Marmaduke had fortunately escaped the hands of these unrelenting enemies, and as Paulden tells us, lived to see the return of the King. Had he not broken prison he would have assuredly been executed, on the plea urged in the following, that he had assisted the foreigners, the Scots.

To the Honourable my honoured Friends Robert Jenner and John Ashe, Esquires, These.

Knottingley, near Pontefract,
20th Nov., 1648.

GENTLEMEN,—I received an Order from the Governor of Nottingham, directed to him from you, To bring up Colonel Owen, or take bail for his coming up to make his composition, he having made an humble Petition to the Parliament for the same.

If I be not mistaken, the House of Commons did vote all those [to be] Traitors that did adhere to, or bring in, the Scots in their late Invading of this Kingdom under Duke Hamilton. And not without very clear justice; this being a more prodigious Treason than any that had been perfected before; because the former quarrel was that Englishmen might rule over one another; this to vassalise us to a foreign Nation. And their fault who have appeared in this Summer's business is certainly double to theirs who were in the first, because it is the repetition of the same offence against all the witnesses that God has borne, by making and abetting a Second War.

And if this be their justice, and upon so good grounds, I wonder how it comes to pass that so eminent actors should so easily be received to compound. You will pardon me if I tell you how contrary this is to some of your judgments at the rendition of Oxford: though we had the Town in consideration, and blood saved to boot; yet Two Years perhaps was thought too little to expiate their offence. But now, when you have such men in your hands, and it will cost you nothing to do justice; now after all this trouble and the hazard of a Second War,—for a little more money, all offences shall be pardoned!

This Gentleman was taken with Sir Marmaduke Langdale, in their flight together:—I presume you have heard what is become of *him*. Let me remember you, that out of the [same] Garrison was fetched not long since (I believe while we were in heat of action) Colonel Humphrey Mathews, than whom this Cause we have fought for has not had a more dangerous enemy;—and he not guilty only of being an enemy, but he apostatised from your Cause and Quarrel; having been a Colonel, if not more, under you, and then the desperatest promoter of the Welsh Rebellion amongst them all! And how near you were brought to ruin thereby, all men that know anything can tell; and this man was taken away by composition, by what order I know not.

Gentlemen, though my sense does appear more severe than perhaps you would have it, yet give me leave to tell you I find a sense among the Officers concerning such things as those men, to amazement;—which truly is not so much to see their blood made so cheap, as to see such manifest witnessings of God, so terrible and so just, no more reverenced.

I have directed the Governor to acquaint the Lord General herewith; and rest, Gentlemen, your most obedient servant,

OLIVER CROMWELL.

How suggestive are the words of this remonstrance against mercy! "Now,—when you have such men in your hands, and it will cost you nothing to do JUSTICE", you hesitate to take their lives! Oliver, in so many words, forbids such hesitancy, and continues his urgent cry for "justice."

The following is his letter to Fairfax referred to above. To Fairfax, his cry is for "impartial" justice. He seems, as knowing his correspondent, to lay stress on its impartiality, but the prisoners and their royal head himself might well pray to be delivered from such. Thus, not only did he direct the Governor to acquaint the Lord General, but he took care to do so himself.

For his Excellency the Lord General Fairfax.
Knottingley, 20th Nov. 1648.

MY LORD,—I find in the Officers of the Regiments a very great sense of the sufferings of this poor Kingdom ; and in them all a very great zeal to have impartial Justice done upon Offenders. I must confess, I do in all, from my heart, concur with them ; and I verily think and am persuaded they are things which God puts into our hearts.

I shall not need to offer anything to your Excellency : I know, God teaches you ; and that He hath manifested His presence so to you as that you will give glory to Him in the eyes of all the world. I held it my duty, having received these Petitions and Letters, and being so desired by the framers thereof,—to present them to you. The good Lord work His will upon your heart, enabling you to it ; and the presence of Almighty God go along with you ! Thus prays, my Lord, your most humble and faithful servant,

OLIVER CROMWELL.

To the Lord General he thus enlarged fully upon the "manifest witnessings of God," of which he had said but a few words at the close of his communication to Robert Jenner and John Ashe. According to this Cromwellian doctrine, whatever is successful, can claim by reason of its success, that the hand of God is fighting for it : a doctrine very comforting to a successful thief of any kind. For some two months longer, Fairfax listened to such specious words : those two months, however, showed him their hollowness.

The Lieutenant General's notes from Knottingley have been preserved in pairs. The two last are dated November 20th : the two next are dated November 25th.

The first is an urgent appeal for the payment of the dues to the Garrison at Hull, concerning which the

Lieutenant General wrote on November 13th (see page 188). The letter had been taken into consideration by the House, and an order made on Saturday, November 18th, but insufficient thinks Cromwell, or insufficiently obeyed.

The result of his dissatisfaction is the following letter to an official in whose power it seems to have laid, to forward the matter.

For my noble Friend Thomas St. Nicholas, Esquire. These at London.
Knottingley, 25th Nov., 1648.

Sir,—I suppose it's not unknown to you how much the Country is in arrear to the Garrison of Hull :—as likewise how probable it is that the Garrison will break, unless some speedy course be taken to get them money ; the soldiers at the present being ready to mutiny, as not having money to buy them bread ; and without money the subborn Townspeople will not trust them for the worth of a penny.

Sir, I must beg of you that, as you tender the good of the Country, so far as the security of that Garrison is motioned, you would give your assistance to the helping of them to their money which the Country owes them. The Governor will apply himself to you, either in person or by letter. I pray you do for him herein as in a business of very high consequence. I am the more earnest with you, as having a very deep sense how dangerous the event may be, of their being neglected in the matter of their pay. I rest upon your favour herein ;—and subscribe myself, Sir, your very humble servant,

Oliver Cromwell.

The next letter—which darkly refers to the impending Trial and Execution of the King—was addressed to Colonel Hammond, who had charge of his Majesty (that Person !) in the Isle of Wight. Colonel Hammond was not so tractable in the hands of the would-be regicides as they had hoped he might have been, and the letter shows the specious reasoning by which the Lieutenant General vainly endeavoured to overcome the scruples of his friend of such ancient standing.

To Colonel Robert Hammond : These.
Knottingley, near Pontefract.
25th Nov., 1648.

Dear Robin,—No man rejoiceth more to see a line from thee than myself, I know thou hast long been under trial. Thou shalt be no loser by it. All things must work for the best.

Thou desirest to hear of my experiences. I can tell thee : I am such a one as thou didst formerly know, having a body of sin and death ; but I thank God, through Jesus Christ our Lord there is no condemnation, though much infirmity, and I wait for the redemption. And in this poor condition I obtain mercy, and sweet consolation through the Spirit. And find abundant cause every day to exalt the Lord, and abase flesh,—and herein I have some exercise.

As to outward dispensations, if we may so call them: we have not been without our share of beholding some remarkable providences, and appearances of the Lord. His presence hath been amongst us, and by the light of His countenance we have prevailed. We are sure, the good-will of Him who dwelt in the Bush has shined upon us; and we can humbly say, We know in whom we have believed; who can and will perfect what remaineth, and us also in doing what is well-pleasing in His eyesight.

I find some trouble in your spirit; occasioned first, not only by the continuance of your sad and heavy burden, as you call it, but by the dissatisfaction you take at the ways of some good men whom you love with your heart, who through this principle, That it is lawful for a lesser part, if in the right, to force [a numerical majority &c.]

To the first: Call not your burden sad or heavy. If your Father laid it upon you, He intended neither. He is the Father of lights, from whom comes every good and perfect gift; who of His own will begot us, and bade us count it all joy when such things befall us; they being for the exercise of faith and patience, *whereby in the end we shall be made perfect* (James i).

Dear Robin, our fleshly reasonings ensnare us. These make us say, heavy, sad, pleasant, easy. Was there not a little of this when Robert Hammond, through dissatisfaction too, desired retirement from the Army, and thought of quiet in the Isle of Wight? Did not God find him out there? I believe he will never forget this. And now I perceive he is to seek again; partly through his sad and heavy burden, and partly through his dissatisfaction with friends' actings.

Dear Robin, thou and I were never worthy to be door-keepers in this Service. If thou will seek, seek to know the mind of God in all that chain of Providence, whereby God brought thee thither, and that Person to thee; how, before and since, God has ordered him, and affairs concerning him: and then tell me, Whether there be not some glorious and high meaning in all this, above what thou hast yet attained? And, laying aside thy fleshly reason, seek of the Lord to teach thee what that is; and He will do it. I dare be positive to say, It is not that the wicked should be exalted, that God should so appear as indeed He hath done. For there is no peace to *them*. No, it is set upon the hearts of such as fear the Lord, and we have witness upon witness, That it shall go ill with them and their partakers. I say again, seek that spirit to teach thee: which is the spirit of knowledge and understanding, the spirit of counsel and might, of wisdom and of the fear of the Lord. That spirit will close thine eyes and stop thine ears, so that thou shalt not judge by them, but thou shalt judge for the meek of the Earth, and thou shalt be made able to do accordingly. The Lord direct thee to that which is well-pleasing in His eyesight.

As to thy dissatisfaction with friends' actings upon that supposed principle, I wonder not at that. If a man take not his own burden well, he shall hardly others'; especially if involved by so near a relation of love and Christian brotherhood as thou art. I shall not take upon me to satisfy; but I hold myself bound to lay my thoughts before so dear a friend. The Lord do His own will.

You say: " God hath appointed authorities among the nations, to which active or passive obedience is to be yielded ". This resides in England in the Parliament. Therefore active or passive resistance &c.

Authorities and powers are the ordinance of God. This or that species is of human institution, and limited, some with larger, others with stricter bands, each one according to its constitution. I do not therefore think the Authorities may do *anything*, and yet such obedience be due. All agree that there are cases in which it is lawful to resist. If so, your ground fails, and so likewise the inference. Indeed, dear Robin, not to multiply words, the query is, Whether ours be such a case? This ingenuously is the true question.

To this I shall say nothing, though I could say very much; but only desire thee to see what thou findest in thy own heart to two or three plain considerations. *First*, Whether *Salus Populi* be a sound position? *Secondly*, Whether in the way in hand, really and before the Lord, before whom conscience has to stand, this be provided for; or if the whole fruit of the War is not like to be frustrated, and all most like to turn to what it was, and worse? And this, contrary to Engagements, explicit Covenants with those who ventured their lives upon those Covenants and Engagements, without whom perhaps, in equity, relaxation ought not to be? *Thirdly*, Whether this Army be not a lawful Power, called by God to oppose and fight against the King upon some stated grounds; and being in power to such ends, may not oppose one Name of Authority, for those ends, as well as another Name,—since it was not the outward Authority, summoning them, that by *its* power made the quarrel lawful, but the quarrel was lawful in itself? If so, it may be, acting will be justified *in foro humano*. But truly this kind of reasonings may be but fleshly, either with or against: only it is good to try what truth may be in them. And the Lord teach us.

My dear Friend, let us look into providences; surely they mean somewhat. They hang so together; have been so constant, so clear, unclouded. Malice, swoln malice against God's people, now called "Saints," to root-out their name; and yet they, getting arms, and therein blessed with defence and more! I desire, he that is for a principle of suffering would not too much slight this. I slight not him who is so minded: but let us beware lest fleshly reasoning see more safety in making use of this principle than in acting! Who acts, if he resolve not through God to be willing to part with all? Our hearts are very deceitful, on the right and on the left.

What think you of Providence disposing the hearts of so many of God's people this way, especially in this poor Army, wherein the great God has vouchsafed to appear! I know not one Officer among us but is on the increasing hand. And let me say, it is after much patience, here in the North. We trust, the same Lord who hath framed our minds in our actings is with us in this also. And all contrary to a natural tendency, and to those comforts *our* hearts could wish to enjoy as well as others. And the difficulties probably to be encountered with, and the enemies, not few; even all that is glorious in this world. Appearance of united names, titles and authorities; and yet not terrified, we; only desiring to fear our great God, that we do nothing against His will. Truly this is our condition.

And to conclude. We in this Northern Army were in a waiting posture; desiring to see what the Lord would lead us to. And a Declaration is put out, at which many are shaken: although we could perhaps have wished the stay of it till after the Treaty, yet seeing it is come out, we trust to rejoice in the will of the Lord, waiting His farther pleasure.—Dear Robin, beware of men: look up to the Lord. Let Him be free to speak and command in thy heart. Take heed of the things I fear thou hast reasoned thyself into; and thou shalt be able through Him, without consulting flesh and blood, to do valiantly for Him and His people.

Thou mentionest somewhat as if, by acting against such opposition as is like to be, there will be a tempting of God. Dear Robin, tempting of God ordinarily is either by acting presumptuously in carnal confidence, or in unbelief through diffidence: both these ways Israel tempted God in the wilderness, and He was grieved by them. Not the encountering difficulties, therefore, makes us to tempt God; but the acting before and without faith. If the Lord have in any measure persuaded His people, as generally He hath, of the lawfulness, nay of the *duty*, this persuasion prevailing upon the heart is faith; and acting thereupon is acting in faith; and the more the difficulties are, the more the faith. And it is most sweet that he who is not persuaded have patience towards them that are, and judge not: and this will free thee from the trouble of others' actings, which, thou sayest, adds to thy grief. Only let me offer two or three things, and I have done.

Dost thou not think this fear of the Levellers "that they would destroy Nobility," has caused some to take up corruption, and find it lawful to make this ruining hypocritical Agreement, on one part?

Hath not this biased even some good men? I will not say, the thing they fear will come upon them; but if it do, they will themselves bring it upon themselves. Have not some of our friends, by their passive principle (which I judge not, only I think it liable to temptation as well as the active, and neither of them good but as we are led into them of God, and neither of them to be reasoned into, because the heart is deceitful),—been occasioned to overlook what is just and honest, and to think the people of God may have as much or more good the one way than the other? Good by this Man, against whom the Lord hath witnessed; and whom thou knowest! Is this so in their hearts; or is it reasoned, forced in?

Robin, I have done. Ask we our hearts, Whether we think that, after all, these dispensations, the like to which many generations cannot afford,—should end in so corrupt reasonings of good men; and should so hit the designings of bad? Thinkest thou, in thy heart, that the glorious dispensations of God point out to this; Or to teach His people to trust in Him, and to wait for better things, when, it may be, better are sealed to many of their spirits? And I, as a poor looker-on, I had rather live in the hope of that spirit, and take my share with *them*, expecting a good issue, than be led away with the others.

This trouble I have been at, because my soul loves thee, and I would not have thee swerve, or lose any glorious opportunity the Lord puts into thy hand. The Lord be thy counsellor. Dear Robin, I rest thine,

OLIVER CROMWELL.

Having now done all in his power to organise the siege at Pontefract, Cromwell seems to have found he was but acting the part of an idle man : while knowing what was proceeding, or about to proceed, in London, he felt it more profitable to his cause, and perhaps necessary for his ambition, to transfer himself thither. To London he accordingly went, leaving the conduct of the siege in the hands of Major-General Lambert, who arrived before Pontefract on December 4th, and apparently received from Cromwell those strict charges as to the "exceptions from mercy" which, in the close, he was compelled to make.

As we shall see Cromwell here no more, it may be as well shortly to summarize the events planned while he was at Knottingley, which occurred during the next few weeks.

Parliament having rejected by the large majority of 90 the Remonstrance of the Army against the admission of prisoners to mercy, and their Petition for "Justice," that is, that the prisoners should be tried and executed; and having after three days' debate decided by a majority of 46,—129 to 83—more than three to two,—that the King's Concession, in the treaty of Newport were a ground of settlement of the dispute between the King and Parliament, the military leaders boldly took matters into their own hands. The debate had been an all-night sitting: the decision was reached at five o'clock on Tuesday morning, December 5th. Cromwell was then on the road to town, having left Pontefract on the Monday ; and he reached London on the Wednesday, a few hours after Col. Rich's horse and Col. Pride's foot had taken possession, the former of Palace Yard, and the latter of Westminster Hall, to guard the Houses.

The object of the change of guard was soon apparent. As the members assembled on Wednesday, every one of the "majority" who came thither to attend his parliamentary duties was seized. Forty-one members were soon in safe custody, lodged in a neighbouring tavern, hard by, called "Hell"; and when on the Thursday, more were added to the number till it reached above a hundred, lo! the minority had become a majority; the Army had its will; events followed as a matter of course ; the concession made to Duke Hamilton was rescinded, and the various steps taken which resulted in the trial and execution of the King at the close of the following month.

Meanwhile, at Pontefract, the Major-General's arrival to release the Lieutenant-General, had other consequences of considerable interest to us. The Major-General brought in his train a small company of news-correspondents, some of whose letters have, by the merest chance, been preserved to our time. The principal writers were Thomas Margetts, who appears not to have held military rank and who, at the close of the siege, took up to Parliament the news of the surrender, Cornet John Baynes, cousin, and Robert Baynes, younger brother to Captain Adam Baynes, a man of good family of Knowsthorpe, near Leeds, for which town he was M.P. to Oliver's Parliaments in 1654 and 1656.

Capt. Baynes is sometimes called the first M.P. for Leeds, a description perfectly true, but exceedingly misleading. For when he is so styled, the natural conclusion is that he was one of a long series of M.P.'s for that town, which was not the case. After his time no member was returned for Leeds till the Reform Act of 1832. Nor was he Member for all Oliver's Parliaments: he had no seat in "the Little Parliament" of 1653, which was Cromwell's first experiment, a Parliament of 144 members, including 5 elected by the co-optative choice of the House.

The Rump Parliament, as purged by Col. Pride, continued sitting till 1653, when Oliver by his own act, "Take away that Bauble," dissolved it. The "Little Parliament" called in its place, contained no Members for any City or Borough, except London. Each English county returned 2 or more: Yorkshire had 8, Wales 6, Scotland 5, and Ireland 6. The five co-optative members were:—The Lord General (Oliver Cromwell), Major-Generals Lambert, Harrison, and Desborough, and Colonel Matthew Tomlinson.

The Parliament of the following year, 1654, continued this disfranchisement of Pontefract and so many other Boroughs, but instead of the former two Members for Yorkshire, it allotted six to the West Riding, and four to each of the other Ridings. There were also two members for York, one each for the ancient boroughs of Beverley, Hull, Richmond and Scarborough, and one each for two newly created boroughs, Leeds and Halifax, in each of which Independency was supposed to be very strong. In this Parliament, and in the next, Capt. Baynes sat for Leeds.

The second Parliament which had Capt. Baynes for a member, that of 1656, contained the same number of members from Yorkshire, as did that of 1654, with the addition of a colleague to Adam Baynes for Leeds; thus we may assume that it expressed Cromwell's settled conviction of what was best for the country.

The Protector died in Sept., 1658, and a revulsion followed. The Parliament called by his son, Richard, in the following winter, restored the ancient boroughs, discontinuing, moreover, the novel writs to Leeds and Halifax. This Parliament, to which as Lord Lambert, General Lambert was returned as M.P. for Pontefract, having lasted a twelvemonth only, passed an Act for their own dissolution, and also for the dissolution of the Long Parliament, which had never been formally dissolved, except by the fact that Cromwell turned them out, locked the door, and put the key in his pocket. Their Act for Dissolving the Parliament of 1640, thus practically ignored all three Parliaments of the Protectorate.

So much seems necessary to be explained as to the history of Cromwell's Parliaments, in elucidation of that of Capt. Adam Baynes, as showing what manner of man *he* was whose determination to know all that was passing before Pontefract, caused the following batch of letters to be written, and whose careful methodical habits led to his preserving them for our edification.

About fifteen years ago, the Surtees Society announced their intention to publish his correspondence; but their determination remains to be carried out; doubtless the volume whenever it shall appear will throw much light on the history of these times.

It is but proper to add that the policy of the bloodthirsty letters, of which he was the recipient, was not at the Restoration adopted towards Capt. Baynes, who retired to his estate, and died in peace in 1671.

The letters addressed to Capt. Baynes were preserved in

his family till recently, and shortly after the publication of Carlyle's Cromwell, they were printed in Tait's Edinburgh Magazine, forming the basis of a series of articles under the title of the "Roundheads before Pontefract." But although they throw much light upon the course of the siege of Pontefract, Carlyle seems to have found them of no use for his purpose, and so far as we are aware they have not, till now, been reprinted, though extracts from them appear in the Surtees volume 39. They supplement, very acceptably, the account given by Capt. Thomas Paulden; and as he could hardly have been aware of their existence, they furnish an excellent circumstantial proof of his accuracy, so far as they extend. Thus we have Paulden's account from within, and the weekly report of three newswriters (for practically such they were), from without. That these, when brought together after the lapse of two centuries, should tally with most minute circumstantiality, is evidence of the truth of both.

The first of the series, written on Twelfth day, shows the besiegers still waiting for the Guns.

TO CAPTAIN ADAM BAYNES, AT THE KING'S HEAD, IN GRAY'S INN LANE, LONDON. THESE.

Cousen,— . . . . . There's nothing here of concernment yet happens. The Guns will be here next week. Our men are raising new batteries. I hope all will be ready for the Guns when they come. The Major-General is not yet returned to Pontefract from reducing part of the Militia. All good people here are glad, and desire to hear of speedy justice, delays being often dangerous. Nothing else at present. I rest,
              Yor assured Lo Couzen,
                  Jo. BAYNES.

Pontefract, Janry 6th, 1648 (1648-9).

The terse ejaculatory style adopted by Cornet John Baynes, for that was the rank and position of the writer, betrays his want of familiarity with the pen. He can be pictured painfully thinking out a sentence, exhausting his subject, and waiting for fresh inspiration which came with a new subject only.

The "speedy justice", longed for by all "good people"

was the trial and execution of the King, since delays were dangerous, as had been proved in the case of Sir Marmaduke Langdale.

The next letter, written the same day from Pontefract, for the same post, which it seems was once a week (on a Saturday to reach London on Monday), refers mainly to the same subject, the trial of the King. " The unlucky hole" was still to cause much trouble.

THOMAS MARGETTS TO CAPT. ADAM BAYNES.

SR,—Being at York at the coming of the other week's post I did not receive yours till the post was gone, so that I did not write to you then; neither is there anything considerable happened in these parts since. The Ma: General is not returned from the disbanding Colonel Rodes and Colonel Cholmley's Regiments of Horse, the work having proved very difficult and troublesome; yet by this time the business is well nigh over. There is no visible disquiet in these parts, nor anything tending thereto, if this unlucky hole were but reduced, which, I fear, may be too long yet, and will be the utter undoing of this poor country, besides the continuance of our miserable hard duty in this extreme unseasonable weather, more than all the forces of the kingdom besides.

We have lately had several Councils of war here for the trial of offenders, wherein we have proceeded to the execution of exemplary Justice upon some, to the great satisfaction of the country and reformation of the army here. Enclosed is a copy of some charge against Lionel Copley: how true it is I know not, but no less is believed; and he that put it forth is an honest man. (See Appendix F.)

The well-affected in these parts do greatly rejoice (the malignants are as much troubled) a.t your gallant proceedings against Charles Stuart: you see the Lord and he are not independant: let them all fare alike; private enemies are more dangerous than publique. I think they have gone a more ready way to undo themselves than all human wit could have imagined.

Strive to answer the providence of God in this thing. 'Tis good indeed to follow or come after Providence; but 'tis as good to keep close to it as not to lag. So seasonable a blow to the many seasonable words (which sure is not far off) would set the business much forward: expedition in this would prevent many corrupt meditations [mediations] which other monarchs will send to turn Justice aside, lest it might prove an ill precedent to them in future. I think the agreement of the people needs more time to consider then this, for almost all are agreed upon this: the other relates to future settlement, and will require much wisdom and caution: the one is as the pulling down of an old house, the other is the building of a new. We would fain be doing something in these parts while we are together; when we are gone into larger quarters (as when this Castle is taken) we shall be in a worse condition to testify our concurrence with you, at least from time to time; but being at this distance, and having so late and imperfect relation of affairs, prevent our oftener appearing to you. The poor people in these parts are afraid of Jocky again, hearing rumour as if they were preparing for a second Invasion; and I perceive that is the great hope of this besieged enemy. For my part, though I am apt to believe that they are as great enemies to this late . . . . . of the Army as can be, and would most willingly find a most plausible way of entrance, yet I think at present they are not much to be feared. I confess I have no intelligence from thence. Their

new Parliament begun the 4th of this instant, and certainly something considerable will be done, both in relation to the first Engagement and also to some future service. I wish they were well watcht, both in this and that kingdom, that we may not suffer for want of discovery or true understanding of their proceedings. I pray, Sr, present my service to Cap. Bradford, and accompt me,
Yr affectionate friend and servt.

THOS. MARGETTS.

Pontct 6º Jan.

P.S,—We find in the list of the King's Jury there is no officer of our brigade mentioned for those of the army : Is it not a little disobligement ?

Mr. Margetts complains that the duty of the besieging troops "in this extreme unseasonable weather" was more than that of all the forces of the Kingdom besides ; and perhaps the harshness of the duty made him the more sanguinary and bitter towards those who had been made prisoners : so as by putting them mercilessly to death to prevent a future rekindling of the struggle.

But he rejoices in "justice" also, "exemplary justice," upon offenders in the Army. Indeed the truculence of the whole letter produces an unfavourable impression of the writer. The days of "Brother Roundhead" and "Brother Cavalier" were evidently gone.

Jocky was a by-name for the Scottish Nation, whose new Parliament had met two days before the date of the letters. The writer thought, and thought correctly as the event proved, that the Scots, if they had the power, would rather advocate the King's cause ; and therefore, like Cornet Baynes, he urges speed : because "Delays are dangerous" says one ; lest mediation may be made, says the other.

The P.S. throws some light on the packing of the jury that was to try the King. This Brigade even complained that they had no representative upon it.

Only Mr. Margetts wrote by the next post, that of Saturday, January 13th, and from his letter it appears as if

Capt. Adam Baynes had recently been before Pontefract; he had probably gone to London to assist in the urgent business then in hand,—the trial of the King,—even if only as a spectator.

THOMAS MARGETTS TO CAPTAIN ADAM BAYNES.

Sr,—The Ma. General lately returned hither from the disbanding of two Militia Regiments of Horse, and is now again gone to the disbanding of Coll. Bethel and the foot regiments lately before Scarborough, wherein 'tis hoped there will not be much difficulty, unless want of money retard the work. He is very active and painful upon this public service, and if affairs succeed well in the south, these miserable destroyed parts and the whole kingdom will reap the fruit thereof. This enemy is yet resolute and keeps us upon hard duty, but I hope in a short time he will appear but foolhardy. Our guns and mortar pieces, together with the ammunition, is now come into this Town, and they will play very shortly. They now and then drop away out of the Castle, but are still very active with their great and small shot to prevent our work.

The proceedings in relation to Charles Stuart are well enough resented by the well-affected in these parts, and are glad the business goes on so fast, as it probably tends to the preventing of malicious designs and loss of Justice: 'tis true they are upon a very tickle and high point, and had need of a great deal of caution, though you are upon a sure foundation; and so long as you continue upon these principles you will keep the enemy in a maze, for they know not what to do, in regard they can never act but where they have corruption for the ground. Constancy in the work, and tenderness as to those not altogether (yet near) satisfied would gain advantage of more complying interest. I received yours this week and thank you. The post was late before he came. The Ma. General gone before about disbanding to York. Coll. Lilburne gone to London and most of the other officers out of town, except Coll. Bright (who you know dissents), so that your other letter to the Council is not yet delivered, but I shall get it delivered and consider as (soon as) I possibly can; indeed we never had a Council of public affairs since you went, we have so few actors. Our news here is very little at this time, therefore, I remain,

Your most affect. friend,
THO. MARGETTS.

Pont. 13 Jan. 1648.

Col. Lilburne had gone to London at this time. He was one of the regicides, and signed the death-warrant of Charles I.

From this letter we learn that Col. Bright dissented from the proposed trial of the King, and that notwithstanding the appearance of legality to be given to the proceedings, his execution was clearly determined upon, so that all the pretence of legal forms was a mere sham.

Note also, that there were before Pontefract so few actors, that there could not be a Council of Public Affairs.

Every one that could get away, was at the common centre of attraction.

With regard to the action and progress of the siege, we learn definitely from this letter of Mr. Margetts, that "The Guns and Mortar-pieces" came to hand between January 6 and January 13.

There is no letter by the next post, and one from the affectionate friend and servant Mr. Margetts only, by that of January 27th, two days before the King's sentence. It is as follows :—

THOMAS MARGETTS TO CAPTAIN ADAM BAYNES.

SR,—I received none from you this post, but that by the last post I received two days ago, it being sent from the Major-General, in whose it seems it was enclosed, and for which I thank you. We have little news here; only Wednesday the enemy made a sally upon our nearest guard to them, beat them up, took 14 prisoners, and killed 3 or 4, and then were forced in again.

Mr. Beamond, Parson of Kirby, is apprehended for holding secret cypher intelligence with the enemy in the Castle; the matter is clear, and I think the gallows will shortly have him. The Major-General is yet upon his troublesome disbanding work of Col. Bethell, is expected the beginning of the next week, but it may be longer first. For that you wrote concerning Ma. Rokeby, I confess it was the first I ever heard of it, but upon enquiry since, I perceived there hath been such a rumour (but they arise many times upon slight grounds), and I cannot conceive any good grounds for it, nor do I believe it. I shall enquire further, and in what you desire in relation to that business I shall be ready to serve you, as Sr,

Your very affectionate friend and servant,
THOS MARGETTS.

Pont., 27 Jan., 1648.

"There comes not out a man," the boast of two months ago, thus seems to have been somewhat premature. For there come out, not only a man, but a party, who must have been pretty strong, inasmuch as they kill three or four, and make prisoners of fourteen. They were "forced in" it is true; but they seem to have left no prisoners in the hands of the besiegers. This was sally No. 1; we shall hear of a second presently, on which a subsequent letter throws a most interesting light.

It was the misfortune of Mr. George Beaumont, vicar

of South Kirkby, to be detected holding cypher correspondence with some—surely his parishioner of Hague Hall was one—and according to the practice of the Parliamentarians, and the foretelling of Mr. Margetts, " The gallows shortly had him." It is alleged to the infamy of Major-General Lambert, that before he was executed, he was tortured to force him to confess the secret of the cypher ; but he was resolute, and would not accept deliverance from torture at the price. He was hanged on Baghill in the sight of the Garrison. He left a widow and four children, and is said to have been a cousin of Sir Thomas Beaumont, of Whitley, also a confirmed Royalist. The date of his execution is said to have been Feb. 18th, 1649 ; and the Parish Register of South Kirkby has the record of his burial under that date. To him succeeded as officiating minister, Mr. Samuel Drake, son of Nathan, and afterwards Vicar of Pontefract ; but, as a fact, Mr. Drake was never duly appointed Vicar of South Kirkby.

The news of the execution of the King reached Yorkshire during the week, probably on Friday, Feb. 2nd, for the post was stayed on the day of the execution, that it might carry on the morning of the 31st, the news of the prohibition of any Proclamation of Charles II. Such a hint was hardly necessary to the " Castilians." They at once proclaimed the new King, and shortly struck coins bearing the mottoes HANC DEUS DEDIT ; and POST MORTEM PATRIS : PRO FILIO. Of these, we shall speak presently.

The Post, which left Pontefract the day after the arrival of the dire news, bore three letters to Capt. Adam Baynes, one from each of his three correspondents. Of these, we consider that of Mr. Margetts first. It is as follows :—

THO. MARGETTS TO CAPT. ADAM BAYNES.

SR.—On Thursday last afternoon, Capt. Bradford came to this Town, by whom I received your letter, but by the post I received none from you ; neither have I yet received the agreements. I perceive Capt. Bradford did leave some memorandums with you at his coming away, wherein there was something concerning my particular : I only request your careful remembrance thereof.

Little news here. Malignants talk much of the King's death : well affected are well satisfied. Malignants plot privately to relieve this Castle, and gather together in woods as we are informed, but we have sent Parties to apprehend and prevent them. The enemy hold out resolutely in hopes of relief ; but I believe would come to fair terms, for they would have another summons. The Ma. General hath now done disbanding, and returned hither, but at present is saluting his Lady at Corbrook. Yesterday the enemy sallied forth to beat us out of our Trenches near Swillington tower, killed us one man and were beaten in again. Our Mortar pieces have made some work among them, and I believe will make more. They have heard of the King's death, and seem to be more resolute upon it, but I believe it will make some of them slink.

I remain, Sr,
Your assured friend and servt
THOS MARGETTS.

Pontct 3 Feb.

This is the first time the "Mortar pieces" were mentioned as in use. As we have seen, they came into the Town just before the 13th January, and must therefore have taken more than a fortnight to get into position. But the importance of the fact was such, that not only Mr. Margetts, but Cornet John Baynes, announced it to their correspondent in London. Where this first "Mortar Piece" was fixed cannot now be ascertained, but according to the military man—the Cornet—only one was at this time in play.

It will be observed that there are three distinct gradations in the feeling with which the news of the King's execution was reported to have been received, varying with each writer's own sentiments. Mr. Margetts, who entirely approved it, reports "Malignants talk much of the King's death : well affected are well satisfied." Cornet Baynes, who also approved it, but apparently had his doubts as to the wisdom of the step : "That the King is executed is good news to us ; only some few honest men, and all the Cavaleirs bemoan him." Robert Baynes, more of an outsider, says " The King's death is very harshly digested by most, and almost all the country." This last was doubtless the real feeling, except in the Army itself.

The following is Cornet John Baynes's second letter. It gives his version of Sally No. 2, the "little sally" of February 2, Candlemas Day; but says nothing of prisoners.

CORNET JOHN BAYNES, TO CAPTAIN ADAM BAYNES.

Cousin,—Yours, by Capt Bradford, I have received, but none yet by the ordinary post. That the king is executed is good news to us; only some few honest men, and all the Cavaleirs bemoan him. It will be well if the Court proceed to execute justice upon Hamilton, Goring, &c. I am persuaded that when that is done, if it be not deferred too long, it will be so far from provoking the common enemy that they will be altogether discouraged, and will not dare to appear in tumults any more.

They of this Castle do us daily some harm: one of our morter-pieces has begun to play, and I hope hath done some execution. All our guns are not yet in a capacity of battering; only one or two play now and then at the battlements. The rogues within have no shells for their morter-piece, but yesterday they shot out of the same piece a very great stone, which fell into the next chamber to the Major-General's but hurt none. Yesterday also they made a little sally, (after they heard that the King was beheaded), but were forced in again: they slew us one man.

When you have received the money of Dr. Slane, and what you receive, I pray you let me hear.

Mr Dawson is well, and hath received of Mr. Welburne £40, as your proportion of the benefit of the voyage: it came to more; but in regard some hazard was passed ere the bargain was perfected and the money paid, he hath only allowed that. Thus letting you know that all friends are well, I rest,

Your assured Lo Cousen,

Jo. BAYNES.

Pontefract, Feb. the 3rd, 1648.

I pray you excuse me to Dr. Slane. Present my service to him. I should have written to him this post, but am just now going to muster one of the Militia Regiments.

A tolerably fair business production, but written by fits and starts in the Cornet's usual fashion.

Singularly enough, during the recent excavations at the Castle some partially rounded stones were found—not boulders, but rounded artificially, which were perhaps intended for the mortar for which there was no shell.

In this letter, as in others, we see exactly the process that was adopted to manufacture public opinion, or to represent public opinion to be in favour of "Justice." For these correspondents were evidently instructed to clamour for execution upon Hamilton, Goring, &c., so as to strengthen the hands of those who were already determined what end to make of the matter, if it were possible.

The third correspondent by this post, has little but horse news to tell; of which, however, he is very full. From him we learn the curious fact that a race was pending, in which Captain Baynes had a competing horse. The course, as we gather from subsequent letters from Robert Baynes, was at Clifford Moor, near both Tadcaster and Wetherby.

ROBERT BAYNES TO CAPTAIN ADAM BAYNES.

BROTHER,—I have received two letters from you, the later by Lieutenant Leavens, wherein you give me answer concerning your horse. There is 7 or 8 horses to run, but we shall (I think) come in a good place at the worst. Your man, Henry, hath no mind to ride, for he is above weight; so I think I shall get Corp. Rooke. Your old gray gelding is dead, being almost rotten with colds. Gilbert Cowp' desireth me to pay him for his Tythes; he saith though they be put down for the future, yet he hopes you will pay that which is by past. I desire your answer. My uncle desires you would send him some garden seeds, according to this note enclosed. I would know what I shall do with the young horses when it is time to (man)ure the ground. I heard neething of your letter to me and Mr Allott, but I shall speak to him the first opportunity I have. I need not write any news because you have better intelligence; only this, that the King's death is very harshly digested by most, and almost all the country. Thus hoping of your health and welfare, desiring much to see you, I remain,
Yours in all brotherly affection,
ROBT. BAYNES.

Pont., Feb. 3, 1648.

Probably this letter, as not clamouring for Justice, and not praising and commending the King's death, was not so readily producible as the other two.

As throwing light on these letters, the following extract from a weekly newspaper of the time comes in opportunely. It is styled "The Kingdome's Faithfull and Impartial Scout," and the date of the particular copy is Feb. 2 to 9, 1648.

Munday, Feb. 5. The Intelligence from Pontefract is this: the beseiged have lately made two sallies forth, but repulsed without any great losse to us; in the last they killed but one man of ours, and we took two of thiers prisoners, one of which had a small parcell of silver in his pocket, somewhat square; on one side thereof was stampt a castle with P.O. for Pontefract, on the other side was the crown with C.R. on each side of it. These pieces they make of Plate which they get out of the country, and pass among them for coyn. They cry they will have a king whatever it cost them.

P.O. is a mistake for P.C. in A of the following list; "C.R. on *each* side of it" is an inaccuracy.

For there appear to have been four varieties of these Pontefract siege coins, two of which belonged to the reign of Chales I.; and two, besides a duplicate in gold, to that of Charles II. Specimens of each are in the British Museum; and in Pontefract, Mr E. Foster, of the Castle Museum, is the possessor of one each of B, C and D: while singularly enough, a trial block in lead of the reverse of the first was found among the *debris* while clearing out the ruins of the Kitchen in 1882. It also is now in the Castle Museum. On examination it will be seen that the impression on this trial piece was first struck on the other side, but that the later impression almost obliterated the first.

The varieties are

A. (Ruding xxix, 10) A circular die, generally impressed on an octagon, or a lozenge, though it sometimes occurs on a circle. The reverse has a triple tower with a streamer from the middle of the central and highest tower. In the field above are the letters P. C., one on each side of the central tower. To the proper right of the Castle is the abbreviation OBS (for obsidio, a siege) and to the left is a hand, extended from the side of the tower, and holding a sword. Below is the date 1648. The different examples of this piece like most of the siege coins show great variations in weight. There are seven in the British Museum, the first three being octagonal and weighing 80·6, 95 and 68·9 grains respectively, one circular, weighing 86 grains, and three on a lozenge, weighing 87·2, 88, and 65·7 grains respectively.

The design is the same in each shape, but there are minute variations, which show that the two were struck from different dies.

B. (Ruding xxix, 11) is another circular die, but almost always on a lozenge. It has for reverse the usual Castle with OBS to the proper right, and the date 1648 at foot, but the space on the sinister side is occupied with the

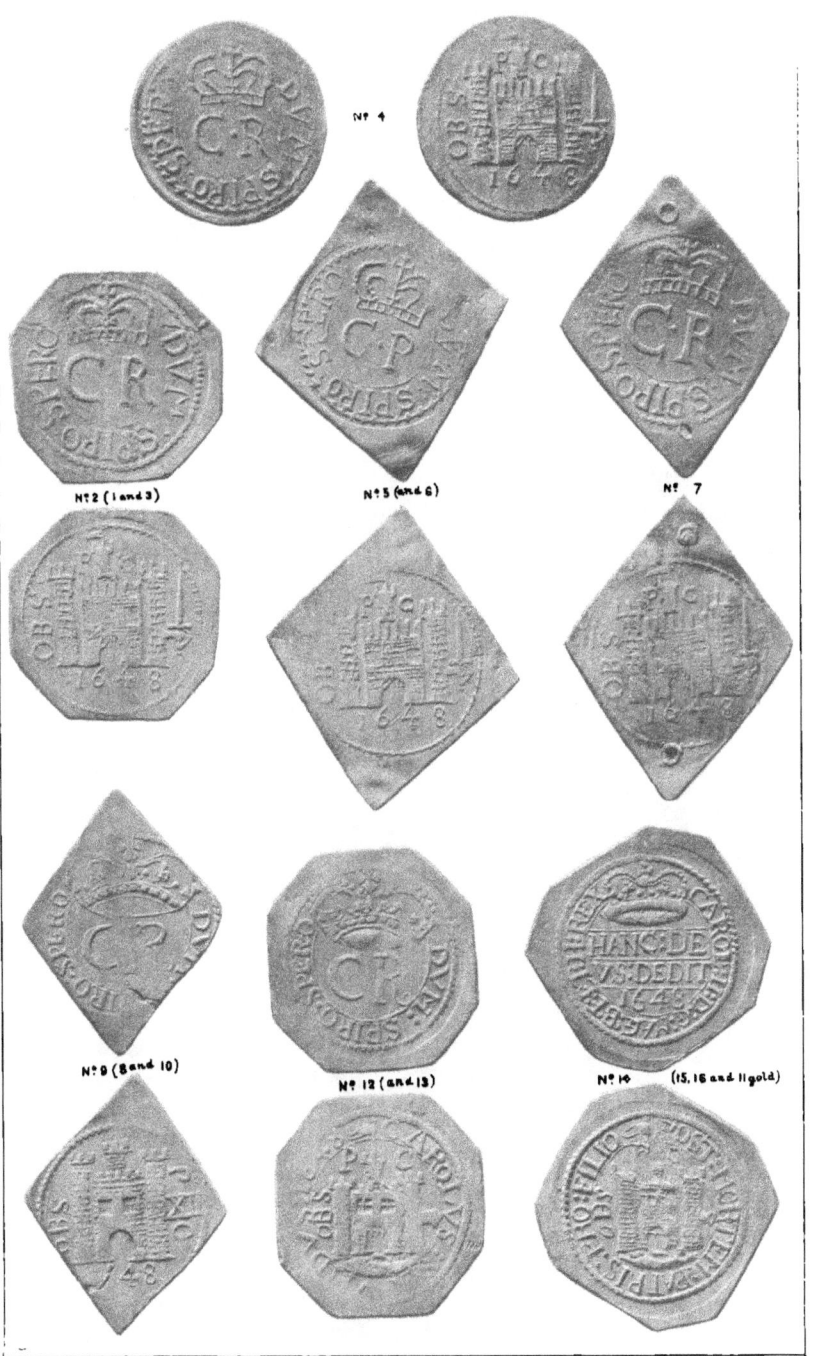

PONTEFRACT SIEGE PIECES.
(FROM THE EXAMPLES IN THE BRITISH MUSEUM.)

Early part of Siege, two varieties............1, 2, 3, 7; 4, 5, 6.
Middle or Trading Period........................8, 9, 10.
Early Charles II.....................................12, 13.
Final Period..14, 15, 16, & 11. *(Gold.)*

letters P.C. to indicate the place where it was struck, and the numerals XII to express the nominal value. Mr Edwin Foster's example weighs 103 grains. This is the only siege coin which, according to the common practice of Queen Elizabeth and the Stuarts, has its value impressed on it. Its weight is generally 66 to 94½ grains, though one example on a circle of silver, was found to weigh only 58¼ grains. Those in the British Museum, Nos. 8, 9, and 10, weigh respectively 83, 75·4 and 66 grains, but Mr. Edwin Foster's weighs as much as 103 grains.

A and B belong to the time of Charles I, but C and D were evidently coined after the King's Execution.

C. (Ruding xxix, 12) is like A, a circular die on an octagon. It has on the reverse a triple tower with a forked streamer from the central and highest. In the field, above the Castle, are the letters P.C., on either side of the central tower; to the proper right of the Castle is the abbreviation OBS, and on the left the projecting mouth of a cannon in place of the sword-holding hand, as in A, or the XII as in B. There is also a foreground in front of the Castle occupying the exergue. The legend is CAROLVS: SECVNDVS : 1648.

This coin is figured by Fox, but with several inaccuracies as if the drawing had not been copied from the coin, but evolved out of the imagination of the engraver, with only a verbal description to guide him. Those in the British Museum (Nos. 12 and 13) weigh respectively 84 grains and 70·2 grains, but Mr. Foster's weighs 56 grains only.

The obverse to A, B and C, is common in general design, with the slight variations we have indicated as showing that the different types did not proceed from the same die. The general idea is a central C.R. surmounted by an arched crown, which is a terminal to the surrounding motto DVM : SPIRO : SPERO.

D (Ruding Silver xxix, 13 ; Gold xix, 3.) But there is

a much finer specimen, a later coin, in which the efforts of the besieged culminated. Like A and C, it is struck from a circular die, on a piece of silver cut octagonally, but the reverse is not so successful as the obverse. The design is the Castle as a tripled tower; the central and uppermost tower being much smaller than the other two, while all are very rudimentary. The dexter side of the upper tower, bears a forked streamer as a finial to the surrounding motto, POST : MORTEM : PATRIS : PRO : FILIO. The upper field has the letters P. C. on either side of the central tower. To the right of the Castle is the abbreviation OBS, and to the left a cannon's mouth as in C. The obverse is a crown, much resembling that on the obverse of the others, but with the central and surmounting cross rather less sharply cut, and again acting as a finial to a motto, CAROL^s : II : D : G : MAG : B : F : ET : H : REX. The field is occupied by three lines containing a second motto, and the date, thus :

HANC : DE
VS : DEDIT
1648.

The reverse, which is given by both Buck and Fox, has been adopted as a design for the Pontefract Bank Notes.

Mr. E. Foster possesses a good example of this elegant piece in silver. It weighs 75 grains; and there are three in the British Museum, Nos. 14, 15, and 16, weighing respectively 74·4, 98·7 and 70 grains. The gold specimen there, No. 11, weighs 94·1 grains.

It may be noted that A has the symbol of an outstretched sword; this represents the early conditions of the siege, an occasional hand to hand conflict. B stamped with XII represents the trading period of the siege. C and D with a cannon, represent the conditions under which fighting was resumed.

It is remarkable that although we know that Sir Gervase Cutler, took in 1644 a quantity of silver to the Castle to be coined, no coin is known to be in existence that was coined during that siege. On the other hand, while there are these four varieties of Pontefract Siege Coins of 1648, there is no evidence whence the Garrison obtained their silver.

For three weeks the Baynes correspondence from before Pontefract Castle ceases; it is then resumed by Thomas Margetts, in the following malignant strain. The writing of this letter is formal, as if written to order : it well represents the "clamour" of the people for "justice." The last paragraph is autograph, and hurriedly written.

THOMAS MARGETTS TO CAPTAIN ADAM BAYNES.

Sr,—We perceive there are long demurs in the execution of Justice upon the rest of the great and notorious offenders, but hope by this time some of them are past demurring. These parts are yet quiet, and we hope will be kept so till this Castle be taken, which, though it be not certain, yet now we hope will not be long. If Jocky will not be quiet, we fear the late disbanding of forces, particularly in these northern parts, and the design of sending so many out of England into Ireland, may give advantage to the enemies' designs in these two nations, especially in so tickle a time as this, wherein (as I conceive) we have more need have all the well affected of the kingdom, either in arms or in readiness, and put in a posture of defence. Besides the standing army, I think likewise it would much conduce to the preservation of the peace of this nation if an act of Parliament were past for the calling in and seizing on of all malignants' arms, and for the preventing and punishing all disaffected priests that, in their preaching, meddle with civil affairs, thereby stirring up and provoking the people to contention, division, parties, and factions, and so demonstrating themselves the greatest (by their advantage of preaching) Incendiaries of the people.

I have written several times to you, but have received none from you these month or 5 weeks.

I am, Sr.,
Yo servant,
Thos Margetts.

Pont., 24 Feb., 1648.

"Jocky" was not quiet: nor did "Jocky" intend to be quiet, while these unhappy events were being enacted, overleaping, as they were doing, all "Jocky's" wildest intentions or expectations. "Jocky" remembered well how that he had delivered up the King to the English Parliament under a promise of good usage, how that the Parliament to which

Charles had been so delivered had been "purged," and how that its Rump had in the name of the whole compassed the death of the Monarch. "Jocky" as representing Presbyterianism had henceforth no belief in the English Independency that had committed that act. Hence "Jocky," now and henceforth, would be loyal to the King and his line; would, as the Pontefract Garrison had done in England, proclaim a new Monarch. It was no longer only DUM SPIRO SPERO, (while I live I hope): henceforth it was to be also, as on the latest siege coin, POST MORTEM PATRIS PRO FILIO. (After the death of the Father, we are for the Son).

The next post took up another letter from Mr. Margetts, who from its contents was evidently in some sort of office connected with the Paymastership of the Army. And now we have the first hints of a possible surrender by the brave little Garrison. Hope of release, there had long been none. But as there was no English Royalist army in the field, if "Jocky" came not, and there was no sign that "Jocky" was likely to come, there was nothing for it but starvation in due course, or surrender. Which surrender, was on the whole the better course, while terms might be had.

But what are the terms? Not yet revealed, at least so far as the following letter shows :—

MR. THOMAS MARGETTS TO CAPTAIN ADAM BAYNES.

SR,—I received yours this post, and perceive yours hath failed to me, as mine to you. This enclosed if you please to peruse and take the pains to deliver to Mr. Cox, will give you satisfaction what I have received by assignment; viz., 6 weeks pay (as you inform me) in Mr. Mabbot's hands, and the assignment of a month's pay, brought down by Capt. Bradford. And beside that, I never had any Assignment from the Committee for the Army. The Marshall Generall, Mr. Mather, is likewise in the very same case with me. Pray Sr. assist to get an assignment for us both together for our whole arrears, to make us up equal with the rest of the general affairs of the Army. If you please to deliver the enclosed to the Judge Advocate of the Army, and receive his answer thereto, and return it to me, you will do me a great favour, for if I have had assignments it may be he hath received them. I pray you enquire likewise of the Marshall General of the Army, whether he have not from time to time received our Marshall's Assignments: therein you will do us both a great respect.

This day we enter into a Treaty for the surrender of this Castle. They were not summoned: the overture was made by them; so that it will come the easier.

though I believe there will be some tugging before any be agreed to be delivered to mercy. We cannot give a certain judgement what the issue will be, but we believe if the Treaty break, they will be broken within, too. Morris, in his letter of overture saith, they are not ashamed to live, nor afraid to die, and they give out they will die with their swords in their hands like men, but certainly they are brought into a low condition. We are all quiet in the Country yet, till next storm come. I am sorry to hear of differences beginning at home; we shall never cease till we have destroyed ourselves. The will of God must be done.

Sr I am,
Yr very affec ser
THOS. MARGETTS.

Pontct. 3 Marc. 1648.

The fragment of Morris's letter, here preserved, exhibits well the dignified character of the man. They were "not ashamed to live," as having done nothing worthy of shame ; "they are not afraid to die," but will die with their swords in their hands, like men ; the extremity of which fate, however, ultimately befell but one of them, the fifth out of the excepted six.

This account of the preliminaries to the capitulation differs somewhat from that of Boothroyd, who, however, gives no authority, though it is possible that Colonel Morris's son is the source from which he derived his inspiration. For it is affirmed that Colonel Morris had a son born during the siege, some say in the Castle, and for that reason named Castilian. This son became (see page 164) Town Clerk of Leeds, and is said (Surtees xl, 15) to have written an account of the siege, which cannot now be traced. This missing narrative of Castilian Morris, we have little doubt was incorporated into Boothroyd's History, with additions by that writer himself, who is probably responsible for such inaccurate interpolations as that Rev. George Beaumont was "Chaplain to the garrison," and "rector" of South Kirkby.

The following is the narrative to which we refer (Boothroyd, 291) :—

> The besieged, having lost many of their brave comrades, and many others being confined by sickness ; their provisions almost spent, and having no prospect

of relief, at length offered to treat for the surrender of the castle, on honourable terms. They however declared, "that unless the terms were such as they could in honour accept, they had provisions for some time; that they were not afraid to die; and if compelled, they would sell their lives at as dear a rate as they possibly could."

Lambert receiving these hints, answered by throwing letters over the wall, in which a stone was wrapped, " that he knew they were gallant men, and that he was desirous to preserve as many of them as he could, but that his hands were bound, and he was obliged to except six of them, whose lives he could not preserve, nor could he mention their names till after the treaty was signed by the governor. As to the rest, he said, he was content to release them, that they might return to their own homes secure and unmolested, and that he would do them all the good in his power, by applying to parliament for an easy composition, for their delinquency."

On receiving this answer, Col. Morrice called the officers in the castle together, and it was unanimously agreed, not to deliver up any person without his consent." They therefore replied to General Lambert, "that they were sensible of his kindness and civility, and would gladly have embraced his offer, if they could have done it with honour; but declared that they could never be guilty of so base a thing as to deliver up their companions.

———

There is also a discrepancy between Capt. Thomas Paulden's account of the death of his brother William and that of Dr. Boothroyd, who, however, gives no authority for his assertion, and we do not find it elsewhere. He says that the brother died in the Castle of a high fever, a few days after the attempt upon Rainsborough,—that is, in November; Boothroyd says that his death was almost a month before the surrender in March, the King's death having taken place two months before. There is thus a difference of three months between the two accounts, but the balance of probability is again in favour of Capt. Thomas Paulden.

———

This seems a suitable place to show how far the demands upon the Pontefract garrison, differed from those so recently made to Colchester. In each the phrase was the same; and the talk, of " delivering to mercy." But in the case of Colchester—Hear Lord Fairfax himself.

" * * After four months seidge they [at Colchester] were necessitated to surrender, & yt upon mercy, they being betweene 3 & 4000 men. Now by delivering upon mercy is to be understood, yt some are to suffer and all ye Rest to go free: so those forementioned p'sons onely, were to suffer, and all ye Rest freed: So, Immediately after o'r entrance into ye Towne a Councell of war being called, those forementionod p'sons were condemned to die, ye Rest to be Quitt. Yet this being resolved I thought fit to manumitt ye Ld Capell, ye Ld Norwich, &c. over to ye parlam't being the Civill Judicature of ye Kingdom (consisting yn of Lords & Commons) as ye most prop' Judges of their Cases, being considerable for estates and Familys. But Sr Charles Lucas & Sr Geo. Lysle being meer soldiers of Fortune and falling into or hands by ye chance of war, execution was done upon ym. And in this Distribution of Justice, I did nothing but according to my Commission, & ye Trust reposed in me."

Thus, at Colchester the "delivering to Mercy" meant that the main body of those surrendered should receive Mercy, while the excepted should suffer as scape-goats. At Pontefract, however, the phrase "delivering to Mercy," meant a different thing. The six by name were to be delivered to Mercy, that is to the hangman: it is Col. Bright, alone, who in a subsequent letter changes the phrase, and truthfully calls the deed, a delivery to so-styled "Justice"; the besieged themselves considered that on their part, a compliance would have been Murder.

The following, sent by the same post from Col. Bright, is a business letter, which, however, gives a few more particulars of the overtures from the "General," as Col. Bright calls Morris.

We have already learnt from Capt. Paulden (see pp 152 and 153) that Col. Bright was at the head of the Commission ultimately appointed to treat for the surrender. It could hardly have been in more merciful hands, and it is not improbable that to his generosity and good feeling, the garrison really owed the slight concession—temporary though it turned out to be in the case of Morris and Blackborne—which the excepted six at length obtained.

Colonel Bright's letter, though dated the same day as that of Mr. Margetts, was evidently written later, and contained later news.

COLONEL BRIGHT TO CAPTAIN ADAM BAYNES.

CAPT. BAYNES,—Yours I received, and thankfully acknowledge your respects and care in the procuring equal encouragement for my regiment with others ; but except you be pleased to take the trouble in getting the 1012li. 10s.

charged upon Herefordshire, I shall have little fruits of that assignment. You may put my hand to the warrant. I have acquainted Colo. Maulyverer, who desires you to do the like to his. If you could procure me a bill of Exchange to receive 1012li. 10s. of Mr. Beale of York, it would be a special favour, of which you put me in hopes. We have sent ten troops of horse into Leicestershire, there to remain upon free quarter till the warrants be satisfied. This day one of the Castillians brought a letter from the General to the Major-General, the substance whereof for . . . . which were granted, the Commissioners named on our part; but it being so near night we cannot expect their return till to-morrow. This is all the progress that is made, to-morrow will produce more. I wholly rely upon your endeavours for our monies from Herefordshire : shall say no more but that I am

Yor real friend and servt,
J. BRIGHT.

3 March, 1648.
Your trouble is desired in the delivery of the enclosed according to direction : I am ignorant where he lodgeth.

It is, to say the least, unfortunate that Col. Bright's letter has perished exactly where it would have been interesting to us, and of substantial aid to our enquiry; for the hiatus appears to mean that the passage has gone, or is undecipherable.

The next letter in order of date is from the brother of Captain Adam Baynes. It is again full of horsey news, but the writer manages to tell us that that day, March 9th, was the day to parley for surrender : and that it was known that six will have to be surrendered to mercy—Mercy is still the term used ; Justice, is the thing signified : Justice being the hangman's rope : and it is difficult to recal a more brutal act than this shameful requirement, which had evidently been left as a charge from the Lieutenant-General, when he left Pontefract for London three months before.

ROBERT BAYNES TO CAPTAIN ADAM BAYNES.

BROTHER,—I recd yours the 6th Instant, with some colleflower seeds, but I heard nothing yet of Capt. Beare, but shall enquire of him. Gilbt Cowper hath been about me again several times, and saith he hopes you will not hold his right from him by the sword, and such like expression. For the young horses, I ride the bay colt. I have taken up the white colt a month ago, and I have sold two other, so there is but 4 of the worst left, which, if you think good, I shall get to run upon the common at Eastfield, because they scarce deserve cost of grassing. For Joseph there is moneys and Clothes sent him already. The horse course at Clifford was put off for a month by the Maj.-Gen. order, therefore is not altogether resolved to run, because we shall run upon great disadvantages. Coll. Bright was about me 6 weeks ago to be his Ensign ; but in regard I must have neglected all other occasions to have attended the place, and the pay being so small, I desired to be excused, but he is yet very importunate with Cornet Baynes to have me, of which I thought to inform you. They are this day to parley for the surrender of the castle; I hope they will agree about it, for the soldiers and gentlemen will have good terms, they surrendering 6 to mercy. Thus, hoping you are in health, as all our friends are here, god be praised, I remain,

Yor. ever lo. brother,
ROBT. BAYNES.

Pontefract, March 9th, 1648.

Gilbert Cowy, of a previous letter (Feb 3rd, see page 211) is evidently the same as he now called Cowper, the *y* having been misread as a contracted *per*, or perhaps the contracted *per* having been in the first instance read as *y*. It may be remembered that Boothroyd makes a similar misreading to this latter, having repeatedly substituted the incorrect word Pi*x* for the name of Pi*per* Tower.

Three letters of the 10th from three different correspondents, reach Capt. Baynes in due course. The shortest, though perhaps most ferocious, we take first.

CORNET JOHN BAYNES TO CAPTAIN ADAM BAYNES.

COUSIN,—Yours of the 6th February and your last are come to hand. . . . This day the Castillians' commissioners and ours do treat about a surrender; what the event will be I know not, and therefore I will not so much as conjecture, knowing, withall, that Colonel Bright and others will give you more certainty in it. I only wish that some of these cavaliers may go the same way (living and dying) with Goring, &c.; for that they have loved a life to be with their comrades rather in Hell (as some have said) than in Heaven with the Roundheads. I should have, may be, said more, but that I now am going to muster Ma. General's regiment; therefore I rest

Your assured Lo. Couz.
JO. BAYNES.

Pontefract, March 10, 1648.

I have writ by this post to Dr. Slane, and have renewed my desire to him to pay you what moneys he hath received for me, which by letter yesterday to me he promised.

The Royalists—indicated by the phrase "Goring, &c.," were executed on the day before. The &c. included Duke Hamilton, Earl of Holland and Lord Capel. Goring himself was, however, saved by the casting vote of Speaker Lenthall.

THOMAS MARGETTS TO CAPTAIN ADAM BAYNES.

Sr, ... I acquainted you by the last that we were upon treaty with the Castillians then, but 6 being excepted to be delivered to mercy, they refused to treat any further, since which time we threw some papers tied to stones over their walls, to put all the unexcepted persons upon a way to redeem themselves by delivering up the castle and the 6 prisoners within 14 days. This paper coming to the Governor's ear, he sent out two gentlemen, viz.: Colo. Roger Portington, and Capt. Thomas Paulden, to the General about it, and after the delivery of their message, and some discourse, they agreed to treat again this day. They pretend honour and conscience will not let them deliver up any: it will be murder, they say, in them, and the first precedent of that kind in England; but I believe the thought of self-preservation will make them deny their honour, forget their conscience, and put them upon some way of satisfying us and accepting of reasonable terms. What the issue will be, God knows; but I think the business will be done, though indeed they are able, if resolute, to hold out a great while still. I pray you present my humble service to Col. Lilburne and Col. Rokeby, and acquaint them with this case of the castle.

Sr.,
Your affec Friend to serve you,
THOS MARGETTS.

This is the only mention of Colonel Portington, who had been in the Castle during the whole of the siege. As became his rank, Col. Bright gave him precedence. On the previous occasion six men went to treat " of whom I was one," says Capt. Paulden; at this time, there were only two, as witnesseth Colonel Bright. Though, indeed, it might have been that only two took part in the negotiations, the other four being in Colonel Bright's eyes, as it were witnesses. In which case, we must assign the most active part of the negotiation as recorded by Capt. Paulden, to have been taken by Colonel Portington. Similarly on the side of the besiegers, the names have been preserved of only Col. Bright and Lieut-Col. Crooke.

The diary-like statements of these letters thus correspond exactly with the account written by Capt. Thos. Paulden himself above fifty years afterwards. Mr. Margett's prognostication was, however, falsified. The "thought of self-preservation" did not "make them deny their honour." And the shame remains on the Cromwellians that this "first precedent of that kind in England" should have been proposed by them.

COLONEL BRIGHT TO CAPT. ADAM BAYNES.

GOOD CAPTAIN,—I have received yours by this post, and do really approve

of those deductions for those uses, and conceive therein you have been as good a husband for us as we should have been for ourselves. I have sent the Bill of Exchange this day to York to get it accepted. Collo. Maulyverer is fully acquainted with what you writ concerning his business. It's hoped this castle will not hold out: some papers were thrown in which have begot some divisions amongst them. This day we are to meet and resolve to insist upon six persons to be delivered up to justice. Both our Mortar pieces have played this week; little execution to any within the castle, saving the ruining of some Rooms, by which means firing is more plentiful among them than usual; in truth, so extreme strong is the castle timber, that if our granadoes break through one story it goes no further. This is all the news that these barren parts affords. Many thanks for your care in the managing of our affairs. I rest,
Y' faithful friend to serve you,
J. BRIGHT.
Pontefract, 10 March, 1648.

What Mr. Margetts calls "delivering to Mercy", Col. Bright more truthfully calls "delivering to Justice": but perhaps the estimate in which the Garrison held the contemplated act was the more completely accurate. They considered it would be "MURDER." Slightly to paraphrase an expression in Col. Morris's letter offering surrender, what the Besiegers were not ashamed to ask, the Besieged were ashamed to grant.

———

"Both our Mortar pieces have played this week"; *i.e.* they arrived about January 10, the first was at work in about three weeks, but the second required very nearly three times as long.

———

The next week Capt. Baynes had letters from two only of his correspondents, who however, have important news to communicate, for the end was coming fast.

CORNET JOHN BAYNES TO CAPTAIN ADAM BAYNES.
COUSIN,—This is the last day of treaty with this enemy. Yesterday they concluded upon a surrender upon Monday next, but could not well agree about delivering the six excepted persons to mercy. The Castillians propound to leave the said six in the Castle, and our Commissioners plead to have them delivered into our hands; for if they be left in the Castle they may, before we can be possessed of them, do us more harm than we can imagine. They are not yet nominated to their Commissioners, but it is concluded that, after the Sealing of the Articles, they shall know them by names. How they will this day agree I know not; but our Commissioners are resolved to keep close to what we have propounded, and not to yield to their Terms. Morris is one of the excepted. . . . . . . Next week I shall be at York, whither you may please to direct your next. I rest, Your assured Lo. Cousin,
JO. BAYNES.
Pontefract, March 17th, 1648.

This day the Ma. Gen. meets the Scotts Commissioners, and invites them to dinner.

And now at length it has become known that Morris himself is one of the excepted, of which Mr. Margetts did not seem to be informed.

The following is the second letter:—

THOMAS MARGETTS TO CAPTAIN ADAM BAYNES.

Sr,—I received yours by Colonel Lilburne's man, and also yours by the last post. Yours to the Council we read, and considered and appointed Lt. Col. Carter and Ma. Smithson to return our present to you thereupon. Those you mentioned to the Major Generall which should have been imparted to the Council never were; for I spake to the Ma. General of it last night, and he tells me that he remembers not that he ever received any such thing; but I perceive you mistook in your direction, for you directed the Ma. General's letter to Colonel Bright, and his to the Ma. General; so that it never came to light (as I conceive little of that nature will through those hands). I cleared you on the point of carelessness in your agitation before the officers, and in it they were satisfied. We are just now going to treat with the Castillians, and this day (I think) we shall either agree or break off the Treaty. Therefore I can add no more, but the great sense I have of those many bonds of engagement you are pleased to lay upon him who is,
Sr,
Yor most affectionately to serve you,
THOS. MARGETTS.

Pont., 17 Mar., 1648.

Although Colonel Bright was even at the head of the Commission to treat with the Garrison, he seems not to have had the cordial confidence of Mr. Margetts. And perhaps he deserved that it should be withheld; for, like the Lord General himself, he was evidently engaged upon a work of which he liked neither the means nor the end; and yet he knew not how to disentangle himself from the engagements into which he had entered. As many another "Reformer" has done, he found himself carried on involuntarily to a Revolution from which his best feelings shrank in horror. But this expression of Mr. Margetts clearly shows that there was nothing of the hypocrite about Col. Bright: his sentiments were well known to his companions.

The surrender being thus practically determined upon, we may thus arrange in order the steps in the negotiation:—

MARCH 3.—This day "one of the Castillians" brought an overture.—J. BRIGHT.

MARCH 3.—We enter into a treaty.—THOS. MARGETTS.

MARCH 9.—They are this day to parley, but must surrender six to mercy.—ROBT. BAYNES.

MARCH 10.—This day, the Commissioners do treat about a surrender.—Jo. BAYNES.

MARCH 10. —The treaty of the 3rd failed, because six were excepted to be delivered to mercy. But we afterwards threw some paper tied to stones over the walls, in consequence of which Col. Portington and Capt. Paulden renewed the negotiations, and are to treat again this day.—THOMAS MARGETTS.

MARCH 10.—This day we are to meet.—Jo. BRIGHT.

When we met we told them that we came to capitulate, but could not deliver ourselves up to execution.—CAPT. PAULDEN.

MARCH 17.—Yesterday, they concluded upon a surrender, on Monday next; the six are not yet nominated, but they will be nominated when the articles are signed, and Morris is one.—Jo. BAYNES.

MARCH 17.—This day we shall either agree or break off.— THOMAS MARGETTS.

At this point the correspondence with Capt. Baynes ceases to guide us; and for the occurrences of the next few days we must use Paulden's letter. It will be seen that there is a slight discrepancy between the accounts given by Margetts, the civilian, and by Cornet Baynes. The former says "This day (March 17) we shall agree, or break off": the latter that "yesterday" that is on March 16, "they concluded upon a surrender on Monday next. The six not yet (March 17) nominated, but Morris is one". But whichever of these was correct, Clarendon (see pp. 172, 173), was wrong in many of his details. No reprieve of "six days" could have been allowed, afterwards voluntarily shortened by the garrison to five; for only three days intervened between the close of the negotiations, and the actual date of the rendition, fixed in the Articles. Again, Clarendon makes two of the excepted to escape on the second day, two on the fourth, and two to remain cooped up, while he says nothing of the death of Smyth. As Paulden tells us, three remained in the Castle at its surrender, who all escaped on the night next after the Parliamentarian forces had taken possession.

It is at least singular that the "authorities" give different dates for both the surprisal and surrender of Pontefract Castle. The surprisal is as often said to have taken place on the 6th of June, as on the 3rd—the Market-day—which we know to be the correct date; while the date of the surrender is stated with even greater variation.

We have seen that the letters of the correspondents of Capt. Adam Baynes all declare that the agreement and articles fixed "Monday next" as the day of surrender—which would be March 19; Dugdale, however, states that the surrender took place on the 21st, while the 1747 edition of Capt. Paulden's letter, while claiming that "The Chronology of Sir G. Wharton which is now added, will be of Use to the Curious in settling the Dates," increases the confusion by fixing that particular date as March 22nd. Clarendon's account fairly collated would also give the 22nd, and perhaps Sir G. Wharton deduced his date from Clarendon; but Boothroyd, who is never accurate if there is any possibility of making a mistake, and who sometimes seems to go out of the way to create confusion, says that "The next morning" (that is, after the death of Smyth) "March 24th, 1648-9, the Garrison pretended to rejoice, and sent the Governor word that as their six friends had made their escape, they would surrender next day. At the hour appointed, the

Garrison marched out of the Castle." As, however, the next day was Easter Sunday, March 25, that particular Sunday indeed when "the Lord sat in the Lady's lap," the surrender on that day as a preconcerted arrangement is improbable on the face of the narrative. Had surrender been so near, it would have been postponed till the Monday.

Among these very various statements we believe that Boothroyd had the truth, but that in an effort to be precise, he interpolated a date in the wrong place. For we conclude on all the evidence that March 24th was the date of the actual surrender. It may be noticed that Major-General Lambert in his letter of March 22nd, says only that he has "agreed to the Rendicon"; while the Aldermen of Pontefract, whose petition was sent up that day "per Mr. Margetts," also speak of "the Rendicon" as something yet to be completed. Moreover, it will not escape notice that the correspondence of March 24th, narrates the break-up and scattering of the besieging forces, which would not have taken place before the actual surrender.

We therefore incline to accept the 24th as the correct date, and to assert that the morning of Saturday, 24th March, Easter Eve, the last day of the old year, witnessed the final surrender of the fortress.

The following are the dates of the concluding stages of the capitulation, as gathered from Paulden:

MARCH 17 (Saturday).—They went out and concluded; and having signed the articles, learned the names of the six excepted.—CAPT. PAULDEN.

MARCH 18 (Sunday).—Morris and Blackburn escaped; Smyth killed.—CAPT. PAULDEN.

MARCH 24.—Castle surrendered.

MARCH 25.—Austwick, Ashby and Floyd escaped.—CAPT. PAULDEN.

END OF MARCH, OR BEGINNING OF APRIL.—Morris and Blackburn taken, too late for the Lent Assize.

It is remarkable that none of the historians mention the circumstance, and we learn it only from the depositions after Morris and Blackburn were in custody on a charge of high treason, that Morris's servant Peter or Peters, one of the first to enter the Castle with him when it was surprised, escaped with him; but thenceforward he disappears. Nothing else seems to be known of Peters.—Dugdale in his Visitation Pedigree had said that two servants of Morris escaped with him, but as he also said that two other excepted persons escaped, while it was known that only Blackburn got through with Morris, the statement attracted no notice.

The siege being over, those who had hitherto been Capt. Baynes's correspondents at Pontefract were scattered with their troops, other actors coming upon the scene. Where they went to may be gathered from the next letter, from Col. Lilburne, the regicide, who was one of the signatories of the King's Death Warrant. The proceedings against him in October, 1660, on the charge, may be seen in the State Trials Vol. I.

It is as well to notice that he and Lambert conclude their letters with a phrase not yet entirely out of use among the uneducated, "This is all at present" : " No more for the present." In the nineteenth century the stereotyped phrase of a class, this appears here as the stereotyped phrase of men of position, even of Major General Lambert, the third in the Kingdom, the future Lord Lambert, M.P. for Pontefract, and a candidate for the Protectorship after the death of Oliver.

COLONEL ROBERT LILBURNE TO CAPT. ADAM BAYNES.

SR,—I give you very kind thanks for your letter by this post, and your readiness to accommodate those gentlemen (my friends) with that money ; but I have one suite more unto you (which I hope Mr. Beale nor Mr Goldsmith will think much at), and that is to desire you to pay unto Mr. Jacob Towley, at the Golden Leg, Cheapside, London, one hundred pounds for my use and to charge it upon me here, for I am shortly to return, and know not how to be supplied with money unless you help me to this return ; which I hope, if possible, you will do it for me, and let me receive two words from you by the next. Mr. Margetts being come up with the news of surrender of this castle will (I know) acquaint you more

fully with particulars than I can write, that I shall not need to trouble you with repetitions, nor would I willingly be the relater of the bad success your horse had at Clifford Moor. The chief news is now that the grand jury at York, the judge, and committee, and all most all this county, are about petitioning to get this castle pulled down. Our forces are sent several ways to quarter ; viz. : Major Generall's, part to Lincolnshire, part to Darbyshire, and I think your troop is one that goes to the latter ; my regiment, part in Rutlandshire and part in Leicestershire, and my major about Newark ; Col. Rookeby, part in Darbyshire, three troops in Leicestershire, and two in Lancashire ; Col. Bright's regiment about Chesterfield and Rotherham, Col. Fairfax in the West Riding, Col. Mauleverar in Nottinghamshire, Col. Wastall's in the North Riding, and the loose companies in the East Riding, and one troop there, and one about Doncaster, and one in Cleveland. This is all at present from
     Your very assured friend and servant,
                Rob. LILBURNE.
Pontef., 24th Mar., 1648.
Capt. Baynes.

"Your troop is one that goes to the latter" implies that Capt. Baynes was in Lambert's division.

The part of Colonel Lilburne's letter mostly concerning us is his reference to the efforts that were being made for the demolition of the Castle. The Assize Jury at York—the Spring Assizes being then on—the Committee for the West Riding, the Aldermen of Pontefract, each sent up petitions, all having but one cry " Down with it." But the truth is that the Castle had long outlived the reason of its construction ; such a stronghold, while useless for good, was a continual source of evil. When General Overton was Governor, he had acted very tyrannically by sending for people whom he suspected, to come to the Castle, and then detaining them. Morris, as Governor, did the very same thing, as we shall shortly see ; and there was no reason to suppose but that the fortress would continue to be a cause of disquiet to the neighbourhood as long as it remained fortified. A Palace and residence for royalty, it had long ceased to be : and even before the Reformation, we read of royal visitors passing through it,—presumably along Castle Chain—and going to lodge at the Priory. Before it was re-fortified, it had been in the charge of a woman—a " She-Keeper"—

and after the second siege it afforded no suitable accommodation for the garrison, who were compelled to lodge in the town, holding themselves in readiness to come up to the Castle when required. The lodgings for the soldiers—which must have been erected under the shelter of the walls of the quadrangle, had long been destroyed ; and it contained no room in which a number of men could live, except the Main Guard. This, however, was not available for prisoners also, as we see from the action of Col. Morris in confining Col. Cotterill and some thirty others in the Magazine, and keeping them there for eleven weeks, in a horrid condition at the idea of which our every sense now revolts. To this we shall presently recur more fully.

The following is the petition of the Mayor and Aldermen, as entered in the Pontefract BOOKE of ENTRIES, the Contemporary Minute Book of the Pontefract Corporation. The date is not preserved, but it was evidently adopted and signed before the "Rendicon." It appears to have been taken up by Mr. Margetts, when he carried the news of the surrender —

To the supreame authority of England, the Co'mons assembled in Parliament.

The humble Peticon of the Major Aldermen, and all the well-affected Inhabitants of the Towne of Pontefract.

HUMBLY SHEWETH

THAT the Towne of Pontefract since the beginning of these unhappy warres hath beene greatly impoverished and depopulated through the setting and continueing a Garrison in that Castle w'ch hath occacioned two severall tedious and chargeable Leagures to the great effusion of much pretious blood, the utter ruinating of no lesse then 200 dwelling houses and upwards (whose confused heapes are lively and speaking Monuments of the Enemies cruelty and yo' Peticoners' misery) the incredible decay of tradeing and comerce, the unavoidable hinderance and interrupcon of Tillage, The totall undoing of many well-affected p'sons and families, the sadd devastacon of the place of publiq : worshipp amongst us. All w'ch damages sustenied by yo' poore Peticoners amounts unto the full value of 40000*li*. and upwards, yet hath God through his blessinge upon the unwearied paines of o'r forces there, once more opened a doore of hope for o' Recovery of that Garrison.

MAY it therefore please yo' Hono'rs seriously to consider the sadd desolacons of o' poore Towne, the past and p'sent pressures, yea unsupportable burthens of yo' poore Peticoners by meanes of the said Garrison, And to appointe the same (imediately upon the Rendicon) to be wholy razèd downe and demolished. And further to allott so much of the materialls of Lead and Timber towards the repaireing of o' place of publiq: worshipp and reedifijng of an habitacon for a Minister as shall amount unto 1000*li*. That so the true cause of o' former miseries and future feares being removed. Yo' Peticoners may both, be incouraged and inabled to serve yo' hono'rs in all yo' just and equitable comaunds w'th theire lives and fortunes

And yo' Peticoners shall daily pray &c.

SIGNED in the name and by the consent of the Aldermen and all the well affected in the Towne of Pontefract.

By me
EDWARDE FIELDE, Major.

This petition was accompanied by the following letter from the Major General, as copied into the same record with this heading :—

MAJOR GENERALL LAMBERT'S Letter to the Parliament concerning the Surrender of Pontefract Castle, relateing something further to the Peticon of the Towne of Pontefract:

Mr. SPEAKER,

After a long and heard winter Seige against the Castle of Pontefract, with great difficulties to the Soldjo's, and heavy burthens upon the poore Country, I have thought fitt to agree for the Rendicon of the said Castle upon the Articles and tearmes inclosed, and though they might seeme better for them than yow might expect by reason of theire long and wilfull keeping thereof against yow to the hazarding and incouraging of more troubles iu the Nation. Yet the continuall cries of the poore distressed Country together w'th theire owne condicon (being in a capacity of holding out at least two moneths longer) considered, I hope they will appeare so reasonable, as they shall receive yo' approbacon which I humbly begg. I shall not need to trouble yow with any more p'ticulers. I have sent this Gentl: Mr. Margetts, (who is acquainted w'th the whole proceedings) to attend yow w'th this account and what els further yow shall desire to be informed of concerninge this busines, I shall referr to his relacon.

I have likewise taken upon mee the boldnes to p'sent unto yow the humble desires of the Majo', Aldermen and well affected Inhabitants of the Towne of Pontefract, who earnestly pray for the demolisheing of that Castle, and though I shall not undertake to advize yow herein, yet I must be witnes with them that I conceive their Peticon conteines nothing but truth, and that this Castle hath beene occacon of ruine to diverse Families in that Towne, besides the great losse and p'judice to the Country adjacent who have suffered equally w'th them in all p'ticulers (except so absolute destruction of theire houses, and therefore I shall humbly offerr it as my opinion that yo' granting thereof will not onely bee a great satisfaction to the well affected of those p'ts, but wilbee of advantage to them in avoiding the like evills. But humbly Submitting to yo'r further co'maunds, I remaine, Sr

KNOTTINGLEY
MARCH, 22o, 1648.

Yo'r very humble and
faithfull servant
JOHN LAMBERT.

For the hon'ble William Lenthall, Esq.
Speaker in Parliament.

According to Whitlock, all these documents reached

London on March 24, his statement being under that date, " Letters received that Pontefract Castle was surrendered upon articles ; six persons were excepted, whereof three escaped, that the soldiers and officers were to go to their homes, first subscribing an engagement not to advise, act, or take up arms against the Parliament or Commonwealth of England ; and that they had two months' provisions and 40 barrels of powder in the Castle."

Here we may note, by the way, that the first news received with regard to the six excepted was that "three escaped," which implied that three were in the hands of General Lambert. We know such was not the case ; but it is well to note the statement.

The intelligence seems not to have been delivered to the House until March 27th (Tuesday), probably as soon as the news arrived that the surrender was a fact, and not an intention; and that the forces of the Commonwealth were actually in possession.

The following is from the Journals of the House :—

Die Martis, 27o Martii, 1649.

A letter from Major-General Lambert, from Knottingley of 22 March, 1648, was read.

Articles agreed upon for the rendition of Pontfract Castle were read.

RESOLVED by the Comons assembled in Parliament That this house doth approve the Articles made and agredd upon for the Rendicon of Pontefract Castle.

The humble Peticon of the Majo' Ald' and all the well affected Inhabitants of the Towne of Pontefract was this day read.

RESOLVED by the Comons assembled in Parliament That the Castle of Pontefract be forthwith totully demolished.

ORDERED by the Com'ons assembled in Parliament That it be referred to the Committee of the westridd' of the County of Yorke to take care that the said Castle of Pontefract be forthw'th totally demolished & levelled to the ground, And the materialls thereof to be p'served from being imbezelled, And by sale of so much of them as wilbee necessary to satisfy in the first place the charge of demolishing & levelling the same. And that so much of the remainder of the materialls as shallbee of the valewe of One thousand pounds be alotted to the Towne of Pontefract towards the repaireing theire place of publiq : worshipp and reedifijng an habitacon for a Minister.

A letter from the General, of 26 March, touching Major General Lambert was read.

ORDERED by the Com'ons of England, That £300 per annum, and of inheritance out of the demesnes of Pontefract, upon a true survey thereof at a full value as the same were in 1641, be settled upon Major-General Lambert and his heirs for ever, in respect of his many great and eminent services performed, with much care, courage, and fidelity by the said Major-General in the northern parts, as well against the Scots' army the last summer, as against the forces of Sir Marmaduke Langdale and others, and in reducing the Castle of Pontefract, being the last garrison in England held out against the Parliament; and in respect of his extraordinary charge therein, he not having been allowed any pay as Major-General.

ORDERED that £50 be given to Mr. Margetts who brought the news of the surrender.

ORDERED that this vote be sent with a letter of thanks and respect from the House to Major General Lambert, and likewise to the Yorkshire gentlemen that sent up these petitions, and that Mr Challoner prepare it.

It cannot be denied that these Resolutions and Orders are tolerably comprehensive. Shortly they are, (made, as we might say, at the first sitting of the House after the Easter holidays, this present Tuesday being Easter Tuesday),

(1). The articles of Surrender of Pontefract Castle (on Easter Eve) are approved.

(2.) The Castle is to be demolished.

And then in descending scale, a letter from the General (Fairfax, but not *Lord* General) having been read,

(3.) Major General Lambert is to have £300 a year, in land of inheritance—rather better for him than a "perpetual pension"; for if he could not sell the land, he could raise the rent.

(4.) £50 to be given to Mr. Margetts.

(5.) And a letter of thanks to the successful general, and the petitioners.

There is added the confession, on the records of the House of Commons, that the Castle of Pontefract was "the last Garrison in England which held out against the Parliament."

Three remarkable letters from Major General Lambert, (two to Capt. Adam Baynes, and one to the Cornet), reflect his feelings and state of mind. The first, in the full flush of the good news of the £300 a year, was by the earliest (Saturday) post, in these terms; (and we have to rely upon the version given in *Tait*, for the original has disappeared from the Baynes's MSS.) :—

MAJOR GENERAL LAMBERT TO CAPTAIN BAYNES.

SIR,—I am glad to hear that Pontefract Castle is to be demolished. I beseech you make it your business to expedite that work, and, if possible, procure the votes and orders to them that are to see it done to be sent down by the next post. I pray you advise with the Judge Advocate [Margetts] therein, and neglect no time to expedite it (as well you know) very much concerns the quiet of these parts. I have no more for the present, but remain

Your assured loving friend,

31st Mar., 1649. J. LAMBERT.

As we learn subsequently, there was a second letter of the same date to the Cornet, who acted as clerk to the committee, more especially concerning "business"; *i.e.* £300 a year in land of inheritance. But the "large letter" has not been preserved.

During the following week, while the formal preparations for the Demolition were being made, and while those formalities left the Major General with some spare time on his hand, having a shrewd sense of what was due to his own personal interest, he seems to have used his opportunity to make inquiries into the reality of the "land of inheritance" offered him, and to have found the result to promise the proverbial "Much Cry, but Little Wool." The ultimate outcome was his settlement at Badsworth; but this present letter to the Cornet, shows some of the reasons for that result :—

MAJOR GENERAL LAMBERT TO CORNET JOHN BAYNES.

SIR,—I write to you a large letter the last week concerning business; but not being rightly directed it was returned to me again this week, which I have here enclosed sent you, and give you thanks for your care and pains in my business. I have made enquiries into the Queen's Revenues about Pontefract, and find it to be a very distracted thing, there being very little demaine land; but so much as is I intend to get surveyed, and to bring the particulars thereof with me when I come up, which I intend to do very shortly. I also purpose to make inquiry of some other demaine lands belonging to the same revenue here in the north, that it may be, with convenience, the want of the other may be supplied.

[But of this] I desire you to advise with my friends above. And if you have so much time, to return me an answer by the next post : which is all at present from Yr assured friend,

April the 7th, 1649. J. LAMBERT.

The writer does not more particularly specify who were his " friends above," nor was the Cornet's answer preserved. That this communication itself should have been among Captain Baynes's correspondence, perhaps implies that the Cornet had passed it to his cousin, the Captain, who with his usual method endorsed it, and placed it with his other documents.

We close this part of the correspondence of the future M.P. for Pontefract, and candidate for the Protectorship, with the following of the same date. It shows that during the week's interval, the formal order for the Demolition of the Castle had arrived. And it leaves the actors standing around the doomed " Palace," as Morris afterwards called it, with weapons uplifted, as it were, ready to strike " upon Monday next."—" Which is all at present" from the Major General.

MAJOR GENERAL LAMBERT TO CAPTAIN BAYNES.

SIR,—I have received yours (for which I give you thanks,) and also the order for demolishing of Pontefract Castle, and have great assurance of the effectual and speedy demolishing thereof; all men declaring much freeness for the effecting thereof. Upon Monday next the workmen begin, and, first, they are to take down the great tower. Sir, I desire you to continue your intelligence: which is all at present from

Your assured friend to serve you,

April 7, 1649. J. LAMBERT.

With this, the letters from Pontefract concerning the siege cease, the scene closes, and the curtain falls. Might not the stage direction be, " Left scrambling"; for the whole throws a sinister light upon the meaning of Cromwell's hint to Colonel Hammond (see page 198), " I know not one Officer among us but is upon the increasing hand," by way of " Land of inheritance" for instance.

To the particulars of the Demolition, and the circumstances attending it, we shall come shortly. Meanwhile we take up the history of the escaped Governor, and his Cornet Michael Blackburn.

Of Michael Blackburn we seem to have had a first glance on May 23rd, 1645, (see page 77) when Michael Blagburne, Clothier, and tenant to Major Beaumont, came to the Castle with news. He was, as we shall see presently, an Almondbury man, which tallies well with this account of him.

Morris and Blackburn, accompanied by Peters (or was he a Peter), and possibly many others, broke through the lines of the besiegers on Sunday, March 18th, and made their way westward towards Royalist Lancashire, in the hope and expectation of being able to get to sea, as Langdale had already done. But their hope was disappointed, and their expectation failed, since they retained the liberty for which they had fought so hard, (and which they understood to be guaranteed to them by the fact of their success in their sortie) for less than three weeks, Whitelock entering their capture as taking place on April 4th.

After their apprehension, they were sent to the county gaol of Lancaster, till counsel was had as to what should be done with them; but ultimately when the Summer assizes were drawing near they were brought to York, and there kept in safe hold, with what surrounding conditions, Morris himself shall tell us in due course.

The Baynes letters contain no hint of the news of their capture; so that probably the intelligence had not reached the writer when the letters ceased. But in view of their expected apprehension, how the destruction of the prisoners was to be compassed let the next tell. It is from Mr. Margetts, now Judge Advocate General, and is one of the last of the Baynes correspondence.

Having returned to Pontefract, from thence he forwarded the following :—

THOMAS MARGETTS TO CAPTAIN ADAM BAYNES.

SR,—Since my last, dated on Saturday, at York, I understand by Colonel

Rokeby that the 99li. 11s. [a misreading of the original ; the last 1 should be 5] charged for me upon Norfolk is an overcharge, as well as another sum charged for him, and the Marshalls of the North with the Norfolk Committee either have or are about to make appear to the committee for the army, so that that money is not likely to be received there but to be charged somewhere [else]. You may please to remember that 99li. 11s [15s] is part of the money 1 received from Coll. Rokeby at Bedford, and which he is to receive again ; therefore I earnestly desire that upon the discharge mine may be charged with his.   *   *   *

    I pray remember the business of Lieutenant Wrench, and get a Commission for his Trial either here or by Council of War, that he may have justice and his enemies may not be his judges. Understanding since my coming hither that a Commission was sent to Ma Genl Lambert at his last going to London for the trying of Morris [Marris], I desire you will please to move the Ma. General to authorise and appoint some fit persons here to meet and consult about the preparing of a charge and examination of witnesses in order to his Trial, against his running [coming] down, and to give order for his sending for, to that purpose if he so think fit. And if so, 1 humbly offer that Major Cotterell may be one.

    Desiring you to present my most humble services to the Major-General,
. I remain, Sr,
Your most affectionate friend to serve you,

Pontct, 19 July [Junij] 1649.   THOS. MARGETTS.

" That his enemies may not be his judges," in the case of Wrench ; " That Major Cotterell may be one" in the case of Morris. To save Wrench ; to destroy Morris.

The result was that some sort of Order was procured by virtue of which a magisterial hearing took place in the Pontefract Town Hall on Monday, July 30, the Court probably sitting in Petty Sessions, or perhaps the ordinary Petty Sessional business being over, when with no prisoner present, a series of depositions were taken and forwarded to York, where they may still be seen. To put it in the usual familiar form, we may " report it" as :—

    Monday, July 30, 1649. Before Edward Feild, Mayor, Mr Ald. John Scurr, Mr Ald. Mathew Franck, and Mr. Ald. John Cowper, justices of the Peace.

These four acting Justices were four of the five who had been elected by the fraction of the Corporation, who acted after the siege under Governor Lowther : the fifth was John Ramsden. Skurr was the senior, and had been mayor in 1646-7. Frank and Cowper followed Feild in the Mayoralty.

But before we enter upon the depositions now taken before the Pontefract Bench, with regard to the seizure of the Castle, it may be as well to give those parts of Fox's narrative which he has intermingled with Boothroyd's. The latter was almost entirely from Clarendon, but with a few words interpolated—by way of explanation or elucidation—here and there, and with a remarkable fatality, generally incorrectly, as we have seen. Fox must, however, have had some addititional means of information, which, unfortunately he fails to specify, and this is especially to be regretted, as there is internal evidence that where there is a variation in the two accounts of this particular transaction, Fox is correct. Throughout his additions there is an intensely local colouring, and where we have been enabled to compare it with original documents, we have found his details generally supported. But bearing in view the intention of these volumes that they should be Collections towards a history rather than a history itself, while we gave Clarendon's and Paulden's accounts when dealing with the history of the siege, we have reserved Fox's for contrast with these depositions as an account of the seizure.

The following are the passages that in this connection deserve extract. The particulars he gives with regard to the projected attempt in September, 1646, to which we have already referred (see pp. 147, 148) will be found in the Appendix. (See Appendix E.)

These additions in Fox's account, are over and above what is to be found in Boothroyd:—

At length the appointed time for the execution of this adventurous exploit drew near. Morrice prepared a scaling ladder at his own house, in the month of April, 1648, and had it secretly conveyed to Mr. Austwick's Lathe. It was constructed broad enough for two men to mount abreast. Eight soldiers being won over to assist him, a night was fixed, and the corporal and a centinel was to be upon the guard according to his premise, at the place intended to be scaled. He, however, was intoxicated at the time, and another guard, ignorant of the attempt, supplied his place. The party amounting to 300 infantry and 50 horse arrived, and Morrice when he had effected the securing of the ladder, mounted with a soldier, and began to scale the walls, when the sentinel gave the alarm and fired upon them. The colonel encouraged them to carry the design into execution, but the Pauldens and others refusing, and the soldiers appearing on the ramparts, they fled from the place precipitately, leaving the ladder in the ditch, and though fired upon by the garrison they lost not a single man. The troops dispersed into the country; and half of the horse marched to sir Marmaduke Langdale, who had then taken Berwick and Carlisle. Morrice and the rest betook themselves to the woods, sending out scouts to gather intelligence of the attack. Having brought them information that though the design was at present frustrated, yet no suspicion rested on Morrice or his associates, they returned home to concert other measures, so determined were they on the reduction of the fortress. Morrice on being told by his wife that Cotterel did not in the least suspect him of being accessary to this assault, boldly and with much confidence repaired to the castle, and requested Cotterel to give him a sight of the ladder; and on beholding it he expressed his surprise in such a way, and conducted himself with so much dissimulation that the governor was certain he could have had no concern in it.

As an incidental illustration of the probable accuracy of this narrative, we find as a positive fact that Mr. Austwick had such a Lathe near the Castle, for in the Fee Farm Book of 1650, we find his heirs possessed of 11 acres in the Chequers " called the willowe tree flatt." The piece is now generally called Willow Park. The whole account, which is very circumstantial and picturesque, bears critical examination, and while we cannot doubt its accuracy, we feel great regret that we cannot prove its authenticity. The scaling party consisted of, in round numbers, 50 horse and 300 infantry; and on the failure of the enterprise, half the horse is said to have marched to Sir Marmaduke Langdale in the north. This quite tallies with what we know : Capt. Timothy Paulden, who was in this party, was killed shortly afterwards at Preston ; Capt. William Paulden remained, and had a share in the honour of the successful exploit; while Capt. Thomas Paulden, with his party of twenty-two horse was in the neighbourhood when the Castle was surprised, and entered almost immediately after Morris took it.

It may moreover be remarked that the Austwick family parted with all their possessions in Pontefract during the Protectorate, and as the knowledge that this lathe ever belonged to them would have soon faded out of living memory, we incline to the belief that these interpolated additions are taken from some contemporary document, or documents written by a contemporary, which are not now in existence.

There is also one circumstance in which this account differs from that of Clarendon, adopted by Boothroyd. Clarendon says (see p. 170) that Morris was in bed with the Governor at the time the attempt was made to scale : this second account, that he led the scaling party, and on the failure of the attempt, escaped " to the woods." All the details favour the present as being the correct version, and we shall see that such was the account given by Col. Cotterel himself.

How the tale came to be set on foot that Morris was in bed with Cotterel at the time of the attempt, there is no evidence to show. It was possibly only a reflection of the statement (p. 260) that he had slept at Knottingley with Col. Thomas Fairfax and Col. Forbes, three in a bed.

The following is the account of the seizure, of the constitution of a Council of War, and of other matters of interest, with regard to the doings of the daring band, and of their organization at the time, and after, the seizure. Very few of the names are those of Pontefract people :—

On the day fixed, Morrice and captain William Paulden, disguised like country gentlemen with swords by their sides, came with the beds, attended by nine others dressed like plain country men and constables to guard the beds, &c. When they reached the castle, which was about six o'clock in the morning, they enquired of the centinel for Major Morrice who had promised to meet them there. The sergeant on guard being one of the soldiers won by Morrice to his plan, immediately went to the governor, who had a short time before retired to his chamber, and informed (*him*) of the arrival of the constables, and that major Morrice would be here in the course of half an hour. Cotterel bid him take the keys and let in the constables ; and when the major came, to bring him into his chamber, and having thus spoke, he composed himself to sleep, accoutred as he was with his sword by his side.

When they had gained entrance into the main guard, the beds were thrown down and a crown piece was given to the soldiers on duty there, to fetch ale. As soon as they had departed, Morrice and his associates drew up the drawbridge, unsheathed their swords, and after informing them that they had a commission from the king to secure the castle, he thus spoke to his men, of the guard, pointing singly to each, ' you and youre are for me and his own.' *(sic.)* The captain perceiving eight of his men to be for Morrice, and being inferior in strength began to be afraid, when Morrice promised fair quarters to those who offered no resistance. They then tamely submitted to him, and he cast them into a dungeon close by, thirty steps in depth, capable of containing between two and three hundred men.

Meanwhile the rest were buried in sleep, little aware of the stratagem and its contents (? *success*) when captain Wm. Paulden and two others, guided by a confederate, proceeded to the apartments of Cotterel. Awakened by the noise on the staircase, he started up and drew his sword ; and on captain Paulden entering, and telling him he was his prisoner, he without speaking made a thrust at the captain, and defended himself bravely, until wounded in the head and arm he began to be faint. He made another desperate push at the captain, and his tuck coming in contact with the bed post it broke in two. He then begged for quarter which was readily granted him. Paulden having taken him prisoner, was conducting him downstairs, when Morrice met them. He told Cotterel to fear nothing, and comforted him with the assurance ' of good usage, and that he would procure pardon from the king for his rebellion.' He was then cast with as many more as they could find into the dungeon amongst the rest. In the castle was found a great quantity of salt and malt, 4000 stand of arms, a good store of ammunition, some cannon and two mortar pieces. Morrice then ordered his chaplain, Mr. Chas. Davison, to commence prayers and render thanks to God for their success, and notice was sent to captain Thomas Paulden then in the wood close by. This assault was effected on the 3d June, 1648, at half-past eight o'clock in the morning. Morrice gave the plunder of the money to the eight soldiers as he had promised, and kept the castle gates shut and the portcullis down until Saturday (read *Tuesday*) the 6th June ; when he gave public notice to all assembled, ' that he had secured the castle for the service of his majesty, and by virtue of his commission declared, no townsman should be molested if they remained at home.'

The basis of these three paragraphs is Paulden's letter, which may be found *Ante*, (page 150); but many little details are interwoven, which come from some independent source that we have hitherto failed to trace. It is remarkable that the dungeon *thirty* steps in depth, figures in these narratives persistently, although in the depositions to which we shall come presently, it is, correctly, said to be forty-two steps down.

If we could be sure that the words "his chaplain" were not an unauthorised interpolation, it would be interesting; but both Boothroyd and Fox so habitually add phrases which they intend to be explanatory, but which only import error, that every word of their narrative has to be weighed and examined before it is received. We have met with nothing else to show that Mr. Charles Davison was Morris's chaplain. Later on, he is said to have officiated as town's minister in place of Mr. Ferrett; and elsewhere, that he was one of those who was concerned in the attempt with the scaling ladders.

The whole of the last three sentences is an addition to Paulden, but they contain what must be a mistake, which we have corrected : Tuesday is miscalled Saturday.

The same mistake is continued in the next paragraph, for Capt. Paulden himself (see page 150) says he came "immediately, and it being Market-day, we furnished ourselves with all manner of provisions from the Town."

The subsequent paragraphs contain a great deal to be found nowhere else, though they open, as we have said, with a mistake in the date,—a confusion between Saturday the 3rd and Tuesday the 6th.

On the 6th of June, captain Thomas Paulden arrived at the castle with thirty horse. On their march towards the castle they were joined by various parties, so that when they had entered, the garrison consisted of 500 men.

Morrice furnished the garrison on this Saturday [probably should be *the* Saturday,—that is the day of the seizure] with all manner of provisions from the town, paying for some from his private purse, and promising payment for some which according to his abilities he performed, to the gentlemen who assisted him in the surprisal of the castle. He gave £60 to Mr. Glatberts. [No such name occurs on the Church Registers; nor is it met with in the subsequent names of officers.]

As soon as the parliamentarians learnt of Morrice's conduct, they plundered his house and took away goods and stock amounting to more than £1000, as well as £1800 in bonds and bills.

His house was at East Hague, South Kirkby; and as we shall see, when he came to Pontefract, he came on horseback, putting up his horse at Mr. Ald. John Tatham's.

When Morrice had secured the castle, it was not stocked with provisions sufficient for one month, but he plied diligently and gathered a great deal; and when it was publicly known that the castle was in his hands, a great number of noblemen flocked to him to aid him against the parliament.

The soldiers unanimously elected Morrice as their governor, yet being aware that there were gentlemen of rank and distinction in the castle, who might look upon him with a jealous eye, he refused it; at the same time presenting sir John Digby to their notice; but he deeming himself unequal to the undertaking, submitted himself to be made their *nominal* governor, whilst Morrice was considered as the *real* governor, and this was negatived to by none.

There is no suggestion on the depositions that this was the case: all concur to give the leadership, both nominal and real, to Morris.

Morrice on the 16th June, granted a safe escort, to Mr. Tennet, (read *Ferrett*) the minister, to depart from the town, and Mr. Charles Davison officiated in his place. On the 17th he constituted a council of war, and orders were made for the better government of the garrison. The council consisted of

Sir Philip Monckton,   Major general Byson, (? *Byron*)
Col. Anthony Gibby,   Colonel Roger Portington,
Lieut. col. Michael Stanhope,   Lieut. col. Emanuel Gibby,
Colonel James Washington,   Captain Wm. Paulden.
Colonel John Morrice, Governor and President.

This council of war, being nominated by the governor, and by him, and us whose names are hereunto subscribed, it is unanimously approved. We do hereby oblige ourselves to obey all orders,—that every gentleman and officer, upon leave desired, shall have liberty for his or their advantage, to serve in this or any other of his majesty's garrisons.

Signed,
Robert Portington,   John Cooper,
Thomas Crathorn,   Leonard Reresby,
Raphael Ashton, (? *Relph*)   Edward Webb,
Wat Saltonstall, or Norbington,   Jo. Battley,
John Benson,   Alan Austwick,
Robert Heron,   William Palmer,
Henry Dunbar,   William Bamford,
William Slater,   Jo. Horsfall,
Edward Skepper,   Tim. Paulden,
Francis Reresby,   George Bonevant,
Edward Monckton, (? *Edmond*)   William Wentworth,
Thomas Man,   Nicholas Manris,
Otho Wosewkeille,   John Corker,
Thomas Webb,   Gervace Nevil,
Cecil Cooper,   Jo. Grymsdyth, (? *Grimsditch*)

On the other side were written
Geo. Metham,   Josh Constable,
Mar. Colmundley,   Fras Aiswright,
Robt Riddell,

Few of these names occur elsewhere. Col. James Washington was a Pontefract man, a branch of the family at Adwick, from which the American General was descended. Alan Austwick was a son of the owner of the lathe in which the scaling ladder had been concealed: George Bonevant was the former governor of Sandal, at first credited by the Parliamentarians with the seizure;

Nicholas Manris is probably intended for Nicholas Morris, a younger brother of the governor; Grymsdyth was probably Grimsditch, at that time of Knottingley, or Cridling Park, but of Hertfordshire extraction, and there are besides some other few Yorkshire county names, but the great majority are those of strangers.

The appearance among the members of this council, of several, afterwards taken prisoners on July 5th, at Willoughby Field (see page 179)—shows that the narrative belongs to an early part of the siege; between its date and July 20th, such important events had taken place, and such changes had been made, that to call it "this council" is hardly justifiable.

This council agreed on the following articles of war; dated July 20th, 1648:—

First:—It is ordered and agreed upon—That after the arming of the governor, colonel John Morrice, and his regiment of foot; colonel Vernon shall have the supernumerary fixtures for the arming of his regiment, for the use of this garrison, and to re-deliver them fixt again, to the governor, when he shall demand the same.

Secondly:—That major Edward Gower, command as major of all the horse belonging to the garrison, and have authority from them for that purpose.

Thirdly:—That captain William Gower command as major of the foot quartered in the town of Pontefract.

Fourthly:—That no constables or other persons brought into the garrison for want of their assessment, shall be detained upon any pretence whatsoever, having given satisfaction to the treasurer for their assessment, without especial order from them.

Fifthly:—That if any be brought in, or monies brought in for the use of the garrison, he or they shall give notice to the governor or treasurer within four hours.

Sixthly:—That sir Hugh Cartroll muster most of all the foot.

Seventhly:—That colonel Roger Portington, and colonel James Washington, be assistants to the new treasurers, sir Hugh Cartroll and Mr. Nevil.

Eighthly:—That if any officer, gentleman, or soldier be negligent upon any duty, commanded him by his superiors, or go from his guard without order, or any ways be disobedient to him, in the lawful martial commands, he shall forfeit a day's pay, and be disarmed at the head of the troops, or company wherein he serves, and shall be imprisoned twenty-four hours, and the day's pay be disposed of to his fellow-soldiers.

Signed,

John Morrice,
V. Cromwell,
Richard Dyson,
Edward Gower,
Roger Portington,
Urian Legh,

Wm. Gower,
Radclif Buckerfield,
Gervace Reresby,
Edward Jones,
C. Congreve.

It is remarkable again that neither of these names, except those of John Morris and Roger Portington, corresponds with either of those in the former list, while they resemble them in being mostly those of strangers to the locality. The Sir Hugh Cartroll (!), however, who figures here, appears subsequently, (see page 246), as Sir Hugh Cartrit. It might be thought that he was one of the Carterets of Jersey, but that Clarendon (who, as Mr. Hyde, knew the Carterets well, and would not have mispelled their name,) calls him Sir Hugh Cartwright (see *Ante* page 170.) It is not unlikely that he was the Capt. Cartwright who was in the second siege, (see page 105,) as adjutant to the Governor, Sir Richard Lowther, (see page 21.)

The following is another insertion in the old narrative :—

On the 26th of August, the governor of our castle agreed with the mayor and aldermen of the town about the corn, "that the castle should have a seventh part, and the townsmen to bring it near to the castle," and the governor imposed upon the town to quarter 1000 men, or pay for each four-pence per day. He was compelled to levy this heavy charge; for although the horse had been sent away on the 3rd July with sir Philip Monckton and other commanders into Lincolnshire, where they were routed by the forces of col. Rossiter, and had sustained a great loss; yet, such great numbers flocked to him, that he could not provide for them so well as he could when the horse attended him, as they assisted him greatly in procuring provisions and gathering contributions.

It were to be wished that the opening sentence of this paragraph had been less obscure. "About the corn" is very indefinite. It might have been the corn now just harvested, or it might have been that which was brought to market, this 26th August, being Saturday the market day. But there is no evidence for either supposition, and there is no other reference whatever to "*the* corn."

The next insertion is as follows :—

Disturbances had also burst forth in the garrison, a duel between Mr. Byford and Mr. Bunckley had taken place, and a misdemeanor had been committed, therefore Morrice deemed it prudent to call a council of war to quell all strifes, and enact other orders; a council then assembled on the 7th October, which was composed of the following gentlemen:—

Major John Morrice, Governor, President,

Sir John Digby,
Sir Hugh Cartrit (? *Cartwright*.)
Col. Washington,
William Paulden,
William Saltonstall,
Mr. Reresby,

Mr. Redhead,
Capt. Benson,
Capt. Thos. Paulden,
Capt. Ashby,
Capt. Marritt,
Capt. Palmer.

It was ordered upon the debate of the duel, that Mr. Bunckley continue in the marshall's custody, and lieut. col. Ashton be confined to his chamber for acting as one of the seconds.

That Mr. Taylor for a misdemeanor depart the garrison.

That no gentleman, officer, or soldier fight any duel; and whoever is challenged, to forbear to fight, and make the governor acquainted with the same, resigning himself to him, or appealing to the board for satisfaction, upon pain of death.

In the afternoon another council of the same persons was held, when it was ordered—

That every officer, gentlemen, and soldier of the garrison take an oath for the defence of the same.

On the 9th of October, the parliamentarian troops entered the town.

This concludes the additions made by Fox to Boothroyd's narrative; and now we can consider the depositions of the various witnesses at the magisterial examination.

The first witness,

William Foster, of Pontefract, saith, that he knoweth John Morrice; and that the said Morrice, immediately after surprizall of the castle, tooke upon him to be governor and commander in cheife of the said castle; and that, within one weeke after the castle was taken, the said Morrice sent muskettiers to take this informant, and carried him downe and imprisoned him in the dungeon six weeks. In which time the said Morrice, in this informant's presence and heareing, said that if he had 1,000*l*. in gold he could not tell itt, he was soe overjoyed, for he had now brought the worke to passe that he had beene about two yeares, meaneing takeing of the castle. He further sayth that diverse of the lord generall's forces and souldiers being taken att Ollerton, and brought prisoners into the castle, and one of them being stripped and to be putt into the dungeon, the said souldier being unwilling to goe into the dungeon, the said Morrice did sticke the said souldier in the backe, and said that he must goe in, and if the Parliament were there themselves they should have no better place nor usage. The said Morrice did make out commissions and appointed officers and souldiers under him; and he saw a draught of a commission wherein one Ashby was made a captaine under Morrice, and it did mencion that the said Morrice derived his power from the Prince. He hath heard him say to the men that assisted him, and were att takeing and surprizeing of the said castle, that every one of them should have and weare a gold chaine that they might be knowne from others, for that their noble and gallant act of takeing the castle.

Now, on the face of it, the very opening statement of this witness was in any case not legal evidence, and probably not a correct statement of facts. He says that

Morris " immediately after the surprisal of the Castle took upon him to be governor and Commander-in-chief of the said Castle." How could he have known anything about it, except by hearsay, and hearsay is not evidence, when he was in the town, and not " taken to the Castle" for " within one week" ? When he comes to what had happened in his own sight and hearing, we can depend upon him, but he evidently *knew* nothing of what happened during those first few days, when " the portcullis was up," and all communication with the outside utterly cut off.

William Foster appears to have been a Pontefract man, but we do not trace him, either in the Fee Farm Book of 1650, or the Church Registers, unless he were the William Foster, blacksmith, who, on 7 June, 1654, was " solemnely marryed" to Elizabeth Loryman, widow. In that case, he was a son of Bryan Foster, also a blacksmith, of Pontefract. In the Rate Book of 1657, he was assessed at 4d. The name was common, it was frequently spelt Fostard, and there was at the time a Richard Fostard, living in his own house in Northgate.

The Ashby referred to by this deponent was evidently Major Ashby, one of the excepted, who was walled up in Piper Tower at the surrender. A subsequent witness gives his Christian name as Alexander.

The second witness,

Richard Lile, of Pontefract, grocer, saith, that he heard Morrice saie that, the Wednesdaie before the castle was surprized, being the fast daie, the said Morrice was in a chamber in the house of Mr. John Tatham in Pontefract, and intended to have surprized the castle that night, but that a regiment of the lord generall's foot being to quarter in the towne that night caused him to deferre it.

This second witness Richard Lile, grocer and mercer, who deposed to the fact of Morris's lodging with Mr. John Tatham, had his shop in front of St. Giles's Church, on ground now partially covered by the south aisle. The

Church was then almost surrounded by houses. We shall find his name recurring as having lent his beam and scales for the weighing of the lead taken off the Castle roofs. In 166—, he was in so large a way of business as to require to issue farthings for the convenience of his customers. After him, his son carried on the business, and in 1701 was a warden of his company ; but before his death he became so reduced in circumstances that he had to receive town pay, and ultimately died a pauper. (See Book of Entries, pp. 353, 374).

This Wednesday, thus deposed to by Richard Lile, would have been May 31st, "being the fast day." This is the only allusion that occurs to the religious fasts of the Independents, and is almost certain evidence that the intruding vicar, Joseph Ferrett, was of that sect.

This Richard Lile was afterwards (in 1657) elected Alderman in place of the very Edward Feild, mayor, before whom he now made his deposition, but he submitted to the fine of £30 rather than accept the office.

Mr. John Tatham was a Royalist ; had been in the Castle during the first siege, and was an unlikely person to have turned upon Morris. It seems rather ungenerous of Richard Lile to have brought his name into question in the matter, for the old man was now ill, and near his end. He died on 26th Feb., 1651-2.

The next witness,

Richard Tailor saith, that Major Morrice before the surprizeing of the castle was an officer in service for the Parliament against the King's partie, and did duty as other officers did. He saith also that Major Morrice ledd forth the forces that went against Ferrybridge against the Parliament's forces soe farre as the Newhall, and then gave order and command to Major Bonnyvant, an officer under him, to march and lead on the said forces to Ferribriggs. He saith that Major Morrice did direct and issue forth warrants for listing of men, levying of monies and provicion for the said castle, and likewise sent out warrants to fetch in severall persons as prisoners, and there detained them untill they lent moneys; and commaunded the gunners and other officers and souldiers under him to dischardge their gunnes and muskitts against the Parliament's forces then before the castle.

Richard "Tailer" was the tenant of "a house and an Orchard, Brooke's land, sometimes Sir John Dixon's, priest," according to the Fee Farm Book of 1650. It was owned by Calisthenes Brooke, and perhaps the ownership by a person of that name, which was that of the foreman of the jury who afterwards tried Morris, his "enemy" as the governor publicly declared, may account for the appearance of this witness against him, at this time. He does not say whether he was in the Castle as a prisoner, or how he acquired the knowledge of Morris's acts to which he testifies. He is described as a "labourer" on the Church books, and it is more than likely that it was he who was sent to fetch in the nearly-hanged John Garforth. (See *Post*.)

Thomas Acaster, of Pontefract, being with others upon the guard, Morrice came to them, and did incourage them, and said, "Stand to it, ladds, against our enimies (the Parliament's soldiors then approaching neare the castle), for if wee be taken, I myselfe shal bee pulled in peeces before any of yow."

Thomas Acaster, unlike Richard Tailor, declares his position at the time he was witness of that of which he now bore evidence. He was within the Castle, as one of the garrison, willingly; for there were no pressed men; and while in that capacity Morris encouraged him with words that deserve to be written in letters of gold, in commendation of the manly fearlessness and self-sacrifice of the governor, who knew that he had set his own life upon the cast, while his followers would be spared in the day of surrender. We would that we could read between the lines here, and believe that this deponent was covertly saying what he could to rouse some feeling of admiration at the conduct of his former commander; for from Thomas Acaster's stock sprang John Akister, the benefactor, who by will dated 27th March, 1733, proved 8th June same year, made a bequest of three bushels of good wheat to be given yearly to poor widows of Micklegate, two to those of Tanshelf, and two to those of Carlton, near Snaith. In Pontefract and Tanshelf the value is still given in flour; and in Carlton, it has been converted into a rent-charge of £5 payable to the parish almshouses by Lord Beaumont.

Thomas Acaster lived through the Commonwealth, and died 26th August, 1658, the month before the Protector. His age was then recorded as sixty-eight. His wife, Elizabeth, survived him only six weeks. Her death occurred on the following 4th October.

<small>Richard Clement, of Pontefract, saith that Major Morrice did cause him to be taken prisoner into the castle, and forced him to pay 5l. for his libertie; and he did see the said Morrice lead upp a partie of horse with his pistoll in his hand against Leiftenant Generall Cromwell's forces being to enter the towne of Pontefract.</small>

The case of Richard Clement differs from all those whose complaints or accusations had been previously heard. He had been arrested, and confined in the Castle, and when thus seized and taken away from his home, his honeymoon was hardly expired; for "24o Aprilis, 1648, Richard Clement & Sarah Wilson, both of this parish, were solemnely marryed in the chappell of St. Giles, with the consent of their respective parents, then and there present; their purpose of marriage having been published according to order three severall lord's days before, and none objecting.— Jos. FERRETT, mi'ster," is the witness borne by the Pontefract Registers. It appears that he was priced by Morris at £5 only, not a high figure when Lieut. Farray was valued at fourteen times as much.

His name occurs on the Church Register as having died on 2nd Feb., 1658-9.

<small>Mary Metcalfe, of Pontefract, saith that Michaell Blackburne was a souldier in the castle, and coronett to Captaine William Paulden. She knew that the said Blackburne was one of that party at Doncaster when Coll. Rainsbrough was slaine, and she heard that Lftent. Autwicke and Marmaduke Greenfeild was there also.</small>

This is all that comes to light at present about Marmaduke Greenfield.

John Bennington, gent., saith, that Major Marrice did give order to Captaine Alexander Ashbie, a captaine then under him, to seize and fetch this informant goods from his chamber in Pontefract into the castle, and that he did see the said Ashbie kill a soldier for the Parliament in the street in Pontefract the same daie the castle was surprized. He saith further that one Mr. William Ramsden of Langley tould him that Michaell Blackborne, his late servant, tould him that he was one of those that runne throughe with his sword and murdered Colonell Rainsbroughe at Doncaster.

Nothing is met with of this witness.

Leiftenant Thomas Farray, of Pontefract, sayth that Major Morrice issued forth warrants in his owne name as governor of Pontefract Castle for raiseing of horses, levying of money and provicions for the said castle, and for seizeing of the goods of anie townesman that was gone away with the Parliament's partie; and he heard the said Morrice say that he drew forth the forces that went against Ferrybrigges as farre as Newhall orchard himselfe, and that the said forces went against Ferribriggs by his owne appointement. He saith that the said Morrice sent for him and kept him prisoner about a fortnight, and told him that he should pay to the said Morrice 70*l*., otherwise he would plunder all his goods and burne his howse. He saith, further, that the said Morrice did committ one John Garforth prisoner into the dungeon, and by a councell of warre, condemned him to be hanged, for giveing intelligence to the Parliament's forces; and, in pursuance thereof, the said Garforth was carryed to the gybbett, went upp the ladder, the rope putt about his necke by the execucioner, and there soe stood a certaine time, being mooved to make his confession, but afterwards was suffered to goe backe. He saith that when Lieftennant Generall Cromwell was to enter the towne of Pontefract, this informant did see the said Morrice draw upp his force, both horse and foot, against the said Parliament's forces, endeavoreing to resist their entry.

This is the first mention of Garforth's case; we shall have his own evidence shortly.

The name of this witness, Lieut. Farray, occurs in the Church Registers in the following February, when 17th Feb., 1649-50, "Dinah, ye daughter of Thomas Farray, of Pontefract, grocer, by Jane his wife, was publikely baptized, being an infant borne the eighth of this instant." When the child died on 23rd November, 1654, Thomas Farray was described as " yeoman."

Marie, wife of John Tatham, of Pontefract, gentleman, saith, that in May was a twelvemoneth John Morrice did sett upp his horse at this infts husband's house in Pontefract: that there did sometimes some souldiers come from the castle to the said Morrice and keepe him company, he then being in armes for the Parliament against the King, and was a leiutenant-collonell to Collonell Forbes, and received pay from the Parliament accordingly, and did duty as other officers did in the leaguer before l'ontefract, when the castle was held against the Parliament by Collonell John Lowther, governor. And, att other times, one—— Ashbie, ——Flood, and John Smyth, souldiers under Major Cotterall, who was then governor for the Parliament. And one John Battley kept him company, then an inhabitant in Pontefract, and imployed afterwards by the said Morrice after the surprizall of the castle, as an advocate for him. She further saith, that the castle was attempted to be taken by ladders about 16 dayes before that itt was taken, but by what persons she knoweth not; onely she saith that Mr. Charles Davison was att this informant's husband's house, the day before the castle was attempted soe to be taken by ladders, and that she hath heard that he was one of them that did attempt the same. She, further, sayth as she hath heard the said Major Morrice confesse, that he with Peter, his servant, an Irishman, did first enter into the castle, when itt was surprized the last summer, and that the said Peter did then shoot and wound Major Cotterall, the then governor, after that the castle was surprized. She, further, saith that the said Morrice, accompanied with Sir Hugh Cartwright, Gervas Nevill, Sir Richard Baron, and others, mett att this informant's husband's howse, and sent out warrants into the country for levying of monies, raiseing of men and arms and provisions of corn and victuall for the said castle. The said Morrice did severall times in her presence declare that he did enter the said castle for the use of the King and the enemies against the Parliament, and that for them he did hold the same, and would doe to the uttmost of his power.

The wife of John Tatham seems to have been peculiarly bitter against Morris, and now gives an apparently indisputable clear piece of evidence that he was on May 9th, 1648, " in armes for the Parliament against the King."

But her tale cannot be reconciled with the statement of Clarendon and others that Morris had been dismissed the service of the Parliament when the army was " remodelled," and that on account of his dismissal he nourished those feelings of resentment which led him to surprise Pontefract Castle.

And yet this deponent is most particular and circumstantial. She declares that " he was a lieutenant collonel to Collonell Forbes, and received pay from the Parliament accordingly, and did duty as other officers did in the leaguer before Pontefract " in 1644-5. If her statement could be true, there could have been no dismissal; for he would have been in the Parliamentary service in Ireland, 1641-2, in the siege of Pontefract Castle, 1644-5, and still an officer of the Parliament in 1648. We must, therefore, receive her whole deposition with hesitancy ; especially as we notice that she speaks of Colonel *John* Lowther, as being the governor of the Castle.

As already mentioned, her husband, a vintner, son of William Tatham and Margaret Ward, and baptised on Christmas Day, 1600, died in 1651. She herself died 10th November, 1657, "about the age of four and fifty years, and her Corps was interred in the Coyre of the Parish Church of Pontefract, the eleventh day of the same moneth." We have failed to trace her descent, and the date of her marriage to John Tatham ; but, judging from the ages of their children, it was during the winter of 1624-5. That she and very many of hers should have been buried in the Choir of the Parish Church of Pontefract, shows the position which they held in the Parish.

John Garforth, of Pontefract, saith, that Major Morrice did send one Richard Tailor, a soldier under him, to fetch the informant prisoner to the castle; and, when he came there, Morrice chardged him with severall false accusations, and caused him to be tried by a councell of warre, where the said Morrice, as president, gave sentence against him, and adjudged him to be hanged. And, in pursuance thereof, caused this informant to be guarded with horse and 100 muskettiers, with matches lighted, to the gallowes on Bagghill, and caused him to climbe the ladder, and putt a rope about his necke : whereupon this informant desireing the spectators to sing a psalme with him, in the time the psalme was singing, one Captaine Browne brought a reprive for eight dayes, and soe from thence they kept him in prison 7 weekes longer, and then whipped this informt out of towne, and charged him not to come to the towne againe upon paine of death.

This was the nearly-hanged John Garforth to whom we just referred, and who, whether deservedly or not, so narrowly escaped the hangman's noose. We can say nothing about him, but that there is an innuendo of a remarkable character concerning him in an unusually imperfect registration, which occurs in the Church Registers against his name on January 10th, 1654-5. ". . . ., the . . . . of John Garforth, of Pontefract, Husbandman, a child of about . . . of age, departed this life, & . . . corps was interred in the . . . . . of Pontefract, aforesaid, ye same day." As there is an absence of entry where the payment of the dues should have been registered, it rather appears as if Garforth had slipped other things beside the hangman's rope, and that he was one of whom Mr. Ferrett complained as witholding his "dues" from him.

———

This evidence shows that there was some sort of permanent gallows erected at this time on Baghill. Doubtless it was upon that gallows that the Rev. George Beaumont was hanged by the Commonwealth soldiers. The Royalists grimly *threatened* to hang their man; the Roundheads bettered the instruction, and carried the threat into execution.

———

Gervase Cooper, of Pontefract, draper, saith, he havinge two cowes taken from him and carried into the castle by the sayd Marris' souldyers, and that when the Parliamentt's forces entred the towne he obtayned favour of Coll. Farefax to goe with a drumme unto the castle to procure his cowes againe. And the officers of the castle then told him thatt none but Marris could lett him have them againe; butt he, the said Marrice, toold this informantt, that he should not have his cowes againe if K nge Charles should write his letter to him to deliver them: and sayd further thatt he would not leave a house standinge in Pontefract: and thereupon commanded to give fire to a morter peece, and shott a granado into the towne, and soe did twice after, whilst this informantt was in the castle: and sayd thatt he would not deliver the castle, although the King's partye in England were destroyed, he would hoold and keepe itt untill he had releefe from the Prince, for he had beene a yeare plottinge to take itt, and he was able to keepe itt three yeares.

There were several families of Cowpers at this time in the town: and it is difficult to ascertain their exact relationship to each other. There was a Stephen Cowper who married Jane Taytame on 29 May, 1592, and had a large family, one of his sons being the John Cowper among the Aldermen who took these depositions, and another being the Boniface (Bonny) Cowper, whose place of business, or shop, is mentioned during the second siege (see page 88.) A Robert Cowper, perhaps his brother, on 28 July, 1594, married Anne Barwick, and had among other sons, a namesake who founded the hospital now in the Butts. Our Gervase might have been the son of either. He was made an alderman in 1657, when Richard Lile refused to serve, and, with his namesake John, was at the Restoration adjudged unfit to serve his Majesty, and ejected from his office.

These Cowpers were all Puritans, and no connection of the John Cooper or Cecil Cooper who formed part of the Council of War in the Castle (see page 243,) and who were sons of Sir Roger Cooper, as we learn from the list of prisoners taken at Willoughby Fight (see page 179), and one of whom was doubtless Capt Thomas Paulden's "Old Friend Jack Cooper" (see page 153.)

> Mary, wife of John Smyth, sayth that Morrice caused her husband, being master of the magazine under Major Cotterall, to be called forth of his bedd, and be putt a prisoner into the dungeon, where they kept him eleaven weekes. And she heard the said Morrice then say that he had beene about that plott 2 yeares; and that he hoped within a moneth to have ten castles more, and that Yorke was theire owne already. And she heard him say that there was two and twenty men there that surprized and tooke the said castle, that should, every man, have a gold chaine with a peece of gold hung in the same, that they might be knowne from all other people in England for their service in taking the said castle.

This evidence of Mary Smith is more interesting than it appears at first sight, to say nothing of the fact that she extends the time in which some of the prisoners were confined in that horrible receptacle to eleven weeks. From June 3rd to August 19th, all the summer months, those unhappy people were detained in that underground cellar, night and day. And the date thus roughly assigned helps us to ascertain the reason why the imprisonment should have then terminated. August 19th was on the Saturday which closed the week that had witnessed Preston Fight, which finally destroyed the hopes of the Royalists. After that disaster, it was evident that little remained for Morris, his followers, and his supporters, but strict siege, and that henceforth they would seek to get rid of every unprofitable mouth. On which account this ubiquitous John Smith, roused up on that eventful June 3rd from his sound sleep, probably after a night's watch, would have been at last discharged.

Master of the Magazine formerly, he had afterwards been its occupant for eleven weary weeks, with nothing to vary the monotony of his existence, but the good fortune which sent him down those forty-two steps with a knife in his pocket. That implement he had been able to use to such good purpose that now in this year of grace One Thousand Eight Hundred and Eighty-Four, two hundred and thirty-six years afterwards, the name which he then carved on those sandstone walls can be read in clear distinct letters, as he there engraved it. Unhappy John Smith!

But even this witness, John Smith's wife, could not confine herself to the truth. Nine or ten were those who seized the Castle: in naming two and twenty she is thinking of the party who went to Conisborough at the end of October.

> Alexander Stileman, gentleman, of Pontefract, saith, that after the attempt of takeing the castle by the ladder, he tooke one Mathew Adams prisoner, and brought him to Pontefract castle, who told him that Morrice was cheife in the plott for the attempt by the ladders. And he heard the said Morrice say that he had 3 times attempted the takeing of the said castle, and, if he had failed, he would have attempted itt six times more but he would have had itt. Hee saith, also, that the said Morrice did, immediately after the surprizall of the castle, commaund Gilbert Hough, Henry Sprowston, and other cannoners, to be brought into the castle, and to traverse the great gunns, and to give fire upon Captaine Browne's horse, a captaine for the Parliament, that appeared in Pontefract feild before the castle. And he heard the said Morrice say that that very day Yorke, and all, or the most, of the holds in England would be surprized. Hee saith, further, that the said Morrice gave order for the parties that went to Ollerton against Ferrybriggs, and takeing of Captaine Todd and his company att Turne-brigg, and shewed letters that Tinmouth castle was betrayed, and other places, and caused bonefires to be made, and great gunns to be shott of for joy upon the report of takeing Newcastle, Boston, and Lincolne.

Alexander Stileman, called in the Church Registers on 24th March, 1650-1, a "habberdasher," was evidently one of Colonel Cotterel's garrison. But yet he does not say that he was put into the dungeon.

The mention of this Henry Sprowston suggests that

another name in the Magazine at the Castle, that was used as a dungeon, is not BROVgTON, as it is generally read, but PROVSTON, and a careful examination shows that such really is the case. The Christian name is James. Prowston was a rather common name here at the time, which might be easily, and was sometimes, mis-pronounced Sprowston.

Ollerton against Ferrybridge is evidently Allerton-by-water, or Bywater.

This Turnbridge, where it may be remembered that (see page 38) the besiegers in the former siege, had a storehouse which the besieged attacked, and from which they fetched " 40 new paire of bootes, with other p'visions," appears to have been similarly used as a base, by the attacking party, in this 1648 siege.

William Tatham, of Pontefract, jun., saith that, in May was a twelvemoneths, Major Morice did frequent the house of John Tatham, his father. He knoweth not by what authoritie Sir Phillip Mountaine, Kt. and the rest of the officers or souldiors went from the castle to Willoughbie fight.

William Tatham, jun., was a reticent witness. He knew that Major Morris did frequent his father's house in May; but he did not know by what authority General Monckton, and the rest went to Willoughby fight: how could *he* know? The eldest of his father's sons, and then between nineteen and twenty years old, he was probably the Tatom, jun., who was in the Castle during the 1644-5 siege in Sir Richard Hutton's list, and his family was one which during the seventeenth century supplied many Mayors to Pontefract. John Tatham, his next younger brother, is described in 1656, as a tanner; Robert Tatham, the third, in 1657, as a yeoman; and Boniface Tatham, the youngest, in 1660, as a vintner: each on the occasion of his marriage. This William, John, and Boniface all died early, leaving no children to perpetuate the name, but Robert lived to have a family, and to be Mayor of Pontefract three times. He died in 1694, and with him the name died out in the Corporation. There are curious particulars on record in the Book of Entries concerning his dealings with the town lands.

This concludes the depositions taken in Pontefract: but Mr. Margett's hint being attended to, care was taken that Colonel Cotterell should be heard. And well for us that he was sought out, and that his deposition should have been preserved, for it thoroughly corrects several of the inaccuracies which have been welded into the hitherto received accounts of the seizure of Pontefract Castle.

The deposition of Colonel Cotterell and the next witness could not be procured in Pontefract, when the Pontefract witnesses were heard before the Borough Bench, but their depositions were taken at York on the following Thursday (August 2nd) before Sir Robert Barwicke, Kt.

Colonel Cotterell must have unconsciously exaggerated when he says that the struggle and resistance on his part to Capt. Paulden and Morris's man Peters, lasted a quarter-of-an-hour, for by the evidence of the next witness the Colonel was brought down into the dungeon "imediately after theire comeing in." In the circumstances of such a struggle, the time might well have appeared longer to him than would have been indicated by a clock.

But his evidence altogether disposes of the alleged treachery of Morris in seeking his friendship, and that he was in bed with him at the time of the arrival of Capt. Paulden and party to seize the Castle. It is clear that Morris came with the attacking party, and that when they sent to Col. Cotterell the message that Col. Morris would come shortly, the handful of men who had a hand in the exploit were quite sensible of the humourous accuracy of the grim joke they were perpetrating in sending such a message. Morris would truly be there in half-an-hour's time, as truly as he was there already.

The tale that Colonel Cotterell had Morris for a bed-fellow evidently sprang out of a confused relation of the circumstance at Knottingley to which Colonel Cotterell refers in his evidence.

Major John Cotterell's deposition was

"That at and before the 3rd day of June, 1648, this ext was governor of Pontefract Castle, and garrison souldiers then belonging to the same, beinge deputed thereunto by authoritie from Major-General Lambert. And, by authoritie in that behalfe derived from the State, he had the charge of the said castle and garrison for the service of the Parliament and Commonwealth of England. And he saith that upon the said 3rd of June, betwixe six and seaven of the clocke in the morning, this ext haveing beene upon duty the night before, and haveing then newly repaired to his lodging chamber, presently there came in two men with swords and pistolls in theire hands, whome he then knew not (but afterwards heard theire names to be Paulden and Peters) who being asked by this ext, "Who comes there?" they answered that the castle was surprised for the King, and that this informer was in the hands of gentlemen: he might have quarter, if he pleased. But refusinge, with his weapon drawne, they fell upon him and wounded him both with sword and pistoll, and after a quarter of an houre's dispute or there abouts, growinge faint with much bleeding, was disabled to make farther opposicion; whereupon the said two men seised upon this informer, and led him into the castle yard, where he mett John Marris, comonly called Major Marris, who had formerly beene active in the Parliament service, and had assisted in the reduceing of that place to the obeidiance of the Parliament of England, when it was holden by one Lowther, formerly governor for the King. And, upon that meeting, the sayd Major Marris sayd " I am now governor of this place for the King," or words to the like effect. And the informant askinge him if he would put him into the dungion, Marris answered, with oathes and great execracions, that if both speakers of Parliament were there they should in. To which place he thereupon commanded this informant to be comitted, where this informant found then newly comitted to the same dungion about the number of thirty officers and souldiers, till that time under this deponents command. And, after he had continued in misery in the sayd place about three days and three nights, he was by order from the said Marris removed to another prison in the said castle. And the sayd Marris, after that, had the title and name of governor, and commanded the souldiers and guards in the sayd castle. And this deponent was inforced in the behalfe of the prisoners formerly under his command, as well for theire subsistance, as for theire exchange, to make his addresse to the sayd Marris, as governor; in whose power and sole command that garrison then was, from and after the time of his sayd surprisall. And the sayd Morris did constitute and appoint officers under his command for the raisinge and disciplyninge of men for defence of that castle and garrison against the authoritye of the Parliament of England. And he heard the sayd Marris say that he had beene about the surprysall of that castle any time for 2 yeares then past. And he further said, that himselfe with Col. Furbus and Col. Thomas Fairefax (who lately revolted from the Parliament and was in Scarbrough Castle) did lodge together at Knottingley in one bedd, about that time the late King came to Doncaster in a hostile manner; and that they there continued expecting command from the said King to surprise the said castle from the hands of Col. Robert Overton, then governor for the Parliament. And this informant also knoweth that there was formerly attempts made to take the castle in the night time by rearinge of ladders, which was duringe this deponent's said governement discovered and prevented. And this informer heard the sayd Marris after the surprisall aforesaid say that he was there in person when the sayd ladders were reared, and intended himselfe to be the first man that should enter, and that he then had the chiefe command of that party. And he saith, that duringe the time of his durance as prisoner in the said castle (beinge about thirteene weeks) he well knoweth that the said Marris commanded in cheife in the said castle, as governor; and did walke the rounds and commanded severall locks and barrs to be layd upon the dores where this informer was in durance. He knoweth not Blackburne by that name, but may perhaps remember both his persons (*sic*) and some of his actions when he seeth him."

Col. Cotterell seems to have been kept in the dungeon three days,—that is, while the portcullis was up, and the new garrison were organizing themselves; after that, he was removed to less rigorous confinement.

Col. Cotterell extends the time in which he was confined in the Castle to thirteen weeks, though his case might have been exceptional, as being a prisoner held for exchange. Other witnesses have charged eleven weeks only, corresponding to the date of the Preston Fight.

Col. Cotterell's pronounced belief was that Colonel Forbes and Major Morris had been at one for some years; that Major Morris commanded under Colonel Forbes, for the Parliament, against the Castle in the Druke siege; and that with Colonel Fairfax, who had also been in that siege, and had been indeed of the parleying party on behalf of the Parliament (see page 143), all three were ready to make a united attempt on the Castle for the King, even as far back as when his Majesty came to Doncaster. That visit was in August, 1645, a few days only after the surrender of Pontefract Castle by Colonel Richard Lowther at the close of the second siege.

How, therefore, is it, that Morris should be selected from the three as having been peculiarly treacherous? It really seems, on a careful examination of the facts, that all three belonged to the more moderate party, who, with Col. Bright, and so many others, could not constrain themselves to go the lengths which the Independents ultimately did; and who, when it was too late, felt compelled to pass over ultimately to the side of the Royalists.

For in none of these original documents can we trace the slightest evidence of the truth of the common allegation, that Morris was inveterate against the Parliament, because he was passed over in the re-modelling of the army.

Indeed taking the testimony of these witnesses as they stand, if their witness is that of truth, the possibility of such a course of conduct on the part of Morris for such a reason is absolutely negatived.

(1) Mary Tatham bears witness that Morris was among the besiegers during the second siege, that is in the spring and summer of 1645.

(2) Colonel Cotterell, on the other hand, testifies that in company with Col. Thomas Fairfax and Col. Forbes, he had been earnest to seize the Castle from Colonel Overton, at the time the King visited Doncaster, that is in August, 1645.

(3) He was in custody for an attempt in the autumn of 1647.

(4) He repeated his attempts till he was finally sucesssful in June, 1648.

(5) General witness is borne in August, 1649, that he had declared that any time during the previous two years he had been plotting to carry out the scheme of August, 1645.

Thus the change in his course of conduct took place during the latter part of the summer of 1645, long after the "new modelling" of the army had been a fact. And looking to Morris's antecedents, his principles, and his connections, it is most likely that the abolition of the Book of Common Prayer, and the establishment of the Directory, which took place in that August, had revealed to him, as it did to so many others, the abyss into which the Independent faction, now becoming predominant, were about to plunge the country.

Colonel Thomas Fairfax, and his son, Major William, consistently served the Parliament, while they thought the Parliament was acting constitutionally. Indeed, Major Fairfax, when dying of a wound received at Marston, alluded in his will to his unrequited services for the King *and* Parliament, and left his arrears of pay to his father, then Lieut.-Col. Thomas Fairfax. The latter, like Col. Morris, had come to have his doubts, and had he survived (he was buried at York Minster, 16 Dec., 1646) he would probably have thrown in his lot with Morris to the bitter end.

His great second cousin, it may be remembered, withdrew his hand at the last moment—too late to prevent the evil—at the trial of the King. He was present the first day, and afterwards, according to his wife's testimony, delivered in open Court, "had too much wit to be THERE!"

The second deponent "Before Sir Robert Barwicke, Kt," is the bearer of a well-known name, never hitherto traced to its owner. On the walls of the steps leading to the Magazine are several names cut in the stone, John Smith and John Grant being each repeated several times. John Smith, as we have seen, was the Master of the Magazine; John Grant, as we shall now see, was "the" gunner. Each, as it were, a non-commissioned officer.

This witness concurs with Colonel Cotterell that the nine or ten who seized the Castle, drove " about thirty officers and soldiers " down into that " darke place " ; and like every one else, he knew of no one in authority except Morris.

Gunner Grant had good cause for saying that the Castle was "unhappily" surprised, but he gives no hint of how long his confinement lasted.

He is evidently mistaken about Blackburn, firstly in alleging that he was one of nine or ten who did the actual deed of seizure, and secondly in giving him the rank of Major. He must have confounded him with Captain or Major Ashby.

The information of this John Grant, who describes himself as " late under the command of Major Cotterill, late governor of Pontefract Castle," is

" That he beinge the gunner of the said castle, as it was a garrison held for the Parliament, under the command of the said Major Cotterill, governor of the same. And whilst the same garrison was soe under that command, it fell out unhappily upon the 3rd of June, 1648, that it was taken by surprisall, by Major John Marris, and others under his command, and of conspiracy with him. And, immediately upon theire entry, this deponent, and about thirtie more of the officers and souldiers of the sayd castle who continued faithfull to the Parliament, were by command of the said Marris comitted to the dungeon in the said castle, beinge a darke place about forty-two steps within the earth. And, imediatly after theire comeing in, Major Cotterill was also brought thither sore wounded in severall places of his body. And this deponent saith that the said Major John Marris was commander-in-cheife of those souldiers who were actors in the said surprisall; and that he did from thence forwards continue governor and commander-in-cheife of the said castle and garrison for the King, and held the same against the Parliament of England, until it was by force regained after a long siege. And this deponent, further, saith that he well knoweth him commonly called Major Blackburne, who was likewise an actor in the said conspiracy, and ayded to surprise the said castle, and continued there in the same under command of the said Marris ; and uttered in this exts hearing many railing words against the Parliament, and affirmed that he had gon forth upon parties and killed severall men."

This closes the depositions ; but a week afterwards, on the following Wednesday, Morris and Blackburn were themselves brought before Sir Robert Barwicke, Knt., and Mr.

Thomas Dickinson, for the ordinary magisterial examination, apparently as a preliminary to a committal to the Assizes.

Michael Blackburn is first heard, and describing himself as late of Coldhil, in the parish of Almondbury, he says

"That he was servante to Sir John Ramsden, and waited on his chamber till the tyme of his death, and that he was not present at the surprising of the castle and garrison of Pontefract, in June was a twelmonth, by Major Marris, nor did then know him; but he came into the castle in the same month of June, and received within few days after his coming into the said garrison a commission from Sir Marmaduke Langdale as cornet of Capt. Palden's troop; and, at that tyme when Col. Rainsbrugh was slaine at Doncaster, he went forth with the same party, but came not to Doncaster by reason that his horse tired; and he sayth that he was one amongst the rest that continued the holding of the said castle and garrison under the command of Mr. Jo. Marris; and, being questioned touching his leaving of the said castle and garrison, he sayth that he, with Col. Marris and his man, did about March last ride through the forces which had then long besieged them in the said castle, and came into Lancashire where they were apprehended."

This may be considered merely a plea of "Not Guilty," for there is no doubt that Blackburn was one of the four who seized Rainsborough.

The same may be said of Morris's reply,

"That he did not surprise the said castle and garrison, for it was delivered to him, the gates being opened to him, and he going into the same without resistance; and he was from thenceforth governor of the same, as his commission from the Prince of Wales, which he hath to shew, will expresse at large, and he did there comand in cheife the soldiers of the said garrison according to this said comission, for all the tyme he held the said castle against the forces of the Parlament."

The York Summer Assizes were now approaching, and Justices Thorpe and Puleston were the Judges appointed to preside. Their conduct to the prisoners, and particularly that of the last named to Colonel Morris, almost surpasses belief. It will be seen that he proceeded to such lengths as to threaten the unfortunate man at the bar with personal violence; and that he ordered him to be put in irons in his presence, and even before the verdict was pronounced. We wish we could see anything in the account that would show some alleviating circumstance; but there is very little doubt that the narrative is correct, which we print from Somers's Tracts (3rd Collection vol. I, London, 1751), itself taken from a contemporary tract of which it gives the following title :—

An exact Relation of the Tryal and Examination of JOHN MORRIS, *Governor of* Pontefract-Castle, *at the Assizes held at* York.
Together with his Speeches, Prayers and other Passages immediately before his death, August 23. 1649.
Whereunto is added the Speech of Cornet BLACKBURNE, *executed at the same time.*
Printed in the year 1649.
(*Not in the State Tryals.*)

The note "Not in the State Tryals" appears to intimate that this "Tryal" was not in the folio edition, so called. It was subsequently published in Cobbett's Collection, and in Howell's. In those Collections the reprint was nearly verbatim, but it was preceded by the following heading :—

The Trial of Colonel JOHN MORRIS, Governor of Pontefract Castle; at the Assizes at the Castle of York, before Mr. John Puleston, and Mr. Baron Thorpe, Justices of Assize, for High Treason : 1 CHARLES II. A.D. 1649.

And then follows the text of the "Exact Relation."

Colonel *Morris* being demanded to hold up his hand, refused, and the Indictment was read against him for Treason for levying War against the late King and the Parliament upon Stat. *Ed.* 5., (an evident mistake, corrected in the later Editions of the State Trials, which copy this, into 25 Ed. 3.) The Court desired him to plead *Guilty* or *Not Guilty.*

Col. *Morris.* My Lords, under correction, I conceive this Court hath not power to try me in this case, I being a Martial man, I ought to be tryed by a Council of War.

Court. Sir, What do you say, Are you guilty or not guilty ? This is the second time you have been asked : Sir, if you will not answer the third time, we shall know what to do, Are you guilty or not guilty ?

Col. *Morris.* My lords, I still conceive I ought not to be tryed here, if I have done any thing worthy of death, I appeal to a Martial Court, to my Lord *Fairfax*, Major General, or a general Council of War : You have not any precedent for it, either for you to try me in this way, or me to suffer by it.

Court. Are you guilty or not guilty ? This is the third time.

Col. *Morris.* My Lords, if your Honours will force me to plead, I conceive I am not guilty.

Court. How will you be tryed ?

Morris. My Lords, I was never at any Bar before, I am ignorant herein.

Court. Tell him what to say. [*Upon that, some near him, told him,* By God and the Country.]

Col. *Morris.* By God and the Country.

This commencement of the Trial sufficiently shows what a mockery was the "Justice" invoked upon the prisoners, who, notwithstanding their exceptions to the jurisdiction, are forced to plead, under an implied threat.

It must be borne in mind that this is a Reprint of the "Exact Relation of the Tryal," as printed at the time. It was no "news" furbished up to serve a subsequent purpose.

———

After that, challenge is made for Colonel *Morris* to except against any of the Jury.) [*Master* Brooke, *a great man for the Cause, comes first returned, to be sworn as Fore-man of the Jury*]

Colonel *Morris*. My Lords, I except against this Brooke.
Court. Sir, he is sworn, and you speak too late.
Col. *Morris*. My Lord, I appeal to himself, whether he be sworn or no.
Brooke. Sir, I am not to answer you, but the Court. My Lord, I did not kiss the Book.
Court. Sir, that is no matter, it's but a Ceremony.
Col. *Morris*. My Lords, I beseech your Honours that I may except against him, I know him, as well as I know my right hand, to be my Enemy.
Clerk of Assize. Sir, he is recorded sworn, there is no disputing against the Record.
Col. *Morris*. My Lords, I must submit to your Honours:

Of this jury, evidently packed so as to procure an adverse verdict, the first man called is excepted against by the Prisoner, when he came forward to be sworn. According to his own confession, he had "not kissed the Book," that is, he was not sworn; but all exception is overborne by the assumption that if he were not sworn, he ought to have been; and would have been, had he been sufficiently alert: any how, "Kissing the Book" was no matter, and was but a ceremony; he was recorded as sworn, and as it was permitted to no one to dispute the Record, whether or no he had kissed the Book it was too late for objection, and there was nothing for it but submission.

———

The "Exact Relation" proceeds :—

After that, Colonel *Morris* challenges sixteen Men, and my Lord *Puleston* thinking Colonel *Morris* tedious in excepting against so many, answers, Sir, keep within your compass, or I will give you such a blow as wll strike off your head.
Col. *Morris*. My Lords, I desire nothing but Justice, for by the Statute of 14 *Hen*. 7. fol. 19. I may lawfully challenge thirty-five men, without shewing any cause to the contrary.
Court. It is granted.

It is to be hoped that at least this threat of "Such a blow as will strike off your head" was metaphorical, rather than intended as literal. For surely such a threat of personal violence was never before uttered by an English Judge to a prisoner before him on trial for his life.

The Sheriff for the year was Sir William St. Quintin, who seems to have been a worthy second to Justice Puleston; the foreman of the Grand jury was George Eure, Esq., and the following was the jury ultimately impanelled: Richard Brooke, of Birstal, foreman, Thomas Reynolds, Thomas Thomlynson, Sampson Darnborough, John Yonge, of Rocliffe, William Robinson, Henry Peele, John Rookesby, John Clerke, William Johnson, William Oldridge and John Hewan. The date of the trial was Thursday, August 16th.

After a full Jury, the Indictment read, and Evidence for the State very full, that Colonel *Morris* was Governor of *Pontefract*, which *Morris* being very modest and civil, did not contradict any thing, until his time of answer.

Col. *Morris*. My Lords, I humbly desire a Copy of my Indictment, that I may know what to answer, I conceive I may plead special as well as general.

Court. Sir, you cannot by the Law.

Col. *Morris*. My Lords, I conceive there is a point of Law in it, and I humbly desire to have Council; for I conceive by the Law, being attainted for High Treason, I ought to have Council by the Statute 1 Hen. 7. fol. 23.

Court. Sir, I tell you you cannot have it.

Thus the Copy of his Indictment was refused him, and that so peremptorily, that he was not permitted to have Counsel to argue the point whether it should be allowed him or not. But he proceeds temperately,

Col. *Morris*. Then, my Lords I conceive I am not any way guilty to (*of* in the State Trials) the Indictment, for Treason, my Lords, it is said to be against the King, his Crown, and against his Peace, whereby, my Lords, I can make it appear, I have acted only for the King, and nothing against him, which may appear hereby by (*here by* in the State Trials) my Commission. *The Court looks upon it, and answers,*

Court. Sir, you are deceived, this is false, it is from the Prince.

Col. *Morris*. My Lords, It is very well known, my Lord *Fairfax* hath his Commission derived from the Parliament, and upon that he grants Commissions to his Officers, which is all one and the same. The Prince hath his from his Father, and I have mine from the Prince, which is full Power, he being Captain General of his Majesty's Forces.

This argument, which would appear to most people conclusive, was quietly ignored, without answer, and the questioner continues,

Court. Sir, have you nothing else to say?

Col. *Morris.* My Lords, under Correction, I conceive it is sufficient, for by the same power, all Judges, Justices of Peace, your Lordships, your Predecessors, and all other Officers, did act by the same power, and all process and writs of Law, were acted, and executed, in his Name, and by his Authority.

Court. His power was not in him, but the Kingdom, for he was in trust for the Kingdom ; the King's Highway, and the King's Coin being so called, is not his own, but his Subjects, and his Natural power, and Legal power, are different.

The prisoner did not take advantage of what now seems a very obvious defect in this reasoning of the Court. If the King had been, according to their own phrase, merely in trust for the Kingdom, to act for the Kingdom, then his acts as trustee should have bound the Kingdom ; and therefore the acts of those who acted under his Commission, when done by virtue of that Commission, were legal and valid. But Morris applies himself to the latter part of the speech only.

Col. *Morris.* My Lords, under Correction, I conceive his Legal and Personal power, are undevisable *(sic)*, all one, and cannot be separated.

Court. Sir, all is one, if the King bid me kill a man, Is this a sufficient Warrant for me to plead ? No, Sir, it is unlawful ; Sir, have you no more ?

Col. *Morris.* Sirs, I beseech your Honours give me leave, I am upon my Life.

Court. Speak what you will, Sir, you shall be heard.

Heard ! Yes, certainly ; in one sense of the word, heard. Morris replies,

Col. *Morris.* Your servant, my Lord ; then my Lords I conceive I have acted nothing against the Parliament, for that which I acted, it was for the King ; and since the abolishing of Regal power, I have not meddled with any thing against the Parliament, for that Act was but inacted the 14th of *July* last, and before that time an (corrected to *and* in the State Trials) Act of abolishing Kingly-government, that princely Palace which I kept by his Commission was demolished ; my Lords, I beseech your honours, that my Commission may be read, to give satisfaction to the Court.

The Princely Palace was Pontefract Castle.

My Lord *Puleston.* Sir, it will do you no good, you may as well shew a Commission from the Pope, all is one.

Col. *Morris.* My lords, I desire your Lordships to do me that Justice.

My Lord *Thorp.* For my part I am willing, if my Brother be not against it.

This was a fortunate word, as it threw the onus of the implacable malevolence of the Court upon Puleston, who, however, was equal to the emergency. He fell back at once on the allegation that their judgment had already been given. This point was not noticed by the Editor of the State Trials, who altered " held " to " hold."

My Lord *Puleston.* Sir, we held (*hold* in the State Trials) it for law to be void, it is to no purpose.

Col. *Morris.* Then if your Lordships be not pleased to do me that justice that it may be read, I desire it may be restored me again. [*Upon that, Colonel* Morris *received his Commission unread.*] My Lords, it seemeth strange, that your Honours should do that which was never done the like before, never any of your Predecessors ever did the like; I wish it may not be to your own and your friends wrong, that you make yourselves precedents of your acting, and my self of suffering. But, my Lords, I do not speak for saving my own Life, for (I thank my God) I am prepared, and very willing to part with this lump of clay. I have had a large time of repentance, it being twenty-two weeks since my imprisonment; and I am sorry for those which are like to undergoe the same sufferings, if your Lordships take away my life. And though I do not speak any way in glory, indeed at this present there is a cloud hanging over our heads, I desire there may be a fair Sun-shine to dispel it. And though there were a world of plots in the Kingdom when I took the Castle, there is not wanting the same now, only the time is not yet come; and as I was to be the fire-brand to *Scarborough,* so he (meaning *Bointon*) to *Tinmouth,* and that to others; and though you take away my life, there will be others which will take up the Lintstock to give fire, though I be gone.

A manly protest, and a prediction which came to be verified in due season. For the regicides actually had to make this very plea, that their acts were done under the authority of the then Supreme Authority, a plea which provoked the rejoinder that what they did was not done even "by one Estate; they were not an eighth part of the Commons, they were but a Company of Men, supported by the Sword": the allusion being to the condition of the House after Pride's Purge. (See page 200.)

Morris makes a strange mistake here, when he says he had been imprisoned for twenty-two weeks. The utmost of time could not have been so much as even twenty weeks. (See page 227.)

The personal dispute, and reply from the Bench, which followed this speech, seem very remarkable and unseemly, to say the least. The Judge—Puleston presumably—forgets his dignity so far as to say

Court. Sir, you have little hopes to talk of any fire to be given here, having received such a total rout in *Ireland.*

Which gives occasion to the prisoner to make quite as remarkable a reply. For he boasts that he had news of what was passing in Ireland, of a date a day later than that of the Bench: their news he told them, was fourteen days old, his was of thirteen days only.

Col. Morris. My Lords, I should have been unwilling to have contradicted your late news concerning *Ireland*; but since you have given me a hint of it, you must give me leave to let your Honours know, that I received Letters from the Marquis of *Ormond*, dated the 3d of *August*, and yours is but the 2d, wherein he pleases to let me understand of the great care he hath of me, and that whatsoever shall befal me here, the like shall be to those which he hath Prisoners there, which (as he saith) are good store. Therefore, if your Lordships did not at all value my Person, yet methinks you should have some care of it for your own friends goods (*good* in the State Trials).

The Marquis of Ormond, it may be remembered, gave Morris his Major's Commission. (See page 174.) But the Court declines argument, and continues

Court. Sir, have you no more to say?
Col. Morris. My Lords, still I appeal to my Commission, which I conceive is sufficient to defend me withal in what I have done, notwithstanding your power to the contrary.
Court. It is nothing at all, we have power to try you here.
Col. Morris. Then, my Lords (under correction) Laymen may as well be tried at a Martial Court: which, if granted, those excellent Acts of *Magna Charta* and the Petition of Right would be destroyed.
Court. But you are not looked upon (*on* in the State Trials) here as a Soldier, we shall do what in justice belongs to us.

This finally closes the question of Morris's Commission; and the prisoner proceeds to another objection.

Col. Morris. My Lords, still (under correction,) I have taken the Oath of Allegiance, and I conceive in that I was bound to do as much as I did or have done, though I had not had any Commission at all. And I beseech your Lordships that you will do me justice, and not incline to the right hand of affection, or the left of (*to* in the State Trials) hatred, but to have an ear for the accused as well as for the accuser: Neither have I acted any thing contrary to my Allegiance, which Allegiance I was as (*as* omitted in State Trials) willing to pay to the Son, as well as to the Father. Now for my (*the* in the State Trials) Allegiance I owe to any person or authority, but to these, I know none.

POST MORTEM PATRIS, PRO FILIO, was, it will be remembered, the proud motto of Morris's coinage during the siege:—After the death of the Father, we are for the Son. A declaration, first made in Pontefract, afterwards in Worcester; and frequently adopted as a motto at both PONTEFRACT, and "THE FAITHFUL CITY."

And now Lord Thorpe once more interposes, and finally closes the Plea.

My Lord *Thorp.* Sir, if you have any thing else to say, speak for yur self, for this is not much to the purpose.

Col. *Morris.* My Lords, 'tis true, since you have rejected that authority which I acted by, I might as well have held my tongue at the first, and spake nothing, were it not for the satisfaction of the hearers ; but if it must be so that you will make me a precedent, you must do with me as you did with my dear and honoured Lord, [*meaning the Lord of* Strafford] making an Act for the future, that this my suffering shall not be a precedent to any Soldiers hereafter. Besides, my Lords, this same Statute which you alledge against me is, if that any shall act againstthe King, 'tis Treason, which I have not done ; but contrary, for him, and by his authority. And there is an Act ot 11 *Hen.* 7. *cap* 1. That *whosoever they are that shall aid or assist the King at home or abroad, shall not be questioned at all*

My Lord *Thorpe.* 'Tis true, Sir, but *Henry* VII. then stood in a fickle condition, and being an Usurper, made that Act for his own safety ; sometimes Duke of *York* ruling, sometimes Duke of *Lancaster*, and others contending, therefore it was enacted.

Col. *Marris.* My Lords, but this same Act of *Henry* VII, was later than that of *Edward* III, which you have laid against me, and as yet never repealed, untill this last Act of 14 of *July*, before which time I had delivered up the place.

My Lord *Thorpe.* Well, Sir, it seems you have not any more (*to say*, added in the State Trials.)

Here the misspelling of Morris's name makes its appearance, once more, singularly enough. It might have been thought a mere Printer's error, but that we have already seen that in spelling the name of this family the use of *a* instead of *o* was by no means unusual, even in official documents (see page 148.)

The next question, to Blackburn, appears in The State Trials only : the original, in Somers's Tracts, has only the sentence commencing " After he had answered "; which makes the " he " refer to Morris. In the State Trials, " he " refers to Blackburn, whose name is mis-spelt " Blackston " in the second addition to the State Trials.

[What have you to say, Blackburne ?] After he had answered, the Court commands Irons to be laid on them. [Cornet Blackston being condemned at the same time.]

All the editions continue :—

Col. *Morris.* My Lords, I humbly desire that we may not be mannacled ; if you make any doubt of us, that we may have a greater guard upon us.

Ly (*sic*) Lord *Puleston.* Sir, you that have made such attempts through such guards as were of purpose set to receive you, ought to be lookt to now. Yet if Master Sheriff please, I am content.

The Judge's reference appears to be to the prisoners'

having forced their way through the besiegers; and his willingness to concede this one demand was possibly a result of his already having had a communication with the Sheriff on the subject. Morris ineffectually appeals to the officials:

Col. *Morris.* Master Sheriff, I desire that this mannacling may be forbore: if you please to clap a guard of a hundred men upon us, I shall pay for it. This is not only a disgrace to me, but in general to all Soldiers, which doth more trouble me than the loss of my life. Master Sheriff, what do you say?

Master Sheriff. Sir, Irons are the safest guards.

Col. *Morris.* My Lords, hitherto (I thank God) I have not done any unsoldiery and base act, and to begin now I will not do it to save my life, and though you look upon me *Sampson*-wise, I vow to God, I would not touch the pillars though it lay in my power, to injure you, therefore I still beg pardon that I may not be mannacled.

Under-Sheriff. Come, Sir, it cannot be helpt, we are commanded.

Col. *Morris.* My Lords, I beseech you grant me this favour, it is not my life I beg, but to forbear this mannacling, which shame, and dishonour, doth more trouble me, than the loss of my Life.

Under-Sheriff. It must be done, and upon that, did it, and carried him away.

The scene is pitiful, for the two were prisoners still upon trial, and although the verdict was a foregone conclusion, it had not yet been delivered.

After dinner [they were brought again, and] the Jury brought in their verdict, [who found them both] guilty of Treason.

The two clauses within brackets were omitted in the State Trials.

The Exact Relation continues, and thenceforward to the close of the Trial, it is adopted literally by the later editions:

Col. *Morris.* My Lord, I am here found guilty of Treason by that villain *Brooke*, whom I know to be mine enemy, and the first man that I did except against: in which I conceive I have received hard measure, for none could have found me guilty of Treason, had they gone according to the Letter of the Law. which they did not.

My Lord *Puleston.* Sir, you speak too late, you are not to dispute it now.

Col. *Morris.* Neither would I, my Lord, if this were a Court of Chancery, but being a Court of Law, bound up in express words and letter, I conceive I ought to dispute it, and my business better weighed.

My Lord *Puleston.* Well sir, you are found guilty, therefore hold your peace.

Col. *Morris.* If I must suffer, I receive it with all alacrity and chearfulness, and I thank God I shall die for a good cause, and the testimony of a good Conscience, for which had I as many lives as there are Stars in the Firmament, I would sacrifice them all for the same.

Court. Sheriff, Gaoler take them away, or Ile take you away.

Col. *Morris.* Well, I beseech God bless King Charles, and fight for all those that fight for him, or have fought for him.

So the "Trial" ended much as it had begun. The first altercation closed with a threat to the Prisoner; the last with a threat to the Sheriff or Gaoler. The Judge who would give the Prisoner such a blow as should strike off his head, was in the end as ready with a threat to " take the Sheriff away!" But the undaunted Morris has the last word, in a prayer for the King, and for all those who would fight for him.

There is no mention of any further particulars as to the sentence. Carlyle says that Morris "lost his head," but that expression seems to have been but loose and, as so frequently with that writer, inaccurate. The usual death at York was by hanging; and such there can, as we shall shortly see, be no doubt was the sentence in this instance.

Thus concludes what may be called the First Part of the " Exact Relation." The Second is headed

The Confession of Colonel JOHN MORRIS, *and some passages betwixt the Prison and place of Execution.*

But the later Collections of State Trials conclude the First Part thus :—

After he was condemned, col. Bethel writ to the General and his Council of War, that Morris might be reprieved; but col. Pride opposed it, urging, "That it would not stand with the justice of the Army, nor the safety of the Commonwealth, to let such enemies live, the Parliament having adjudged him worthy of death, and given instructions to the Judges accordingly."

This allegation of Colonel Pride—the hero of Pride's Purge—is most striking. He asserts—as a reason that leniency should be refused—that previous to the Trial, the Parliament had judged Morris worthy of death, and had given instructions to the Judges accordingly. If this were true, no wonder that Puleston set his face like a flint, that even Thorpe ignored all Morris's Pleas: the Judges had received their instructions—he was " worthy of death."

The application to the General would probably have been

looked upon favourably, had it not been for this interference of Colonel Pride.

Anyone tolerably conversant with Scripture cannot fail to notice, how full all these seventeenth century documents are of Scripture language. This is only one instance out of many.

The State Trials head the Second Part with the following title :—

The SPEECH of Colonel John Morris, Governor of Pontefract Castle, at the place of Execution at York, August 23, 1649.

But neither version takes any notice of a nearly successful attempt at escape made by the two prisoners, for a notice of which, this seems the most convenient place.

The last letter we shall quote from the Baynes correspondence to which we have made such frequent reference—presented to the British Museum in 1856 by Rev. Adam Baynes, and of which there are eleven volumes (Addl. MSS., 21,417—21,427)—is one from Cornet John Baynes. He says, under date York, August 21, 1649, "Morris and Blackburn were near escaping last night; they had got over the Castle wall, but were taken ere they got over the moat. To-morrow they are to be executed, *with about thirty other prisoners.*"

The writer was wrong in his date, for the execution took place on Thursday, August 23rd ; though it is possible that it might have been delayed a day from the original intention in the expectation of a reprieve, or on account of the accident to Blackburn. It seems singular that neither the Exact Relation, nor the account in the State Trials makes any reference to this attempted escape.

Fox, indeed, records it, but he makes it happen before the trial, while this Baynes correspondence is clear: it was "last night."

Another account says that Morris got down safely, but that the rope broke with Blackburn—he was a little older, and presumably somewhat heavier than Morris—and that he fell and broke his leg. In this strait Morris refused to avail himself of his opportunity, would not desert his comrade, allowed himself to be re-taken, and virtually suffered for his generosity.

The determined policy of the Army, which now entirely had the upper hand, was "Death to the Leaders." And to this ruthlessness may be attributed the utter collapse of the Royal cause: a collapse which, however, lasted only until a new generation had time to grow up. In little more than ten years the Prince and his fellow exiles were welcomed home with almost universal rejoicing.

A loyal Tract of the same date (printed in the year MDCXLIX.) extant in the Bodleian, incidentally adverts to this Trial of Colonel Morris.

The Tract, which is really a sort of Indictment against all the prominent leaders, including Colonel Pride, who is denominated the Drayman, the House of Commons being stigmatised as his "Drayhorses," has for Title "Anarchia Anglicana, or the History of Independency. The Second Part. Being a Continuation of Relations and Observations Historicall and Politique upon this present Parliament, Begun Anno 16. Caroli Primi. By THEODORUS VERAX (CLEMENT WALKER). Psal. 88. Virum Sanguinum & dolosum abominabitur Dominus."

In speaking of the refusal to allow Morris his exception of Brooke, the Pamphleteer says:—

The Court (knowing *Brook* to be the principal Verb, the Key of their work) answered &c.

Again, when mentioning the threat to Morrice (as he

calls him), to keep within his compass, THEODORUS VERAX remarks :

> Here you see the Judges (which ought to be of Councel with the prisoner in matter of Law) endeavouring to out-face, and blind the prisoner with ignorance of the Law, being a Martial-man.
>
> * * * * * *
>
> These Usurpers have got the old tyrannical trick, *To rule the People by the Laws, but first to over-rule the Laws by their Lawyers ;* and therefore *Ut rei innocentes pereant, fiunt nocentes judices ;* that true men may go to the Gallows, Thieves must sit on the bench.

This pamphlet also interposes some very pertinent remarks upon Colonel Pride's contention against Morris, in this way :

> Col. *Pride* opposed it, urging, *That it would not stand with the justice of the Army* (you see now who is the foun-(tain *omitted*) of Justice) *nor the safety of the Commonwealth, to let such Enemies live, the Parliament having adjudged him worthy of death,* (without hearing) *and given instructions to the Judges accordingly.* (O serviceable Judges !)

On which THEODORUS VERAX observes

> So the General was overborn by this Drayman. This fellow sitteth frequently at the Sessions house in the *Old Bayly*, where the weight of his Slings turneth the scale of Justice which way he pleaseth.

Whitlock's Memorials (page 405) under date August 20 (being the date on which the news of Morris's Trial reached London by letter) gives the following report :—

> Letters from *York*, that one *Morrice*, and one *Blackbourn*, were arraigned before Baron *Thorp*, and Judge *Puleston, for levying War against the Kingdom,* they pleaded *not guilty*, but desired *as they were Marshal Men, that they might be tryed by Marshal Law*, which was denyed to them.
>
> *Morrice* at last said, *he would be tryed by God and the Country*, and 17 *Witnesses* proved foul Crimes against him. He had two Sheets of Paper written with Matters of Law, and Statutes, many of which he pleaded, and urged the case of the War betwixt the two Houses of *York*, and *Lancaster*, the difference of which, from his Case, was shewed by the Judges.
>
> Then he produced a Commission from the King, when he was Prince, the Judges told him that the Prince was a Subject as well as he, and must be tryed by the same Law.
>
> He was found guilty of Treason, and manacled with Irons, at which he said, *What, a Martial Man Ironed ? the like President was never before known.*
>
> He desired to have a strong Guard, saying, *Let me be damned if I escape*, but it was denyed, so was a Copy of his Indictment, and to have Councel, or to be exchanged.
>
> He and *Blackbourn* were both condemned.

Incidentally it may be noted that the Commission to Morris was here said to be " from the *King*, when Prince," thus granting the right of succession : and, moreover, the manacling of Col. Morris and his fellow prisoner is mentioned *after* the delivery of the verdict.

But, as a whole, though written adversely to Morris, the account seems to be a tolerably correct summary of facts.

The following is common to the Exact Relation, and both Collections of State Trials, with a few very slight verbal corrections, which we have interlined :—

When he was brought out of prison, looking upon the Sledge that was there set for him, lifting up his eyes to Heaven, knocking upon his breast, he said, I am as willing to go to my death, as to put off my doublet to go to bed, I despise the shame as well as the Cross, I know I am going to a joyful place ; with many like expressions.

When the Post met him about St. *James*'s Church, that was sent to the Parliament to emediate for a reprieve, and told him he could not prevail in it, he said, Sir, I pray God reward you for your pains, I hope and am well assured to find a better pardon than any they can give, my hope is not in man but in the living God.

The "Post" here means the special messenger ; the word was not yet restricted to the ordinary carriage of letters.

At the place of Execution he made this profession of his faith, his breeding, his cause he had fought in :

Gentlemen, First I was bred up in the true Protestant Religion : having my education and breeding, from that honoured house my dear Lord and Master (honourable *in State Trials*) *Strafford*, which place I dare boldly say, was as well governed and ruled as ever any yet before it, I much doubt, better than any will be after it, unless it please God to put a period to these distracted times : this Faith and Religion I say I have been bred in, and I thank God I have hitherto lived in, without the least wavering, and now I am resolved, by God's assistance, to die in.

Those pains are nothing, if compared to those dolours and pains which Jesus Christ our Saviour hath suffered for us : when in a bloody sweat he indured the wrath of God, the pains of hell, and the cursed and shameful death which was due to our sins ; therefore I praise the Lord that I am not plagued with far more grievous punishment, that the like hath befaln others, who undoubtedly are most glorious and blessed Saints with Christ in heaven ; it is the Lord's affliction, and who will not take any affliction in good part when it comes from the hand of God, and what shall we receive good from the hands of God, and not receive evil ? and though I desire, as I am carnal, that this Cup may depart from me, yet not my Will, but thy will be done : Death brings unto the godly an end of sinning, and of all miseries due unto sin ; so that after death there shall be no more sorrow, nor cry, or pain, for God shall wipe away all tears from our eyes, by death our souls shall be delivered from thraldrom, and this corruptible body shall put on incorruption, and this mortal immortality.

Therefore blessed are they that are delivered out of so vile a world, and freed from such a body of bondage and corruption, the soul shall enjoy immediate Communion with God in everlasting bliss and glory, it takes us from the miseries of this world, and society of sinners, to the city of the living God, the Celestial *Jerusalem*.

I bless God I am thought worthy to suffer for his Name, and for so good a cause, and if I had a thousand lives, I would willingly lay them down for the cause of my King the Lord's Anointed ; the Scripture commands us to fear God and honour the King, to be subject to every Ordinance of man, for the Lord's sake, whether to the King as supreme, or to those that are in Authority under him : I have been always faithful to my Trust ; and though I have been most basely accused for betraying *Liverpool*, yet I take God to witness it is a most false aspersion, for I was then sick in my bed, and knew not of the delivering of it, till the Officers and Soldiers had done it without my consent, and then I was carried (*prisoner* in State Trials) to Sir *John Meldrum*, afterwards I came down into the country, and seeing I could not live quietly at home, I was persuaded by Colonel *Fairfax*, Colonel *Overton*, Lieutenant Colonel *Fairfax*, whom I
(Forbes *in State Trials*)
took for my good friends, to march in their Troops, which I did, but with intention still to do my King the best service when occasion was, and so I did ; and I pray God to turn the hearts of all the soldiers unto their lawful Sovereign, that this land may enjoy Peace, which till then it will never do : and though thou killest me yet will I put my trust in thee, wherefore I trust in God he will not fail me nor forsake me.

Except from the narration of Clarendon, which in this point will not, as we have already seen, bear critical examination, there is no reason for supposing but that Morris is here telling the exact truth : And that his being taken prisoner by Sir John Meldrum, and afterwards dismissed, either on parole or exchange, was really the correct history of the termination of his first service. For at this time, the contest between the rival parties had not developed the amount of bitterness which entered into it, when the Independents obtained strength, and gained the upper hand. In August, 1644, when Sir John Meldrum took Liverpool, Presbyterians and Independents were united against Romanists and High Churchmen, many of the more moderate Churchmen rather inclining towards the former party, and in some instances joining with them temporarily. The alliance did not, however, last ; as the Independents became stronger, these "moderate" Churchmen, and even the Presbyterians themselves, grew disgusted, and returned to the ranks of the Royalists, though only after their vacillation had so strengthened the aggressive and more unscrupulous faction, that these latter were able to act without them, perhaps, in fact, better pleased that such should be the case.

Then ensued the policy of Plunder for the Army officers, and that of Death to the officers of the Royalist Army, of which this trial of Colonel Morris and Cornet Blackburn was but a conspicuous example.

The correction of "Forbes" for "Fairfax" in the two Collections of State Trials was warranted by the facts. Two of the three officers named by Morris, saw their mistake as quickly as he, but when too late. (See page 264.)

The narrative continues,

Then he took his Bible and read divers Psalms fit for his own occasion and consolation, and then put up divers prayers, some publickly and some privately, the publick was this that follows:

A PRAYER.

Welcome, blessed hour, the period of my Pilgrimage, the term of my Bondage, the end of my cares, the close of my sighs, the bound of my travels, the goal of my (sins *in State Trials*) (gaol *in S. T.*) race, and the heaven of my hopes ; I have fought a long fight in much weakness, (haven *in State Trials*)
I have finished my course though in great faintness, and the Crown of my joy is, that through the strength of thy grace, I have both kept the true faith, and have fought for my King's, the Lords Anointed's cause without any wavering, for which, and in which I die ; I do willingly resign my flesh, I despise the World, and I defy the Devil, who hath no part nor share in me ; and now what is my hope, my hope Lord Jesu is even in thee, for I know that thou my Redeemer livest, and that thou wilt immediately receive my Soul, and raise up my body also at the last Day, and I shall see thee in my flesh with these eyes and none other : And now, O Lord, let thy Spirit of comfort help mine infirmities, and make supplication for me with sighs and groans that cannot be expressed ; I submit myself wholly to thy will, I commit my Soul to thee as my faithful Redeemer, who hast bought it with thy most precious Blood ; I confess to all the world, I know no name under heaven by which I may be saved, but thine my Jesu, my Saviour; I renounce all confidence in any merits save thine ; I thankfully acknowledge all thy blessings, I unfeignedly bewail all my sins, I stedfastly believe all thy promises, I heartily forgive all my Enemies, I willingly leave all my Friends, I utterly loath all earthly comforts, and I entirely long for thy coming, Come Lord Jesus, come quickly, Lord Jesus receive my Spirit.
The Private were to himself, his hat being before his eyes ; after this he put up divers (*short* added in State Trials) Ejaculations : As, I know my Redeemer liveth ; Father unto thy hands I commend my spirit, for thou hast redeemed it ; O God, thou God of Truth, Lord Jesus receive my Spirit ; and many of the like, and so he yielded to Death.

It has already been noted how largely Scriptural language entered into the ordinary conversation of the men of the seventeenth century; and it might have been expected that on such an occasion as this, the words of a religiously-minded man would have been more charged than usual, with phrases from religious formularies. But we were hardly prepared to find that Colonel Morris's quotations are taken indifferently from the two translations of the Bible, which were current at the time: from the Breeches Bible, as it is called, which was for so long the ordinary Bible of the people, and from King James's Bible, which was issued when his father was but a lad, and which had at the time almost superseded its predecessor.

It might have excited less surprise had the words of the "Puritan Bible" been in the mouths of the opponents of the King; but here Colonel Morris makes use of an expression, found in that volume and nowhere else, and substitutes it for the equivalent found in King James's Bible.

The elements of Colonel Morris's Prayer, "Let thy Spirit of Comfort help mine infirmities, and make supplication for me with sighs and groans that cannot be expressed," are to be found scattered in the Book of Common Prayer, and in ROMANS viii. 26 (King James's version,) but for the *sighs that cannot be expressed*, reference must be had to the Breeches Bible.

In King James's version, the text is *groans* that cannot be *uttered*; and it is interesting to notice that Morris used both the "sighs" of the Puritan Bible, and the "groans" of the Authorised Version, while he adopted the "expressed" of the former edition, in preference to the "uttered" of the later version.

In his preliminary examination before the Magistrates at York, Blackburn declared himself to have been of the parish of Almondbury, and by the courtesy of the Vicar of Almondbury (whose "Annals of Almondbury" are so well known) we have been supplied from the existing Registers of that parish with a list of above fifty entries referring to persons of the name of Blagburn or Blackburn, between 1607 and 1650. Careful collation of these makes it evident that there must have been at least four—or perhaps five— families of Blackburn in that parish at that time, located respectively at Armitage, Cold hill, Hall bower, High house, Newsome, Quarry hill, and Field end, though some of these names may have been, and very probably were, second names for the same place.

The entries referring to Cornet Blackburn seem to be : Michael Blagburn (father), buried 12 Feb., 1624-5, whose children were—

Bapt.
26 May, 1614, Dorothy
20 Oct., 1616, Grace
(day torn out) Dec., 1619, Michael (the Cornet)
29 Sept., 1622, Mathew
17 July, 1625, Sarah (posthumous)

And there is moreover at Somerset House the registered will of Edmund Blackburn, clothier, of the Armitage in the township of South Crossland. This is dated 8 Nov., 1656, and was proved in 1659, in P.C.C. by Mathew Blackburn, his brother, who may be the Mathew born in 1622. Mathew's will was proved in July, 1665.

Of the mother of Michael Blackburn we learn nothing, nor do we trace anything of his own marriage or of that of his brother Mathew. His father appears to have died when he was only five years old, and this corroborates the description which Drake gives of him (see page 77) when he calls him a Tenant, not the *son* of a Tenant ; Coldhill, being adjacent to Hall bower, the seat of the Beaumonts.

But we note that, in his short address below, the Cornet says that his Parents *are* of a honest quality and condition. Now, if we could be sure that a mistake was not possible here, the expression would have tended to show that his father was still alive at the time of his trial. But the probabilities are either that " were" was reported as " are" ; or that the expression " Parents" was understood for " Relatives," a not unusual use of the word.

We have now concluded the account given in the " State Trials"; but the " Exact Relation," which concerns itself with Blackburn as well as with Morris, has appended

THE SPEECH OF CORNET MICHAEL BLACKBURN, IMMEDIATELY BEFORE HIS DEATH. August 23, 1649.

It is expected I should say something, and indeed it is my desire to say something, and but a little. I am not a Gentleman by birth, but my Parents are of an honest quality and condition ; I was brought up in the Protestant Religion, and in that Religion I have lived, and in that I now die ; I have some five or six years since engaged in this War, wherein I had no other End or Intention but to do my King true and faithful service, according to my duty and the dictate of my Conscience ; I have not done so much service as I desired, but I have been always faithful to him, and wish I could have done him more ; and for his Son, the King that now is, I wonder any man of this Kingdom should have the boldness or impudence to lift up his hand against him, to keep him from his Crown whereof he is Heir apparent, and hath as good right and title to it by his Birthright, as any man living hath of his Inheritance or Possession ; I pray God bless him, forgive all my Enemies, and Lord Jesus receive my Spirit.

This statement of Blackburn's position in life is exactly borne out by the particulars we have been able to collect of him, his opening avowal that he was " not a gentleman by birth," seeming to be intended as a contrast to that of his fellow-prisoner, a gentleman brought up in the household —as one of the family—of the Earl of Strafford.

The five or six years since, as he says, he engaged in the War, may easily be taken to refer to some short time before 1645, when, as Michael Blagborne, he was named by Nathan Drake, as coming to the Castle (see page 77.) And knowing as we now do what was the strength of his loyalty to the royal cause, it is curious to recall the almost supercilious terms in which Nathan Drake couched his few remarks concerning him.

For nearly five years the system of proscription, of which the trial of Colonel Morris and Cornet Blackburn was so outrageous an instance, had been in force. It seems to have begun in the autumn of 1644, but was then confined to the native Irish who were found armed in England; a measure which Carlyle says was " not uncalled for"; the "not uncalled for" ordinance being one promulgated by Parliament on 24th Oct., 1644, *to hang* any Irish papist taken in arms in this country. Commenced, however, against the "Wild Irish," the scope of the measure and its spirit were extended, till at length the ruling authorities had, as we have seen, brought themselves to instruct the Judges that such an one was "Worthy of death"; and the Judges had brought themselves to take the hint, and with a packed jury ready to follow the lead, mercilessly ignore each plea, and resolutely overbear the victim that was once within their toils.

The following, which we find in the aforenamed contemporary Tract, "ANARCHIA ANGLICANA," hardly seems language too strong for use concerning the mockery of "JUSTICE," which was then prevalent. And it exhibits the light in which out-spoken Royalists regarded the farce of Morris's Trial, while the foretelling and fore-judging shows what was thought of the partiality of the Assize tribunal:

> The mungrel, hypocritical, three-headed conquest [explained in the margin to be "1 Councel of War. 2. Councel of State. 3 Parliament."] we live under hath dispoyled Justice of her ballance, and left her in a Military posture, with a Sword to strike, but no scales to weigh withal : Our licenced News Books (like Ill-Boading-Birds) fore-told and fore-judged *Morrice's* death a month before; He dyed resolutely.

The following Chronology of events in the life of Colonel Morris may be useful as being a direct refutation of the slanders that have been put forth concerning him, which are evidently inconsistent with these well-ascertained facts.

1619 or 1620.—Born, just before the commencement of the records of the Church Registers at South Kirkby, which open in 1621.
    Page to the Earl of Strafford (page 149.)
1636.—Ensign to the Earl of Strafford's foot (see page 174.)

1641.—Captain in Sir Hy. Tichburn's regiment (see page 174.)
1641.—Wounded at the storming of Rosse Castle.
1642, June 2—Major by Commission from the Earl of Ormond (page 174.)
1643.—Married Margaret, daughter of Dr. Dawson, Bishop of Cloufert, who was then aged 16. (She died, as the wife of Jonas Buckley, on 28th October, 1665, in her 38th year) (page 165.)
 Served in the Royal Army under Lord Byron, and was at the fight at Nantwich, where he is said to have been the only field-officer who brought any of his men from the field (page 174.)
1644.—At the defence of Liverpool from Sir John Meldrum (page 278), but taken prisoner at the surrender, and liberated on parole or exchange.
 His eldest son, Robert, born this year (page 165.)
 Retired to his own estate (pp. 174 and 278.)
1645.—Persuaded by Col. Forbes, Col. Overton and Lieut.-Col. Fairfax to serve in their troop (page 278.)
 His daughter, Mary, born (page 165.)
 At the sieges of Pontefract and Sandal against the Royalists (page 260.)
 Aug.—At Knottingley, with Col. Forbes and Col. Thomas Fairfax, ready to seize Ponfefract Castle for the King (page 260.) (Before the fall of Sandal.)
1646, Aug 2.—His daughter, Jane, baptised at South Kirkby.
1646, Sept.—Made an unsuccessful attempt to seize the Castle (page 147.)
1646-7, Jan 21.—Released from custody on the charge.
1647, Nov. 15.—His son, John, baptised at South Kirkby.
1648, May.—Another unsuccessful attempt, at which Col. Morris headed the party, and was first on the scaling ladder.
 May 31, the Fast day.—Col. Morris came to Pontefract, intending to surprise the Castle (page 247.)
 June 3.—Effected the surprise.
 June 16.—The intruded Vicar, Joseph Ferrett, had a safe conduct to depart the town.
 Aug. 9.—Cromwell paid a flying visit to Pontefract, on his road northwards.
 Aug. 17.—Battle of Preston.
 Oct. 9.—The Parliamentarian troops enter the town.
 Oct. 23 (cir).—Seizure of 200 or 300 head of cattle at Knottingley (pp. 187 and 192.)
 Oct. 27.—The Rainsborough sally (page 184.)
 Oct. 29.—Death of Rainsborough (page 184.)
 Nov. 1 or 2.—Cromwell arrives before Pontefract (page 189.)
 Nov. 9.—Cromwell summons the Castle (page 190.)
 Dec. 4.—Cromwell leaves Major-General Lambert in charge of the siege (page 199.)
1648-9, Jan. 10 (cir).—The Guns and Mortars arrived before Pontefract (page 206).
 Feb. 2.—Col. Morris proclaims Charles II. as King.
 Feb. 3.—The Guns play upon the Battlements (pp. 209, 210.)
 March 18 (Sunday).—Morris and Blackburn escape.
 March 24.—The Castle surrendered on the last day of the old year.
1649, Aug. 16.—Morris and Blackburn tried.
 Aug. 23.—Morris and Blackburn executed.

Much effort was made to save Col. Morris, and it was hoped that he might have escaped from Lancaster Castle where he and Blackburn were confined : the Governor was indeed accused of undue lenity towards him ; but the many watchful determined eyes upon him frustrated all the efforts of his friends in his favour. The Baynes correspondence sufficiently shows with what perseverance he was followed throughout the three months during which he awaited trial, and with how much personal malignity he was regarded by the less generous of those against whom he had acted, and who had reason to dread his bravery and ability.

The final scene is slightly glanced at in a letter among the Clarendon State Papers in the Bodleian Library. It is endorsed,

To my honble Vncle Sr J. B., Knight of the honble order of the Bathe : thes. [Probably Sir John Byron, like Morris, an excepted person.]

The document, which is dated August 31st, 1649, will be found towards the beginning of the volume. The series is unfortunately arranged, the Old Style documents being translated as it were into N.S. This letter is O.S., and being bound up with N.S. documents of a later date, runs risk of being overlooked ; for it must be sought in the volume which commences in Sept., 1649. In the Calendar it is vol. 2, page 20.

After mentioning Irish affairs, with which it mainly deals, the letter continues

Colonel Moris, that kept Pontefract castle, was hangd, drawne & quartered att Yorke. his indictment was for Surprising one of ye kings castle & holding of it against the king, hee pleaded his commission from the King. yt would not serue. * * * * * * * * *

Yor most dutifull &
obedient nepheu
R. F.

This is the only statement we have met with in reference to the actual mode of execution of Morris, for to Carlyle's "lost his head," we attach no importance whatever. The account in the Clarendon Papers is however very probable, death in that manner being, during several centuries, the horrible doom of those convicted of High Treason.

We have thus traced the termination of the career of Colonel Morris and Cornet Blackburn as possible leaders. We slightly diverge to show what was the fate of the conquered commonalty. Morris, when he seized the Castle for the King, drove the garrison into the Magazine, where they were confined for eleven weeks : a fate horrible enough to contemplate even at this distance of time. . But none of the witnesses complain that the confinement of that number of men in so contracted a space caused death or sickness among them. Miserable as was their condition during those summer months, the large ventilating shaft of four feet by seven would have helped materially to alleviate its horror. And the unhappy prisoners would, at least, have been able to congratulate themselves that they were not as others. The Roundheads similarly imprisoned their captives, but their places of imprisonment were the holds of ships, and the ultimate destination of very many of them was the Plantations. That is to say the unfortunate men were transported to the colonies, in a condition of slavery. Sold to the highest bidder, *en masse*, or granted away to some Petitioner, who would make use of them as labourers, care was effectually taken that they should not again make their appearance. " Being in a friend's hands," as says Oliver Cromwell, " there need be no fear of their being ever employed against you." And there could be but one termination to the system, although there might be a difference, more or less harsh, in the way in which some of the unhappy prisoners were treated.

But the greater number of them having been quietly killed out of the way by the ordinary hardships of forced labour, the planters at length by experience, ascertained at the cost of the lives of those first experimented upon, that white men could not bear the strain ; and when the supply of these captives failed, the importation of negroes was the natural recourse of the cultivator. Negro importation thus supplied the demand caused by the cessation of the stream of white captives which flowed throughout the middle of the seventeenth century.

Conversely, we may say that this Cromwellian system of sending prisoners of war "to the Plantations," as it was euphemistically styled, was the direct parent of the system of slave hunting. Imported black captives, who could endure the climate, were the natural successors of imported whites, to whom out-door labour, under the tropical heats, was fatal.

The Tanner MSS., in the Bodleian, have preserved a most instructive letter of Oliver Cromwell on this subject which Carlyle has faithfully reproduced without a word of reprobation. Nay with something very like approbation: "Doubtless" saith he," the request was complied with !"

Let us see what the request was :—

For the Honourable William Lenthall, Esquire, Speaker of the Honourable House of Commons : These.

SIR, Dalhousie, 8th Oct., 1648.

Upon the desire of divers Noblemen and others of the Kingdom of Scotland, I am bold to become a suitor to you on the behalf of this Gentleman, the Bearer, Colonel Robert Montgomery ; son-in-law to the Earl of Eglinton. Whose faithfulness to you in the late troubles may render him worthy of a far greater favour than I shall, at this time, desire for him : for I can assure you, that there is not a Gentleman of that Kingdom that appeared more active against the late Invaders of England than himself.

Sir, it is desired that you would please to grant him an Order for Two-thousand of the common Prisoners that were of Duke Hamilton's Army. You will have very good security that they shall not for the future trouble you : he will ease you of the charge of keeping them, as speedily as any other way you can dispose of them ; besides their being in a friend's hands, so as there need be no fear of their being ever employed against you.

Sir, what favour you shall please to afford the Gentleman will very much oblige many of your friends of the Scottish Nation ; and particularly your most humble servant,

OLIVER CROMWELL.

"Two thousand of the prisoners" taken at Preston : of that Scotch army of which Duke Hamilton was the Commander: of that very body to strengthen whose efforts, Colonel Morris's feat was conceived : in fine, of the exact parallel to the Garrison driven down into the Magazine of Pontefract Castle.

They were simply *given away into Slavery!* For as Carlyle says, in his naive manner, " Doubtless the request was complied with !" Doubtless ! " The Bearer" was " son-in-law to the Earl of Eglinton;"—by the bye, he was the Earl's *own* son, his youngest son, and the less said of the subsequent " faithfulness" of the family to the Commonwealth the better, from the Cromwellian and Carlylean point of view. For even this bribe of " two thousand of the common prisoners," as a gift, did not secure their absolute fidelity. The prisoners were " doubtless" soon " used up," and the grant forgotten, till it was disinterred from the Tanner MSS. by Cary, from whose " Memorials of the Great Civil War," Carlyle extracted it. It does not appear in the original edition of the "Letters and Speeches."

Similar acts followed the Battles of Worcester and Dunbar. Indeed, the ravages made by the War in this and other ways were so great, that in many parishes at least one third of the popular surnames disappeared between 1645 and 1660. That is to say, if careful reckoning is made of the surnames of those registered as heads of families in the lower walks of life, in the former year, it will be found that a third are unrepresented in the Church Registers of the same parish in 1660 and subsequently; they have absolutely disappeared from the native homes of their forefathers.

There seems to be a general conspiracy to hide these horrors, for the ordinary histories absolutely ignore them ; and it is only in some of the by-paths of historical study, that the reader meets with the particulars. Hume, for instance, although as a Scotsman one might have thought he would have been touched by the sufferings of his country-men, makes no reference whatever to the subject. But yet the facts are indubitable. The Parliamentary History (xx. 72) tells us that after the Battle of Worcester :—

> Most of the common soldiers were sent to the English Plantations; and 1500 of them were granted to the Guiney Merchants, and sent to work in the Gold mines there.

More fortunate were the "large numbers" which Wells, in his History of the Bedford Level, states to have been employed in draining the great level of the Fens. But most fortunate perhaps were those referred to in the following entry in the Churchwardens' accounts of the parish of St. Margaret, Westminster, the Parish Church of the House of Commons :—

> P'd to Thos. Wright for 67 loads of soyle laid on the graves in Tothill Fields, wherein 1200 Scotch prisoners, taken at the fight at Worcester, were buried; and for other pains taken with his teeme of horses, about mending the Sanctuary Highway, when Gen. Ireton was buried .. .. xxxs

And, while yet the Worcester "mercy" was fresh news, under date Oct. 2nd, 1651, Cromwell, in a letter, also preserved in Carlyle, replied to Rev. John Cotton, of Boston, who had described to him, what was being done with some of the Dunbar prisoners.

This Reverend John Cotton had been the Minister of Boston, who emigrated to New England, and transplanted the name of the Lincolnshire town which he had left, to his new home. He had thus written on "Twenty-eighth of Fifth" *i.e.* July, "1651," and his letter would have been on mid-ocean while the Battle of Worcester was being decided.

> The Scots whom God delivered into your hands at Dunbar, and whereof *sundry were sent hither*, we have been desirous, as we could, to make their yoke easy. Such as were sick of the scurvy, or other diseases, have not wanted physic and chirurgery. They have not been sold for Slaves to *perpetual* servitude; but for six, or seven or eight years, as we do our own. And *he that bought the most of them*, I hear, buildeth Houses for them, for every Four a house; and layeth some acres of ground thereto, which he giveth them as their own, requiring them three days in the week to work for him by turns, and four days for themselves; and promiseth, as soon as they can repay him the money he laid out for them, he will set them at liberty.

Thus far the Christian Minister, honestly endeavouring

to lighten the burden of the expatriated survivors; and rejoicing that the Scots who had been delivered into Cromwell's hand had been fortunate enough to meet with a fate less hard than the *perpetual* servitude,—the life-long slavery, to which that successful General had practically condemned them.

The perusal of these narratives of horror is necessary to make us tolerant of the use to which the Magazine of Pontefract Castle was put during those eleven or thirteen weeks.

It must be a sad awakening to those who have looked upon this civil strife as having been so largely one of principle, to find the leaders grasping on all hands, at either "Lands of Inheritance" at £300 a year, or at "Prisoners" by batches of Two Thousand at a time, even although they were worth, in some cases, only *half-a-crown a dozen*, which was the actual price given for numbers of them.

But perhaps the special interest of Colonel Robert Montgomery in his twenty guineas' worth of Scottish captives, might have been materially quickened by the fact of his elder brother, the coming Earl of Eglinton, having married the eldest daughter of the defeated and shortly-to-be executed Marquis of Hamilton. We should rejoice if we could find that, with his interest awakened in that manner, he gave liberty—Scottish liberty—to the unhappy men whose fate was thus influenced by the victorious General, who first conquered them in battle, and then did his best to consign them to perpetual slavery, as a means of "preventing them from troubling" him any more.

WE HAD REACHED thus far with our Collection: had, as we thought, completed all we should have to say with regard to Colonel Morris, and were commencing with the account of the Demolition of the Castle, when information arrived of the existence in the Bodleian, among the Clarendon State Papers, of a MS. history of this third siege. As, on enquiry, we found that this really was the case, and as the document appeared to have been hitherto absolutely unknown, we have had it copied with care, and now add it to what has hitherto been said.

In some respects, it will be seen to contradict, and we are inclined to think, with truth, what has been the usually received history; in many respects it confirms, with additional circumstances, the account given in the letter of Capt. Thomas Paulden; but it throws an altogether unexpected light upon Morris's relations with those within the Castle.

From it we learn that the assertion that Colonel Morris was a friend, or even on friendly terms, with Colonel Cotterell, was a fabrication. Hence all the allegations of personal treachery made against Morris, fall at once to the ground; while the account given by Clarendon, (see pp. 168-9) was evidently founded upon an entire misapprehension, a confusion between the governor,—Colonel Overton,—and his successor or deputy,—Colonel Cotterell.

It is true that Morris was on friendly terms with the Governor of Pontefract Castle; but he knew little of Colonel Cotterell, the Governor of 1648. Morris's friend was Colonel Overton, who was himself one of the *via media* party, who, however well-inclined they might have been to see Presbyterianism prevail, were by no means well-inclined to see Cromwell's party get the upper hand, but were waiting for an opportunity to reveal themselves, when their so doing would not be utter destruction.

Had Colonel Overton remained governor of Pontefract Castle, it appears as if the seizure of the fortress would have been effected with his consent; or rather, that at the favourable moment, he would have declared for the King: That favourable moment being at the end of 1646, when it was hoped that the Scots would so pronounce; or in the summer of 1648, if the Scots had defeated the Cromwellian army.

But, however, the MS. will show all this in due course, for Col. Overton had been transferred to the Governorship of Hull, in November, 1647, and henceforth, Morris had no friend at the head of affairs in Pontefract Castle. Colonel Cotterell's deposition had prepared us for this: but still it is somewhat astonishing to have even Clarendon's History of the Great Rebellion thus shown to be so largely at fault in the particulars concerning the seizure of Pontefract Castle, for which it has been hitherto the principal authority.

The document now unearthed seems to have been written by Capt. Thos. Paulden, and to be the complement to his account of the seizure of Rainsborough, which we have already given (see pp. 149—154.) How this remarkable document can have escaped notice so long, is a matter of wonder, especially as Capt. Paulden's letter concerning the seizure of Colonel Rainsborough has been printed and re-printed, over and over again, and has been read with much interest by several generations. But it may be examined in the Bodleian by anyone interested in the subject, its reference no. being **Clarendon State Paper 2978.**

The document now discovered commences thus,—more abruptly than does what is usually called Capt. Paulden's letter:

> After the first warre in a manner was ended and his late ma'tie was come to the Scotts then before Newarke, and it was hoped they would have declared for him, my Brother had some meetings w'th C. Marris (a Confident of Overtons then gouernor of Pomfrett castle) wth whom he had formerly contracted an acquaintance whilest hee had serued against the King in the seige of Sandall, and had some assurance of his good affections to his Ma'tie as well from his zealous professions to that purpose as also some good offices hee had done vs in that siege. and finding him very ready to entertaine any proposall whereby hee might redeeme his reputation w'th the King and his party, w'ch hee had deseruedly lost by some late actions, hee propounded the surprize of Pomfrett as a thing faisible to him by reason of his intimacy w'th Overton and a service considerable to his ma'tie if the Scotts should then declare as many did beleeue they would; w'ch proposition hee chearefully embraced, and promised that hee would open a Sally-Port whensoeuer the King should thinke it convenient for his service; & my Brother promised to pr'pare what number of men might bee necessary for that designe.

So far as can be gathered from this very unpromising opening sentence, the writer seems to intend to say that while he was engaged in the defence of Sandal, he made acquaintance with Morris, who was among the besiegers. And this is consistent with what we have hitherto learned; with what Morris asserted in his last speech, that he had been persuaded by the two Fairfaxes and Colonel Overton, to serve in their troops, as the best way to do service to the cause of Monarchy. All, however, at this time, depended upon the line taken by the Scots; and when they decided upon surrendering the King to the Army, on receiving their arrears of pay from the Parliament, they entirely cut away the ground of any hope that the Royalist party might have had of maintaining an independent position. The Parliament, by its Army, then had the King in virtual imprisonment, to await the time when by its instrument, Colonel Pride, the officers should assume the mastery, in mockery, as it were, of the "Self-Denying Ordinance" of three years previously. Colonel Pride's seizure of the King in the Isle of Wight, and his forcible detention of so many of the membrrs of the majority as were sufficient to turn that majority into a minority, were only two single steps in the same determined course.

Capt. Paulden continues:—

But the Scotts crossing our expectation and deliuering the King, made that attempt vnseasonable till such time as Duke Hamiltons designe was in some readynesse, & Sr Marmaduke Langdale was dispatched into Scotland to com'aund such English as shonld repayre thither; but soone after Col. Overton was remooued from Pomfrett to bee gouernor of Hull and major Cottrell made gouernour of Pomfrett w'th whom Marris had little or no acquaintance nor any such trust as might render him vsefull in that designe of opening a Sally-port. therefore wee was then to thinke of some other way to bring the businesse about, and it was not long before wee made an acquaintance w'th some in the Castle who had formerly seru'd the King and were then compelled to serue the Parliam't for protection from some that persecuted them for actions done in the warre. Jt (1) was two of these persons onely w'th whom wee treated who assured vs that they knew fiue more w'thin the Castle who were very ready to hazard their liues to serue the King.

The figures within brackets refer to additions by the writer, which add much to the apparent genuineness of the whole.

From this particular addition, we learn that the two were Lieut. Ashby, and one Copley. This might have been the Lionel Copley against whom we have already found Mr. Margetts (p. 204) in possession of some charge, to which he hesitates to give the credence which he cannot altogether withhold. Mr. Copley was probably deranged sometimes; and it is on record (SURTEES vol. XL., p. 125) that a true bill was found against him by the Grand Jury "for having at Rotherham, on 25 Sept., 1664, beaten one Richard Firth, put a bridle into his mouth, got on his back, and ridden him about, for half-an-hour, kicking him to make him move." Possibly the charge in 1649 was for some similar absurd extravagance : and his behaviour, as recorded by Capt. Paulden may have been the consequence of the same mental defect. That is, supposing that the Lionel Copley was the "one Copley."

So the designe was form'd that a ladder should bee made & the place of the wall assign'd where the Corporall that was our friend should sett a Sentinell that was true to vs at the night & houre appointed, and so accordingly (hauing receiued a Com'and from Sr Mar: Langd: to doe it as soone as wee could) wee pr'pared ourselves and the night appointed randeuouzed in a wood some fiue miles from the Castle some three score horse & 100 foote resoluing if the surprize succeeded to march imediately to Wakefeilde to take a troope of horse of the ennemy w'ch was then all the horse the Parliam'nt had in the County.

This brings us to the second of the series of attempts on the Castle, which concluded with the exploit of June 3rd. At first—during Overton's governorship—Morris intended to open a Sally-Port and so admit the Royalists. But owing to Overton's being transferred to Hull,—which was in November, 1647,—and the deputy-governorship, or lieutenant-governorship being given to Cotterell, this design could not be perfected; and the resolute party had to attempt to effect their purpose by a scaling ladder.

Comparing this with the account already printed (see page 238) we notice considerable discrepancy in the numbers. Fox says 300 infantry and 50 horse: Paulden gives us three score horse and 100 foot, which antecedently seems the more probable.

There is no hint of the position of the wood in which the horse and foot "randevouzed"; but the distance, five miles, was rather more than that between Pontefract and Colonel Morris's house.

To this purpose wee marched towards the Castle about 8 aclocke or nine in the euening being then the latter end of May or beginning of June and Came to the place of the wall appointed, about breake of day w'th our Ladder, & calling softely to the Sentinell wee found ourselues answered by another then wee expected who gave the Alarum to the garrison, & before wee could reare our ladder we saw the Gouernor & Soldiers vpon the wall. it being by this time growne a little light they begunne to fire their musketts & wee to runne away leauing our ladder w'ch was very heauy behind vs. wee Jmagined then that wee had beene betrayed by some w'thin, but afterwards wee learned that this was occasioned by our Corporalls falling drunke in the euening and another Corporalls being putt on the guard, and consequently another sentinell then ours.

Capt. Paulden is slightly at fault in the matter of the date of this attempt. It was on 18th May. Dates are not his strong point, by any means, but it is remarkable that he committed this particular slip, inasmuch as he subsequently says that the successful attempt of 3rd June was on the Saturday fortnight after the unsuccessful attempt with the scaling ladder. He thus remembered the particular that the occurrence was on the "next Saturday fortnight"; though he did not remember the exact date from which the Saturday fortnight was to be calculated.

The drunken Corporal (see page 150) was Corporal Floyd, afterwards excepted from mercy : who was one of those who hid in the passage under Piper Tower, and ultimately got safe away.

<small>The foot dispersed & shifted for themselues, & the horse marched some 7 miles together ; & the most of them thinking it in vaine to expect a second opportunity, marched pr'sently for the North to Sr Mar. Langd: & came safe thither. Col: Marris, my Brother, and some 13 or 14 more, gott into a wood. they hoped to bee secure till they could know where the mistake was ; and to that purpose we sent a Spy to Pomfrett who brought vs backe word the same day that no man was taken nor any one either w'thin or w'thout the castle discouered. that the corporall was very sensible of his errour in being drunke & desired to redeeme it by any hazard wee pleased to putt him upon. This encouraged vs to resolue vpon a second attempt & C. Marris to that purpose rid pr'sently to the Castle w'th 2 other, two w'ch belonged to the garrison who had beene w'thout w'th vs, who p'tended they had beene in the Country & had heard that there was some plott ageinst the Castle & therefore had made what hast they could to their garrison. This the Gouern' lookt vpon as a piece of diligence he ought to thanke them for & told them that hereafter he would haue all his garrison ly w'thin the castle (whereas before they onely lodged w'thin the castle that were vpon the watch & the rest lay in the towne), & in order to it issued out warr'ts pr'sently into the Country to Com'aund them to bring in bedds for a hundred soldiers.</small>

There is again no hint of the position of the wood in which Colonel Morris and his companions found refuge, except that it was evidently to the North of Pontefract. Capt. Timothy Paulden was one of those who "marched presently for the North," leaving his two brothers, Capt. William, and the writer, Capt. Thomas, to continue their attempts on the Castle ; though, as we shall learn from this MS., he was in arms there, again, during some parts of June and July.

The "Spy sent to Pomfrett," we learn from Fox to have been Morris's own wife (see page 239), who brought him the information which encouraged him to go boldly to the Castle, and inspect and investigate for himself.

The " issuing out warrants" for beds was just one of those exactions which made the presence of the fortress so terrible an infliction on the neighbouring country. As we gather, the hundred beds were requisitioned from the neighbouring villages, so many from each.

> This opportunity of bringing in bedds wee thought might serue vs, & accordingly it was ordered that on the Satturday fortnight following (w'ch was the time limited for some townes to bring in bedds) wee should try what could bee done for the gaining of the place, & therefore desired them w'thin so to order there businisse that all our friends might bee upon the guard that night.

A very necessary precaution; and considering what had already happened with the drunken corporal, the Colonel might have had warrant for adding the injunction that the men should be kept sober.

> so the day being come Col. Marris went w'th fowre men carrying a bed, my Brother w'th other fowre, & three others as from another towne come to compound for theirs. C. Marris & my Brother had swords, the rest onely daggers & Pockett pistolls.

There need be little doubt but that this circumstantial account represents the exact truth; Morris and Paulden with three helpers, each brought two beds, and three others came as pretending to wish to pay instead of obey the requisition. There were thus eleven in the party, besides Colonel Morris and Capt. Paulden, the two ringleaders; and not either eight, nine, ten, or twenty-two as has been variously stated. For notwithstanding his haziness of language, easily misinterpreted, we gather that Paulden means to say that he and Morris were each one of the four, and not with the four, in the sense of addition to them. For " with," we must understand " among."

The particulars of their arms may also be relied on, as may be the statement that there was no disguise, at least of the leaders, Col. Morris (persistently called Marris) and Capt. Paulden.

upon their appearance at the gates and saying they had brought bedds according to ye warr'ts sent them, the draw-bridge was lett downe by their friends and they entred to ye 2d gate, w'ch likewise hauing ye wickett opened by ye sentinell they entered to the maine guard & there threw downe their bedds to rest them, & Marris throwing out a Crowne to the souldiers desired fowre or fiue of them to goe fetch ale for the rest to drinke his health ; and they being gone out, all pr'sently draw their pistolls and askes the rest of the guard if they would have q'rter & told them the Castle was for the King, w'ch they hearing accepted q'rter & rendered themselves prisoners w'thout further resistance & so were put in hold.

How often must the Paulden brothers have talked this tale together during the subsequent siege : how often must this writer, Thomas, have pictured the party coming through Micklegate, and approaching the Castle gates, which extended nearly to the bottom of Spink lane. But they could not reach even the first gate : they were kept at a distance by the wide and deep moat, as it was sometimes called—though there is no evidence that it contained water—the graft, as is the proper name—that is a pit, from which the natural earth has been removed, as from a grave—which separated this, the West Gate, from the road which led to it. The rock was cut sheer away, leaving a gulph below, now again filled up with made earth,—only an uncertain foundation, as the buildings at the two corners of Spink Lane, which partially rest upon it, testify to this day with extended perpendicular cracks through their walls.

The few details which the writer of this document gives us, furnish a very complete description of the character of this entrance to the Castle. It appears that the Drawbridge being let down the party passed over, through the first gate, and along a passage at the end of which was a second gate, each gate being apparently provided with its wicket, as we gather from the use of the word "likewise."

There is no intimation as to how the portcullis was worked, by whom, or from what apartment ; but at the second gate the party was received by a sentinel, who admitted them to the Ballium by a wicket. To their right was then the Main Guard, the building which to this day bears the Lancaster arms on its front; and under those arms they passed, entering an oblong room supported by a Timber Post,—surely the counterpart of a similar post which then stood in the Round Tower, and round which, it was fabled that King Richard II dodged his murderers, while fighting for his life.

This part of the tale is to a great extent new, but the rest has been often told, though not with the present particularity. Morris seems to have been the leader, and as such, and therefore the paymaster, he here threw down a crown for drink for the soldiers whom he found on guard; and we may easily suppose that the "four or five" volunteers who fetched the liquor were not the "friends" of the new-comers, and were indeed innocent of all knowledge of what was about to be done. These "four or five" having gone out, the drawbridge was raised, by which means their return was cut off, and the adventurers had "four or five" fewer possible opponents. Their course was then quick, sharp, and decisive :—

<blockquote>Under which King, Bezonian? Speak or die!</blockquote>

The Garrison soldiers seem to have made little demur, they accepted quarter, and were soon "put in hold."

<blockquote>The Gouern'r was newly gone to ly downe to repose himselfe. My Brother went to his chamber (whilst the rest some of them guarded the prisoners, others the gate, & others went vpon the walls to secure the sentinells there who yet knew nothing of what was done below) & found him asleepe vpon his bed, & waked him, told him the Castle was taken for the King, & offered him quarter; but hee replyed nothing but raising himselfe vpp takes his rapier w'ch lay drawne by his side & makes a passe, & my Brother vpon it shootes him into the thigh & offered him q'rter againe, w'h hee refused still fighting, till hee had receiued three or fowre wounds more & contracting all his strength & making a violent passe hitts vpon the Bedstocke w'th his rapier & breaks it in three or foure pieces & being faint w'th losse of blood falls downe & askes quarter w'ch hee had & afterwards was recouered of his wounds.</blockquote>

The band had their work still cut out for them. They

possessed the Main Guard, and the Main Guard only; but though only a mere handful, yet knowing their own minds, they felt themselves equal to a host. The sentinels on the walls had not as yet learnt what had passed; and some of the party at once took precautions to prevent their learning anything until it was too late for them to make use of their knowledge. They were quickly disarmed, one after the other: but while this was being done, "my Brother," Capt. Wm. Paulden, and one other, (who, as we know from Colonel Cotterell's deposition (see page 259) and other sources, was "Peter" or "Peters," "an Irishman," "Morris's servant," as he is variously described) went to Colonel Cotterell's chamber, where they found him, after his night-long watch, asleep on his bed, with his sword by his side. He was treated as the sentinels were being dealt with, quickly disarmed, in his case after a struggle in which he was wounded, and then driven down into the dungeon, heated with his unwonted exertions that summer morning, bleeding from his wounds, and breathless with astonishment and indignation at the fate which had befallen him.

While Capt. Paulden was doing his part above with Col. Cotterell, Col. Morris had charge below, and was ready to receive the disarmed and bleeding governor when brought down. As we learn from his deposition, Col. Cotterell hesitated at first to descend those awful steps, and obeyed only when peremptorily ordered by Morris. Thus Clarendon's tale of Morris being in bed with the governor is thoroughly exploded; both his own deposition, and Capt. Paulden's narrative of the circumstance, from the two opposite points of view, concur at least in this, that far from being in bed at the time, Morris was in the chief command of the party.

It may be noticed that Colonel Cotterel's weapon is here called a "rapier"; in the Rainsborough letter it is called a "long tuck." Probably the former was the better name, and technically, more correct; an observation which helps us to the conclusion that the document now in hand is later than the Rainsborough letter, and increases our astonishment that it should have remained unknown, even after the death of the writer, and at a time when the earlier letter was being "Reprinted for the Benefit of the Widow."

The narrative continues:—

This was all the blood that was spilt in recouery of that place w'ch being mastered by onely eleuen they imediately dispatched a messenger to two & twenty horse w'ch was in a wood some fiue miles distant to come away im'ediately into the castle w'ch accordingly they did & entered priuately into the Castle so that yet nothing was knowne in the towne of the surprize.

Here again is mention of the un-named wood some five miles distant. The twenty-two—Thomas Paulden's troop—could easily have entered without the knowledge of the townspeople, by coming the way of either the Darrington road, the Ferrybridge Road, or the Road from Knottingley: but as they could have come by only the first named way, without the knowledge of the troops of horse at Knottingley, we are constrained to the opinion that they entered the Castle from the south.

This narrative ought to leave no room for doubt whether the party consisted of eleven, including the two officers, or eleven besides them. Notwithstanding Capt. Paulden's apparent statement that four helpers came with each of the beds, we cannot but believe that his language is mistaken, that there were indeed but eleven in all, and that the four in each case included the officer in charge. Capt. Paulden, it will be presently seen, made the same confusion when enumerating the party that attacked Colonel Rainsborough; and is frequently at fault in these minor matters of dates and numbers as in the very next paragraph.

And now it was to bee considered whether wee should w'th those twenty horse adventure to surprize three troopes of horse w'ch then quartered in security at Knottingley three miles of, & had their horses at grasse w'ch made it more faisible, or else fetch in provision out of the towne it being then the height of the markett w'ch was kept that day. & it was thought more necessary to gett in provision & men w'ch wee might doe both sufficiently in an houre or two to keepe it 3 monneths. and it was vrged that if wee should attempt the quarter at Knottingley & fayle wee should very probably loose the castle againe w'thin 3 or 4 dayes. So that it was resolued wee should goe into the towne & declare the castle to bee for the King, w'ch wee did & in an howres time had aboue 100 men in the castles whom wee knew faithfull & provisions for three monneths. this was in the latter end of June or the beginning of July.

According to the narrative given on page 241, the portcullis was kept down from the time of the seizure till the following Tuesday (June 6th), though of that fact — probable enough as it might appear—Capt. Paulden's narrative says nothing. On the contrary, the party seem to have had no mistrust whatever of the loyalty of the town's people; but, directly they had secured the Castle, after a short debate, they went into the town, declared what they had done, and within an hour had a hundred men in the Castle, and were provisioned for three months. By this statement, the writer evidently wishes us to understand that the Royalists had not only plenty of money, but had also the good-will of the inhabitants of Pontefract.

The troop of horse, which in the early part of the document (see page 295) was mentioned as quartered at Wakefield, had now become three at Knottingley; and the small party of twenty-two, after full debate, did not consider it wise to attack them till the place had been fully garrisoned and provisioned.

But the Parliamentarian horse did not give them much time to reconsider their determination. Directly they learned what had happened they made off for York to Col. Lambert with the intelligence; and from York the news was sent to London, distorted as we have already found it. (See page 159.)

The three troopes w'ch was then all the horse that were in the County being all armed marched away towards Yorke where they mett Lambert who then com'aunded in cheife in the north. hee marches backe w'th them to Ferri-briggs & then sends a Trompetter to the Gouern'r C. Marris to demaund by what authority hee had scazed on the Castle & for whom hee kept it, offering indemnity to all if they would deliuer it into his hands. but it was answered that hee had Com'ission from his highnesse the Prince of Wales, & kept it for the King.

All this seems to have taken place during Saturday, the day of the seizure.

Some two dayes after, these three troopes faced the Castle, w'th whom wee had some skirmishing, being then encreased to the number of nigh upon 80 horse & great numbers of foote came euery day to offer their service, many of whom wee turn'd backe because wee could not tell how to arme them nor how to quarter them in any place in security. but in a monneths time or lesse wee had encreased our number to aboue 300 horse & 7 or 800 foote, severall gentlemen of Condicon coming out of Nottinghamshire and' Lincolneshire to vs; as Sr Rich. Byron, Col: Mich: Stanhop, & out of other Parts of Yorkeshire, as Sr Philip Monckton, the two Col Portingtons and others.

The case of Sir Philip Monckton is another illustration of the policy of Cromwell towards his prisoners. In a MS. lent by the then Lord Galway to Dr. Milner, and quoted in the History of Doncaster, Sir Philip says of himself, " I suffered many long and chargeable imprisonments during His Majesty's excitement, and *had been sent a slave to Jamaica*, if God had not prevented it by Oliver's death.

The " two Col. Portington's" were Col. Robert and Col. Roger. They had been in the Castle together during the first siege, Robert being then a Lieut-Col., and Roger a Captain, each in Colonel Gray's list (see page 22.) Roger remained till the close of this third siege, being one of those who with Capt. Thomas Paulden, the writer of this account, went out to treat (see Mr. Margetts's letter, on page 222.) Robert was taken prisoner at Willoughby. - The family was settled at Barnby Dun.

& now the Ennemy begunne to bestirre themseues & raise forces; as Sr Hen: Cholmeley to Levy a regim'nt of horse & Sr Ed: Rhodes another, Coll: Fairefax a regiment of foote & Bright another, and Bethel & others begunne to raise forces in the East Riding, Rossiter & White in Lincolnshire & Nottinghamshire, though all of them had obliged themselues to the Contrary as much as words & oathes could doe; & not onely so, but had promised to raise men for the King when they should see any visible force to secure them, & J belieue at that time when they promised they really intended to performe it. but J am confident the dessigne was new form'd aboue & they was to receiue Comissions from the Parliam'nt, and not subordinate to Cromwells, but in the meantime to suppresse the Kings party, & afterwards if Cromwell had beene beaten to haue joyned w'th Hamilton.

These few lines give a very clear idea of the state of parties at the time, as presented to the mind and retained in the recollection of Capt. Thomas Paulden. And its witness is borne out in every point; that there were then three parties, the High Royalist and Episcopalian ; the moderate Royalist and Parliamentarian, generally a Presbyterian; and the Republican and Independent, " Sectary," as he was called. The first headed by the Prince of Wales and Sir Marmaduke Langdale ; the second headed by General Fairfax, uncertain whether to give way to their Royalist instinct or their Presbyterian sentiments, and vacillating till too late. Had Hamilton gained the day at Preston, there is little doubt these would all have joined him, but meanwhile, the Parliament, even the Rump, was endeavouring to keep them in hand, by promise of independent commands, independent that is of the Lieutenant-General, the acknowledged leader of the Republican Party. Cromwell's unscrupulousness turned the balance ; by the execution of the King and the capable leaders, and the transportation of the defeated common soldiers to the Plantations, he made peace—by a virtual No Quarter. And having used the Moderates and the Parliament to extirpate the Royalists, he ultimately found it a comparatively easy matter to destroy the Parliament and " Take away that Bauble !"

But to return to Capt. Paulden :—

The Reasons that make mee beleeue this are not onely drawne from their oathes & promises w'ch they gaue seuerally to those that treated w'th them, but also their refusing to march w'th Cromwell to that ;battle, w'ch must necessarily decide ye businesse of the Kingdome ; & when they was able to haue brought him 5000 horse and foote to haue joyned w'th him, w'ch was almost as many as hee had when hee fought, yet they refused and busied themselues in the siege of a small castle of very inconsiderable consequence in comparison of winning or loosing that day, w'ch was likely to put an end to the warre.

That battle was the Fight at Preston, Wigan, and Warrington, which practically broke up the moderate and Presbyterian party.

---

this induces mee to beleeue that they did not wish very good successe to

Cromwell & his army; & J am confirmed the more in it when J consider the astonishm'nt they was all in, when they heard the newes of Hamiltons defeate.

This remark is another illustration of the fact that Hamilton's defeat had quite destroyed the hopes, nourished till then by the moderate party, of weakening Cromwell's influence.

Astonishment = stunned surprise.

But to returne to the disposall of our small forces at Pomfrett w'ch amounted about the beginning of August to nigh 400 horse & 800 foote, whereof 300 (3) horse marched away to Doncaster (Sr Hen. Cholmley, Sr Ed: Rhodes, & C. Fairefax, being then at Leedes w'th a more considerable force) to q'rter there; the towne of Pomfrett being almost eaten vpp & wee so straitned that the foote were ready to mutiny for want of meate.

It may well be wondered at how even the reduced number of 800 foot and 100 horse could have been quartered in Pontefract Castle. But it must be remembered that the season was summer, when a bivouac on what may be called the Barrack Square would not have been without its alleviations; but the journey to Doncaster was a disastrous one, as we shall shortly see.

In this paragraph, Capt. Paulden was once more wrong in his dates. The expedition was in the beginning of July, not in August.

---

they had not quartered aboue 4 or fiue dayes at Doncaster, but they was invited to march into Lincolneshire w'th promises of great numbers of horse that would come into them, & that Boston should bee deliuered to them, & that (3) one gentleman was ready to march to meete them w'th 500 horse; but none of these promises was made good, onely they tooke Lincolne where ther quartered a troope of horse & a Company of foote of ye enemy, where they gott some armes.

This reference (3) evidently indicates the 4th note, which informs us that "my Lord Beaumont" was the gentleman indicated.

Vpon their advance into Lincolneshire the Ennemy marches from Leedes to Ferri-briggs, & there leaue some 500 foote & two troopes of horse & march w'th the rest (w'ch was 500 horse & 300 dragoones) after ours into Lincolneshire. this wee gaue them intelligence of, & they considering that it would bee very hard for them to march away & not fight either Rossiter & White who was 600 horse, or else Cholmeley & Rhodes w'ch were a greater force; & some of Rossiters Vanguard appearing, they resolued to fight Ross: & White before the Yorke-shire forces ioyned w'th them, w'ch they had intelligence they would doe w'thin fiue or 6 houres; & therefore drew vp resoluing to expect Rossiter. who p'sently appeared, & w'thin halfe an houre after engaged each other, where it was very handsomely disputed on both sides, but ours being ouer numbred being not aboue 400 horse & the ennemy aboue 600, at last were putt to the worse, and almost all killed or taken prisoners. J doe beleeue there was not 20 escaped of the field.

The tactics of the Parliamentarians were thus plainly perceived by the writer, Capt. Thos. Paulden, who remained behind in the Castle.

Sir Henry Cholmley, Sir Edward Rhodes, and Colonel Fairfax, who were at Leeds with a superior force, having news of the doings of the Royalists in Lincolnshire, started from Leeds for Ferrybridge. Then, leaving at that place the tired troops they had brought, they took up fresh soldiers. Continuing their journey, they accomplished two days' march in one, and going to the assistance of Rossiter and White, completed the rout of the Royalist party.

How naive, simple, and open-hearted are these memoirs, written probably half a century after the date of the occurrences of which they treat. The Cavaliers were doggedly determined to fight at a disadvantage rather than not fight at all; being unwilling, with two bodies of the enemy near at hand, to submit to the hardship of not fighting at least one of them. When such was their spirit, and enthusiasm, and recklessness, no wonder that in the absence of supreme generalship, they soon met with a reverse. For this Willoughby Fight was indeed a shocking disaster, and almost utter annihilation. As Capt. Paulden says, hardly 20 escaped from the field.

The list of Royalist officers taken prisoners, we have already given (see page 179).

J haue heard some impute the losse of the day to our want of Colours, being thereby made incapable of Rallying when they were dispersed in the charge, as the enemy likewise was rather more then lesse; but they rallying to their Colours & wee mistaking the ennemy for our owne party were taken by small numbers. J haue heard the Enemy confesse they had more men killed then wee.

This confusion occasioned by "want of Colours" seems a very probable aid to the disaster, though on occasion their absence was not without its advantage. It is well known —mentioned indeed in his own Memoirs—that even General Fairfax, at Marston Moor, was able to save himself, through the want of a distinguishing uniform; when being entirely surrounded by the Royalists, and cut off from his own men, he " took the signal " " out of his hat," and so " passed among " the enemy " as one of their own commanders."

Wee had no better fortune about the same time at Ferri-briggs, w'ch wee resolu'd to storme when they was march't into Lincolneshire w'th most of their strength. To that purpose a Councell of warre was called in the Euening, & there resolu'd that in the morning by breake of day wee should fall vpon it; but before the Councell was risen there comes two or three men one after another & brought vs word that they was marching away towards Yorke. vpon this there was shuffled vpp an order to march p'sently w'th our horse & foote, & fall vpon their reare, w'ch accordingly wee did imediately; but found them not quitting the towne but in a posture ready to receiue vs. & now wee was at a stand what to doe hauing no guides provided who knew the Avenues of the towne, nor no body that would vndertake to giue vs orders. yet in a Confusion wee diuided ourselves into seuerall bodyes & attempted to breake into their Barricades, but was repuls't w'th the losse of about (5) 100 men killed & others wounded.

Here again, reckless bravery did not compensate for want of cool judgment in those who had the command; and bad intelligence incited the Garrison to what proved to be an imprudent ill-considered act. The fresh troops kept better guard at Ferrybridge than their immediate predecessors had been accustomed to do; and while those anxious to make that onslaught had expected them to be on the move towards York, they were really in a posture ready to receive attack; while, on the other side, there was no one to decide how that attack could be best delivered.

The note (5) gives many interesting particulars of this sally, which appears to be that already referred to when Major Morris led the party as far as New Hall, and then gave up the command to Col. Bonivant (see page 251.)

But some 4 or fiue dayes wee recouered some part of our reputacon at a passe called Olerton boate where wee fell vpon two of the Enemies troopes wch was of Gene'l Fairefax his life guard, who was accounted the best horse in the Army & had the boast neuer to haue beene beaten. our numbers & theirs were neare vpon equall, and the dispute was very sharpe they worsting vs in the two first charges, but in the third wee breake them, routed them, killed, tooke & drowned most of them, tooke both their colours, wounded Browne who com'anded them very desperately in the body. Sr Rich. Byron com'anded the Reformades in this action & my Brother the rest.

This corruption of Ollerton Boate for Allerton-By-Water is of a kin to that of Hope and Anchor into Haulpeny (see page 60). Capt. Paulden seems to have been an active energetic commander, and to have borne an important part in every action; although conversely, it might be said that his brother would not have felt so much interest in this, or any other particular action, had not Capt. William Paulden held the command.

Fiue or 6 dayes after this, Cromwell marched downe through Nottinghamshire into the North, where C. White joyned w'th him & marched w'th him to Pomfrett; where hee entered the town and plundered it & then marched northward. C. White & ye Nottinghamshire and some part of the Yorkeshire forces accompanying him one dayes march, & then tooke their leaue & returned towards Pomfrett, dividing themselues into three bodyes, & quartered one (6) at Ackworth, another at (7) Fetherston, ye 3d at (8) Ferribriggs, w'thin two miles on euery side.

We have already referred (see page 179) to this visit of Cromwell to Pontefract. The wounded Rossiter appears to have been left behind in Lincolnshire.

The very interesting local information contained in this paragraph, has, we think, never hitherto been made known. The notes (6), (7), and (8) further tell us that Colonel White and Colonel Hacker quartered at Ackworth, Colonel Fairfax and Sir E. Rhodes at Featherstone, and Sir Henry Cholmley at Ferrybridge.

about a weeke after, wee heard of Hamiltons defeate. & after, wee heard that it was so cleare a victory that Hamilton had surrendred himselfe & all hee had left to Lambert at Tossiter. then wee begunne to thinke what was fitting to bee done seeing that wee could not hope to keep the Castle if wee should admitt that number of men w'ch was in the towne into ye castle being about 900 horse & foote besides ye garrison of ye Castle. it was resolued to treat w'th the enemie to desire passes to goe to their homes, to all that would take them, w'ch they granted; & so all was dispersed sauing 500 foote & my Brothers troope of horse & some gentlemen that stay'd, in all making about 60 horse. w'th these wee resolu'd to keepe the Castle & New-hall, a great house w'thin thrice muskett shott of ye Castle, till such time as wee could send to know his ma'ties pleasure, then Prince of Wales.

Tossiter = Uttoxeter.

It seems that practically, at this time, the town of Pontefract was besieged, as well as the Castle; the Royalists in the town numbering about 900, those in the Castle more than half that number.

Throughout all their trial, it will be noticed that the garrison constantly kept in mind the duty of looking for instructions from the Prince. And, indeed, through a letter from Rev. F. Drake, vicar of Pontefract, under date August 26, 1716, to Mr. Thoresby, we learn with reference to Mr. George Beaumont, "condemned and executed by a Council of War at Pontefract in 1648, by Judge Advocate Margetson," in whom, we presume that we recognise Thomas Margetts, one of the correspondents with Capt. Baynes—that "his crime was his loyalty and steady adhesion to his Prince in all misfortunes, in the worst of times, *and conveying letters from the garrison of Pontefract Castle to King Charles the First at Oxford.*" The fact is probably true, although Mr. Drake errs in the circumstantial details; for Charles the First was then in close custody, if not under trial. The letters must have been for the Prince.

Very likely it was at this time that the prisoners were released from the Dungeon: though Colonel Cotterell may have been detained a fortnight longer, in the hope that he might be exchanged. And now, probably the women were sent out, including, perhaps, Morris and his infant son born in the Castle, and named on that account Castilion.

It is at least unfortunate that we can trace no more of Castilion Morris, for the circumstances of his birth, and its date, might have thrown some light on our history. It ought to be well known that he was Town Clerk of Leeds, for Thoresby in his Diary, under date May 13, 1703, says that he spent part of that day

Perusing a MS. of our late Town-clerk, Mr Castilion Morris, wherein are both historical notes of his own time, and the History of Pontefract Castle, which his father, Colonel Morris, held out for King Charles the latest of any in England. • This part was designed for the press, only prevented by the author's death.

As Thoresby, a few weeks before, says that he had been " sent for by Mrs. Morris about Mr. Morris's MS. designed for the press," it is evident that the two entries bear a mutual relation. The question then arises, and it is one to which we regret not to be able to give a definite answer, What became of these MS.? They seem to be at present irretrievably lost, but it is not impossible they may yet see the light.

But to return to our document, which continues,

This being done, & all our men hauing taken passes, the Enemie marched quietly into the towne, September ye 9th 1648, as neare as J can remember. the same day they brought downe some foote w'thin Carabin shott of the Castle & there made a Baricade, & planted 3 foote Colours, & brought a horse guard vpon the south-west side of ye Castle, & placed them vpon Bag-hill.

From this day then, September 9, when the Parliamentarian troops took final possession of the town,—Fox (see page 246) says October 9, an evident error,—Capt. Paulden dates the commencement of the siege.

---

the next day wee made a sally w'th 100 foote & 40 horse, (9) the foote vpp to their Barricade & ye horse towards their horse guard. The foote entered their Barricade, Kill'd some, tooke others & their 3 colours, & beate them vpp to the markett place. our horse likewise beate their horse-guard but catch'd few, they running away betimes.

The foot notes inform us that this sally, and the five which followed were " Commanded by my Brother," whose troop was indeed now the only troop left in the Castle.

---

fiue or 6 dayes was spent in getting in corne w'ch was then shorne & ready for getting in, w'ch dayly occasioned some skirmishing but nothing considerable. after wee had gott in what corne was w'thin our reach, wee made a sally with (10) 30 horse vpon their horse guard & surprized them, tooke 30 prisoners & 40 horse. some 3 nights after wee beate vpp a quarter (11) some 7 miles of, &

tooke a Lieuetennant & most of his troope. this putt their horse to great duty, (the Nottinghamshire & Leicestershire horse being marched away); they was vpon 48 houres duty & then durst not ly w'thin a dozzen miles for feare of beating vp.

There is no allusion whatever to the arrangement which had been made a fortnight before (see page 245) with the Corporation, as to the supply of corn.

---

in the meane time wee gott in euery night both corne & cattle more then wee spent. wee meddled little w'th their foote but resolued to weary out their horse if possible, & to that purpose wee made another attempt vpon their horse-guard at Bag-hill, w'ch (12) wee thought to have surpriz'd w'th 24 of our horse but found them 60 horse w'th their Colours in very good order expecting vs w'th some foote marching vp ready to backe them; w'ch made vs resolue to charge them before their foote could gett vpp to them; w'ch wee did, & they receiued vs more gallantly then hitherto any had done. but some of their front falling w'th our pistolls they begunne to turne aside and breake, and being to passe through a narrow-gapp & a deepe ditch wee did the more execution vpon them.

This was the third successful attack upon Baghill, and the importance the garrison attached to keeping the enemy away from that position will be understood from a consideration of its physical features. Baghill is a limestone ridge, on a sandstone foundation, which running parallel with the western part of the south face of Pontefract Castle, at a distance of about 150 yards, commanded the main approach to the fortress. Behind Baghill is a table land of some considerable extent, the greater part of which has been cultivated since the Conquest; and still further away were the Chequer Fields, on which was fought the battle by which Sir Marmaduke Langdale raised the first siege. The whole, although so near, was out of sight of those in the Castle, except from the Towers. From the Ballium, nothing could be seen but the bare ridge against the sky. On this ridge was fixed the gallows, to which John Garforth was taken by the Royalists in the early days of the siege, as detailed in the depositions against Col. Morris (see page 253), on which the Parliamentarians were now threatening to hang Sir Marmaduke Langdale, and on which, in the following February, they did indeed hang the Rev. George Beaumont, for the offence to which we have just referred. (See also page 208). This gallows must have been most conspicuous, both from the Castle, and from the neighbouring country; and it was doubtless the model from which was taken the wall-engraving of a gallows, ladder and rope, which is still to be seen on the staircase to the Dungeon. It was itself within sight, from the mouth of that horrible receptacle; and any prisoner allowed to pass to the top of those forty-two steps, must have seen it facing him against the bright summer sky.

> wee tooke & wounded their Lieuetenant, Kill'd their Coronett, tooke their Colours, & few escaped ˸vnwounded. this was Major Euers his troop now Ld. Euers. their foote that was coming vp to them fled backe to the towne.
> This made the Enemie resolue to quitt that guard, & make their horse-guard in the Parke stronger w'ch was vpon ye north east side of the Castle. this left vs more liberty to forrage vpon the South west.

In reading this, it must be borne in mind that the Park then extended to what is called Skinner Lane; and that its boundary in this direction was very near to the Castle; not half a mile away, as is the case at present. While Baghill was in the possession of the besiegers, the besieged could forage to the south-west, only with difficulty.

> some few dayes after wee resolued to try what might bee done vpon their great horse guard in the parke; & because wee imagined them very strong wee sallyed all the horse wee could make, w'ch amounted to 50. their guard consisted of 150 drawne (13) up in 2 bodies, w'ch wee charged & routed, & followed to their Barricades, tooke the captaine that co'maunded them, & killed about 40.

The note adds that there were in all, 240 parliamentary cavalry engaged on this occasion.

> about this time w'ch was (as neare as J can guesse) in the latter end of October, came C. Rainesborough w'th his regim'nt of foote out of ye South hauing a co'mission from Cromwell to comaund in cheife against the Castle in stead of Sr Hen: Cholmeley who would not obey Cromwells order, aleadging that hee was not vnder Cromwells com'aund but had his Com'ission imediately from the Parliam'nt.

This mission of Col. Rainsborough was thus, as indeed we have already seen (see page 182) a part of the struggle between the Parliamentarians, at the head of whom was General Fairfax himself, and the Cromwellians headed by the Lieutenant-General.

The Admiral-Colonel Rainsborough had just been put ashore by the Fleet, which in this final struggle had declared for the King ; and as he was a firm supporter of the Cromwell party, an effort was made to advance him to the command against Pontefract. Cholmley, however, who was in command of the rough militia,—by the nomination of the anti-Cromwellian party,—refusing to give way, Colonel Rainsborough had the discretion to remain at a distance, though within reach, until superior authority had decided the difference between himself and Sir H. Cholmley. And this difference and jealousy between the Commanders gave the garrison the opportunity, of which they were not slow to avail themselves.

---

whilest this was in disputing Rainesborough quartered w'th his regiment of some 800 at Doncaster, whither wee sent a Spy to learne how hee kept his guards (desiring if possible to pr'uent his besieging vs, hauing as wee thought a more easy enemy to deale w'th) who returning told vs that he kept a strong guard vpon the Bridge & another strong one in the middle of the towne, but none but one sentinell at the South & west Auenues, w'ch made vs imagine it possible wee might surprize him that way. And to that purpose wee marched out (14) two & twenty of our best horse at 10 a clocke at night, & by breake of day came to Mexborough, a village where there is a ferry ouer the riuer. there wee refreshed our horses & reposed ourselues as a party of Cromwells horse come from the Army, till eleuen a clocke at noone. this village was fowre miles from Doncaster. thence wee dispatched a faithfull messenger to Doncaster for Jntelligence & appointed him to meete vs at night at a place where wee intended to quarter, w'ch was w'thin two little miles of Doncaster. & accordingly hee came & told vs they were very secure & had not any allarum nor suspition of an enemie, & acquainted vs w'th other particulars of their guards & q'rters. so by breake of day the next morning wee mounted, & by sunne rise came to the Barrs of the towne where there stood a Sentinell who demaunded whence wee came. Wee told him from Gen'r'll Cromwells army come vpon businesse to C. Rainsborough. so hee bid god speed vs well (15).

This again adds details, but introduces a few differences. The former account says that the party left Pontefract at midnight ; this, that their departure was at ten o'clock. But all the differences are merely of such a character as to shew that the writer was telling no set tale. In the former letter he says they rested at Mexborough till about noon : now that it was till eleven o'clock at noon. In the former he speaks of their second resting-place as Conisborough, a mile from Doncaster: now, as two little miles; though it is really four. But in this newly discovered letter particulars are added of the message brought by the spy from Doncaster, of the entry of the party into that town, and of the manner in which the different bands carried out their share in the adventure.

> before wee came neare the towne wee had divided our horse into 4 parties, 6 to fall vpon the backs of the guard at ye Bridge to make good our retreate, 6 to fall vpon the maine guard, 6 to ride the streets to pr'uent ye enemies making a head, & 4 to Rainsboroughs lodging. & all succeeded according to our wishes; both their guards was surprized, & their foot all runne out at their backe doores in their shirts, & not any man offered to make head against vs sauing Rainsborough himselfe, who when hee was brought downe into the streete & saw himselfe & his lieuetenant & ye Sentinell at his doore prisoners to three men, & one that held their horses, w'thout any party to second them, begunne to escape from them & cry Armes, armes.

The day was well selected for such an adventure. It was a Sunday, when the almost universal tradition allows a later hour of rising than usual: not only on account of the Day, but also on account of the heavier labour of the previous day, in preparation.

It being Sunday, moreover, the Bible-signal, which was taken to Conisborough (see page 151) was the less likely to be noticed.

> a Coronet w'ch was one of our fowre running after him, & not willing to kill him, catcht him by ye wast-coate; & in the struggle Rainsborough gott his sword & Rainesboroughs Lieuetenant his pistoll, but Rainsbor' was throwne downe & one of our Troopers runne him into the throate w'th his sword, whilst my Brothers Lieuetenant runne Rainsborough his Lieuet: through, & kill'd him.

The Cornet was Michael Blackburne; the Lieutenant was Allan Austwick.

> in the meane time Rainsb: had gott vpon his feete though wounded, w'th a sword in his hand, & receiuing another thrust through the body by my Brothers lieuetenant fell downe dead: This done wee threw what armes wee found vpon the guards into the riuer, & marched on the rode ye nearest way to Pomfrett, & came at noone day in ye sight of all their horse into the Castle.

This account also, adds a few particulars, which are not to be found in the former. From a comparison it appears that the course of this daring action was much as follows:—

Blackburn and a trooper—perhaps Marmaduke Greenfield—(see page 250) are conducted by Rainsborough's lieutenant to his bed-room, where they turn upon their guide, disarm him, and, having taken the precaution to secure his sword, seize the General also. Bringing both downstairs, where their return is awaited by Austwick and the second Trooper, they bid Rainsborough mount one of the horses, on which Austwick is already seated. He prepares to do so, but looking round as he puts his foot into the stirrup, like a clear-headed man with his wits about him, he sees, as by inspiration, that if the sentinel at hand comes to his assistance there will be three against four, the fourth man being moreover encumbered by the care of two horses besides his own.

Perceiving, with a soldier's glance, the possibilities that may arise from this state of affairs, he gives the alarm to the sentinel,—Arms, Arms, being the call to which his trooper should have responded by immediate action—and attempts to escape his captors.

It would appear, however, that the whole struggle passed so quickly that the sentinel had no time to interfere, before Blackburn knowing that they wanted a live General to exchange for Sir Marmaduke, injudiciously threw down his sword and pistol, in order to seize the escaping man by the waistcoat. A struggle followed, and Rainsborough fell, but while on the ground he was able to reach Blackburn's sword, and so arm himself.

Meanwhile the lieutenant, now as bright and ready as his superior himself, having picked up the discarded pistol, begins to cock it. But before he has prepared it for discharge, Austwick, in command of the party, dismounts and runs him through, while the trooper who had been with Blackburn to Rainsborough's chamber comes to his assistance, and wounds the escaping prisoner in the neck.

Notwithstanding, however, this wound, Rainsborough

retains his feet, still with Blackburn's sword in his hand, and still endeavouring to prevent his daring assailants from effecting his capture, until Austwick, having despatched the lieutenant, turning on the General, runs him through the body, and all is over, without any such alarm as would have been occasioned by the discharge of a pistol.

Thus it appears that Austwick's was the hand that killed both Rainsborough and his lieutenant; that Blackburn seized Rainsborough, and brought him down stairs, and that Capt. William Paulden, in command of the whole party, scoured the streets, and overlooked all.

The note (15) supplements the tale with the distinct assertion that Capt. Thomas Paulden commanded the party that attacked the Main Guard. Such, indeed, we suspected to be the case (see page 155) before this document came into our hands, and we are therefore gratified to meet with the explicit statement.

It is worth while to notice the almost exact parallel between the seizure of Col. Cotterell on June 3, and the seizure of Col. Rainsborough on October 29. One act might have been a mere rehearsal of the other. In each case, two are guided into the chamber of a sleeping man, at early morning, seize him, take him prisoner, and bring him downstairs. But Col. Cotterell was able to seize his sword, and make a resistance, which was provided against in the second case by the precaution of taking possession of Rainsborough's arms, before he was awake, or at least before he was able to pay attention to anything but the packet which the self-styled messengers brought him.

In Rainsborough's case, moreover, the idea of the possibility of resistance did not occur to him till he was in the inn-yard, and saw his captors reinforced by but other two; that in fact only four Royalist soldiers were engaged in his capture, while his own party consisted of three; for surely he had a right to count upon the efficient services of the sentinel. Had he then hesitated, another few seconds would have seen him bound behind Austwick, and emerging from the inn-yard on the way to Pontefract, the rest of the Royalist band falling in, party by party, as the prisoner and his captors took the road. But even notwithstanding his resistance, his capture would probably have been effected; for Blackburn, having gauged his physical capacity, seems to have been taking measures to lift the prisoner bodily on to the horse which Austwick bestrode in readiness. Had the Cornet not dropped his arms, in his anxiety to redeem his promise not to hurt a hair of Rainsborough's head, and so provided the two Parliamentarians with means of effectual resistance, the scheme might still have been successful; for once on horseback, behind an expert horseman governing a well-trained horse, Rainsborough's chance would have been but small. Though only four when they left the inn yard, his captors would have been joined at quick intervals by six from the main-guard, six from the streets, and finally by six commanded by a Major, as they passed the Bridge on the road to Pontefract, having entered the town from the unguarded south; while Colonel Rainsborough would but have had the fortune which befel John Garforth and Lieut. Farrer, abducted from Pontefract, Mr Clayton, Lord Fairfax's steward, taken from Denton, and Sir Arthur Ingram himself, seized in his own house, from the midst of his own own servants. But there would have been this important difference; on Colonel Rainsborough would not have been set a mere money ransom: his life would have been held a safe bond for that of Sir Marmaduke Langdale, at Nottingham. His death was the frustration of the whole scheme by which it was hoped to save the Royalist General.

But, indeed, though these, who were ready to lay down their lives for their friend, knew it not, other active steps were being taken, by which Sir Marmaduke was able to escape from Nottingham ; his escape being managed so adroitly that he was across country, and perhaps on board ship, before his absence was detected.

The virulence of Parliament, or at least the fragment of Parliament, which was then sitting, was so great that on 6th November, the Monday week after the attempt upon Rainsborough, they impotently included Langdale, then in safety, among the " Seven that shall be excepted from mercy "—" whom the King himself, should he bargain with us, shall never forgive."

Miller's History of Doncaster, states that the scene of this daring exploit was at an hostelry on the western side of the Cross, then tenanted by Mr. William Smith.

It would have been hardly necessary to notice that Rainsborough's troops amounted to a little more than a thousand, had it not been that, by an unfortunate mistake, the number was once mis-printed 12,000 ; and notwithstanding that three pages earlier in the same history, it had been correctly stated in words as "twelve hundred," hasty writers have not unfrequently copied the figures which strike the eye, rather than the words which must be sought for, with entire forgetfulness of even the probabilities of the case.

some 3 or fowre dayes after (which was in the beginning of Novemb.) came Cromwell w'th his army out of ye north & sumoned vs ; but wee hauing lately receiued an order from his Matie then Prince of Wales to keepe it, & yt it would doe him more service then, then many such castles would doe at another time wee refus'd to deliuer it, but hee forct vs to quitt the New-hall w'ch wee had hitherto kept ; & pr'sently drew a line about vs, planted two batteries w'th w'ch he beate vs from our gunnes that wee had planted vpon the towers, but afterwards wee gott them into chambers & made so good shotts y't wee killed seuerall of their Canoniers, seuerall times dismounted their gunns, & at last made them that they did not play at all against vs. onely their morter-piece playd for a long time, & blew vp a great part of our building.

The particulars of Cromwell's summons, we have already met with, (see page 190). And Capt. Paulden rather hurries the conclusion. After the exciting events he had recorded, the tamer incidents of the last four or five months of the siege, seem hardly deserving, in his eyes, of being told at all.

after this little was done worth noting, onely a sharpe feuer begunne to rag amongst vs whereof many dyed & few escaped being sicke, besides scuruies & other diseases vsually caused by a close castle & salt dyet.

The sharp fever was probably that which carried off his gallant brother, William. Of three, or four, Thomas only survived this siege.

in this condicon wee kept it till ye March following, 1648, & then hauing receiued an expresse from his Matie, then Prince of Wales, wee deliuered it vpon such condicons as they pleas'd to giue vs, w'ch was to march out & liue quietly at our houses, except 6 persons who were excepted from hauing any benefitt by the Articles, who sallyed out thinking to escape; but one was killed; ye Gouern'r & a coronet escaped through, but was afterwards taken and executed at Yorke Assizes. three more were beaten backe into ye castle where they hid themselues, & escaped the next day.

This is not the only intimation that we have had, that correspondence was kept up with the King. But it now appears that they had at length His Majesty's orders to risk no more, but to surrender although they still had two months' provisions.

This permission of the King gives a reason for what has seemed to some extent unaccountable, and accounts for the overtures made by the Castilians on March 3rd, (see J. Bright's letter, page 220.)

Of some 600 that wee entered into the Castle there came out betwixt six & seuenscore, & many of them sicke & lame hauing beene beseiged almost 7 monneths.

So, honourably, closed this memorable siege.

The following notes are added in the MS. showing the whole to be the original draft of the old soldier's narration; afterwards to be translated as it were into that more scholarly language, of which the writer felt himself to be incapable. As it is, however, and rough diamond as it is we feel that we have the very words of the writer. In the former letter, we all along felt an uneasy doubt that the diction had been manipulated (see page 154). In the present we doubt not but that we have not only the narrative of Capt. Thomas Paulden, but his very words.

The additions are,

1. One Ashby who had formerly serv'd ye King but was then gentleman of the Armes to Cottrell the Gouernour. but after ye Castle was taken for the King was Major of ye Castle. the other was one Mr. Copley who afterwards when ye Castle was taken, through some mistake or fright ranne to the Enemie.

2. Ashby & another.

3. Com'aunded by Sr Philipp Monckton, Coll : Phil : Byron & Col. Rob : Portington.

4. My Ld Beaumont.

5. Major Thimbleby who did not goe against any Barricade but vp some backsides entered ye towne w'th his men w'thout any resistance, but not obseruing his orders (to come vpon the backs of them that mainteined ye barricade & so open it to our horse) but advancing further into the towne was mett by a Troope of their horse, & was taken prisoner & his men killed or taken. & the Enemie knowing by some of the prisoners that hee was ordered to open the Barricade to our horse, pr'sently called to our horse to enter, & imagining that ye Barricade was opened by Mr Thimbleby, marched vpp to ye Barricade w'th some 24 horse or 30 most of them oficers & gentlemen, but when they came w'thin Pistoll shott of ye Barricade they perceiu'd it was the ennemies stratagems to call them, by two or three volleys of muskett shott that came amongst them, & some case shott from 2 drakes. Sr Rich. Byron had his horse kill'd vnder him, his man slaine. Major ower his horse shott, my brother Wil. his horse kill'd vnder him, & another horse shott, my Brother Tim. was shott in the shoulder & ye bone broken, & in ye hand, & his horse shott in three or fowre places, but carryed him of. there were very few in ye party that was not either shott or their horses & some 10 or 12 killed outright.

6. Col. White & C. Hacker.

7. Col. Fairefax & Sr. Ed. Rhodes.

8. Sr. Hen : Cholmeley.

9. My brother Wil com'annded ye horse, who com'aunded ye foote J doe not remember.

10. Comaunded by my Brother Wil.

11. Likewise by my Brother.

12. Likewise by my Brother.

13. This party was likewise com'aunded by my Brother, but after their guard was beaten into their Barricade they came out w'th two troopes more in all, to the number of 240 horse besides some 120 foote that came along in the enclosures. they comming fast vpon vs before wee could make our retreate wee were forced to charge them all w'ch wee did taking ye Advantage of a passe w'ch some of them was gott through & routed them, tooke ye Cap : that co'maunded ye first body, & pursued the rest almost as farre as their Barricade.

14. Co'maunded by my Brother.

15. Major Saltonstall com'aunded 6 to fall vpon their guard at the Bridge : my Brothers Lieuetenant Austwick & his Cor : Blackebourne, & other two was

to light & goe into Rainsb: lodging: my Brother w'th a party of fiue more to see them in, & then to ride ye streets & to second any party that should find any resistance, & J had a party of 6 wth myselfe to fall vpon the maine guard.

N.B. These are References to the Narration.

These appendixes also, contain particulars which may be looked for in vain elsewhere. No 5 imparts the secret of the failure of the attack on Ferrybridge, which was designed to be carried out in a manner similar to that upon Doncaster; namely by entering at the further and undefended side of the post. At Doncaster, as we have seen, that portion of the plan succeeded admirably, and Major Saltonstall, at the head of the party, entered the town from the south, detaching first one Captain, then the other, and he himself going right through the place, seized the arms of the guard at the Bridge, threw them into the river, and holding that post, secured the unmolested departure of all. But at Ferrybridge, Major Thimbleby having obtained access to the town, neglected his orders to attack the guard in the rear, and thereby caused the failure of the expedition and almost its destruction. So great a misfortune naturally made those entrusted with the expedition to Doncaster careful not to perpetrate a similar blunder.

After the notes to various portions of the narrative, the following additions are appended.

I had forgott an action w'ch was done after Rainsborough was killed, before Cromwell besieged vs w'ch was this. wee had Jntelligence of 300 oxen w'ch was guarded by a Troope of ye Ennemies horse at Wentbridge some 3 miles from vs & wee resolued to try if wee could take them & to that purpose wee marcht out some 20 horse Co'maunded by my Brother & some 12 foote to driue. wee found them all in one close feeding & some few men watching them who pr'sently runne & gave ye Allarum to the troope, whilest wee driue ye Cattle away towards ye Castle ye troope followed vs in ye reare. some twelue score or more distant from vs all the way but never firing a pistoll against vs till wee was driuing ye oxen ouer ye draw-bridge, & then they fired their pistolls at some 12 score distance & so returned hauing seeue ye cattle driuen into ye castle, it being fayre moonelight.

In this he gives some few more details with the regard to the seizure of the 300 oxen, but he fixes the *locale* of the operation at Wentbridge, which, in his former letter, he had said (page 150) was at Knottingley. Which is another instance of his disregard of accuracy in matters not dealing with military details.

Persons excepted, The Gouernour C. Marris, Major Ashby, Lieuetenant Awstwick, Coronett Blackebourne, Lieuetenant Flood & Ensigne Smith. Smith was killed in ye attempt to gett through ye enemies guards. C. Marris & Cor: Blackebourne were afterwards taken in Lancashire & hang'd at Yorke assizes by a Jewry at Com'on law. the other 3 who were beaten backe into the Castle are yet all liuing for any thing J know to ye contrary.

This does not add to what we already know: but the "Corporal," "Sergeant Floyd," is advanced in rank, and having become Lieutenant Floyd, is named, as becomes his superior rank, fifth instead of sixth. Probably he subsequently became Lieutenant, and Captain Paulden forgot that he had a lower rank at the time he was "excepted."

He repeats that he has not heard of the death of either Ashby, Austwick, or Flood, and is evidently unaware that Dugdale has chronicled Austwick as having died in 1657, at "Standon" (see Booke of Entries, page 313.)

The MS. has an endorsement in another hand, which shews a singular want of acquaintance with the whole story, on the part of the annotator, who appears to have thought that he could deduce from the narrative the extraordinary statements that Morris had no particular share in the surprisal of June 3rd, and that the Castle was taken by Cromwell himself, when he came in November. And remarkably enough, he had never heard of the death of Smyth in the sally.

Such as it is, however, we print it below, as an example of the way in which inaccurate inferences are sometimes drawn, and lest some one may presently accept the annotation as justified by the facts.

This account differs in many Circumstances from that given in the Hist. of Rebellion B. 11. P. 545, &c.

Particularly it does not appear that Col: Morris, tho' one of the six excepted Persons, had any particular share in the act of surprising the Castle, for that his Intimacy was not with the then Gov'r Col. Cotterell, but w'th his Predecessor Col. Overton.

It also appears that one of the six excepted Persons was killed in a sally.
The account is drawn up by one of those concerned in the Dispatch of
Rainsborough. Lambert is not mentioned ; but the Castle is said to be taken
from the Royalists by Cromwell himself after his Return from Scotland.

With regard to the discrepancies between these
accounts of Capt. Paulden, and that given by Clarendon, it
must be borne in mind that Earl Clarendon died in 1674,
and that his history was not given to the world until nearly
thirty years after his death. It was then published,
however, with the assurance, from an anonymous editor,
writing " within a little more than fifty years since the
murder committed on that Pious Prince," "that they who
put forth this History, dare not take upon them to make
any Alteration in a Work of this Kind, solemnly left with
them to be publish'd, whenever it should be publish'd, as it
was delivered to them."

The volume was Licensed by the Queen, on 24 June,
1703, and the First Volume had received the Oxford
Imprimatur on April 29, 1702, the Second Volume on
September 15, 1703, and the Third Volume on October 16,
1704.

The effect of these imprimaturs and licenses was to
preserve the work from mutilation in subsequent editions,
for any later edition, other than one of literal identity,
would appear to have required a fresh license : but it is
difficult to reconcile the apparent statement of the editor
that the volume was published in the eighteenth century as
left by the author in 1674, with the evident fact that
Paulden's first letter, published in 1702, was used in its
compilation.

Paulden's second letter is, however, as evidently supplementary of all, and therefore most valuable for our present
purpose, since it is full in exactly those places in which the

former accounts had been misunderstood, or had proved to be open to misinterpretation.

In closing the account of the siege operations, and of Paulden's letters, we desire to note that Thoresby (Diary II. 62), July 18, 1710, says that he "visited the two aged virgins, Mrs Pauldens, about 80 years old, (and) was pleased with an account of their *four* memorable brothers, of whom I took notes, as after from Sheriff Baines, of the family at Knowstrop."

Now, Thoresby was not by any means a careless writer, and, moreover, says he "took notes" of these "four memorable brothers." As, therefore, we are unwilling even to suspect that painstaking antiquary of carelessness in this instance, we note his statement, and that, moreover, he seems to say that the Pauldens were of Knostrop, though he might have meant that Sheriff Baines was of the family of Knostrop. If, however, both the Pauldens and Capt. Adam Baynes belonged to this hamlet, (and it is well known that Capt. Paulden's descendants remained there till this present century), this is one more instance of the havoc made in all social relationships by the Civil War. For, in that case, Adam Baynes would have been pushing the siege of Pontefract Castle, while his neighbours, the three Pauldens, at least, were as earnest in its defence. When Thoresby visited the two aged virgins they seem to have been living at York.

Knostrop is at the south-east extremity of the township of Leeds.

THE LEADERS having been put to death, and the common people having been sent to the Plantations, the Buildings, as we shall shortly see, were razed to the ground. And there was but one way to deal with the chief and best among them, that " Princely Palace " of Pontefract Castle. Concerning it, the cry was at once raised, "Down with it, down with it, even to the ground." It had offended too deeply to be spared again, and the unanimity and determination with which its destruction was clamoured for, show how much its existence was feared. It had been spared once, it should not be trifled with now. The army was thoroughly imbued with the Cromwellian spirit (see letter, page 194) " Now when you have such ' a castle ' in your hands, and it will cost you nothing to do justice !"— " Down with it !"

Before the fortress was actually surrendered, that cry as we have seen ascended ; from all quarters, concerted petitions to Parliament poured in, their one burden being a prayer that the Castle should be demolished. It will be remembered that we left the triumphant Roundheads, on Saturday April 7th, with the order of Demolition in their hands and the word in their mouths, on " Monday next " the workmen are to begin. This was by virtue of the Order obtained from the Wakefield Quarter Sessions, and dated Wednesday, April 4th. By which Order the Demolition was entrusted to " Mr. Edward Feilde, now Major of Pontefract, Mr. Robert More, Mr. Robert Franke, Mr. Matthew Franke, Mr. John Ramsden, Mr. Christopher Longe, and Capt. John Ward, or any foure of them."

Although full particulars of the Demolition were published by Gent in 1738, and have been since reprinted, this present Collection would hardly be complete without them. We, therefore, once more put them in print.

A True Accompt *of the Value of all the Materials belonging the* **Castle** *of* PONTEFRACT, *sold: And of the Moneys received, and Debts owing: Also the Charge of the demolishing the same.*

	l.	*s.*	*d.*
IMPRIMIS: Moneys received for Lead	1540	07	02
Moneys received for Timber	0201	07	10
Moneys received for Iron	0037	02	04
Moneys received for Glass	0001	00	00
	1779	17	04
The Charge of Demolishing	0777	04	06
Moneys allotted unto the Town	1000	00	00
The rest due unto the Common-Wealth	0002	12	10
Debts *owing for Materials, which are also due unto the Common-Wealth*			
For Lead	100	09	09
For Timber	042	04	02
For Iron	002	17	08
	145	11	07

The PARTICULARS, *of all the above recited* Accompt *are as, in this* BOOK, *followeth.*

The 5*th of* April, 1649.

The Charges *of the Demolishing of the* Castle *of* PONTEFRACT, *are, in Particulars, as followeth.*

	l.	*s.*	*d.*
I*Mprimis,* An Agreement made with JOHN HARRISON for demolishing the *Round Tower,* for which paid him	080	10	00
An Agreement made, the same time, with THOMAS LAKE, and Others, for the pulling down the *Barbacan* Wall, for which paid	020	05	00
Paid THOMAS THURSTAN, for levelling the Earthen Mount, call'd *Nevill's* MOUNT, and the *Barbican* Wall, from the *Great Stable* to the *Low Draw-Bridge*	010	00	00
Paid JASPER ELLIS, by an Order from the Committee of the 27th of *April,* for Moneys laid out, about the removing the Ammunition from *Pontefract* Castle to *York,* and for carrying it up in *Clifford* Tower	004	04	00
P A I D	114	19	00

	l.	*s.*	*d.*
Lancelot Lamb, and Others, for taking down the Timber from the *King's Tower*, *Queen's Tower*, and *Round-Tower*; and other Buildings about the same	035	00	00
Paid JOHN HARRISON, and others, for demolishing the Two Skreens, from the *Gate-House* to the *Round-Tower*, and thence to the *Treasurer-Tower*	034	00	00
Paid THOMAS TAYLER and Others, for the Timber taking down from the *Chapel*, *Constable Tower*, and all the rest of the Buildings to the *Gate House*	035	02	06
Paid TATTERSALL, and Others, for taking down the Timber from off the two *Gate Houses*	002	00	00
Paid TATTERSALL, JOHN SMITH and Others, for taking down the Timber of the *Treasurer-Tower*, Gascoygne-*Tower*, the Great *Kitchin*, and so to the Great *Hall*	034	05	00
Paid them more for the Great *Hall* Timber, and the *Gate-House* taking down	012	05	00
	152	12	06
Paid SIMON PROCTER for demolishing the *King* and *Queen's Tower*, and all the Buildings betwixt the same, the Sum of ..	104	05	06
Paid THOMAS LAKE, and Others, for demolishing the two Out *Gate-Houses*, and the Skreen by the *Constable-Tower* ..	015	06	08
Paid EDWARD WILLSON for demolishing the *Constable-Tower*, and all the other Buildings from the *King's Tower* to the *Gate-House*: As also the *Treasurer Tower*, Gascoigne *Tower*, the Great Kitchen, and all the Buildings from the Skreen unto the Great *Hall*, the Sum of	201	00	00
Paid EDWARD HANDSON for pulling down the Skreen between the Upper *Gate-House*, and the *Round Tower*; also for the *Guard-House*	001	10	00
Paid JAMES JOLLY for pulling of the Iron from off the three Gates, the two Draw-Bridges; and the Timber of the Low Draw-Bridge taking up	002	16	00
Paid for filling up the Graft at the Low Draw-Bridge, and pulling down Part of the Skreen close by the *Constable Tower*	001	07	04
	326	05	06

Paid three Labourers for removing Timber out of the Fall of a Tower	00	03	00
Paid for taking down the Timber from *Swillington* Tower	01	13	04
Paid JOHN OXLEY, and THOMAS LEE, for smelting of Lead into Pigs	04	01	00
Paid for filling up the Graft at the Upper Draw-Bridge, and the Chapel Walls *pulling* down	04	10	00
Paid SIMON PROCTER for felling down *Swillington* Tower..	08	10	00
Paid SIMON PROCTER more, in regard we did conceive that he had a loosing Bargain upon former work done by him	04	00	00
Moneys expended upon several Messengers sending abroad into several Parts of the Country to seek out experienced Workmen, for the speedy demolishing of the Castle: And also for Moneys expended at several Contracts making: As also Moneys given to Workmen for their Encouragement at the Falls of several Towers: With other incident Charges	20	00	00
	42	17	04
Paid for bareing of Timber from under the Fall of the *Constable-Tower* ..	002	14	00
Paid for two Paper-Books, and to the Justice's Clerks, for drawing the Orders betwixt the Committee and the Trustees	000	10	00
Given to a maimed Workman, that was to return to his own Home at *Malton*, towards his Charges ..	000	05	00
Given to LANCELOT LAMB for his Care and good Service in the Work..	000	10	00
Paid 7 Soldiers, by Order from Capt WARD, for Work done by them	000	07	00
Paid for 5 Stone and 5 Pounds of Iron for making Crows for pulling off Lead	000	14	08
Paid FRANCIS BRADLEY for Crows making, and Shovels Shoeing ..	004	04	00
Paid several Labourers for Work done, as appears by a Note in Mr LONG's Hands	003	11	05
Paid JOHN SMITH for Work done by him ..	002	10	00
Paid Six Carpenters for loading Timber that was secured from burning by the Soldiers, and surveying the rest of the Timber	001	00	00
	016	06	01

	l.	*s.*	*d.*
Paid GEORGE RENNARD for taking Crooks out of the Walls	000	10	00
Paid LAKE and HANDSON for demolishing the Great *Hall*, and the Inner *Gate-House*	037	06	08
Paid JOHN OXLEY, and his three Men, for several Days Work for taking the Lead of the *Castle* down..	005	00	00
Paid for Lime and Workmanship for the two *Draw-Bridges* walling up of either side	001	10	00
Paid RICHARD LYLE for the Loan of his Beam and Weights for weighing of Lead	000	05	04
Paid for Cools to several Guards, to secure the Timber from Burning	000	18	00
Paid several Draughts for leading Timber out of the *Castle Garth*, to secure it from the Soldiers	003	02	08
Paid Labourers for several Bulwarks pulling down, about and near the Castle	000	12	00
Paid two Counsellors their Fees, for Advice how to proceed in Suit, and in whose Names, for Materials sold, and not paid for	001	00	00
	050	04	08

Paid by Mr ROBERT MOORE *to several Workmen, and Labourers, as appears by his Note of Particulars, as followeth.*

For the First Week	01	03	10	For the 7th Week	04	17	04
For the Second Week	05	15	06	For the 8th Week	17	16	00
For the third Week	06	19	09	For the 9th Week	04	00	02
For the 4th Week	14	14	06	For the 10th Week	03	15	04
For the 5th Week	09	16	10				
For the 6th Week	05	00	02		73	19	05

	l.	*s.*	*d.*
Total of all the Disbursements for the demolishing the Castle amounts unto the sum of	777	04	06

April *the* 18*th*, 1649.

LEAD *taken off* Pontefract *Castle, and sold as followeth.*

Sold to the Church-Wardens of *Barnsley* 20 Hundred Weight at	010	02	06
Sold unto Mr *Richard Wilcocke* 20 Hd. Wt. at	010	02	06
Sold unto Mr *Samuel Childe*, of *Leeds*, 40 Fother of Lead, at 11*l* 5*s* comes to	450	00	00
Sold him more 9 Fother, 12 Hundred, and 24 Pounds at the same Price, comes to	107	19	09
He rests indebted for Wood for smelting of Lead	002	10	00
Sold unto Mr *Winter*, of *Hull*, 4 Fother of Lead at	045	00	00
Sold unto Mr *John Skurr* one Web of Lead, 21 Stone, and 12 Pounds at	001	10	00
Sold unto Mr *Edward Rhodes*, 84 Fother of •Lead, 14 Hundred, 2 Quarters, and 5 Pounds at	940	00	00
	1567	04	09
Sold unto *Grace Briggs* 3 Webs of Lead, &c. 9 Hundr. and 13 Pounds at	05	00	00
Sold unto Sir *Thomas Wentworth* one Fother of Lead	11	05	00
Sold unto Lieutenant *Ward* 11 Stone and 5 Pounds at	00	17	00
Sold unto *Bryan Fosteard* 30 Stone of Lead	02	05	00
Sold unto the Lord *Savile* 20 Hun. Weight of Lead at	10	02	06
Sold unto Mr *John Savile*, of *Methley*, 3 Fother and 13 Pounds	33	16	00
Sold unto a Potter 18 Stone and 3 Pounds at	01	07	10
Sold unto *Francis Bradley* 21 Stone Lead at 1*s* 6*d* &c	01	11	06
Sold unto Mr *Robert Moor* 11 Hundr. 1 quarter and 17 Pounds, at 11*s* 5*d* &c	05	15	06
Sold unto Mr *John Clayton* 18 Stone and 4 Pounds at	01	07	00
Sold unto *Edward Field* 43 Stone and 10 Pounds at	02	15	10
	76	03	02
The Total of all the Lead sold amounts unto the sum of 1640 Pounds 16 Shillings, 11 Pence; whereof received in Money	1540	07	02

Moneys owing for Lead to ballance the Account, above written, as follow.

Sir *Edward Rhodes* Debtor for Lead	040	00	00
Mr *Samuel Childe*, of *Leeds*, rests indebted for Lead	057	19	09
Further Mr *Childe* rests indebted for Wood for Smelting his Lead	002	10	00
	100	09	09

The Total of all the Iron, belonging to the Castle, is 79 Hundr. 3 Quart. and 27 Pounds sold at 10s per Hundred, amounts unto the Sum of 40 Pounds, whereof received in Money					037	02	04
Moneys owing for Iron to ballance the Account as abovesaid. Col Overton, by an Order from the Lord General, for the Publick Service for Draw-Bridges for Hull, had Iron Teams delivered him to the Value of in Money					002	17	08

May the 7th, 1649, Money received for Timber, as followeth.

Rec. Coll. *Tho. Rookeby*	07	00	00	William Wright	04	06	08
Mr Birkebecke	01	03	00	Thomas Jackson	01	00	00
William Nicholson	02	01	00	Charles Tootell	00	10	00
William Jennings	01	06	08	John Killingbecke	10	00	00
Mr *Leonard Ward*	23	00	00	Richard Turner	00	18	00
Robert Howson	01	00	00	Thomas Boswell	02	00	00
Thomas Thwaytes	01	04	00	Peter Outhwaite	00	13	00
Richard Smith	00	02	06	John Wattson	09	10	00
William Farrowe	05	00	00	Francis Lee	02	12	00
Grace Brigge	08	00	00	Robert Bawlderton	05	00	00
Philip Austwicke	01	02	00	William Ward	12	00	00
William Hill	00	18	00	Mary Rothwell	00	09	00
Thomas Taylor	04	10	00	Thomas Feilde	00	13	04
Edward Fielde	22	08	00	Rec for *Timber* for the Church	20	00	00
Richard Lyle	02	11	00				
Robert Sutton	03	10	00	Timber for the Wind Mill	02	00	00
William Brame	12	00	00	Rec. of Mr John Skurr	03	00	00
Francis Bradley	01	10	00	John Wildman	02	08	00
Zechariah Stable	04	06	08	Received for the Remainder of the Timber in *Brame* Garth	05	00	00
John Potter	10	00	00				
Tho Jackson and Robert Farrowe	06	15	00				
	119	07	10		82	00	00
The Total of all the Timber sold comes to the Sum ..					201	07	10
Moneys receiv'd for Glass					001	00	00

Debts owing for Timber as follows.

William Farrowe	01	03	04	Thomas Jackson	04	01	06
Col *Overton*, by an Order from the Lord General for the Publick Service of *Hull* for Timber	08	06	00	Richard Cattle	01	17	00
				John Hodgshon	02	08	08
				John Box	02	10	00
				Thomas Eaden	01	10	00
George *Wrigley* by Assignment from *John Potter*	03	00	00	Thomas Boswell	02	00	00
				John Ambler	03	06	08
				Mr John Lambe	02	16	00
Thomas Farrowe	03	00	00	Bryan Fosteard	01	10	00
Thomas Farrowe and Tho Jackson joyntly together	03	05	00	Richard Fosteard	01	10	00
					42	04	02

The 11th of April, 1651.

WE, the Trustees, *authorized by Order of the Committee of the* West-Riding *of the County of* YORK, *for the demolishing of* PONTEFRACT Castle, *by their Order, dated the 4th of* April, 1649, *in Pursuance of an Order of the Honourable* House of Commons, *in Parliament assembled, dated the 27th of* March, 1649, *in that Behalf made; do declare the Account before-mentioned to be a full and true Account of our Receipts, and Payments, and all the Actings concerning that Service. Witness our Hands,*

    JO. WARDE.
    ROBERT MORE.
    MATTHEW FRANCK.
    EDWARD FIELDE.
    JOHN RAMSDEN.
    CHRISTOPHER LONGE.
    JOHN SKURR.

AND THUS was this ancient fortress demolished; and that which had been five centuries and a half perfecting, destroyed to within a few feet of the ground.

Destroyed so utterly that, with the single exception of part of one of the towers of the Porter's Lodge, not one stone was left upon another unless in retaining walls. All was destroyed to within a few feet of the foundations; and then the débris and rubbish being collected and enclosed, a layer of vegetable soil was placed over all, and a garden established above, the foundations of the buildings remaining in position beneath the vegetation.

The only exception to the universal destruction was the base of the Round Tower; but though the actual building was demolished to the very ground, the cased remains of the hill-top which served as its foundation was allowed to remain,—a crumbling ruin. The Main Guard, the scene of the first episode of Colonel Morris's adventure, was however, utilised by being converted into a gaol for debtors and West Riding offenders, the following Order of Sessions, dated 5th October, 1671, fixing the fees payable by prisoners to the gaoler, according to their degree of Knight, Esquire, Yeoman or Artificer.

A Table of Orders and rates of fees and dues allowed by his Majestyes Justices of the Peace for the West Riding of the County of York at Wakefield Sessions in the said West Riding the fifth day of October in the Three and Twentieth yeare of the rayne of King Charles the Second by the grace of God King over England Scotland France and Ireland, Defendor of the faith &c Anno Domini 1671 to be observed and kept concerneing the Gaoler and prisoners within the Gaole held at Pontefract Castle for the Honor of Pontefract and libertyes thereof or parcell of the Duchy of Lancaster in the said West Riding of the County of Yorke of all persons whatsoever that now are or shall be thereunto committed.

IMPRIMIS Every Knight shall pay for his weekly commons at the Table the sume of.. .. .. xiiis. iiijd.
and for his fee being committed by Warrant .. .. .. xiiis. iiijd.
Item every Esquire for his weekly Commons at table the sume of xs. iiijd.
and for his fee being committed by Warrant .. .. .. xs. iiijd.

Item Every Gentleman for his weekly Commons at Table the sume of viijs. and for his fee being Committed by Warrant .. .. .. viijs.
Item Every Yeoman or Artificer for his weekly Commons at Table the sume of .. .. vjs. viiid.
And for his fee being Committed by Warrant .. .. .. vjs. viijd.

And be it hereby ordered that every person or persons of what degree, Estate or Condition soever hee shee or they bee or shall bee beeing and remaining a prisoner within the said Gaole, that shall use or frequent any unlawful swearing rayleing reasoning or other undecent conference of any matter whatsoever at any tyme or tymes, that every such person or persons soe offending shall forfeite for every such defaulte Twelve pence to be levyed and to be bestowed upon the poore men in the Low prison, or else every such person soe offending to be committed to the said lowe prison att the discretion of the Keeper of the said prison or his deputye there.

Alsoe bee it further ordered that every person or persons that shall goe astray without the Libertyes of the sayd prison not having the license or consent of the Keeper of the said prison or his Deputye shall forfeite for every such defalte twelve pence to be levyed to the use of the said poore men in the Low prison else every such person soe offending to bee committed to the said Lowe prison at the discretion of the said Keeper of the said prison or his deputye there for the tyme beeing

Item that every Knight shall pay nightly for his bedd .. .. .. viiid.
Item that every Esq: shall pay nightly for his bedd .. .. .. vjd.
Item that every Gentleman shall pay nightly for his bed .. .. iiijd.
Item that every Yeoman or Artificer shall pay nightly for his bed .. ijd.
Item that every person or persons committed for any offence pay for his ease of Iron at the rate of Twopence in the pound and if they weare no Irons their fee is Twelve pence.
Item that every person or persons that shall have occasion necessarily to go into the Towne of soe many as may lawfully go at large without a Keeper shall pay for every tyme so goeing to the Keeper fowerpence.
Item that all women that shall be committed prisoner to the said Gaole shall pay the rate and fees abovesaid according to their respective qualityes above mentioned.

Wee doe allowe of this Table of fees.
John Kay
Robert Benson
William Lowther Junr
William Ellis.

That which is here spoken of as "The Low Prison" was apparently a kind of cellar entered from the south side of the building.

There were thus three different wards to this gaol; the Low Prison, the Ground Floor, and the Upper Floor, each having its separate class of prisoners. Here languished many, and the proportion of prisoners buried from this "lodge," as it was called, was in some years considerable.

The following entries in the Church Registers show how very soon after the demolition of the main building the Main Guard had become a debtor's prison.

Jan 19, 1654-5. Sir Ferdinando Leigh, prisoner for debt in the gaole of the Ho'r of Pontefract, being about 61 years of age, departed this life, & his corps was interred in the quoire of ye parish church of Pontefract aforesaid, the 21th day of the same moneth.

And again,

Sept 9, 1658. Agnes Holdsworth, widow, a prisoner in the common gaol of the honor of Pontefract, departed this life, & her corps was interred in the co'mon buryall place of Pontefract, the tenth day of the same moneth.

The case of this Sir Ferdinando Leigh is an illustration of the pecuniary straits to which Royalists were reduced during this decade. The heir of an eminent family, seated at Middleton for three centuries and a half, the husband of four wives, each of whom brought him a dowry, he became at length a prisoner for debt, and died before his debts were satisfied. One of his daughters, Frances, by his fourth marriage, was married to Dr Samuel Pulleyn, son of Samuel Pulleyn, archbishop of Tuam, of Pontefract extraction, the contemporary archbishops Pulleyn of Tuam and Bramhall of Armagh being both of Pontefract ancestry.

Among the prisoners evidently of the better class, was also a certain Thomas S—— (probably the Thomas Stockes whose burial is recorded on August 22, 1667,) who during his captivity must have passed many weary hours at a window which then overlooked the town, but which had probably been blocked up for about two hundred years previous to 1871, when, some repairs being in progress, a singular discovery was made. The splays of this window were plastered in the usual way, and Thomas S—— possessing the luxury of a lead pencil, appears to have amused himself with writing on one of the side walls. That writing was in 1871 uncovered, after the lapse of two hundred years, and though unhappily the left-hand side of the plaster was so injured that part of the inscription was illegible, sufficient remained to show its character. We copied all *verbatim et literatim*, and may add that its general appearance could leave no reasonable doubt of its authenticity. It may be noted that the only *v* in the six lines was in the word *salvation*.

> Hee that liueth longest hath the greatest
> of Miseries. Therefore Set the howerly
> of Death and Mortality Before
>   yes. And as thou tenders the Salvation of thy
> Soule, Indeuour to liue without Blame
> thou Bee not Found   atching. 14 July 166 .

Which appears to have been intended to read thus:—" He that liveth longest hath the greatest share of miseries. Therefore set thee hourly the thought of death and mortality before thine eyes. And as thou tenderest the salvation of thy soul, endeavour to live without blame, lest thou be not found watching."

A little distance below this writing was the signature Thos S   , the latter part of the name, as of the date, having disappeared, though it was stated at the time by the workmen who opened it out, that the full date was 1666, a date which corresponds with the record of the burial of Thomas Stockes, allowing him to have languished in prison for thirteen months.

We presume that the unhappy Thomas S———, when on that bright Saturday in July, 1666, he looked out so longingly on the beautiful valley before him, had paid his "Twopence in the pound" for his "ease of iron."

But while the Main Guard thus fulfilled the purposes of a prison, the grounds of the Castle were let out by the Duchy of Lancaster as a Liquorice Plantation: and their dedication to the cultivation of that grateful esculent continued till 1881.

337

WE APPEND a few documents, as either illustrating the use to which the Castle was put in its palmy days, or being circumstantial narratives of events which occurred there.

The first is from page 51 of the 6th volume of the Rolls of the Parliament of 1473 (12 & 13 Edw IV). It shows that the exploit of Colonel Morris in seizing Sir A. Ingram, taking him to the Castle, and holding him for ransom, was not without a precedent nearly two centuries old.

---

57. ITEM, Quedam alia Petitio exhibita fuit prefato Domino Regi in dicto Parliamento, dicto Octavo die Februarii, per Johannem Assheton, Militem, in hec verba.
TO the Kyng oure Sovereigne Lord: Besecheth your Highnes in the moost humbly wise your true and feithfull Liegeman John Assheton Knyght to considre his true and feithfull service, accordyng to his dutie and liegeaunce which he hath at all tymes had and doon to your Highnes, sith the begynnyng of your moost noble and rightwyse reigne, aswell afore your departer oute of this your Royalme, as contynuelly sith, and so at all tymes with the Grace of God entendes to doo. That where as the said John Assheton, the Tewesday next afore the day of the fest of Seynt Martyn, in wynter, the xth yere of your moost noble reigne was in Goddes peas and yours, in and at his Maner and dwellyng place of Holley, in the Towne of Morley in the Counte of York, his wyfe, childer and other his houshold manyall Servauntez, his said wyfe beyng then newely delyvered of child, and liying in child bed, with other dyvers hir susters, gentylwomen and frendes accompayned there and then with hir, the same day, abowte twoo of the clok in the mornyng oon John Myrfeld, late of Pountfrette in the same Counte, Squyer, Richard Ledys, late of Pontfrete in the same Counte Gentilman,

Riottours and evyll disposed persones, then and there accompayned with other Riottours and evyll disposed persones unknowen to your said Besecher, to the nombre of cc persones and moo, arraied defensably in maner of werre that is to witte, with Curays, Corsettes, Speres, Jakkes, Salettes, Bowes, Arrowes, and Long debieffes and dyvers other defensible wapens, and with Trompettes and Hornes blawying openly afore theym with force and armes, ayenst your lawes and peas, the said Maner and dwellyng place assauted, and dyvers howses and walles of stone and plaister therof brake and pulled downe, and the yates of the same Manere and dwellyng place willfully and purpeusely with fyere brought with theym in a Salette thider then and there brent, to oon of the worste example that ever was in thoos parties, and by cause of the which, the said wyfe of youre said Besecher, was in right grete dispare of hir lyfe, and by grete space then after so contynued, and in like wyse the said gentilwomen then with hir accordyng to the lawes of God and womanhede as is aforeseid accompayned, were in grete dispare of their lyves, and also youre said Besecher, and all other then beyng within the said Maner and dwellyng place, put in grete fere of their deth; and your said Besecher theruppon concernyng the said horrible riotte, the malicious purpose of the said Riottours, and the brekying and castyng downe of the said howses and walles of the said Maner and dwellyng place, and the said wilfull and ferefull birnyng, and that his said wyfe so beyng but newe in child bed, and in the bandes of oure Lady, myght not be remeved ne caried oute of the same place withoute jeopardie of hir deth; in salvation of his lyffe, hir lyfe, and the lyfes of all the other that at that tyme were within the said Maner and dwellyng place, come furth and submitted hym to the said Riottours; wheruppon the said Riottours, soore ayenst the wylle of your seid Besecher, then and there toke hym and karied hym with theym from thens to Pontfrette Castell within the same Counte of York, and there kept hym at their owne wille by grete space, to the tyme that by the supplication of his frendes he was enlarged, uppon promys and affirmans by mouth made by hym to the said Riottours in M li to be bounden, that he shuld abide the rule of such persones as they wold be agreable unto.

Wherefore, the premysses considered, it may pleas your Highnes, of your moost rightwyse and haboundaunt grace, by the advis and assent of the Lordes Spirituall and Temporell in this present Parlement assembled, and the Commens of the same, to ordeyne, enacte and establishe, by auctorite of the same Parlement, that the said John Assheton may have as many Writte and Writtes uppon the premyssez, and uppon every parcell of theym, oute of your Chauncery, as in that behalfe may be to hym necessarie, to be direct to the Shireff of the said Shire of York for the tyme beyng, commaundyng the said Shiref by the same Writte and Writtes, uppon the payn of c li, the half therof to your Highnes, and the other half to your said Besecher to be forfeited, to make open and severall proclamations uppon the severall market dayes next after the delyvere to hym of the same Writte or Writtes in the open markettes in the Tounes of Pountfrette and Wakefeld, within the said Counte, that the said John Myrfeld, Richard Ledys, and either of theym, in their propre persone and persones appiere afore your Highnes in your Benche at Westm', at the day and daies of the retourne conteyned in the same Writte and Writtes there to aunswere, and answere in and to all such Writte and Writtes, Bille and Billes, there to be sued, put or declared, ayenst theym or any of theym by your said Besecher, perteyning any of the premisses, in their propre persones, and so to appiere contynuelly the same plee duryng, and not to be admitte to appiere by any Attourney.

And also that it be ordeyned by the said auctorite that the said Shireff for the tyme beyng, truely retourne every of the said Writte and Writtes of proclamation, at the day and daies of retourne specified in the same Writte and Writtes, uppon the payne of every defaulte c li; the half therof to your Highnes, and the other half to your said Besecher as is aforeseid: And that your said Besecher uppon every forfeiture aforeseid, may have an action of dette, by Writte or Writtes ayenst every Shiref defectyf as is aforeseid, afore youre Justices of your Comen Benche, in the which like processe be had as usuelly there is used in actions of dette sued at the commen lawe; and that no Defendaunt therin, in any such Writte or Writtes be receyved to wage his lawe. And if any the said Riottours, so apperyng, plede any relesse, arbetrament, or any other plee, not matier of Recorde, triable oute of the said Shire of York, that then the issue therof to be tried within the said Shire of York, and in noon other place and also that noon Essoyn nor Protection, be allowable nor allowed for any of the said Riottours, Defendauntes in any of the said Writte or Writtes, Bille or Billes.

And also that it be ordeyned by the said auctorite that if the said Riottours and every of theym, appiere not in their propre persones at the day and daies as is aforeseid to be lymyted, that then he and they which then appiere not, stond and be convicte and atteynt of the forseid Riottes, and the other trespassez, and offensez aforeseid, and every of theym; and that the said John Assheton may have, and have theruppon, alsmany and all such Writtes to enquere of his damagez in that partie, as to hym shall be necessarie, to the said Shiref of Yorkshire for the tyme beyng to be directe, and of the damagez in that partie founden and retourned the said John Assheton have like processe and execution in all thynges, as is used in your said Bench in Writtes of trespas, supposed to be doon with force and armes, sued by partie ayenst partie in the same Bench, and in the same convicte or atteynt, by verdit, or otherwise.

Qua quidem Petitione in Parliamento predicto lecta, audita & plenius intellecta, de avisamento & assensu Dominorum Spiritualium & Temporalium, ac Communitatis Regni Anglie, in dicto Parliamento existen' ac ejusdem Parliamenti auctoritate, respondebatur eidem sub hiis verbis,

Soit fait come il est desire.

This document has many points of singular interest

into which the limits we have put upon ourselves forbid us to enter. It must suffice that we put it upon record.

Pontefract Castle maintained its grandeur during the reigns of Edward IV and his two successors, and towards the close of the reign of Henry VIII, in the interval between the suppression of the lesser and the greater monasteries, it became the seat of the Pilgrimage of Grace.

The following is a graphic account of the visit of the Lancaster Herald to the Castle to call those then in arms there to submit themselves. It shows incidentally many particulars of its condition in 1536.

A REPORTE OF LANCASTRE HAROLDE AT ARMES TOWCHYNG THE ORDRE OF THE COMONS IN YORKESHYRE.

The maner, fac'on, and ordreying of me Lancaster Heralde at Armes to o'r Sov'aigne Lorde the Kynge, sent from Scroby, the xxi day of October, by the right honorable Lorde th' Erle of Shrowesbery, Lorde Stewarde of the Kinges most honorable householde and Lieften'nt Gen'all from the Trent Northewards; and the right hon'able Erles of Rutlande and Hunttyngdon, of the Kinge's moost hon'rable Counesaile, to Pomfrett wt a p'clamac'on to be redd amongeste the traiterous and rebellious p'sonnes assemble at Pomfrett, contr'y to the Kinge's lawes.

And when I did approche nere the towne of Pomfrett, I ov'rtoke c'ten companyes of the said rebellious, beinge com'on people of husbandrye, w'che saluted me gentilly, and gave grett honor to the Kinge's coote of armes, which I ware. And I demaunded of them why they were in harnés, and assembled of such sorte; and they aunswered me yt it was for a Comen welthe: and saide if thay did not so, the Comynaltie and the Churche shulde be distroied. And I demaunded of them howe? and they saide that no man shulde burye, nor x'ten, nor wedd, nor have ther beasts unm'rked, but the Kinge wold have a c'rten sum'e of money for ev'ry suche thinge, and the beasts unm'rked to his owne use, w'ch had never ben seene. And I answered them, and tolde them how good and gr'cious Lorde the Kinge had bene to them, and howe longe he had kepte them in grett welthe, tranquillité, and peas ; and also that his G'ce, nor noone of his Counsaile, never intended nor thought no suche thinges and articlez as thai founde them greved wt. And wt suche p'swac'ons as I founde and saide to them, ridinge to the towne, I had gatt graunte iii c or foure hundred of the com'ons to goo gladly home to ther houses, and to abide the Kinge's m'cy, and saide thuy were wery of that lyffe thay ware in.

And I resorted furst to the m'kett closse, wher I shulde have made the p'clamac'on, and Rob't Haske, Capitaigne of the booste, beynge in the Castell, harde telle that I was comen, and sent for me to cum' to hym, and so I did. And as I entred into the furste warde, ther I founde manny in harnés of very cruell felowes, and a port'r wt a white staffe in his hande and at the too other warde gates, evry of them, a porter wt a staff in his hande, accompanyed wt harnest men ; and so I was brought in to the hall, w'ch I founde full of people, and I was co'maunded to tarry to suche tyme as the saide traiterous Captaigne his pleas'r was knowen. And in that space I stoode up at the high table in the hall, and ther shewed to the people the cause of my com'ying, and th' effecte of the p'clamac'on; and, in doinge the same, the said Haske sent for me in to his chamb'r, and yr, keping his porte and counten'nce, as thoughe he had ben a grett Prince, wt grett rigor, and like a tiraunte ; who was accompanyed w'h th' Archbishop of Yorke, and Lorde Darcye, S'r Rob't Constable, Mr. Magnus, S'r X'tofur Danby, and dyvers other.

And, as my duetie was, I saluted th' Archebishope of Yorke, and my Lorde Darcye, shoynge to them the cause I cam thethur for; and then the saide Rob't Haske, wt a cruell and a inestimable proude counten'nce, stretchid hym sellfe, and toke the heringe of my tale, w'ch I opened to hym at large, in asmoche honor to o'r Sovraigne Lorde the Kinge as my reason wolde s'rve me, w'ch the said Capitaigne Haske gave no credens to, and sup'sticiously demaunded the sight of my p'clamac'on ; and than I toke it oute of my purse, and delyve'd it to hym; and then he redd it openly, w'toute revrence to anny p'son, and said it shulde not nede to call no counesaile for th' answer of the same, for he wold of his owne witte, give me th' aunswere ; which was this : He, standyng in the highest place of the chamb'r, takinge the highest estate upon him, saide, " Haraulde, as a mesengere you are welcom to me, and all my company, intendinge as I do; and, as for this p'clmac'on sent from the Lordes from whens ye com shall not be redd at the m'kett crosse, nor in no place amongest my people, which be all und'r my guydinge; nor for feare of losse of lands, lyffe, and goodes, nor for the power w'ch is against us dothe now ent'r in to o'r hartes wt feare but ar all of oone accorde, w't the poynctes of o'r articles clerely intending to se a reformacon, or els to die in thies causes."

And then I demaunded of hym what his articles was? and he said that oone was that he and his company wolde go to Londo' upon pilgremage to the Kinge's Highnes, and ther to have all vile blode of his Counesaile putt from hym, and all noble blod sett up againe, and also the faithe of Criste and his lawes to be kepte, and full restituc'on of Criste's Churche of all wronges done to it, and also the com'ynaltie to be used as thai shulde be, and bade me truste to this, for it shulde be done, or he wolde die for it. And then I requyred hym yt he wold gyve me this in writinge, for my capacité wolde not s'rve me to bere it awaye; and he said, " wt a good will," and called for his othe w'ch he gave to his people, and said the articles were comp'hended w'tin the said othe, and delyve'd it in writeinge to me, and caused me to rede it my selffe; and he said to that he wolde sette his hande, and die in the quarrell, and his people wt hym; and then I p'yed him to putte his hande to the said bill, and so he did, and wt a prounde voice, saide, " this is myne acte, whosoev'r say to the contrary." And also he saide he ment no harme to the Kinge's p'sonne, but to se reformac'on. And I fell downe uppon my knee before hym shewying hym howe I was a messengere, and charged by the Kinge's Counesaile to rede the p'clamac'on w'ch I brought, for my discharge: and he clerely aunswered me yt of my lyffe I shulde not, for he wolde have no thinge put in his people's heads yt shulde sounde cont'ry to his intent; and said at all tymes I shuld have his sauffe conduyte to cum' and goo in message, wearing the Kinge's coote of armes, or els not; and also said if my Lorde of Shrewesbury, or any oy'r of the Lordes of the Kinge's armye, wold cum' and speke wt hym, thay shulde have of hym a sauffe conducte to cum' saffe and goo sauffe ; and also said, " Haraulde, com'end me to the Lordes from whens you cum', and say to them, it wer mette that yai were wt me, for it is for all y'r welthes, that I do ;" and then he comaunded the Lorde Darsie to give me too crownes of vs for rewarde, whethur I wolde or no; and then toke me by the arme, and brought me forthe of the Castell, and y'r made a p'clamuc'on yt I shulde goo sauffe and cum' saffe, wearinge the Kinge's coote, on paine of deathe ; and so toke his leave of me and rētorned to the Castell in high'st honor of the people, as a t'ytour may. And I myssed my hors ; and I called to hym againe to have my hors ; and then he made a p'clamac'on, yt whoso held my hors, and brought hym not againe, imediately bad kylle hym w'tout m'cye ; and then bothe my hors was delyve'd to me. And then he comaunded that xxti or xxxti men shulde bringe me out of the towne, wher I shulde se the least of his people, nor yt I shulde not speke wt them ; for surely I thinke, if I might have redd the p'clamac'on and good words unto people, that all the plowgh com'ynaltie wolde have goone home to yr houses im'ediatlye, for thai say yt they ben wery of yt lyffe thai lede ; and if thai say to the cont'ry, to the Capitaigne's will he shall die imediatly. And this all to be true, I, the said Lancastre, have written yis wt my handes, and true reporte as my othe is.

LANCASTRE HARAULDE.

This report gives us some little idea of the sort of state held in the Castle, in the sixteenth century, and the succession of tests through which a visitor had to pass, from ward to ward, and from porter to porter. Its quaint and minute description is also in character and accordance with what we should expect from the office and position of the writer.

But the Castle is described with a more complete particularity in a survey in 1538, which we reproduce. We presume that the original is in the Public Record Office, but have not been so fortunate as to discover it.

REMAINS OF ROUND TOWER, MARCH 31st 1885.

The view of the Castell of Pontfrect mayd the x and xijth day of January in the xxix yere of the Reign of o'r Sov'aign lord Kyng Henry the Eghte by Sir Henry Savell Knyght, Sir George Lawson Knyght, and Robert Chaloner. By advice of John Forman, Mason, John Tomson, Carpent'r, and Thos. Jackson, Founder.

In p'mis, vj Chambers in the nedder storre of the Dongon Tower, which haithe the walls sore rente and two Dowers of Stone to be amendyd.

Item, In the seconnde storre of the same Tower five Chambers, too wyndowes, and one Dower of Stone, and one Corbell of stone to be amendyd.

It', In Chambers in the thirde storre of the same Tower, callyd th' artelere, w'ch haithe the leeds decayed so that it raynthe into the said Chambers; and also iiij Balkes of tymbers in the said Tower ar Rotten in sander and also wants one Dower.

It', In the said storre one od' dower, and a wyndowe of Mason worke to be amendyd.

It', In the v Chambers of the said storre one vawte of stone, and one Dower of Stone to be mendyd, and xi gyests of tymber is decayed in the same Tower.

It', A Stone to be mendyd that goithe up the same Tower to the leeds.

It', Nevellis Tower wants iiij Corbells of Stone and iiij gyests and too walle playts.

It', The leeds of vj rooys ov' the Dongon Tower to be newe caste and laid, and iiij spouts and dev's gutters and oder leed necessary for the said Tower to the value of vj foder.

It', Unto Nevill Tower, Pip' Tower, and Bakhouse Tower, and the Rovys betwixt the same, vj foder of leed.

It', two toppis of Chimneys in the Kechyn haithe nede to be mendyd.

It', the Rovys of the Bakhouse, Kechyn, pastre, Buttre, pantre, and the haule, xx foder of leed.

It', to the Kings logyng and the qwenes, xvj foder of leed.

It.' vj Chimnethe toppis ov' the Kechyn and Buttre to be mendyd.

It', too foder of leed to the said Tower.

Bords	It'	five thousand foyte of serkyn Bords or above, to the said Castell.
Leed	It'	lxx foder of newe leed ov' and besydes the old leed of the same Castell woll serve to cov' newe all such howses within the said Castell as haith been cov'yd with leed of lait.
Tymber	It'	xx Toone of Tymber wolle serve for the repa'con of tymber worke for the said Castell.
Mason Work	It'	6 pounds in money woll bere the costs of the Masonre of the said Castell.
Iron Gaytts	It'	The said Castell wants Iron gaytts wiche viij Toone of Iron woll mayke.
Wells	It'	in the said Castell is a very fayre well in good reparacon and one other in the Dongon wiche is stopped.
	It'	in the grett Tower is one other decayed.

Artilere

Furst in the hye Tower of the said Castell is remayning of Cheyffe arrows withe heeds unto the nomber of } xj score & iiij cheyfe

It' in the said Tower of Cheyffe arrowes without heeds } xx cheyfe

It' in the said Tower remaynthe Bowes

It' there remaynthe by Estimaçon of arrowe tymber unwrought } one Cartelood

Ordenance

It' in the said howse is remayning v Iron gonnes
It' of Iron Chambers for gonnes to the number of xi.
It' in the said House is remayning 1 gonstones of Iron.
It' in barbyd stakes for Horses to the nomber of xiij Cheyffe.
It' in the said howse of cheyff arrowes with heed lj Cheyffe.
It' in cheffe arrowes without heeds xi cheyffe.
It' in the said howse is x chysts to lay ordenance in, and a Carte } x chysts & a Carte

Howses of Office

It' in the said Castell is a sufficient Bakhouse and Brewhouse savyng there is no Brewyng vessell ne horse-mylne within the said Castell.

From this very interesting document we learn much concerning the structure of the Castle.

The Donjon Tower appears from it to have had three stories, the lower having six chambers, the others five. The upper of these stories, which was called the Artillery, was vaulted in stone, and its roof was leaded. The Donjon Tower had moreover a Neville's Tower, connected with it, no trace of which remains, though indeed, until the recent excavations the same might have been said of the Bakehouse, the Kitchen, the Buttery, and the Hall.

It is curious that the name Neville should here be given to a tower that evidently had some relation to both the Donjon and Piper Tower, since the name was applied at the Demolition to a Mount in the Lower Barbican.

Leland, whose description of the Castle had been written two years before, similarly says of it, "The Castelle of Pontefract * * conteineth 8 toweres, of the which the dungeon, cast into 6 roundelles, 3 bigge and 3 smaul, is very fair, and hath a fair spring." The "six roundelles" would have contained the six chambers of the ground floor.

This present survey tells us, moreover, that the Castle had three wells, "a fayre well," "one other in the Dongon, which is stopped," and one in the "grett Tower" "decayed." Of neither of these, unless indeed it is that which had been "stopped" do we know anything. This may be at the foot of the interior staircase leading to the underground dungeon.

It is also exceedingly remarkable that the Bakehouse, Kitchen, &c., concerning which nothing was known until the late excavations, are here so clearly on record that only a few years ago the document would have been a hopeless puzzle, and its perusal a source of bewilderment, owing to there being nothing that could then be identified as corresponding to the description; though now, there is little described in this survey that cannot be identified.

Whether any of the repairs, thus certified to be necessary, were really effected is not so clear. Apparently they were not: for less than twenty years afterwards, in the time of Philip and Mary, the Great Tower was reported ruinous, as appears by the following, which we have copied from a document in the handwriting of Patience Warde, with his certificate that it was a true copy of the original. It is entitled

A Warr't upon a Commission for Repairing the Castell of Pountfrett.

Philip & Mary &c. To our Trusty & well beloved Sr. Thom's Gargrave Deputy Steward of our possessions belonging to our Hon'r of Pountefret p'cel of our Dutchy of Lancaster in our County of York, Knight, and Will'm Mallett, Rec'r of our said possessions Esqr, and to either of them, Greeting.

Forasmuch as We be credibly informed by the Certificate of you the sd Sr. Thomas, & Willm Mallett, That our Tower called the Gyllott Tower, or the great Round Tower, both within, & without the Walls of our Castell of Pountfret, p'cel of our said Duchy, in our said County, is in great ruine & decay, as well in tymber-work as in Stonework & is likely shortly to fall down, unless some speedy Remedy be had & provided for the same, more & more to our disherison, & losse, as by the Commission, together with the sd [Certificate certified by you the sd Sr. Thomas & Wm. Mallett into our Dutchy Chamber, awarded lately for the View of the State of the same more at large doth appear: We intending ye Repairing, supportation, & amendment of the same our tower, Will & desire you two jointly that in as convenient time as ye well may, ye do see our said Tower now being in ruine & decay as is aforesd, to be repaired & amended in such places thereof as be needfull as well in timber as in Stone, which shall be needfull for the sufficient repairing, & amendm't of the same, Letting you our said Rec'r to wyte our pleasure, that is that you shall disburse & lay out from time to time as much money, as shall be requisite for the necessary repairing, & amendm't thereof. And also, We authorize you, & either of you by these p'esents to take such Stone & tymber meet, & necessary for the Repair of our said Tower in such places hereafter recited.

That is to say the said Stone, as well of the late dissolved Abbey of Puontf't aforesd, as of the decayed Chappell called St. Thomas Hill being distant one quartr of a Mile or thereabouts from our said Castell; And the said Timber Trees to be taken in our Woods of Creedling Sowewood, & Ackworth being p'cel of our said Dutchy, or in such other our Woods, p'cel of the same Dutchy, as the same may be best spared, & most to our Commodity, & availe; And the topps and lopps of the said trees which shall be felled within our said Woods for the Reparation of ye p'omisses. That is to say part of them for the burning of the Lime to repair, support & amend the said Tower; & that ye two jointly do sell the Residue of the said topps & lopps, & bark of the said trees that shall be felled for the same, to our most profit & avayle, And therefore, You our said Rec'r to make Us true Acc't before our Auditor, or Auditors of our said Dutchy for the time being; Letting you, & either of you to wytte that our pleasure is, that upon the same Acct to be made, our Auditor of our said Dutchy shall from time to time upon p'ticular book or books subscribed with yo'r hands make unto you our said Rec'r, due allowances for all such Sums of money as shall be laid out, in & about ye repair of our said Tower. And that These our Lett'rs, shall be as well unto you, & either of you, as to our said Auditors, and every of you a sufficient Warrant & discharge agst Us, & ye Heirs & Successors of Us the said Queen at all times hereafter in this behalf. Given at our Pallace of Westmin'r, under our Seal of our said Dutchy the 3d day of July, in the fourth & fifth years of our Reigns, Anno D'm 1557.

The following memorandum is at the foot of the copy of this interesting document. It also is in the handwriting of Sir Patience Warde, Alderman of London, and the Lord Mayor of 1680-1 :—

Taken out of a Book entitled Liber primus, Temp' Edw 6 & H. 8vi f. 246 b., & in custod. Auditor Ducat' Lanc. P'rused 27th Apr 1709.

p' P.W.

The document, for which we are indebted to the spirit of antiquarian research, and to the love of his birth place which was possessed by Sir Patience Warde, throws many glimpses of light on the condition of the building in the sixteenth century. The Round Tower, as we call it, is said to have been " both within and without the walls " : that is, it was on the line of the walls, and from it, as we know, access was obtained both to the Garth within the inner Barbican, and to the private garden without.

And, moreover, it accounts for the presence of many stones among the ruins, that could never have formed part of the actual buildings, and shows that they might have been at this time fetched from the Priory, or from St. Thomas's Chapel on the Hill. No mention is, however, made of any temporary buildings on the inner sides of the walls, though there must have been such, as a sort of barrack, to accommodate the many men occasionally within the Castle.

Again, this document shows that any project that had ever been entertained by Queen Mary, of restoring the Priory or Chantry, had now been absolutely relinquished, for she deliberately ordered the buildings to be used as a quarry.

That some such hopes had been entertained in the early part of her reign, is well known, and perhaps the following letter, from Mr. Hamerton, of Purston, while giving interesting details with regard to Pontefract, will indicate the direction in which he was inclined to believe that improvement might then have been made. In itself, it is of a most pathetic character.

The copy has been carefully transcribed from the original, in the State Paper Office. It is addressed to Cardinal Pole, at that time, and during her whole reign (they died on the same day) Queen Mary's faithful friend and adviser.

TO THE RYGHT HONERABLE AND MOST REVERENT FATHER IN GOD THE LORD CARDYNELL POULLE TO HYS GOOD GRACE.

May yt please your honerable grace, of your greate mercy, pety, and abundant Charyte, Evyn accordyng to your accustumyd cleme'cy, to reduce into your devote memorie my olde Long and Co'tenuall sute to your noble grace, Tutchyng the reedyfyyng of the churche belongyng to the colege and ospital fundid in the hono'r of the moste blyssyd Trynetys in Pomfret withe in the countey of Yorke. My Lord what can I say there ing that hathe not byn revalyd in former symplecyons to your grace exebetyd tutchyng the same sute, not as my only privat sute, but by the sute of the mayer and all the hole in abbetance (*i.e.* inhabitants) of the same towne, not onely exebetyd to your grace but also unto the kyng and the hyghest under there co'mon seale ou' and besyd the supplecacyons of the poore bede peopyll of the same ospitall et c.

My Lord, as I have sayd before, we had in that towne one abbaye, two collegys, a house of freers prechers, one ancrys, one ernyt, four chantre prests (tor in dede *erased*) one gyld pryst. Of all thes, the in abbytance (*i.e.* inhabitants) of the towne of pomfret ar nother relveyd bodely nor gostly. We have there lefte an unlearnyd vecar which hyryth too prests, for indede he ys not able to discharge the cure other wayes, and I dar say the vicar's levyng ys under fortie markys, the personage hath the pensshonars and suerly too p'tis of the prophety (property) hath the prochers, but this ys a generall infyrmyty and Lord amend yt. Truly there be sume hed prochers, and petty prochers et c and ev'y one catcheth apeece. But the pore nedy me'bers of cryst catchyt none at all.

But my sute to your noble grace at this p'sent ys, most umble (humbly) to desyer your grace that yow wyll have co'passion of the great mesery that this sayd towne of Pomfret ys fallyn into, bothe bodely and gostely, sence the godly fundacyons afore sayd hathe bene so (a *erased*) mysse ordereyd and mysse usyd and the hold sanctures (*i.e.* sanctuaries) of god so petefully defilyed and (petefully *erased*) spoulyd.

thes prymysys tenderly co'sederyd, yf it wold please your noble grace so to p'efarre the co'tinuall sute aforesayd, to the adwanseme't of god's glory And to the co'forth of his poore me'bers, bothe bodely and gostly, so that I your poore supplecant, and many others shall have cause co'tenually to pray accordyng to our abundant dewty for the prosperous estate of our soverant Lord and Lade the kyng and the quene's hyghnes with your honerable grace long to endure by your supplecant and co'tynuall orator, unworthee

JOHN HAM'TON.

The quaint earnest language of Mr Hamerton, the evident sincerity of his appeal on behalf of the "pore nedy me'bers of cryst" is most affecting, notwithstanding the manner in which he manages to spell his words—in a way which, to say the least, modern custom has not sanctioned. As he pathetically says, the diversion of ecclesiastical properties from the purposes to which they had been devoted was a general infirmity in that generation. It led in the next reign to the establishment of a Poor Law.

Mr. Hamerton's enumeration of the recently suppressed religious foundations is also not without its interest. There had been,

One Abbey	The Priory of St. John.
Two Colleges	St. Nicholas and Trinity.
The Friars Preachers	At Friar Wood.
One Anchoress	At St. Nicholas.
One Hermit	At the Hermitage.

The four chantry priests were those of St. Thomas the Apostle, called also Rishworth's Chantry, our Lady's Chantry, and St. Roque's Chantry, in All Saints' Church; and our Lady's Chantry in St Giles's Chapel. The Gild Priest was attached to the Chapel of Corpus Christi.

His object—to obtain the re-establishment of the Trinities—was unattainable in the way he proposed. But it came to pass thirty years afterwards, when John Freeston purchased the property, and re-endowed the charity.

The date of this interesting letter is not given; but it is supposed to have been about May, 1556.

The vicar upon whom such reflections were cast was the last vicar appointed by the monks. As he held the living from 1538 to 1568, well into the reign of Queen Elizabeth, it may be remarked that the unlearned vicar who hired two priests, retained his living through all the phases of the Reformation. His name was John Barker.

With regard to Sir Thomas Gargrave, deputy steward, to whom the warrant was addressed, we find from a document calendered in DOMESTIC ADDENDA (ELIZABETH) vol XII, p 68, —"A List of such who have the government of Castles and seigniories within the County of York," —the name of the "Earl of Shrewsbury, resident in Yorkshire; Sir Thos. Gargrave is his deputy there." This was in 1565. Sir Thomas Gargrave then owned Nostell and Kinsley.

The following is the entry:—

> Therle of Sherewsburie is Stuard of the honor of Pountefrette, beinge a greate Seignorie, & hath thorder of the Castell of Pountefrette & the men theare.

There is a marginal memorandum,

> Pontefrette. Resident in Yorkeshyre, and his deputie theare Sr Thom's Gargrave.

But even a generation before the Castle fell into the state of disrepair which led to the grant of this warrant, we find that it was hardly in a condition to receive the Princess Margaret, eldest daughter of Henry VII, who, in her progress northward to meet her affianced husband—the King of Scotland—in 1503, stopped at Pontefract. She passed *through the Castle* (that is presumably along the Castle Chain) and lodged in the Priory; which is rather evidence that there was at that time a quasi thoroughfare through the Castle yard, for it is plain that the course of the procession was through Ropergate, the Market Place, Micklegate, and forward through the West and East gates of the Castle.

The princess had slept at Scrooby, a manor belonging to the Archbishop, afterwards the cradle of the Pilgrim Fathers, and now in the ownership of Lord Houghton. On her journey, she

Drew to Doncastre. And halfe Way came Sir Edward Savage and with hym Sir Rauf Ryder, well appoynted, and the Folks of ther Liverays, to the Nomber of 60 Horsys, well mounted.

Witqout the said Doncastre was the Mayor, Aldermen, and Bowrgesses on Foot, the wich resayved the sayd Quene. Thys doon, in fayr Aray she entred within the said Towne according to the precedent Custome, and was lodged in the Freres Carmes.

The xiiiith Day of the Monneth, the Quene departed from the sayd Place, right noble accompaned, and the sayd Mayor, Aldermen and Bourgesses were att the End of the Towne, without gowyng any fourther.

After that she drew to her Lodgyng at Pontfret and feyve Mylle from thence cam to hyr Sir John Melton, well arayd and with him eight Men well horsyd making Gambads. Also xiii Horse well appoynted of his Liveray.

Fore Mylle nyer to the sayd Place cam Sir William Gaskyn having in hys Company many Gentylmen of his Hous, and others, to the Nomber of 100 Horsys well apoynted of his Liveray.

Att two Mylle nyer to the sayd Place, Sir John Savyll mett hyr, to the Nomber of xii Horsys well appoynted.

Item, many other noble Sqyers, and Gentilmen of Yorkshire, well mounted and appoynted, and their Servants also, came to hyr.

Att the Intryng of the sayd Pontfret was the Mayor alone on Horsback, with the Baylys, Bourges, and Habitants all a Foot, who resayved the said Queene as the other Precedents.

And ther was the College of the said Place, togeder with the Freres Jacobyns, in Processyon, honestly revested. This don, after the Custome before, she entred within the sayd Towne in fayre Ordre. The wich Thing was very fayre for to se with muche People of the sayd Towne, and of the Contre thereabout.

In the Midds of the sayd Towne wer the Religyous of the Trinite revested, and the Offring hyr the Crosse for to kiss was done by the sayd Bischop in such manner as before.

And so shee past thorough the sayd Town, and thorough the Castell to the Abbay. Wher th'Abbot in Pontificalls, and all the Convent att the Porte of the Church, revested.

resayved her. The wiche kissed the Crosse, and entred within the sayd Church, where she maid her Prayers, and after went to her Lodginge within the sam Place for that Night.

The 15th Day of the sayd Monneth, the Quene departed from Pontfret in faire Company, as at other Tymes before, the Mayor, Aldermen, Bourgesses and Habitants conveying of her. And from thens she went to Dynner to Tadcaster.

But the Castle had, during the next reign, been again made habitable, for here King Henry VIII rested in his northern progress in 1541, after the dissolution of the Priory; and in Pontefract Castle, occurred the circumstances which led to the divorce and execution of the Queen, Katherine Howard.

After the dissolution, the Crown presented absolutely to St. Nicholas Hospital; but, inconveniences arising from that mode of election, the right was transferred by King James's Charter of 1606, to the Corporation. But we have found among the docquets in the State Paper Office one dated 10 March, 1609, (*i.e.* 1609-10) which orders

An almeseroome for John Anderson in consideracon of his old age and blyndnes, in the Almes howse at Pomfret. dated " ut supra prius, per Sir Danyell Dun."

This is at least singular, considering the renunciation by the Crown only three years previously.

Of nearly the same date, in vol. xxxvii, is "a description of the manors of Wakefield, Pontefract, Knaresborough, and Tickhill in Yorkshire, belonging to the Duchy of Lancaster, and of others in Lincolnshire, according to a recent survey, with entries of the nature of the tenures, the occupations and character of the inhabitants, and the feasibility of obtaining increased rents."

The text of the document is as follows :—

The Manor of Wakefeild is neare 3000 li of Copihold rent, rented gen'ally at iiijd the acre.
The very most of it inclosed ground. Meadow and pasture worthe eight or Tenn Shillings an acre p' annu'.
Their fynes upon deathe or alianacon arbitrable.
The proffits of Courts are in lease.
The Stewards make great proffits.
The bettr sorte of the tenn'ts there desire to be made free and thinck foure score yeares fyne no great rate.
The tenn'ts gen'ally riche and traders in clothe, most of them peaceable and quietly disposed.
Therefore I think this Lordshipp may be made A worthie example of proffit to many oth's of like tenure, for I verily thinck they may be drawn w'th some Circumstance to very highe rates.
The hono'r of Pountfrett consists of Eightene Manors, whereof fowre of the best are in joincture to the Queene. therefore not surveyed by me. the Copihold rent of the rest amounts to 400 *li*, or thereabouts.
The rents, there are rated higher than Wakefeild.
Their fynes arbitrable as Wakefeild.
The soile nor ten'tes so riche, yet well disposed, and may be drawn to Condicons, answerable to their abilities, and the benefitt they shall receave.

This was in 1609. Eleven years afterwards, we find from the Dodsworth MS. BBB 151 (vol. 32, as it is numbered), that,—we quote from the translation in Harl. 803—the King had granted to the Queen the whole of the Honour.

Pat. 17 James pt. 1. n. 3.
Out of Queen Anne her Joynture.

The King granted &c. and all o'r mann'r of Pontefract in the county of Yorke & other counties wheresoever that hon'r extendeth & all the demeasnes, castles, mann'rs &c. beeing p'cell or member of the said Hon'r of Pontefract or to the said Hon'r of Pontefract any way belonging, with the appurtenances in the said county of Yorke, viz't all those o'r townes of Pontefract & all those o'r mann'rs of Tanshelfe, Carleton, Aickworth, Allerton, Altofts, Kipax, Warnefeld, Barwicke, Scoles, Roundhay, Elmeshall, Camsall, Ouston, Knottingley, Credling, Beghall, Rothewell, Leedes, Marshden, & Almondbury. And the Wappentake of Staincrosse, the Wappentake of Skiracke, the Wapp'e of Aggbrigg & Morley, the Wappentake of Barkston &c. Dat. at Westminster 11 Octob: 17. Jacobi. (1619).

A few months afterwards in (DOMESTIC, JAMES I, vol. xlv) we find Gilbert, Earl of Shrewsbury, applying to the Earle of Salisbury, as Lord heygh Ths'er (Treasurer) of England, and alleging that Lady Arabella Stuart has informed him that the City of London desire to purchase Houghton, part of the Queen's jointure, and within a mile of Pontefract Castle. This, he protests against, as he believes it "would be a great prejudice to that fair and stately Castle," while on the other hand, he himself is anxious to buy lands for his Brother, Sir Charles Cavendish. His letter is written from Sheffield Lodge, and dated June 29, 1609. It is in No. 153 of the volume.

Nothing came of either of these projects so far as Pontefract is concerned, though later on the money of the Corporation of London was invested in a purchase of the manorial rights of the manor of Knottingley.

During the reigns of Elizabeth, James, and Charles, the Castle passed through many alternations of renewal and neglect. In 1634, it was under the care of a She-Keeper, as appears from

A RELATION OF A SHORT SURVEY OF 26 COUNTIES, BREIFLY DESCRIBING THE CITTIES AND THEIR SCYTUATIONS, AND THE CORPORATE TOWNES AND CASTLES THEREIN. OBSERUED IN A SEUEN WEEKES JOURNEY, BEGUN AT THE CITY OF NORWICH, AND FROM THENCE INTO THE NORTH, ON MONDAY, AUGT 11TH, 1634, AND ENDING AT THE SAME PLACE. BY A CAPTAINE, A LIEUTENANT, AND AN ANCIENT, ALL THREE OF THE MILITARY COMPANY IN NORWICH.

This towne of Pomfret is an ancient Corporation, consisting of a Mayor, 12. Aldermen, & a Recorder; and hath 2 Churches therein; there to lighten o'rselves we lighted at the Star, & tooke a fayre repast, to enable us the better to scale that high & stately, famous & princely impregnable Castle, & Cittadell, built by a Norman vpon a Rooke: which for the situation, strength, & largenesse, may compare with any in this Kingdome.

In the Circuit of this Castle, there is 7. famous Towers, of that amplitude & receit, as may entertaine so many Princes, as sometimes have commaunded this Island. The highest of them is called the Round Tower, in wch that vnfortunate Prince, was enforc'd to flee round a poste till his barbarous Butchers inhumanely depriu'd him of Life: Vpon that Post the cruell hackings, & feirce blowes doe still remaine: we view'd the spacious Hall wch the Gyants kept, the large faire Kitchen, wch is long, wth many wide Chimneys in it; then went we up, and Saw the Chamber of Presence, the King, and Quenes Chambers, the Chappell, & many other Roomes, all fit & sutable for Princes. As we walked on the Leads, wch couers that famous Castle, wee tooke a large, & faire prospect of the Country 20. miles about; Yorke we then easily saw, & plainely discouered, to wch place (after we had pleased the She Keeper our Guide) we thought fit to hasten.

The previous year, there had been a correspondence, also preserved in the State Paper Office, with regard to some necessary reparations, when the Castle appears to have been under the care of Francis Oglethorpe, a member of a family seated for some generations at Carleton.

The subject is commenced by Oglethorpe with the following, and the document can be seen as " STATE PAPERS, DOMESTIC, CHARLES I, VOL. 257, NO. 125."

TO THE HONO'BLE SR FRAS
WINDEBANCK, SECRETARY TO THE KING'S MA'TIE.

May it please yo' honor, his Ma'tye in his last progresse into Scotland takeing veiw of his highnes Castle of Pontefract in Yorkeshire, being the Ancyent Scite of the honor thereof, and being much delighted w'th the pleasantnes of the Scittuation, but disliking the decayes of some of the buildings, and consulting with his servant the porter of the same Castle touching some necessary reparacons to be had about the Church, Stables, and other out buildings, in greatest decay, and advertysed by his said Servant of a Just way to finish the said reparacons, without deminution to his Treasure or revynew, namely by calling in, and collecting all the neglected fynes and forfeitures imposed by his Ma'ties steward of the said hono' upon his highnes Tenants w'thin the same for not doeing their suitts and services att his Ma'ties Courts of the same hono'r. A duty fitt for his said Tenants to have done, and therefore the penalty Justly Imposed, and w'th the same Justice to be Collected and taken, w'ch proposition his Ma'tie haveing taken into Consideracon hath resolved to proceed in the worke, and hath therefore sent for his servant the porter, and given him direccon to procure a warrant drawne upp, for calling In and collecting his Ma'ties said fynes and forfeitures lost by any his highnes said Tenants of or w'thin the said hono'r of Pontefract, for not doeing theire suitt or service at his Courts of his said honor.

The action taken upon this communication led to the following Statement of Reasons why, if any such warrant were granted, certain villages should be excepted :—

Kinge James about the 13th yeare of his Raigne did graunt unto Sr Franncis Wortley power to Keepe certaine Court Leets of certain villages and hamletts w'thin the hono'r of Pontefract under the great Seale of England, and the Seale of the Dutchy of Lancaster for w'ch the said Sr Francis payed a good and valuable consideracon to the late Duke Lenox. Notw'thstandinge the said Graunts the Steward of the Hono' of Pontefract, where the said villages & hamletts did formerly appeare hath since continually fined and amerced such as did not appeare at Pontefract Court, but did not cause such Fines to be levyed in regard of his said Ma'ties Graunt. But nowe of late his Ma'tie beinge peticoned by one Oglethorpe, the Porter of Pontefract Castle, hath given order for a Reference of the busines, to the intent that if the busines bee of such value & consequence as is suggested, the said Fines amongst other things may be levyed and imployed by the said Oglethorpe towards the repayringe & amendinge of Pontefract Castle.

It is desired that those villages & hamletts granted to Sr Francis Wortley for a valuable consideracon as aforesaid may be excepted in the said levy, & exempted if a Graunt for that purpose should passe to Oglethorpe.

1. If his Ma'ties Tennants and subjects upon whom the said Fines and Amerciam'ts are layed, have offended in not appearinge at his Ma'ties Court, it was in obedience to his Ma'ties l'tres patents under the broad Seale of

England and the Seale of the Dutchy of Lancaster, w'ch was to them a sufficient Warrant as they conceave.
2. The Said l'res patents are yett extant and in force, and in case they should not, They desire to be protected by them untill they shall be declared voyde.
3. If the said fines be levyed, it will be a ruine & undoeinge to very many of his Ma'ties poore Tennants and subjects, within the hono'r of Pontefract, who have offended only out of their obedience, as they conceave, and it will besides rayse great sutes & troubles in the Countrey for replevyeinge and protectinge their goods.

In a later undated document—"Francis Oglethorpe, Porter of the Castle of Pontefract to the King"—the writer desires to know, Whether His Majesty continues the purpose to have the Castle and Church repaired, Whether coals should be digged in the Park, and Credling Park be passed away, and States that if the King wished to have the Castle and Church repaired, the Petitioner would upon warrant collect money in arrear sufficient to repair it.

To this letter we have not ascertained the reply; but evidently much was done to the Castle buildings about this time, of which the base still remaining of a colonnade between the King's Tower and St Clement's Chapel is sufficient, if the only and for many years buried, record.

In reference to this hint as to the digging of coals in the Park, we may notice that during the recent excavations, it was ascertained that the dead, buried in the modern Castle Chapel within a few inches of the surface, were buried in coal.

WE HAVE RESERVED for a final article the account of the trial and execution of Thomas, Earl of Lancaster, whose was the first royal blood shed in England; and a recital of the circumstances connected with the murder of King Richard II here, which so soon followed that of Earl Thomas. The fourteenth century was thus the time of the greatest glory of the Castle, and of its greatest shame. The century opened with the great Earl of Lincoln holding his Court in it, with a magnificence certainly equalling, if in some respects it did not surpass, that of the King. It closed with the cruel murder of that King's descendant, within its walls. The Earl died before the close of the first decade, leaving but a daughter, though she was the wedded wife of a prince royal,—the Earl Thomas, whose fateful end was one of the scenes of a long act of bloody crime. She did not much to deepen the happiness of her husband, and may indeed be said to have been in a great measure the indirect cause of his shameful death.

We will not recapitulate, at this time, the circumstances. It must suffice for us to quote, as we are about to do, from Leland, a full account of Earl Thomas's trial and execution, which will be found in the Collectanea, vol. 1, page 462 *et seq.* The historian whose writing Leland thus collected and preserved, was one William de Pakyngton, who was Clerk and Treasurer to Edward the Black Prince, and "did wryte a Chronique yn Frenche from the ix yere of King John of Englande, on to his tyme, and dedicated it to his Lord, Prince Edwarde. Owte of an Epitome in French, of this afore sayde Cronique, I translated carptim the thinges that folow yn to Englische." Thus saith John Leland, evidencing that Pakington had every opportunity of knowing the course of the affair at first hand.

The following is that part of Leland's translation which concerns Thomas of Lancaster. It is a curious admixture of French and English, but we print it verbatim:—

The Nobles of England seing the infinite Covetusnes of the Dispenser, cam to Thomas of Lancastre to treate a meane for it. And after of one assent made Assemble at Shirburne yn Elmede. And sending the Kinges Supplication, and not hard, the Barons went into the Marches of Wales, and destroyid the Dispensars Landes. Then King Edward, at the motion of the Dispensars, banishid John Mountbray, Roger Clifford, Gosseline Dainville, and dyvers other. And after the Barons caullid by brief to a Parlament cam with 3. Battayles yn ordre, having ten colourid Bandes on theyr Sleves, wherefore it was caullid the Parlement de la Bende. And yn this Company were Humfre de Boun Counte of Hereforde, Syr Hugh de Andeley, Syr Roger Damare, (alias Dainmore, et Damory) the whiche had maried the King Neecis, soers: Gilberte de Clare Counte of Glocestre that was slayn yn Scotlande at the Batel of Styvelyne: and these 2. had the 2. Partyes of the Counte of Glocestre by theire Wyves, and were of great Poure at that tyme. Ther cam also with them Syr Roger Clifford, Syr John Montbray, Syr Gosselline Daivil, Syr Roger Mortimer de Werke, Syr Roger Mortimer de Wigmore le Neuen, Syr Henry Tyeis, Syr John Giffarde, Syr Barptolemew Badelesmere the Kinges Steward, that the King had sent to Shirburn yn Elmede to the Erle of Lancastre, and them with hym to treat of Acorde, but he hym self allyid to the Barons with many other of theyr Confederation.

At this Parlament was both Hugh Dispenser the Father, and Hugh the Sunne bannishid out of Englande. And so Hugh the Father depertid oute of England, cursing the tyme that ever he begot Hugh his Sunne, and givyng hym his Malediction. But Hugh Dispenser the Sunne wold not avoide, and felle to spoilling on the Se, and taking out of 2. Dromondes, aboute Sandwich Cost, Goodes to the Value of xl. M. Poundes.

The King after sent for the Dispensers agayn his Barons Wylle. And after stoutely besigid the Castel of Leedys, wher Syr Barptolemeus Badelsmeres Wife lay, partely be cause she denyed Logging there to Quene Elizabeth ; but chiefly by cause Badelesmere was with the Barons agayn him, and wanne the (*sic*) by meanes of Londoners, that were with hym, and intelligens with them withyn. The Barons hering this, both the Mortymers toke Brigenorth, for the wich the King banishid, by Proclamation, Thomas of Lancastre, and Humfrede de Boun, with al theyr Adherentes.

And after the King cumming agayn his Barons with a strong Hoste, booth Mortymer the Uncle, and Mortymer the Nephew, put them self yn the Kinges Grace, and were sent to the Toure of London.

The Barons hering this cam to Pontfract to Thomas of Lancastre, and there gathering theire Poure, assautid the Kinges Castel of Tikhille, but not Wynning yt.

And hering of the Kinges Hoste, went to Burton apon Trent, keping the Bridge to let the Kinges Passage. But the Kinge passid per force, and thens wente the Barons with Thomas Lancastre to Tuttebyri, and thens to Pontefract. And in this Yorney Syr Roger Dainmore dyed yn the Abbay of Tuttebyry.

In this Yorney had Thomas of Lancastre a Traytor with hym callid Syr Robert de Hollande, whom he had taken oute of his Botery, and preferrid to the yerely lyving of 2. M. Markes, whom he had sent yn to Lancastreshire to bring hym V. C. Men, the which he brought not to hym but to the King.

After this Thomas Lancastre and the Barons counselid together in Blake Freres in Pontfracte, and the Barons concludid to go to Dunstanburg, a Castel of Thomas of Lancasters in Northumbreland: but he utterly refusid that Counsel, lest it might have be thought, that he had, or wolde have Intelligence with the Scottes. Wherefore he entendid to remayne at his Castel at Pontfract.

Syr Roger Clyfford hering this, toke oute his Dagger, and sayde that he wolde kille hym his oune Handes in that Place, except he woold go with them.

Then Thomas Lancastre aforce grauntid, and went with them, having yn Company VII. C. Menne, to Borowbridge.

To Borowbridge came Syr Andrew de Harkeley, Warden of Cairluel and that Marches, and Syr Simon Warde to encountre with the Barons. Where Thomas

Lancastre tolde Harkeley his juste Quarel agayne the Dispensers, promising hym, if he would favor his Cause, one of the V. Countes that then he had in Possession. But Herkeley refusid his Offre. Then Thomas prophetied that he wold sore repent, and that shortely, so fair, (sic) and that he should dy a shameful Deth, that is to say, to be hangid, drawen and quartered.

Then Harkeley, whom Thomas of Lancastre had afore tyme made Knight, made his Archiers to shote, and so did the Barons upon the bridge. And emong al other, one gotte under the bridge, and at a Hole thruste with a Launce the renoumid Knight thorough oute al Christentye Humfrede de Boun yn the Foundemente, so that his Bowels cam oute. And Syr Roger Clifford was sore wonded on the Hedde. And Syr William Sulley, and Syr Roger Bernefeld were slayne. And then wente Thomas Lancastre into a Chapel, denying to rendre hym self to Harkeley, and said, looking on the Crucifix, " Good Lord, I rendre my self to the, and put "me yn to thy Mercy."

Then they toke of his Cote Armures, and put on hym a Ray Cote, or Goune, one of his Mennes Lyveryes, and caried hym by Water to York, were they threw Balles of Dyrte at hym. And the Residew of the Barons part were pursuid from Place to Place, and to the Chirch hold was no reverence gyven, and the Father pursuid the Sunne, and the Sunne the Father.

At this Batayle were taken on the Barons parte, Syr Roger Clifford, Syr John Montbray, Syr Wylliam Tuchet, Syr William de Fiz William, and divers others Barons.

And Syr Hugh Dandeley was taken the Day after, and sent to the King, and after was put yn Prison, and should have be put to Deth, but that he had maryed Gilbert of Clares Doughtter the Kinges Niece.

Syr Barptolemew Badelesmere was taken at Stow Parke yn the Manoyr of the Bisshop of Lincoln that was his Nephew.

The King hering of this Discumfiture, cam with the Dispensars and other Nobles his Adherentes to Ponfracte.

Syr Andrew of Herkeley brought Thomas of Lancastre to Pontfracte to the Kinge, and there |was put in a Tower that he had newly made toward the Abbay, and after juged in the Haule sodenly by thes Justices, Syr Hugh Dispensar the Father, Syr Aimer Counte of Penbroke, Syr Edmunde Counte of Kent, Syr John de Britayne, and Syr Robert Malmethorp, that pronouncid his Jugement.

Then Thomas Lancastre sayd, "Shaul I dy with owt "Answer?"

Then certayne Gascoyne toke hym away, and put a pillid broken Hatte, or Hoode, on his Hedde, and set hym on a lene white Jade with owt Bridil, and he than cryed thus, "King of Heven, have mercy on me. For the King "of Herth nous ad querpi."

And thus he was caryed, sum throuing Pelottes of Dyrt at hym, and having a Frerer Precher for his Confessor with hym, on to a Hylle with owte the Toune, where he knelid doune toward the Este, on tylle one Hughin de Muston caussid hym to turne his Face towarde Scotlande : wher kneling, a Villayne of London cut of his Hedde 11. Cal. Aprilis anno D. 1321. And after the Prior and the Monkes required his Body, and got it of the King, and buried it on the right Hond of the Hy Altare.

The same Day were hanggid, drawen, and quarterid thes Noble Men at Pontfract: Syr William Tuchet, Sir William Fitz William, Syr Warine Lisle, Syr Henry Bradeburne, Syr William Cheny Barons, and John Page Esquier.

And straite after Syr Roger Clifford, and John Mountbray Baron, and Syr Goceline Deinville were put to Deth at Yorke.

At Bristow were put to Deth Syr Henry Welington, and Syr Henry Montfort.

At Glocestre Syr John Giffarde, and Syr Roger Elmebruge.

At London Syr Henry Tyeis.

At Wynchelsey Syr Thomas Colepeper.

At Wyndesore Syr Frauncis de Aldenham.

At Canterbyri Syr Barptolemew Badelesmere, and Syr Barptolemew de Asscheburn.

Apon this King Edwarde made Hugh Dispensar the Father Erle of Wynchestre, and Andrew Harkeley Erle of Cairluel, and Robert Baldock Chauncelar of Englande, and apon that disenheriteid al them that wers on the Barons Parte, and confisked all their Goodes, and so went toward

Scotland with a C. thousand Men anno D. 1322. But the Scottes wold not straite, but kept so long in Woddes, Mounteynes, and Mores on tylle Famayne, and then Murmure were yn King Edwardes Hoste.

The King seyng Famyne and Deth yn his Host recoylid.

James Duglas, and Thomas Randol Capitaines of the Scottes seyng this, made a greate Rode into Northumbreland, and destroiyng the Contery aboute went forth to Northalreton, and brent it. And King Edward seyng this, reysid his Host beyond Trent, and they encounterid with the Scottes at Beighlaude Abbaye xv Dayes after Michelmes, and there were the Englisch menne discumfited. And there John of Bretayne Erle of Richemont, Ennemy to Thomas Lancastre, was taken Prisoner, and after delyverid for a great Raunsom went yn to Fraunce, and never returnid in to England agayn.

Straite apon this was Syr Andrew Erle of Cairluel attaynted for Conspiracy with James Duglas the Scotte, whereby the Englisch men for lak of Harkeley ready help, wer vanquisshid yn Batel at the Abbay of Beighlande, and jugid before Syr Arcelyne Luscy, the Kinges Commissioner, to be hangid, drawen, and quarterid at Cairluel, as Thomas of Lancastre prophetied of hym. And this was doone the lastre day of Octobre yn the Yere a 1322. and this Day the Sunne chaungid in the Morning to blody Color, and so endurid to a xi. of the Clok.

As will be seen on careful perusal, Leland has condensed much of the original with considerable vigour. He continues, after an omission which he thus particularises :—

Here folowid a Chapitre of the Miracles that men sayde that God wrought for Thomas a Lancastre. And for Resorte of People to the Monte, where Thomas was beheddid, Baldok the Chauncelar caussid xiiii. Gascoynes welle armid to watch the Hille a certen tyme.

Aboute this tyme was the Castel of Wallengford kepte agayne the King by certeine that were Adherentes to Thomas Lancastre. Wherapon wer taken Syr John Godlington Chivaler, and Syr Edmund Roche person, and

Hogekin Walton Esquier, that was sent to the King to Pontfracte, and after drawen and hanggid at York.

The account of the trial and execution of the gentle Earl is given with much greater fulness by Caxton, who had evidently before him the same original that Leland had, but who used it with far greater freedom.

The following is Caxton's account, slightly abridged in the last sentences of each chapter :—

How Thomas of Lancastre was beheded at Pountfrete, &c. cap 198.

* * * * * And sir Andrew of herkla a fals tirant thurgh the kinges commaundement toke with him the gentill erle Thomas to Pountfrete, & ther he was prisoned in his own castell that he had newe made that stode ayens (*against*) the Abbey, of kyng Edward &c. And so it befell that he was ledde to barre (*brought to trial*) before the kynges Justices barehede as a thief, in a faire hall withyn his own castell, that he had made therin many a fair fest both to riche, & eke to poure. And these were his Justices Sir Hugh spencer the fadre, Aymer of valaunce Erle of Penbroke, Sir Edmond of Wodestocke Erle of Kent, Sir Johan of Britaigne Erle of Richemond and Sir Robert of Malmethorppe Justice and Sir Robert hym acoulped (*acrosted*) in this maner.

Thomas, at the firste our lord the kyng and this court excludeth yowe of all maner ansuere.

Thomas, our lord the kyng put vpon yowe, that ye have in his lande riden with baner displaied ayene his pees, as a traitour.

And with that worde the gentill erle Thomas with an high vois said nay lordes forsoth, and by seint Thomas I was never traitour." The Justice said ayene tho

Thomas our lord the kyng put vpon yowe that ye haue robbed his folk and mordred his peple as a thefe.

Thomas, the kyng also put vpon yowe that he discomfited yowe, and your peple with his folk in his owne reame. Wherfor ye went and fled to the Wode (*Cross*) as an outelawe, and also ye were taken as an outelawe. And, Thomas, as a traitour ye shull be honged by reson, but the kyng hath forgeue yowe that Je wes (*I wist*) for loue of quene Isabell ; And, Thomas, reson wolde also that ye sholde be honged, but the kyng hath forgeve yowe that Je wes for cause and loue of your lynage. But, Thomas, For as moche as ye were take fleyng and as an outelaw the Kyng wyll that your hede shall be smyten of, as ye have well deserved. Anone doth hym out of prece and anone bryng him to his Jugement.

The gentyll knyght Thomas he had herde all these wordes with an high vois he cried sore wepyng, And said Allas

Seint Thomas faire fadre Allas shall I be deed thus, Graunte me nowe blissefull god ansuere ; but all availled hym no thyng. For the cursed Gascoynes put hym hidder and thidder and on hym cried with an high vois O kyng Arthur, most dredfull, well knowen is nowe thyn open traytrie, an euell deth shalt thou die as thou hast well deserved. Tho sette they vpon his hede in scorne an olde Chapelet all to rent and to torne that was nat worth an halpenye. And after they sette hym upon a leue white Palfrey full un semelich, and eke all bare and with an olde bridell and with an horrible noise they drove hym oute of the Castell toward his deth and cast vpon hym many balles of snowe.

§ And as the turmentours lad hym oute of the Castell tho said he this pitonse wordes, and his hondes helde vpon high towardes heven. Nowe the kyng of heven yeve vs mercy For the Erthely kyng hath vs forsake. And a frere prechour went with hym oute of the Castell till that he come to the place that he ended his lyfe vn to whom he shrofe hym all his lyfe. And the gentill Erle helde the frere wonder fast by the clothes and said faire fadre abide with vs till that I be ded, for my flessh quaketh for drede of deth ; And soth for to say the gentill Erle sette hym vpon his knees & turned hym toward the Est, but a ribaude that was called Higone of Mostone set hande upon the gentill Erle and said in despite of hym Sir traitour turne the toward the Scottes thy foul dede to underfong. and turned him toward the north.

The noble Erle Thomas ansuerd tho with a mylde vois & said now fair lordes I shall done all youre Wylle, and with that worde the frere went fro hym sore wepying and anone a ribaude wente to hym and smote of his hede the xi Kal. of Averill in the yere of grace mcccxxi. Allas that ever such a gentill blode &c.

The chapter thus ends with a definite statement of the circumstances and place of burial of the Earl, and the devotion of the people was for centuries afterwards divided between the place of his execution and that of his burial :—

When the gentill erle of his lyfe was passed The priour and the monkes of Pountfrete geten the body of sir Thomas of the kyng and they buried it before the high Auter on the right side.

That is, before the high altar of the Church of St. John the Evangelist, then standing in what is now called the Grange Field.

The Earl's tomb, and the hill at which his execution took place, each became noted for the miracles there performed; and one consequence was that "the hill where he suffered was kept by certeine Gascoines, appointed by the lord Hugh Spenser, the sonne, then living at Pomfret, to the end that no people should come and make their praiers there in worship of the said Earle, whome they tooke verilie for a martyr" (Holinshed.)

Thus hindered in their worship at the scene of his death, the multitude resorted to a painting in St. Paul's Cathedral, London: and a letter dated at York, 8 June, 1323, from the King to the then Bishop of London, is in existence, informing him that it has come to his hearing "that some of the people in his diocese foolishly betake themselves to a tablet set up in the Church of St. Paul whereon is depicted, among other things, the effigy of Thomas, late Earl of Lancaster, which they worship and adore as something sanctified, pretending that miracles are there performed," at which the King is "highly displeased," and commands "an immediate restraint to be put upon the people, to prevent such doings in future."

It is probable that the King used like pressure upon the Archbishop of York; for even so early as 9 Kal. Sept, 1323, we learn from an archiepiscopal mandate issued in due form, that the people of both sexes came to the tomb of Thomas and to the place of his execution, to worship him as a saint "although he had not been canonized by the Apostolic See" from which gatherings, deaths and wounds had been occasioned, "*non absque homiridiis & aliis lætalibus verberibus.*" The Archbishop therefore commanded the official of the Archdeacon of York to forbid such assemblages. The order could have been only partially obeyed, for a second similar mandate issued on the Nones of the following month.

The tide, however, turned, for on Feb 24, 1326-7, after the deposition of the King, and seven months before he met his fate at Berkeley, where he was murdered on the following St. Mathew's day, Abp Melton wrote to Pope John XXII, asking that the particulars of miracles wrought at Thomas's tomb might be enquired into, in order to his canonization.

There is no proof that the Earl was ever formally canonised, but a chapel was erected to his memory on the neighbouring hill, which has even to this day continued to bear the name of "the gentil Erle," as St. Thomas's Hill, although every trace of the building has long since passed away.

The following completes Caxton's account of the gentill Earle, the noble Erle, the good Erle ; as he variously delights to style him :—

Of the miracles that god wrought for seint Thomas loue of La'castre; wherfor the kyng let close the churche dores of the Priorie of Pountfret for no man shold come therein to the body for to offren. Capitulo ducentesimo primo.

And sone after that the good erle Thomas of lancastre was martred a preste that longe tyme had bene blynde dremed in his slepyng that he shold gone vn to the hille ther that the good erle Thomas of lancastre was done vn to the deth and he shold have his sight ayene and so he dremed iii nyghtes sewing (*ensuing* or *following*) & the prest let tho lede hym to the same hylle & when he come to that place that he was martred on, devoutely he made ther his praiers & praid god & seint Thomas that he must have his sight ayen, & was in his praiers he laid his right honde vpon the same place yt the good man was martred on, & a drope of drye blode & smale sand cleved on his honde & ther with striked his yien, & anone thurgh the myzt of god & of seint Thomas of lancastre he had his sight ayen & thanked tho almyghty god & seint Thomas. And when this miracle was knowen amonge men the peple come thidder on every side & kneled & made hir praiers at his tombe that is in the priorie of Pounfret and praied that holy martir of socour & of helpe & god herd hir praier.

Also ther was a yonge child drenched in a Welle in the toune of Pountfrete & was dede iii. daies & iii nyghtes & men comen and laid the dede child upon seint Thomas tombe the holy martir, & the child arose ther from deth to lyfe as many a man it saw, and also moch peple were oute of hir mynde & god hath sente hem hir mynde ayene thurgh vertue of that holy martir, and also god hath yeven ther to to creples hir goyng & to croked hir hondes & hir feet and to blynde also hir sight, & to many sike folke hir hele of diverse maladies for the loue of his good martir.

Also ther was a rich man in Coundom in gascoyne, & such a maladie he had that all his right side roted & fell awey from hym that men myzt see his lyuer & also his hert & so he stanke that vuneth men myzt come nye hym. Wherfor his frendes were for hym wondre sory. But at the last as god wolde they praied to seint Thomas of lancastre that he wollde pray to almyghty god for that prisoner & behight to gone to pountfrete for to done hir pilgrymage that the martir seint Thomas come vn to him & annoynted ouer all his sike body, And ther with the good man awoke & was all hole, & his flessh was restored ayen that before was roted and falle away. For which miracle the good man & his frendes loued god and seint Thomas ever more after. And this good man come into Englond and toke with hym iiii. felawes & come to Pounfrete unto that holy martir and did hir pilgrymage but the good man that was sike come thidder all naked sauf his breche. & when they had done they turned home ayen in to hir contre & tolde of the miracle wher so ever they come.

And also ii. men haue be heled ther of the mormal thurgh helpe of that holy martir, though that evell be hold incurable.

When the spencers herd that god did such miracles for this holy martir, they wold be leue it in no maner wise, but said openlick that it was grete heresie such vertue of hym to beleue. And when Sr hugh the spencer the sone saw alle this doynge, anone he sent his messagier from Pountfrete ther that he duelled to the kyng Edward that tho was at Gravene at Skipton for cause that the kyng shold un do that pilgrymage. And as the Ribaude the messagier wente toward the kyng for to done his message he come by the hulle on the which the good martir was done to dethe and in the same place (he was taken ill of a sore disease, and died) ere he came to York.

And whan Sr hugh the spencer herde this tydyng some deel he was adrad, and thought for to vndone the pilgrymage yf he myght by any maner way, and to the kyng wente and said that they shold be in grete sklaunder thurgh oute all cristendome for the deth of Thomas of lancastre yf that he suffred the peple done hir pilgrymage at Pountfrete.

Se ye church was shut up agst ye franchise of holy church, & the Monks were set to their wages, & 14 armed Gascoines kept the hill that no pilgrim might come by that way.

All these precautions were, however, but temporary: the sense of the wrong that had been done to the Earl was too powerful to be restrained; and the judicial murder at Pontefract, of Thomas, Earl of Lancaster, had no small share in causing the deposition and murder of his kingly cousin, which so soon followed.

A few words remain to be said about the second great catastrophe with which the name of Pontefract has been associated.

It is remarkable how very much of the popular English History is drawn from Shakspeare ; and, of course, his picturesque version of the death of King Richard II, which has not the slightest historical basis, has received a very general credence, and become mixed with all the traditions of its supposed scene. For those who accept it with so little reservation, do not reflect that the object of the dramatic poet was to produce that which was most fitted for reproduction on the stage, and not necessarily to represent historic truth.

But the fact is, that almost all the personal history which Shakspeare adopted in his play of Richard II., is so highly coloured as to be absolutely inaccurate. Even the opening line,

Old John of Gaunt, time-honoured Lancaster,

was but a poetical figure, for its subject died when only fifty-eight. And again, Richard's second wife, whom Shakespeare represents as a full-grown, intellectual woman, in 1399, who addresses her ladies as "girls," and conducts herself in every way as a staid, considerate matron, was really only a child of 7 years old when she became Richard's affianced wife in 1396.

Similarly, for the sake of stage effect and stage action, Shakespeare adopted the theory of Richard's death which best served his purpose, not necessarily that which was most accordant with historic truth. Of these theories, there were three, (1) which probably very nearly represented the truth, That Richard was starved to death by his keepers, his food being prepared for him below, and sent up to him by the lower servants, but withheld from him by those more immediately about his person; (2) That he voluntarily starved himself, in grief and mortification at the reverse of fortune which had befallen him; and (3) last in point of time, and even from a foreign source, That he was killed with brutal violence by Sir Piers Exton.

On this subject, we reproduce some remarks from the Appendix to " Pontefract, its Name, its Lords, and its Castle," page xxi.

The fountain and origin of all the accounts of the murder of Richard II by Sir Piers Exton, is a French Chronicle, of which indeed many copies exist abroad, but which is rare in this country. It appears to have been an outcome of the anxious desire of the French King, father of Richard II's young widow, to prove that King to be really dead, that Isabella might be again married; and it seems to have been scarcely known in England, till given by Holinshed in 1577, from whom Shakspeare copied. The date of the murder given by the Chronicler is moreover manifestly incorrect, for Richard's death took place on Feb. 14, 1399-1400.

The following is from a translation in the British Museum (A.C. 8116 11) of the French Chronicle to which we refer :—

Item. It is true that on the day of the Kings, when King Henry had taken the field, without London, with all his people who were about to combat the lords who had risen to support King Richard, he commanded a Knight called Sir Peter Exton, to go and deliver straightway from this world, John of London, called Richard, for it behoved that the sentence of Parliament should be accomplished. The Knight having taken leave of King Henry, rode to the castle where he found King Richard confined, who was seated at table awaiting his dinner; and Sir Peter called King Richard's esquire tranchant, and forbad him on the part of King Henry to dare to taste any more the King's meat, saying " he might let him eat alone if he chose, for he should never eat again." The esquire returned to the room where King Richard was seated, who was unwilling to eat because he was left alone, and his esquire would not perform his office as usual. " What is the news?" said the King. The esquire replied " I know of none except that Sir Peter Exton is come; what tidings he has brought them I know not." King Richard then begged the esquire to carve him some meat and taste it, as was his duty. The esquire went down upon his knees before the table, and begging King Richard's pardon, hoped he would excuse him, for they had forbidden him by King Henry's order; upon which King Richard went into a passion, and seizing one of the table-knives struck the esquire on the head with it, exclaiming "Cursed be Henry of Lancaster and thou." As he uttered these words, in rushed Sir Peter Exton to the room where King Richard was, with seven men, each man having a lance in his hand. It is true that King Richard perceiving Sir Peter Exton and his seven armed men, put the table back from him and springing io the midst of them, wrung an axe from the hands of one of them who came there to murder him, with which King Richard right valiantly and vigorously defended himself, and in so doing slew four out of the eight men; when Sir Peter leaped upon the chair where King Richard usually sat at meals whilst he was in prison, where he awaited, his axe in his hand, till the King came near to him. The King defended himself so well that it was great marvel how he could so long make head against them for they were all armed; but King Richard defended himself right vigorously like a good and loyal knight, till at last in defending himself, he retreated towards the chair where Sir Peter Exton was, who gave him his death blow, for he smote him such a blow on his head that King Richard fell backwards on the ground. The King exclaimed "Lord have mercy on me," after which he gave him yet another blow on his head. And thus died noble King Richard without confession, which was a great pity, and he that saith otherwise doth not speak discreetly. When the King was dead, the Knight who had given him his death blow, went to sit him down beside the corpse, and began to weep, saying "Alas, what is that we have done? we have murdered him who has been our sovereign lord the space of twenty-two years. Now I have lost mine honour, and I shall never go into any country, but I shall be reminded of it." On the morrow the corpse of King Richard was carried to Pomfret, and there was he interred like a poor gentleman. God have mercy on him.

The Chronicler evidently thinks Leeds in Kent, to be

the scene of the murder, (Sir Bartholomew Badlesmere's stronghold—see page 352) for he makes Sir Peter Exton ride to Leeds from London before dinner time; he believes, moreover, Leeds to be close to Pomfret, to which place he represents the corpse of the dead King to be carried the next day; and he declares the King to be there buried; mistakes avoided by Holinshed, with better local knowledge. But their existence in the original shews how utterly unreliable it was, and yet this is the tale which unthinking historians have produced and reproduced with wearisome iteration. Holinshed, however, with the carefulness of a true historian took care to shew the light esteem and inferior regard in which he held the statement of the French Chronicler by carefully placing it last in order, and by incorporating it into his history only with this preface, "Another writer which seemeth to have great knowledge of King Richard's doings, saith," &c The followers of Holinshed omit to notice all this careful discrimination.

But to draw a parallel from our own times, what would be thought of the discretion of a Chronicler who was now publishing a detailed account, never hitherto heard of in England, of the secret doings of the court of Queen Anne or King William III., nearly two hundred years ago. And yet that is what his copyists quietly assume Holinshed to have done.

And now, bidding the reader who has accompanied us thus far, a hearty farewell, we conclude our pleasant task,—a task requiring, however, considerable investigation and research.

Where an original authority has been in existence and accessible, we have in every case endeavoured to inspect it, and in most cases have succeeded in doing so; and where we have found the generally received statement inaccurate, we have usually recorded it, with its correction, in order that no one else might be misled by the inaccuracy.

The generous reader will, therefore, not assume that the very frequent contradiction in which we have been compelled to indulge has arisen from needless captiousness.

APPENDIX.

THE DRAKE PEDIGREE.
A (See page 3).

The Drake Pedigree, preserved in the family, commences with William de Schipdene, as by deed of 33 Edward I. He had two sons, John and William, the former of whom is named in a deed of 35 Edward I, and took the name of Drake. He had a son, John Drake, of Shibden, who is named in Northowram in the Poll Tax of 1379, and was living 2 Hen. IV. Unless a step in the pedigree is here omitted, the marriage settlement of his son, John Drake, of Southowram, with Cecilia, daughter of John Prosser, of Thornton in Bradford-dale, is dated 1443. Their son, William, married Christabella ———, and had a son, also a John Drake, of Halifax, who, by his will dated 1544, and proved on 2 May that year, directed that he should be buried in the middle aisle of Halifax Parish Church.

At this point the Halifax registers are most useful, and from them it is gathered that JOHN DRAKE had

(1) Thomas, of Shibden Hall, (2) William, of Horley Green, to whose widow, Alice, administration was granted 8 June, 1565, (3) Gilbert, who married Margaret Holgate, and, like Thomas, had a family, (4) EDWARD, of Southowram, and many other children.

Gilbert had descendants at Horley Green and Northowram, who did not intermarry with those of Edward. But EDWARD DRAKE, of Northowram, married Agnes Brugge at Halifax, on 8 Feb., 1545-6, and died in August 1551, leaving four children,—Michael, Thomas, Gilbert and WILLIAM.

Michael Drake, of Damhead in Northowram, had a large family; Thomas died unmarried; Gilbert had a family by each of two wives; as had WILLIAM, (will proved at York, 15 March, 1621-2). His first wife brought him ten children, of whom NATHAN, the Diarist, bapt. 17 Dec. 1587, seems to have been the second surviving son, his elder brother, Joseph, being five years older.

TURNBRIDGE.

B (See page 38.)

Earlier mention of this place may yet be discovered in private hands, but the earliest we have been able to gather, is in a petition presented to Parliament in 20 Hen. VI. (1442.) The Commons of the Counties of York, Lincoln, Nottingham, and Derby, in that year, presented that

"Ther is, and of longe tyme hath been an usuall and a commune passage fro dyvers and many parties of the said countees, unto the citees of York, Hull, Hedon, Holdernes, Beverley, Barton and Grymesby, and so forth, by the hie see by the costes, unto London and elles where, with all maner of shipps charged with wolle, leed, stone, tymbre, vitaille, fewaille, and many other marchandises, by a streme called the Dike, in the counte of York, that daily ebbith and floweth, over whiche streem ys made a brigge of tymbre called Turnbrigg, in the parisshe of Snayth, in the same counte, so lowe, so ner the streem, so narrowe, and so strayte in the archees, that ther is, and of long tyme hath been, a right perilous passage, and ofte tymes perisshinge of dyvers shippes; and atte every tyme of creteyne and abundaunce of water, ther may no shippees passe under the seid brigge, by the space of half a yere or more," to the great injury and inconvemence of the neighbourhood, as well as to the diminishing of the King's revenue.

The Petitioners therefore pray the Parliament to beseech the King to grant, with the concurrence of Parliament, license to any persons of the said counties, to take down the said bridge and build another five yards longer, and a yard and a half higher, with a moveable leaf in the centre for the passage of vessels; to prohibit persons stopping the course of the stream by stones, or piles, or any other "disceyte," which, in this sense, seems to mean contrivance; and to confirm to the shipmen passing along the said river, the right they had of old time enjoyed, of having towing-paths on the banks of the said river.

This petition appears to have been granted in all points, but we do not trace what was then done, and it is possible that the troubles of the next few years might have had an injurious effect upon the projected undertaking.

A century afterwards (1536) the hamlet is mentioned by Leland (COLLECTANEA) III 46):—

" Dun, sive Dano, * * * fluit vero per Dancastrum, op. nobile, & apud Turnebrige, fessum, se abscondit in alveo Aere fluminis."—(The Don flows through Doncaster, a noble town, and at Turnbridge, exhausted, buries itself in the bed of the river Aire).

Which seems to be a graphic description of the then condition of the sluggish Don, now diverted, and kept within bounds.

THE OATES FAMILY OF PONTEFRACT.
C (See page 84).

There were evidently at least two families of Oates at Pontefract in the seventeenth century, quite distinct, although intermarrying. The first of the name in the Pontefract Registers is one Wyll Oyets, buried 30 June, 1592, who left young children (including a son Richard, baptised 9 Sept. 1591); but the connection between him and either of the subsequent bearers of the name does not appear.

His namesake, if not son, William Oats or Oyts was elected mayor in 1623, but died in May, 1630, before his wife Frances, who survived till 27 November, 1637. He had four children :—

(1) William, born before 1585, who married Isabel Frank, 26 Feb., 1621-2, and was Alderman in 1627, when his son Richard, was baptised. He was elected mayor in 1633, but as he died in 1643 or 1644, his burial is not recorded in the Church Registers, which are defective between 1642 and 1647.

In his Will, (dated 28 August, 1643, proved 24 March, 1645,) he describes himself as " William Oates, of Pontefract, Alderman"—he leaves half his lands, &c., in Pontefract to his wife, Isabel, for her life, the house he dwells in, and the house his brother Richard dwelleth in, in the Newmarket, with the lands and appurtenances, to his son Richard, remainder to his brother, Richard, of Pontefract, Alderman, remainder to the heirs of his son, Richard, for ever—to his kind friend, William Stiles, £5—to Mr George Fothergill, vicar of Pontefract, whom he desires to preach at his funeral, £5—to his niece, Isabel Oates, £5—to his sister, Mary Maie £10—to Edward Field 40/-—Boniface Cowper 20/- and Nicholas Smithson for their former service—to the Poor of Pontefract £30, at the discretion of his brother Richard Oates, his brother Robert Frank, and the Mayor and Vicar of Pontefract. To his servant, Ann Hodge, xxs. Residue to his wife and son. His brethren, Richard Oates and Robert Frank, to be supervisors, and to each eleven shillings to buy them rings.

" My niece, Isabel Oates," subsequently married William Oates, founder of another family at Pontefract.

As the will thus names his wife, Isabel, and his son Richard Oats, generally called junior to distinguish him from his uncle, and elsewhere his wife and son as if there were only one, and as there is no repudiation of any other, it is probable that his eldest son, William (bapt. 6 Jan., 1624-5) predeceased his father.

William Oats's widow continued his business, and was the Isabel Oats, who issued the Pontefract tokens which bear that name. She died 25 March, 1664, and her will was proved July 20, 1665, when administration was granted to Henry Eyre, M.D., who had married her sister, Alice.

(2) Marie, bapt. 19 Sept, 1587, buried 6 May, 1588.

(3) A second Marie, baptised 11 June, 1589, who had married (? Richard) Maie before August, 1643, when her brother William made his will as above.

(4) Richard, the Royalist, bapt. 9 Sept, 1591, who was in the Castle at the time of the first siege, had been mayor in 1643-4, and filled the office again in 1645. For his loyalty to the King, he fell into disgrace with the Parliament, but endeavoured to make his peace in 1646, taking the Covenant on Oct. 21, and the "Negative Oath" on Nov. 13, on which date Colonel Robert Overton, the then governor of the Castle, vouched for him alleging that he had lately lived quietly and conformably in the town, and for the most part of the time executed the office of mayor (a most interesting fact to know, as the mayoralty of that year has hitherto been ascribed to Gervase Shillitoe.) He petitioned on Nov. 24, 1646, to be allowed to compound; and attached to the documents in the Record Office is a certificate from Wm. Oates, setting forth that his father-in-law, the petitioner, is too weak and infirm to travel to London to present his petition personally. The permission to compound was given, and Richard Oats survived ten years, dying on 31 Oct., 1656, administration to his estate being granted by P.C.C. to Sarah his widow. This must have been a second wife, for his first wife had been Isabel   , whose daughter Isabel (bapt. 21 Dec., 1623) married a namesake William Oates in 1644, 5, or 6. With regard to the year we can only say that she appears to have been unmarried in 1643, when her uncle William bequeathed £5 to her, but that she was married in 1646, when her father, Richard, petitioned for leave to compound, and her husband vouched for him, as his *father-in-law*.

"Richard Oats, junior," (an ironmonger) son of Ald. Wm. Oats and his wife, Isabel, bapt. 20 Nov., 1627, died while mayor on 29 March, 1657. His will dated six days before his death, with a codicil signed the following day, was proved in 1658, when administration was granted to Isabel, his mother, power being reserved for Elizabeth, his relict. He had married twice, (1) Mrs Frances Goodyer on 17 June, 1651, who died the following 5 March; and (2) Elizabeth Kelham, daughter of Ald. Wm. Kelham, who as his widow, took William Adam, of Hardwick, for her second husband. One cause of perplexity in this descent was introduced by Dugdale, who in his Kelham pedigree, called this, the first husband of Elizabeth Kelham, William instead of Richard; but there can be no doubt of the facts being as we have given them. Richard Oates had two children, each by his second wife; William born 8 July, 1655, died 27 March, 1658; and Dorothy, a posthumous daughter born 15 June, 1657, nearly three months after her father's death.

It is remarkable that a document connected with each of these two brothers thus chronicles a fact which has hitherto absolutely escaped notice. All the published lists of the Vicars assume that after Mr. Wm. Stiles resigned in March, 1642, there was a vacancy in the Vicarage of Pontefract till Mr Ferrett by some means possessed himself of the position, which would be in 1647. But here is Mr. Ald. Oates making his will in August, 1643, and while remembering with

£5 his "kind friend William Stiles," the late vicar, giving an equal sum to Mr George Fothergill, the then Vicar, whose connection with the place no one has ever yet hinted at, although it indicates a reason of kinship why half a century afterwards Mr. Marmaduke Fothergill should have taken so loving an interest in the Church of Pontefract.

The composition papers of the second brother, on the other hand show that (he had not only been mayor in 1643, but that) during some subsequent time he had "acted as Mayor," though the phrase is indeed vague enough to allow of his having been only deputy-mayor or acting ex-mayor. But the two facts, interesting as referring to the troubled times between the two sieges, are new. (See also Appendix F.)

Thus this family died out.

But there was another apparently distinct family, the head of whom, William Oates, married Isabel, daughter of Richard Oates, the Royalist, brother of the William Oates who married Isabel Frank.

This William Oates (whose name is always, at least by himself, spelt with the final *es*, the other family generally contenting themselves with Oats) is described in the 1650 Fee Farm Book, as of The Leaden Porch. He had married Isabel Oats before Nov., 1646, and was mayor in 1654. At the Restoration, although willing to take the oaths to the King, he was ejected from his Aldermanic office, as having been "illegally" elected. He remained out of the Corporation till 1674, when being re-elected Alderman he was again mayor in 1676 and 1682.

Mr William Oates's house, The Leaden Porch, was a residence in the Horse Fair, still existing in its main features. It is the house on the south side, which is next above the Wesleyan Chapel. Just without the line of circumvallation of the sieges, it seems to have escaped demolition at that time, and was even in 1650 in good habitable condition for a person of repute and financial ability, such as there is every reason to believe belonged to this Mr William Oates, gent. The name of " Porch" adhered to the property even to the last generation by whom it was used as a school. It has been divided into tenements, the more easterly of which is now kept as a shop. The lower apartments of this portion still contain highly ornamental ceilings, of an evident Restoration design, of which acorns and oak leaves are very prominent features.

It was under Mr. William Oates's auspices that the Borough obtained the Charter of 1676, which is ornamented with an excellent and elaborate portrait of Charles II.; but his election in 1682 seems to have been secured by means which exceeded legitimate intrigue (see Book of Entries p. 144) and against which Richard Lyle entered his sworn protest. His children, whose names are in the Church Registers were :—

(1) Rebecca, born 26 Dec., 1647; (2) Deborah, born 6 July, 1650, married 19 Dec., 1670, with Daniel Sykes, who was buried 8 Sept, 1697; she re-married with Francis Mason, of Crofton, and died 15 Jan., 1730, aged 80 years ; (3) Richard, born 21 May, 1652, married Isabel (whose surname is not recorded) died 1 Feb., 1686-7 ; (4) Anne, bapt 3 Dec., 1654 ; (5) William, bap. 3 Sept., 1658, who was made Alderman in 1693, but vacated in 1697, by going to live at Brotherton. This William, as residuary legatee and principal executor, obtained possession of the original of his father's will, for which he gave a receipt dated 4 Oct., 1686, but failed to return the document : so that the Will office at York has a copy only. He sealed his receipt with a bend charged with a crescent for difference, between three garbs (or perhaps *cat* sheaves) 2 and 1. (6) Isabel, bapt 10 June, 1661. There were probably two earlier ; Sarah, who married Robert, son of Christopher Long, on 28th June 1663, and another who married Wm. Ramsden. Rebecca seems to have been the wife of Robert Ward, and Anne to have been unmarried at the date of her father's will. The youngest child was (7) John, baptised 12 May, 1663.

Mr. William Oates was buried 17 May, 1685, and his will dated 5 July, 1683, was proved 16 March, 1685-6. The following are its principal provisions :—

He desires to be buried in Pontefract Parish Church " as near my dear wife as may be."

He leaves lands in Tanshelf and Carleton to William (5) ; to Wm. Burgesse " half an acre in Crossland in Carleton Low Field, which his father gave to me ; " he names his grandchild Sarah Ramsden ; he leaves Clay Dike Close to his son Richard Oates (3) ; to his son William (5) The Leaden Porch in Micklegate ; to his daughter Anne (4) " All the licorice and licorice buds" growing " in a certain garth", and £100 ; he forgives his son Richard (3) the £100 lent to " him to buy iron with, since his coming out of Sweden" ; also " all my tithes and tithe rents within the vicarage of Halifax, and rights under various leases thereof from the Prior of l'ancrage" (probably St. Pancras, Lewes) ; he gives to his Executors "the sixteenth part of the Shipp at Hull, called the Prosperous primrose, and my lease of the Town's Closes ;" he bequeaths to the poor of Pontefract £6/13/4, and those of Tanshelf 6/8 ; to the poor of Wath and Norton Coniers, [in the parish of Wath in Richmondshire,] *"where I was born, and some while brought up,* £3 to be distributed by my nephew, Matthew Oates" ; " to my nephew and neices Nathaniel Wood, Jane Wood, Rebecca, Debora, Sarah and Mary Wood, 50/- a piece" ; " to my sons-in-law Mr. Robt. Long, Mr. Wm. Ramsden, Mr. Daniel Sykes (2), and Mr. Robt. Ward each 20/- for mourning rings" ; " to my brother Henry Oates and nephew Matthew Oates 20/- each" ; " to Wm. Burgesse, a broad 20/- piece of gold " ; and the residue to his son William (5), and daughter Anne (4).

Light is thrown on some parts of this will by the fact that administration of the goods of Thomas Wood, of Gatefulforth, was granted by P.C.C. in 1659, (fo 178) to Wm. Oates, gentleman, who was assigned guardian to Jane, Rebecca, Deborah, Nathaniel and Mary Wood, and to administer the effects unadministered of Katherine Wood, deceased, to whom a previous administration had been granted in 1658 (fo 68.).

The arms borne by this family, as used by this last William Oates, prove that the Pontefract Oateses claimed no affinity with those of Meanwood.

THE BADSWORTH BELLS.

D (See pages 114 and 116).

The bells of Badsworth Church were re-hung during the summer of 1884, and the opportunity being taken to examine them carefully, it was ascertained that, contrary to the statement of both Boothroyd and Fox, quoted on p. 114, only two of the bells date after the Restoration. The following description of them appeared in the PONTEFRACT ADVERTISER at the time :—

The peal consists of four bells, and each is a very fine example. The treble is of the Pre-Reformation period, at least four hundred years old, and is very probably the remnant of the old peal, which was taken away after one of the Northern risings in the sixteenth century, when as a punishment for the bells having been rung to excite the people to take part in the insurrection, all but one were removed from so many church towers. That which now remains bears the inscription :—

PERSONET HEC CELIS DULCISSIMA VOX GABRIELIS

The letter used is so very compressed that, for instance, the *b* in "Gabrielis" having little or no upper part, looks like *v*, as does the *p* in "personet," for a similar reason.

The translation of the inscription seems to be "May this sweetest voice of Gabriel sound throughout the heavens," from which it may be inferred that the bell was the "Sanctus" bell, rung at the moment of the consecration of the elements in the Mass, so that those of the parishioners who were not able to attend the service in person, might at the supreme moment unite their prayers with such as were present.

This bell bears a very good conventional rose, with eight petals and eight stamens, arranged around a central calyx, the whole being on a square block. It has also a bell-founder's mark, similar to one on the old bell at All Saints', Pontefract, and to that on the great bell at Hemsworth, consisting of a shield containing a central cross with the foot forked. At the fork, the point of division is encircled by the letter O. The centre of the stem has an arm projecting on the sinister side, from which depends a bell at rest; a letter R in the dexter is probably the Christian initial of the original owner of the stamp, which seems to have been used in the Nottingham foundry for some generations. The O may stand for Oldfield, the family name. With slight variations this stamp is of very frequent occurrence on similar bells of the sixteenth and seventeenth centuries.

The second bell contains a very elaborate floral ornamentation, concealing the founder's mark, S.S. Ebor. It bears the inscription :—

GLORIA IN EXCELSIS DEO 1683
IH HH WH CHVRCH$_S$
WARDEN^S

And this manner of placing the word "Churchwardens" in two lines, is very usual with the York foundry.

The third is also dated, and bears— [soule
I sweetly toling men do call to taste on meate that feeds the
1669.

The couplet is in one line, and each separate word is on a separate block. The date is in a distinct line and falls under the word "men."

On this bell is a founder's mark which we have seen nowhere else. The usual shield has become of a heart shape, the two lobes being occupied with the initials H.O., a bell hanging between them, and filling the point of the heart. This also appears to belong to the Nottingham foundry, with perhaps Henry Oldfield as the founder.

The fourth, like the first, is of earlier date than the Pontefract bell. As with the third, the separate words are logotypes, but the execution is very coarse and imperfect; the figure "2" in the date, and the final "s" in "excelsis" being reversed. Its inscription is as follows:—

GLORIA IN EXCELSIS DEO IHC ANNO DNI 1582

This bears as a founder's mark, what is sometimes called a folyfott or fylfot. On this bell it is a narrow-limbed Greek cross, each limb of which is bent to the right, at right angles. This mystic symbol (sometimes also called a gammadion, from its resemblance to the Greek letter *gamma*) whose meaning is quite unknown, is not unfrequently met with on Church Bells in Yorkshire and neighbouring counties, but the example at Badsworth is the only one, to our knowledge, in this neighbourhood.

In the Badsworth instance, however, the fylfot has only three rectangular arms, there being no return at the foot. The initials G.H. are connected with it.

These initials are perhaps those of Gilbert Heathcote, of Chesterfield, who died soon after Aug. 4, 1558, as we have been since informed by J.T.F., of Bishop Hatfield's Hall, Durham, in answer to an inquiry through that useful periodical *Notes and Queries*.

OTHER DOCUMENTS CONNECTED WITH 1645-8.

E (See pages 218, 222 and 147).

After the body of this volume was in type, while looking over some of the articles comprised in the Gough collection in the Bodleian, we discovered (in the volume marked No. 41 York) bound up with a copy of the first edition of Paulden's Letter (In the Savoy, printed by Edward Jones, MDCCII), a copy of Buck's print of Pontefract Castle, and two fly leaves, each with letterpress on one side only of the paper, referring to a History of the Town and Castle of Pontefract, then in preparation.

There is no clue to the identity of those who had the undertaking in hand, or to the intended publisher, and moreover no printer's name is attached to the Prospectus; but as the general character and style of the typography are those which prevailed about 1700, it is probable that the History was that prepared by Mr. Castilian Morris, which Thoresby perused in 1703, and to which we have referred at pp. 217 and 310. The MS.S. are now lost, and there is but small likelihood of their recovery.

It will be noticed that the date of the seizure by Colonel Morris given in this document is 1647, in error for 1648.

There's now in the Press, and shortly will be Publish'd *The* HISTORY, *of the* TOWN *and* CASTLE *of* PONTEFRACT, from their Original to the Entire Demolition of that Memorable Fortress,
BY A GENTLEMAN.
In this the Publick will be oblig'd with several Historical Events in the late Civil War, not taken Notice of by my Lord *Clarendon*. *Eachard*, or any other Writer. An exact JOURNAL of the First and Second SIEGE in 1644 and 45, Printed (*Literatim*) from the Original MS. taken upon the Spot by a Gentleman, of the Garrison: Who also gives a full LIST of the *Gentleman Voluntiers* that serv'd in it. The Surprize of the Castle for the KING by Coll. *Morrice* in 1647. The bold Attempt upon Rainsborough at Doncaster by Capt. Paulden, who commanded that small but brave Detachment. Several LETTERS which pass'd between the Governour *Morrice*, *Cromwell*, *Fairfax*, and the other Commanders, during the Time of the Last Siege, from their Originals. With a Copy of the Original articles of Rendition, sign'd by General Lambert, &c. The Tryal, Behaviour, and Dying Speeches of MORRICE and BLACKBURN at their execution at *YORK*, from Coll. *Morrice's* Son's Papers. To these will be added, a curious

Copper-Cut of the *CASTLE*, as it stood beleaguer'd by the Parliament's Forces, from a Draught, still kept in the FAIRFAX Family, with the different Coins struck at the same time, in that most Remarkable Place.

In the same volume (Gough, Yorkshire collection, vol. 41) is bound up a M.S. copy of a letter to Baldwin's London Weekly Journal, No. 798, Saturday, March 15, 1777, referring to an attempt upon General Lee, parallel to that of Capt. Wm. Paulden upon Rainsborough, and in another volume labelled Yorkshire, No. 34, in the same collection, is a second copy of Buck's print, one of Jolluge's map, the engravings from Archæologia vol. vi., and some originals by Mr. Toms. These last are but poor, and appear to date about 1750. Two of them show a small shed erected on the Western roundle of the Donjon, which is curious, inasmuch as it was in that roundle that the late excavations show a sort of cellar to have been at some time. This cellar might thus have been in use a hundred years after the Demolition of the Castle.

The following is a copy of "Major General Lambert's propositions to Sir Hu : Cart : and others, the 7th of March, 1648," being presumably the document fastened to a stone, and thrown over the wall. It also has been preserved in the Bodleian, but among the

CLARENDON PAPERS, 2739.

Gentlemen,

Yo'r owne condicon is best knowne vnto you within, J conceiue you cannot be ignorant how improbable it is you should have releife from without, which beinge seriously considered you cannot but as reasonable men iudge how preiuditiall yf not destruction vnto yo'selves the wilfull and obstinate keepings of this Castle against all visible authority in the kingdome wil be to the great oppression of the Country the dayly losse of Christian blood which doubtlesse will cry loud for Justice ; vpon consideracon thereof and conceiuinge that those propossitions may be kept secret from you, which hath beene tendered to you all upon surrender of the Castle, (some few p'sons not above sixe excepted) who have beene faithlesse to their former trust or guilty of other notorious and bloody crymes) J thought fitt to vse those meanes to lett you know my intentions, and once more to make you an offer of faire termes which yf they shalbe by you neglected or refused you may both before god & man appeare to be guiltye of yo'r owne destruction ; If therefore you or any of you shall deliver the Castle withall the Armes and provisions of warr into my handes within fowerteene dayes after the date hereof you may expect these condicons followinge

(1.) All who shall act and be asistinge in the deliu'y of the Castle) exceptinge the number above menconed) shall have libertye to martsh (*sic*) away with their goodes & necessaries which properly belongeth vnto them & shall have passes and protections to goe & live quietly at their owne home or habitacon, or passes to goe out of the Kingedome yf they shall desire it within two monthes after the rendition thereof and all those who have estates and desire to Compound I shall to the vttermost indeavour they may be admitted to Composition;

(2.) To all those who shall neither act nor yett oppose shall have faire q'rter, & not be pillaged nor plundered;

(3.) That all others who shall oppose deliu'y therof shal be deliu'ed to mercy, and satisfye for all the blood which hath beene vnnecessarily spilt;

I shall make good these Condicons to all who shall make themselves Capable of them.

March the seaventh,
1648.   J. LAMBERT.

Endorsed: For the two Coll' Portingtons, Coll' Wheatley, Leiut-Coll' Ashton, Sr John Digby, & Sr Hugh Cartwright, this.

There are moreover in the Tanner MSS (Bodleian) several documents relating to the attempt of Sept 1646. Vol. 59 No. 597, is a Letter from Poyntz, dated at York, Nov. 27, 1646, without endorsement, enclosing "a breife relation from Capt. Bayard, of Coll' Copley's regiment, concerning the betrayal of Pontefract Castle"; and reporting that Poyntz had ordered the apprehension of the conspirators, and had sent troops to the garrison. The "breife relation" is

"That Phillip Anne, Esq., reported that h'b' Lady Savile had sent to ye Kinge to know his Ma'ties pleasure about ye supprisall of Pontefract Castle, for now they had an instrument readye that would effect it for ye King, and names Leift Colonell Morris."

The margin contains

"The names of those who are instruments for ye betraing of Pontefract Castle, as followeth:—Phillip Ann, Esq., Mr Michaell Anne, Leift-Coll. Morris, Mr Sam Saville."

This letter is printed in Cary's Memorials, but the compiler makes no reference to the examination of George Holgate, of Stapleton, as to the Annes and the surprising of Pontefract Castle. This latter, No. 344 in the same volume 59, is as follows:—

The examinacon of George Holgate of Stapleton
          taken ye 4th of Decemb, 1646.

He sayth that about 10 days ago he had conference wth Mr. Philip Anne at his ye sd Mr. Holgates house at Stapleton, whither ye sd Mr. Anne resorted & lodged one night (having th *erased*) being yen newly come out of Pomfret Castle upon his parol w'th his keeper where he stood comitted for refusing ye negatiue oath. And ye sd Mr Philip Anne then told ye sd Mr. Holgate that Michael Anne his sonne came to him to ye said Castle & wished not to come abroad out of ye same by reason that there was an intention of surprisall of ye sd Castle, & yat ye Lady Savile had or should send to his Ma'ty to know his pleasure whether he would allow of ye surprisall thereof, yea or no, & yat ye instruments employed for ye doing yereof were to be one Maior Marris.

         (Signed.)   GEO: HOLGATE.

This Lady Savile was the widow of Sir Wm. Savile, of Thornhill, and mother of Sir George, created Baron Savile, of Elland, and afterwards Viscount, Earl, and Marquis of Halifax.

Of the son of Mr. Samuel Savile we shall have somewhat to say in connection with the next note.

THE BAYNES CORRESPONDENCE.
F (See pages 203, *et seq.*)

Since the body of this volume was in type, we have had the privilege of inspecting the documents themselves, (21,417-27 Add. MSS), and are now able to make some exceedingly interesting additions.

We find also, that the copy which we used was not absolutely verbatim, but that many alterations had been made, in order to round and complete the sentences of the different correspondents. John Baynes's seal, still preserved on the original letter, was a tower battlemented, a second smaller tower issuing therefrom, on the top of which is an eagle with opened wings. On each side of the tower is a letter slightly defaced, the two letters being possibly the initials of the writer, J.B.

As curiously corresponding with our remark in the text of page 203, as to John Baynes's style, we notice that his writing varies so much with his different sentences, that not only does he appear to pause, but that it might almost be imagined that he took up a fresh pen for each.

From careful collation of the copy with the original documents, we supply the following corrections:—

Page 204, 17th line of Mr. Margett's letter, "a.t" should be "against." There should have been no hesitation as to the word: it is perfectly legible, and written in full.

Page 204, last line but 2, "this late . . . . of the Army," should be "theis late cuts of the Army."

Page 206, 2nd paragraph. "The proceedings in relation" was originally "Your proceedings" but altered by the writer. Similarly " tis true they are " was originally "tis true *you* are." "In regard" three lines lower, is a less important correction for "*for*." The last line but two should read "get it delivered, and considered as soone as possibly can" &c.

Page 207. "Only Wednesday last," is a correction for "Saturday," as is in the next paragraph "Parson" for "minister": Mr. Beaumont was the duly inducted vicar, and therefore Parson, not merely minister. The last line should read "to serve you, as *becomes*, Sir."

Page 209, 3rd line, "I only request *you* careful remembrance," should have been "*your*."

Page 210. The running of this letter into one paragraph hardly does justice to Cornet Baynes's style. The original is in four, respectively commencing "Yours," "They," "When," and "Mr. Dawson." And evidently there was much stopping and thinking between each. The writer must have had a great dislike for these obligatory epistolary communications, and his next letter, written five weeks afterwards, breaks off with a similar excuse to that in the P.S. to this present: he can write no more, for he is about to muster one of his regiments.

Page 211. In Cornet Baynes's letter, "Cowy" is clearly "Cowp'"; "for the future" should be added after "put down." The missing word was probably "manure." The letter reads "to . . ure the ground. I heard *noe*thing," not "something."

Page 215. The letter of Mr. Margetts is in a formal, stiff, hand-writing, as if written to order. It represents the pretended "Clamour" of "The People" for "Justice." Only the last two lines are autograph.

Page 216. The 10th line of the letter of Mr Margetts should be "with the *rest of the* general affairs of the Army. If you please *to* deliver" &c.

Page 217, 3rd line. "Morris" is spelt "Marris," as usual.

Page 220, 1st line, should be "Hertfordshire," not "Herefordshire." The 4th line originally read "of Beale, of York," "Mr." being interlined. The 8th line is "whereof for a Treaty, which were granted, & Commissioners" &c. The last line is in the original "I *being* ignorant." In Robert Baynes's letter on the same page, the name is "Capt. Brear," not as printed.

Page 221, last line of the body of the letter, insert "the" before "Ma General."

Page 222. This which appears as a letter from Mr Margetts, is a postcript to his letter of 10 March. The word "prisoners" is an instance of the absurd way in which conjectural emendations are sometimes made. The original speaks of "delivering up the Castle and the 6 within 14 days": that is, the six excepted. The transcriber not knowing the circumstances, interpolated "prisoners," and a very incorrect deduction might be made from the sentence as corrupted.

Page 223. The original of the 9th line is "firing is more plentye amongst them then usually," an example of the modernizing process through which the letters have passed.

Page 224, 3rd line of the letter should be "our present *answer*"; and the 10th line reads "care*full*ness" not "carelessness."

Page 228. Colonel Lilburne's letter, 2nd line, reads "*those* gentlemen" not "*the* gentlemen"; and page 229, 5th line, "country" should be "county."

Page 234. It is important to notice that Major General Lambert's letter to Captain Baynes is not now in the series. His letter to Cornet Baynes, who had by that time become Clerk to the Committee who were making the financial arrangements, should have "But of this" before "I desire you.

Pages 236-7. The copy of the Judge Advocate's letter is especially corrupt. "99li 11s" in two places, should be "99li 15s." "Else" should follow "charged somewhere." "*The* Council of War," should be "*your* Council of War *above*"; "*Morris*" should be "*Marris*"; and "running," which we always mistrusted, should be "coming." The date "19 *July*" should be "19 *Junij*."

We append some other letters of interest, which we found among the mass of documents, which fill eleven goodly volumes, and contain an enormous amount of interesting matter.

Nos. 7 and 8 are two letters from Wm. Stiles, Vicar of Leeds. He had been Vicar of Pontefract till March, 1642, when he resigned to go to Hessle, near Hull, and it is not known how the spiritual necessities of the town were attended to during the interval between his departure and the settlement of Mr Ferrett, in Nov. 1647. In the will of Mr. Alderman Oates, dated 28 August, 1643, mention is made of Mr George Fothergill, Vicar of Pontefract, but that vicar is ignored by both Boothroyd and Fox. He might, indeed, have held the appointment in some such way as Mr. Ferrett did afterwards, but Mr Oates's will almost conclusively proves that he was virtually Mr. Stiles's successor.

It is, however, evident from these two letters, that Mr. Stiles was, so early as 1645, settled at Leeds in some ecclesiastical capacity. But he is not usually reckoned Vicar of Leeds till 1652. Probably the troubles at which he hints were too many for him at this time, and he resigned his position, being re-appointed in 1652, after the death of Peter Saxton, who is well ascertained to have been minister there for the last five or six years of his life.

The Mr. Weobley alluded to was probably the Weobley who was for some time Lecturer at the Parish Church, Leeds.

Much Honored Sr

The reason of my deepe, & long silence, hath beene partly out of an vnwillingness to interrupt y'u in y'r weighty affaires, partly out of an indisposision in myselfe, hauing beene a greate while together much troubled w'th a very sore cold, soe y't J hope y'u will not thinke me negligent or vnmindefull, of y't greate respect I deseruedly owe you. J confess it was my purpose to haue troubled you w'th a l re a weeke, or a fortnight since, but I was compelled to enter vpon a course of phisick, w'ch retarded y't purpose. J am glad Collonell Gill is come vp to London, he will (J know) inform y'u truly how things goe w'th vs & is very much y'r friend. Sr, Whilst I indeauored to reconcile both parties (according to y'r constant desire) J well perceiue J haue offended both parties, J meane in reference to y'r businesse, but ye Lord knowes y't what J did, it was intended well, & since y'u haue beene pleased to approue of what J did, J shall sitt quietly downe, and leaue the success of all to All mighty God: Mr Alanson is now admitted as a member of Mr Todds Church, whereby, J well foresee y't Mr Alderman & he, doe intend J shall haue as little comfort from that party as may be. J beleiue by y'r favour, & furthurance they expect to doe greate things, & hope to haue an absolute conquest ouer such as appeared for y'u. truly J doe not at all feare them, neither shall J giue them any just occasion of offense, besides, J builde soe much vpon y'r wisdome, & sincerity, y't y'u will haue a speciall regard of y'r friends, whome they look vpon (though w'thout cause) (*sic*) them as theire enimies. J perceive ye Com'issioners haue putt Mr Skurr besides his augmentation, & am much affraide, it will prejudice ye augmentation we haue at Leeds & this day speaking w'th Cornett Lademan about it we agreede to ioyn in one address to my Lord Widdrington if y'u approue of it for w'thout your consent J shall doe nothing as to y't p'ticular & therefore J pray y'u let me haue y'r counsel & direction what is fit to be done. J am knowne to some of the commissioners & therefore if it could be settled vpon me, w'thout any further trouble, J should be heartily glad, but if a certificate be required when J am able to stir a brode J shall procure it but ye halfe yeare is nere dew at Christmass soe if vnless you stand my friend J am at a losse. pardon J beseech you this boldness, & rather then this request shall proue (*sic*) any way to reflect vpon y'u, J shall earnestly Desire it may fall to ye ground. Mr Webley hath gone away w'th ye Surety of it ever since my co'ming, saue onily J detayned a small portion of it ye last time to defray some charges appertining to ye vicarage & wh't euer he hath had he hath had it by my good will & ye only reason why J appeare in it now, is a iealosy y't my meanes will be full as shorte as may be by those y't are in power w'th vs. y'u see how Liberally J express my Selfe, & my co'fidence is y'u will kepe what J write solely to y'r self, & to deale plainly J doe really intend y't as Mr. Webley takes halfe of ye paines soe he shall haue half of ye profitt if his cariage be such as doth become ye Gospell. J shall ad noe more but the remembrance of my vnfained respect to you, & my hearty prayers to God, both to protect & direct y'u in all y'r Godly vndertakings.

        Yr affectionat Friend & seruant,

            WM. STILES.

Leedes, Decemb. 19th (45).

Worthy Sr

  J haue receiued an order for ye augmentation y'u write of, from ye Commissioners at White-Hall, but since ye receipt thereof J am certified y't except J haue another order from ye committee for iriages of parishes (sa *erased*) J am not to receiue it. J doe not remember ye title of yt ordinance though I confess I haue seene it, but J am informed yt vpon sight of my order from ye aforesaide commissioners yt committee will grant me an order whereby J may be putt into a capacity to receive ye monies now due. J heare yt Sr. John Thorogood or Sr. Thomas, J know not well whether is one of ye Gentlemen of ye Committee. Sr. J am as loth, to putt y'u vpon trouble as any man in ye world but if y'u will doe me ye favour to lett me know how ye case stands as to ye particular J shall take it as a very greate fauovr & shall send vp my order to y'u when y'u shall command me Dr Deveuers is w'th ye High-Sheriffe & ye last time J saw him was tellinge me of his negligence in writing to you but I suppose y'u will heare from him shortly: Sr. we in ye country are alltogether, in ye Darke as to parliamentary proceedings, if y'u would hinte som things y't may safly be communicated y'u would much oblige

        Yr seruant & affectionate friend,

            WM. STILES.

Leedes,
Decemb. 29th (45.)

No. 9 of the volume is a letter from Mr. Margetts, dated York, 16 June, '46, and asking that a reply may be sent to him "at Mr. Alderman Skur's house in Pontefract, to be left with the PostMr of Ferribrige to that purpose." Mr. Skurr lived in Ropergate. This fixes Mr Margetts with some knowledge of Pontefract long before he made his appearance here in company with the besieging army.

No. 14 is the appointment of Capt. Lawson to the Company lately under Colonel Boynton, in Scarborough Castle, "he having revolted." Dated 6 Aug, 1648, signed Fairfax. (See page 269.)

No. 15 is a letter from Fairfax to General Overton, Governor of Hull, informing him of the appointment of Capt. Lawson. Undated.

Nos. 26 and 27 deserve copying, as we have hitherto had Mr Margetts only by the weekly post of 12th January. No. 26 adds something to the race episode.—It is,

Lov'd Brother,
haveinge so fit an opportunity, I thought fit to Certifie you yt Clifford Course is within 14 dayes aft'r Candlemass. Therefore, I desire to know yo'r pleasure concerneinge yo'r horse whether he shall run or not. I ca'not informe you what horses will be there only Mr Chambers gray horse, which run last yeare is come thither againe. Henry is alleeady gone to Compton, because wee now pay our quarters, therefore thought it more convenient for his heates (?) Thus not haveinge others (?) at p'sent to trouble you withall, wishinge for yo'r healthe and prosperity.

Pontefract 12th January,   I remayne,
    1648 (1648-9).   Yo'r ever lo: brother,
                                                ROBT. BAYNES.

All our freinds at Higfield, Eastfield, and els where are in good health.
    Idem, R.B.
For (Comissary *erased*) Capt. (*written above*) Baynes, these.
Endorsed : my brother, Jan the 12.

The seal is imperfect: all that is clear being a reversed R.

This "Eastfield" is a sly reminder of a certain Mrs Martha, who was thought to be likely to be Adam Baynes's second wife, and of whom we shall have somewhat else presently.

No. 27, by the same post, is a letter from Jo. Baynes, which thus concludes:—

* * noe newes worthy yo'r notice. the Ma Gen. is gone about disbandinge more of the militia. Collo Lilburne tooke post last Thursday for London. he wilbe with you before this. The Gunns are now come to Pontefract. by the next I hope to lett you know wt execution they doe.
  For Capt Adam Baynes,
    Att the King's head in Gray's Inn,
      these. London.

No. 30 is another from Jo. Baynes, written from York, the following week. It supplies that which was wanting on page 207.

* * Pontefract Castle yet in Capacity to dispute with us a longe time. they devise new waies to p'iudice us, & doe us much harme, but att last I hope we shall pay them home for all.

Many men not satisfied with the Army's proceedings (though God give never soe good event) and with Justice to the life on C.S., yet I hope the work begunne will be effected. I pray God give unity, faith, fulnesse & Courage to those appointed to that end, that we may not be frustrate in our expectations of soe good, warrantable and necessary a worke.

This is all att p'sent, only desireinge you to direct yo'r nxt to Pontefract, to my Quarters there, restinge
      Yo'r assured Lo Couzen,
Yorke, Janu'ry 20th, 1648 (1648-9).   Jo. BAYNES.

No. 31, from the same, and of the same date, is in reference to a projected marriage of Adam Baynes to Mrs Martha Cudworth. Its contents rather imply that he was a widower, and had had much trouble with the health of his first wife. John Baynes warns him that Mrs Martha is consumptive, as two doctors declare; but as the sequel proved, John Baynes must have been imposed upon by those who did not wish the young lady to be sacrificed to Capt. Baynes, but who did not care to have to refuse his alliance, for Mrs Martha Cudworth was one of three co-heiresses, the youngest of whom married Dr Nathaniel Johnston, who christened one of his children Cudworth. The second, Martha, upon whom (as the intended heiress of Eastfield, which her family had possessed for 400 years) Adam Baynes thus had his eye, ultimately married Samuel Savile, who was concerned in the attempt upon the Castle, as recounted in the last note. It is remarkable that this poor lady lived to be a centenarian, or nearly so. Her marriage took place on October 7, 1651, at Tankersley, and she lived 76 years afterwards, dying on December 29, 1727. She was buried at Mexborough on the following January 4.

No. 44, though not immediately connected with Pontefract will be of interest.

JOHN COWPER, OF DONCASTER, TO HIS HONERED FREIND, CAPTAINE ADAM BAYNES.

Doncaster, the 9th of February. 1648 (1648-9).

Nooble Captaine, after my best respects remembered, wishing you much healthe & happinesse etc. the experience I have had of your many neighbourly curtissies and loving kindenesses imboldenes me to desire you to add one more to the rest which is you would be pleased to use meanes if you can to procure me A license to draw wine heare at Doncaster upon reasonable tearmes, and what you lie unto about it I shall thankefully repay you. I acquented this bearer, Mr Routcliffe, what I write you, & intreated him if he could to be assistant unto you in it, my wife remembers her kindely unto you, and desires you to do what you can in this, and thereby you should ingage both her and me to be (ever *interlined*) your most humble servants till death,

JOHN COWPER.

To his honered freind
  Captaine Adam Baynes.

No. 45 shows Col. Bright once more especially urgent for himself, that his lot and that of his fellows may fall in good counties. The endorsement is evidently a receipt for the £3 referred to in the letter.

Capt. Baynes,

Yo's with the two warrants I rec'd and thankefully acknowledge yo'r paines and saw therin litle advantage will yr be to mee as yett, ther being sevvll ordrs of ye maior Genells to be first satisfied: I pray deliver this (enclosed *interlin d*) to Mr Coxx (*sic*) and give him three poundes wch shalbe repayd you att yo'r retorne, or to any in theise pts who'ver you please to appointe to receive ye same, upon yr assignments for ye Army's. I hope by yor meanes Care wilbee taken that o'r lotts fall in good Countyes. I know you have from sevrall handes ample account of wt these barren p'ts affordes, soe shall trouble you noe further.

Pontefract,   I remaine,
  10th Feb,   Yo'r well freind to serve you,
    1648 (1648-9).   J. BRIGHT.

Feb. 24th, payed to Mr Coxn (*sic*) according to this letter, the sume of 3lb. Witness Coll. Lilburne & the dorekeper.

No. 52 is from Capt. Bradford, who has not hitherto appeared in proper person, but who, as we know already, brought down an assignment of a month's pay to the forces.

The Talbot in Gratious meane in Gracechurch Street.

Sr Beinge uppon a dirty cold guard before Pontefract, I cannott but salute you, & tho I know yow to be better accommodated, yet doe I not envie your happines but rather wish you a happy and longe continuance of yr employment.

I desire you to procure a coppy of my Lord Gen'lls warr't remaineinge with Capt Blackwell, the Treasurer att Whitehall w'ch did authorise him to pay to me for the use of the militia forces the thousand pounds Mr Lovell returned for me,"& to send the same unto me, Major Gen'll thinkeinge that the same is charged uppo' his accompt, tho' I thinke that he is not named in it. I lately sent to Hull to enquire of the Chirurgeons this (?) but cannot heare of them. You had neede to send to Mr. Hollis, att the Talbot in gratious, to know whether they be shippt & whether gon, & by wt Mr. present my Service to Mr Cox, & desire him to place our Assignem'ts uppo' cleare countyes. In this last monthes Assignem'ts, Lestershire refuses Coll' Bright. for that the Maior Gen'll is forced to send two troopes of horse to quarter uppo' them. I desire you to p'sent my humble service to my Collonell & maior Rookeby, w'th my respect to yo'r selfe p'sented, I rest,

Sr yo'r most humble Servt,
24 Febr, 1648 (1648-9),   W. BRADFORD.

No. 55 is a pitiable letter from Mrs Cudworth and the poor Martha, who little knew the report that Jo Baynes had made of them to the Captain.

The handwriting is a beautiful clear and formal hand, though probably (alas!) all written by the mother, except the timid postcript wrung out of a sorrowful heart.

COSEN BAINES, my best respects attend yow. These Few lynes are humble suiters in the behalfe of my cosen Smith, his wife and poore children to help them of, with theire sequestration. Good Cosen doe what you can for them, I know one word of your mouth to the Generall and Leeftennant Gennarall will cleare 'him, for all the Country will witnes with him that he was never in armes for the Kingis partie, If you would have him to come to you, he shall upon your letter Good Cosen, helpe now or never, and we shall all of us ever be bonnden to pray for your health and happines, and in the menetyme restith,

Yo'r Cosen to com'aund till death,
East feild, this   SUSAN CUDWORTH.
2o March, 1648 (1648-9).
Cosen I pray you lett us have yo'r
helpe herein. it is the humbe suit
of your servant
             MARTHA CUDWORTH
Direct to Willi Sims at Wakefeild
your letter per net post if you can

No. 60 is another pitiful letter from one Ellen Wiggins, a widow, of Leeds, dated 8 March, asking for Capt: Baynes's intercession with Quarter Sessions to obtain for her a yearly maintenance, her husband having been slain in the service of the Parliament, under Capt. Baynes.

Much honored Sr. you haue giuen me soe great and good experience of yo'r readines to Commeserate the teares and sad Condic'on of me A poore distressed Comfortles widdow : that I am hereby emboldned and necessetated further to be troublesome vnto yow. employments are soe very scarce and all kind victualls soe extraordenary deare that J and mine are in great danger of perishinge by famine if some releife and mainetenance be not afforded vnto vs, J haue shifted w'th my father and litle ones as long as possible J can and J am per force put vpon this extremity for I haue none soe pitty full and Faithfull as yo'r selfe to addresse my selfe vnto and J doubt not but yo'r goodnes is soe sencible of my great necessity and sad Condicon that yow will make me what helpe yow can. yow know very well it is not possible for me to come to London to wait and attend soe long and vncertainely as J must to see what may be procured there.

Therefore my humble suit to yow is that yow would be pleased to Certefy it vnder yo'r hand by a L're to the Justises at our generall quarter Sessions that my husband was slaine beinge in office vnder yow and that yow would be pleased to Certefy allsoe my sad and distressed Condic'on to them and moue them to helpe me w'th some yearely mainetenance and allowance, for J haue noe way as J Conceiue to seeke for releife but this. Good Sr. lett me heare from you w'th all possible speed for the Sessions are suddenly, that soe J may make A tryall what God will doe for me in this way. J take leaue and rest

Yo'r distressed and troublesome
seruant ELLEN WIGGINS.

Leeds 8 March 1648 (1648-9).

Robert Baynes's letter of the following day, (pp. 220-1) has a P.S. which shows how Ellen Wiggins's letter obtained access to the "nooble captaine." The P.S. is as follows:—

> I have heare Jnclosed sent you a ltter from Widdow Wiggins desireinge yo'r l're to the Justices at the quarter Sessions w'ch will be the latter end of this month here, as allso another l're from Martin Jles. I was forct to open it for wrappeing it, in his roome. Martin Iles is an ill friend to the Mane rideinge, solicitinge the Maior Gen and Comittee to ioyne it to the towne, yt so they may assese it at their pleasure, but I hope they will (* doe no good in it) will preuale nothing.   *erased

Idem R.B.

There was evidently an intrigue on foot, the result of which was expected to affect the assessment of " the towne " (*i.e.* Leeds). But we have no space to enquire into the particulars, restraining ourselves to the statement that No. 68 is from Wm. Stable, evidently in authority at Knowstrop, in the absence of Captain Baynes, and that he deals more fully with the attempt then being made to alter the rateable chargeability of Leeds. Martin Iles was the person most exclaimed against in the matter by both parties. No. 68 is dated 15 March, 1648 (*i.e.* 1648-9).

No. 71, from Col. Lilburne, has a seal, 3 water bougets with a label of 3 points, in very fine condition; No. 74 is a letter from Wm. Stable's son Richard; and No. 76 is one from Wm. Stable (Knowstrop, 23 March.) But we observe none at this part of the volume worth copying, before No. 85, which is from the unfortunate cousin Smith, whose estate was in such danger.

He appeals as follows to what he appears to think the vulnerable part of Capt. Baynes :—

SR,—

I make still bould this one tyme with you in pursuit of my former petition for yo'r assistance. Good Sr lett me have yo'r helpe, and this my note shall, I engage me at yo'r returne into the Countrye to passe my estate unto you untill you be satisfyed whatsoever it cost you. Sir, you are the only help I have under God in this busenes, and without you I my wife and Children are utterly undone. S'r I pray you if it be possible let me have two words from you by the next post directed to William Sim's howse at Wakefeild, as alsoe whether I need to come up to you or noe. S'r, my unckle, my Aunt & Cozen Martha remembereth their respectes to you hopeinge it will not be long before they see you in the Countrie, soe makeing bould at this tyme as I have done alwaies to trouble you. I rest,

East feild, this Yo'rs to Com' to his power,
30 March, 1649. EDWARD SMYTH.

No. 86 is from Jo. Baynes, dated York, 31 March, 1649, in which he says :—

The Assizes end this day, Never Judge had so gen'rall a good report as Judge Thorpe. he hath taken very great paynes, & wearied almost all the Lawyers keepeinge them from 6 or 7 in the morninge till as late or later att night in the Court.

No. 93 is a letter from Col. Robert Lilburne, under date York, 3 April, 1649, in which we have definite news of Colonel Morris, his servant Peter, and his Cornet Blackburn, who escaped on March 18 (see p. 229).

. . . . . . Morrise & 2 more (being going to ye Ile of Mann) was taken & are now att Lancastr The Scotts are of Laite much spoken off, yt they are p'pare- ing many forces, & speakes big words, & people begin to feare them. The Last weeke (att Malton) on a Markett (*interlined*) vizt. Capt Denton & one Mounton, but ye other I know not day 4 Cavil'rs proclaimed ye Pr' King, and was nott app'ehended Though Col Be came imediately into ye Towne, & was acquainted w'th it. I am told p'paracon is makeing to begin to pull downe Pontefr' some day this weeke, w'ch is glad newes to very many. . . . . .

No. 110 is from Robert Baynes at Leeds, April 20, 1649.

Brother,—
> I have recd yo'rs of the 10th Instant. I am afraid I shall scarce buy any thinge at Pont Castle, but at the full vallue in regard it is wholy bought up by one or two yt will make their best profit of it, but shall try what I can doe. . . .

He may have tried, but he did not succeed. All fetched the "full value" which Robert Baynes did not intend to give. No. 134 shows Mr. Margetts to have been a Bedfordshire man. No. 186 is from a royalist John Baynes:—

> To my approued and euer honored
> Friend Capt Baynes this present.

——ght hon'bl
> Acknowledgeinge my selfe soe farr Engaged to the memorie of your hon'bl Family vnto w'ch I haue relation as beinge sonn to the late Baynes of Sellett Hall neere Kirby Lonsdale, whoe in the's distractions is vnfortunately slaine besides 3 of my brothers by w'ch meanes J am left destitute of all Comfort. Sr, J was taken Prisoner att Taunton & brought vp to the honnorable Parliament as a prisoner at warr, by Sr. Tho: Wrath the 3d daie of June in ye yeare 1645. And then Committed to prison as being one of his late Ma'ties officers : & about 9 weekes after J procured an Exchange which was accepted of : yet notwithstandinge Contrary to the lawe of Armes J haue beene detained vpon false actions of debt ; And throwen into a Dungeon double Irond vpon the bare boards for ye space of 23 months in the Jnfamous Goale of Newgate w'thout any offence more than attemptinge to get [liberty ; as for my allowance 't was *obulum per diem*, and sometimes a peice of rawe liuer w'ch the Goalers fed their Fox w'thall ; theise J have endured w'th *patientia per vim*. And now haueinge Contracted all my buisines into the some of betwixt 30 and 40ls for an absolute freedome : w'ch some my Cozen ye Lady Bellasys J am enformed will aduance ye halfe. And if your honnour will be pleased to putt your helpe therein my Endeuours shall not be wanting to sacrifice my life in your hon'rs seruice, if J maje haue such Commaund as J am Capable of vnder you : J humblie desire your honnour will please to Countenance me nowe beinge vpon ye redemption of one vsed worse then a slaue in Turky : the bearer can in perticuler relate, more then J am able to express by my guill, therefore to be tedious in matters w'ch jmploreth to such sence J conceive jmpertinent, espetially to one of your gallantry, soe J leave it to your hon'rs discretion & humblie subscribes my selfe
> Sr. yr. hon'rs most Faitbfull servt
> JOHN BAYNES.

Newgate 13o June '49.

No. 194 is a further letter from E. Smyth, with regard to his composition which seemed then to be nearly settled. It is dated Eastfield, 22 June, 1649. He concludes:—

> . . . noe newes Save only Mr. Barnbye and my Cozen Martha are quite broake in Suuder one reason is they cannot get a Docto' in all the Countrie that will undertake to cure him of the (Symples). . .

The link between Capt. Baynes and the Cudworths, and therefore, the Smyths, may perhaps be found in connection with the facts that (1) Ducatus Leodiensis (Sykes's Pedigree page 36) says that Susannah, daughter of Edward Binns, of Horbury, married William Paulden, father of the three captains, that (2) Hunter (S. Yorkshire II, 270) gives Susan Cudworth as the daughter of Thomas Binns, of Thorpe, and that (3) Thoresby in his Diary (II, 62) says he took notes (see page 324) of the Pauldens in 1710, from the then Sheriff Baines, of Knowstrop. For, together, they say that the Cudworths were cousins to the Pauldens, of whom Sheriff Baines had some special notice apparently as a matter of family record.

No. 225, the last for which we have room, shows the uncertainty as to the place from which Lambert was to receive his £300 per annum. Now that the war was nearly over, the leaders of the successful party seemed to be concerned with little but buying, and acquiring. Well might Cromwell declare (see p. 198) " I know not one officer among us, but is on the increasing hand!"

Deare Sir

J rec'd yo'rs by this last Post of all, but haue not yet rec'd that by the former Post though J haue laid out all J could for it. By the last Post J did not write vnto you because J had not one word worth a L're.

The Com'tee of Leicestershire haue refused to pay Cap: Oates and Cap: Cowper the money desired for disbanding so that the bills of Exch' charged on you for that money are taken in againe. J should be glad to heare whether the 99l. 15s. charged for me vpon Norfolk & the other for the Marscall are fixed there or remoued to some other place, and when we may expect it, for J owe that money to Col· Rokeby hauing rec'd it from his at Bedford and he is sollicitous to me for it. J doe not perceiue that the Ma: Gen'll is writt for to come vp, or if he be it is not hasty for it is thought not this three weekes, he is now at Ledston and hath appointed a meeting of officers in a Counsell of Warre there on Thursday next. J pray when the next assignm'ts are given out remember me & the Marshall, & that you will please to giue notice when you think it wilbe, J shall take care to satisfie the Ma: Gen'll the money Mr. Mather hath rec'd of him, so that you may pay his two moneths pay to Cornet Baynes.

J vnderstand that Col: Fairfax & Lt. Col: Crook are gone vp to London partly about buying the wood in Pontefract Park, w'ch will be a great preiudice to the Ma: Gen'll if that Park be in his graunt of 300l p' ann' imperpetuu', & did yesterday acquaint the Ma: Gen'll what J heard, who said it would be a pr'judice to him if the Park should be his. what course he will take in it J cannot tell, but J thought fitt to mention it to you, and J am sure if you can well tell how to pr'uent Col : F: it will be good seruice to the Ma: Gen'll and very well accepted, so J leaue it to yo'r further inquiry & consideration. J have nothing at all of newes and therefore rest,

Sr
Yo'r very affec : freind & serut
Tho Margetts.

Pont'ct 7. July 49.

Pontefract Castle on the West Riding of YORKSHIRE.
Granted by WILLIAM the Conqueror to HILDEBERT de LASCY, Repaired by QUEEN ELIZABETH but totally demolished in 1648, is thus transmitted to Posterity by the Society of Antiquaries, London. 1734.

SUPPLEMENT.

THE ADDITION of a series of Photographs to the present volume, as an after-thought when the work was completed and the Index far advanced, necessitates some little explanation, which can now be given only in this place. The Views of the Castle, Church, and Hall, will speak for themselves as a faithful and permanent record of the buildings, in the spring of 1885; but we feel that we ought not to allow the remainder to go forth unaccompanied by a few words which may do somewhat (1) to reconcile what appear at first sight to be irreconcilable differences; (2) when such differences are only apparent, to attempt to point out how they may have arisen; and (3) to indicate as nearly as possible how it has come to pass that the truth has been put forth under such very varying aspects.

In the remarks we are about to make, we purpose firstly to comment upon the published engravings of the Castle, occasionally contrasting them with the different siege plans; and then to consider these latter in comparison with each other.

There had been two earlier efforts to preserve to posterity a view of Pontefract Castle, but each of them—by Buckley Wilsford, and by Buck, respectively,—was confessedly taken from memory only. The first serious attempt was made by the Society of Antiquaries in No. 44 of their Vetusta Monumenta (published 1735, and reissued by Marsden under the patronage of the Marquis of Rockingham, in 1776.) That engraving from a drawing then in the office of the Duchy of Lancaster was a spirited production; and we have reproduced it from a photograph, by means of the autotype process.

But it should be borne in mind that the ultimate result was arrived at by three stages. There was firstly the drawing, one of a series preserved for many years (we should probably be correct if we said for centuries) in the Office of the Duchy of Lancaster; secondly, the engraving published by the Society of Antiquaries; and thirdly, Marsden's improvement which we have reproduced.

Alterations and amendments to suit the current notion of the picturesque were doubtless introduced at each stage; though what "embellishments" were made by the engraver in 1735 we cannot at present say, the original drawing having disappeared from the Duchy Office, where no trace of it now remains. We know, however, that the 1735 print received in its turn several "improvements" at the hands of Mr Marsden, each "improvement," however it may have added to the artistic value of the print, being almost necessarily a further deviation from the now lost or misplaced original. For that drawing we are bound to say we have enquired in vain, not only at the Duchy Office, which was certainly its original depository, but also at the Public Record Office to which the great bulk of the Duchy documents and papers were removed some years ago. We cannot, however, altogether divest ourselves of the hope that it may yet be discovered among the many documents and papers in the Record Office yet unindexed and unregistered.

The drawing, as thus modernized by the two engravers who succeeded each other with an interval of very nearly half a century between them, seems at first sight and to the casual observer, to present insuperable difficulties. And yet we venture to say, and doubt not that we shall be able to make good our assertion, that on close examination the print will offer very many more points of resemblance to what the original may fairly be presumed to have been, than it will of dissimilitude.

Not many words are necessary to show how this must have been the case. For, so far as the general character of the drawing is concerned we have to remember that it was an official production, or at least accepted for official purposes by those who had every means of knowing to what extent it corresponded with the original. That it served those official purposes for some time, as long indeed as the buildings themselves remained without much alteration, is probable; and that it was afterwards preserved with official instinct, at least till 1735, was the natural outcome of the conditions.

To what extent the less important details of the engravings deviated from strict accuracy, our only present means of judging are a partial examination of the foundations of the various towers and walls, and an acquaintance with the ordinary laws of mechanics. That in its main features the ground plan is remarkably accurate can be proved by comparison with the five-ft. ordnance map of Pontefract. But it is nevertheless clear that there are several points in which the representation of the elevation differed to a considerable extent from the view of the buildings that would have been presented to a spectator who examined them from the point of sight taken by the engraver. This point was at a spot about eighty yards south-east of the Porter's Lodge, in what is now cultivated ground behind the All Saints' School, but which was evidently at the time of the drawing, only a part of the waste under the Castle walls, though afterwards utilized and taken possession of by the townspeople some time before the enclosure of the Outer Barbican.

For in the first place we must remember that the draughtsman naturally gave greater prominence to the larger features of the building, than he did to those that were less important,

that he perhaps lowered walls or raised towers, as he wished the one to cease to conceal, the other to cease to be hidden; while misled by the name of Queen Elizabeth, added merely for the purpose of description, the engraver of 1776 has even ventured to introduce figures clothed in a dress such as never could have appeared before the building he has represented. But although he has taken this and many similar liberties in order, as he appears to have thought, to translate what he saw before him into the language of his time; yet on the whole he has left us much which we cannot fail to recognize as a truthful representation, especially when considered in the light thrown upon the subject by the recent excavations. This we will shortly proceed to demonstrate, showing at the same time in what respects the engravings of 1735 and 1776 differed from each other.

The drawing is of the Castle at a very early date, probably that part of the fourteenth century when Thomas of Lancaster was at his zenith, and long before John of Gaunt was a power in the land, or his son Henry had conceived the project of usurpation which led him on step by step to the murder of his cousin and sovereign within its walls. It represents probably the results of that activity which set in, in Pontefract, in 1278, when the coming to age of Henry de Lacy closed a succession of minorities such that there had been an interval of only six years out of thirty during which the Honour had not been held by a minor. As that six years, the short "reign," as it may be called, of Edmund de Lacy, witnessed the establishment of the Black Friars (the only church in England we believe, dedicated to St. Richard, the godly bishop of Chichester, whom Edmund had been so fortunate as to have for his tutor), so the reign of Henry de Lacy, the great Earl of Lincoln, coincident as it was with the glories of our English Justinian—the Greatest of All the Plantagenets, witnessed the resumption of a building fever in both Castle and town, which did not cease till it had transformed each. But although the Castle was, during the continuance of that building era, much enlarged and almost entirely reconstructed, it did not, at the time represented in the engraving, cover nearly as much space as it ultimately embraced. When the draught was made, it is evident that there was no Outer Barbican, as it has been called; neither was there East Gate, or drawbridge, at least from that direction: on the other hand, there then existed many buildings which had no later representatives, (among which we may specify the residences of the dean and four canons, for St. Clement's was at the time still a collegiate chapel,) while the small party of five so dramatically figured in the right foreground are literally under the Castle walls—outside—and if they are supposed to belong to the Castle, would have had to undergo a short journey before they could enter the actual precincts of the establishment.

The outer wall appears, moreover, to have been somewhat lowered, it is easy to see for what pictorial effect, while it must be remembered that when deprived of battlements this wall would have been, then as now, little more than breast-high to those within, although it represented a height of ten or twelve feet to those without.

The 1776 print displays to the right the figure of a bareheaded gentleman approaching his lord with eloquent humility, the successor of a similar group of medieval retainers in the 1735 print, between whom and the Castle Wall the artist of the original or the engraver of 1735 figured some five or six sheep, which in the 1776 print have been transferred to the upper right. Above the group in each case, is a short wall, running south, towards the foreground, and then turning to the west and continuing in that direction to the end of the View. This latter is interrupted by a projection diagonally forward at about a fourth of the distance, to enclose a trapezium, the object of which was to enable an inmate of the Castle standing at or near the diagonal, to command with ease the whole or any part of the wall. The wall, thus truthfully represented, is, in its main features, standing to this day; and, although strangely overlooked by each of the siege plans, which here depict a perfectly straight piece of masoury, the projecting section may still be examined. It will be found to bear evidence of having been substantially, as represented on the engraving; two set-offs as a base, and four or more courses of masonry. These are still perfect in two places, though almost everywhere else, the casing-wall has been despoiled, not only of its battlements but of most of the worked stones. Of what is lost, the engraving gives us, as we cannot help believing, a truthful representation, with the one exception that the later engraver reduced the number of the courses, thus by consequence magnifying the size of the stones employed, and practically making them of an almost impossible weight. In the 1735 engraving, this defect does not exist in anything at all like the same degree.

How much skilful constructional design was exercised in the creation of this wall, will appear when it is considered that to produce it, the inclined plane of the lower part of the hill on which the Castle was built, must have been quarried away to form a perpendicular wall; that the side of the quarry thus formed must have been made to extend in an irregular line; and that the resulting zig-zag so produced, which in the whole included at least a dozen deviations from the horizontal, must afterwards have been cased, the casing being carried upwards so as to form a battlemented screen wall, rather more than breast high.

It is by no means necessary to suppose that all this was done at once: according to the conception of some one individual. On the contrary, there is every reason to believe that one generation improved upon the plan of another, and that the work was really produced by stages. That which we now see before us is, for instance, the fourteenth century fortress, which takes no account of the Outer Barbican or of the East Gate, while it makes no attempt to represent the Main Guard, like these other two features, then non-existent.

For it may be noticed that the outer wall appears to have continued to the west beyond the limits of the engraving. This we doubt not it did; and that, as continued, it included the Main Guard or its predecessor, and the several other buildings connected with the West gate. These were each and all erected upon a solid platform carved for the purpose out of the original rock, by a similar process or successive processes to that which we have already attempted to describe.

Meeting this outer wall at nearly a right angle, is what is called in Siege Plan No. 1, a Flanker Wall, extending from the S.W. roundel of the Round Tower; and it is again greatly in favour of the correctness of the old engraving that it is the only one which gives that Flanker Wall accurately, each of the "Plans" continuing it to the south to enclose the Outer Barbican, which there is no evidence that it ever did. There is moreover at this point a difference of level of eight or ten feet which all other plans ignore, even in a manner palpable and intrusive, but which is represented with tolerable accuracy on the more ancient drawing. And this very difference of level would have been sufficient to have rendered such a continuation of the Flanker Wall unlikely, if the clear evidence of the present remains did not prove it to have been impossible.

This Flanker Wall contained a gateway, like the difference of level ignored entirely in Siege Plan No. 1, and of which there are now no remains, every trace having been recently obliterated in the erection of the present Lodge and its approaches. Further excavation, however, may unearth some evidence yet underground. The Flanker Wall is represented as reaching to the bottom only of the set-off; but in fact, as the Photograph of the Remains shews, it really had some considerable height. Siege Plan No. 3 seems to give the most faithful representation of it; while that which we have styled No. 1 is here even more inaccurate than the print, though perhaps for the same reason, an attempt to lower the walls in order to display the buildings.

It is interesting to notice as an illustration of the degeneration which may arise through copying from a copy, and allowing the engraver in each case to give play to his fancy, that whereas the 1735 engraving exhibited the two sections of the Round Tower which are on the inner side of the Flanker Wall as nearly flat, and without any set-off, that of 1776 rounded each excellently and placed set-offs upon them both, as may be seen on our Photograph. But the real state of the case differs from each of these representations: for in truth and in fact only one of the sections, the roundel to the east, had a set-off, as may be seen to this day; while the more westerly section not only has no set-off, but is nearly flat, being, in fact, merely a straight containing wall to a capacious cesspool, intended to receive the drainage of the chambers above.

Each of these engravings, however, displays, with what all the evidence of the remains, and of the documents we have already quoted, shows to have been perfect accuracy, the mode of approach by which, even down to the last day of its existence, those who entered the Castle were conducted to the Ballium.

Having passed over the Drawbridge, and through a second gateway —"also by a wicket," as graphically described by Capt. Paulden (see page 298) and having left the Main Guard to the right, and the King's Stable to the left, the visitor would have been required to pass by the Middle Gate, through this Flanker Wall, in order to be admitted to the Barbican of the old print, the "Inner" Barbican of the Siege Plans. The description furnished by this engraving corresponds indeed, exactly with that of the report of the Lancaster Herald in 1536 (see page 342) who having passed through the first ward (in which was the Main

Guard), and having found there "many in harness of very cruel fellows," had to enter by "two other ward gates," the gate in the Flanker Wall being the second of the three. This gateway is, however, as we have pointed out, entirely and completely ignored in Siege Plan No. 1, which makes the Flanker Wall impassable, and transfers the "Middle Gate" to the centre of the Barbican Wall. But its existence is indicated, though with no details, on Siege Plan No. 3.

Unless, therefore, we can suppose a middle state, in which this gateway was blocked up, and a Tower Gate made in Barbican Wall, every evidence of which on the Wall itself has been since destroyed and in which, moreover, the difference of level between the Barbican proper, and what was afterwards the outer enclosure, was temporarily destroyed, though restored at a later date, we can attach no weight to the "evidence" of this part of Siege Plan No. 1. It looks at present very much like a mere development from the Artist's inner consciousness.

But if there had been any kind of gateway in the present Middle Wall, (the outer wall of the Prints), it is clear that it must have been a staircase-gateway, in order that it might deal with the difference of level of some ten feet, which is about the perpendicular height of the shelf of rock that is cased by what has since been called the "Inner" Barbican Wall; and a staircase-gateway, of such capacity, one would think, could hardly have been absolutely spirited away without leaving many indications of its presence, easily recognisable, even in the present condition of the Wall. None, however, can be clearly discovered, though the wall has been in places so altered and adapted, that only after excavation could a positive judgment be formed on the subject. But on the other hand, when the Outer Barbican was enclosed from the waste, the newly formed enclosure became what was practically the Farm-yard of the establishment, and there must then have been some method of easy communication between it and the two inner wards. Any such is, however, still to seek; for very slight indications of any possible means of communication from one to the other are at present discernible.

We return to the Flanker Wall. Passing the Middle Gate in it, the visitor, who would have faced the rising sun, found another short screen wall to his right, intended probably to conceal his movements from those outside ; and at its termination he would have come upon a small gabled building, called in the Siege Plans (improperly so, as we believe, and only in default of a better name) the "Stable" and the "King's Stable." For the King's Stable which was clearly (see page 63) in a line between the Main Guard and the Round Tower was, we conceive, the building part of which still faces the Main Guard (and not the Main Guard itself, as we were at one time inclined to think). Not only, however, do the two Siege Plans thus miscal this building, but they misplace it, bringing it down to the Barbican Wall, while, moreover, each makes its entrance face the south, with no intimation whatever that there was, at that point, the great difference of level to which we have already referred ; and by which, without a staircase or its equivalent, interior or exterior, any entrance from below would have been absolutely impossible.

Taking all these various circumstances into consideration, here, again, therefore, we are compelled to acknowledge the greater accuracy and complete superiority over those subsequently published, of the Print issued by the Society of Antiquaries a century and a half ago. To say the least, it represented at this point a possible state of things, which neither of the others did.

Turning his back, for a moment, to the gabled building, whatever it may have been, the visitor would have faced what from a line of view somewhat to his right, the Prints indicate as two roundels of the Round Tower. One only, however, answers that description: the first, that nearer to the Flanker wall, is merely the hollow well of a quadrangular cesspool, and it is neither circular nor oilletted; the second is the casing of a scarped rock, which by means of oillets the print incorrectly indicates as hollow. This second roundel, however, though circular, is not a hollow structure at all. It is nothing but a solid rock, cased.

The 1776 print moreover represents each of these constructions as having set-offs, which in 1735 were given to neither, and pictures the Flanker Wall as reaching only to the level of the lower ridge of the set-offs. But considering that the apparent diminution of the height of the wall, thus produced, might have been intentional in order to improve the view, we are again inclined to put faith in the earlier artist, who is certainly correct in his indication of the position of the wall, and in showing as neither of the Siege Plans does, the bases of two distinct erections between the Flanker Wall and the retaining wall of the platform, which is in a direction almost perpendicular to it. He errs, however, in the one point we have indicated; he gives two roundels to the east of the Flanker Wall. For the constructions are clearly (1) a roundel to form a solid bastion as foundation to a building above, and (2) a nearly flat casing wall to conceal the cesspool. And it should be borne in mind that this cesspool, though difficult of access, is still open to the sky, as it was when the print was published, and as it has been since the Demolition.

The cavity in the thickness of the wall, to which the name of cesspool is the only one applicable, gave at one time some considerable difficulty to those who wished to describe the place—a difficulty, which completely baffled the learned Mr King, the authority of a century ago, whose ponderous volume on "Ancient Castles" was at the commencement of this century a *sine qua non* in the formation of a library. He says "After you have ascended a ladder against the inside of the wall, for a few feet, you then look down into a dismal square cavity about 14 or 15ft deep, or rather more, but only about five or six feet square; which cannot be conceived to have been applied to any other purpose than that of a dungeon; since there is neither loop, nor door beneath; or any outlet whatsoever; nor does there appear the least possibility of there ever having been any; nor could it from its shape and dimensions, have served for a staircase, or, for drawing up timber and machines of war, or for any other purpose than that of a place of severe confinement. In short, it reminds one of the description, given by Sallust, of the Tullianum in the ancient Capitol at Rome: and as it even now very well answers to that description, it must have done so still more, before the upper part of the building, with the arches, was destroyed."

This description, together with Mr King's accompanying plate (in Archæologia vol vi), were copied verbatim by both Boothroyd and Fox; but the recent excavations having unearthed the Lancet doorway by which the cesspool was emptied, have made thoroughly apparent the purpose for which the receptacle was intended, and for which doubtlessly it was used for many generations.

Long before Mr King had seen it, Gent had been in a similar difficulty. He duly figures this cesspool on his engraving, and in his lettering describes it as "11, Horreum Spatiosum." evidently with a vague notion similar to that which Mr King afterwards possessed. But Boothroyd while reproducing Gent's engraving with even its lettering and references, makes one remarkable exception: he transfers this reference (No 11) to the Barn in the Outer Barbican (History of Pontefract 163, 164), thereby leading the reader, who might have seen Gent's volume also, to infer that he himself could not perceive any such cavity as that to which Gent refers: which perhaps was, in fact, the case. Thus each successive writer has added difficulty to difficulty, and contributed to obscure the original ground work of truth.

Little but the core of one end of the Flanker Wall now remains; and the southern side having been deprived of all its casing stones by the disintegrating effect of the winter sun to which it has been exposed from the south-west, is given with some effect, in the accompanying View of the Remains of Pontefract Castle (Taken 31 March, 1885).

On the inner side, however, where the wall had a northerly aspect, and where it had been during several generations partially buried by the accumulating soil, its condition is remarkable. It exhibits three states; in the upper courses the casing has entirely disappeared; while, in the more protected parts, the lower courses are still nearly as perfect as when the workmen placed them in position, probably six centuries ago. But a diagonal line across the wall, and therefore across certain particular stones, shows an intermediate condition, and exhibits in a striking manner the contrast between the perfect remains which have been preserved underground for several centuries, and those other portions of the construction which, not having been buried under the sloping artificial hill which concealed and protected the foundations of the Tower, have been exposed for many generations to the wind and rain.

It may be observed that on each side of the Flanker Wall, the engravings represent a rectangular bastion, having a battlement common to it and to the roundles which face the spectator. If such bastions ever existed, and we are inclined to believe they did, because, although we can perceive that considerable alteration has been made by successive copyists, we do not credit the original artist with any unnecessary creation,—that to the east has entirely disappeared; but the core of such an erection is still to be seen on the western side, and may be faintly discerned in the Photograph of the Remains, as a quadrangular centre to the circular roundel.

Since neither of the later engravings gives the faintest indication of any such construction, we are disposed, here again, to find evidence of an unsuspected accuracy in the medieval drawing.

Advancing towards the Great Gateway, as did the Lancaster Herald in the time of King Henry VIII (see page 342) the visitor passed to his left a retaining wall, which separated him from a platform of which, however, (the wall being in the engraving again dwarfed for our convenience) we are allowed to obtain a tolerably clear and distinct view. This platform is called in Siege Plan No. 1, "The Bowling Green"; though it is not sufficiently evident why that name was given to it. What was thus afterwards the Bowling Green is represented in the Engraving of the Society of Antiquaries as a rectangular enclosure, apparently of three grades of height, to which admittance could have been obtained from the opposite direction through a well-studded door, provokingly closed. This doorway appears to be at about the point where the recent excavations ceased in that direction, that is at that angle of the fortification which is nearly in a line between Piper Tower and the King's Seat; and if any slight remains of it exist, they are still buried.

The Great Gateway or Porter's Lodge is represented in the Engraving of the Society of Antiquaries as being approached between two curved walls, and as being faced by two semi-circular towers or quasi-bastions, concerning which there is no hint in either of the Siege Plans, on account of what appears to be the simple fact that they had been levelled before the sieges, and that that generation knew nothing of them. But as the excavations prove these to be correct representations, it is evident that the artist who figured them must have flourished at least previous to the seventeenth century, which knew nothing of them; and that no draughtsman later than the seventeenth century, could have represented them, except from an original which existed before that date. That original we conceive to have been the drawing from which the Society of Antiquaries took the engraving published by them in 1735, which thus exhibits so many features that had been absolutely hidden, to say the least for a very considerable time before the sieges.

The bases of the two curved walls which bounded the approach have however now been uncovered, and might easily have belonged to small ornamental towers exactly such as the print represents, that to the east having the wider sweep. Moreover the platforms on which the two semi-circular quasi-bastions stood are still in position, though the superstructure has quite disappeared; while the base of a similar semi-circular erection of rather larger radius which still remains in front of Piper Tower, having also been destroyed though not so thoroughly as those in front of the Great Gateway, serves to indicate clearly what kind of erections formerly stood in this latter position.

The small distance between the fore-building and the Tower, is however just sufficient to allow of a narrow slipe between them, to increase the accommodation of which the buttresses of the Porter's Lodge may have been mutilated.

It is remarkable that neither of the artists of the Siege Plans gives the slightest indication of either of these buttresses, though the fragment which still remains could never have been less than it is at present, and must at all times, after the removal of the forebuilding, have been quite as prominent as now.

There is one peculiarity about the construction of the curved walls, as shown in the engravings, which deserves notice. The inner of the two is represented as with but a small radius, and a solid basement; while the outer one, which is also considerably the higher, appears to have been in part built upon arches, at least three of which are represented by the artist. The recent excavations, however, were not at this point pursued so far as to show whether any of these, or any parts of either of them, remain beneath the surface.

To the east of these arches is figured a series of five steps or platforms, which might have been only the upper part of a casing wall; and there is also a group of three small gabled buildings, as to the intent or purpose of which there is no hint. These appear to have extended nearly to the then outer wall, and there is no indication in either of the Siege Plans of their existence. But as each of the Plans represents a building called indifferently the Great Lathe or the Barn, as occupying a somewhat corresponding position inside the Lower Wall, it may well be that this Great Lathe was the successor of the three buildings in the ancient drawing, removed into the new Barbican, at the time or after it had been taken in and added to the Castle grounds.

At the North Eastern angle of this enclosure — *THE BARBICAN* as distinguished from The Barbican of Siege Plan No 1—the difference of level between outside and inside is cleverly denoted in the engraving, the wall being shown clearly to be a retaining wall only. And the difference is, at this present, one of at least twelve feet, the inner level having been probably somewhat raised by the destruction of a Tower, now unrepresented, but which seems to have adjoined Constable Tower and to have given admittance to the Barbican from a small platform in front of the larger Tower.

This small Tower was the forerunner of the subsequently erected East Gate and its Drawbridge, which continued to the Demolition, which are figured on each of the Siege Plans, but of which the Print shows no trace, though their remains are still in the ground beneath the present road way. And as the Print absolutely ignores them, the only conclusion which can be drawn is that which we have already inferred, that they were of later date than the drawing

It is noteworthy that the wall running southward at this point, and its

continuation in that direction, constitute the present township boundary, as marked on the Ordnance Map, and as governing all local taxation. The group of five, in the 1776 print, are in fact standing in what is now the township of Pontefract, while the dog advancing towards them from the west in the foreground, which did not exist in the 1734 print but was added in that of 1776, is in the extra-parochial Castle Precincts, on land now enclosed, but which these drawings show to have been at the time an open roadway.

Constable Tower itself is represented on the engravings as a hexagonal building, entered from the Inner Ward or Ballium, at about half its height from the ground. But the two parallel oillet-holes in that part which the engraver figures as a lower story (like the similar apertures in the Round Tower) must be considered as due to his imagination only, for the basement of the Tower was nothing but solid rock, scarped and faced, unless indeed the Constable Tower could have been a hollow bastion built in advance of the rock. The present appearance of the remains, however, does not favour any theory that such was the case, while the construction of the adjacent Norman wall seems to preclude its possibility.

The engraving shows to the East of the building which we thus identify as Constable Tower, an octagonal segment, which it presents as level with the entrance to that Tower from the Ballium, as leading to a similar entrance to King's Tower, but as at a considerable height from the level of the foreground. Such, it must be constantly borne in mind by any one trying to understand the construction of the Castle, was the actual condition of the lower six, eight or ten feet of each of the Castle walls which faced the south: each was a scarped perpendicular, cased with stone; so that if the casing wall had been penetrated, only the solid rock would have been reached. This casing was in some parts very strong—near to Constable Tower, it may be even now seen to have been lined or backed with rough slabs of yellow marl, placed with one of the shorter ends outwards; and some feet of its base was generally concealed by a composition of clay and broken sandstone, which became naturally so covered with herbage, as to have the appearance of a grassy mound. A real wall was built above, which from below could not have been distinguished from a mere casing; but this upper wall was probably of no great height, so that though each appeared to be a wall some fourteen feet high when looked at from below, it was to those within, a mere battlemented screen of but six feet or even less. Considering which, it is easy to understand how John, the younger son of Henry de Lacy came by his death.* And it follows that undermining such a wall was almost an impossibility; for having completely penetrated what appeared to be the foundation, any miners would discover that they had reached but solid rock, and that a single blow of their tools would by its percussion betray their whereabouts.

At this point, however, that condition of the structure had not been developed at the time represented in the engraving. The rock, then unbuilt upon, but cased and with no further defence, was the site upon which was afterwards built the latest St. Clement's Chapel, that which existed till the Demolition, the eastern end of the plot being converted into an irregular chancel, abutting on the King's Tower. In this Chapel, a construction of Queen Elizabeth's time, or later, and on this site, were buried Sir Jervas Cutler, Capt. Paulden, Lieut. Smyth, and others who died during the sieges while the investment continued. But in ordinary times St Clement's Chapel, whichever its site, had no ecclesiastical right of burial, which was

* The great Earl of Lincoln lost each of his two sons by a violent death. Edmund was drowned in a draw-well in the Red Tower of the Castle at Denbigh; John fell over the battlements of Pontefract Castle.

possessed only by the neighbouring monastery, by the Parish Church, by St. Richard's Church from the thirteenth century, and by that of the Trinities in the fifteenth.

While every construction in this the Norman line of the south front of the Castle site, can thus be identified, Round Tower, Staircase, Great Gateway, Constable Tower, site of the Jacobean Chapel, site of King's Tower; very few of the buildings represented as in the Ballium can be pointed out as being the same with those in existence at the time of the sieges. Exception may perhaps be made in the case of the tower to the north-west of King's Tower, which has what appears to be intended for a Decorated doorway. This may have been Queen's Tower, and as (except a railed communication, consisting of a short flight of steps, preceded and followed by a short landing) there are in the Prints no indications of the range of buildings that afterwards connected it with the King's Tower, we may fairly assume that those buildings are of a later date, an assumption which the appearance of their remains recently uncovered clearly warrants.

But although this may have been the Queen's Tower or its predecessor, more probably it was a Tower, part of the base of which is still on the north side of the Norman Chapel, at a level some four feet higher, and to make room for which the Norman Chapel was levelled. The flooring of its lower room is still represented by Norman tiles, alternately purple and gold, the heraldic colours of Henry de Lacy's Earldom of Lincoln, OR ; a lion rampant, *purpure*.

The engravings place on the garth, three other buildings which have now entirely disappeared, leaving no trace of their purpose. These are (1) a small isolated structure having two single-light windows on the eastern side, and four on the south. It is not clear whether the artist intends to indicate a louvred roof, or a second building between this isolated structure and the Hall : but its position east and west gives much of an ecclesiastical character to the building, and this is increased by the addition of a cross to the east end. (2). To the south-west is a low hexagonal tower, nearly corresponding in design with Constable Tower ; and (3) there is an indication of a third building of still smaller height, only the upper part of which emerges. Of the first building, nothing more can be said ; but the second is in the position which would be occupied by a tower over the ventilating shaft of the magazine, while the third corresponds to the position of a supposed tower over its entrance, and is still represented by the remains of a circular staircase, a few steps down on the right hand of the descent. Careful examination at that point will also show that to allow of the construction of the upper part of the present staircase, a wall some 4ft thick of such a building has been cut through. No suggestion can be at present made as to what these buildings were, and only a conjecture can be offered as to the remaining erections which so gracefully fill the back ground. An octangular building with a square central tower occupies the site of Swillington Tower, which Thomas of Lancaster is said to have newly built (*i.e.* rebuilt) shortly before his death in 1321-2, and therefore, after the date we have assigned to the drawing. The building which appears on the print of the Society of Antiquaries, may thus be considered the thirteenth century Swillington Tower.

The two quadrilaterals which fill the upper centre are (1) one, of which a spacious square garderobe chamber, lately opened out, was the lower story. This was the Red Tower. And (2) a second to which a turret staircase, also recently opened out, would have led. This appears to have been on the site of what was afterwards Treasurer's Tower, and to have formed part of the eastern wall of the Hall, before it was converted into a Kitchen; but when that conversion had been made it became part of the line of division between the Kitchen and the latest Hall.

These two quadrilateral towers were connected by a walk which was sheltered by a screen wall, along the top of the old Norman wall of which so much has been for so long concealed. In front of this Norman wall may be seen the long, single-storied * building at this time a Hall, but which as we have pointed out, was afterwards converted into a kitchen. When the débris was removed in 1882, many tiles from the roof of this building were found in the rubbish. They were thin plates of Knottingley limestone, and specimens are in the Castle Museum.

The Hall was approached on the western side between two pinnacled buttresses, part of the more easterly of which can still be traced. This communication from the garth led to the main state entrance to the Hall, from the direction of the Keep, which was blocked when the Hall was converted into a kitchen, but the approach to which was at this time (cir. 1300) thus safe guarded. The entrance to this Hall from the garth was a few feet to the East, where in the 1734 engraving the door-opening extends to the ground, and where during the Kitchen period, advantage was taken of the convenient position to insert in the flooring a 3-inch water pipe of hammered lead, part of which was discovered in its bed during the recent excavations. In the south wall of this building, were two windows: and the interior distinctive masonry of each of these three openings can still be partially traced, though the face of the outer wall is now quite blank, being indeed a mere casing of a much later date.

And beside these two entrances to the Hall, from the south and from the west respectively, the engravings indicate one of a more stately character, from the east, from the direction of the state apartments in the two towers

---

* We viewed * * the large faire Kitchen, wch is long, wth many wide Chimneys in it."—Diary of Some Tourists in the North.—Lansdowne MSS 213, fo 318b.

on the south-west platform. The façade containing this entrance was flanked at its southern angle by a cylindrical tower on which, apparently under the supposition that it was a bell tower, the 1776 engraver has placed a plain elongated cross.

The whole of this front, however, disappeared when the latest Hall was built, and when the Hall of these engravings became the Kitchen of the establishment. It was in this apartment, that the seventeenth century Royalists set up their forges and their coining apparatus, the débris of which was found here when the rubbish was removed in 1882.

Behind this thirteenth century Hall, and beyond the broad Norman wall against which it was built, is a louvred structure, which we suggest to have been a second St. Clement's Chapel with its conventual buildings for four canons; in use during the time to which this engraving belongs, after the Norman Chapel was destroyed to permit of the construction of the King's Tower, and before a Chapel was erected on the octagonal site which alone was identified with its name in recent generations. This Chapel and its accompaniments would thus have been buildings exterior to the original Norman wall, but between it and the graft or moat. They probably remained till the Dissolution caused the confiscation of the revenues of the Chapel, which were after 1538 let to farm, and by Queen Elizabeth absolutely alienated, except so far as being subject to a payment of 6/8 per annum.* There was however probably

---

* Richard Jackson, in 1548, had a lease of the property for 21 years, at £6/10/- per year, which Queen Elizabeth renewed for a similar term, and in 1588 granted to Edmund Downing and Miles Dodding, at a rent of 6/8. These sold it the same year to Humphrey Mildmay and Thomas Crompton, who in the following year released it to Charles and Francis Jackson, who sold it almost immediately to John Bramhall. John Bramhall's son Peter sold part in 1615, to Richard Thwaites, and

an interval of more than half a century between the destruction of this medieval Chapel, about 1540, and the foundation of the Elizabethan or Jacobean structure on the octagonal segment in the eastern corner of the garth. The smaller building to the south of the Hall is indeed not unlike a Chapel, and it is possible that after examination it may prove that it was really the Castle Chapel; but on the whole we are at present inclined to look with favour on the suggestion that the Chapel had been rebuilt outside the Wall, on the site we have indicated.

Finally, the square battlemented tower behind the Porter's Lodge may be intended for Gascoigne Tower, that which contains the King's Chamber, and which, according to the evidences afforded by the excavation, seems to have been at one time converted into a cistern, or perhaps a bath. There is no intimation of the bakehouses and stables lately opened out at this angle, and it is probable that they did not exist till at least the time of John of Gaunt.

From the point of sight taken by the draughtsman, any view of Piper Tower would have been obstructed by the Round Tower, and it should be added that he gives us not the slightest indication of moat or ditch, either wet or dry.

There are still three buildings in these engravings, outside the Castle proper, which require identification; but in the absence of the original, and without a knowledge of the manner in which they have been manipulated by the engraver, we hesitate to name more than one of the three. That to the extreme left appears to be intended for a Church; which the 1734 engraver considers should have a solid four-square tower, surmounted by a thin spire, while he of 1776 gives it a broach steeple. In each case, however, the idea seems to be that St. Giles's in 1616 disposed of the remainder to Henry Frank, in whose family it has remained.

Church was the building intended. This, however, we cannot accept; for since in every other single respect we find the idea of relative distance adhered to in this remarkable drawing, we do not see why it should be deviated from in this one instance; and as St. Giles's Church is quite out of line, and besides being half-a-mile off, was behind the crest of the hill, while the Church of the engraving is only on the side of the ascent, and not nearly at the top, we cannot think that St. Giles's Church was intended. Nor is it the Church of the Trinities; firstly because Sir Robert Knolles's foundation did not exist at the time we have demonstrated to be represented by this print; and secondly because it also was out of the line.

Therefore, especially when noting that the body of the Church in the engraving runs north and south, and that the tower is at the north end, we can only suggest that the insertion of so inaccurate a building was a mere freak of the engraver, to be accounted for if ever the original should be traced. But we feel perfectly justified in asserting that no church ever existed on the spot thus indicated in the engraving, or (except that of the Trinity, subsequently) even near it, unless, indeed, it were the lost church of St. Michael, Foulsnape, which we consider to have been connected with the Bede-house. There is, however, a bare possibility, though no document has yet been exhumed which gives colour to the supposition, that St. Michael's Church might have been here, and that when it was secularized, as secularized it had been long before the Reformation, (whether by absolute alienation, or through absorption by some other religious community, is uncertain), the ecclesiastical duties of St. Ellen's and St. Michael's were combined in the same building, as they always had been performed by the same priest. Casual notices of the foundation are to be met with between about 1220 and about 1460, but there is nothing of later date, and no account of the original foundation, all record of which seems to have disappeared

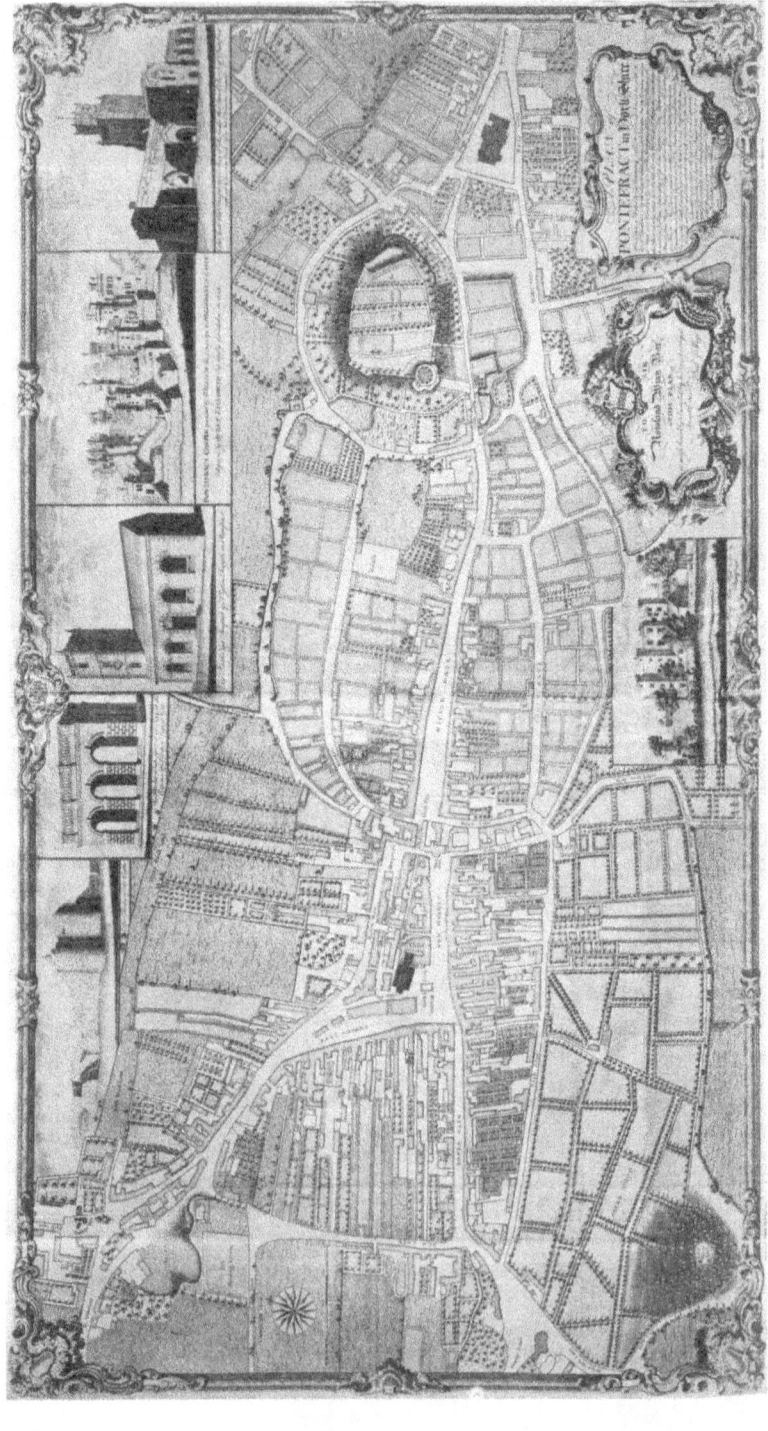

almost as thoroughly, as has the record and history of the Chapel of St. Nicholas, Cobcroft, in the parish of Womersley, which, like the Church of St. Michael, Foulsnape, was certainly in full action in the thirteenth century, but of which nothing more is known.

The ruined structure on the hill to the left of the engravings is a difficulty, almost equally with the church, for it is represented as being on the crest of Monkhill itself, where no building of the kind is known to have existed. But singularly enough, remains of just such an extensive erection in just about that spot have been recently disinterred. We may therefore fairly surmise, without much play of the imagination, that the artist has represented a building of the thirteenth or fourteenth century that has now utterly disappeared, and the very memory of which has passed away.

With regard to the third isolated building, we have less doubt. It has often been thought to represent All Saints' Church, but, on the principle we have laid down, that cannot be; for firstly All Saints', likewise, is out of the line of view ; and secondly, that Church was never at all like the building depicted in the engraving. In this case, however, we consider that the structure is not far to seek.

And to begin with, it may be observed that it is under King's Tower, with only a narrow roadway between, which the 1776 engraving entirely ignores. Now at the time represented by this engraving there was just such a building attached to St. Nicholas Hospital, which was dedicated to St. Ellen, and in which a priest had to officiate four days a week, the other three days being appropriated to the Chapel of St. Michael, Foulsnape. We are inclined therefore to think that the engravings give us a fair idea of the appearance which St. Ellen's Chapel presented at the close of the thirteenth century, a building of the type of a Hall Church, a parallelogram, with no aisles and no chancel.

It may indeed be objected, as throwing doubt on the accuracy of the representation, that this building, as figured in the later print, (that which is, perhaps, best known), has transoms to each of the two windows, which would be a manifest anachronism: for such transoms could not have existed in a thirteenth century building. But the fact is that, as may be seen in the reproduction now issued, there were no transoms in the 1735 engraving, which represents the windows as of good thirteenth century design, and entirely corresponding with those of the Kitchen within the Court-yard. This, as confirmatory of our theory of the date of the drawing, is exceedingly important.

Nor is it less satisfactory to find that on examining the site which the engraving thus assigns to St. Ellen's Chapel, we discover there a building of exactly the size and shape figured : a parallelogram of 30ft by 15ft, which might well be successor to the aisle-less chancel-less building of the engraving. Its site, moreover, still belongs to St. Nicholas Hospital by the same title of immemorial ownership through which the Trustees possess the Hospital itself. This is another remarkable corroboration of the correctness of our opinion on the point.

Though it so happens that any one seeking for an example of such a chapel as that which is thus represented as of St. Ellen, would have but to go to Wakefield to find an ecclesiastical building, in the shape of a parallelogram, with no aisles, with no constructional chancel, and in other respects the near counterpart of that represented in our engraving, even if of slightly larger dimensions. It was known as the "Chapel of our Lady on Wakefield Bridge ;" and though subsequently rebuilt, that Chapel is still on the old thirteenth century lines. In their general appearance, indeed, these two buildings must, at one time, have borne a very considerable resemblance to each other. At Wakefield, however, the Chapel was entered from the west, and its south side had three windows, while at Pontefract, although the south side had that number of openings, only two were for windows, one of them being used as a doorway : at Wakefield, the original Chapel had the fortune to be renewed, and succeeded by an ecclesiastical building ; but at both St. Nicholas, Cobcroft, and St. Ellen's, Pontefract, a stable or workshop was erected upon the old lines.

But between the dates of the two engravings which we have compared, in 1742, a Plan of Pontefract was issued by Mr Paul Jollage, which while representing the main features of the town with an accuracy tolerable but unfortunately not too strict, occupies the vacant spaces with engravings of a few of its noteworthy buildings, some being so absurdly inaccurate as to be little better than caricatures. One, of the Round Tower, is very bad ; that of the Castle Buildings is good, we may say singularly good, and one of All Saints Church is superior to many which have been issued of that building. The engraving of the Castle, in the main follows the 1735 engraving, from which, however, it differs in several points in the very respects in which the 1776 engraver "improved" upon him of 1735. As Mr Marsden afterwards did, Mr Jollage placed a slight foreground in front of the wall, but no dog : his Hall windows are, correctly, without the transoms which Mr Marsden introduced ; his roundels are without setoffs ; in the retaining wall between the Round Tower and the Porter's Lodge, he suggested a doorway which Mr Marsden afterwards correctly disallowed ; and he effaced the buildings outside the line of the fortress. Finally, in the description at foot, Mr Jollage retained, from the 1735 print, the word "totally," the use of which Mr Marsden afterwards discarded, when he had viewed the Remains.

It is very curious that Mr Jollage thus anticipated Mr Marsden in so many respects ; but the actual truth may be that the latter, while adopting many of these "improvements," exercised an independent power of selection, and refused to accept, or be bound by them all.

In all probability, however, each was guided by the drawing itself, which was then, as it is not now, producible. And in justification of our hope that the drawing from which the artist of 1735 drew inspiration may still be found, we note that when in 1753, a similar engraving of Sandal Castle was published in Vetusta Monumenta II xl, it was heralded by the following remark : "This Print was engraved from a drawing taken in the reign of Queen Elizabeth, and *still preserved* in the Dutchy of Lancaster, with several other draughts of Antient Castles, 6 of which *have been already published* by the Society in the 1st vol. of their Vetusta Monumenta." This evidently implies that the "draught" of Pontefract Castle was in existence so late as 1753. We cannot therefore resist the impression which we have already expressed that it is now in the Public Record Office, under the care of the Master of the Rolls, and among the unexamined and uncatalogued documents transferred from the Duchy Office in 1868. The officials at the Record Office, however, at present know nothing of it.

Thus concludes what we wish to say concerning the different engravings of the Castle itself ; it remains that we should say a few words with regard to the various published Siege Plans.

Of these, three have been given to the world, which we now reproduce, that which we have called No. 1 being the earliest in publication. It is by one of the Basires,* it has no date,

* There seem to have been four engravers of the name of Basire ; three of the name of James and one of Isaac, the name Basire and the occupation of engraver having been coupled for four generations. The earliest was Isaac, an engraver of maps, who flourished in the early part of the eighteenth century. His son James became engraver to the Society of

and it was published in 1750, or a year or so later; that published by Boothroyd in 1807, and afterwards adopted by Fox, with slight alterations, not always amendments, was the second in order of publication, and that issued by the Surtees Society from the Drawing in the possession of Lord Galway may be called No. 3.

No. 1, which is a bold well-executed production, from a plate about 30 inches by 20, professes to be "from a drawing found in the possession of a descendant of the Fairfax family of Denton"; but nothing is known of the original. A letter in the British Museum (Addl MSS., 6210) from Francis Drake the antiquary, and dated York, Nov. 21, 1753, speaks of it as recently published. The writer referring to it says "The drawing of Pontefract," ["Published by Soc. Ant. Vol. 1, No. 42, Vetusta Monumenta" is added incorrectly by another hand] "was taken from one still in the Fairfax family, and was done at that time to let the General, who was at that time in the South Countrey, see how the Siege was carried on." This is a very probable explanation; but if it is the correct one, it does not express the whole truth, for the works are all named as they were held by the various commanders in the last Siege, that of 1648-9, and not at that in which General Fairfax commanded.

It may well be, however, that the drawing was roughly taken for the siege of 1644-5, and adapted for that of 1648. The besieging works were, of course, at each siege in the same positions, as shown by the present evidence

Antiquaries in 1760, and died in 1802. A second James died in 1822, and a third, born in 1796, who, like his father and grandfather was the engraver to the Society of Antiquaries, died so recently as 1869. The Siege Plan, which bears no date of publication, may probably be attributed to the first James, and as it was published before he became engraver to the Society of Antiquaries, it may have helped to secure him the appointment.

of the ground itself, a soft sandstone with, in most places, only an inch or two of surface soil; and the trenches where there were any such, which were hollowed out of the solid, still exist at a short distance from the surface.

In the first siege, that raised on March 1, 1644-5, by the battle in the Chequers (see p. 29), the works had been few, the principal being that " in Mr Lund's back yard," which battered down Piper Tower; and few of those represented on Basire's plan could have existed before June 1645, as is evident from the detailed list we have given in the Index (pp. xxxv, xxxvi.) Indeed as we have already pointed out, the drawing itself, if taken on the spot, was taken with no pretence at exactness, and is incorrect in many details, mistakes being made which could have been possible to no one who knew the ground. For instance, within the walls, the road from Southgate to the Porter's Lodge is represented as being a straight ascent, with no hint of the great difference of level between the two Barbicans: the names of King's and Queen's Towers are transposed; there is no Main Guard, or any building on its site; the Flanker Wall starts from the wrong angle; and even a prominent object like Mr Warde's house on the opposite side of the graft (see p. 28), from which the besiegers attempted to mine towards the Round Tower, and whence Mr Warde communicated by word of mouth with the besieged (see p. 109), is entirely ignored.

There are many other minor inaccuracies of detail: while the ground plans, without the walls, (not only of New Hall, but of All Saints Church and even St. Giles's Chapel) are misrepresented; the arms are figured without the label of Lancaster (the helmet. that of a sovereign, would indicate one of the early Edwards); most of the works are at points which were never occupied; and even the "Deus" on the siege coin is represented by " Dius". But yet the print, if only a concoction (and it is to be feared that its pretended origin is very apocryphal) was sufficiently accurate for its purpose, which was to give a realistic idea of the Siege to the general public of the eighteenth century, not over careful as to details, but principally anxious to have within their reach something which might tend to bring more nearly home to them, a condition of things which had inflamed their imaginations. For to them Col. Fairfax, or the great General himself, were equally but names; Cromwell's fort or Cromwell's foot was equally definite; while Forts, Works and Guards were one and the same thing. To such complacent absence of knowledge, Basire's print with its bold lines, and its houses all facing the spectator, was exceeding realistic: while the important fact that its supposed trenches cut bodily through the two streams at four different points was a detail of not the slightest consequence and which disturbed in no degree the equanimity of the student.

The style of the engraving was less unnatural than that afterwards adopted by Mr Jollage, which had all the unreal primness of those Dutch landscape gardeners, who were patronised by King William and the early Georges; and the ground plan itself, although a little out of perspective, is by no means bad. It represents the two streams which give its peninsular character to the tongue of land on which the Castle and Town are built; and the streets themselves are depicted with fair accuracy, especially on the west or town side, although the thoroughfare opposite Neat Market (now Beastfair)—Blue Bell Yard, we presume—is represented as a street of houses, which it never was. The siege works themselves are, however, transparently inaccurate, when considered in relation to the ground plan; and the trenches are in some instances represented as being in places where such could not have existed. This species of inaccuracy, which it possesses in common with No. 3, though developed differently, we shall attempt to account for later on.

No. 2, Boothroyd's print, published in 1807, was a well-intentioned attempt to correct what was manifestly amiss in Basire's. But in his correction, the draughtsman seems to have drawn considerably upon his imagination. Finding that certain of the works could not have occupied the position assigned to them, he transfered them to what he imagined to be their proper place; and then in order to display a connection between them, which probably never existed, he depicted the trenches as going not only across streams as his predecessor had done, but through hills and behind elevations which would have effectually prevented any attempts at bombarding the Castle from some of the forts. His references are (1) the Round Tower, (2) the Red Tower, (3) Treasurer's or Pix Tower (he means Pi*per*, but misreads the contraction, and in his mis-reading has been servilely followed by men who must have known better, had they exercised their critical faculty for a single moment), (4) Swillington Tower, (5) Queen's Tower, (6) King's Tower, (7) Constable's Tower, (8) East Gate House, (9) South Gate, (10) Main Guard, (11) Barbican, (12) All Saints' Church, (13) St Nicholas' Hospital, (14) Major General Lambert's Fort Royal, (15) Horse Guard, (16) Horn Work, (17) Pinfold Guard, (18) Main Guard, (19) School House Guard, (20) Fairfax's Royal Horn Work, (21) North Horn Work, (22) Colonel Bright's Fort, (23) Lieutenant General Cromwell's Fort, (24) Colonel Dean's Fort, (25) Tanalian Guard, (26) East Guard, (27) Baghill Guard. And to these numberings it will, perhaps, be found convenient if we adhere.

His plan of the town is as accurate as possible for his own time; but as it is a copy only slightly altered of Hepworth's, published in 1777, it represents the buildings as they were at that date, or later, and not as in 1645 or 1648. Bearing in mind, however, this initial defect, which is no imputation of general inaccuracy, it was not distorted as Jollage's and Basire's were; and we have accordingly made it the basis for a plan of the works, such as our own personal investigation of the actual soil has in almost each case

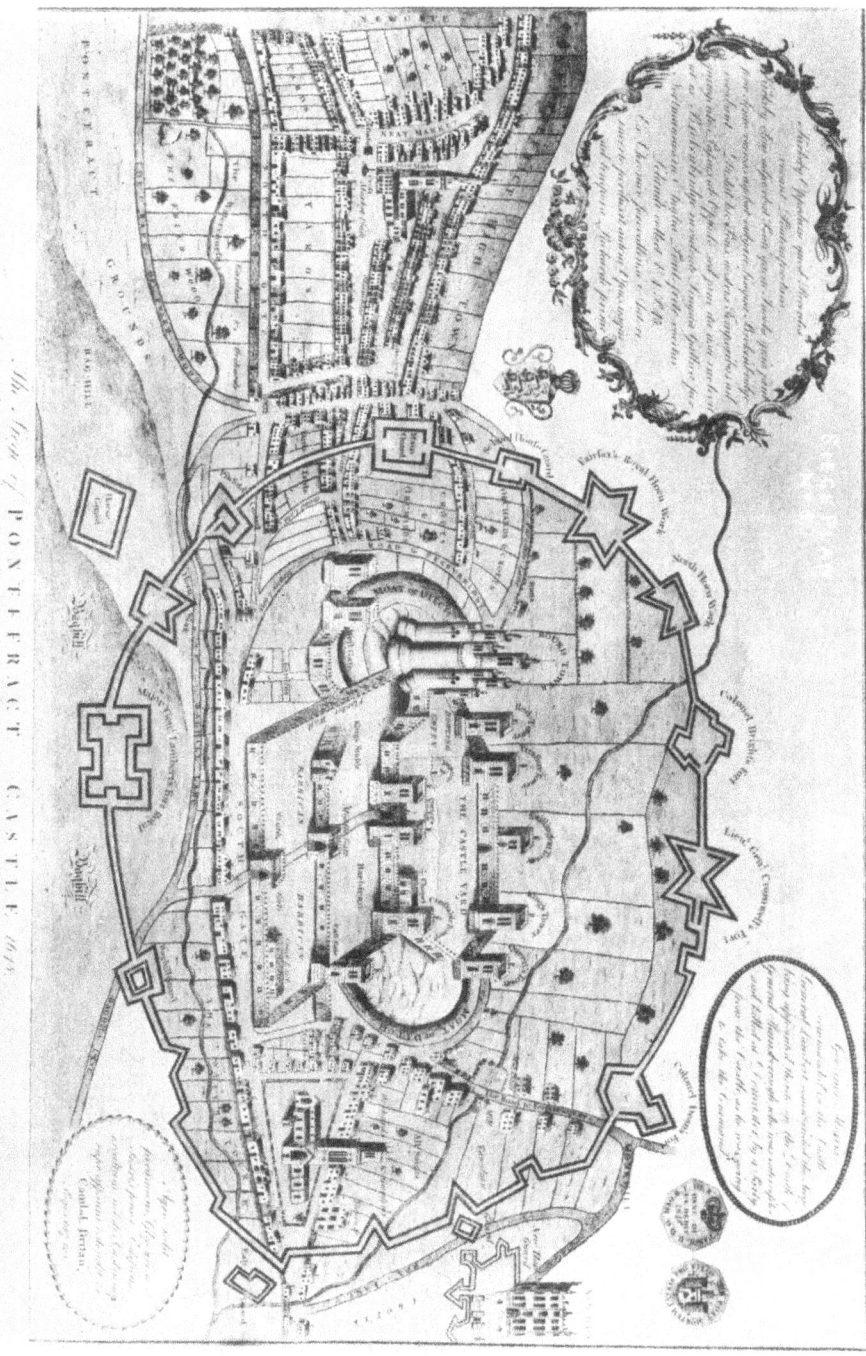

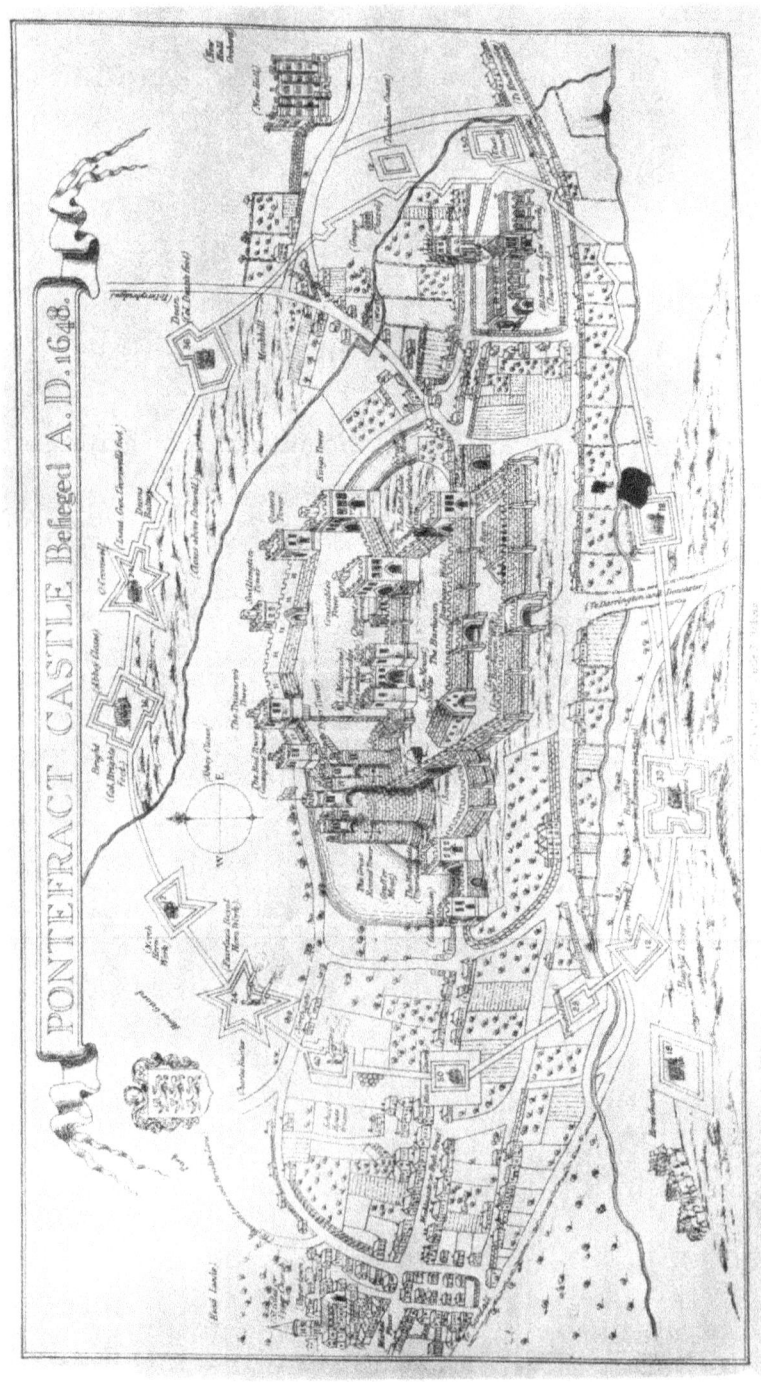

PONTEFRACT CASTLE Besieged A.D. 1645.

From the original at Serlby Hall, Bawtry. By Permission of the RIGHT HON. LORD VISCOUNT GALWAY, Lineal Descendant in the 7th Generation of COL. PHILIP MONCKTON (see pp. 179, 243, 245, and 320).

1. The Great Round Tower.
2. The Red Tower.
3. The Treasurer's Tower.
4. Swillington Tower.
5. Queen's Tower.
6. King's Tower.
7. Constable's Tower.
8. Porter's Lodge.
9. The Stables.
10. The Barn.
11. The West Gate.
12. The East Gate.
13. The Barbican.
14. Mickle Gate.
    The Great Street that goes down to the Castle from the Town.

The Hill to the South is call'd Baghill.
That on the North side is Monkhill.

ascertained their real position to have been; and we shall accordingly find ourselves called upon to speak more fully upon his Siege Plan in a final section. It is, however, so bad and faulty, that no mere criticism will meet the circumstances. We shall be compelled to contrast it with the facts, in a more forcible manner.

Siege Plan, No. 3, is from a copy of a draught which has been in the possession of Lord Galway, and his ancestors, for several generations. Although published latest, (by the Surtees Society, in 1861) it was probably the earliest drawing; for, as we have intimated, our faith in the history of No. 1 is not implicit.

The original, which by the kind permission of Lord Galway we have examined carefully, and now reproduce, appears to have had at least three stages. The nucleus was probably a draught of the Castle, slightly conventional. This however could not have been drawn from the Castle itself, as it represents each of the Barbican Walls with buttresses which never existed, and it shows no Main Guard, a building which has stood on the multangular base from at least 1500 till now, and which must have presented itself to anyone sketching the building *in situ*. But this part of the drawing appears to us to have been the original of No. 1 (Basire's), in which, however, the buttresses were properly omitted, and the details much "improved," being still further conventionalised by the incorrect addition of embrasures to the walls, even to those which as we have seen were mere casings of solid rock. Numbers are also placed above the various buildings corresponding with a list in the space at the upper corners of the drawing, and which are different to those afterwards adopted by Roothroyd. Lord Galway's list of references is:—

1 The great round Tower
2 The red Tower
3 The Treasurer's Tower
4 Swillington Tower
5 Queen's Tower
6 King's Tower
7 Constable's Tower
8 Porter's Lodge
9 The Stables
10 The Barn
11 The West Gate
12 The East Gate

13 The Barbican
14 Mickle Gate : The Great Street that goes down to the Castle from the Town.
The Hill to the South is call'd Baghill : That on the North side is Monkhill.

This list is repeated on a slip affixed to the canvas at the back of the drawing, with the single difference that on the latter, Bag hill is given as two words.
None of this writing has, however, come up well in the Photograph.

To the buildings of the fortress itself, Lord Galway's drawing also added the nearest siege works, and these were connected by Trenches; but the drawing shows no signs of the more distant works, or of any other trenches than those supposed to connect each work with its immediate neighbours.

Such a Ground Plan of the Castle with the besiegers' trenches alone seems to have been the original intention of the drawing; and it must have been full of interest to the descendants of Sir Philip Monckton, of whose doings at the last siege it was so lively a reminder; because, even if originally drawn with reference to the 1645 siege, it equally answered for that of 1648, with the early part of which Sir Philip Monckton's memory is associated.

But there is a very singular circumstance with respect to its condition, which well deserves notice. The original label in red ink (referring to this ground plan only, as we have already said) was
"PONTEFRACT CASTLE,
Besieged A.D. 164 ... "
And the three dots show that the draughtsman doubted what should be the unit. " 5 " was afterwards added at some much later date, for the character of the figure 5 is of quite

fifty years later, and it is also traced in a slightly darker shade of colour than that used in "164." But a keen eye can easily detect the difference; while the dots with which the blank was originally supplied, show in addition that the "164..." was not a mere momentary hesitation, but was at one time intended to be the permanent representation of the date.

To judge from the character of this lettering, the drawing cannot be of a date much if any earlier than 1700. The A in Pontefract is very wide at the base; the s in Besieged is long-shaped, and forms a double letter with the i, the dot being common to both. The e is very narrow at the top, the sector being hardly a fourth of the diameter, while the top of the figure 1 which covers a very acute angle, terminates in a point. And most of these are indications of an eighteenth rather than a seventeenth century style.

This was the first stage of the drawing. The second introduced considerable confusion, and a destruction of one of the unities; for to the design, now with the label presenting the date definitely as 1645, were attached the names of the commanders in 1648, while to make the whole correspond the better with this addition, the date of the Plan in the Surtees Copy was also altered to 1648.

Several subsequent alterations were made; the earliest addition to the group of buildings within the Castle walls being a distorted plan of the town, each part of which taken by itself is tolerably accurate, though its relation to the rest is, so to say, not perfect. For instance, Broad Lane and the Trinities were each represented with fair accuracy, but they were made to face each other from opposite sides of Micklegate, although a distance of quite a hundred yards separates them; and there are many other similar incongruities in the plan, attributable in each case, as we venture to think, to the attempt to fix theoretically the position of the streets of a town on a Siege Plan which was not prepared or attempted to be prepared with the necessary mathematical accuracy.

But there was still another and more remarkable addition, which we could hardly think to be placed without authority, and as a mere matter of guesswork, but yet we seek in vain for the source from which the information could have been obtained. We allude to the various numbers (12 18 24 28 30 36 40 50 150) which were at the same time added to the various works, apparently to show the supposed strength of the force in each case; and the different symbols which were intended to indicate whether the work was occupied by foot or by horse; whether it was a battery; and if so, whether there was a store of ammunition. According to this guide, (which we doubt not to be trustworthy, although we fail to trace the authority) besides one outlying in that part of the Park, which was divided into closes by the Park Act of 1780, and where all traces of the encampment have been long since ploughed up, the only Horse Guard was that at Baghill, and the only batteries were that near the School House Guard, and the Fort commanded by Col. Fairfax, each symbolised by a couple of cannon, vomiting a volume of smoke towards the Round Tower. But Lord Galway's plan is silent as to the "Forts" held by Col. Bright, O. Cromwell and Col. Dean, according to Basire, though it indicates the positions supposed to be held by those commanders. These useful additions were probably filled in by tradition some time after the original sketch of the Siege Plan itself.

But at a still later stage in the history of the drawing, some of the streets of the town were placed on it in the discordant unharmonious fashion to which we have alluded, and the several Towers of the Castle were named, adopting Basire's inaccuracy of Queen's for King's; while a compass had been at some time added which, however, points several degrees west of the true North; and an earl's helmet had been inserted over the original shield with the unlabelled three lions of England, the arms of the King.

Notwithstanding all this, there are very many minute touches of accuracy

SUPPLEMENT.

about the drawing which show that the draughtsman had much local knowledge, a fact which makes us the more surprised at the indications of inaccuracy, which should have been shown by no one who knew the place well. For instance, what is called Grange Chapel is figured as it never could have existed, and certainly not in the Cromwellian period; since the building intended to be represented would have been the Church of St John, which was a part of the Priory, and which shared with the whole of the conventual buildings a common destruction, so complete that unless in the wall of the enclosure, and in the fabric of the New Hall, not a stone of the whole remains; and this destruction had taken place long before either of the Sieges. Thus the building, in fact, never existed alone, and while it was in being, it could have presented no such appearance as that given to it in this drawing; for at least the lower part of the south side of the structure would necessarily have been concealed by the buildings connected with the Cloister of the Priory; and when they were destroyed it would have perished with them: for each was but a part of the same whole.

The representation here given of the Chapel must therefore be altogether apocryphal, or symbolical, and yet as we shall see, a later drawing not only adopts it, but still further "improves" upon it by adding a south porch. The houses about St. Nicholas Hospital, and its Chapel (which is indicated by a small cross at the east and west ends) are indeed placed with some accuracy, though it must be confessed that St. Ellen's Chapel itself is much too far to the north. This is in great and gratifying contrast to Basire's print, in which the whole of this quarter is, as we have pointed out, so distorted as to be utterly unrecognizable, while it makes no attempt to indicate even the position of Grange Chapel.

There is, however, still one other independent Siege Plan, which has not hitherto been published, but which we are now able by the courteous permission of the Society of Antiquaries to include in the present Collection. It bears its history on its face, professing to be an exact copy of an original drawing in the possession of Mr. Recorder Frank, a prominent member of that Society in the middle of the 18th Century. That original seems to have been framed and glazed, and to have belonged to Dr. Drake in 1745. It was possibly the same which Gent "had seen" in 1730, had "had" in 1735, but had parted with to Dr. Drake during the next ten years.* Dr. Drake is stated in Gough's British Topography, to have shown the Society of Antiquaries "such an one" framed and glazed in 1745, which may thus be the drawing which afterwards came into the possession of Mr Frank. But wherever he obtained it, Mr. Frank fortunately presented a copy to the Society in 1759, but he appears to have retained the original in his own possession, and nothing is now known of it. It has long disappeared from Campsall, which is much to be regretted; for, so far as we can judge from the copy, and supposing this to be "exact," and not "improved," it seems to have been a very careful production, and in some respects more accurate than the drawing belonging to Lord Galway, or than Basire's print. It is more accurate than the former in the absence of buttresses to the Castle Walls, and differs from the latter in (correctly) omitting the embrasures; while it excels both in its general plan of the town, which is worked out with very considerable accuracy.

---

* History of York, 1730, p. 251: —"It had a stately Castle * * * of which I have seen a fair prospect, as also of the Town, beautifully done in Vellom, resembling its antient glory." —Annales Hullini, 1735, p. 168:—"I have a Prospect of the Castle, the antient Inheritance of the Duke of Lancaster, then a most beautiful Structure." Gent enumerates the Towers, King's, Queen's, Constable's, Swillington's, &c., but does not mention Piper's.

Indeed, except that it ignores the approach to the Castle from the South, by Baghill Lane or Darrington Road, as it was indifferently called, and represents Baghill as continuous, it includes every feature which either of the others presented. It has "Grange Chappel," though the building is placed too far to the south, and never could have had a south aisle with such windows as are represented; for they would have overlooked the cloisters, and interfered with the monastic cells on that side. Nor could it have had any Porch, as the Cloisters themselves would have practically been the Porch to the Church. The Grange Chapel, as it is called, is thus certainly, like the corresponding building in Lord Galway's drawing, only conventional; a pure draught upon the imagination.

In the Castle yard, moreover, two cannons are exhibited, which are on neither Lord Galway's plan nor that by Basire, and the Market Cross is represented, as in Basire, by an obelisk, surmounted by a small cross, and not by the Market House, which existed at the date of the drawing. A gallows is figured at the Hemp Cross; there is an attempt to represent a "Butts" at the end of Back Northgate, and the whole is headed "The Seige of Pontefract Castle, Dec 25, 1648."

Mr. Frank's drawing has, in addition, the figures denoting the numerical strength of the besiegers at the various works, which are not on Basire's print, and in which it entirely agrees with Lord Galway's; thus evidencing a common origin; it has Skinner Lane and Paradise Lane, neither of which is on Lord Galway's drawing; while it accurately places the trench of the School House Guard on the old road, which nearly bisected the present square within the Militia Depot, a road which was the boundary of the townships of Tanshelf and Pontefract, but of which, as using Hepworth's later plan, Boothroyd knew nothing.

But Mr. Frank's plan rivals both Basire's and Lord Galway's in the extraordinarily incorrect position which it also assigns to the South Porch of the Old Church,* as may be seen by the comparison we are now enabled to institute, of the Print with our own recently taken View.

All three Plans, however, agree in the number and names of the Besiegers' works, in ignoring Piper Tower, and in the relative positions which they assign to the other Towers of the Castle, except that Basire reverses the position of those called King's and Queen's. Each with equal inaccuracy, shows the Chapel of St. Clement to the

---

* In the library of the British Museum (K xliv 43b) is a View of the Old Church, intended to embody Gent's account that the lantern was ornamented with "the effigies of eight Apostles standing on pedestals, joined to the several corners, while the four corners of the square were enriched with the effigies of the Four Evangelists." The print is before letters, and was probably never published. In any case, this is the only copy extant, so far as we know; it represents the chancel with a small cross at the east end, none being on the south chapel, which is figured as with three bays. This print appears to be the original of the view of the Church in the plans both of Lord Galway and Mr Frank, each of which places the south Porch much too far to the west, and cramps the most westerly window of the south aisle excessively. This Museum print gives the small turret at the S.W. corner, and what may be intended for an entrance to it from the lean-to roof of the north aisle. But it represents the whole with general accuracy, though it places above the tower an intended octagon lantern, *five* sides of which are towards the spectator, each such side being represented with two figures on it, with their arms in various attitudes, one holding a sword, others in the attitude of benediction, more or less defined, &c. The engraving bears a blank inscription tablet, enclosed within a wreath, and it gives the double staircase; though like the turret with proportions somewhat attenuated.

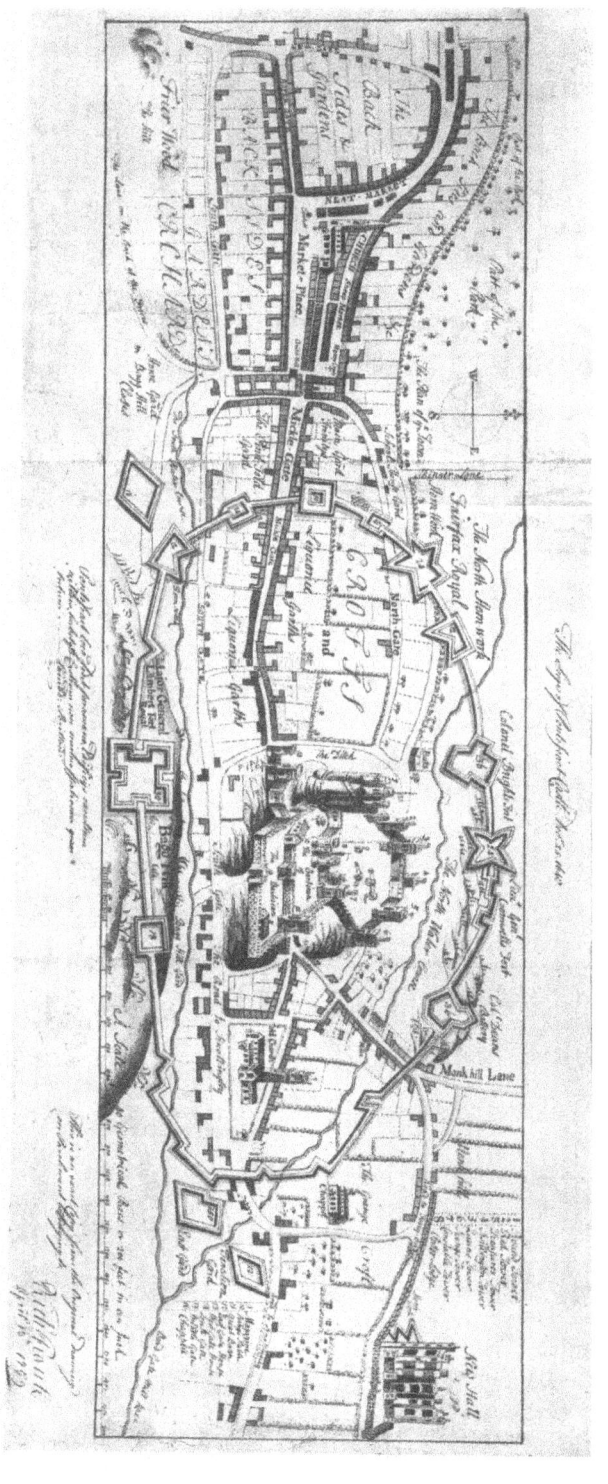

FROM THE DRAWING PRESENTED TO THE SOCIETY OF ANTIQUARIES ON APRIL 15TH 1759, BY RICHARD FRANK, F.S.A. OF CAMPSALL HALL, RECORDER OF PONTEFRACT AND DONCASTER.

From "A Comprehensive Dissertation on the Ancient and Present State of Pontefract" in the Appendix to "Historia Conpendiosa Romana," by Thomas Gent. (See pp. 417–418.)

A South Prospect of the ancient Castle of PONTEFRACT, Churches, &c.

A South West Sketch of All-Saints.

A Skeech of the Ruins of the Old Church, dedicated to *All-Saints*.

Sic transit Gloria Mundi.

A. A Sketch of the Market-Cross, before it was finish'd at the Top, &c.
B. Grainge-Chapel, built near Pontefract.
C. A smaller Sketch of New-Hall.

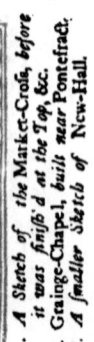

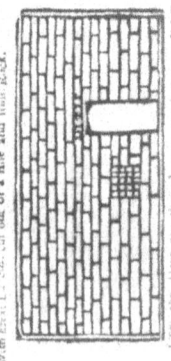

SUPPLEMENT.

west of Constable's Tower; while only Lord Galway's is at all accurate with regard to the distance between the last named Tower, and its eastern neighbour, and each appears to place Swillington Tower immediately outside the Castle Wall.

But finally, Mr Frank's drawing is dated Dec. 25, 1648, a date inconsistent with the facts of the siege. For Cromwell never had a fort before the Castle, and certainly not on that day, as he went to London early in the month and returned no more, while the Guns, as we know, (see p. 210,) were not in position till the beginning of February. The Surtees copy of Lord Galway's drawing changes the word "fort" as given by Basire, to "foot," with even less apparent reason: for Cromwell had always been a horse soldier, and as Lieutenant-General of the kingdom, it was not likely that he would have been at the time in command of a body of foot; though indeed it must be remembered that one regiment of foot before the Castle was known as the Lord General's foot, i.e. as belonging to Lord Fairfax himself (see p. 192). But there was no pretence that he was there to command it.

In this respect, we note that Lord Galway's View is perfectly accurate, while it most carefully indicates one point, which each of the others left obscure: the Royal Horn Work, called "Fairfax's," without qualification, both in Basire's engraving, and in Mr Frank's drawing, as if named after the Lord General himself, is correctly marked in Lord Galway's drawing as "*Charles* Fairfax's." This was the Colonel Fairfax, son of the first lord and brother to the second, upon whose promised help the Royalists had counted with confidence, but who, at the supreme moment, raised a regiment of foot to act against them (see p. 303); and whose troops were quartered in the town during the siege. This was the Fairfax, who, as we learn from a note of Roger Dodsworth's, supplied him with his copy of the Pontefract charters, which he had himself obtained from Boniface Savage. The appearance of his name on this drawing is thus an instance of careful discrimination by some one who knew of, and wished to provide against a latent mistake likely to mislead any one who had not the benefit of local knowledge. That it has misled many goes without saying; but the fact is that Lord Fairfax's movements during almost every day of the time occupied by the last siege of Pontefract Castle can be well accounted for; and it is perfectly certain that he was not on the ground at the time, far less in charge of any of the works, even though the regiment which was called after his name might have been there.

Before concluding these remarks upon the Maps and Plans, we must notice that the painstaking Thomas Gent published without date, about 1750, an 8-page tract, containing a small engraving of Grange Chapel, as he seems to have been the first to call it. This tract is frequently to be met with bound up in various volumes; and as it is with no particular assigned place, its appearance rather favours the supposition that towards the close of his life, when he was really hard bestead for means to supply his ordinary wants, Thomas Gent issued his volumes in whatever way he thought most likely to catch a stray customer. For instance, our own copy of the volume *Historia Compendiosa Romana*, which is lettered at back "History of England," and is without the 8-page tract, contains only to page 50 of the Appendix, pp. 23 to 43 of which is the Compendious History of Pontefract. In the Museum copy the tract to which we refer precedes page 23, while at the end of the volume is a tract on Judas Iscariot dated 177-. So that that particular volume could not have been completed till after that date. The Museum Catalogue, however, gives 1741 as the year in which the volume is printed, while ours is dated 1739, though it can be easily seen that the imprint in this case is on an erasure.

Gent's drawing of what he called "Grange Chapel," could have been nothing like the original, which as we have stated was a conventual building; and as it had a range of cloisters to the south, it is evident that it could have had neither Porch nor low windows on that side, and the drawing can be only the result of a draught upon the artist's imagination.

The same 8-page Tract also gives a "South Prospect" of the Castle, very much like Mr. Frank's as afterwards adopted by Boothroyd: and was the first to transfer 11 ("Horreum Spatiosum") which should have been above the cesspool in the Round Tower to the Barn in the Barbican, translating the title into "Spacious BARN." It has besides, an engraving of the "Ancient Hermitage," consisting of a masoned wall with a doorway and a barred window, the transom over the doorway having the inscription D.I.T.I.S. (Deo in Trinitate : Jesu the Saviour.) This is now however, walled up, and there is not the smallest indication of its existence.

Gent gives also a view of All Saints Church with the Porch too far to the West, as in the British Museum View, and with *three* stages to the Tower; although the following description appended allows for only two. "The Height of the Steeple to the first Battlement is 28 yards 1 foot 5 inches : From thence to the second Battlements, 7 yards 3 quarters ; and 8 yards more to the apex of the Cross or Spire." Thus self-contradictory have been so many of these early views.

As this present Collection includes a copy of Jollage's Map, it seems necessary to add to what has been already said concerning the vignettes which accompany it, that its Plan of the Town is very good, bringing out clearly its Danish type with the accompanying plateau to the west ; but though the groups of buildings are drawn with very fair accuracy, the enclosures outside seem to be generally depicted with more endeavour at picturesqueness than accuracy; while some of the few names it gives are applied with extraordinary confusion, transferring "Wakefield Road" from Penny Lane to Halfpenny Lane ; Bondgate Wash from Knottingley Road to Monkhill, and calling Church Lane, Salter Row. The Plan has, however, a very distinct merit, and is by no means an inartistic production. Imprints at foot (which however, are so much reduced by the photograph as almost to require a magnifying glass) state that it was "Surveyed and Drawn by Paul Jollage 1742," and "Engraved by John Pine."

The production was dedicated to Sir Rowland Winn, and if published at or soon after the date it bears, to the fourth Baronet, the second Sir Rowland of that name, in lineal succession, who was then in mourning at the recent decease of his wife, Susannah Henshaw, a descendant of the great statesman, Sir Thomas More, whose portrait, painted by Holbein, is to this day, perhaps the most celebrated of the remarkable collection at Nostell.

We should note that this Map fixes the site of the old "Presbiter Chapel," at Pontefract, within whose walls was buried the Cromwellian minister, Joseph Ferrett, who seceded soon after the Restoration, (April, 1661), and established in Tanshelf Court, a separatist congregation which was afterwards removed to Newgate, to the site marked in Jollage's Map. But no memorial seems ever to have been erected to one who is frequently but inaccurately alleged to have been "ejected" in 1662, and to have been one of the memorable Two Thousand. The simple fact is that he resigned his position as Minister of Pontefract, sixteen months before the historical St. Bartholomew's day.

It may be as well to state that observing a statement that there had been at some time, a view of Pontefract Castle in the Ashmolean Museum, we have made application there and been assured that no such drawing is known to be in the custody of the Trustees.

Having thus considered the various Plans and Maps, and pointed out their individual inaccuracy, we come in due course to indicate the real position of the various Siege Works as proved by actual excavation. And in order to do this, it will be first convenient to say a few words as to the general arrangement of the town, which is well shown on Boothroyd's Plan (No 2). Its original design is of a type common to many English towns of Danish origin, which seem to have been planned for strategical purposes by an organized body of military invaders rather than to have grown in a natural way, to meet the gradually increasing wants of their inhabitants. The nucleus of a typical Roman town was a central cross, where two streets crossed at right angles, as at Worcester and Doncaster, Oxford and Gloucester. But the typical Danish town as constantly consisted of a main street debouching at the centre of one end on a wide open area, otherwise entered at the corners alone; both main street and area being flanked by one, two or three concentric streets, which do not communicate throughout their whole length; while the spaces between these main lines are partitioned into long plots, the lines of division having in each case an angular twist "like a dog's hind-leg," in the direction away from the point to be strategically defended. Such are Pontefract, Knaresborough, Northallerton, Thirsk, and Wakefield, all Danish towns in this kingdom of Northumbria.

In Pontefract, the original town and the seat of population in Saxon times had been at Bondgate, near the Old Church, and generally to the east of the Castle area, within the angle of confluence of the converging brooks. To this was added, apparently in the eighth or ninth century, a distinct town, of the type we have indicated, the main street of which received the name of Micklegate, the Great Street—for in these Danish towns a " gate " is a "street." (And accordingly in the deed by which Sir Robert Knolles purchased the property on which he intended to build Trinity Hospital, the land was said to be *in magno vico*.) This Micklegate was flanked to the north by Northgate and Paradise Lane, the position of which is much distorted on Basire's print, while it disappears altogether in Lord Galway's; to the south it had Garden Lane, or Southgate as it has been differently called at different times. If therefore Micklegate be somewhat roughly compared to the body of a saurian, the parallel thoroughfares to it would correspond with the legs of the animal; and the central tableland which formed the area would be its head. This area, rather of the shape of a truncated triangle, originally extended to Salter Row, the whole of the buildings in what was in the original plan of the town a central space, having been erected by legalised encroachments in and subsequent to the reign of Henry III, after there was no longer what may be called military occasion or necessity for so large an open space in that position.

This *Place*, for such it was, a wide open table land, extended nearly due east and west, and had its main entrance on its eastern side, where by a considerable ascent the high table land was reached. At the south-eastern corner of the open area was the Moot Hall, the seat of the secular authority, civil or military; while at the opposite end of the table land was the Cross, probably the preaching place for the town and neighbourhood before the erection of a Church; and ever since, the seat of the religious observances of the upper part of the town.

But besides this main entrance, the plateau was entered only by the four corners; and its feeders were Gillygate, Ropergate, Tanshelf Street, and the Woolmarket, each of which admitted the people from one or more neighbouring townships. For it is a remarkable fact, shewing that the town did not grow, but was built on a plan, that neither of the roads by which these out-dwellers thus came to the central meeting place, this chief town of the Wapentake of Osgoldcross, had any communication whatever with each other outside the borough, even though they had for miles a parallel course. When they had passed the Borough boundary, however, crossroads ran from one to the other; though these might have been of later origin. and have been intended to subserve the convenience of a later time.

Thenceforward, after this establishment of a settlement on the western table-land, with that curious instinct with which the habitable portions of English towns shift their location in a westerly direction, the smaller or Old Town about All Saints' Church became the less popular district, and by degrees a mere appanage of the newer western portion of the town.

For the purposes of the seventeenth century Blockade, however, the central point was the Castle, which was erected upon a talus, isolated by a natural valley, which almost surrounded it on and on three of the four sides separated it from higher ground. Thus it was that there was, towards the north, south and west, a segment of a circle, at a distance of from thirty to two hundred yards from the Round Tower, which was at the same altitude as the Castle buildings, but which was separated from them by the natural valley. This was the scientific position for a seventeenth century line of circumvallation, and accordingly the works of the Cromwellian besiegers were placed on those parts of this line where a point-blank shot at the Castle could be best obtained. It naturally followed that just the very positions which were suitable for the besiegers of 1644, were equally suitable for those of four years afterwards, to say nothing of the not unimportant fact that the later comers found the rock excavated ready for their purpose. For if even the opening had been filled up, the trench or cavity made by the earlier besiegers had but to be emptied of the rubbish which had been cast into it, to become after a few minutes' labour, as good a work as that which had, in the first instance, required days or even weeks of almost unremitting toil, to excavate a peculiarly hard and stubborn rock, nowhere naturally covered with more than a few inches of soil.

On this line accordingly the Castle was encircled by a series of at least ten works, most of which, though not all, are given on the Siege Plans. The principal of these were defended from a rear attack by Guards outside the lines, a little higher up the hill behind, or just beyond the crest, where that was possible ; while in the other direction the Works themselves sent forth advance posts towards the Castle.

Thus Major-General Lambert's Fort Royal (No. 14), at Baghill, had a Horse Guard (15) which Boothroyd figures with tolerable accuracy, as he also does the East Guard (26) and the Tenalian Guard (25) ; while the Horn Work (16) (which on the other plans was nearly in its proper place, but which he places too far to the south) had the Pinfold Guard (17) throttling the sextuple cross-road where Gillygate, Baxtergate, Harrop Well Lane and Slutwell Lane converged upon Southgate ; and what Drake calls the Upper Trenches (p. 48) throttled Micklegate, and defended the Main Guard (18) ; while the School House Guard (19) throttled Finkle Street. and defended the Great Work behind Mr Lund's ; and a " Work " at the end of the Abbey Close, some hundred or six score yards from the Castle, too distant to be included in either sketch, guarded Lady Balk Lane, and defended the Work above Denwells (23).

Both Lord Galway's and Mr Frank's Plans are almost absolutely accurate with regard to all these Works, except the last named which of course they do not give, and except the Tenalian and East Guards, both which they place too near together ; each other position of the Besiegers has evidently been in each case laid down with exceeding carefulness by one who well knew what he was doing ; the works are quite accurately placed in reference to the Castle itself, and in the case of Lord Galway's plan, they only appear to be inaccurate when they are considered in relation to a

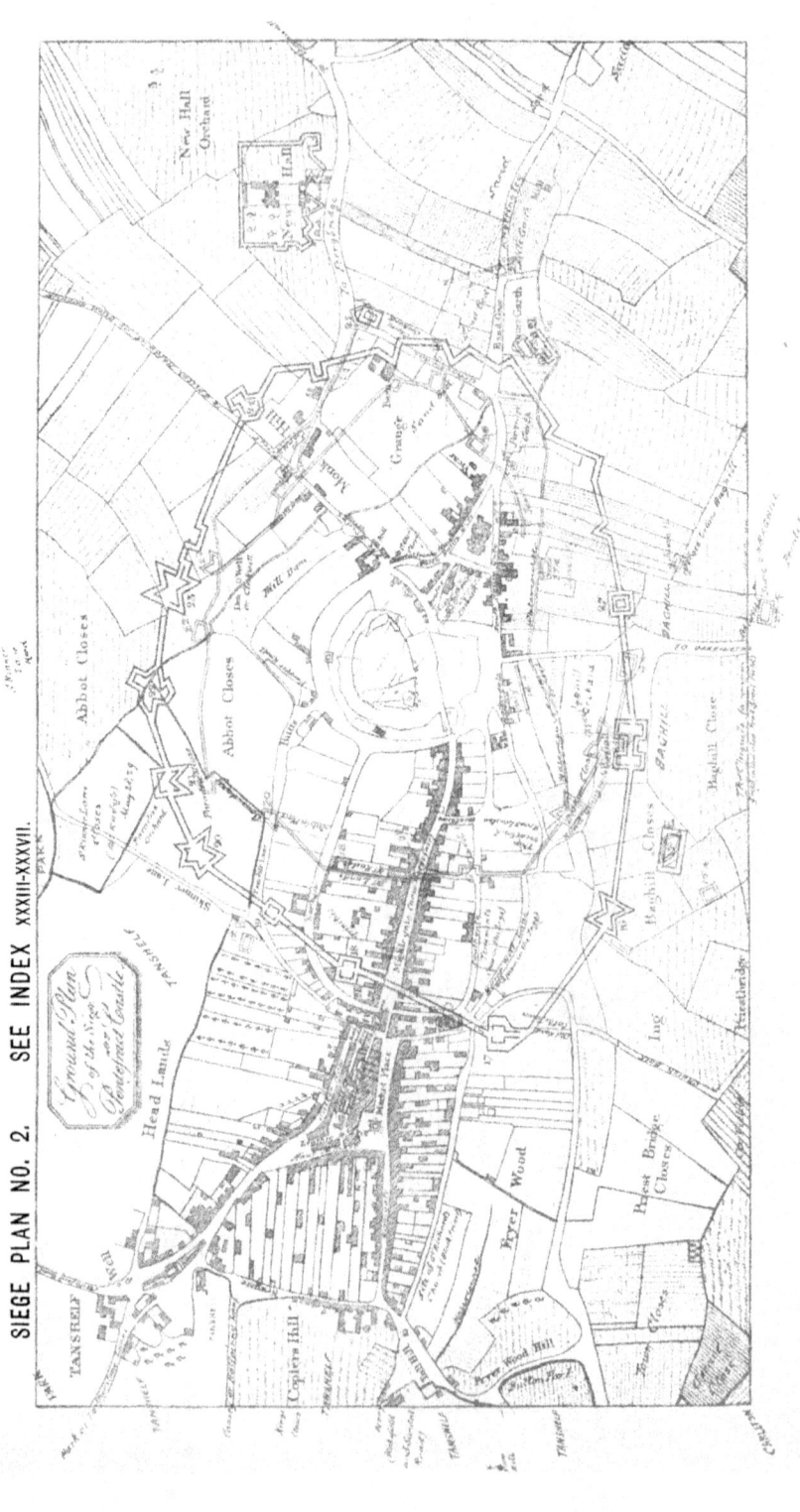

SIEGE PLAN NO. 2.   SEE INDEX XXXIII-XXXVII.

ground-plan which their designer never contemplated.

When they undertook the Siege of Pontefract Castle, which was practically a virgin fortress, almost the first thought of the Besiegers was to make their position particularly strong in the Micklegate, from the immediate neighbourhood of which their first attack was to be delivered.

And accordingly, as may be seen from the minute account contained in Nathan Drake's Diary, the attacking force had two sets of trenches in Micklegate, the Upper Trench and the Main Trench; which position they subsequently strengthened by the addition of a sentry house in advance towards the Castle. That there was no Battery in the line of Micklegate itself, is certain; for in that case, the buildings of ancient construction still remaining between those trenches and the Castle, could not have outlasted the siege and continued till now, as they have done. They would have been demolished either by the Besiegers themselves as a preliminary to their attack, and to make a clearance of the ground in their front; or as a consequence of the fire itself. This their continued existence would, therefore, have been in any case, clear undeniable evidence that the firing took another direction.

And thus the artist of Mr Frank's Drawing, who, when he commenced his work, evidently had the advantage of a tolerably accurate Plan of the town as a groundwork, an advantage which his predecessors did not possess, but who, from internal evidence,* was as

---

* For instance, Mr Jollage correctly partitions off from Grange Field, a long rectangular slip, which, in his time and for many years afterwards, was used as a liquorice garth, but which is now again merged in the Field. Mr. Frank's Drawing ignores this garth, although it existed in his time, and is, moreover, given by Boothroyd. —Mr. Jollage incorrectly represents a path bordered with trees as dividing diagonally the plot to the east of Friar Wood Steps; this also Mr. Frank

clearly independent of Mr. Jollage's Map, correctly placed the Main Battery(18) on the land behind Mr. Rusby's house, the position given to it by Basire also. This latter, however, confused the Battery in that position with the Main Guard which crossed Micklegate at a much higher point, and which, at first, like each, if not all, of the other Guards, was very little more than a simple Barricade. For most of the mistakes made by the draughtsmen of these Plans, have arisen from their having omitted to notice that the Guards were *outside* the line of Works; or that, as it may be otherwise phrased, the line of Works was defended by a line of Guards.

But between the Castle and the position chosen for the principal Battery—that is, at the northern end of the plot the southern portion of which was occupied by the houses of Mr Lund and Mr Rusby (pp. 87 and 90), the side of the hill had been converted from a steep slope into a series of terraces or steps, each some six or eight feet higher than that next below; the terraces themselves corresponding with the lateral boundaries of the various properties into which the land on the north side of Micklegate had been divided, when the town had been planned some seven or eight centuries before. And upon the particular plot apportioned between Mr. Rusby and Mr. Lund, upon that part of it which was immediately facing Piper Tower, the Besiegers placed their chief and only effectual Battery; that to which, after it had received little short of a thousand shots (823 are Drake's exact figures, see p. 24), Piper Tower suddenly succumbed.

This Battery and a Work connected with it, which together appear

ignores.—And there are other similar differences between Mr. Jollage's Map and some of the Plans, which any one making use of Mr. Jollage's Map would almost infallibly have adopted. The absence from Mr. Frank's Drawing, of any and all of these differences is we think, evidence that it was of independent origin.

to have passed under the name of the Main Battery, extended to Northgate, a street concentric to Micklegate, and were defended more especially by the School House Guard (19), which like the Main Guard in Micklegate, had been but the development of a Barricade at Skinner Lane End, at the back of the plot containing the School House.

The position of this School House Guard was peculiarly advantageous. It was placed at the junction of two boundary roads which it throttled ; Skinner Lane, which separated Pontefract from the Park, and a road between Pontefract and Tanshelf which led from the town to the Headlands, through what is now the Militia Depot. This road has been since diverted.

The position received its name from the School House, behind which it was placed ; and a curious mistake respecting it, is made in some of the Siege Plans, arising apparently in this way. Lord Galway's Drawing had indicated its site by placing the name "School House Guard" behind the Battery. But as that drawing was not clear with regard to the two concentric roads to the north of Micklegate, a misinterpretation of this symbol occurred, not altogether to be wondered at under the circumstances. And owing to that misinterpretation, the name was transferred by each of the subsequent transcribers except Mr. Frank, to the Battery itself, which is called by both Basire and Boothroyd, the School House Guard ; the latter enlarging his exaggerated extension of the lines, to include what he thought to be the site.

Much further to the north, at the other extremity of Skinner Lane, was Skinner Lane Head, as Drake calls it (p. 40) apparently to distinguish it from Skinner Lane End. Skinner Lane Head is at the junction of Skinner Lane with a short lane called Lady Balk Lane, which leads to a road called Lady Balk. This Lady Balk itself, from which the only recently formed lane derives its superfluous title (for "Balk" signifies that strip, two furrows broad, at the side of a close, which was the way by which its further end was reached), adjoined the upper extremity of that large tract called the Abbey Close, where, in the very early days of the first siege, the Besiegers, as a practical defiance of the Garrison, "set up their colours," only, however, to have them beaten down by the Besieged, by means of their Cannon on the King's Tower. The marks of this outlying Guard, which was too far away to be included in our Plan, are still to be seen in the irregularities of the pasture of the extreme portion of the Abbey Close, just below the brow of the hill ; and the spot can be effectively pointed out from the Castle. The position was excellently well chosen, being defended on three sides by hedges, while the fourth side faced the Castle. It communicated easily, by means of the Lady Balk, with the road from Castleford and from Tadcaster. And somewhere not far from it, but a little to the West of Skinner Lane, i.e. in the Park, was the Great Horse Guard of the last Siege (page 312) ; though, as the land was, about a century ago, made arable, all traces of the position have long since been removed by the plough.

The Main Battery (18) was connected with the next Work (20) by trenches drawn across Northgate, and owing to the subsequent levelling of Northgate at that point, their bases are now within a very few inches of the surface.

This Work (20) was very nearly to the north-east of the Main Battery, and was called, at the later siege, Fairfax's Royal Horn Work, the prefix Royal having reference only to its size. In Lord Galway's Drawing it is represented as a second Battery. The heavier Battery (18) was on the land, between Micklegate and Northgate ; but this was on the road called Paradise Lane, which was the third of the three elliptical concentric lines, and almost in the position now occupied by the end of Jubilee Place. The remains of this last Work are still come upon whenever the road that passes over the locality is disturbed.

The position of Paradise Lane can be well seen on Mr. Jollage's Map, and Mr. Frank's Drawing gives it with some carefulness; but in Basire's it is much distorted, apparently to give the greater prominence to the Castle; while in Lord Galway's it is ignored entirely, or merged in Northgate. This is very singular, for it must always have been an important landmark to a map maker, inasmuch as it encircled the town proper, which it separated from the land reserved for meadow and pasture.

The Work next in order (21) was to the north-east of Fairfax's Royal Horn Work (20). It was called the North Horn Work to distinguish it from another in a corresponding position to the south (16). This seems to have been the Work at Paradise Orchard "all along the hedge" (p. 79), advantage being taken of an existing angle in the hedge for aid in its construction. It, like No. 20, was on the boundary line between Pontefract and Tanshelf, which was then probably clearly defined, especially round this outlying piece of the township of Tanshelf within the bounds of Pontefract, a boundary which has now entirely disappeared. The Union Workhouse covers part of the site, and another portion has been thrown into an adjoining enclosure; but there are still some remains of the Paradise Orchard, which appears to have extended over the lower portion of the plot.

The next Work (22) was at the "bottom of the Abbey Close"*;

* The Abbey Close originally included the whole breadth of the land north and north-east of the Castle, from Monkhill Lane across to Skinner Lane; from Paradise Lane almost to that part of Lady Balk which bounded the Hospital Estate of Spital Hardwick. This came down as far as Lady Balk and a short zig-zag hedge which, as it were, divided the properties diagonally.—This zig-zag is a remarkable feature, and must have existed for ten or twelve centuries. It

as Drake phrases it. We read first of the occupation of this ground on April 27, when the other side of the hedge was "lined with musqueteers;" but on May 16, and again on May 19, Drake notices it as a "New Work," in that position (pp. 69 and 75). So slowly and tentatively were these works constructed. This New Work was on the further side of the brook, was the mark of the termination of several of the Danish half-acres which were allotted to the early settlers, along the road to Hardwick, St. Ive's Well, (so called after a 7th century Abbess Hiua, or Hiva, a contemporary of Ethelburga), and Fairy Hill (more correctly Ferry Hill). The longitudinal divisions between each of these half-acres have, however, long been obliterated, though the butt ends remain. Very early, also, as another part of the Danish settlement, long before the monks obtained their grant, the plots about Knapper Knoll fell to private hands, as afterwards did in another direction the cit-rivuline plots called Paradise Orchard, Paradise Close, Skinner Lane Close, and the Mill Dam. Of these, Paradise Orchard and Close are in Tanshelf, an indication of allotment before the two townships were divided; Skinner Lane Close is an exhausted brickfield, in Pontefract but not touching Pontefract, being surrounded either by Tanshelf, Pontefract Park or the Brook. The plots to the east had been gradually enclosed and so acquired separate names. What is now known as Denwells was at the time of the sieges undergoing the process. It had been named, but was not enclosed.—That which remained of the Abbey Close, all these being subtracted, belongs to the lay Rector, the Earl of Harewood; for except one or two well-known plots, the ecclesiastical land of Pontefract has been kept together in three groups, belonging respectively to the Earl of Harewood, Lord Houghton and University College. It was at the very extremity of the most northerly plot of Abbey Close that the Parliamentarians erected their defiant flag.

where the besiegers had the slope of the hill behind them. In the last siege, it was called "Col. Bright's Work," and all the Siege Plans except Boothroyd's fix it with tolerable accuracy. He, however, with an extraordinary defiance of the probable, apparently catching at Drake's word "bottom," accepting it literally, and being unaware of the extent of the Abbey Close at the time of the siege, locates the Work on the brook, with the stream flowing through it. The others were each and all more fortunate in their selection of a site.

In the third and last siege, the next Work (23) received the name of Oliver Cromwell; and the Plans, except that of Mr Frank, agree that it had two horns on each face, with an enlargement to the east, that might help the communication between it and a Work named in Lord Galway's Plan Dean's Battery, but unnamed in either of the others, and unnumbered in all. No. 23 threatened Swillington Tower; and during the first siege many attempts were made by the Besiegers to establish an approach through the intervening closes, while on the other hand, most gallant, and it may be added successful, efforts were constantly put forth by the Besieged to thwart their assailants.

But as these small Works, like the various "Sentry" houses, were not part of the regular Plan of the third siege, neither Lord Galway's View nor Basire's mentions them. It is indeed possible that an endeavour to incorporate them into his plan, led the artist of Mr Frank's Drawing into several inaccuracies; for almost every one of the positions as given by him, not only of the Works, but also of the Castle Buildings, east of this point and of Baghill, is incorrectly placed. We have already pointed out that although that View is fairly accurate in regard to the town, it yet omits all mention of the Darrington Road, which is cut through Baghill to the south; and shall note, as we proceed, some of its other more glaring omissions and inaccuracies; but we may at once say that from this point of Cromwell's Work (23) it represents all to No. 27 in so distorted a fashion, that it ceases to guide us with regard to any of the Works.

Only Lord Galway's View gives the name of Dean to the small redoubt near No. 23, but all agree that the next in order, however much they may disagree about its exact position, was Dean's Fort (24). This is very erroneously placed by Boothroyd to the east of Monkhill High Street, and behind the Hill; it is much too far to the north, even in Lord Galway's View, but it seems to have been correctly placed by Basire, as illustrated by the Drake record.

Basire's ground plan however, at this point, is so defective as to be confusing. As we noted with regard to part of Lord Galway's Drawing, its Siege Plan is good, even where its Town Plan is defective. That is exactly the case with this part of Basire's Plan. The earthworks, which could have been figured only by some one on the spot at the time, or before they were obliterated, are fix d with almost absolute accuracy; while the ground plan of the fields and closes, open to any one to make at any time, is just as ludicrously inaccurate. For instance, and it is only one such out of very many, there was an old road, now absolutely blocked, which led from the Ferrybridge Road to Spital Hardwick; from, in fact, the Priory to the Farm belonging to it. But after the Dissolution this road fell out of use, the traffic passing into the Monkhill Street at a point some yards to the south. Thus the two roads enclosed a triangular patch, which is shown in Lord Galway's Drawing, and in those of both Boothroyd and Jollage, while Basire omits all notice of what must have been a remarkable feature. The main road was lately lowered here to the depth of ten feet, so that the old road which is private property, now terminates in a small precipice; and its having been ignored by Basire is not only a remarkable illustration of his inaccuracy at this point, but it tends to show that the Works were all well within it, and that it did not present itself between the Besiegers and the Castle.

Indeed this portion of Basire's Map is altogether inaccurate ; he has not only compressed everything, but he has divided the Priory enclosure into six parallel slips running east and west ; which is a pure invention, for it never was so divided ; and he has evidently considered that the two enclosures between Monkhill Street and Box Lane were in one. But, in regard to the Plan, he has been accurate where all others have failed ; he has almost exactly hit the Besiegers' lines, which crossed Monkhill High Street just where he has indicated, considerably to the south of the points where the Ferrybridge roads met that to Spital Hardwick. That this was so is incidentally evidenced by the continued existence of the old houses which were outside the line ; and which, had they been within it, must have been sacrificed to one of the many exigencies of the Besiegers.

The construction of Colonel Dean's Fort (24) seems to have been watched with much natural anxiety by the Garrison ; and Nathan Drake has given us several particulars with regard both to the Work itself and to some advanced redoubts in connection with it. He says that it was begun on May 10 " in manner of a haulf moone " (p. 65), was attacked on the 16th, and again on the 18th, when " Capt. Smith with 30 Souldyers went up by Denwell Lane to the outworks upon the back of Munkhill, and beat them from those workes, and so went along theire trenches, and cleared them as he went, to theire first lower Worke." Ten or twelve days afterwards, he relates (pp. 86 and 87) how a "Triangle Work" was made between it and Swillington Tower (from which, however, the Besiegers were temporarily driven the next day by help of a "little drake" planted upon the tower itself). On June 10th, he continues his narrative, and shows how that the construction of another was commenced : and on July 14th, how that these were connected, and that port holes were made in them for the use of the musqueteers (pp. 136, 137.) But as the soil there is deep, all indications of the operations of the Besiegers would have been obliterated when the siege terminated and the cultivation of the ground was resumed. Thus no trace of either of these Works would have presented itself to the beleaguering force at the last siege, and therefore neither of them is shown on any of the Siege Plans, which really refer to the latest siege when Col. Morris held the command of the Garrison.

In connection with the attacks on this Work in advance of Swillington Tower, it may be noted that the firstnamed attacking party (p. 70) went out from the Castle "*over the Bridge* towards Munkhill." Now the meaning of this expression has been variously misunderstood, from want of that local knowledge which could be obtained only by careful observation on the spot. In Lord Galway's Drawing an attempt has been made to realise the idea by the representation of an actual bridge across the road, between the buildings under the King's Tower and Halfpenny House (The Hope and Anchor) ; though this, which was the result of a pure misapprehension, seems not to have been the conception of the original artist, but to have been a subsequent addition. The Bridge, over which the party of the Garrison went, was a levelling up of the road across the bed and banks of the brook, and it extended from St. Nicholas Hospital to the corresponding part of the bank on the opposite side of the stream. This higher road, to which Drake gives the name of The Bridge, was some ten feet higher than the lowest part of the valley ; and as we have had a recent opportunity of learning, it was laid across the brook and its shelving shores upon oaken piles about four feet long. Several of these were disinterred lately, when the sewerage works were in course of construction, and some of them are still preserved in the Castle Museum.

The Trench across the Monkhill Street, which appears to have been at last made so deep, so wide, and altogether so formidable as to be impassable for horsemen, was at first but a weak place. On April 29, (p. 59), a party from the Castle easily drove out of it a company of Sir John Savile's men, who had possession of the district from New Hall to Monkhill. But on May 18, "about 20 horse" attempting to assist in Capt. Smith's sally over the Bridge, had to return foiled, for they could not pass the Trenches (p. 71) of whose enlargement they seem then to have learnt for the first time. And only ten days afterwards, the position had been made so strong by the Besiegers, and was so well guarded, that the ten or twelve Sandal men who had remained behind, of those who had brought relief to the Castle, attempting to make their way back by a circuit, probably through the Abbey Close, were suddenly faced by a guard of the Besiegers before they had passed the Hospital. The determination to prevent their further progress, was indeed so great, and the power of the Besiegers so evident, that after one of the party had been wounded the rest were obliged to take counsel with discretion and return, in order to renew the attempt at a point possibly more easily penetrated.

From the Monkhill Street, the line of Trenches was continued across a plot of cultivated ground to the west of Grange Field, and which being one of the banks of an ancient river has a very steep incline. It then entered the Grange enclosure, where the Besiegers took advantage of the presence of a building called the Grange Lathe. This was a fragment of St. John's Church, or of some other building connected with the monastery, perhaps the Chapter House, which the Besiegers used as an occasional cover, placing their trenches to the south of it. At the Grange Lathe, "Many officers and souldyers" of Sir John Savile's company drew fire from the garrison on April 26 ; but on May 16 it was the scene of a more direct contest. On that day (p. 69) a small party of the garrison having sallied and attacked the Besiegers at the Old Church, these latter took refuge in the Grange Barn, on which the sallying party quickly took possession of a thick Orchard of trees right opposite, whence across Grange Lane they faced the party of the besiegers in the Grange Lathe, interchanging shots for some half hour, but not venturing on a direct attack. This was, however, merely a reconnoitre ; and having by its means ascertained the weakness of the position, two days afterwards, on the following Sunday, a force of 70 from the garrison made another sally as part of a concerted operation, when they fell upon and killed a company of officers sitting after dinner in the Grange Barn, and "toasting the higher house of Parliament." But there was no battery here, the position being too low.

We have already pointed out the differences in the treatment afforded to "Grange Chapel" by the different artists, and it is singular to note the remarkable unanimity with which they agree to differ in regard to it : one places it as a chapel within the lines ; another as a chapel without ; a third calls it a Barn, and entrenches it from the Besiegers ; while Basire, the fourth, makes no mention of it, whether as Church or Barn. As in regard to the point at which the trenches entered the Grange Field, it is singular that this last alone is right in his treatment of the lines defending the Grange Lathe. For although he does not indicate a building, he makes them diverge, in order to entrench the position, which they must have done, since, as we have seen, the sallying party had to make a complete detour in order to attack it. It is noticeable that at this point, Boothroyd once more most glaringly defies the probable ; placing the Barn within trenches as if it were to be defended from an enemy at New Hall ; while he brings the trenches themselves through or over a perpendicular cliff twenty feet high.

This formidable cliff which Boothroyd thus ignores, was in fact the quarry from which the monks obtained much of the stone they used in their buildings; and these were constructed under its shelter from the north. The surface of this cliff was moreover the cemetery of the monastery—the quadrangle of the Cloisters being reserved for the Priors—and on that part of the cliff which still remains, the Cluniac monks of St. John the Evangelist repose in regular ranks,* on the top of the rock. This is in each case slightly hollowed for the reception of their remains, which are covered by about four feet of soil. The soil being used as garden ground, and the cultivation seldom more than a foot deep, the dead lie beneath, practically undisturbed by any change that may take place on the surface.

The platform which sustained the Battery against the Church, clearly was in this direction, as we gather from isolated remarks with regard to it. But neither of the Plans attempts to fix its locality, probably because, in fact, they all deal with the last siege. The data concerning it are that it commanded the Church; that it was commanded by the King's Tower; that one of the cannon from Queen's Tower, some twenty yards to the north of King's Tower, had formerly killed one of the enemy in the Work at Monkhill which was therefore so much to the north of the platform; and that its construction involved some labour, and required a waggon load of planks from the town. Together, these indications would be satisfied as to locality only by a point to the west of Monkhill; and its most probable position seems to be at the head of what was afterwards called Box Lane Close, where Basire seems to locate the New Hall Guard, and

* Fountains was built on the model of Pontefract; and the locality of its cemetery being unknown, we suggest that it may be probably found in an arable field to the north of the church, which occupies at Fountains, a similar position with regard to the monastic establishment, which is occupied by what is now known to be the cemetery.

Boothroyd fixes the Tenalian Guard (25). For it seems feasible that each would have made his selection, as a consequence of having allowed himself to be guided by indications of some military Work on the spot, even if he had no clear indications of its exact character. And that it is thus probable that the position showed, for a time, such marks of military occupation as to justify and further the idea that a Work had been there; the Tenalian Guard, says one, the New Hall Guard, says another: each an evident guess, though, indeed the latter might have been a name applicable to the circumstances of the last Siege.

But this being almost the only point which would answer the required conditions, we think we do not err in placing there the Platform from which the Church was battered.

This is also the position which seems to have been occupied early in April, by a Barricade, which was partially destroyed by a party sallying from the Castle without orders on April 14th who daringly drove the enemy out, and pulled the place to pieces, before the approach of cavalry, in face of whom they retired. And it was the Barricade here, at Cherry Orchard Head, towards which was directed the Trench commenced by the Scots from Bondgate Mill Dam, to which we shall shall have occasion to make further reference.

The two older Plans each agree that the next redoubt was strengthened by a Tenalian Guard, though they disagree as to its exact position. Lord Galway's View places it full in Grange Lane (Box Lane, as it is called) though almost touching the trenches which defended New Hall. Mr. Frank's Tenalian Guard is placed inaccurately to the south of the Knottingley Road, while Boothroyd goes to the other extreme, and, as we have already said, places it at the upper end of the Cherry Orchard, on the road to Ferrybridge. So far as we have been able to ascertain, there are now no indications in the land, of the position of this Guard, and it is evident from the frequent sallies up Grange Lane made by the Garrison that the trenches did not cross that road, at least up till May 18th. Thus far the representations made by the two earlier drawings are corroborated by the facts, recorded by the eye-witness, Nathan Drake.

But once more, the position with respect to the Trench, which is given by Basire to the Tenalian Guard (25), has the more antecedent probability, because in his drawing the Tenaille and the Guard appear to supplement each other, as should be the case ; and the enclosure wall, which seems to have been destroyed needlessly, would not have been recklessly pierced, if the construction of the Tenalian Guard at that point could have assisted the Besiegers in their endeavours to hinder the sallies of the beleaguered Garrison up Grange Lane. For those sallies were not repeated after the successful attack upon the enemy at dinner in Grange Lathe ; which looks very much as if one result of that attack had been the discovery by the Besiegers of their weak point, and the consequent construction of the Tenalian Guard, even at the sacrifice of part of the wall of the Grange Field.

All the Plans are unanimous in placing no Work on any plot of land, east of Grange Lane, and bounded by Ferrybridge Road and Knottingley Road to the north and south respectively. So that were it not for Drake's Diary, we might suppose the besieging operations in this "quarter" to have been *nil.* That eye-witness however, tells a different tale. Let us recall it.

Immediately east of the point at which the brooks converge, and south of the road to Knottingley, here called Bondgate, or "The way to the boundary," which it is—was a long narrow garth, the name of which like that of Bondgate, carries the mind at once to the pre-Norman centuries, and the Danish settlement. It was called Coney-garth or King's enclosure, a name, which through all the later changes, and even till now, has adhered to it, or at least to that portion, west * of the Mill Garth.

The plot had, however, long before the time of the sieges been divided into two, which were separated by a short lane. The lower or eastern portion was called the Mill Garth, and contained that East Mill of Pontefract, which had been given to the Monks of St. John by the lord in 1159, as the West Mill, near the Hospital—that is, west of the Priory,— had been appropriated to them by his father in 1090.

From this Mill Garth, a party of Scots, who had come as a reinforcement to the Besiegers, commenced a Trench on April 20, intending as it appeared to the Garrison to continue it towards their Barricade at Cherry Orchard Head, near New Hall, and therefore across part of the plot east of Grange Lane. But two days afterwards, news coming that Sir John Savile was approaching with his troop, the plan was changed, the Scots left, and the construction of the Trench was discontinued, while its existence is altogether unrecorded on any of the Siege Plans.

The next mention we have of a Work in this quarter is on April 27th, when one is mentioned, indefinitely, as being " below the low church." The Work, however, but imperfectly discharging its function, it had to be supplemented by the Tenalian Guard. It seems to have been designed to defend the cross road at the end of

---

* " It is a singular coincidence, possibly the resultant of a general law, that the name of Northumbria which was given in Saxon times to a very wide extent of territory, came ultimately to belong to its extreme portion only, and that the name Taddenescylf, which was similarly given to a large district including what is now Pontefract, the Park, Tanshelf, Monkhill, Hardwick, and Carleton, became at length confined to Tanshelf alone."— From PONTEFRACT AND ITS NAME.— R. HOLMES, 1877.——Coney Garth is another example. The original name again adhered to the western portion.

Grange Lane, as it was called by Drake; Box Lane as it and the adjoining close were subsequently styled after the name of their owner, a certain well-known John Boxe.

Now, all the Plans except Boothroyd's, concur in placing this East Guard (26) upon the peninsula within the confluence of the two brooks; Lord Galway's Drawing fixing its position to the north of the Knottingley Road, and the others to the south, but each placing it in clear relation to the Old Vicarage, a prominent building distinguished by its three gables, and more than a century ago converted into three private houses.

There was, however, another work in Coney Garth itself, of which there still remain evident signs, which Mr Frank seems to have considered was the Tenalian Guard, but which both Basire's Plan, and Lord Galway's Drawing consent to ignore. This was probably the position selected, in the second place, for the East Guard; which not being found to answer its purpose, was abandoned by the Besiegers, who ultimately fixed their Guard somewhat nearer to the Castle, so as to be able to command the point at which North and South Baileygates converged.

Thus the East Guard (or Barricade) gradually crept closer towards the Castle. At first in the upper end of the Mill Garth, behind the short lane which separates the Mill Garth from Coney Garth; then nearly in the centre of the latter, guarding Grange Lane; finally in the plot to the east of the Vicarage, "close by the Low Church" (p. 69). And this last East Guard—if it was so called at all till the latest siege—was for long the nearest position which the Besiegers could maintain. It was however but a weak place, and not only supplied no real defence, but was unfortunate either in its *soi disant* defenders themselves, or in the way in which they were handled; and it may be remembered that even as late as June 11th, when Capt. Munroe made an attack upon it from Mr Kelham's house, (27‡), on the opposite side of the street "they all runne away at his first charge."

This house of Mr Kelham's, (27‡) a post much in advance of the Baghill Guard (27) is then first mentioned, on June 11 (p. 97) when the enemy were driven from it. The Garrison next held it, in their turn, for some days, as an advanced post from the Castle, and a position by means of which they could obtain grass from the meadow behind. In order to effect this object, they first cut a trench to the Church, through Mr Tatham's Orchard, by which they could gain easy access to that building; they then on the other hand constructed a "blind of boughs and sods" from the Church to Mr. Kelham's house, under cover of which they easily passed to and fro; and while the enemy were so plied with shots from the steeple that they durst not even look out, the garrison party coolly went into the closes at the back of Mr Kelham's, and fetched in "near a hundred burden" of grass (p. 103). It was not likely, however, that this could last long, even if the grass withstood the demand, and on June 15, the Besiegers contrived to dig a trench behind Mr Kelham's, "to prevent our men from getting of grass, where they got before," (p. 106); and a day or two afterwards managed to continue their trench through two little closes to the east of Mr Kelham's, and thus effectually excluded the Garrison from the pasture.

But this was all done at a late date. The Main Work at this side was the Baghill Guard (27); in advance of which, somewhat between it and Mr Kelham's, was an actual work at which there were some important contests, though (probably because no advantage was taken of it at the last siege) it is not mentioned on either of the Plans. It was, however, a much contested post, and the centre of a deal of skirmishing during the latter part of the second siege, as we shall shortly have occasion to show.

The site (27†), and the adjacent Orchard, belonged to one Zachary (not Zechariah) Stable or Stables*, and a

---

* Little would Nathan Drake, the Diarist, at this time of siege (1645)

little explanation as to the relative positions of the plots will help much to the understanding of these final scenes in the proceedings of the Siege, and of the relative positions of the various Works of the Besiegers.

The crofts or plots of property to the south of South Baileygate had in medieval times numbered five, to the east of which were three garths—Parsnep Garth, which must have been a modern name or a corruption, and which is bounded on two sides by the southern water course; Coney Garth,

have imagined that thirteen or fourteen years afterwards, his elder daughter should become the wife of the only son of this Zachary Stable, then a boy of eleven. But such was the case (p. 5.) ——There is nothing to show that Zachary Stable was any but a distant relation of his close neighbour (p. 126) Mr Ald Stable, who belonged to a wealthy Pontefract family. Zachary Stable, whose antecedents and origin we have not ascertained, had married in 1624 with Mrs Barbara Skipton, an heiress of that family, and probably through her, had become a man of some property. He had a family of five children, only one of whom was a boy, the future husband of Elizabeth Drake. One of his daughters, Hester, reached womanhood, and died in 1653, aged 23; but an elder sister, Sarah, was married in 1657 to Thomas, son of John Routh, of Pollington, who became the head of a large group of Rouths, who held property in South Baileygate for some three generations. Zachary lived till 1678, when he was buried " very aged" (p. 5) dying intestate. His widow survived, and took out administration on Jan. 20, 1679-80.

It adds somewhat to the interest to know that the wife of Peter Redman, the tanner, whose hides were " stolen" by the besiegers (pp. 92, 93) was also a Skipton, probably a cousin of the wife of Zachary Stable. (29 Nov, 1638, Peter Redman and Elizabeth Skipton were married by license.) Their properties thus adjoined.

and Mill Garth; these three being suburban, rather than town plots.

Each of the five town crofts had been originally a union of so many Pre-Norman half acres, the old lateral boundaries of which, north and south, still remained. But some of these crofts had been additionally sub-divided by new boundaries running east and west, and Mr Kelham's property was the fourth—or part of the fourth—reckoning east from the Darrington road. Zachary Stable's, which was the third, had been so sub-divided; and of one of the sub-dividing or cross boundaries the besiegers made use in their attempt to establish a new work. Neither his house nor his orchard had received mention in the Diary, till the siege was drawing to its inevitable close, and the death hand-to-hand grapple was about to commence. Then on the night of June 4th, 1645, the Diarist informs us (p. 92) that the besiegers began "a New Work near to Zachary Stable's Orchard Head," of which he speaks as of a well-known site. He at first describes it as being about 120 yards from the previous work (27) capping the slope; an estimate which after the work had been more clearly developed in depth, and perhaps after the site of the upper work had been altered, he subsequently reduced by just a third. Its locality (27†) is fixed by the narrative of the events of St Barnabas day, when four parties sallied from the Castle to engage in its attack, the tactics of the besieged being on that occasion very similar to those they had employed in the earlier undertaking against the Grange Lathe. Having isolated it, they concentrated their forces upon it to its destruction.

The whole of the Garrison seems to have been, in one way or another, actively concerned in this enterprise, but four parties were directly engaged in the attack. The first, as a necessary preliminary, took possession of Mr Kelham's house. This was in order to prevent any possible communication between the work to be attacked, (27†) and the East Guard (26). The second closed upon it, as if to seize it; but instead of delivering their attack, they diverged to their left, and passing along an accommodation road, which then lay between the rear of the houses in South Baileygate and the meadows, stationed themselves behind a hedge (now destroyed) the shelter of which had enabled those in the "New Work" (27) to communicate with the "low work" (27†). A third directly attacked the work itself, while a fourth held themselves in reserve in the Orchard hard by. The result of this well-conceived strategy was as in the case of the Grange Lathe ; the party attacked found themselves absolutely isolated, and virtually at the mercy of their resolute opponents. They were almost exactly like so many rats in a hole or rabbits in a burrow, with enemies daringly attacking them on their front and sides, while assistance and help were absolutely cut off from the rear. The result was that while "about 40" were killed outright, eleven of the besieging party were captured, and they so "soare wounded" that they could not even " get out over the work" at the back, as eight or nine of their more fortunate fellows were able to do (p. 98.) The loss of the Besieged was almost nominal.

This " New Work" (27) as the Diarist calls it, and persists in calling it, Baghill Guard as it was afterwards styled, seems to have been constructed partly in furtherance of a design to attack the Church, which had become practically an advanced post from the Castle, and partly to prevent a similar exploit to that which resulted in so substantial a relief to the Garrison on May 27 (p. 81). On that occasion a party from the Castle went through the houses to the south of the Church, up the closes to Baghill, that is to the eastern portion of the ridge, as the context shows ; and while those in charge of the Work on Baghill (14) had their attention distracted by a direct attack upon Primrose Garth (14*), the company commissioned for that purpose received near a hundred cattle from the hands of a detachment of Sandal men, and drove the greater portion of the herd into the Castle.

Drake describes the Work on the day its construction was commenced, June 2, as being " like a half-moon in the closes below Baghill over against the Church," which description exactly answers to the site (27). There are indeed two sites which may be fixed upon for this " New Work" ; but as there were probably works at each, we have indicated them as 27 and 27*, the latter being established in order to prevent the Garrison from making use of the accommodation road in the manner already explained. The Work which was furthest from the Castle is probably that which Drake describes as 120 yards from the Low Work. It also answers the description which he gives of Moody's Close (p. 96) ; it was separated from the Darrington Road by the breadth of only a single plot ; but it is just beyond the limits of our map (Siege Plan No. 2). It was a plateau sheltered on three sides, and open only on that which faced the Church, which it effectually commanded. The second is nearer, but lower down the hill, and commanded Mr Kelham's house rather than the Church, enfilading the hedge behind which the Garrison concealed themselves during the attack upon the "low work." Its site is even now marked by two fine elms which still bear on their seamed stems, the marks of the conflict, the Castle cannon having (perhaps when during the attack on the Upper Work William Ingram (p. 101) "shot twice through it with cannon balls, and once with case shot, with into and round about it") left on them scars, which in the course of years have now widened into gaping wounds. All Pontefract probably does not possess a more remarkable reminiscence of its memorable sieges than that afforded by this pair of venerable elms, which, now that these siege-scars have been pointed out on them, will, we trust, be treated as historic.

Each Work (27 and 27*) was defended by a hedge to the left, right and rear ; a favourite position with the Besiegers (p. 94), who were glad to nestle in the end of one of the long Danish half-acres, common round Pontefract. The lower of the two (27*) was in close communication with the work in Primrose Close (14*), to distinguish them from which, each of these other two later Works was so constantly called by Drake the "New Work." The Work in Primrose Close is, however, not named on the Siege Plans, though Drake is most clear concerning it as being in "a little round close called Primrose Close under Baghill" (p. 81), and its remarkable omission in the Plans ought to have been sufficient in itself to show that these have no claim to be looked upon as infallible.

As the Baghill Guard (27) was a New Work in relation to that in Primrose Close, so the Work on Primrose Close (14*) was a Lower Work (p. 61) with reference to the Fort Royal (14). The description is especially definite, and Primrose Garth (contents 1r 13p) remained very nearly as it had been in the siege times, till 1877; when under that name, it was carted bodily away to make room for the Swinton and Knottingley Railway, which now runs at a level several feet below the site from which the Parliamentarians for so many weary weeks, watched the Royalist garrisons of Pontefract Castle. One side of "the lane, by Primrose Close, under Baghill," (p. 80) has also disappeared with the Garth, but the southern side, that bounding Bottom Close and Baghill Orchard, remains in pretty nearly the condition which it presented two centuries ago.

The great Work on this Southern side was a Fort Royal (14) to which the name of Major Lambert was given at the third siege. But it may be noted that Drake persistently calls both this and Cromwell's Fort (23) a Triangle. He gives very clear particulars with regard to No. 14, indicating the style of its construction in the rainy summer of 1645. These show that it differed materially from what the later Besiegers found to be necessary for the winter campaign of 1648-9, which Mr Margetts anathematised so bitterly (p. 204). In the earlier siege, it was a Triangle, walled with stone, and filled with earth (pp. 60 74), and the Garrison conceived that there was a little Work within it, for officers to sit in under shelter (from the rain) (p. 60). But as its position is correctly marked on all the Plans, we need make no further allusion to it.

We can place satisfactorily but one Work between the Fort Royal (14) and the Main Guard in Micklegate (18); though all the Plans agree that there were two, styled respectively the South Horn Work (16), and Pinfold Guard (17). But the site of this latter we believe to have been fixed erroneously, as we shall explain in due course.

Each Plan indicates the existence of a bivouacking Horse Guard (15) in Chequer Field, in rear of No. 14; or, as Boothroyd alone places it, between No. 14 and No. 16. The last named is, however, clearly wrong; misled probably (as with the Tenalian Guard and the East Guard) by evidences of the disturbance of the soil at the place he indicates. With Boothroyd we place a Work (15) on the face of the hill in the second close; but we agree with the others in supplementing it with a bivouac in the rear behind the hill, (15*) which would have been concealed from the Garrison, and of which there is now no trace in the arable land. But neither of them was the effective Work on this side, that which was probably in the mind of the constructor of Basire's Plan, when he figured his Horn Work. This seems to have been identical with the lowest Work under Broad Lane End, (which then extended into Southgate) twice referred to by Drake (pp. 81 and 95), and which was commanded from the burnt houses by Elizabeth Cattell's, (p. 81), which were near Walkergate. It seems to have been in the upper part of the Close, (16) which we fix as the site also of the negotiations which preceded the Treaty of Surrender (p. 143). This Close (Bottom Close as it is called by Drake) is bounded to the south by the southern water course, and to the east by Baghill Orchard; and these two enclosures entirely fill the space between the watercourse and Baghill Lane. It is singular that this watercourse is given correctly by all except Boothroyd; though on the other hand the last-named depicts the plots themselves with accuracy, while each of the earlier plans presents a fanciful and bewildering distortion of almost every enclosure.

A word or two as to the southern watercourse may not be out of place here, as helping to the understanding of the contour of the ground on this side of the town; which had a natural influence on the position of the Siege Works. Its principal branch takes its origin in what by an extraordinary misnomer has been of late years called the Priory. This stream was in medieval times carefully protected by the Black Friars, whose house and church (of neither of which there is a vestige above the surface) were on its banks, and who had cause to complain, and did complain not without result, of its scanty supply of water.

All the Plans, except Boothroyd's, agree in depicting the stream as flowing directly eastward, though with many fanciful windings after it left the grounds of the Friars, till it ultimately joined the northern stream at Coney Garth; but Jollage and Boothroyd totally suppress it until its emergence from under the Darrington Road, where they represent it accurately. The stream, which was of considerable importance, to judge from the many wells which it fed, receives from both right and left, principally from the right—many smaller streams; for the ground, which seems to be slowly rising * throughout the valley, is full of water.

---

* To show how the land is rising it is sufficient to point out that in The Ings this stream is quite lost, and can be reached only by penetrating through a mass of clay, some inches in depth; and that in the Knottingley Road, at a point between Parsnep Garth, Coney Garth, and the Grange Field, there are remains of a Roman Road, six feet below the surface, and of course nearly as much below the present level of the bed of the northern stream. This was

This stream is very clearly defined through the Black Friars. It was at one point utilised as a boundary between the Friar Wood, and their garden; and had throughout its course a well-constructed and well-preserved bottom, with good sides of masonry. After it has passed under the road which connects Southgate and Friarwood Lane (and which on the six-inch Ordnance map is called Friarwood Street, though the town has never adopted the name) the stream gets lost, but its course may clearly be traced by the remains of its ancient sides, which are frequently turned up, and give colour to the erroneous idea that some of the buildings of the Black Friars were in that plot. The underground course is due east for about 20 yards, after which it seems to turn to the south, but a line of wells is the only indication it gives of its position until it has passed through Harrop Well Garth, or The Ings, as that close has been lately called. It is here a broad but shallow underground stream, the overflowing of which was till lately utilised as a Bath; and just before it passes under Baghill Lane it receives a second stream which rising partly in Ox Fields, and partly in the Town's Close, brings down an almost equal body of water. The united brooks then pass under Baghill Lane, where they supply what is on the Ordnance Map called Harewood Well, probably a corruption of the old name Harrop; and on the eastern side of the road the waters were used a century ago (much subsequently to the siege days) to feed a long fish pond that was so prominent a feature, as for some time to give a name to the close, which was known as the Canal Garth. Similarly the close on the western side of the road, which receives the two brooks, (from Ox Fields, and Friar Wood, respectively) was called for a long time Pond Garth. Its site is now under the embankment of the new railway.

---

displayed during the recent drainage excavations, and it had been seen in the course of similar works about thirty years ago.

Both canal and pond have been, however, long since destroyed, and the waters now pass along their original eastern course at the foot of Bottom Close, in some strength, until they reach Baghill Orchard, and an adjoining piece of grass-land. Having bounded the orchard to the south for some yards, the stream makes an abrupt underground divergence across the grass land, perhaps directed underground by design in order to increase the value of the ~~Orchard as a~~ meadow. The stream having flowed underground in a north-east direction through this close to its western boundary, passes under the Darrington Road, and resumes its eastward course. Thenceforward all the Plans give its direction with tolerable accuracy; but all fail to notice that just before it reaches Parsnep Garth, which it bounds, it once more makes an underground dip for a space of about five yards, as we have indicated on the Siege Plan. Here, however, the process by which the stream is diverted underground can be examined, and it is seen to be entirely artificial, the object being evidently to convert into one what otherwise would be two meadows with an open stream between them, which would be a constant source of danger to grazing cattle. The stream has accordingly been ingeniously bridged over, the grass being encouraged to grow above it.

To the south of this stream, and west of Baghill Orchard, is the meadow called by Drake Bottom Close, and afterwards known as Canal Close. In this meadow was placed the South Horn Work (16). This seems to have communicated with the Main Guard (18) in Micklegate, by the line of the open street, the houses serving as a shelter from the fire of the Garrison. Although this Work (16) was intended to command Walkergate (Poppin Lane as called by Basire, using a very temporary name); yet a party coming to the upper part of Walkergate from the Castle (p. 81) prevented those at the Baghill Work (14) from affording their fellows in the Bottom Close any effectual relief. This seems to show that the shelter afforded by the "burnt" houses was still so very considerable, as to make their continued existence most useful to the Garrison.

But properly to carry out the tactics of the Besiegers, there must have been an intermediate Work in Southgate, to prevent a future interference of this sort by the Garrison; for the Besiegers who as we have seen, constantly locked the door directly the steed was stolen, doubtless here repeated the tactic they had adopted in the case of the Tenalian Guard and of that at Baghill. But all is so altered in this direction that we fail to discover any evidence of the existence of any such Guard here. That it was not at the Pinfold, where Boothroyd places it, hardly requires pointing out; for that site was far out of view of the Castle, and even behind an elevation then much larger and steeper than at present. As an aggressive Work it would have been absolutely useless at that spot; for if there were any Work at all there it could have been intended only to protect the rear.

The Pinfold occupied a piece of ground, now vacant, where Baxtergate and Gillygate jointly debouch. Boothroyd evidently knew the position; but made the mistake of supposing it to be included in an imaginary line of circumvallation. On the other hand, Basire indicated the site of the Pinfold itself correctly, but was misled into giving its name to a Work which must have been distant at least a furlong and a quarter, and was even on the other side of a steep hill.

Reasoning from analogy, it is very probable that the Besiegers really had a Guard in this position in the rear of their line, and to protect their communications. Like (19) and (25) it was probably placed where it could best command and defend some crossroad, which in this case was sextuple, as may be seen by a reference to Siege Plan No. 2, or even better on Jollage's Map. This latter is, however, somewhat confusing, as it gives Baghill Lane as the name of the road (now out of use) which led from the Pinfold to Baghill, across what is called the Ings. The correct name of the lane was Harrop Well Lane, and only its eastern portion was known by the name which Jollage, in error, gives to the whole.

But the superficial features of Southgate have been materially altered since the time of the Sieges. Then a passenger from the Pinfold towards Walkergate would have had to ascend quite a steep incline for some fifteen or twenty yards, and afterwards to descend a still more considerable declivity before he began the final ascent by which he would have been compelled to approach the talus on which the Castle was erected.

The crest of this steep hill has, however, altogether disappeared, and the bed of the valley has been raised. The side of the road, which was formerly a hill, is now six feet of solid sandstone, cased and concealed by what appears to be a wall of masonry, but which is really only a casing of a few inches thick; while but a few yards further the level is maintained by a filling up of the valley to the extent of at least eight feet at the lowest point, the artificial road being supported and kept in position by strong buttresses. This was done in the last century partly to make a level road for the stage coaches, and partly to give a uniform appearance to The Ings, and the grounds attached to Mr Joshua Wilson's house. A group of houses on the north side of The Ings which appear in both Basire's Plan and Lord Galway's Drawing, and each of which for many years conferred a right of voting by burgage tenure, were also demolished, and the name Garden Lane, which it probably deserved, was given to the road. There was then no necessity for the Wakefield and Ferrybridge coaches to ascend the hill and enter the town. The thoroughfare was through Southgate, thus made more easily passable by coaches.

The position which we assign to the Guard (17) is exactly where this artificial road resumes the natural level. But all is now so altered that we fail to note the slightest indication at this point (17 ?) of what must have been the Work of the Besiegers, who would have communicated with the Work in the Horsefair, by means of the lane by the side of the present Wesleyan Chapel.

And thus we have carefully and painstakingly gone over every foot of the ground. Our great difficulty has been to ascertain how much and what to receive of former statements. Rejecting nothing unnecessarily, we have had to be constantly on our guard against the reception of anything without proof, or inference so clear as to be almost equal to proof. How we have succeeded we must leave to others to say. We only trust that nothing we have advanced, however opposed it may appear to some foregone conclusion, will be dismissed lightly, and without a full consideration of the evidence which has seemed to us so strong as to warrant the adoption of the opinions we have expressed.

IN ADDITION to the various circumstances of Col. Morris's life which we have collated in the Index, (pp. xv, xvi) we have since discovered his will, made a few days before his trial, while he lay in York expecting the assizes. Its terms show that he was by no means the obscure adventurer he is so frequently represented as being. It is as follows :—

Will of John Marris. In the name of God, Amen. I, John Marris, of South Elmsall, in the county of Yorke, Gentleman, being of good and perfect remembrance, Praised be Almightie God. First I co'mend my Soule into the hands of Almighty God, And my bodie to the Earth from whence it came. And for my personall Estate, I give and bequeath in manner following, vizt., All my Lands, Tenements and hereditaments which now I have, or of right ought to have, I give and bequeath to Robert Marris, my eldest sonne, TO HAVE AND TO HOLD to him, and his heires for ever. And if he dye without lawfull issue of his body to be begotten, Then to the next heire that shall survive him. But if it happen that my said sonne Robert shall live to have and to enjoye the same, and to have issue of his bodye as aforesaid, That then my Will is, that he shall pay to his Brother Castilion, and to his Sister, Marye, the Sume of Three hundred pounds a peice of good and lawfull money of England. And if it happen that my now wife shall have another child, Then my mind and Will is that my said Sonne, Robert, shall pay unto Castilion and Mary, his said Brother and Sister, but two hundred pounds a peice ; And other two hundred pounds to that Child which shall please God, my Wife shall bring forth. And further residue of my personall Estate, vizt., Bonds, Debts, Debenters, or any Goods and Chattells, properlie belonging or to belong unto me, my Will is that the Third part thereof shall be unto my Wife, Marjory (Jur) Morris, and the residue equallie to be divided amongst my said youngest Children. And if any of them die, to the Survivor or Survivors of them. And if the Bond of Mr Ridges be recovered, That then my Brother Edward, my Sister Elizabeth, my Sister Anne, and my Cosen Anne Burbidge, shall have out of the same bond Twentie pounds a peice.

IN WITNESSE whereof, I have hereunto putt my hand and Seale The Eight day of August, in the yeare of our Lord God, One Thousand, Six Hundred, fortie and nyne. John Marris. Witnesses:—Christopher (Jur) Stones, Rich. Alline.

Nothing was done with regard to the Probate for some years, but on June 15, 1655, administration of goods was granted in the Prerogative Court of Canterbury to Margery Morris relict of John Morris, Gentleman, of York. This was without the production of the will ; but after the Restoration full Probate was applied for, the will was produced and proved by Marjory Morris, the widow of Colonel Morris, and Christopher Stones, one of the witnesses, the administration being duly granted to " Margt. Buckley, al'Marris, relict, now wife of Jonah Buckley, gent." These two documents clearly prove the identity, and disprove the disparaging allegations so groundlessly made against Colonel John Morris, otherwise Marris, or Marries or Morrice.

INDEX.

(Part I—General; Part II—Castle and Town;
Part III—Siege Works.)

PART I:—GENERAL.

ABBEY of Pontefract, Princess Margaret rested there in her progress northward 354, Queen Mary, by warrant, orders its stone to be used in the repair of Potefract Castle 349
Abbot Mr 20 34
Acaster Thomas, his evidence against Col. Morris 249 (See Akister)
Accommodated, peculiar use of the word 59
Ackworth 96, Timber from, to be used in the repairs of Pontefract Castle 349, Rector of, in the Castle in 1644-5 23, Besiegers' forces quartered there in 1648 under Col. White and Col. Hacker 308 320
Adams Matthew, one of Morris's confederates in the attempt of May, 1648 256
Adcherman, Cornet (See Matthewman)
Aiswright Francis 243
Akister John 249 (See Acaster)
Aldenham, Sir Francis de, executed at Windsor 365
Ale wives or Sutlers 54 63 104
Allerton Bywater (corrupted into Ollerton 257 and Ollerton Böate 308,) Expedition to, ordered by Col. Morris 256, Which was intended to be an attack on the rear of Ferrybridge *ib*, Who commanded there 308, Commonwealth soldiers taken there and brought into the Castle 246 308
Allott Mr 21 23 211
All Saints' Church, reached from the East gate of the Castle 158, (See also Low Church and Works.)
All to rent and to torne 368
Almondbury, Cornet Michael Blackburn, belonged to this Parish 236 264

Ambler John, did not pay for some timber he bought at the Demolition 332
Ammunition of Pontefract Castle removed to York at the Demolition 326
Anarchia Anglicana, or the history of Independency, quoted 275 283
Ancient (See Ensign)
Andelay, Sir Hugh 362
Anderson John, allowed an alms-room at St. Nicholas Hospital 355
Anne, wife of James I, manors in her jointure named 356
Anne, Mr Philip of Frickley 157, In the Castle in 1644, 20 34, Concerned in the attempt of Sept. 1646, 147 383 384
—— Mr Michael, his son, 21 34 147 157 384
—— frater 34
Antrobus Lieut. 20 34
Apple pickers shot or shot at 107 117 133 137 138 140
—————vend their fruit at 4, 5, or 6 a penny 138
Archbishops, two contemporary, of Pontefract ancestry 335
————of York owned Scrooby 353
Arkesham (see Axholme) Isle of 113
Arksey 113
Armagh, abp of 335
Arms in the Castle, when seized by Col. Morris 159
Artillery, the name of the third story, in the roof of the Round Tower of Pontefract Castle 345 347, Its contents 346
Ashbourne, Sir Bartholomew de, exe-

GENERAL INDEX.

cuted at Canterbury 365
Ashby Alexander 247 251, Gentleman of the arms to Col. Cotterell 320, One of Col. Morris's correspondents in the Castle 153 252 320, Made a Captain by Col. Morris 246, and Major of the Castle 320, Commissioned to seize goods in Pontefract 251, Killed a Parliament soldier in the street 251, One of Col. Morris's council 246, Excepted at the rendition 153 247 322, Hid in a sally port and escaped 153 158, Ultimate fate at present unknown 322
Ashingdon William 164, His daughter Annabella married Castilian Morris ib
Ashton Sir John, seized at Howley and brought to Pontefract Castle 337, His petition ib
——— Ralph Lieut.-Col. taken prisoner at Willoughby 179
——— Raphael ———, one of Col. Morris's council 243, Imprisoned for acting as a second in a duel 246
Aske Robert, leader of the Pilgrimage of Grace 342
At, for (th)at 113
Atkinson Mr 20 34
Attempt to surprise the Castle, in Sept. 1646, 147 238 383, Do. in May, 1648, 170 174 295, How it failed 150 238, Was probably made from the Baghill side 239
Attitude of Parties in Aug, 1644, 278, How and why it changed ib, Do. in June 1648, 304
Audesley or Audley, Cornet 21 34
Austwick, Alderman Thomas 21 33 140 238
———, Allan his son, Paulden's Lieutenant in the attempt on Rainsborough 250 314, Was commander of the four that seized Rainsborough 320, Dealt the fatal blow to both Rainsborough and his lieutenant 314, One of Col. Morris's council 243, Excepted at the Rendition 153, 322, Hid in a sally port 153 158, and escaped 153
——— Philip, bought some timber at the Demolition 331
Autterway Aunchiant. (See Ensign Ottoway)
Axholme, Isle of 113 178

BABLE, little cannon at Baghill, so styled 76 77
Badlesmere, Sir Bartholomew 362 363 364, Executed at Canterbury 365
Badsworth Bells 380
Baghill, Mr Beaumont hanged there 208, probably at a permanent gallows 253 254, Caricatured in a wall engraving in the Magazine 312 (See Works) Under Baghill=Primrose Close 80 (see also 92)
Baldock Robert, Chancellor of England 365, Set armed men to guard St. Thomas's Hill 366
Bamford Cornet 20 34
——— William 243
Bands of our Lady, between confinement and churching 338
Barker John, an unlearned vicar 351, Retained the living through all the stages of the Reformation 352
Barnby Dun 303
Barnsley, Churchwardens of, bought some lead at the Demolition 330
Barthrome (Bertram) Capt 81
Barton Serjeant 70 81 97 99
Barwick (in Elmet) 54
——— Sir Robert 258 263
Bates Capt William, Taken prisoner at Willoughby 179
Battery began 24 37
Battley Lieut 20 34
——— John, one of Col. Morris's council 243 252
Baumforth, Mr Thos. 21 23, Sent to Newark 62
Baune Nicholas, killed 40
Baynes Capt Adam 200 201, His correspondence, passim from 203
——— Cornet John 200 209, His letters 203 210 221 223 385 386 390 394 395
——— Robert 200 211 220 385 386 389 394
Beale Capt 21 33 41 42 48 50 71
——— Mr Paul, of York 220 228
Bease, old plural for beasts 50
Beaumont Mr George, vicar of South Kirkby, not merely minister but Parson 386, Detected in correspondence between the Garrison 207, and the Prince 309, Hanged on Baghill 208 311, and buried at South Kirkby 6, not chaplain to the Garrison 217
——— Lord, disappoints the Royalists 305 320

GENERAL INDEX.

Beaumont Richard 21
——— Major Sir Thomas 21 33 77
——————————— one of his tenants 77
Bees Capt 178
Bell, a presbyterian minister, a means of the arrest of Col. Morris 175
Bellasis Lady 395
Belwether (called Wm. Wether) leads attacks 44 45, Fetches in a Barwick suttler 54, Sent towards Newark 64, Returns 69, Goes to Newark 76
Belv General, the Scots' great general, 141
Bennington John, his evidence against Morris 251
Benson Mr 34, Capt. 21 22 41 42, With others went to Sandal 68, Was one of Col Morris's council 246
——— Was this John? 243
——— Robert 334
Berkeley 370
Bernefield, Sir Roger, slain at Boroughbridge 364
Berwick 149 239
Besieged, loss of, 18 145
Besiegers, loss of, 18 145, Their soldiers refused to charge 37, Increasing their strength rapidly 44
Best Capt. 20 34
Bethel Col. 190, Raises forces against the Royalists though he had promised to help them 303, His militia disbanded 206 207, Interceded for the reprieve of Morris 278, Probably Col. Be' 394
Bett them from their cannon 29
Bible, why Capt. Paulden's messenger carried one 151 314, Col. Morris quotes both the Breeches Bible and King James's version in one sentence 280
Biggleskirke Thomas 21
Binnes Mr 20 23
Birkbeck Mr, bought some timber at the Demolition 331
Blackfriars, Pontefract 363
Blackburn Michael, a clothier, came to the Castle during the 1644-5 siege 77, Called Blackston in error 271, An Almondbury man 280, From Coldhill 281, His own account of himself 264, Was Servant to Sir John Ramsden ib, Was Capt. Paulden's Cornet 250 264 314 320, and one of the party that seized Rainsborough 250 251 264 314, Excepted at the Rendition 153 175 322, Charged through the Besieged and so escaped 175 236 319 322, Captured in Lancashire 236 264 319 322, Attempting to get to the Isle of Man 394, Brought to trial 276, Ordered by his judges to be ironed 271, His attempt at escape 274, His recapture through a fall which broke his leg 275, His speech at the gallows 282, His execution 285, An unpretending man, since Col. Cotterell was not acquainted with his person 259, While Gunner Grant called him Major, confounding him with Major Ashby 263
Blackwell Capt., Treasurer at Whitehall 392
Bland Major 50
——— Sir Thomas 21 33 140
Blockley Cornet killed in a sally 74
Blundeville, Lieut Edward 179
Bohun, Humphrey de, Earl of Hereford, 362, 363, Killed at Boroughbridge 364
Bolderton Robert bought some timber at the Demolition 331
Bonevant, Capt Geo, Governor of Sandal Castle in 1644-5 49, Col. Morris's exploit at first attributed to him 49 159 160, Alleged by the Parliamentarians to have been a groom 160 162, One of Col. Morris's Council 243, Led the attack on Ferrybridge 248 251 307
Bonfires towards Doncaster 137, On Sandal Castle 78 92 96 111 112 122 124 130 134 136 137, On Round Tower 78 80 92 96 122 124 130 134 136 137 142, Between Wentbridge and Doncaster 130, On the Towers 81 83 111 112, In Westfield 131
Booth Mr Alderman Edward 62
——— Mr Wm, keeper of Pontefract Park 39, Sent away to Newark 62
Boothroyd quoted 38 217 218 221 226
Boroughbridge 363 364
Boston 256 305
Boswell Thomas, bought some timber at the Demolition 331, But did not pay for it 332
Boughs and Sods, how used by the besiegers 61 103 125
Box John, did not pay for some timber bought at the Demolition 332

GENERAL INDEX.

Boynton Col. Matthew, 153 269 389
Bradburn Sir Henry 365
Bradford Capt. 208 209 210 216 391
Bradley Francis, engaged in the Demolition 328, And bought some lead there 330, and some timber 331
——— Dr (clericus), rector of Ackworth 21 23 33, preached 66
Brame William, bought some timber at the Demolition 331
Bramhall Abp, 335
Brampton, Mr Ellis of, seized 38 178
Brandlin Col, his regiment routed by the Royalists 38
Brear Capt, 220
Bridgnorth 363
Briggs brothers 31
Briggs Col. 185
——— Grace, bought some lead at the Demolition 330, And some timber 331
Bright Col, one of the Commissioners for the surrender after the siege of 1644-5 143, Raised forces though he had promised to help the Royalists 303, On duty before the Castle in the 1648 siege 190, A Commissioner for the surrender of the Castle after the third siege 152 219 222, Was one of the moderate party who dissented from the execution of the King 206 261, His letters to Capt. Baynes 220 223 391, Mistrusted by the extreme men 224, Where his regiment was quartered after the siege 229
Bristol, some of the adherents of the Earl of Lancaster executed there 365
Britany Sir John de, one of the judges of the Earl of Lancaster 365 367, Taken prisoner by the Scots at Byland 366
British Museum possesses examples of each of the six Pontefract siege coins 212
Brooke Calisthenes 249
——— Master, foreman of the Jury which tried Morris 266, The principal verb 275
Brotherton Marsh 124 125
Broughton (see Prouston)
Browne Capt. 22 34, Killed in the Barbican 27, Lieut exchanged for Mr Ogle 37
——— of Wakefield, his charitable expression 41

Browne Capt. brought a reprieve for Garforth 253
——— a parliamentary officer defeated at Allerton Bywater 308, Who had been previously shot at 256
Bruerton Col. (Sir William Brereton) 78
Buchanan Mr (clericus) 20 33
——— Mr (Scotus clericus) 20
Buckerfield Radcliffe 244
Buckingham, Duke of 154
Bullett 18lb. weight 25 114
Bunckley Mr 245 246
Burchell Mr 20 23
Burials in the Church of St. John 73
Burley Mr (clericus) 21 33
Burton Mr 20 21 23, Robert 20
——— upon Trent 363
Butchers, two seized, with horses loaded with flesh 41,
Button Park 46
Byard Capt. Thomas 179
Byford Mr 245
Byland battle at 366
Byram House, Cromwell quartered there 189
Byron Sir Gilbert 179
——— Major General Sir Richard 243 252 303, Commanded the Reformadoes at Allerton 308, Called Phil. 320, Had his horse killed under him at Ferrybridge 320

CANNON number of, fired against the Castle, Jan. and Feb. 1644-5, 24, Number shot from 1 May to 4 June, 92
——— or Bable, at Baghill 76 77
Canterbury, Sir Bartholomew Badlesmere and Sir Bartholomew de Ashburne executed there 365
Cape Lieut 20 34 Capt 34
Capel Lord 219 221
Carisbrooke Castle 177
Carleton 96 125 131
Carlisle 78 83 149 239 363, Andrew de Herclay made Earl of 365, Attainted of conspiracy and executed 366
Carlyle's detraction of Col. Morris 176 177 183
——— quoted,177 183 184, His inaccuracy 183 184
Carr Ben 68, Ellen 68
Carriage from the town, how drawn, 70
Carter, Lieut-Col 224

GENERAL INDEX.

Carteret (see Cartwright) Sir Hugh 181 244
Cartroll (see Cartwright)
Cartwright Capt 21 34 105 118 245 One of his soldiers deserts 128
———— Sir Hugh 170 181 244 245 246 252
Carwike Mr 21 23
Case shot (16 dozen bullets) 74
Castilians, made overtures 220, Why? 319
Castle, provisioned during the interval between the first and second sieges 38, Stores at the seizure by Col. Morris 159
Castleford Bridge 53
———— Road 68
Cattell Richard, did not pay for some timber he bought at the Demolition 332
"Cattle or Castle" 84 85
Cattle Laith 28
Cattle sent out to feed near Swillington Tower 44, a relief of 97 got in 81, 300 seized by Morris's garrison at Knottingley 150 177 179, or Wentbridge 321
Cavendish Sir Charles, an applicant at second hand for permission to purchase the Manor of Houghton, part of the Queen's jointure 357
Cawood 44 69
Caxton quoted, 367
Cellom (see Kelham)
Chadwick Capt 21 33
Challoner Mr 233
Challoner Robert, one of the Commissioners to "view" the Castle 345
Chapel, Constable Tower, &c., demolished 327 328
Charles I (see The King)
Cheny Sir William 365
Child Samuel, of Leeds, bought some lead at the Demolition 330, But did not pay for all *ib*
Cholmley Sir Henry 150 179 181 182 305, Raised militia forces though he had promised to aid the Royalists 303, Quartered at Leeds 305 306, At Ferrybridge 308 320, His weakness as a commander 185 187, His intended supercession by Rainsborough, and its consequences 185 312, His troop of horse disbanded 190 204
———— Col. Mar. supposed to be slain at Willoughby 179, One of Col. Morris's Council 243
Churchwardens' accounts of St. Margaret's, Westminster, quoted 289
Clare, Gilbert de, Earl of Gloucester, 362 364
Clarendon's account of the taking of the Castle by Morris 167, And of the seizure of Rainsborough 171, But is very inaccurate 173 174 226 240 252 291 323
———— History, account of, 323
———— Papers, in the Bodleian, quoted 285 291 292
Clarke Capt, a prisoner in the Castle 128
Clayton Capt 187
———— Mr, Lord Fairfax's steward, seized at Denton 182 188 317
———— Mr John, bought some lead at the Demolition 330
Clement Richard, his witness against Col. Morris 260
Clerke John 267
Clifford Moor, Race there 211, Postponed 220, Date fixed 389, Who lost 229
Clifford Sir Roger 362 363, Wounded at Boroughbridge 364, And taken prisoner *ib*, And executed at York 365
Clithrow Mr 21 34
Clough Capt 21 33
Cluniac monks of Pontefract, their history almost unknown 46
Coal, the question of digging in Pontefract Park 360
———— Burials in 360
———— Measures, lime stone, sand and sandstone, in one curtilage 44
Coining not mentioned in the Diary of the 1644-5 siege 74
Colepepper, Sir Thomas, executed at Winchelsea 365
Colchester 177 182, Delivered to mercy 218
Collinson Lieut 22 34
Collins Dr 34
Colours, their absence a disadvantage at Willoughby 306, An advantage at Marston 307, Parliamentary officer dressed "All in Red" 64 99, Another with a Red Scarf 100, And another in Buff 45
Comforthes or Comforth for Comfort 50 77 81 113

GENERAL INDEX.

Committee of Lords and Commons at Derby House, letter of Cromwell to 192
Complimentary letter from the Governor of the town 88
Congreve C 244
Conisborough 151 184
Conspirators of Sept. 1646, sent to London in custody 148, and referred to the Northern Council *ib*
Constable Capt 20 33
———— Josh 243
———— Sir Robert, in the Castle at the Pilgrimage of Grace 342
Cooke Lieut 21 34
Cooper Cecil 243 255
———— Gervase, his evidence against Col Morris 254
———— Capt John 153 179 243 255, Capt Thomas Paulden's "old friend Jack" 153 255
———— Sir Roger 179 255
Copland Sergeant 70
Copley Major 21 33 140
———— Lieut-Col (Parliamentarian) 143
———— Lionel 204 294, Had been a royalist correspondent, but by mistake joined the besiegers 320
Corbrook 209
Corker Mr (clericus) 21 33, Went to the Prince, and procured the aid of Sir Marmaduke Langdale 30
———— John, one of Morris's council 243
Corn, agreement with the Mayor and Aldermen about 245, The Garrison fetch in as much as was within their reach 310, And more than they "spent" 311
Correr Mr 22 34
Cotterel Colonel, governor of Pontefract Castle, immediately before the third siege 149 240 252, Did not then know Morris or Blackburn 260, Seized and shot by Peter 252, Taken prisoner 150 159, And put in the dungeon 150 241 259, Kept there for 3 days 259, To be brought as witness against Morris 237, His evidence against him 259, His seizure, as it were, a rehearsal of that of Rainsborough 316
Cotton Rev. John of Boston, his description of the considerate treatment received by the Dunbar prisoners sent to the plantations 289

Council, for the Government of the Garrison during the third siege 243
Coventry Thomas, lord, 156
Cowbeck Capt, supposed name of a Parliamentarian officer, all in Red 65
Cowper Gervase (see Cooper)
Cowper Gilbert, wants his by-past tithes, even if tithes are put down for the future 211 220 221
———— John 179 243 255 ; Jack 153 (See Cooper)
———— ———— of Doncaster 391
———— Mr John 237 254
Cowy (see Gilbert Cowper)
Cox Mr 216 391
Crathorn 243
Craven in Skipton 372
Cremona, Prince Eugene's exploit there, compared to the surprise of General Rainsborough 149 154
Cridling Park 244 360
———— Sour Wood, timber to be applied to the repair of Pontefract Castle 349
———— Stubbs 95
Croft Capt, 20 33 41 48
Cromwell Lieut-Gen 112 139 305, "Views" Pontefract on his way to the North 179 308, Returns and quarters at Byram 189, At Knottingley 189, Took possession of the town 251, Summons the Castle 190 318, His correspondence from before Pontefract 191, Never bombarded the Castle 191, Leaves the Siege to Major Gen Lambert 199, Capt Thos Paulden brought before him and denies his name 153, Applies for the gift of 2000 prisoners from Preston for Col Robert Montgomery 287
———— V 244
Crooke, Lieut Col 153 222 396
Cudworth Mrs Martha and her suitors 390, Marries Samuel Savile *ib*, Mrs Susan intercedes for her cousin Smith 392
Culverin 159
Cuthbert Lieut 21 34
Cutler Col. Sir Gervase 21 33 41 42 48, Jonathan, his man, 44 45 94, Brought his plate to the Castle to be coined 74 138 215, His death 119, And will 120, Burial in the Castle Chapel 120 146, Remained buried

during the interval between the second and third sieges 146 174, Removed to Silkstone, when the Royalists regained possession in 1648 120
Cutler Lady 111 119, detained in the Castle after her husband's death 120, Enticed out, searched, and driven back 123, Finally allowed to go home 124

DAINVILLE Sir Josceline 362 365 Dalhousie 287
Damory Roger 362 363
Danby, Sir Christopher, in the Castle at the Pilgrimage of Grace 342
Dandeley, Sir Hugh, taken prisoner at Boroughbridge 364
Darcy, Lieut-Col 20 33
—— of Hornby, Lord 20
—— Lord, in the Castle at the Pilgrimage of Grace 342
Darnborough Sampson 267
Darrington to the West Field 76, Into the town 96, Baghill Lane, towards, 127
Davison, Mr Charles, Morris's chaplain 241 243 252
Dawson Mr 210
—— Quartermaster, killed, 42
De Lacy burials at Pontefract 73
Demiculverin, brought against the Castle 25 114 129
Demolition of the Castle 153, Account of the 326, Petition for 325
Deunis Major 21 33 50
Dent Capt, wounded 61
Denton 182 188 189 317
Depositions against Col Morris 246, Are still at York 237
Derby 80 89 91 96, Earl of 153
Deserter came into the Castle 62 63 113
Despencer Hugh, the father 362 367, One of the judges of Thomas of Lancaster 365, Made Earl of Winchester 365; The son 73 362, Banished, but refused to leave the Kingdom 362, Had a grant of the Honour of Pontefract 369, Sent messages to the King to "undo" the pilgrimage to the tomb of Earl Thomas 372, Placed armed men on guard there *ib*
Diary, Nathan Drake's, description of 17 26 injured by rain 76

Dickinson Mr Thos, Morris and Blackburn examined before 264
Dickson Wm, wounded in the cheek 81
Digby Sir John, according to Clarendon's account, put in charge of Pontefract Castle after its seizure by Morris 170 242, Went to Nottingham to confer with Sir M. Langdale as to the surrender of the Castle 181, One of Col. Morris's council 246
Dighton Major 384
Divine Service held in the Hall 143
Dixon Sir John, priest 249
Dobson Richard 21
Dodsworth M.SS. quoted 356
Dolman Marmaduke 179
Domestic State Papers quoted, Elizabeth 353, Charles I 358, James I 357
Dominican Friars in procession met the Princess Margaret 354
Doncaster 38 95 111 123 124 130 136 151, Troops of horse came in from 68 93 96, Surprise of Rainsborough at 151 251 313, 300 horse from Pontefract quartered at 305, The Princess Margaret rested there 353, The Carmelites there 354
Douglas James 366
Drake Nathan the Diarist 21 23, Description of his diary 17 26, His persistent faith in the justice of his cause 55 56, And his particularity in his details 55 145, His old-fashioned language 154, Contrast between his diary and Paulden's letter 154, The Diarist held no military rank 4, And did not, after the siege, resume his military life 146
—— Family, memoir of 1-16 377
—— Samuel, minister of South Kirkby 208, Vicar of Pontefract *ib*
—— Sir John Savile's 25, Planted at Baghill *ib* 61, Little one belonging to the besieged planted on top of Swillington Tower 79 87, One belonging to the besiegers planted in Market Place 136
Drinking healths after dinner 70
Drum a, came from Newark 133, Sent in with a note 139, With provisions for the prisoners 142
Duel in the Castle and orders thereupon 245 246
Dugdale's Visitation, quoted 35 164 165 175 228
Dunbar Henry 243

GENERAL INDEX.

Dunbar, prisoners taken at the battle sent into slavery 289
Dunstanburg, in Northumberland, why Thomas of Lancaster would not go there at the request of his council 393
Dutchman The, played his cannon 105 126 138, Wounded 138, His final shots 142 144
Dyson Richard 244

EADON Thomas, did not pay for the timber he bought at the Demolition 332
Earl of Shrewsbury, steward of the Honour 353
Eastfield, the common there 220, "Our friends" there 389
East Hague 242
East Hardwick 96 97
EasterDay 41
Eden Col, a commander with a Buff coat and a Black scarf, supposed to be 45, or Lieut-Col 65
Egerton Magdalene, daughter of John, Earl Bridgewater, Lady Cutler 119
Eglinton, Earl of 237, Had married the eldest daughter of Duke Hamilton 290
Elizabeth Queen (See Isabella)
Elland 156
Ellis Jasper, removes the ammunition from Pontefract Castle to Clifford Tower, York, 346
—— Mr, of Brampton, seized and brought into the Castle 38 178
—— William 334
Ellison James 20
Ellyate James, the little gunmaker of York, wounded 31
Elmbridge Sir Roger, executed at Gloucester 365
Elmsall North 164
Elvidge Capt John 179
Empson Mr 20 34
—— senior 21
—— Lieut. 111
"Encouragement" 74
Escort through the Park 59, To Baghill 64
Eugene Prince 149
Eure George 267
—— Major, his horse defeated by the Garrison 312 (*now* Lord Eure)
"Excepted" Six, The 153 222, (the word *prisoners* is used incorrectly by the copyist, see note page 386) 223
Exchange of Prisoners 90
Execution of the King, how the news was received by different parties 209 210 211
Exton Sir Piers 374

FAIRFAX, Col Charles, raised forces against the Royalists at the third siege, although he had promised to act with them 303, His regiment was quartered at first at Leeds 305, Afterwards at Featherstone 308 320, And then in the town during the siege 190 192 254, But in the West Riding after its termination 229
—— Ferdinando Lord, summoned Governor Lowther 32 36, But returned to York without drum or trumpet 37, Made another visit 102, Expected to pay a third visit 139
—— Sir Thomas, his son, afterwards Lord 37, Report that he had been defeated by General Goring 133 135 141, Appointed military governor of Pontefract Castle, after its surrender 147, Lord General 186 188 192, Letter of Cromwell to 195, Admits Colchester to mercy 218, His commissions were as Captain General for the Parliament 267, His "life guard" defeated at Allerton Bywater 308, His steward abducted from Denton 182 188 317
—— Col Thomas, one of the Commissioners to treat of the surrender of Pontefract Castle 143, Was confederate with Morris in the design to seize Pontefract Castle in Aug. 1645, 260 261, Revolted from the Parliament at Scarborough 260, Died in December 1646, 262
—— Major William, son of Col. Thomas, killed at Marston 262
Farmarie Mr 21 34
Farram John 20
Farray Thomas (a grocer of Pontefract) Lieut, his evidence against Col Morris 251, Had been requisitioned for £70 *ib* 317
Farrer Robert, Thomas and William (the names seem to have been confused) bought some timber at the Demolition 331, But did not pay for

GENERAL INDEX.

all 331 332
Farrow (? Farrer) See Works
Fast day of Royalists was on Friday 135
———— of Independents was the last Weduesday in the month 247 248
Favell Lieut (Capt Hemsworth's Lieutenant) 20 48 49 57 70 114 118
Fawkes Guy, besiegers likened to 32
Featherstone 125
———— some of the besieging forces quartered there under Col Fairfax and Sir E. Rhodes 308
Fee Farm Book of 1650 quoted 249
Fees payable at the Gaol 333
Feilding Daniel 21
Fell Colonel, one of the committing magistrates of Col Morris 175
Fellows=Comrades 371
Fenton Mr 21 23
Ferrett Joseph, the Commonwealth minister of Pontefract 243, Probably an Independent 248
Ferry bridge in the Lowther siege, *passim*, Besiegers march over 28, Besiegers beaten back towards 29, Their reinforcements came from 32 96, Mr Ellis seized between Wenthill and 38, Wounded men are taken over 43, Detachment through the Park to 58, Horse litter came from 63, Three or four loads of goods sent towards 67, Besiegers drive sheep and cattle towards 68, Two waggons went towards 74, Three do 88, Four do 105 107, Many go 109 13 or 15 wains go through, towards Doncaster 111, and return next day *ib*, Companies of the besiegers stayed there 125, Fortified 135 ; In the third siege, attack on by the Castle Garrison 248 251 307, Some of the besieging forces quartered there under Sir H. Cholmley 308 320
Fether Serjeant 20
Field Edward, mayor 231 237 248, Bought some lead at the Demolition 330, and some timber 331, was one of the Demolition commissioners 332
———— Thomas bought some timber at the Demolition 331
Fignates (Faggots) for a Barricado 126
File, about 6 men 99 100 117
Fines Capt 178

Fire on Sandal Castle 74 76 78 (See Bonfire)
Fitz Randall Edward 179
Fitz William, Sir William, taken prisoner at Boroughbridge 364, And executed at Pontefract 365
Fleming Lieut 21 23
Flood Capt 22 34 42 70 98, Sallies from the Lower Gate 41, Sent to fetch in the messenger from the Scots 51, Wounded while receiving a parleying party 52, Commanded one of the detachments that covered the relief 81 83, Not on the nominal lists
Floyd Sergeant excepted as one of the royalist correspondents 153 252, Hid in a sally port and escaped 153 158 296, Called Lieutenant 322
"Folks of their Liverays" 354
Fooled by them 124, Played the Fool 107
Footmen reported to be at Ferrybridge 76
Forbes Colonel William brings a summons 36, Sends for a reply 37, Wounded before the Castle 27 32, In command 41, Confederate with Col Morris in the project of seizing the Castle in Aug. 1645, 260, 261, Col Morris alleged to have been his Lieut-Col 252
Forman John, mason, assisted in the " view" of the Castle 345
Forthis=Forth this 112
Fosteard (Foster) Bryan bought some lead at the Demolition 330, But did not pay for some timber 332
Fosteard Richard did not pay for some timber he bought at the Demolition 332
Foster Mr 21 22 34
———— William, his deposition against Morris 246
Fothergill, Marmaduke, established a Lectureship at Pontefract 16
Fotheringay 73
Foundations of Pontefract, List of those suppressed 352
Fountains Abbey on the plan of Pontefract Priory 72
Fourpence a burden 86
———— a journey 31
Fox George, historian of Pontefract, quoted 238 240 242 243 244 245 383, Had some source of information

GENERAL INDEX.

which he fails to specify 238 383
Foxcroft Anthony, wounded while receiving a parleying party 52
" Foxt" with strong ale 79
Frank Ald John 84
―――― Ald Mathew 237, One of the Demolition commissioners 325 332
―――― Ald Robert 19, One of the Demolition commissioners 325, Did not sign the final account 332
Free Quarter, Parliamentary horse on, till warrants satisfied 220
Freeston John purchased the endowment, and restored the Trinities 352
French Quartermaster 20 23
Furness Fells 175

G T., one of the besieged footmen his encounter in the Freales 45
Gambads 354
Garforth John abducted 253 317, Put in the dungeon 251, Condemned to be hanged 251, 311, But reprieved 251, Gives evidence against Morris 253, A remarkable entry relating to him in the Church Register *ib*
Gargrave Sir Thomas, deputy steward 348 353
Gascoigne Mr 21 34
―――― Sir William 354
―――― Tower demolished 327
―――― or Red Tower, the later locus of King Richard's murder 155, Timber taken from 327
Gascons, Fourteen set to watch St Thomas's Hill 366 369 372
Gawthorpe Edward 20
Gent Thomas 325
Gentlemen Volunteers, List of 20–1 33-4
Gerard General 112
Gibby, Colonel Anthony 243
―――― Lieut-Col Emanuel 243
Gibson Lieut. 22 34
Giffard Sir John 362, Executed at Gloucester 365
Gilbraith Lieut-Col 48 70 (name not on the nominal lists) commanded the second covering detachment at the time of the relief 81 83, As Colonel commanded a sallying party 98, Was one of the Treaty committee 143 144
Glatberts Mr 242
Glented=glanced 62
Gloucester Earl of, Gilbert de Clare 362

Gloucester, Some of the adherents of Thomas of Lancaster executed there 365
Godley, near Halifax 3
Godlington Sir John 366
Golden Leg, Cheapside 228
Goldsmith Mr 228
Goole 105
Goring General 112 133 135 139 141 210 221
Gower Capt Wm 244
―――― Major Edward 244, His horse shot under him at Ferrybridge (not ower, as copied) 320
Granado shot into town 254
Grant John 262, His name on the walls of the Magazine *ib*
" Grass for the Cattle" a continual trouble 86 91 92 94 101 112
Graven (See Craven)
Gravener Mr 20 34
Gray Mr (surgeon) 34
―――― Col 20 21 22 33 42 49
―――― of Warke, Lord 20 22
―――― Gilbert 21
Great Guns, all the three 81
Greathead Capt 187
Green Sauce 66
Greenfield Marmaduke 250 315
Grimethorp 163
Grimsditch, Lieut John 179 243 244
Grimstone Capt 20 33, Went to Sir M. Langdale 52, His man tortured by the Besiegers 52
Grinfield Sir Richard 120
Grinoway Castle relieved 77
Guards at New Hall relieved every tenth day 64 75 86 95
Guill=Quill 395
Guinea Merchants, had a grant of 1500 prisoners after the Battle of Worcester 289
Guy Fawkes, besiegers likened to 32
Gybson (See Oyston)

HACKER Col 185, Quartered at Ackworth 308 320
Halifax Earl of, Savile 156
Hallyfax Robert 20
Hamerton John of Purston, letter from 351
―――― Mr (1st division) 20 34
―――― (4th division) 21 34
―――― frater 34
Hamilton Col thought to be killed 50
―――― Duke, his intended invasion

GENERAL INDEX.

149, Beaten at Preston 151 305 308, Surrendered to Lambert 180 308, Beheaded 180 200 210 221, Two thousand of his army given to Col Robert Montgomery 287, Presbyterian colonels who had promised him help 303
Hammond Col. Robert, Cromwell's correspondence with 196 235
Handson Edward, employed in the Demolition 327 329
Hanson Thomas sent to Sandal for news 69, Returns from a second journey 77, Was —? 80
Harborough 111
Hardwick (East) 96
Harebread Mr 34 140, Ensign Harbert 20
Harington Cornet (1st division) 20 34
——— Cornet (3rd division) 21
Harkeley Sir Andrew de 363, A false tyrant 367, Who had been knighted by Thomas of Lancaster 364, But took him prisoner *ib*, Was made Earl of Carlisle 365, Was attainted for conspiracy with the Scots, and executed 366
Harris Capt 21 33
Harrison John demolished the Round Tower 326, and the screens from the Round Tower to the Gate House, and to the Treasurer Tower 327
Harwood Capt took the news of Willoughby Fight to the House 179
Hatfield 105
Hats and shoes 73
Hats or heads 54
Healths drunk after dinner 70
Heaton Peter 21
Helmsley, bombardment commenced with cannon from 30
Hemsworth Capt 114 118, Name not on the nominal list 48, Attacks trenches at Ald Lund's house and the Great Trench 48, Relieves and maintains the Church 105, One of the Treaty commissioners 141
Henry VIII, King, visited Pontefract 355
Hereford Earl of, Humphrey de Bohun 362 363
Heron Robert 243
Heslam John 20
Hewan John 267
Hey Mr 20 23
Higford Mr 20 23

Higgins Elizabeth, wife of the Diarist 3, Her father Francis 3
Higher House of Parliament, a Presbyterian toast in 1645 70
Hill Quartermaster, taken by the Garrison 49
——— William, bought some timber at the Demolition 331
Hilton Capt (Baron) 21 33
Hirst Mr clericus 21 33, preached to the Garrison 95 130, One of the Treaty commissioners 140, 143 144
"Hit," not "Shot" 138
Hitchin Mr 21 23
Hodgson Mr 21 34 140
——————Capt John, his memoirs quoted 124
——— John, did not pay for some timber he bought at the Demolition 332
Holdsworth Agnes, died in the prison at Pontefract Castle 335
Holgate George, father-in-law of the father of Col Morris 163 383 384
Holinshed 374 376
Holland Earl of 221
——— Sir Robert de, a traitor to Thomas of Lancaster 363
Honour of Pontefract consisted of eighteen manors 356
Hopgood Mr 20 34
Horselitter came in from Ferrybridge 63
Horse, How the besieging horse was harassed by the garrison during the third siege 311
Horse Racing, depending among the besiegers 211 220 229 389
Horsfall Capt of Storthes Hall 21 34, Went out to Sandall Castle 64
——— Jo 243
Hough Gilbert, a cannoner 256
Houghton Lord, owner of Scrooby 353,
———, City of London desired to purchase the Manor of 357
Hoult Lieut 20 34
House of Commons; The Journals record that Col Morris was in custody of the Sergeant at Arms in the winter of 1646, 147 148 174
Howley 337
Howson Robert bought some timber at the Demolition 331
Huddleston Capt 20 33
——————Major 20 33
Hull 90, Iron taken at the Demolition

GENERAL INDEX.

for the public service at 331, And Timber 332
Hunter's South Yorkshire quoted 157 174
Huntingdon, Earl of 341
Hurt=wounded 101 104
Hutchinson Mr 34
Hutton Col Sir Richard, Knt, 20 21 33 41 48 140 142 143 257

ILES Martin 393
Inaccurate endorsements 17 322
Ingram Sir Arthur, surprised in his own house, and brought to the Castle 182 187 317
———— William, gunner, shot through Mr Lund's house top 48, And other places 92 94 96 101 111 117, His last shots 142
Ink of the Diary becomes paler on May 9, 65
Intelligence party start for Sandal and Newark 59 64 69 76
Investment completed 50
Ireton General, his burial referred to 289
Iron Gun originally outside the Upper Gate 51, Fetched in 51, Played to Baghill 67, Shot into the town 78 Replaced in its old position 79, Played three times 81, Fired 84, Shot to the works behind Mr Rusby's and Mr Lund's 87, With 14 dozen musket bullets 90, To the new works behind Baghill 92, To the upper work above Zachary Stable's 94 101, Into the Market Place 94 96 111, Shot into the town 105, Through a house on the Bridge 109, Placed in the Garden within the Gate House 116, Played thence from the Mount to the Church *ib*, To their Lower works against the Church 117, To the Church again 118 119, Returned to its old position 142, Its last shots 142
———— at Scarborough dismounted 80
Irons put upon debtors in gaol 333 395
Isabella, Queen of Edward II (called Elizabeth) 362
Ivers Major 187

JACKSON Mr 21 34
———— Mr Charles 20

Jackson Thomas, bought some timber at the Demolition 331, Did not pay for all 332
———— ————, founder, assisted at the Survey of the Castle in 1538, 345
Jacobin Friars (See Dominican)
James I, rested at Pontefract on his way to take possession of the crown 53
Jenner and Ash, letter of Cromwell to 194
Jennings William, bought some timber at the Demolition 331
Jocky, a bye-name for the Scottish nation 204 205 215 216
John XXII Pope 370
" John of Gaunt, old," died when but 58, 373
Johnson or Johnstone Mr 20 34
————, William 267
Jolly James, engaged in the Demolition 327
Jonathan, Sir Jarvis Cutler's man, his skirmish near Baghill 44 45, His exploit at Monkhill 94
Jones Edward 244
Jubbe Wm, taken prisoner 79, But escaped 80

KATHERINE Howard visited Pontefract 355
Kay John 334
———— Mr (See Key)
Kelham Mr, (a doubtful alderman) 19, On the nominal lists 33 35, His house to the South of the Church 97 103 113, Trench to his house 106
Kendrick James 20
Kent Edmund Earl of, one of the judges of Thomas of Lancaster 365 367
Kerby's son 77
Key Mr (clericus) 20 33 95 130 140
Killingbeck, Ensign or Antient 70 98 Called Lieut 81
———— John, bought some timber at the Demolition 331
King The (Charles I) sends letters into the Castle 69 77, Reported as coming to relieve it 78
King's Army The 134 137
King's Library (Brit Mus.) E 446 quoted 159 161
———— Tower 345 360, Lancelot Lamb and Simon Procter assisted in the Demolition of 327, Edward

Willson, of the Buildings between King's Tower and the Gate House 327
Kinsley 353
Kirkby South 156 163
"Kissing the Book" but a ceremony, the formal ruling of the Court at the trial of Col Morris 266
Kitchen Capt maintains the Church 111 118
———— Great demolished 327
———————— named in 1538, 345
Knaresborough 44 245, Cannon from, brought to Pontefract 30
Knottingley 70 95 125, a messenger for Doncaster taken there 137, Morris lodged there in one bed with Col Forbes and Col Thomas Fairfax 260, Seizure of 300 Cattle there 150 155 187, Seizure said to have been at Wentbridge 321, Cromwell quartered there 189, Three troops of horse there 302, City of London purchase the manorial rights 357
Knowsthorpe, near Leeds 201

LACY Robert de, appropriated the Parish Church of Pontefract to the Priory 47
Lake Thomas, demolished the Barbican Wall 326, The two out Gate Towers and the screen by the Constable Tower 327, The Great Hall and the Inner Gatehouse 329
Lamb John, did not pay for some Timber bought at the Demolition 332
———— Lancelot, engaged in the Demolition of the Castle 327, Was paid extra for good service 328
Lambert (Major-General) sent against Pontefract Castle 152, Siege entirely left to him 199, M.P. for Pontefract in 1653, 202 228, His treaty with the Garrison 218, His letter recommending the Demolition of the Castle 231, £300 a year in land settled on him 233, His letters from Pontefract 234 235, Commander-in-chief in the north 302
Lancaster Castle 175
——————— Herald, visits Pontefract Castle 341
——————— Thomas, Earl of 361, Taken prisoner at Boroughbridge 364, and brought to Pontefract ib, Tried, condemned, executed, and buried in the Priory 73 365, His effigy in St. Paul's Cathedral worshipped, and he himself at Pontefract 369, Miracles wrought at his tomb 370 371
Langdale Sir Marmaduke 30 32 52 75 89 125 136 139 141 149 161 204 239, Defeats the Besiegers in the Chequers 29, Sends letters into the Castle 77 135, Taken prisoner and brought to Nottingham 151, Escaped 156 318, Had been in danger of being tried for his life 182 196 318, Threatened with hanging at Baghill 311, Despatched to Scotland to command the English in the Army there 294, Led the High Royalist and Episcopalian party 304
Langwith John 20
Lapidge Richard 94
Lassell Lieut Henry 179
Lathom Hall 77
Lathome Lieut. 20 34
Lathom of Carleton, a maternal ancestor of Colonel Morris 164
"Laws of God and Womanhood" 338
Lawson Sir George, a commissioner to "view" the Castle 345
Layborne Capt 20 33, Sent out to view 32, Takes Mr Ellis 38
Lead of the Castle to whom sold 330
Leaguer Ladies, taken prisoners and dismissed 74
Leavens Lieut 211
Ledger Lieut-Col, and Lieut-Col Lee brought in from Turnbridge 38
Ledstone Hall 156
Lee Capt Arthur 179
———— Francis, bought some timber at the Demolition 331
———— Thomas, engaged in lead melting at the Demolition 328
Leeds, 3000 Scots quartered at 44
———— in Kent, besieged by King Edward II 362, Not to be confounded with Leeds in Yorkshire 376
———— "the first M.P." for 201
———— Richard engaged in the abduction of Sir John Ashton 337
Legh Uriau 244
Leicester, the King took 91
Leigh Sir Ferdinando died in the gaol of Pontefract Castle 335, His daughter Frances married Dr Samuel Pulleyn ib
Leland, the antiquary 27, Quoted 91

GENERAL INDEX.

347 353 361 379
Lennox Duke 359
Lenthall, Mr Speaker 221 231 287
Lieutenant Colorel "The" 59 95
Lilburne Col Robt, 206 222 224, His letters to Capt Baynes 228 229 393 394
Lile Richard 247, Elected Alderman 248 (See Lyle)
Lillhole Kate 60
Limestone, sandstone, sand and coal measures in one curtilage 44
Lincoln 256 305
—— Earl of 361
Liquorice cultivated at Pontefract 156 157, Origin of the liquorice trade mark 156, Stored in the Dungeon 157, Plantation at the Castle 336
Lisle, Sir Warren 365
Lister Mr (clericus) 21 23 33
——Mr Richard 21
Liverpool, Morris at the siege of 278
Local Subjects, This volume restricted as much as possible to 156
Locking the stable door after the steed had been stolen 86
London, City of, reported dissentions in 111, Desire to purchase (Glass) Houghton 357, Purchased Knottingley ib, Sir Henry Tyas executed there 365, Picture of Earl Thomas worshipped in St. Paul's Cathedral 369
Long Mr Christopher, one of the Demolition Commissioners 325 328 332
Lonsdale Capt 34
Loss of Besiegers in Col Lowther's sieges 18
—— of Besieged do 18
—— on both sides in the second siege 145
Low Countries, how a surrendering garrison marched out 132
Low Prison at the Castle, what it was 334
Lowther Col Sir Richard, Governor of Pontefract Castle 20 32 33 237 245, His reply to the summons 36 107, Called John 252
—— Capt Gerard, his son, 21 34, Speaks with General Poyntz 132
—— Robert, his brother 20 21 22
—— Thomas a soldier 58, His encounter with Lieut Thomson 68 And with another Lieutenant 78,

Wounded, and loses his leg 78
Lowther William junr., J.P. 334
Lucas Sir Charles 219
Lucy Sir Asceline 366
Lumsdall Capt (Scots) 20
Lund Ald 21 33 35 140, His back yard 24
Lyle Richard (see also Lile) lent his beam and weights at the Demolition 329, And bought some timber 331
Lysle Sir George 219

ABBOT Mr 216
Madockes Mr 20 23
Magazine used as a Dungeon, which see
Magnus Mr in the Castle at the Pilgrimage of Grace 342
Maid shot in Mr Tatham's orchard 53, buried at the Church 54
Main Guard 150 157, Utilised by conversion into a gaol 157 333, Part of it now a Museum 157
Mallet, William King's Receiver of the Honour of Pontefract 348 349
Malmsthorpe Sir Robert, one of the judges of the Earl of Lancaster 365 367
Malton workman from, employed in the Demolition 328
Man Thomas 243
Manchester 80
Mankenhole Mr, high sheriff's chaplain 20 24 33
Manris (See Morris) Nicholas 243
Margaret Princess, daughter of Henry VIII visited Pontefract 353
Margetts Thomas, a Bedfordshire man 395, His letters to Capt Baynes 204, 205 206 207 208 215 216 217 221 224 236 386 396, Judge Advocate General 309, Rewarded with £50 for bringing up the news of the surrender of the Castle 233
Market Cross, proclamation to be made there 339 343
—— Place, Princess Margaret's procession passed through 353
Markham's Life of Fairfax 153
Marris Mr Richard, steward to the Earl of Strafford 157 164, Buried at Wentworth 157, Monumental inscription still there ib
—— (See Morris) Nicholas 243
Marritt Capt 246 (See Morritt)
Mary Queen (1557) orders the mate-

GENERAL INDEX.

rials of the Priory and of the Chapel of St Thomas to be used in the repair of Pontefract Castle, thus showing that any project for their restoration had been abandoned 350
M.S. in the British Museum quoted (12,482 Addl) 166
Masham Mr (clericus) 21 33
Massey Mr 20 34, Sent out on a parley 90
Mather Mr Marshall General 216
Matthews Col Humphrey 194
Mathewman Cornet 20 34 (Adcherman)
Mauleverer Col 190 192 220 223 229
Maullett Capt killed on the top of the Round Tower 28 (See Morrett)
Maurice Prince 78
Mayor and Aldermen, Petition of, for the Demolition of the Castle 230
———— Mr (Shilitoe) 21 33
Meldrum Sir John 89, Took Liverpool in August 1644, 278
Melton Abp 370
———— Mowbray 107 110
———— Sir John 354
Metcalf Mr 34
———— Mr Cuthbert 20
———— Mr John 20
———— Alexander sick of the gout 120, a rogue named Metcalf who waited upon him 120
———— Mary, her evidence against Morris and Blackburn 250
Metham Geo 243
Methley Bridge 95
Mexborough 151 313
Micklegate, Princess Margaret's procession passed through 353
Midday dinner in the Grange barn interrupted 70
Middleton (in Rothwell) 335
———— Col 33, Or Lieut-Col 20
———— Lieut 99
Miller's history of Doncaster quoted 303 318
Mines of the besieged 32, of the besiegers *ib*
Miracles at the tomb of Thomas of Lancaster 370
Mirfield John, one of the abductors of Sir John Ashton 337
Miscryed by the boy 137
Mollett (see Morrett and Maullett)
Monckton Capt Edmond 179 243
———— Sir Phillip 179 243 245,

Called Mountain 257, Narrowly escaped being sent as a slave to Jamaica 303, Commanded the Royalist troops quartered at Doncaster 320
Monks (Early) The Pioneers of agricultural progress 48
Monks Sergeant, wounded 50
———— Lieut 99
Montfort Sir Henry 365
Montgomery (Lord) his brother 70
———————— Colonel, Commander of the Scots 50
Montrose Marquis of 141
Moore Robert 20
———— Lieut engaged in two sallies 42 97, Shot through the arm 43, Sent down to the Church 116 118
More Ald Robert 19, One of the Demolition Commissioners 325 329 332, Bought some lead 330
Morley 337
Morrett Capt (or Mollett) 21 33 (See also Maulett and Marritt)
———— David 21
Morris Castilian, born during the siege 163, Town clerk of Leeds 310, His marriage 164, His MSS 217 310 (See also the Preface to this volume)
———— Col John, a South Elmsall man 156, His social position 162, His arms 163, Descended maternally from the Lathoms of Carleton Hall 164, Brought up in the household of the Earl of Strafford 149 157 277, Hunter's account of him 174, Dugdale's 175, Clarendon's 167, This latter inaccurate in several respects 173 174 226 240 252 323 ; Morris received his Ensign's commission from Earl Strafford 174, That of Captain from Sir Henry Tichburne *ib*, And that of Major from the Marquis of Ormond *ib* 270, But being taken prisoner at Liverpool 278, Served the Parliament *ib*, Especially at the Siege of Sandal 293 ; His subsequent change of front coincided with the establishment of the Directory 262, Not because he was passed over in the re-modelling of the Army 261, Summary of his attitude towards the Castle *ib*, Served under Forbes, Overton, and Fairfax 278 293, Was confederate with Col Forbes and

GENERAL INDEX.

Col Thomas Fairfax in a design to seize the Castle, in August, 1645 206, Concerned in one against it in August, 1646 148, When he was taken into custody, but dismissed on payment of Fees *ib*, Was a friend of Overton the Governor 293, Who was privy to his design 291, Which was to admit the confederates at a sally port 293, Why that design had to be abandoned 294, Had chief command of the party who attempted a seizure in May, 1648 260, By means of scaling ladders 149 260, Why that attempt failed 149, His wife visited the Castle to ascertain if suspicion had arisen 239 296, Was no intimate of Colonel Cottrell as frequently alleged 259 294, Devised a further scheme which was successfully carried out 150 300, This exploit recorded in the Church Registers 158 ; Was Governor of the Castle 254, By commission from the Prince of Wales 264, From the moment of the seizure 246 259, And President of the Castle Council 243, For the thirteen weeks that Cottrell was prisoner 260 263, And till the surrender 264, Also President of the Council of War that tried John Garforth 253, How he exhorted and encouraged the garrison 249, And acted against Cromwell's forces 250 251, Issued warrants as Governor for seizing horses, money, persons, provisions, and goods 248 251, And led the forces against Ferrybridge as far as Newhall 248 251 307, His house plundered 242, He furnished the Castle with provisions 242, Seized and brought Sir A. Ingram into the Castle 182 187 317 337, Seized Capt Clayton steward to General Fairfax 182 187 317, And sent out a party to seize Col Rainsborough 313, That he might be a hostage for the life of Sir Marmaduke Langdale 151 ; On the death of the King, proclaimed his son 208, And struck coins with the superscription of Charles II. *ib*, After nine months siege makes overtures for a Surrender 220, His accompanying Declaration 217, Excepted at the Rendition 153 322, But charged through the enemy and escaped *ib*, In company with his servant Peter, and Cornet Blackburn 236 264 319 322, Under promise that if he could escape for five miles, he should be free 175 236, Captured in Lancashire 236 264 322, Ten days after 153, While seeking to get to the Isle of Man 394, Imprisoned at Lancaster Castle 175, Depositions against him 246, Brought to trial 264, The "Exact Relation" of his trial 265, At York Assizes 319, Objects to be tried by a Civil Court 265, Pleads under compulsion *ib*, Challenges sixteen of the Jury 266, Copy of the Indictment forbidden him 267, And counsel not allowed him to argue the point 267, His Commission from the Prince rejected 269, Although he pleaded that the Prince was the King's Captain General 267, And that he owed allegiance to no one but the King and Prince 270, Ordered to be put in irons by the Judges 264 271. Though he offered to pay for a guard of even a hundred men 272, Found guilty 272, Col Bethel fails to obtain a reprieve 273, He attempts escape 274, But refusing to desert his comrade, who fell and broke his leg 275, Was retaken *ib*, And executed 279, His speech 277. And prayer at the gallows 279, Is hanged, drawn, and quartered 285, Buried at Wentworth 157, His family 164 165, His widow re-married with Jonas Buckley 165, Chronology of his life 283

——— Mathias, the father of Col Morris, his pedigree 163
——— (See Marris) Richard, steward to the Earl Strafford 164
Mortar Pieces 160, With shells 192 206, Reached Pontefract between Jan 6 and Jan 13 207, First used against the Castle in the third siege 209, Projected round stones 210, From the Castle 254, Against it 223, Blew up part of the buildings *ib* 318
Mortimer Sir Roger de Werk 362 363, De Wigmore 362 363
Motherby Thomas 21
Mountain Major 21 33, His man helps to take Mr Ellis 38

Mowbray Sir John 362, Taken prisoner at Boroughbridge 364, And executed at York 365
Munroe Capt John 21 34 57 70 104 105 141 179, Sent out to View 32, Sallied from Swillington Tower 41 48, Commanded a covering party from the Lower Gate 81 83, Led out the first company 97, Maintained the Church 102 118
Munson Capt John 179
Musgrave Capt 20 34
Musten Mr 22 34
Muston Hugh de 365 368

NASEBY 105, News of the Battle there reached Pontefract 107
Naylor Cornet 20 34
Nevil Mr Gervas, in Lowther's sieges, 21 34 141, In the third siege 243 244 252
Newark 140 of the Garrison go to 30, Attempts to communicate with 59 64 69 111 128 132, News from 62 91 111 133 134 141, The Scots before 293
Newcastle 256
New Hall, about a musket shot or two from the Castle 150, Held by a small garrison *ib* 309, Reached from Eastgate 158, Abandoned by the Garrison 190 318, Morris led the forces that attacked Ferrybridge as far as New Hall Orchard 248 251 307 (See Part II.)
New Well water 67
Nicholson William bought some Timber at the Demolition 331
Nicholas St, Hospital of, the right of presentation vested in the Crown after the Dissolution 355, Till transferred to the Corporation *ib*, The Crown presents *ib*
Northallerton, the Scots burn it 366
Northampton 112
Norton Mr 34
Norwich Lord 219
Nottingham, the prison of Sir Marmaduke Langdale 151 182, His escape thence 156 190 318, Parallel between Pontefract and 182
Nostell 353
Nunn or Nunns Cornet 21 34

OATES Ald 21 33, The Family 84 379

Oates Isabel (née Frank) 84
—— William, has a lease of Denwells 27
Officer (Parliamentary) in Buff 45, In Red 94
Ogle Mr exchanged for Lieut Browne 37
Ogleby Capt 41 42 48 81, His name not on the nominal lists 48
—— Lieut 81
Old Style, Time reckoned by, in the Diary 107
Oldridge William 267
Oley Mr (clericus) 20 33, Preached 66
Ollerton and Ollerton Böate (See Allerton Bywater)
"Or from thence, or—" 81 83
Oreton in Furness Fells 175
Ormond, Marquis of, gave Morris his Major's commission 174, And was in communication with him the month of his death 270
Ottoway Ensign, or Ancient 70 98 117 118
Outhwaite Peter, bought some Timber at the Demolition 331
Overton Colonel, their Governor 84 90, Governor of Pontefract 111 112, Sends for Lady Cutler 123, Vacillates with respect to the treaty 141 142 143, Was Governor of the Castle after its surrender 260 261, And when Morris first conceived the design of seizing it 293, Was one of the *via media* 291, Had persuaded Morris to serve in his troop 278, Was transferred to Hull 292, Had he remained Governor, the Castle would probably have been seized with his consent *ib*, Had some iron delivered to him at the Demolition for the public service of Hull 331, And some timber 332
"Overquart," across 91
Owen Colonel Sir John 193 194
Oxen as beasts of burden ; fourteen and a horse used to draw a carriage 70, Eight to four carriages 134
Oxford referred to 111 194, Paulden's narrative reprinted there 148
Oxley John (2nd division) 20, (3rd division) 21, One of his name engaged in lead-melting at the Demolition 328 329, —— Joseph 21
Oyston Dr, (not Gybson) a physician among the besiegers 128

PAGE John 365
—— Pakington, William de 361
Palace, that princely 235 268 325
Palmer William 243, Capt 246
Papers and Letters taken at the Castle, referred to the Committee for the King's Cabinet Letters 147
Parish Church, the Garrison habitually attended service there 90
Park, Parliamentary Horse Guard there 312, Its extent *ib*
Parker Mr 34
—— Sergeant 99
Parley, a "gentleman of ours" shot during a 66
Parliament de la Bende 362
——————— dissensions in 111
——————— the Rump 201; Higher House of Parliament, a Presbyterian toast in 1645 70, Journals of the House of Commons, their record of the imprisonment of Col Morris in 1646, 147 148 174
Parsnips fetched in 132
Pattison Mr 26 27
Paulden Brothers, Thoresby speaks of four 324
——————— Thomas, a captain of foot 149, His first narrative of the seizure of the Castle 149, The mistakes in it confirm its truth 156 158, His fuller history 293, Compared with his first letter 323, Frequently inaccurate in dates 295, But can generally be corrected by internal evidence 155 296, Commands that party in the attack on Rainsborough that seized the Main Guard 155 316 321, One of Morris's council during the siege 152 246, One of the Commissioners for the Treaty of Surrender 152 222, Brought before Cromwell 153, How he escaped *ib*, His age 155, Date of his death unknown 158, but between 1702 and 1719 *ib*
——————— Timothy, a captain of horse 149, One of the Council 243, Wounded at Ferrybridge 320, Was Major to Col Boynton 153, Killed at Wigan *ib*
——————— William, a captain of horse 149, A leader in the surprise of Pontefract Castle 150 239 240 293, One of the two who seized Col Cottrel 259 299, Was one of the Council 243 246, Projected and carried out the capture of 300 cattle at Knottingley 321, Had his horse shot at Ferrybridge 320, Had part of the command at Allerton Bywater 308, Attacked the advanced works of the besiegers 310, And made five other sallies 310 311 320, Laid the design to seize Rainsborough and hold him hostage for Sir Marmaduke Langdale 151, Had charge of the party at his seizure 151 316 321, Died of a fever in the Castle 153 218 319
Paul's St Cathedral 73, Earl Thomas's likeness worshipped there 369
Peele Henry 267
Pembroke 186
——— Aylmer Earl of, one of the judges of Thomas of Lancaster 365 367
Percey Lieut 20 34
——— Mr, senior 21 34
——— Mr, junior 21 34
——— Mr, frater 34
Perry Lieut, dismounted one of the enemy's scouts 43, Assisted at an improvised sally 44 55
Pert Capt, at Lincoln, plundered by the Royalists 178
Peter or Peters, Col Morris's servant 228 236 258 259 264, An Irishman (probably connected with him in consequence of his service in Ireland) 252
Pickering Mr (clericus) 21 33
Pilckliffe Richard 21
Pilgrim Fathers, nursed at Scrooby 353
Pilgrimage of Grace 341
Pilkington Capt 21 34
Plague in the town 137
Plantations, Royalists sent to the 286 325, The practice of sending prisoners there was the direct parent of negro slavery 287
Playing the Fool 107
Pocket Pistols at Scarborough dismounted 80
Pocklington Colonel 179
Pole Cardinal, letter from Mr Hamerton to him 351
Pontefract not Pomfret 154, Borough Disfranchised by Oliver Cromwell (For References to Places within the Town or Castle, and Works, see Parts II and III of Index.)

GENERAL INDEX. xix.

Pontefract Park District 68
——— Priory, Tithes of Pontefract appropriated to 14 47
Portington Lieut-Col. Robert 20 33, Colonel 243 303, Commanded some of the horse which quartered at Doncaster 320, Fought and made prisoner at Willoughby 179
——— Capt. Roger 20 34, Colonel, One of the Council among the garrison 243 244, One of the Treaty Commissioners 222 303
Post Mortem Patris, Pro Filio, the motto of both Pontefract and Worcester 270
Post, weekly between Pontefract and London during the Third Siege 204 205 207
Potherbs, a woman gathering, shot 78
Potter John, bought some timber at the Demolition 331, But all was not paid for 332
Pouke Thomas 20
Povntz General 102 103 111 141 143 146, Summons the Castle 107, His good will to the Garrison 108 120 132, Asks to speak with the Governor 131, Sends in a message 139, And his Trumpet to fetch the Commissioners 144, The House of Lords requested that he should be appointed Governor of Pontefract Castle 147
Prayers From, to the Watch 91
Preales (See Freales)
Precedent, "The First in England" 222, None for trial of Col. Morris by Civilians 265, Nor for Ironing a Martial man 276
Presbyterianism of Scotland *versus* English Independency 216 304
Presently=at the present time 84 85 107 114, and also Immediately 113 139 298
Preston, Duke Hamilton defeated at 151 181, The Commonwealth garrison liberated from the Dungeon in Pontefract Castle after the Fight at 255
——— General 175, Mr 20 34
Pride Col, his "Purge" 180 200 201 293, Opposes the reprieve of Morris 273, Seizes the King 293
"Priests," Mr Margetts's plan of dealing with those that were "disaffected" 215
Prince Maurice 78 80

Prince of Wales, Morris's commission to seize the Castle was from him 246 264 267, And the garrison looked to him for instruction to maintain 254 318, Or surrender 319
Priory of Pontefract, Tithes of Pontefract appropriated to 14 47
Proclamation of Charles II, as King, prohibited 208
Proctor Simon, assisted at the Demolition of King's and Queen's Tower 327, and Swillington Tower 328
Prouston, as carved in the Magazine, mis-read as Brougton 257, mis-pronounced as Sprowston *ib*
Puleston Judge 175, At the trial of Col. Morris 264 265, Whom he threatened to iron 264, His otherwise outrageous conduct 266
Pull down Pontefr'=Pontefract Castle 394
Pulleyn Dr Samuel 335
——— Archbishop of Tuam 335

QUARTER Sessions were authorised to order the Demolition 325

RACES, Horse, depending among the Besiegers during the third siege 211 220 229 389
Radcliffe Sir Edward 20 33
——— Sir Francis 20 33
——— Mr 20 23 33, Capt. 42
Raids by the Garrison to Wenthill, (query Wentcliffe near Ferrybridge) Turnbridge (twice) and Doncaster 38
Rainsborough General sent to terminate the siege 151, With 800 troops 313, Or 1200 151 318, His headquarters fixed at Doncaster 151, His disposal of his forces there *ib*, What emboldened the Royalists to attempt his seizure 151 182, Their object 317, Had been an Admiral 182, His seizure and its circumstances 314, Parallel between it and that of Col. Cottrell 315, How the command of the attacking party was divided 320 321, Rainsborough's death frustrated the scheme of his captors 317
Ramsden Ald. John 237, One of the Demolition Commissioners 325 332
——— Capt 21 33
——— Col. Sir John 21 33 41 42 48, Blackburn at first supposed to be his

Tenant 77, And in his deposition claimed to have been his body-servant 264, Appointed to treat 140 143, His endurance while in the gout 144
Ramsden Wm, of Langley 251
Randall Thomas 366
Rapier 299, or Tuck 150 241
Ratcliffe (See Radcliffe)
Reaser Mr 21 34
REBELS defied 77, Hypocritical and treacherous 49
Red, all in 99, Red Scarf 100
Redhead Mr 246
Redman Capt 22 34, Killed at the Bridge 38 39
Reformadoes 140 308
Relative pronoun frequently omitted by the Diarist:
   A ould meare of ours (which) was turned forth to grasse 62
   Trenches (which) was made there 71
   We saw one officer fall upon Baghill (who) was shot from the Round Tower 101
   All other ammunition (which) was within the work *ib*
   From that work (which) was taken *ib*
   A man shot (who) was going down 103
   Killed a woman (who) was bringing ale 104
   To two troops of horse (which) was there 107
   Shot a cow of ours (which) was feeding 111
   Twelve pieces (which) was lost 112
   At those (who) was making *ib*
   All (which) was lost 113
   Letter (which) was sent from their Governor 142
   Letter (which) was sent from Newark *ib*
Relieving the Sentries and Guards an opportunity to attack 55 56 94 103 105 117
Religious Foundations of Pontefract, List of those Suppressed 352
Rennard George, engaged in the Demolition 329
Requisitions from the Castle 296
Requital by the Dutchman 138
Reresby Francis 243, Gervase 244, Leonard 243, Mr 246

Reynolds Thomas 267
Rhodes Sir Edward, raises militia forces, though he had promised to help the Royalists 303, Commanded in the third siege 150 179, Stationed at Leeds 305 Was advancing towards Willoughby when the battle took place *ib*, Quartered at Featherstone 308 320, His regiment disbanded 204, Bought some lead at the Demolition 330, But did not pay all the value *ib*
Rich Capt. John 179
Richard II 361, His second wife was only a child, and not a woman as represented by Shakespeare 373, Whose account is in other ways not in accordance with historical fact *ib*, Three theories of Richard's death *ib*, It is probable that he was starved to death 374
Richmond Earl of 2, one of the judges of Thomas, Earl of Lancaster 365 367, Taken prisoner at Byland 366
Riddell Robert 243
Ridge of the hill in the Park 76
Ringing the Church Bell as an alarm 113
Risby Capt. John 179
Roads calculated for horse traffic, not carriages 70
Rob an Orchard, soldiers on both sides agree to 141
Roberts Major George 179
Robinson Wm 267
Roche Sir Edmund 366
Rokeby Major 207 392, Col. Thomas 222 229 236 237 396, Bought some timber at the Demolition 331
Rolls of Parliament quoted 337
Rooke Corporal, proposed jockey of Capt. Baynes's horse at the Clifford Moor Races 211
Rookesby John 267
Rookes Mr 21 34
Rosemary in the hat (a badge to be worn during an encounter) 37
Rosse Castle 175 177
Rossington 95
Rossiter Col. 139, Raised forces, though he had promised to help the Royalists 303, Fought and conquered at Willoughby 178 179 245 305 306, But wounded and left behind in Lincolnshire 308
Rotherham 123

GENERAL INDEX.   xxi.

Rothwell Mary, bought some timber at the Demolition 331
Roundheads before Pontefract 203 (See also under Baynes and Margetts)
Rump Parliament 201 216
Rupert Prince 30 39 130
Rusby Ald. 21 33 (See also Part II)
Rutland Earl of 341
Ryder Sir Ralph 353

SAFFE come and sauffe go 344
St Nicholas, Thomas, letter from Cromwell to 196
St Quintin, Sir William, high sheriff at Morris's trial 267, Ordered him into irons 273
Salisbury Earl of, lord high treasurer 357
Sally made by Capt. Smith 40, By two horse-men 40, By 90 men 40, Under Capt Washington and Capt Beale (horsemen) 41 42, With Capt. Smith (foot) on Easter Day 42, Into Middle Street ib, To Baghill (twice) 42, To Monkhill 43, To Newhall 44, To the Trenches 48, To Baghill ib, To Newhall 49, To Monkhill (twice) 51, To Monkhill 55 56, From Swillington Tower in two directions 57, To the Work below the Low Church 58, To Monkhill ib 59, 61 69. To the Low Church ib, To the Abbey Close ib, General sally 70, Sally to Newhall 73, Sally to get in 97 beasts 81, Gallant sallies 97 113, Gallant sallies in the third siege 150 209 210
Salt, plenty in the Castle at its surprise 150, Why Capt Thomas Paulden loved it 153
Saltmarsh Capt William 179
Saltonstall Major Walter 179 (or Norbington) 243, Called William 246, Commanded a party in the attack on Rainsborough 320 321
Samond Capt 144
Sand, sandstone, lime and coal measures within one curtilage 44
Sandal Castle, Sir John Savile attacked in three sallies by a party from 49, Attempts by the Pontefract garrison to communicate with 59 117 132 134, Capt Horsfall went forth to 64, Two messengers sent to 65 (of whom Thomas Hanson was one), Their return 69, Hanson and another sent there again ib, Hanson brings news from 77, Capt Washington and Lieut Wheatley sent there 78, Their return 81, Sandal soldiers 81 84 96 120, Skipton horse reported to have gone by Sandal 136, Enemy send parties to 134 136, Messengers sent to 128 (twice) 132 134 (See Bonfires), Castle thought to have been surprised by a party from 159
Sanderson Cornet 21 34
Sandstone, limestone, sand, and coal measures in one curtilage 44
Sandwich 362
Sauce, Green 66
Savage Sir Edward 353
Savile, Baron, of Elland 156, Bought some lead at the Demolition 330
——— John, of Methley, bought some lead at the Demolition 330
——— Lady, wife of the 3rd Bart., and mother of the 1st Baron, concerned in the attempt of Sept. 1646, 147 156 383 385
——— Lieut. 21 34
——— Samuel, concerned in the attempt of Sept 1646 148 156, Not of the Thornhill branch of the family 157, His son married Martha Cudworth 390
——— Sir George, 1st Bart, 156, The principal cultivator of liquorice at Pontefract ib, His crest, an owl, used in the liquorice trade mark ib
——— Sir Henry, "viewed" the Castle officially 345
——— Sir John, his drake 25, He brought a force from Sandal 43, Had been attacked and defeated by the Sandal garrison 49, Came to Newhall 53 58, One of his men killed at Monkhill 54, 16 of them driven away by 3 (or 4) of the garrison 55, Skirmish with a party of them 56 58 59, They lined a long hedge and a deep ditch with 60 or 70 men 61, Skirmish with them ib
——— 354
——— Sir William, 3rd Baronet, 156
Scammenden Stephen 20
Scarborough Castle 78
——— 44 78 80 89
Sconce set up for safeguard 116
Scotch march, Manner of 94
Scotland King of, affianced to Princess Margaret 353

Scots, 3000 at Leeds and other places 44, 600 came to Newhall 50, Were defeated repeatedly in one day 51, Sent a drum to the Castle *ib*, But fired upon those who came to speak with him 52, Strengthened their trenches *ib*, Went away as they came, through the Park *ib*, but left company behind 53 ; Their first work in the Monkhill High Street 70, They return in full force 130, 131, Their action in surrendering the King fatal to the Royal cause 293 294
Scot Major John 179
——— Thomas 179
Scrooby 341 353
Scurr or Skurr Ald John, the senior magistrate of the Pontefract Bench that took depositions against Morris, 237, Was one of the Commissioners at the Demolition 332, Though not authorised by the Order of Sessions 325, Bought some lead at the Demolition 330, And timber 331, Lived in Ropergate 389
Seaton Mr 22 34
——— Capt. 20 33
Seizure of the Castle by Col. Morris 149, At first attributed to Col. Bonivant 159 160, Early account of it which reached London 160 161
Selby 44
Self-denying ordinance 293
Senior Thomas 20
Sergeant-at-arms receives the conspirators of Sept. 1646 into custody 148 156
Sermon on Easter day, April 6, 41 ; April 13, 44 ; May 11, 66 ; May 18, 70 ; Whit-sunday, May 25, 79 ; June 1, 89 ; June 8, (the last preached in the Parish Church) 95 106 ; July 6, 130
Seventeenth century writings redolent of Scripture phraseology and language 274 280
Shakespeare, much of the popular history drawn from his writings 373
Shaw Capt. 21 33
Sheffield 96
——— Lodge 357
Sherburn, besiegers driven beyond 29, The Barons assembled there 362
Shillitoe Mr (mayor) 21 33
——— George 21
Shooting and shouting 94 102 107

"Shot" contrasted with "played" 112 113 118, and with "hit" 139
Shrewsbury Earl of 341, Steward of the Honour 353
———————, Gilbert, a letter from, quoted 357
Shrove Tuesday 28 32
Sidlinges=Sidelong 96
Siege (First) commenced 25 26, Second siege begun 25 38, At first thought to be only to confine the Garrison 39, Closed by capitulation 144, The third virtually commenced on Sept 9, 1648, 310, Ended also by capitulation 227 319, By direction of the King *ib*
——— coins struck in the Castle 208, List of them 212
Signals suspected to pass from some traitor within the Castle 69 70
Sikes Mr, (clericus) 21 33
Silkstone 119 120
Skepper Edward 243
Skipton Castle 77
——— horse 136
Slane Dr 210 221
Slater Wm 243
Sleeping soldiers shot on the Round Tower 89, And in the Lower Barbican 92 116
Sling pieces used by the besieged 28 43 50 52 54 59
Smith Ald. 20 33
——— John, employed in the Demolition 327 328
——— ——— his wife Mary's evidence against Col. Morris 255, Master of the Magazine under Col. Cottrell *ib*, Imprisoned there by Col. Morris *ib*, His name still to be seen on its walls 256 262
——— Lieut (1st div) 20, Capt-Lieut 34, Had his lip cut with a stone 28, Makes a sally 40 41 42 57 69 70 81 83 98, Relieves and maintains the Church 107 118
——— (2nd div) 20 81, Lieut to Capt. Munroe 57 112 118
——— Mr Wm, the host of Rainsborough at Doncaster 318
——— Richard, bought some timber at the Demolition 331
Smithson Major 224
Smyth Edward, in trouble, 392 394 395
——— Ensign John, excepted as one of the Royalist correspondents 153 252

GENERAL INDEX.   xxiii.

322, Killed in the attempt to escape 153 322
Snaphanches 81 83 100 101 107 111 112
Soldiers joyful and merry 67 109 136
Somers's Tracts quoted 264 *et seq*
"South Yorkshire" quoted 157
Speed in artillery practice of the Besiegers and of the Garrison 114 115
Speght Cornet 20 34 48 49, Capt. 50 78
Spence John, killed in the Barbican 27
Spencer (See Despenser)
Sprowston, a cannoner 256 (See Broughton and Proston)
Spurgeon Cornet (See Speght)
Stables (should be Stable) 20 33
—— Mr Richard, His prentice in the Castle was wounded while getting grass 92
—— Zachary 5, bought some timber at the Demolition 331 (See also under Works)
Stage Trick of the Besiegers 121
Standeven Capt (2nd div) 20 34
——————- (3rd div) 21 23
—— Stephen 21
Stanhope, Lieut-Col. Michael 243 303
Stapleton Mr 20 34
—— Mr Brian 21 23
Steele Walter 20
Steeple of the Church 26 100 104 116 118
Stileman Alexander, his evidence against Morris 256
Stiles Wm, Vicar of Pontefract till March 1642, letters from him to Adam Baynes 387 388
Stocks Thomas, prisoner in the gaol of Pontefract Castle 335, Reminiscence of him there 336
Stone throwing 78 113
Stow Park 364
Strafford Earl of, Col Morris had been page to the 149 175
Strickland Mr 21 34
Stringer Mr 21 34
Stuart, Lady Arabella 357
Styvelyne Battle of 362
Sulley Sir William, killed at Boroughbridge 364
Suppressed Religious Foundations of Pontefract 352
Surnames prevailing in each parish changed largely in the seventeenth century. Why. 288
Surrender of the Castle after the third siege, negotiations for 181, Took place on Easter Eve, the last day of that year 227
Survey of Pontefract Castle, 1537-8 345
Survivors of the third siege were only six or seven score out of 600, 319
Sutlers female 54 63 104
Sutton Matthew 20
—— Nathaniel (a barber) killed 61
—— Robert, bought some timber at the Demolition 331
Swift Peter 20
Swillavant Capt. 21 34

TADCASTER 29 53 355
  Tailor Richard 253, His deposition against Col. Morris 248
Tankersley 391
Tanner M.SS. in the Bodleian quoted 287
Tanshelf 127, the lane there 76, Wind mill there 128, Belonging to the Corporation of Pontefract 129, The manor in the jointure of Queen Anne 1619, 356
Taptoo beat 67 117 118
Tatham, Mr Ald. John, A vintner 20 33, His orchard 53 103 104, Morris lodged with him 157 247 251, Evidence of his wife, Mary, against Col. Morris 251, William, his son 20 23, In his deposition "knows nothing" 257, Particulars of the family *ib*
Tattersall Employed in the Demolition of the Gate Houses 327, Of other Towers and Buildings *ib*
Taunton 120 133
Tayler Thomas assisted in demolishing the Chapel, Constable Tower, &c., 327, And bought some timber 331
Taylor Mr, to depart the Garrison for a misdemeanor 246
Tennet Mr (See Ferrett)
Thanksgiving, Day of 122 189
"The" occurs in Drake's Diary for "they" 57 74 75 78 79 80 81 93 125 127 128 130 131, Sometimes corrected 81 93
Thimbleby Major, his unfortunate disobedience at Ferrybridge 320 321
—— Mr John, senior 21 23 34
—— Mr John 20 23
Thomlynson Thomas 267
Thomson Lieut, taken prisoner by Thomas Lowder 68

Thoresby 163, His pedigree of Col. Morris 164 165, Letter from Rev. F. Drake to him 309, Perused M.SS concerning Pontefract 310, Where are those M.SS *ib* (See Preface to this volume)
Thornhill 156
Thorpe Judge 175 264 265 394
"Three very good hogs" 58
Throngest=most crowded 55
Thurley Cornet, shot in the arm 68
Thurstan Abp. 72 73
——— Thomas, demolished Neville's Mount and the Upper Barbican Wall 326
Thwaites Thomas bought some timber at the Demolition 331
Tickhill 95 355 363
Tickle time 206 215
Tindal Lieutenant-Col. 21 33
——— Mr George 21 34
——— Mr William 21 34 140
Tinmouth Castle (See Tynemouth)
Tobacco "prohibited" 80
——— pipes frequently found (broken) near Pontefract 82
——— smuggled into the Castle 120
Todd Capt. and his company taken at Turnbridge 256
Tofield (or Tokefield) Mr 20 34
Tomb of Thomas, of Lancaster, in the Priory Church at Pontefract 73 369
Tomson John, assisted to "view" the Castle 345
Tootell Charles, bought some timber at the Demolition 331
Touchet Sir William, taken prisoner at Boroughbridge 364, And executed at Pontefract 365
Towley Mr Jacob 228
Towton, battle of 73
Treaty of Surrender at close of second siege 139 to 144, At close of third siege 181 to 227
"Trent northwards" 341
Trinities, Church in the, Mr Hamerton's pathetic appeal to Cardinal Pole for its restoration 351
True list of the Knights, Gentlemen, and Volunteers in the First Siege 20
Tuam, Abp of 335
Tuck 150 241, or Rapier 299
Tulley Capt. goes with 140 horse and men to strengthen Newark 30
Tupman widow, her house at Monkhill 62

Turnbridge (beyond Snaith *and not beyond Ackworth*) 38, Raids on by the Besieged 38, Capt. Todd and his company taken at 256, Used as a base by the besiegers 257, Petition to Parliament concerning its bridge 378
Turner Richard bought some timber at the Demolition 331
Tutbury 363
Tuxford 93
Two and twenty engaged in the attempt to sieze Rainsborough 151 313 321
Tyas Sir Henry 362, Executed in London 365
Tynemouth Castle 256

UNDERMINING attempted 32
   Unlucky hole 204
Unpossible 140
Upper Gate, description of its position 157
Uttoxeter 308 309

VALENCE Aylmer of, Earl of Pembroke 367
Vapouring, 10 of the enemy's soldiers came vapouring 64, (Compare Braving up 56)
Vaughan Colonel 21 33
Vavasour (Vaucer) Capt. 20 33
Vermuyden Sir Cornelius 105
Vernon Colonel 244
Villeroy Marshal 149
"Volley" spelt "Valley" 122
Volunteers list of, in the Castle on 25 Dec. 1644, 33 34
——— true list of the Garrison in the First Siege 20 21

WADE Capt. taken prisoner by the besieged 48
Wain loads of wounded men carried away 43 49
Wakefield 76 295 302 355 356
——— Ald. Joshua 19 27
Wales Prince of 303 304 309, Ultimately ordered the surrender of the Castle 319
Walker Capt. Joshua 26 81 100 103 118, Killed one of the enemies 80, His snaphanches 81 83 100 111, Maintained the Church and Steeple 100
——— Thomas 20

GENERAL INDEX.

Wallingford 366
Walton Hodgkin 367
War-cry " Arms " 49 81 152 314, " A Prince " 75 81, " A Cromwell " 78, " Horse " 135
Warde Capt. John, his house was along the ditch 28 32, His assurance to the Garrison 109 110, Was one of the Demolition Commissioners 325 332, And ordered seven soldiers to receive extra pay 328
—— Lieutenant 41 42 48 70 81 98, His name not on the nominal list 48 103, Shot in the arm when going down to the Church 102, Which Warde was he 103, A Lieut Ward bought some lead at the Demolition 330
—— Major 21 33
—— —— Old 70 71
—— Mr Leonard bought some timber at the Demolition 331
—— Patience, his copy of a warrant for the repair of the Castle 348 350
—— Sir Simon 363
—— William, bought some timber at the Demolition 331
Wards, for-and to-, bearing no reference to the name Warde 51 109 131
Washington Capt 21 33 49, Horse sally under (twice) 41 42, Goes towards Newark 76 111, Towards Sandal 78 81 82, Returns 80
—— —— Col. 107 108
—— —— James 243 244 246
—— —— Mr and Mrs (of Pontefract) 133
Wastall Col. 229
Wasthill Mr (a lawyer) 143
Waterhouse Capt. of Netherton 22 26 34
Watson John bought some timber at the Demolition 331
—— Wm 20
" We " Did it include the Diarist? 101 113
Webb Edward 243
—— Thomas 243
Welbeck 96
Welburne Mr 210
Welington Sir Henry 365
Well New, Water of, and a suggestion regarding it 67
Wells, Three in the Castle in 1538, 346 347
Welshmen, fellow-feeling among 130

Wench keeping a cow 80
Wentbridge, hill on this side 29 128, A strong guard there 131
—— 300 oxen said to have been captured there 321, (But see Knottingley)
Wenthill, Mr Ellis seized near 38, Its position (probably Wentcliffe) *ib*, Reinforcements to the besiegers came over Wenthill 95
Wentworth Col. Sir George 21 33 41 48 109 110 140 142 143 144
—— Lieutenant-Col. 21 33
—— Major 21 33
—— George 20
—— Sir Thomas, bought some lead at the Demolition 330, Had been privy to the attempt at seizure in Sept. 1646, 384
—— William 243
——s of North Elmsall, Col. Morris descended from 164 165
Werke, Sir Roger Mortimer de 362
West Chepe, an ancient township merged into Pontefract in 1250, 39
Westchester, (Chester) news of the battle or siege at 54 78 89 (?)
Westminster Parliament at 149, Gatehouse at 153
Wether William, alias Bellwether, leads attacks 44 45, Fetches in a Barwick sutler 54, Goes to Newark 76
Wharton Sir G, his ' Chronology ' inaccurate 226
Wheatley Capt. 20 33 42
—— Lieut. 20 34, Goes towards Newark 76, To Sandal 78, Returns 81, His exploits 81 82 83 98, Maintained the Church 109 118
—— Lieut-Col. 20 33, Was one of the Commissioners to treat 140
White Col. 185, Had promised to help the Royalists 303 305, But joined Cromwell 308, Quartered at Ackworth *ib* 320
—— Lieut Robert 179
Whitelock's Memorials, Account of Col. Morris's trial from 276
Wigan defeat of Royalists at 152 181
Wiggins (Widow) in distress 392
Wigmore, Sir Roger Mortimer de 362
Wilcock Richard bought some lead 330
Wildman John bought some timber at the Demolition 331
Wilkes Mr 20 23

xxvi.   INDEX.

Wilkinson Ald. John 21 33, his house in Micklegate 64, houses near 105
——— —— Thomas 19 21 33, Killed at Barbican gate 43
Willoughby Field 179 244 257, A decisive overthrow 306
———— —— Lieut 70 99 104 113 118
———— —— Sir Francis, Morris was senior captain to him, at Dublin, in 1642, 174
Willson Edward engaged in the Demolition 327
Wilsford Buckley 165, His arms still exist in Pontefract 166
Wilson Mr 20 23
———— a trooper taken prisoner by the Garrison 42
Winchelsea, Sir James Colepepper executed there 365
Winchester, Hugh Despencer made Earl of 365
Windebank Sir Francis, letter to, concerning Pontefract Castle 358
Windsor, Sir Francis de Aldenham executed there 365
Winter Mr, of Hull, bought some lead at the Demolition 330
"Witness" preferred by the Diarist to "Evidence" 139
Woodstock Edmund of, Earl of Kent, one of the judges of Thomas, Earl of Lancaster 365 367
Worcester battle of, Sundry prisoners taken there sent into slavery 289
Wortley Sir Francis, authorised by James I. to keep certain courts leet 359
Wosewkeille Otho 243

Wrench, a Parliamentarian captain, a means of the arrest of Col. Morris 175, Or was he Lieutenant? 237
Wright Capt. Anthony, 179
———— Thomas, paid for providing 67 Loads of soil to bury 1200 Scotch prisoners taken at Worcester 289
———— William bought some timber at the Demolition 331
———— a, wounded on the Round Tower 66
Wrigley George, assignee of John Potter 332

"Y" in M.SS of the 15th and 16th century frequently mis-read as "z" 138
"Yearly" for "early" 59 60 70 128
Yonge John 267
York 33 37 44 68 369 390, The headquarters of the besiegers 37 43 95 96 102 103 142, How the news of the seizure of Pontefract Castle reached York 159, Col Morris tried at the Assizes there 153 264, York expected to surrender the same day as Pontefract 255 256, Ammunition removed from Pontefract to Clifford Tower 326, Archbishop in the Castle at the time of the Pilgrimage of Grace 342, Thomas of Lancaster brought there after the Battle of Boroughbridge 364, Some of the adherents of Thomas of Lancaster executed there 365 367
———— Richard duke of, buried at Pontefract 73

PART II :—CASTLE AND TOWN.

ABBEY Close 56 94, Their work side in the bottom of it 75, 480 men came in single file through 86, At this time bounded by Pontefract Park 87

BACK Closes and Town field behind Baghill 125
Back side or Back yard: Mr Lund's 24 62 63, At Trinities 45, Mr Rusby's 104 122, Ald. Stable's 126
Baghill (on the south side of the Castle) 25 40 and *passim*, Sallies to 42, Port hole upon 64, Character of the ground 75, Chequer field to the south 75 83, Round Tower commanded 76, The Bable at 76 77, Primrose Close, under 80, Closes by or below (over against the Church) 81, New work there 90 92, Further side of 102, Back closes and Townfield behind 125, Bottom close, the scene of the treaty 143 (See Works) Gallows there 253 254

Baghil', lane going up to (at right angles to Baghill Lane) Barricado there 84 126
——— Lane, towards Darrington 127
——— top 81, Old dike there 45 57, Lined with musqueteers 51 to 55, Old hedge there 43 45 74, By their works 84, Also lined with musqueteers 51 to 55, Store of ale brought into the triangle work 61 63 (See Works)
Bailey gate 46
Bakehouse Tower 345
Barbican, some of the garrison shot in the 27 28 32 60 68 122, Three hogs seen out of, and fetched in 58, New Mount within 51 52 70 81, Garrison assembled there 101
——— Gate, (a sally port 81 133,) Ald. Thomas Wilkinson, killed there 43, Work just against 131 139 142, Contracting parties met there 143, No present trace of 44 126 (See Works)
——— Low 70, Sleeping men shot there 92 116, Covering party lined the walls 70, Over which the two forces could communicate 96, And over which a rogue escaped 120, Demolished by Thomas Lake 326
———, Trench in the, man shot while working in it 63
——— Upper, Wall demolished by Thomas Thurston 326
Barley Market Place, plague there 137
Battlements 37 63, round about the Castle 101
Battley's (Mr Robert) barn and new house 64
Bell at the Church 113 115
Blind Hardwick 97
Bondgate 46 57 Mill dam there 51, Cannon from King's Tower to 105
Booths, The 83 158
Booths Wm. (in the Park) 39 96
Bottom Close under Baghill 143
Breach made in the wall 37
Bridge towards Monkhill 70
——— between the Market Place and Micklegate 38 39
Broad lane end (on the Baghill side of Micklegate) 58, Commanded by Elizabeth Cattell's burnt house 81, Trenches below 45, Works below 64 81 95, Close under Baghill, and a little above Broad Lane End (the scene of the treaty) 143 (See Works)
Burnt houses 39, At Monkhill 62, Near Elizabeth Cattell's house 81, Halfpenny House 140
Butts overlooked by the Treasurer Tower 40

CASTLE, To be neither garrisoned nor demolished, but made untenable 148, The greatest and strongest Castle in England 149, Demolished 153, Col. Overton was Governor in Aug. 1645 260, and till Nov 1647, 294 295. Col. Cottrell succeeded him 259, Side towards Monkhill 84 85, Pontefract Field before the 256
——— Chain 353
——— Dikes 123
——— Gate (the Porter's Lodge), Mount before 51 52 81, Was within the Barbican 70 (See Gate, Upper and Lower)
——— Wall, breach attempted 31, Mines without 32, Closes about 50, A little house under 60
——— Yard (See Low Barbican) Traverses within 32, Filthy pond in the 68, Garrison assembled ready for assault or sally in 126, Correspondence read in 142
Castleford Road 68
Cattell's (Elizabeth) house in Walkergate, fired 28, And the burnt houses thereabouts 81, Not far from Broad Lane End *ib*
Cattle Laith 28
Causey Lane 60 76
Chapel in the Castle 120
Chequer Field, Battle there 29, separated by some closes from Baghill 81 105, The town field behind the hill 125, Facing the Castle 127 256 311
Cherry Orchard head, near Newhall, 51 70, Side 74
Church Balk Lane 29
——— Lower, fired at 25, Taken in the first siege 26, Double staircase there 26, In possession of the besiegers 40, Who left those killed there unburied 58, Their lowest works by 70, Closes over against 90 92, Steeple of 26 100 113 116 117, An advanced guard of the besieged there all night 100 102 104 105 *ib* 107 109 111 *ib* 112 113 114,

Day time only 116 117 Houses on north side of 99 101 116, Do. south side of 81 116, Church Top 113, Lantern 114, Lantern struck 115, Ten of the enemy came vapouring there 64, Works below the 81 97, Blinds from Mr Kelham's house to the 103, Battery planted against 113 115 116, Besiegers entered 113, And make a Work there, digging up dead men's corpses, 119

Church Upper 58 247
———— Yard 26 113, Cow feeding there shot 111, Upper side of the 116 (See Works)

Clerkwell 41

Close, Abbey 56 69 94 112, Up the closes 111 112, Below Baghill over against the Church 81 90 92, By and under Baghill 81, About the Castle Walls 50, Under the Castle within reach of Baghill 54, Near Swillington Tower 80 95, Primrose Close, a round Close under Baghill 61 80 81 126, Man killed there 92 94, Two little closes near the work below the Church 107, At Monkhill 55, Hard by Monkhill 56, Above Denwell 86 111, Under the Headlands 105. Below the town 27, At west end of the town near Clay dike 125, Round the town 121 131 135, Bottom Close under Baghill 143

Commencement of First Siege 26, of Second Siege 38, Of Third Siege 310

Constable Tower written for Swillington 27, Demolished by Thomas Taylor and Edward Willson 327 328

Cowper Bonny, his shop in the Market Place 88

Cutters up of Clottes 27

DARRINGTON Lane (another name for Baghill Lane 29

Denwell or wells, Right of the inhabitants to bleach clothes there 27, Sometimes called Clerkwell 41, A resting place between Monkhill and the Castle 56 58, A triangle work in the closes above 86 87 111, Lane 70 111, Separated from Swillington Tower by the length of a hedge 132 (See Works)

Dikes, Castle, horse turned into, to feed there 123

Ditch, (or Moat) Warde's house along the 28

Donjon or Round Tower, the chambers therein in 1538, 345 347

Drawbridge Lower, Man shot entering at 91, Cannon shot entered through 122, One less successful 126 129, Barbican Wall, which extended from the Great Stable to, demolished by Thomas Thurstan 326, Graft filled up there 328
———— Upper 150 157, Graft filled up there 328
————s, Both to be demolished 327, And walled up 329

Dungeon ; garrison imprisoned in the Magazine 150, Which was the cellar under the Norman Hall 157, Forty-two steps led to it 263, not thirty 150 241, Garrison kept there eleven weeks, or above 255 286

EAST Gate at the top of the Booths 158 (See Lower Gate)

England's house (in or near the Chequers) 29, The battle began at the long hedge leading from *ib*

FARRER William, his door 125, Under Monkhill 129

Featherstone Lane 60 76

Four hundred people at least within the Castle, where did they all sleep? 72

Frealles (see Preales) 32 45, Their south side was just beyond eyeshot of the Castle 46, But could be seen from the King's Tower 127

GARDEN within the Gatehouse 116 117 118

Garth of the Castle 329

Gate House, (Castle Gate, or Porter's Lodge), Screen to, from Round Tower demolished by John Harrison 327, Chapel, Constable Tower and rest of the Buildings to, demolished by Thomas Tayler *ib*, Lake and Handson demolish the Inner Gatehouse 329, Except one fragment 333
———— Lower (facing East) Sally from 41 48 81 126 129, Messenger from the Scots came to 51, Exposed to Monkhill 52 61 96, To Baghill 61, The house there 96 115, called also the Castlegate 116, Trench from it to the

Church, through Mr Tatham's orchard 103, Work made before it by Garrison 113, Point blank shot through 122, One less successful 126, Parliamentarian in trenches killed from the top 133, Was at the top of the Booths 158
Gate House (facing Baghill) Col. Forbes's drum sent down to 37, a Sally Port in the Barbican 133, at which 97 cattle were got in 81
—— ——s Two (Upper and Lower), Tattersall employed to take off their Timber 327, Thomas Lake and others complete their demolition *ib*
—— Upper (facing Micklegate) 126 Outwork above 51, man shot there leaning on a gun 91, Iron gun originally on platform there 51, And after three changes 51 79 116, Finally replaced in its old position 142
Graft (or dry Moat) bullets fetched from 31, At the low Drawbridge 327, At the upper Drawbridge 328
Grange Barn, or Lathe 55 69 71 72 99, Midday dinner there 70
—— Field 46
—— Lane 51 56 70 75
—— Lathe side 104
Greave Field, part now called Cattle Laith 28
Guard House demolished 327
Gyllot Tower (Gaol), another name for the Round Tower 348

HALFPENNY house 31 41 85, Burnt 140, Probably the present Hope and Anchor 60 85 86, Was under the Castle Wall 60, A little house between it and the Wall burnt *ib*
—— lane, in Tanshelf 60
Hall, The, Conference in 140, Service in 143, Demolished 327 329, The Buildings connected with it in 1538, 345
Hardwick, Blind, Spital, East and West 96 97
Headlands, Closes under the 105
High Street to Monkhill top, "by Scotte's" 70
—— from the Church to the Castle 113
—— called Middlestreet 42, And Micklegate 64

"Hope and Anchor," corrupted into "Halfpenny" House 60 85 86
Hospital (St. Nicholas's), shot from Swillington Tower to 27, Mine within towards the King's Tower 32, One of the Sandal men wounded at its door 84 86
Houses burnt (See Burnt Houses)

JACKSON Mrs, her door in the Market Place 55

KELHAM Mr 33 35, His house near the Church 97 103 113, Trench south of 106
King's Chamber 67
—— Close 127
—— Tower 32 37 40 44 64 69 74, Cannon from played to Mrs Oates's 81, to the Market Place 91 107, To Baghill Lane 127, To New Hall yard 86, To Baghill or the close under 92 107, To Bondgate 105, To St Thomas's hill 112 125, To Monkhill 112 114, To the Church steeple 118, To the Town 126, To the Freales 127, To the Church 128, To the New Hall 142, Flag of defiance set up on *ib*

LANE to Baghill 84 126
Long hedge from England's house to Baghill top 29
Low Church (See Church)
—— Park House 68
Lower Barbican wall 96
—— Gate, (See Gate)
—— Town, still at liberty, 38, Fired 50, Wood fetched from 76
Lund Mr, his back yard 24, Cannon fired from at the west end of the Castle *ib*, Trench commenced before Mr Lund's 39, Powder explosion there 42, Great trench there attacked by Capt Hemsworth, and little work by Lieut Favell 48, House top shot through *ib*, One of the besiegers killed there 53, Consultation of besiegers there 54, His back premises extended to North Street 62, And were between the Trinities and Mr Rusby's *ib*, A man killed in the trench behind his house 64, And one in the Barn behind 65, Iron Gun shot into the works behind Mr Lund's house 90

MALFAY Gate, the mediæval name of part of Southgate 46
Market Place, Cannon shot into the 28 42 55 56 69 81 91 96 126 142 144, Towards the 64, Six cannon brought into the 30, A volley of shot in the 64, Enemy drawn up in the 111
Market Place Upper 128
—————— Barley, plague breaks out there 137
Mayor's (Mr) barn in Northgate burnt 64
Micklegate or Middle Street 42, That street 40, Called High Street 64, Mr Battley's new house there *ib*, Mr John Wilkinson's on the other side *ib*
Middle Row 84
Mill, Water-, under the Castle 78 93, An officer shot at the Mill door 78, At Monkhill 94 112 ; Stone Windmill near Westfield, 128 ; Mill Dam at Bondgate 51
Moat by the Round Tower 32
Monkhill, on the north side of the Castle, 25 40 & *passim*, Houses below fired 28, Lower end of, fired 50, Slight attack upon 51 58, Upper end of, fired 51, Sally to the top of 51 56, Scots there fired upon those sent to receive a parleying party 52, Sally to 55, Closes at *ib*, Closes hard by 56, Unordered Sally to 58, Poor Kate Lillhole's house on 60, A long hedge there, and a ditch lined with 60 or 70 men 61, Widow Tupman's house there burnt 62, Half moon at 65, An alarm at the new work there 69, A bridge towards 70, Outworks at the back of *ib*, High Street to Monkhill top *ib*, First works in the High Street there *ib*, By the Castle Side towards 84, A soldier in the works killed from Queen's Tower 92, Mill there 94 112, Cannon planted against the Church *ib*, William Farrer's under 129
Monkroyd 47
Moody's Close, near Baghill 96
Mount (Nevill's 52) in the Barbican 70, before the Castle Gate 51 52 79, Near the Lower Gates 61 62 81, The earth mount called Nevill's mount, demolished by Thomas Thurstan 326

NEVILL's Mount, (see Mount)
—————— Tower, its condition in 1538, 345 347
Newhall 25 27 40 & *passim*, Cherry Orchard 70 94 112, Sand bed below the Hall 44, Barricado at hedge at Cherry Orchard Head near 44 51 Sally to 49, 600 Scots come to 50, Left the same way they came 52 ; Sir John Savile and his company replace them 53, Had ale brought them by a Barwick woman 54, Were attacked by some of the Garrison 56, 150 soldiers came from over Ferrybridge 56, A sentry receive a night attack from the Garrison, and run towards New Hall 57, A troop from Doncaster came to 68, Attack upon by the Garrison 73, About five hundred men come to 76, Works below the Church were a Guard to New Hall 81, The sallying party *would* go up to New Hall *ib*, Relieved by a strong guard of horse 96, Relieved every ten days 104 131, Relieved with 320, 105, Relieved with 140 Scots 131, Final shot from King's Tower into 142
New Hall Yard fired into from King's Tower 86
Nicholas (St) hospital 60 97, Shot into from Swillington Tower 27, Mine from towards the King's Tower 32, At its door 84 86, Reached from the East Gate 158
Northgate, sentry houses at the lower end of 28, Besiegers set fire to their own work there 80, Another house there burnt 84, Sally into 41 42 48 57, Escort party came back through 59 ; (North Street), Sentries there 62, Two barns of Mr Shillitoe's and Mr Robt Battley's burnt 64, Other houses burnt there 78, Some of the Garrison went to get apples there 137
North side of the Low Church, about the Star 99
Nursery, The 68

OATES Mr, Leaden Porch 40
—————— Mrs, her house in the Market Place, a conspicuous mark, 40 80 81 84, Her kiln-house near the Upper Church 58
Old Church, strong house near, taken

CASTLE AND TOWN.

possession of by the besiegers in the third siege 190
Orchard, Cherry at Newhall 70 94 112
———, Mr Tatham's, close by the Lower Castle Gate 53 93 103
——— Paradise 62 63 84 86, Drake from Swillington Tower shot towards 79, Probably the same as 137
——— thick of trees, opposite the
——— Zachary Stable's 92
Grange barn 69
Outwork belonging to the Garrison above the Upper Gate 51 142, Belonging to the Besiegers against Barbican Gate 131 139 142

PARADISE Orchard 62 63 137, Drake on Swillington Tower shot towards 79, The hedge there *ib*, Work there *ib*, Man killed in Mr Rusby's closes under 84 86
Park, The 40. Reinforcements came through 32 50, Returned same way 52, Cannon shot to 28 40, Besiegers' horse drawn up in the 37, Wm. Booth's in the 39 96, Hedges betwixt the Well and 40, Detachment of besiegers through, to Ferrybridge 58, Intelligence party accommodated to 59, Horse assembled in the evening there 68, Its extent 68. From Darrington to the West Field, and so to the 76, Trumpet sounding in the 94, To Ferrybridge through 105 107
Parsnip Garth 109
Penny Lane 60
Piper Tower fall of 24, Way through rammed up with earth 30, The only tower that gave way 31, Its condition in 1538, 345, Not named at the Demolition because already down 330
Pits sunk within the Castle 32
Platform (leads) by Treasurer Tower Nicholas Baune killed there 40, The cannon was on the Leads *ib* 105, The Dutchman was cannoneer 126 138 142, And fired the last shot from 144
Pond in the Castle Yard 68
Porter's Lodge, or Gatehouse, part still remaining 333
Portholes were above the reach of a man's head 133, But shots passed through them 50 66

Primrose, a little round close under Baghill, so called 61 80 81 92 94, Now deported 61 82
——— Cottage 61
Priory of Pontefract, received the appropriation of the Tithes of the Parish 14, Princess Margaret passed through the Castle and lodged at the Priory 353, Thomas of Lancaster buried there on the right-hand side of the high altar 365-368, Closed on account of the miracles there 372
Pudding Middings, old name for Church Lane 41

QUEEN'S Tower, Shot from to Monkhill 92, Named in 1538 345, Lancelot Lamb and Simon Proctor assisted in its Demolition 327

RATTEN Row 84
Red, or Gascoigne Tower, the later locus of King Richard's murder 155
Redman (Peter) his tanpits 92
Ropergate End 127, Princess Margaret's procession entered the Town through 353
Round Tower *passim*, Bonfire on the top of 78 80 92 96 122 124 130 134 136 137, Flag of defiance set up on 142, King Richard II. died there 153 155 358, Called the Donjon in 1538 345, Its then condition *ib*, Called the Great Round Tower in 1557 348, And the Gyllot Tower *ib*, Its then condition *ib*, Said to be within and without the walls *ib*, Demolished by John Harrison 326, As were the screens therefrom to Gate House and Treasurer's Tower 327, Lancelot Lamb assisted in its Demolition 327, Casing of the foundation alone left 333
Rusby's Mr 40, cannon shot to *ib*, His lathe (being a sentry) and part of his house burnt *ib*, Lowest trench there 59 62, Trench behind 64, Sentry house over against 79, Trenches against 80, His closes under Paradise Orchard 84 86, Works behind his premises 87 90, Works in his back yard 104 122 140, Houses against shot through 105, A man killed within Mr Rusby's Barricado 129

CASTLE AND TOWN.

ST. NICHOLAS Hospital (See Nicholas St.)
St. Thomas's Chapel, stones therefrom ordered by Queen Mary to be used in the repair of Pontefract Castle 349
———— Hill, enemy ran away over 73, The back lane on the north side of 112, King's Tower played to 125, Stones ordered to be brought from the Chapel there, for the repair of Pontefract Castle 349, The Earl of Lancaster beheaded there 365, Miracles wrought there 366 369
Sallyport ; In the Barbican 81, The chaplain met Lady Cutler there 123, Mrs Washington came there to speak with her husband 133, Original plan of the seizure of the Castle in 1646 was that Morris should open a 293, Why that plan was abandoned 294
———— under Piper Tower rammed up with earth 30, Austwick, Ashby, and Floyd hid there 153, Recently cleared out 158
Salter Row 84
Sandal Road 60
———— men who relieved the Castle 81, Attempted to return 84, (See Sandal Castle in Part I.)
Sandbed below the Hall 44
Sandhill near the Bridge at the top of Micklegate 49 57
Schoolhouse, Barricade at back of 51
Screens from Round Tower to Gate House and Treasurer's Tower demolished 327, And that by Constable Tower ib
Skinner Lane 68 87 312, End, sentry at 40, Head, besiegers' colours set up at ib
Spittle Hardwick 97
Stable, Between Baghill and the Castle 63
———— Wall from the Great, to the Low Drawbridge 326
———— Alderman, his back premises bounded by a hedge 126
———— Zachary, his orchard head 92, The upper work above 94, His house near the Church 98
Star, on the north side of the Low Church 99
Stone Wind Mill 128
Swan Hill Flat 29
Swillington Tower *passim*, Sally from 41 48 57, An ox put out to graze near Swillington Tower killed from Monkhill 61, Half moon to prevent sallies from 65, Green sauce gathered without 66, Belwether and Hanson, the messengers, met there 69, Drake planted on 27 79 87, A little poor wench shot while keeping a cow, under 80, Upper side of 86, New work over against 87, Work behind *ib*, Close near 95, Another work begun there 96, It contained 70 men 131, Was separated by the length of a hedge from Denwell Lane 132, Two triangle works to the North of 137 ; Demolished 322

TANSILL (Tanshelf) lane 76
Tanpits, Peter Redman's 92 93
Tatham Mr, his orchard close by Lower Castle Gate, a young maid shot there 53, Trench through to the Church 103
Thomas (St.) (see St. Thomas)
Towers in the Castle, all towards Baghill could be seen from the Mount in the Barbican 70
Town field behind (or before) Baghill (See Chequer Field)
Traverses within the Castle Yard 32
Treasurer's Tower, Nicholas Baune killed at the platform there 40, The fire at the top of Micklegate reached by shot from 64, Two men in the Park killed by cannon from 76, Platform was on the leads by the 105, Shot from into the Market Place 126, Screen between it and the Round Tower demolished 327
Trinities 53 62, Backside (between Northgate and Micklegate) 45, Mr Hamerton petitions Cardinal Pole for its restoration 351, The Religious from, in procession, met the Princess Margaret 354
Tupman Widow, her house 62

VICAR'S Closes 68

UPPER Gate (See Gate)
———— Park House 68
———— Town 38 51-58 *passim*

WAKEFIELD'S Mr, The houses behind 27

SUPPLEMENT. xxxiii.

Wakefield road 60
Walkergate, Elizabeth Cattell's house was there 28 81
Wall of Castle strengthened with earth 30, Undermined 32
Warde's house, works along the ditch from 28, Opposite the Round Tower 32
Water Mill below the Castle fired 78, And the houses thereabouts *ib*; Robbed of its iron 93, Prisoners taken there 94, Grass there 112
Well, position of, not yet discovered 30
—— hedges between Denwell, and the Park 40
Well, New 67
West end : Of the Castle opposite Mr Lund's back yard 24 ; Of the Church 26 ; Of the Town 134
Westfield 125 127 128 129 130 131 134 136, Soldiers marching from Darrington to 76, Behind the hill in

the 132, Trenches there 136, General reported to be there *ib*, Report that all the soldiers were to be encamped there 137
Wilkinson Mr John, his house in Micklegate 64 105
Willow Park 75 239
—— Tree Closes 75
—— —— Flat 239
Wind Mill, Pontefract Stone-128
Wool Market, present name of the Barley Market 137

YARD : Traverses within 32, Filthy Pond there 68, Wounded boy walks up and down the Castle Yards 92, The Garrison sports, plays and shouts there 109, 136, Ordered there ready for assault or sally 126, Correspondence read in the Castle Yard 142

PART III :—SIEGE WORKS.

(The bracketed figures refer to the Works on the large Siege Plan.)

WORKS OF THE BESIEGERS :—
(At the first siege :—)
In Mr Lund's back yard 24, From Warde's house along the ditch 28, Mine below that house, under the moat, and towards the Round Tower *ib*, Below Warde's house 32, Within the hospital towards the King's Tower *ib*
(At the second siege ;—)
Guards (See Plan) [A] At Skinner Lane Head ; [B] School House ; [C] Upper Trenches ; [D] Pinfold Guard ; [E] Horse Guard at Baghill ; [F] Baghill Guard ; [G] East Guard ; [H] Tenalian Guard ; [I] New Hall Guard
On June 2, 1645, the Works were twenty-six in number 90. The following are named in Drake's diary :—
Barricades : At a corner of a hedge near Newhall 44, Called also Cherry Orchard Head 51 ; At the Back of the School House [19] *ib*, In Baghill lane [14*] 84 ; Another in the lower lane 126 ; One at Will Farrow's door under Monkhill 125 ; And one at Mr Rusby's 129

Half Moon works, at Monkhill, [23 a b, d,] against Swillington Tower 65 69, Below Baghill, over against the Church [27] 90 92 94 98
Mines 32
Sentry houses at the lower end of Northgate 28, Fired by the Besiegers themselves 80 ; Upon Mr Lund's back premises 62, At Skinner Lane End 40, Over against Mr Rusby's 79, At lower end of town 40 57, At Widow Tupman's at Monkhill 62, And one nearer the Upper Castle Gate 142
Sentry lathe at Mr Rusby's, and two others, attacked and burnt 40
Triangle work at Baghill [14] 60 63 74, In closes above Denwell [23] 86 87, Two more [a, b] on the north side of Swillington Tower 136 137
Works on S. ; [14 14* 14† ;]
The hedge and the dike all along Baghill 51 55, Night work of 100 men, half the way in the old dike 57, Trench on Baghill 58, And all along the hill 59, Difficult to work on account of the stone 58 ; — Night work of 300 men 59, Trenches al-

SUPPLEMENT.

most finished *ib*, And other works which they had made under the hill, betwixt it and the Castle *ib*, Their chief work was a triangle walled with stone and filled with earth [14] 60 74, It was blinded with boughs 61, And it was supposed to contain a Drake 61 63 ; It had a port-hole 64, And was above the Round Close 81, Called Primrose Close 61 80 81 92 94 ; There was a lower Barricado in Baghill lane [14*] 84, Another in the lower lane 126 ; 34 Guards on Baghill 64, and 42 Guards 75 ; Another work near to Barbican Gate 139 142 ;—Moody's Close 96, Trench along the hedge against Ald. Stable's back premises [14†] 126, Which was full of portholes to shoot out at *ib*

Works on S.W. : [16 17]
Trenches below Broad Lane End [17] 45 64, Lowest work under Broad Lane End [16] 81 95

Works on W. : [18]
Trench at Alderman Lund's house 39 48, In Middle Street 42, Called also the Great Trench 48 ; The Upper Trenches [C], Were nearer the Bridge *ib* ; Trenches on Mr Lund's back premises 53 63 104 122 140 ; Enemy's powder set on fire at Mr Lund's 42, Great Trench there attacked by Capt. Hemsworth 48, Mr Lund's housetop shot through *ib* ; Trenches above the Castle towards the town 60 ; The lathe or barn behind Mr Lund's 62 65 ; Trenches about Paradise Orchard, Trinities, Mr Lund's & Mr Rusby's 62, The great iron gun shot into the works behind Mr Rusby's and Mr Lund's [18] 87 90, Men killed at the relieving of the guards there (twice) 64 ;—Mr Rusby's lathe was a sentry 40, The lowest trench there 59, There was a trench behind (twice) 64, And a sentry house over against 79, There were trenches against Mr Rusby's 80, And a Barricado there 129 ; A sentry house nearest the Upper Castle Gate 142

Works on W.N.W. : [19, 20, 21, 22, A] Sentry houses at lower end of Northgate 28, Attacked 57, Fired 80 ; Sentry at Skinner Lane End, 40, Barricade behind Schoolhouse [19 B] 51 ; The hedge at the bottom of the Abbey Close lined with musqueteers 56, New work at the bottom of the Abbey Close [22] 69 75 ;—A work at Paradise Orchard all along the hedge [20, 21, 22] 79, Colours set up at Skinner Lane Head [A] 40

Works on N.W. : (Pontefract side of the road) [23 24 a b c d]
Divers hedges lined, between the well and the Park 40, Denwell still at the disposal of the garrison 58, Guards at Monkhill 63, New work in manner of a half-moon [23] 65 69 70, Called a Triangle 86 136, Against Swillington Tower 65 69 87, Outworks at back of Monkhill up by Denwell Lane [a] 70, First lower work there *ib*, Was in the High Street by Scotte's *ib*, Another work begun, near Swillington Tower [b] 96, Fence all along the hedge side from the work against Swillington Tower into Denwell Lane 132, Works made up betwixt the two triangle works [c, d] 136, They made portholes there 137

Works on N. : (The road, and the Monkhill side of the road)
Trenches beyond Halfpenny house 41, Sir John Savile's men beaten from the houses to their Works 55, And to their Trenches 56, First trench there 59, Sir John Savile's men beaten from the hedge at Monkhill into their Works [24] 61, Sentry house in Widow Tupman's house at top of Monkhill 62, Trenches there impassable for horsemen 71, A man killed in the works at Monkhill from the Queen's Tower 92, Platform constructed for cannon at Monkhill 112, Lantern of the Church fired at from it 114 115 116, Barricado at Will Farrow's door under Monkhill 125

Works on N.E. :
Barricado at the corner of a hedge near Newhall [I] 44, Called a Work 49, Bulwarks from to Monkhill top 51, Sir John Savile's quarters about Newhall 58, Guards at Newhall strengthened by 42 men 75, Grange lathe was occasionally used by the besiegers 55 69 70 99

Works on E. : [26, in three positions] Sentry houses at lower end of town 40 57, Scots began a trench from upper end of Bondgate Mill Dam towards the Newhall Barricade 51, 52, Work below the Low Church (in Coney Garth) [26] 58 69 76 81, Was then the lowest there 70 97

Works on S.E. : [27 27* 27† 27‡] New work like a half-moon in the closes below Baghill over against the Church [27] 90 91 92, Which was also called " the upper work above Zachary Stable's" 94 101 ; It was shot at by William Ingram with his Iron gun, from the Castle Gate 92 94, It was close to the hedge 94 ; A lower work at Zachary Stable's orchard head, [27*] 92, It was " about 120 yards" from the half-moon [27] in the closes below Baghill 92, And on the other side of his house from the Church 98, It was a low work 95, And their lowest work 98, Taken by Capt Flood *ib*, But not held by the garrison 100, There was a hedge between the works [27 and 27*] 94 98, The low work [27*] had one little place for entrance, narrow and low *ib*, Which the enemy would gladly have enlarged 109 ; Another work [27†] "Was about 80 yards" from the work taken by Capt Flood [27*] 101, The Iron Gun shot Cannon Bullets and Case shot through it *ib*, 100 burdens of grass obtained by the garrison from near the low work 104, Trench on the south side of Mr Kelham's [27‡] to hinder that practice 106, Trench continued through two little closes 107 109 ; 27* was then the lowest work near to the Church 116, 27† shot into by the Iron Gun 117 ; Works in the Church 119

Works and Trenches in West Field 134 136 137

THE TRENCHES AT THE SECOND SIEGE :

March 22. The enemy fell a trenching in divers places [as foundations for Works], but especially before Ald. Lund's house ; [that is halfway up Micklegate].

April 6. The besieged sallied ; went by the Halfpenny house to the Trenches at Monkhill.

Same night. They fell upon Northgate, and so into the Middle Street, *above* the trenches. [C]

April 7. Men in the trenches killed by musket shot from the Round Tower.

April 14. First mention of trenches below Broad Lane End. [17 ?]

April 16. The trenches at Mr Lund's, and the Upper Trenches [C] attacked.

April 20. The Scots fell a trenching from Bondgate Mill Dam towards their Barricade at Cherry Orchard Head. [I]

April 22. They made those trenches stronger, but did not run them further on.

April 26. After much lining of the hedge and the old dike at Baghill, the besiegers came at night and commenced a trench as foundation for their work. [14]

This day and the next, being beaten from their work below the Church, [26], the besiegers run to New Hall.

April 27. A hundred men were working in the trenches at Baghill, but went not far forwards by reason of the stones there.

April 28. Trenching at Baghill continued by at least 'three hundred men.

April 29. The trench at Baghill was almost finished. Sir John Savile's men beaten from their first trench at Monkhill. The lowest trench in Micklegate was that near Mr Rusby's, (and west of Mr Lund's).

May 5. There were trenches about Paradise Orchard, Trinities, Mr Lund's and Mr Rusby's.

May 18. There was a trench at the upper part of High Street, Monkhill, which was impassable by horsemen.

June 13. A trench made by the Garrison from the Lower Castle Gate, through Mr Tatham's Orchard.

June 15. A trench made at the south side of Mr Kelham's. (27‡)

June 16-17. A trench made through two little closes there.

June 21. The trench made by the garrison on June 13, used by the besiegers.

July 1. A trench run all along the hedge against Ald Stable's back premises. (14†)

July 10. Trenches run near the Castle.
July 14. Trenches in the West Field.
WORKS OF THE BESIEGED :—
(At the first siege :—)
Two Traverses in the Castle Yard *ib*,
Mines under the Castle Wall 32
(At the second siege :—)
Guard between the Lower Gate and the Mound 61, Trench in the Barbican 63, Trench from Lower Castle Gate through Mr Tatham's Orchard to the Church 103 113, Blinds from the Church to Mr Kelham's 103, New work before the Lower Castle Gate 113, At the Barbican Gate 131
BATTERIES OF THE BESIEGERS:—
Long Drake at Baghill
Fired at the south side of the Castle 25, Against the Round Tower 61, Loaded with case shot 63, This Little Buble (but query Bauble) played three times 76 77
Demiculverins
At Newhall 25, From Monkhill to the Church 25 113 114 115 117
BATTERIES OF THE BESIEGED :—
From the ROUND TOWER only Muskets were fired *passim*. But four Sling Pieces were shot to Baghill 54 ; From the TREASURER TOWER ; And the Platform there 40 138, Which was at its side 64, A Cannon was fired to Mr John Wilkinson's house (near the Bridge *ib*, To the Park 76, The Dutchman played his Cannon to Headlands 105, And into the Market Place 126 142 144 ; He makes a requital to the Park 138. From SWILLINGTON TOWER : Five Drakes fired to the Hospital 27, The little Drake placed there and twice shot towards Paradise Orchard 79, Shot six times to the new Work over against Swillington Tower 87. From the QUEEN'S TOWER : One man at Monkhill killed 92. From the KING'S TOWER : The Cannon beat down the colours at Skinner Lane Head 40, Was shot to the sand-bed below the Hall 44, To Mr Lund's house 54. To the Market Place 64, Fired as a signal 69, Shot to Monkhill 77, To Mrs Oates's 81, To New Hall Yard 86, To the Market Place 88, 91, To the New Work against the Church 92, Towards New Hall 101, To Bondgate 105. To Baghill 107, To the Market Place *ib*, To Monkhill 112 114, To St Thomas's Hill 112 125, To the Church Steeple 118, Into the Town 126, To Baghill Lane 127, To the Freales *ib*, To New Hall 142
The Great Iron Gun (William Ingram gunner 48, 92, 94, 96, 101, 111, 142) Which was originally outside the Upper Gate 51, Having shot through Mr Lund's house top 48, Was fetched in on April 21 to be placed on the Mount 51
Having been played to Baghill 45 67 74, And into the town 78, It was placed in its old position on May 26, being Whit-Monday 79 ; It was then played ro the sentry house over against Mr Rusby's *ib*, Three times to the works in the town and about the town 81, Was fired to Baghill 84, And shot to the works behind Mr Rusby's and Mr Lund's 87, With 14 dozen large Musket Bullets 90 ; It was shot to the new Work under Baghill 92 94 101, Killing a muster maister, and a common soldier 93 ; It was afterwards shot into the Market Place 94 96 111, Into the town 105, And through a house at the Bridge 109, It was placed in the Garden within the Gatehouse on June 24 116, When it played to the Church *ib*, 118 119, And to the lower works against the Church 117
It was returned to its old position outside the Upper Gate on July 17 142, Whence it made its final shots *ib*
(One of the missiles projected by this gun, weighing 32 lbs and measuring 1ft 7½ins in circumference, with a diameter of rather more than 6 ins, was found embedded in the soil at Baghill in May, 1876, when the Swinton and Knottingley Branch Railway was in course of formation. It was of moulded iron.)
(At the third siege :—)
Major Lambert's Fort Royal [14] 61, Trenches near Swillington Tower 209, Barricade within carbine shot of the Castle with three foot colours 310, Horseguard on Baghill *ib*, Each attacked by the Garrison and broken up *ib*, Horseguard in the Park 312,

SUPPLEMENT.

Order of Construction of the various Besiegers' Works :—

Jan. 17, 1644-5.—Cannon planted in Ald. Lunn's back-yard (on a retaining wall as a platform)

Mar. 22.—Trenches begun in divers parts of the town, and especially before Ald. Lund's house.

April 13, 1645.—A Barricade mentioned, apparently before Mr Lund's.

—— 14.—A Barricade at Cherry Orchard Head.

—— 17.—A Work at New hall.

—— 26.—Trench made on Baghill as a foundation for the Works (14.) Hitherto a "Work" has meant an occupied building.

—— 29.—There were Works at Baghill (14), and under the Hill (14*).

May 1.—(14) was a Triangle Work, and the lower work (14*) was in the Round Close (Primrose Close.)

—— 6.—The "Triangle Work" (14) still spoken of as if it were the only Work.

—— 9.—There were Works below Broad Lane End (17 ?)

—— 10.—A new Work at Monkhill in the manner of a half moon (24).

—— 14.—There was a Work below the Lower Church (26), and at the bottom of the Abbey Close (22).

May 18.—There were outworks upon the back of Monkhill (24a), and the first lower Work there (24b) was in the High Street by Scott's.

—— 26.—There was a Work at Paradise Orchard all along the hedge (21)

—— 28.—A Barricade was made in the lane going up to Baghill (27).

—— 29.—The enemy made a Triangle Work in the closes above Denwells, near to the upper side of Swillington Tower (24c).

June 2.—They made a Work like a half moon in the closes below Baghill (27*), which, on June 6, was styled the Upper Work above Zachary Stable's.

—— 10.—They began a Work near Swillington Tower (24d).

—— 11.—The lowest Work the enemy had was that near Zachary Stable's Orchard Head.

—— 21.—A Work (25) made against the Church.

July 1.—The besiegers "crossed the lane going up to Baghill" with wood, and ran a trench all along the hedge by Ald. Stable's back side (14‡).

—— 14.—There were two Triangle Works (24c, 24d) on the north side of Swillington Tower.

SUPPLEMENT.

ABBEY Close 420, 423
All Saints' Church, correctly represented in Jollage's Map 410
Antiquaries, Society of, published a view of Pontefract Castle 397
Ashmolean' Museum, no copy of Pontefract Siege Plan there, as asserted 418

BAGHILL Guard 412, 429, Was a New Work on 2 June 431. So called in reference to the Work in Primrose Close 432
Baghill, the Work there was a Fort Royal at the last Siege, but a Triangle in that of 1644 432
Baghill Orchard 432
Ballium, to a great extent covered with buildings in the 14th Century 407

Barbican 400, Was called the Inner Barbican on later Plans ib
Barn, Great 404
Basire, four engravers of this name 410, The first James engraved the first Siege Plan 411
Battery at Monkhill commanded the Church, 427
Blackfriars, founded by Edmund de Lacy 398, Its situation 433
Bondgate 428, Or Old Pontefract 419
Boothroyd Dr., published the Siege Plan No. 2 411
Bottom Close 432, 434
Bowling Green 403
Box Lane=Grange Lane 427
—— Close=Cherry Orchard 427
Boxe, John, 429
Bramhall John, had a lease of St.

xxxviii.   SUPPLEMENT.

Clement's Chapel which his son Peter sold 407
Bridge at Monkhill 425, Laid upon oaken piles *ib*.
Bright's (Col.) Work 424
Broad Lane End, Lowest work there 432 ; Extended into Southgate at the time of the Siege *ib*
Buck, his View of Pontefract Castle was taken from memory only 397
Buckley Jonas, married Col. Morris's widow, 436

CANAL Close 433, 434
Cattell Elizabeth, her house near Walkergate, burnt 432
Cesspool in the Round Tower, A difficulty with King and Gent 402
Chequer Field, Horse Guard there 432
Cherry Orchard Head, erroneously assumed by Boothroyd to be the Tenalian Guard 427, Otherwise called Box Lane Close *ib*, Barricade there *ib*, 428
Clement's (St) Chapel, was Collegiate 399, The Norman building on the Garth 407, The medieval building on the northern ramparts 407, Had no rights of interment 405, Dissolved and the revenues let to farm 407, The successive holders of the property 407, 408, The refounded Elizabethan or Jacobean building near Constable Tower 405, 407
Cobcroft, St. Nicholas 409, 410
Coining evidences found in the Castle 407
Coney Garth 428, 429, 430, 433
Constable Tower 404, 405, 412
Cromwell's Fort, or Cromwell's Foot 412, 417, 424, 432, He never bombarded Pontefract Castle 417
Cross, St Oswald's, the seat of the religious observances of Pontefract 419

DARRINGTON Road 424, 431, 433
Dean's Fort 412, 424, 425
Denwell Lane 425
———— s 423
Downing Edmund and Miles Dodding had a lease of St. Clement's Chapel 407
Drawbridge at East Gate 404
———— ——— at West Gate 400

Duchy of Lancaster Office had preserved the view of Pontefract Castle till 1734 397, And 1753 410, But its present whereabouts is not known 397, Though it may be in the Record Office 410

EAST Gate and Drawbridge 399, 400, 404
East Guard 412, 428, 429, 430
East Mill 428
Ellen's (St) Chapel 408, 409, 410, 415

FAIRFAX Col. Charles, was in command of one of the Pontefract Siege Batteries 417, 423, Had a copy of Pontefract Charters which he supplied to Roger Dodsworth *ib*, His Royal Horn Work 412, 417, 422, 423
Fairfaxes of Denton, said to have possessed the original of Basire's Siege Plan 411
Fairy Hill=Ferry Hill 423
Ferret Joseph, the Cromwellian Minister of Pontefract, not ejected, as generally asserted 418
Flanker Wall accurately represented in the Engraving of the Society of Antiquaries 400, It separated the First from the Second Ward 401, Little of it now remains 403, Its present condition *ib*
Forebuilding to the Great Gateway 403, To Piper Tower 404
Fort Royal 412, 432, Was a Triangle at the first Siege *ib*
Frank Henry purchased the tithes of St Clement's Chapel 408
Frank Richard, the Recorder, his Siege Plan 415, 420, 421

GALWAY'S (Lord) Drawing reproduced by the Surtees Society 411, Was probably the earliest of the Siege Plans 413, Described *ib* to 415.—See Siege Plan No 3.
Garden Lane 419, 435
Gascoigne Tower 408
Gent Thomas, published a View of 'Grange Chapel 417, A South Prospect of the Castle 418, A View of the Ancient Hermitage *ib*, And one of All Saints' Church *ib*, His difficulty with Horreum Spatiosum 402

SUPPLEMENT. xxxix.

Giles (St) Church, was not represented in the medieval prints 408
"Grange Chapel" was St John's Priory Church 415, View of it published by Thomas Gent 417, Differently represented by the different artists 426
Grange Field, the site of the Priory of St John 426, 433
Grange Lane 426, Otherwise Box Lane, 427, Sallies of the Garrison up 428, Tenalian Guard was across it 429
Grange Lathe 426, 428
Great Gateway 403
Great Lathe or Barn 404
Guards The, were in rear of the Works 421

HALFPENNY House=Hope and Anchor 425
Harewood, Earl of, owns the monastic property, and is lay Rector of Pontefract 423
———— Well, a probable corruption of Harrop 433
Harrop Well Garth 433
————— Lane 435
Henry de Lacy (1278-1307), his time an active building era 398
Horse Guard in Chequer Field, Behind Baghill 412, 414, 432
Houghton, Lord, owns the property of St Nicholas Hospital 423

INGS (The) 433, 435
Ive's (St) Well, named after St. Hiua (pronounced Hiva) 423

JACKSON Charles and Francis owned the property of St Clement's Chapel 407
Jackson Richard also had a lease of it 407
John, son of Henry de Lacy, killed by a fall from Pontefract battlements 405
Jollage Paul, his Plan of Pontefract, intermediate in time and design between the two engravings of the Society of Antiquaries 410, Was prim and unreal 412, Contained several Vignettes 418

KING'S (Mr), his troubles to find a possible use for the Cesspool 402

King's Seat 403
King's Stable, near the Main Guard 400
King's Tower 405, 406, 409
Knapper Knoll 423
Knaresborough, ground plan, resembles that of Pontefract 419
Knottingley lime-stone, medieval hall roofed with 407
Knottingley Road 433
Knowles, Sir Robert, the founder of Trinity Hospital 419

LADY Balk and Lady Balk Lane 422
Lambert's (Major) Fort 412, 432
Lancaster Herald's Visit 400
————, Arms of the Earldom of, still represented in the ruins of Pontefract Castle 406
Lathe Great 404
Lund Mr, his back premises the site of the Main Battery 421

MAIN Battery was behind Mr Rusby's 421
Main Guard not represented in the Engraving of the Society of Antiquaries; why 400, Near the King's Stable *ib*
Market Place, Pontefract, Plan of 419
Marsden John, his View of Pontefract Castle 397, 410
Michael's (St) Church, where was it? 408, 409
Mickle-gate=The Great Street 419, No Battery there 421
Middle Wall was formerly the Outer Wall 401, And is a mere casing to solid rock 399, Separated the Outer and Inner Barbicans 401, Is represented with Buttresses in Lord Galway's Drawing 413
Mildmay Humphrey and Thomas Crompton had a lease of St. Clement's Chapel 407
Mill, East 428
———— Garth 428, 429, 430
————, West 428
Monckton, Sir Philip, ancestor of Lord Galway, took part in the last Siege 413
Moody's Close 431
Moot Hall, the seat of the secular authority 419

More, Sir Thomas, his portrait at Nostell 418
Morris's (Col.) Will 436

NICHOLAS (St.) Cobcroft 409, 410
Nicholas (St.) Pontefract 409
Norman Wall round the Ballium 405, 407
Northallerton, How its ground plan resembles that of Pontefract 419
Northgate 422
North Horn Work, 412, 423

OILLET Holes in the Prints, only ornamental 405
Old Church, The British Museum print of 416
Outer Barbican, a late enclosure 398, 399, 400, Practically a Farm Yard to the establishment 401, At a lower level than the Inner Barbican 404
Oxfields (The) 433

PARADISE Lane, site of the Fairfax Royal Horn Battery 422
——— Orchard 423
Parsnep Garth 430, 433
Pinfold 434, 435
Piper Tower 403, Does not appear in the Medieval Print; why 408, Its fall 421
Pond Garth 433
Pontefract, a Danish town 418
Poppin Lane 434
Porter's Lodge or Great Gateway 403, Its buttress mutilated to allow of a slipe between it and a fore-building 404, But ignored in all the Siege Plans *ib*; Approached between curved walls *ib*
Presbiter (old Independent) Chapel, site of 418
Primrose Close 431, 432, The Work there unnamed in either of the Siege Plans 432

RECORD Office, Is not the original Draught of Pontefract Castle there? 397, 410
Red Tower 406, 412, 413
Redman Peter 430
Richard's (St.) of Pontefract, the only Church in England of that dedication 398, St Richard's Church had rights of burial 406

Rockingham, Marquis of, The Patron of Marsden's View of Pontefract Castle 397
Roman Road Remains near the Grange Field 433
Round Tower, on Jollage's map, very inaccurate 410, And represented differently on the two Soc: Ant: engravings 400, Each representation being inaccurate *ib*, The circular roundels had quadrangular cores 403
Routh Thomas, son of John 430
Royal Horn Work (Fairfax's) 412, 417, 422
Rusby Mr, his garden the site of the Main Battery 421

SANDAL Castle, View of, published by the Society of Antiquaries in 1753, 410
Savage Boniface, supplied the copy of the Pontefract Charters in Dodsworth MSS. 417
School House Guard, Its position 422
Scots among the Besiegers 428
Siege Plan No. 1 claimed to be taken from a Drawing in the possession of the Fairfax family 411, Which had been drawn during the Siege for the information of General Fairfax *ib*, It is very inaccurate in details *ib*, Though its plan of the town is by no means bad 412
Siege Plan No. 2, an imaginative attempt to correct the inaccuracies of No. 1 412; Plan of the town accurate, though slightly modernized to date 412, Used for the Frontispiece to this volume, 413, 414
Siege Plan No. 3, is from a Plan belonging to Lord Galway 413, Probably the earliest drawing, though published last *ib*, Seems to have been the original of No. 1 *ib*, Intended for the 1645 siege, but having the names of the commanders in 1648, 414
Siege Plan, Mr Frank's 415, Presented by him to the Society *ib*, Was in some respects more accurate than either of its predecessors *ib*, But is dated with manifest inaccuracy 417
Siege Works were defended by a line of Guards 421

SUPPLEMENT. xli.

Skinner Lane End, and Skinner Lane Head 422, ——— Close 423
Skipton, Mrs Barbara, 430
Southgate 419, 434, Much altered since the time of the sieges 435
South Baileygate 430
——- Horn Work 412, 432, 434
Stable, Mr Ald 430
——— Zachary, His Orchard 429, The Work there 430, His family *ib*
——— The King's, near the Main Guard 401
Swillington Tower Rebuilt by Thomas of Lancaster 406, The object of attack of a series of small Works 424, 425

TATHAM'S (Mr) Orchard 429
Tenalian Guard 412, 420, 427, 428
Thirsk, how its ground plan resembles that of Pontefract 419
Thwaites Richard, had a lease of St. Clement's Chapel 407
Town's Close 433
Treasurer's Tower 406
Trenches at Monkhill 426
Trinity Church had rights of burial 406

UNIVERSITY College, Oxford, owns the property of Trinity Hospital 423

VETUSTA Monumenta, View of Pontefract Castle therein 397
Vicarage, its position 429

WALKERGATE, the burnt houses there 432, 434, 435
Wakefield, how its ground Plan resembles that of Pontefract 419
——— Bridge, Chapel on 409, 410
Wards, Three to the Castle in 1536 401
Watercourses of Pontefract 433, 436
——— pipe of hammered lead supplied the Kitchen 407
Westgate and Drawbridge 400
West Mill 428
Wilsford, Buckley, published a View of Pontefract Castle, taken from memory only 397
Winn Rowland, 4th Baronet, Jollage's Map dedicated to 418
Work, Besiegers', were practically the same at both sieges 410, 420

ERRATA.

PAGE
75, last line but 3, for *enemyes* read *enemeys*.
81, last line but 1 of the small type, *theire men from falling upon* is repeated unnecessarily.
165, line 1, for 1645 read 1635.
174, 1647 occurs twice for 1646 as the date of the attempt on the Castle in which the two Annes and Lady Savile were interested.
203, line 9, for *Vol.* 39 read *Vol.* 37.
204, line 25, for Appendix F, read *page* 294.
261, last line but 9, for 1647 read 1646.

PAGE
296, line 23, for 2 *other, two* read (2) *other two*.
308, Allerton or Ollerton Boate we have since ascertained to be the name of a ferry between Allerton Bywater and Methley.
324, line 20, for *Paulden* read *Baynes*.
367, line 24, for *accosted* read *accused*.
376, line 2, for 352 read 362.
390, last line but 2, before *Samuel Savile*, insert *Samuel, son of*.
423, 2nd col., the 10th and 11th lines from the bottom have been accidentally transposed.

www.ingramcontent.com/pod-product-compliance
Lightning Source LLC
Chambersburg PA
CBHW071732150426
43191CB00010B/1545